McGRAW-HILL SERIES IN EDUCATION

HAROLD BENJAMIN, Consulting Editor

MODERN LANGUAGES

for

MODERN SCHOOLS

MODERN LANGUAGES

for

MODERN SCHOOLS

BY

WALTER VINCENT KAULFERS, Ph.D. 1904-

*Associate Professor, School of Education, Stanford University;
Director of Foreign Languages, Menlo School and
Junior College, Menlo Park, California*

FIRST EDITION

McGRAW-HILL BOOK COMPANY, Inc.

NEW YORK AND LONDON

1942

THE MAPLE PRESS COMPANY, YORK, PA.

To

B. F. K.

I would rather hear kind thoughts and sincere feeling expressed in poor language, than the lack of them in the best.

—BERTHA FRANCES KAULFERS.

PREFACE

Those who, at the present day, would reject an improvement because of the place of its origin, belong to the same school of bigotry with those who inquired if any good could come out of Nazareth.

—HORACE MANN.

Changing a curriculum is like trying to move a cemetery.

—RAY LYMAN WILBUR, PRESIDENT, STANFORD UNIVERSITY.

With the appearance in 1937 of the revised edition of *Modern Foreign Languages and Their Teaching* by Robert D. Cole and James B. Tharp,[1] and the more recent appearance of two scholarly books on methods—Peter Hagboldt's *The Teaching of German* (1940),[2] and Charles H. Handschin's *Modern-language Teaching* (1940),[3] there is little need at the present writing for a critical synthesis and interpretation of the vast number of books, monographs, tests, and articles that have appeared on the subject of curriculum and instruction in foreign languages since Johannis Ludovicus Vives wrote his famous *De causis corruptarum artium*.[4] The afore-mentioned books, together with Coleman and King's *An Analytical Bibliography of Modern Language Teaching*,[5] Oliver's *The Modern Language Teacher's Handbook*,[6] the

---

[1] Robert D. Cole and James B. Tharp, *Modern Foreign Languages and Their Teaching*, D. Appleton-Century Company, Inc., New York, 1937, xxi + 640 pp.

[2] Peter Hagboldt, *The Teaching of German*, D. C. Heath and Company, Boston, 1940, ix + 306 pp.

[3] Charles H. Handschin, *Modern-language Teaching*, World Book Company, Yonkers-on-Hudson, New York, 1940, vi + 458 pp.

[4] Johannis Ludovicus Vives (*né* Juan Luis Vives), Valentian humanist and Renaissance educationist, 1492–1540, *De causis corruptarum artium; De tradendis disciplinis, Exercitatio linguae latinae; De ratione studii puerilis.*

[5] Algernon Coleman and Clara Breslove King, *An Analytical Bibliography of Modern Language Teaching*, Vol. I, xiii + 296 pp., 1933; Vol. II, xviii + 561 pp., 1938, The University of Chicago Press, Chicago.

[6] Thomas Edward Oliver, *The Modern Language Teacher's Handbook*, D. C. Heath and Company, Boston, 1935, vii + 706 pp.

reports of the Stanford Language Arts Investigation,[1] and current issues of *The Modern Language Journal*,[2] constitute a minimum key library[3] which every prospective teacher of modern foreign languages, as well as those already in service, will find of inestimable value.

The aim of this volume is not to duplicate what has already been admirably accomplished, but rather to discuss in practical detail a reconstructed supporting ideology for the teaching of modern foreign languages, literatures, and cultures in American education.   The many evidences of insecurity and confusion lend strength to the conviction that the need is for the development of a creative conception of the nature and function of language in human life, and of ways and means for translating this conception into constructive action.   The viewpoint of the present volume is not that of "teaching foreign languages to students," but that of *helping young people to grow in ability to use a foreign language for worthy life purposes.*   Unless this point is clearly understood, the author's preoccupation with the sociological and psychological foundations of language learning, and with education as comprising *more than formal schooling*, will seem irrelevant indeed. In addressing the chapters of this book to so complex a problem, the author does not presume that a particular body of content, or a special system of teaching, can provide a panacea.   Neither is it the writer's intention to proclaim a "new" method from the housetops.   The germ of many of the ideas supporting the discussions can be found in the writings of great teachers of language from classical to modern times— Quintilian, Vives, Comenius, and M. West—many of whom are quoted in the pages that follow.   The aim is not originality per se, but to select the best wherever it is to be found and, if possible, to perfect its adaptability to the needs of the present and future.   In the references to articles reporting successful classroom practices, the reader will find that credit has been given where credit is due.   The author has taken the liberty, however, of formulating the following criteria as bases for the selection of content and learning activities:

1. Method is important in relation to the life objective that is to be achieved; for people frequently become, not what their objectives are, but what the means they employ subtly transform them into being. Just as the individual who tries to become wealthy by illegal means is more likely to end life as a criminal or racketeer than as a multimillion-

---

[1] Walter V. Kaulfers *et al.*, *Foreign Languages and Cultures in American Education*, Reports of the Stanford Language Arts Investigation, Vol. II, McGraw-Hill Book Company, Inc., New York. In press.

[2] *The Modern Language Journal.* The National Federation of Modern Language Teachers.   Established 1920.

[3] See also Appendix, references 1–156.

aire, so the child who is taught to read, write, or speak a foreign language exclusively by means of proofreading exercises illustrating rules of grammar is more likely to become an amateur proofreader (if he can endure the course long enough) than a critical reader of good literature, a fluent conversationalist, or a "cultured" individual.

2. Knowledge and skill have no significant value except in terms of the uses to which they are put in life, *i.e.*, in terms of the kind of human beings which they enable people to become. The traditional conception that knowledge per se is power contains just enough truth to be misleading. The average sophomore in high school, by virtue of his contacts with books, radio programs, and moving pictures, has more accurate knowledge of the world than Plato or Aristotle could possibly have had, yet few sophomores become Platos. Why?

Again, in an era of unavoidable social and economic interdependence, the effect which the use of a skill has upon other people is of increasing importance. It is significant to observe that the roster of penal institutions and asylums contains names of people with advanced graduate degrees (and the "intelligence" necessary to attain them) as well as *Who's Who*. Do not these facts have significance for teachers of languages and literatures who have long had as their objectives the building of humane attitudes on an international scale? Is it not time that the teachers of foreign languages, literatures, and cultures join hands with those frontier workers in the humanities who are vitally concerned not only with the diffusion of knowledge, but also with the development of the kind of mind-set that will guide the use of knowledge and skill into constructive channels for the solution of the really crucial problems of individual and group life? Certainly a nation that has twice pledged itself to maintain the dignity of the individual as a human being on all the continents cannot afford to neglect the service that the foreign-language teachers of America can perform at home in helping to prepare the citizens of tomorrow for a future in which the mending of men's minds and hearts will be far more important than the mending of their pocketbooks.

In the preparation of this volume, the writer has drawn upon his own eighteen years of experience as a classroom teacher in Spanish, French, German, and general language in junior and senior high schools, evening schools, and junior colleges, and upon his work as curriculum consultant to the Eight-year Study of the National Commission on the Relation of Schools and Colleges. As director of the foreign-language programs in the Stanford Language Arts Investigation (1937–1940) the author acknowledges with sincere appreciation the cooperation of the participating teachers in putting many of the hypotheses advanced in this book to the acid test of effective class-room use. Sincere thanks are also due the following individuals for valuable assistance in the preparation of this book:

To Thornton Clark Blayne for valuable bibliographical and technical assistance in the preparation of the manuscript.

To Dante P. Lembi of the Jefferson Union High School, Daly City, Calif., and to Douglas M. Whittemore of the Menlo School and Junior College, Menlo Park, Calif., for a critical reading of the manuscript from the viewpoint of the teacher in service.

To Professors Holland D. Roberts, William L. Schwartz, and B. Q. Morgan of Stanford University for their friendly suggestions.

To the editors of *School and Society, Curriculum Journal, Journal of Higher Education, High Points, The High School Journal, The Phi Delta Kappan, Education, Progressive Education, The English Journal, The Modern Language Forum, The Classical Journal, The French Review, The School Review, The Modern Language Journal, The German Quarterly, Italica, Hispania, California Journal of Secondary Education, Journal of Educational Research,* and *The Clearing House* for permission to quote from the pages of their magazines.

In writing for graduate students who are preparing to make modern-language teaching their lifework, and for teachers in service who may wish to familiarize themselves with types of content and learning activities that have proved successful in meeting the changing educational needs of American life, the author is mindful of the fact that these needs will change in the future as in the past and that for this reason no final word with respect to the best kind of foreign-language program for any given group of students ever can or should be written. This fact, however, does not preclude the desirability of calling attention to new needs that have seldom been met by conventional foreign-language courses or to time-sanctioned practices that defeat, as often as they achieve, the ends that they pretend to serve. If education is to have anything to do with making human beings behave differently from predatory animals or complacent sheep, then in teaching the arts of communication it is safer to err on the side of faith in the educability of growing boys and girls, under proper motivation and guidance, than to convert man's most significant social invention and most indispensable medium of thought into a mere disciplinary instrument for the frustration or destruction of young people.[1]

STANFORD UNIVERSITY,   WALTER VINCENT KAULFERS.
    July, 1942.

[1] For problems and issues for discussion see Appendix A.

CONTENTS

xi

CONTENTS xiii

APPENDIXES

EDITOR'S INTRODUCTION

Subjects are easier to teach than human beings.

A fact is a fact. It will stay where you put it. It will not go off on a tangent at the flicker of an eyelash—at least it will not do so if it is a proper and well-behaved fact. It will not look out of the window when you are talking to it. It will not smile at you today and scowl at you tomorrow. A fact, if you really have it by the nape of the neck, is always in there pitching for you.

Human beings are not entirely like that. They will work one hour and loaf the next. Sometimes they will fail when according to all appearances they should succeed and sometimes they will come through magnificently for no good reason at all. No doubt the measure of their unpredictability is merely the extent of our ignorance of them, but the truth remains that our knowledge of learners is usually much less than our knowledge of that which we attempt to teach them.

To teach facts is like playing chess according to rules; the pawns and the pieces always move legally. To teach human beings is like playing a game where the pawns occasionally stiffen their backs and fight like queens, or where the knights and rooks and bishops sometimes lie down in the ditch and refuse to fight at all.

Linguistic facts are especially satisfactory to teach. Verbs compounded with *ad, ante, cum, in, inter, ob, post, prae, pro, sub, super*, and sometimes with *circum*, take the dative, or if they do not conform to this rule in certain instances, their very nonconformity is in itself a pleasant fact to impart. When *to teach* is construed with the single accusative of fact, it gives safety and simplicity to the whole task of instruction.

There may be no royal road to learning, but the royal road to teaching was discovered long ago by the first grammar master who found that the rigorous profession of helping children to achieve humanely great goals through use of language abilities could be discarded for an easy trade of teaching language skills for their own sakes.

The present book is designed for teachers who will have none of this royal road. It is for teachers who believe that the arts of communication are not arts at all, but only busywork of tongue and brain, unless they serve those human purposes which are above and beyond all the arts.

The author of this book is a distinguished spokesman for this group. He speaks as a teacher of long experience in helping young people to use foreign languages for achieving life objectives and in helping young teachers to use foreign languages in the task of developing human personalities. Simply, clearly, and precisely he pictures the complex of information, skill, and method which modern language teachers of this faith and persuasion employ.

HAROLD BENJAMIN

UNIVERSITY OF MARYLAND
July, 1942.

MODERN LANGUAGES FOR MODERN SCHOOLS

INTRODUCTION

WHY FOREIGN LANGUAGES ARE SO FOREIGN

Facts that are not frankly faced have a habit of stabbing us in the back.
—SIR HAROLD BOWDEN

Any program of instruction is functional if it actually attains with a maximum economy of time and effort the objectives toward which it is oriented.   Any approach in foreign-language teaching is functional if it is effective in developing ability to use a language for the purpose or purposes for which it is being learned or taught.   Obviously, one cannot discuss any approach to the learning of a language except in terms of the student—his abilities, background, interests, and probable future—the objectives for which the language is being learned or taught, the content and activities in and through which the objectives are to be attained effectively with the least expenditure of time and effort, or the resources of the teacher as the director of the learning process.   The learning environment is also destined to play an important role in determining particular types of activities that can be carried on effectively during the course.   What is possible in a class of five beginning students, meeting around a table in a special foreign-language room supplied with equipment in the way of phonograph records, picture-projection facilities, voice-recording machines, classroom library, and piano, is not possible to the same extent in a class of 40 students regimented in five rows in a boxlike classroom, used the preceding period for geometry and the following period for freshman hygiene.   Neither are the same activities possible in a community devoid of cultural contributions from the country whose language is being studied as are possible in a community rich in environmental resources.   Any discussion of the problem of foreign-language teaching apart from these four considerations is destined to be, from the func-

1

tional standpoint, little more than armchair philosophizing without foundation in reality.

In considering the student in relation to foreign-language study, it is important to bear in mind that almost every human being, except congenital idiots and a small percentage of speech defectives, develops considerable facility in the vernacular as regards pronunciation, vocabulary, and language consciousness, or *Sprachgefühl*, though in the case of low-grade imbeciles and morons *what* is said does not necessarily represent a high level of intelligence in language. The big point is that language, almost irrespective of intelligence (unless intelligence is made synonymous with ability in language), is the natural birthright of every normal human being. Why, then, is the learning of a foreign language so unusual a thing?

The answer is perhaps to be found in a variety of circumstances: Certainly the limited amount of time in which the pupil—especially in large classes—hears and uses the foreign language in school is insignificant compared with the amount of time during which a Spanish, French, German, or Italian child hears and uses his own language daily. Again, a partial answer may be found in the handicap that a firmly established background in the vernacular often imposes upon the development of ability in a foreign language. Although cognates and near cognates, recognizable from their similarity to words in the learner's native language, at times facilitate the comprehension of foreign words, this carry-over from the vernacular is slight compared with the handicap imposed by differences in pronunciation, articulation, inflection, intonation, word order, idiomatic usage, and the like. Once the mind is habituated to reacting automatically in certain ways, its habit patterns tend to carry over from the vernacular into the foreign language. Neither the teacher nor the student of foreign languages, therefore, has a clean slate upon which to begin foreign-language work.

It is also possible that the medium used to short-cut the language-learning process in school—to develop in a relatively few hours language abilities which even in the motivated circumstances of normal life require many years to attain—is for many students as much a handicap as an aid.[1] The terminology of grammar, invented by highly trained and specialized adult minds, schooled in all the techniques of linguistic analysis and classification, is not an idiom easily learned, and seldom correctly applied, by boys and girls of elementary-school or

[1] Ray Yaller, "A Survey of Causes of Student Failure in Language Study," *High Points*, Vol. 20, pp. 12–23, June, 1938.

high-school age. Even such relatively simple terms as the parts of speech seem to cause difficulty in application. Although the definitions of *subject* and *predicate* can be learned and repeated accurately even by seventh graders, the abstractness of this terminology seems to make it almost useless when the pupils attempt to write complete sentences of their own. "When I was young." is still written as a complete sentence by many students who have passed satisfactorily all background tests in formal grammar.[1] For a considerable number of students such grammatical terms as *auxiliary verb, clause,* and *subjunctive,* are as foreign as the foreign language itself. To teach one language to a beginner in terms of another idiom even more abstract and elusive in application is, therefore, as often likely to complicate as to facilitate the learning process. The adolescent mind does not, and cannot be expected to, work as efficiently as the mind of a schooled adult grammarian or teacher of foreign languages. Some writers of textbooks, and not a few teachers, have exceeding difficulty in placing themselves *in loco discipuli*.

A fourth explanation is possibly to be found in the seemingly different conceptions of language held by the beginner on entering the language class, and by the teacher of foreign languages. To most young people who enroll in such courses, language is primarily a medium for the communication of feelings, wants, and ideas, and not an end in itself. As long as the content and activities in and through which the language is practiced contain ideas of interest or significance in terms of the learners' background of experience and needs, the desire to understand and communicate through the language is usually maintained. When the program of instruction, however, becomes primarily a study of grammatical classifications or of syntactical theory, interest and enthusiasm usually wane as soon as the novelty of the course has worn off. Some young people (not unlike their elders in evening-school classes) soon lose interest and drop out; some muddle through half-heartedly, doing just enough to get by; others do the assignments religiously as a chore to earn a grade of *A* or *B*; and a few who find the mechanics of language as fascinating as a crossword puzzle become sufficiently proficient in the essentials of the language to continue

---

[1] T. H. Briggs, "Formal English Grammar as a Discipline," *Teachers College Record*, Vol. XIV, pp. 251–343, September, 1913. Ellen Frogner, "Clarifying Some Facts," *The English Journal*, Vol. XXIX, No. 8, pp. 653–655, October, 1940. L. J. O'Rourke, *Rebuilding the English-usage Curriculum to Insure Greater Mastery of Essentials, A Report of a Nation-wide Survey,* The Psychological Institute, Washington, D. C., 1934, x + 98 pp.

voluntarily into advanced courses. The poverty and sterility of the thought content of the materials commonly used for practice in reading, writing, or speaking in conventional elementary and intermediate courses have been responsible in many cases for an apathetic attitude on the part of secondary-school students toward foreign-language study, to such an extent that it is still rated by a majority of young people among the subjects "most disliked," or "liked least" in high school.[1] To read and discuss material far below the intellectual and social maturity of the learner may be amusing at times, or serve as a relief from formal exercises, but in the long run it is more boring than educative, more satiating than stimulating. The negative psychological effect of subordinating content to form and mechanics, so frequently apparent in elementary textbooks (in which language is concocted primarily to illustrate words and constructions of high frequency rather than to convey ideas or information worth reading, writing, or talking about) is as subtle as it is vicious in its effect upon the morale of students and their achievement in foreign-language courses.

Finally, the aims of the foreign-language program have either been too remote or too unrelated to the immediate objectives of the student to retain his confidence and interest in the course. Except in the case of Latin, few pupils study a foreign language with the primary purpose of improving their English vocabulary, increasing their knowledge of English grammar, or disciplining their minds; yet these objectives often dominate modern-language teaching to such an extent that even ability to read, write, or converse in the language seems to be a secondary or even incidental consideration—at least so it seems to the novice for whom the conventional beginning textbook is often little more than a book on grammar in which the examples and exercises happen to be chosen from the foreign language, and the beginning reader merely a series of supplementary exercises in connected context to illustrate the rules, idioms, or tenses that have been "covered" in the grammar. For whatever content in the way of information or ideas is contained in the average elementary reader is often so meager and heavily diluted with illustrative wordage, or so unimportant or irrelevant to the really significant interests of young people, that it is hardly more than an

[1] Adolph Klein, "Failure and Subjects Liked and Disliked," *High Points*, Vol. XXI, pp. 22–25, January, 1939. See also the earlier studies by S. S. Colvin and Andrew H. McPhail, "Intelligence of Seniors in the High Schools of Massachusetts," *U. S. Bureau of Education Bulletin* 1924, No. 9, 39 pp. William F. Book, *The Intelligence of High School Seniors as Revealed by a State-wide Mental Survey of Indiana High Schools*, The Macmillan Company, New York, 1922, 371 pp.; pp. 159–184.

exercise in decoding, translating, deciphering, or question-and-answer pencil pushing.

Almost every investigation of the foreign-language interests of elementary- and secondary-school pupils has shown that the purposes for which most students enroll in foreign-language classes are, in descending order of importance, as follows: to fulfill college requirements, to speak the language, to read the language, to prepare for travel abroad, to learn about foreign lands.[1]   It is, perhaps, the over-emphasis upon certain of these objectives to the neglect or exclusion of others in conventional courses that has made foreign-language offerings fail to "click" with as large a number of pupils as foreign-language teachers would like to see enrolled in their fields, or with as large a number of pupils as have in the past professed a genuine initial interest in learning a foreign tongue.   The fact is that the mortality rate in foreign-language courses is still among the highest (30 to 40 per cent) for the secondary-school subjects,[2] and the number of dropouts, through failure or by choice, sufficiently large to preclude the organization of a full four-year program in foreign languages even in relatively large institutions.

The fact that foreign-language offerings have not been well adapted to the capacities, interests, and abilities of large numbers of students has been recognized by foreign-language teachers for many years.   Not all teachers, however, have been willing to admit the necessity for modifying the objectives, content, or activities of the classroom.   Until recently the emphasis has been primarily on fitting the students to the courses, and only incidentally on fitting the courses to the students. Such negative factors as the abstract elusive medium through which the language is often taught, the sterility of the thought content of the course, the discrepancy between student objectives and teacher objectives, or between what students consider important and vital in foreign-language work and what teachers feel is "good for them," have often been dismissed with derogatory cries of "soft pedagogy" or "spoon-feeding."   The assumption has too often been that pupils who do not or cannot profit from foreign-language courses as offered need to have their minds disciplined and their study habits developed; that pupils

---

[1] Anne Z. Moore, "Why I Chose to Study a Foreign Language," *The Modern Language Journal*, Vol. XXV, pp. 181–185, December, 1940. See also "Why Pupils Choose the Different Foreign Languages," *High Points*, Vol. X, pp. 41–42, March, 1928.

[2] Adoph Klein, "Failure and Subjects Liked and Disliked," *High Points*, Vol. XXI, pp. 22–25, January, 1939. Basil Thomas Coleman, "An Analysis of the Scholarship Reports of Thirty-three of the High Schools in Greater New York," *High Points*, Vol. XIX, pp. 5–18, January, 1937.

who, because of their mental immaturity, cannot understand or make effective use of the grammatical lingo of the textbooks need to have their English vocabulary and grammar improved; that pupils who have learned good English at home without benefit of grammar, but cannot learn to pronounce, read, write, or speak a foreign language with ease and accuracy by theorizing in English about its phonetic or syntactical composition, obviously lack "language talent" or "aptitude";[1] that students who do not become enthusiastic over translating a foreign classic on the next-three-pages-for-tomorrow plan obviously need to develop a taste for this form of cultural busywork whether they like it or not.   In any case, college entrance requirements presumably do not allow of any important changes in the course of study—even though scarcely three students in a beginning class of 35 ordinarily continue in college in the same language which they begin in high school.[2]   At least, so the arguments ran.

In keeping with this negative supporting ideology, exploratory or general-language courses were to be introduced to weed out the unfit;[3] prognosis tests were to be administered to eliminate pupils without language talent,[4] elementary and junior-high-school teachers were to teach more grammar[5] so that every fourteen-year-old boy on enrolling in Spanish would have no difficulty using the object pronouns correctly after reading in his textbook that "the conjunctive direct object pronouns must precede the auxiliary in compound tenses of the indicative, except in the case of gerunds and infinitives.   For the sake of clarity the prepositional pronouns are frequently employed with the conjunctive object pronouns of the third person, especially in direct address."

[1] Robert Herndon Fife et al., A Summary of Reports on the Modern Foreign Languages with an Index to the Reports, The Macmillan Company, New York, 1931, vii + 261 pp.; pp. 123–124.   V. A. C. Henmon et al., Prognosis Tests in the Modern Languages, Vol. XIV, Publication of the American and Canadian Committees on Modern Languages, The Macmillan Company, New York, 1929, xviii + 182 pp.

[2] E. F. Engel, "Why Do not College Students Continue the Foreign Language Begun in High School?" The Modern Language Journal, Vol. V, pp. 500–503, March, 1932.   Walter V. Kaulfers and Vera E. Whitmann, "Continuance in College of High School Foreign Language," The School Review, Vol. XLVIII, pp. 606–611, October, 1940.

[3] Lilly Lindquist, "A General Language Course as a Pre-requisite to Foreign Language Study," Modern Language Journal, Vol. XIV, pp. 285–289, January, 1930.

[4] Henmon et al., op. cit.

[5] "Report of the Committee on Foreign Languages," The Modern Languages Forum, Vol. XII, pp. 13–18, October, 1927.

All these panaceas for making the foreign language more functional were tried with some success, usually offset by such a material reduction in foreign-language enrollments that the teachers themselves became a little fearful of the wisdom of their remedies.   The result of these efforts to make the foreign-language program more functional by fitting the student to the program and still maintain the *status in quo* gradually led to the development of a new school of foreign-language teaching which has found organized expression in such cooperative curriculum-revision programs as those undertaken by the Eight-year Study of the National Commission on the Relation of Schools and Colleges,[1] and the Stanford Language Arts Investigation.[2] The efforts of the foregoing organizations and of other similarly minded groups of teachers have been directed toward rooting the foreign-language program at the adolescent level more securely in the capacities, interests, abilities, and needs of growing boys and girls, toward making the foreign-language curriculum contribute something more significant to American education and culture than a "ticket of admission to the university," and toward bringing the instructional process in foreign languages into conformity with recent developments in the psychology of learning and research in the psychology of language itself.[3]

In the following chapters the philosophy and psychology of language, and the educational objectives of the newer type programs in foreign languages, are discussed in connection with illustrative samples of content and activities, and with a résumé of outcomes as measured by batteries of tests and other evaluative criteria.   The aim throughout is to stress content and learning activities that will not make the study of foreign languages, literatures, and cultures more foreign to the capacities, interests, and abilities of American students, or to the needs of American life and culture, than physical limitations temporarily cause it to be.[4]

[1] Conducted under the auspices of the Progressive Education Association, 221 West 57th St., New York.

[2] Walter V. Kaulfers, "The Foreign Languages in the Stanford Language Arts Investigation," *Hispania*, Vol. XXI, pp. 13–18, February, 1938.   Walter V. Kaulfers, "Foreign-language Outcomes of the Stanford Language Arts Investigation," *School and Society*, Vol. LII, pp. 235–237, Sept. 21, 1940.

[3] Recent research has been critically analyzed in the April issue, 1940, of the *Review of Educational Research*, "The Language Arts," Vol. X, No. 2, pp. 73–175 See also Walter S. Monroe, Ed., *Encyclopedia of Educational Research*, The Macmillan Company, New York, 1941, 1344 pp.; pp. 446–457, 520–539.

[4] For problems and issues for discussion, see Appendix A.

CHAPTER I

THE PSYCHOLOGY OF COMMON SENSE IN FOREIGN-LANGUAGE TEACHING

So act as to treat humanity in every case as an End, never as a means only.

—Immanuel Kant

Implications from the Social Psychology of Language.—No language has ever come into being except as a vehicle for the communication of feelings, wants, or ideas. New words and phrases are rarely created except in response to a felt need for communicating a concept for which a language symbol does not already exist or for which the existing symbol seems trite or inadequate. Often the very nature of the idea or concept to be expressed tends to determine even the aural form of the language symbol itself. This fact is most readily apparent in such onomatopoeic words as *buzz, cackle, grumble,* and *murmur,* in which the sound of the word imitates the actual physical sound which it is intended to communicate. It is also apparent in the frequent use of central long vowels, as in *keel* and *crane,* to give the impression of length, and of central short vowels to give the impression of brevity, *e.g., slap* or *pen.*[1]

Again the basic thought processes that originally molded the syntactical patterns of the language are revealed in such phenomena as the double negative in certain languages such as Spanish, the position of adjectives, the subjunctive mood, the distinction between the imperfect and preterite tenses, and the like. The Frenchman and the Spaniard, for example, say "a table square" (*une table carrée; una mesa cuadrada*) rather than "a square table."[2] Why? Probably because those who were originally responsible for setting the syntactical format

---

[1] Maurice Grammont, *Traité de phonétique,* Delagrave, Paris, 1933, 480 pp. Otto Jespersen, *Language: Its Nature, Development, and Origin,* George Allen & Unwin, Ltd., London, 1934, 448 pp. Joseph Delcourt, "On the Impressive Possibilities of the English Vocabulary," *The Modern Language Journal,* Vol. XXV, pp. 4–13, October, 1940.

[2] P. G. Wilson, *The Student's Guide to Modern Languages: A Comparative Study of English, French, German, and Spanish,* Sir Isaac Pitman & Sons, Ltd., London, 1930, vii + 190 pp.

of the present-day romance languages saw the *whole before the part, i.e.,* they saw a table, then noticed that it was square. Those who were originally responsible for establishing the objective framework of the English and Germanic languages probably were in the mental habit of noticing the *part before the whole, i.e.,* of seeing something square and then noticing that it was a table. Although these differences in word order were probably just as unconscious on the part of those who originally spoke the language as they are today, they reflect originally *different ways of reacting to the environment,* different ways of thinking. Similarly, the double negative in Spanish is correct, because in terms of the mental process of algebraic addition involved, the greater the number of negatives added, the more emphatic and the stronger the idea of negation. In English, the double negative is considered incorrect, since in terms of our accepted present-day linguistic ideology the mental process is not one of algebraic *addition,* but one of algebraic *multiplication.* Whereas -2 and -2 are *added* to give -4 in Spanish, -2 and -2 are *multiplied* in English to give a positive 4.

All this is intended to show that differences in construction between two languages, as well as differences in form, often reflect original *differences in ways of thinking,* or differences either in mental reactions to the environment or in the environment itself. The sound of a drum is imitated in English by the onomatopoeic word *rub-a-dub-dub,* and in Spanish by *rataplán.* The English expression probably derives its origin from a different type of drum, or from a different way of playing a drum.

Do not these facts have implications for the teaching of foreign languages? The answer of an increasing number of teachers is definitely in the affirmative. The result in many instances has been a shift from the formal approach to what, for want of a better name, may be termed the psychosemantic approach in the teaching of correct usage—an effort to replace formal grammatical rules and explanations, wherever possible, with insights into the past and present ways of thinking which differences in language represent. Although research into the psychosemantic aspects of language has not proceeded far enough to reveal explanations for any and all language phenomena, the body of material is sufficiently large to cover a considerable number of the more common constructions that cause difficulty and to provide helpful clues to many others.

Suppose that the beginning student of French or Spanish puts an adjective in the wrong place—that he writes *une bleue robe, un azul vestido* (a blue dress) instead of the conventional order *une robe bleue,*

un vestido azul (a dress blue).   How shall the teacher enable the student
to develop the insight necessary for him to understand and apply the
principle of language involved?   Shall the pupil be referred to the rule
in the grammar that states that "Adjectives usually follow the noun
they modify when used literally to define, distinguish, specify, or
emphasize some property or quality; but when used figuratively, or as
a merely ornamental epithet, or denoting a quality or characteristic
viewed as inherent or essential to the object, or when forming one
idea with the noun, they usually precede"?   What if the pupil does
not understand the meaning of such terms as *inherent, epithet,* or
figuratively, which are not always an integral part of his own vocabulary?   Will explaining an unfamiliar phenomenon in terms of an
unfamiliar language simplify and clarify the point, or will it more
likely complicate the learning process?   Experience would seem to
show that confusion, or a feeling of uncertainty, results.   To say
that the pupil ought to know his "English" does not solve the problem.   To stop and teach him his "grammar" then and there merely
consumes time which, from the foreign-language standpoint, might
more profitably be devoted to the most important factor in language
learning—abundant practice in actually using the language in some
purposeful and meaningful activity where a desire for correctness is
inspired by a desire to communicate effectively.[1]

Wherever a particular construction causes difficulty, a simple
explanation of the orientation of mind which it originally reflected
is more effective than a grammatical description of the phenomenon.
Grammatical rules rarely, if ever, explain the reason for anything.
They are descriptive, not explanatory in the sense of stating *why.*   If
a pupil asks, "*Why* must adjectives agree in gender and number with
the nouns or pronouns they modify?"—merely repeating the rule certainly does not answer the question, "Why?"   A psychosemantic
approach to usage in terms of insights into the ideology underlying
language phenomena is for most pupils a more meaningful alternative.
It eliminates almost completely, at times, the need for rules phrased
in abstract grammatical terms which young people have difficulty in
understanding and still greater difficulty in applying.   It is in general
a more interesting approach, more likely to be remembered because
it deals with the basic *raisons d'être* which grammatical rules far more
often obscure than reveal.   If a student continues, through some lapse
of memory, to misplace certain adjectives—to say *une carrée table,*

---

[1] Holland D. Roberts, "English Teachers Face the Future," *The English
Journal* (College Edition), Vol. XXVII, pp. 101–113, February, 1938.

un azul vestido, instead of *une table carrée, un vestido azul*—it will usually suffice to ask him the question, "How did those who originally set the pattern of the French (or Spanish) language look at things?   Did they see the object as a whole first, and then notice what it was like, or did they notice first something *square* and then realize that it was a *table?*"

From such examples it is not difficult to develop the general concept of the position of "sense adjectives."   Words such as *green, big, heavy, sweet,* and *fragrant,* which mention some quality that can be seen, felt, heard, tasted, or smelled, or otherwise appreciated through the five senses, generally follow the word (noun) which they describe, since those who originally set the pattern of the Romance languages were in the mental habit of perceiving the thing first, and then noticing what it was like.   Note that no grammatical terms are required for an understanding of the principle involved.   Observe also that the explanation comes closer to stating *why* than the conventional rule, inasmuch as it affords an insight into the basic psychological foundations of language which are usually eclipsed by the grammatical jargon of the conventional textbooks.

As an alternative for the conventional grammatical method of dealing with problems of usage, the psychosemantic approach possesses many possibilities.   Unfortunately, an understanding of this approach requires a thorough foundation in the field of general linguistics, semantics, and the philosophy and psychology of language which ordinarily do not form a part of teacher-training courses below the Ph.D. level.   Moreover, research in general semantics and the psychology of language is not as yet sufficiently developed to afford a suitable explanation for every phase of language.   Nevertheless, this fact does not preclude taking advantage of such resources as are available to date.   Able teachers of foreign languages have always made incidental use of philology and historical grammar, but the possibilities have not as yet been consciously developed.   Scarcely a single elementary textbook in any language is available to date that attempts to explain problems of construction or usage as reflections of *how people think.*

Just as mental processes and concepts often condition the composition of the language in which they find expression, so function determines form.   Indeed, form without function, or language without thought content in the way of information, feelings, wants, or ideas, is hardly language at all.   It is form and little else.   Language as a means of communication exists only when something is communicated to someone. This presupposes a speaker or writer and a reader or listener linked by content in the form of meaning. Where these essentials to any normal communication situation do not exist, it is doubtful if the result can rightfully be termed more than an exercise in form. When the pianist rehearses scales, arpeggios, and the like, he is *practicing*, he is not actually performing music. Similarly, when the tennis enthusiast practices serving or returning rallies from the net, he does not presume actually to be playing a game of tennis. In the same way, when the language student recalls disconnected paradigms, takes down sentences from dictation, or translates material designed primarily to illustrate grammatical constructions rather than to impart information, he is learning or rehearsing forms. He is not functioning in an actual communication situation; for there is nothing to communicate, and no one to communicate to—unless it be to the teacher, who in such cases is far more likely to be concerned with the *way* things are said, than with *what* is said or to *whom*.

Although a certain amount of specialized practice is essential to the development of a skill, whether it be the coordination of mind and muscle in playing a musical instrument, manipulating a typewriter, taking dictation in shorthand, playing golf, dancing, or developing automatic control of the position of the tongue and lips in articulating a foreign language, the part must not be mistaken for the whole, *i.e.*, the skill itself must not be mistaken to represent the function it is to serve. Indeed, it is only to the extent in which control over the mechanics of form is sufficiently automatic to enable the mind to concentrate primarily on *function* that anything approaching mastery is achieved. The violinist who on performing before an audience has to concentrate primarily on how to finger a certain passage, or on what position to use, is not likely to be able to interpret effectively the composition that he is playing. He may even forget parts of the work. Similarly, the speaker whose mind is occupied primarily with vocabulary, pronounciation, or grammar is likely to lose not only the train of his thought, but also his mental rapport with the audience. Indeed, in the case of language, overpreoccupation with form to the point of self-consciousness occasionally leads to stammering or stuttering. Examples of such speech disorders, produced in sensitive children by nagging parents, are not uncommon in speech pathology.[1] One of the chief reasons why more stammerers and stutterers are not produced under the conditions prevailing in some foreign-language classes

[1] Winifred V. Richmond, *Personality: Its Development and Hygiene*, Farrar & Rinehart, Inc., New York, 1937, vii + 279 pp.; p. 183 and *passim*.

is the fact that the children early give up all hope of learning to speak the language and resign themselves to remaining dumb.

The implication of these analogies for foreign-language teaching is not that practice is unnecessary, but rather that the kind of practice which is provided often tends either to eclipse the function which it is to serve, or to bear little or no relationship to the life situation in which the skill is to operate.   As a result, transfer from practice to actual performance is often ineffective.   A specific example may serve to illustrate the point.   A device commonly used in teaching pupils the tenses of verbs, or the forms of irregular verbs, is the conjugation or verb paradigm.   In nearly all textbooks the format is somewhat as follows:

> *haben:* to have
> habe: I have, do have, etc.
> hast
> hat
> haben
> habt
> haben

Because verbs are often outlined or classified for convenience and brevity in this vertical style, the assumption has seemingly been made that "memorizing" verbs in this format is the easiest and most convenient way in which to learn them.   Now this assumption would undoubtedly be true if verbs were used in exactly this format and sequence in reading, writing, or speaking.   The obvious fact, however, is that outside of grammars and dictionaries they hardly ever occur in this order.   It is a grouping as divorced from reality as any earthly phenomenon could possibly be.   Thus, although a beginning pupil can, and often does, develop a mastery of the conjugation, this skill is only very indirectly and incidentally useful in promoting facility and accuracy in reading, writing, or speaking.   In other words, the transfer of training is ineffective, because the language is not learned in the way it is normally used for purposes of communication.   As an abbreviated, classified reference outline, the verb paradigm is a real convenience, but as a practice exercise, or a teaching device it is a classic illustration of the violation of almost every known principle of the psychology of learning.   As an example of nonfunctional procedures still in use in many foreign-language classes, it deserves special analysis.

In the first place, most students enrolled in elementary classes do not have sufficient background in the foreign language itself to recognize the relationship between an isolated part of the language

and its behavioral relationship to the language as a whole.   Unless
the student has already contacted the forms in connected thought
content (where their meaning is indicated in parenthesis, or by cognate
similarities or associations in context), he is likely to be reciting mere
nonsense syllables.   If a beginner, for example, has not previously
contacted the present-tense forms of *to be* as vocabulary in reading,
short dialogues, or the like, the memorization of such paradigms in
French, German, or Spanish as the following:

suis	bin	soy
es	bist	eres
est	ist	es
sommes	sind	somos
êtes	seid	sois
sont	sind	son

is in itself likely to be little more profitable than the recitation of such
nonsense syllables as *pa, po, pu, pe, pi*.   Why?   Because the learner's
apperceptive background in the language itself is inadequate for the
purpose of providing insights into the meanings of these forms in isolation, or into their role as organic parts of the language.   There is little
or nothing in the learner's background of experience to which these
forms can be anchored.   Meaningful associations, except indirectly
through the learner's native language, are almost impossible to form,
with the result that learning is often superficial, ephemeral, and
parrotlike, and about as interesting as memorizing part of a telephone
book.

   In the second place, the vertical format of the paradigm bears no
relationship whatsoever to the pattern in which the forms are most
likely to occur, if they occur in any patterns at all in normal language
situations.   In reading and writing no special pattern is obviously
distinguishable.   In such question-and-answer activity as is usually
undertaken in the name of conversational work in most classrooms,
however, a fairly definite pattern is distinguishable.   It is a horizontal,
not a vertical pattern, in which in the large majority of cases certain
forms are normally associated in couplets in a kind of stimulus (question) and response (answer) pattern.   This skeletal pattern is, in a
sense, the elementary framework upon which a considerable amount of
conversation in normal life is also built.   Questions lead to answers,
and conversation is often an elaboration of a subject in terms of these
verbal stimuli.[1]

   [1] Walter V. Kaulfers, "A Graduated Approach to the Oral Objective," *The
Modern Language Forum*, Vol. XVIII, Yearbook, April, 1933, 134 pp.; pp. 13–20.

It would seem just as logical, therefore, and infinitely better psychology from the standpoint of facilitating the transfer of training from practice to communication situations in normal life, to learn the verb forms, if they require special attention, in horizontal question-and-answer context (preferably short sentences) which emphasizes the meanings of the individual forms and illustrates their functional relationship to other parts of speech.   The following example of the present tense in Spanish is illustrative of a principle that can be applied just as easily, with minor modifications, to the teaching of any foreign language:

No tocar el piano: not to play the piano.	
¿No toca Ud. el piano?	Don't you play the piano?
—(Yo) no toco el piano.	I don't play the piano.
¿No tocan Uds. el piano?	Don't you (plural) play the piano?
—(Nosotros) no tocamos el piano.	We don't play the piano.

Note that the verb endings are associated in couplets in the horizontal stimulus-response pattern which characterizes a large part of question-and-answer conversation in normal life.   The advantage of this association is the reduction of the number of possibilities for confusion. The conventional vertical paradigm, with its list of six variables, offers five possibilities for choosing the wrong form when the paradigm is used as a "reference dictionary" in extemporaneous or impromptu speech.

Note also that the number of forms has been reduced to four. After the pupil has a working knowledge of the basic forms, those variables which he is likely to have relatively little occasion to use himself can be learned as needed by means of a simple transmutation scheme.   For example, when the pupil has occasion to use the familiar *tú* form in Spanish, or comes across it in his reading, he can be shown how to derive it simply by adding an *s* to the ending ordinarily used with *Ud.* (you)—a fact that holds for all regular and irregular verbs in all tenses except the preterite.   Comparable possibilities hold for *vosotros* in Spanish and for the familiar forms in German and French. Using a known form of high frequency as a basis for deriving a less frequently used form is in the long run preferable to learning a complete conjugation in which the possibilities for confusion increase almost geometrically with the number of variables involved.   The primary purpose here, however, is not to short-cut the learning process, although it does so in effect, but rather to make possible bonds of association into which other language elements can be tied in the terms of their function and importance.   To classify language into isolated parts, and then to teach each part as if it were the equal of every other, is likely to tax the organizing and integrating capacities of even the ablest minds, for until the part can be seen in relation to the whole, organization is difficult, if not impossible. The beginning student is hardly able, like the skilled grammarian, to see the panorama of language from a mountain peak. He is scarcely in a position to distinguish even foothills from mountain slopes.

As a device, the question-and-answer exercise facilitates the transfer of training from practice to normal usage. If practice is to be effective, one pupil should ask the questions and another pupil should answer them; or if choral recitation is used to provide practice in large classes, the pupils on one side of the room may ask the questions of the pupils on the other side, or the girls may ask the questions of the boys, etc. In this way, mere parrotlike repetition without regard for the meaning of the material recited is reduced to a minimum. After the pattern of one question-and-answer paradigm has been learned, the procedure can easily be extended by analogy to other tenses.

Attention is called to the fact that the negative construction is always used at the start since it represents a more complete basic pattern. It is much easier later to leave out the negatives when an affirmative construction is desired, than to convert an affirmative sentence into a negative one by adding an element to an established language pattern, for the result in the latter case is always an unusual degree of originality on the part of the pupils in inserting the negative adverb *no* in almost every conceivable place except the right one.

The principles discussed above are still frequently violated in current foreign-language teaching and in a large majority of foreign-language grammars. The trouble obviously lies in the organization of the textbooks and courses of study. A very elementary course in child psychology, or in the psychology of learning, should suffice to show that a majority of foreign-language curriculums, and a considerable number of basic textbooks, are written primarily from the standpoint of logical classifications within the subject itself and only incidentally from the standpoint of how young people learn. The persistence of this tendency suggests the desirability of reviewing a few common-sense principles of the psychology of learning[1] in terms of their application to the teaching of the foreign languages.

[1] For a more comprehensive discussion of the psychology of language and learning see George W. Hartman, *Educational Psychology*, American Book Company, New York, 1941, vi + 552 pp.; pp. 197-223, 285-345, 433-516. John Madison Fletcher, *Psychology in Education*, Doubleday, Doran & Company, Inc.,

The Principle of Reference to Experience.—The unknown cannot be appreciated or understood except in terms of the known. This principle is so axiomatic that almost everyone makes use of it consciously or unconsciously in everyday life. How, for example, would a father explain to his son the meaning of the word *papaya*, assuming that the former had grown, picked, and eaten the fruit and that the latter had never seen one? Obviously his explanation would depend upon his son's age, and upon his resources in vocabulary. Perhaps, too, the explanation would involve comparisons and contrasts with the size, shape, color, and flavor of fruits already familiar to the child. This process of explaining the unknown in terms of the known illustrates the principle of *reference to experience*. Like most obvious things, this principle is taken so much for granted that it is at times completely forgotten. Thus one often finds children trying to learn the working principles of a foreign language in terms of a technical terminology more difficult for them at times than the foreign language itself. Enough evidence is available to show that, although almost anyone can memorize the definitions of the parts of speech and of other grammatical concepts, relatively few adolescents can apply this knowledge effectively in their *own* original writing or speech. The level of abstraction and generalization represented by nearly all generic grammatical terms is simply beyond the normal level of insight which most young people of elementary- and secondary-school age possess.

In studying a foreign language the high-school student often finds himself in a position comparable to that in which a five-year-old child might find himself were he to ask his father, "Daddy, what is a cow?" and receive the reply, "A cow is a ruminating, herbiferous, quadruped mammal, in which the lacteal glands are abnormally developed." Such an answer would be scientifically exact, unquestionably true, and in this case, absolutely useless![1] Not a single key word is within the experience vocabulary of the child in point. Now, if the father were to follow the precedent set by some teachers, he might berate the

New York, 1934, xx + 524 pp.; pp. 144–224, 381–406, 469–497. Charles E. Skinner, Ed., *Educational Psychology*, Prentice-Hall, Inc., New York, 1937, xxvi + 754 pp.; pp. 59–87, 88–113, 167–191, 297–324, 325–353, 705–734. J. R. Kantor, *An Objective Psychology of Grammar*, Indiana University, Bloomington, Ind., 1936, xvi + 344 pp.

[1] W. Wilbur Hatfield, "What Grammar? and How?" Public Relations Committee, National Council of Teachers of English, 211 West 68th St., Chicago, Ill., 1937, 4 pp. (mimeographed).

mother or the kindergarten teacher for not having taught the child these words. Or, being resigned to their shortcomings, he might stop before answering the question, and teach the child the meaning of *ruminating, herbiferous, quadruped, mammal, lacteal, glands, abnormally,* and *developed*—and most likely lose *both* the cow and the child in the process! If the child did not respond to this procedure, the father might conclude that the child took after its mother, or was simply lacking in intelligence. Obviously, none of these conclusions would be true. Neither would the equally plausible conclusion be justified that a five-year-old child was too young to learn what a cow is. The fault obviously lies in the fact that the *medium* of instruction in this example does not conform to the principle of reference to experience, and a different approach is desirable. The foregoing analogy to foreign-language teaching is hardly exact, but the underlying principle is identically the same.

Reducing to a minimum the use of technical nomenclature which merely complicates the learning process by adding more unknowns to the situation is a possible alternative. For example, instead of saying "the first person singular subject pronoun is omitted, etc.," it would be much easier all around to say "the word *I* is omitted, etc." What else could the first person singular subject pronoun be? The assertion that grammatical terminology is more exact, easier in the long run, and shorter and more convenient is, from the standpoint of most children and adolescents, only a half-truth.

When problems of structure or usage cannot be explained in ordinary English in terms of how people think, or learned directly through practice in imitation of correct models, then such alternatives as the foregoing are still possible to bring the medium of instruction within the experiential background of the learner. The following examples may suffice to make the principle clearer:

Instead of saying the "definite article," say "the word *the*," or, if it seems desirable to have the students learn the more important grammatical terms incidentally (just for their cultural value!):

"the word (definite article) *the*," etc.

Note that in the latter case the statement becomes an illustrative definition of the term *definite article*, without complicating the function of the explanation, which would be just as effective and clear without the grammatical labels in parentheses. This procedure has been followed successfully in several of the latest series of textbooks, to the satisfaction of both pupils and teachers alike, as measured by economy in learning and by outcomes in the way of ability to use the language.   The time and effort so often consumed in "explaining the meaning of the explanation"—in theorizing in English *about* the language—have been profitably allocated to more abundant and meaningful activity in the language itself.

The principle of reference to experience applies not only to the teaching of correct usage but also to such phases of language as pronunciation and vocabulary.   Students can often be made cognizant of subtle differences in pronunciation—especially of the vowels and consonants—by comparing the pronunciation of certain identical cognates in the foreign language and in the student's native tongue. For example, the teacher of French might say to the class, "I am going to pronounce our word *rose* to you in English, and the French word *rose*, in French.   Will you listen to any differences in the sound or pronunciation and tell me, if you can, just what causes the differences?"   Under the teacher's guidance the pupils are enabled to hear and see for themselves the difference in the formation of the *r*, and the absence of the diphthongal glide in the *o*—a characteristic of vowels in many foreign languages.

Although sensitivity to differences in sound is prerequisite to reproducing them correctly, the ability actually to do so requires practice, especially when the relative position of the lips, tongue, teeth, jaw, or soft palate is different from the position that these organs are habituated automatically to assume in the case of sounds which, to a novice in the foreign language, might seem to be identical with certain sounds in his native tongue.   Here experience is an unwelcome intruder.

If the difficulty with the pronunciation of the French *o* in *rose*, or of the vowels in general, is one of diphthongization, merely telling the students not to diphthongize, or to avoid changing the sound of the vowel, is not likely to yield effective results.   The concept is foreign to the learner's experience.   Where reference to experience is difficult or impossible, *direct* experience under guidance is the only alternative; but this guidance must be in terms that can easily be translated into action.   Thus, saying to the students "be sure to avoid moving the jaw, tongue, or lips while sounding the *o*, *e*, etc.," is often a more intelligible and effective way of preventing diphthongization than a verbal description of the nature of the sounds, or a discussion of the theory of diphthongs.   Since relatively few sounds in a foreign language have an exact equivalent in English, the principle of reference to experience in pronunciation is applicable chiefly in terms of contrast, *i.e.*, in terms of differences between the foreign sounds and their nearest approximations in the vernacular.[1]

In reading and vocabulary building, the principle of reference to experience plays a significant role. It is estimated that the average high-school student on beginning the study of Spanish can easily recognize the meaning of at least 750 words by virtue of their similarity to English cognates.[2] The proportion in the other Romance languages is probably not significantly different. This initial stock of cognate words provides an effective nucleus in terms of which the meanings of words that are not cognate can often be explained, suggested, or defined. Thus if the pupil has not previously made the acquaintance of the words *país* (country) or *mundo* (world), a sentence containing these words might well carry parenthetical cognates after them to suggest the meanings of the nouns:

El país (nación, república) más grande del mundo (globo) en área es _____.

Note that the cognate words are intended merely to suggest the meanings of the terms preceding them, not necessarily to define them or to provide synonyms. If this function of the parenthetical cognate is clearly understood by the student, the principle of reference to experience can often be applied effectively to facilitate the comprehension of reading matter, and of short talks by the instructor, without danger that the cognates will be mistaken for synonyms. Although every new word occurring in context cannot be treated in this manner, the possibilities are greater than generally supposed. A more effective use of this technique in beginning readers in the Romance languages would often make possible the use of more idiomatic vocabulary constructions at a relatively early level, and of more mature informational content, without the necessity of much vocabulary thumbing on the part of the student or frequent distractions of the mind from the thought expressed in the foreign language. At the intermediate level, the parenthetic use of noncognate words of high frequency which have already been assimilated into the pupils' passive vocabulary may be made to serve a similar purpose. Although it is undesirable to clutter printed matter with too many mechanical aids that distract

[1] Walter V. Kaulfers, "An Inductive Method of Teaching Pronunciation," *The Modern Language Journal*, Vol. XIII, No. 8, pp. 610–619, May, 1929. Walter V. Kaulfers and Dante P. Lembi, "An Inductive Approach to Italian Pronunciation," *Italica*, Vol. XVII, December, 1940, pp. 150–157.

[2] Minnie M. Miller and Geraldine Farr, "Student Recognition of Some Spanish-English Cognates," *The Modern Language Journal*, Vol. XXIV, pp. 216–220, December, 1939.

the eyes in reading, this procedure is probably preferable to diverting the eyes from the context entirely to the side or bottom of the page, or to the vocabulary at the end of the textbook.   The latter practice interrupts not only the normal movement of the eyes in reading, but also the train of thought itself.   Material that requires too frequent resort to this practice becomes in reality more an exercise in deciphering or decoding than anything that can properly be called reading.

The Principle of Insight.—The fact that the part can be understood and appreciated only in terms of its organic relationship to the whole has already been indicated on the preceding pages.   A person who, for some strange reason, has never seen an automobile or heard of one is not likely to be able to identify either by name or function any of the parts of the car, even were he to see them lying in neatly classified groups on the floor of a garage.   It is doubtful, too, if one or two years of practice in naming the various parts of a car, and in fitting them together according to the directions of a textbook on automechanics, would enable him subsequently to drive more efficiently or safely than a person who in the actual process of learning to drive had acquired, as he needed to use them, the names of such functional parts as are essential to handling an automobile effectively and economically.   Specialized training beyond this point might be useful, and even indispensable, to a garage mechanic or to an individual who is interested in supervising or making his own repairs; but it should be remembered that automobile mechanics do not always drive better than conscientious individuals with an equal amount of actual driving experience.

This illustration is not without implications for the teaching of a foreign language.   No amount of theorizing about the mechanical parts of a language and no amount of practice in fitting individual parts together according to rule will in themselves lead to proficiency in using a language as a means of communication in actual life situations, whether these be reading, writing, or speaking.   If such activity were effective in a truly functional sense, teachers who have majored in foreign languages in school, and have taught the language for ten to fifteen years by methods not unlike those indicated above, should be at least as fluent and proficient in the language, which they teach for five to six hours a day, as a native Frenchman, German, Spaniard, or Italian.   The fact is that those who use these methods are more likely to be deficient than proficient in actual ability to speak or write. Why?   Because neither their training nor their experience has afforded adequate practice in using the language as an organic whole.

From these observations the conclusion might easily be drawn
that accuracy and proficiency in a foreign language can be achieved
by using it as best one can, depending upon trial and error for guidance.
Obviously, this is not the case. The point is that individual parts
can be mastered, and yet little significance achieved in the way of a
ready command of the whole. It is also possible so to overemphasize
the part that its relative significance is distorted or the learner is
bewildered by a maze of details. What would be the value, for example, of a perfect pronunciation if the learner had no vocabulary with
which to say or understand anything? A mastery of all the individual
parts does not in any sense guarantee a mastery of the whole, for the
latter is always more than the sum total of its parts. Just as hydrogen
and oxygen, when variously combined into a unit, are no longer just
hydrogen and oxygen, but water, hydrogen peroxide, etc., so in language the thought group—usually a combination of two or more words
—often determines the meaning of the individual words of which it is
composed, and represents in itself a concept different from that contained in any one of the component parts. The words *out* and *look*,
for example, can be combined in different ways to yield concepts
quite different from those contained in these words individually:
outlook, look-out, look out!

Although the traditional grammatical approach in foreign-language
teaching has been greatly modified in recent years, the method still
has a strong foothold in many schools. A reorientation of the foreign-
language curriculum in keeping with the principles of modern psychology would involve the following changes in organization and
procedure:

1. Abundant opportunity, from the start, to hear and use the language as a vehicle for the communication of meaningful information
and ideas to an audience of one or more readers or listeners.

2. Opportunities to practice the language in meaningful context
in easy emulation of correct models or examples.

3. Supplementary explanations and exercises only when needed to
facilitate or fix elements of vocabulary, structure, or usage.

The need for these exercises can be determined in three ways: by
the difficulties which the pupils have in pronouncing or phrasing the
language, by the mistakes which they make, or by the questions which
the pupils themselves ask to clarify language problems in their own
minds. The sequence of this procedure is almost the opposite of the
traditional piecemeal approach to language, which begins with the part
(often with the individual letters of the alphabet), and gradually

proceeds to the synthesis of the parts into disconnected sentences, void of real thought content, or "reading lessons" written primarily to emphasize vocabulary or grammatical elements rather than to convey ideas or information worth reading, writing, or talking about.

In an increasing number of schools and colleges, the very first exposure of the beginning student to a modern language is in terms of an illustrated talk by the teacher, with the aid of a vocabulary of cognates written on the board, on such informational topics as *Les Contributions de la France aux sciences et aux inventions; Las contribuciones de España a la música: composiciones, formas y ritmos musicales, instrumentos, famosos músicos (artistas) etc.; Deutschland—Geographie und Klima.* Such talks are then followed by carefully constructed completion exercises, written and oral questions, and résumés in the foreign language stressing information of significance and interest in the talk. Special practice in pronunciation or language usage is introduced only as needed to facilitate the accurate use of the language. Pronunciation, vocabulary, grammar, and syntax are learned in terms of an informational topic and, although special practice on certain phases of the mechanics of the language is afforded from time to time, such isolated practice is introduced only *after* the pupil has seen the part in relation to the whole, and on the basis of need as revealed by the questions which the pupils themselves ask, or by their difficulties in pronunciation, word order, and the like.

The introduction of new topics in elaboration of some unifying theme serves to increase the pupils' vocabulary, provides automatically for the learning of new idioms and constructions, and enriches the program with cultural information of value in developing desirable attitudes, interests, and appreciations in daily life. The introduction of one or more readers as soon as the students have acquired a sufficient background in vocabulary, pronunciation, and the rudiments of word order to be able to read for content, serves to develop the language abilities still further in terms of materials having some bearing upon human behavior in the present and future.

The mechanics of this type of approach are discussed in greater detail in Chapter VII in connection with a sample unit based upon stenographic notes taken in a typical beginning class.

The Principle of Learning to Do by Doing.—Perfect practice makes perfect. The development of accuracy and proficiency in the functional use of a language in school is not unlike the development of ability to play a musical instrument. One can "pick up" a certain amount of ability to play a harmonica, guitar, or piano, just as one can "pick up" a language through informal association with people who use it.   In both cases, however, the proficiency developed depends upon the amount of opportunity to play the instrument or to use the language and upon the accuracy of the models that the learner has accepted as worthy of emulation.   If a person who has taken a fancy to playing the guitar as a kind of musical hobby is fortunate enough to be able to rely on the tactful and sympathetic advice of an expert guitar player, his progress will probably be more rapid, and his technical proficiency more professional, than if he had to rely purely upon observation or trial-and-error learning.   Similarly, the individual who "picks up" a language by association with friends or natives will progress in proportion to the amount of opportunity for practice, his own level of insight and desire to learn, and the adequacy of the guidance that he needs to reduce the waste involved in trial-and-error methods.   In both cases, however, although economy and accuracy in learning are achieved through effective guidance in emulation of correct models or examples, the skill itself is achieved only to the extent to which it is actually practiced or exercised—*i.e.*, we learn to do by doing.

Although practice makes perfect only to the extent to which it is perfect practice, foreign-language teaching is often severely unbalanced in the direction of preguidance for perfection, to the neglect of actual doing or practice.   So much time is often consumed in theoretical preguidance to prevent error or to achieve perfection the very first time, that the opportunity actually to use the language sufficiently to develop a command of it as a tool or skill in reading, writing, or speaking has been inadequate even for an understanding of the basic principles of language which such practice is intended to illustrate.   Reading a book on *How to Play the Guitar* or *How to Sing*, or *How to Play Tennis*—or even memorizing it—never has of itself developed an expert guitar player, an opera singer, or a tennis champion.   Similarly, memorizing the grammar of a language has never of itself developed ability actually to use the language as a functional medium of communication; for grammar is no more language than Spaulding's manual is tennis.

Overemphasis on theory at the expense of practice may even have the adverse psychological effect of making the learner self-conscious to the point where self-confidence is weakened.   This is not infrequently the case in foreign-language classes where emphasis on theory, form, and mechanics is so disproportionately stressed at the expense of practice that the learner becomes *self-conscious in language* rather than *language conscious.* It is possible, for example, so to envelop the learner at the start with rules and explanations for the pronunciation of every letter of the alphabet, that he is afraid to say anything for fear of violating some law or being corrected by the teacher every time he opens his mouth.   Overcorrection is a negative deterrent as regards both the building of confidence in language and the development of a feeling for language, or *Sprachgefühl.* It is symptomatic of a disproportionate emphasis on theory in relation to practice.   It is indicative also of a "perfection complex" on the part of the teacher—a failure to realize that no skill is ever learned without error, whether it be singing, dancing, tennis, or typewriting. The function of the teacher is not to assume perfection as a uniform standard, but so to adjust the content and activities of the learning program to the students' levels of insight that the possibilities for error will be reduced to a minimum.   Each error or mistake, if interpreted as a *difficulty to be overcome* rather than as a violation to be punished, can then form the basis for a positive attitude on the part of the pupil toward learning from his mistakes—as most intelligent people do—rather than of a negative attitude of dissatisfaction or discouragement.

Although only perfect practice makes perfect, perfection is more an ideal than a reality.   It is achieved only to the extent to which the learner has insight into what constitutes perfection and uses this ideal as a criterion for judging his own departures from it.   When these departures are accepted in his mind as difficulties to be overcome—as obstacles or handicaps to the attainment of a standard which he has accepted and is anxious to attain—then learning to do by doing is intelligent, purposeful learning, rather than blind trial-and-error activity.   In the case of pronunciation, insight into what constitutes a pronunciation worth attaining is not achieved merely by theorizing about the pronunciation of the language, however helpful occasional explanations may be, but by abundant opportunity to hear excellent pronunciation, and to reproduce it under intelligent guidance.   Unless the ear is first sensitized, the learner has no criterion in terms of which to judge his own efforts. Unless he knows how to form the sounds that cause difficulty, he is helpless to overcome his own deficiencies. It is in the latter connection that explanations, phonetic or physiological, may be exceedingly helpful; but the two most important factors in the learning process itself will always be the development, through abundant opportunity to hear the language, of a discriminating ear for its sounds or sound patterns, and ample opportunity to pronounce the language in emulation of desirable examples. In other words, the learning process starts with doing in emulation of concrete models; guidance in the way of explanations is offered only as needed to facilitate progress in the direction of a socially acceptable norm. This principle applies obviously to other phases of the language-learning processes besides pronunciation.

The Principle of the Transfer of Training.—The principle that practice makes perfect only to the extent to which it is perfect practice implies more than accuracy in the mechanics of form. It is possible to practice a skill perfectly in a technical sense, and yet in a way so different from that in which it is actually to be used or applied, that the transfer of training from one situation to another is imperfect. Tennis enthusiasts who are accustomed to playing on "fast" cement courts, for example, usually find that their game is handicapped when they change to lawn courts, for the rebound of the ball is slower and at a somewhat different angle, and speed in covering the court is likely to be more difficult to attain. The same situation holds for a great deal of conventional activity in foreign-language classes. Verbs are often practiced in isolation in vertical paradigms unknown in actual life; the vocabulary of the classroom and textbooks is different from that which the students are likely to encounter in normal language situations; and oral and written work is often in the form of insipid disconnected sentence exercises, rather than in the form of meaningful topics or subjects such as normally form the basis of reading, writing, or conversation in daily life. For these reasons, students who do superior work in mechanical translation exercises in class, or in answering questions posed by the instructor, often do badly when it comes to writing a letter of their own to some actual correspondent, or in phrasing original questions in the normal give and take of ordinary life situations. Their classroom experience has been too much of the proofreading or word-matching type, often in terms of linguistic exercises in which the mind-set is primarily on form and mechanics, rather than on the communication of information or ideas through any form of language that is appropriately effective at the time. Practice may be perfect in such cases, but the results are not always functional because the transfer of training is handicapped by marked differences between the learning situations and the circumstances in which the skill is to operate in actual application. Transfer is most likely to occur to the extent to which there is an identity or close similarity of component elements, or an ability on the part of the learner to generalize the application of what he learns. Moreover, transfer cannot be taken for granted, for the ability to see applications is limited by the student's level of insight, background of experience, or previous conditioning in this direction.

The Principle of Motivation.—It is not difficult to find examples in daily life of activities which to one person represent a pleasurable hobby and to another a boresome task. This fact is faced by every hostess on planning an evening of entertainment for her guests. The same situation is faced by every teacher in every school. It is this difference in attitude or mind-set which determines whether for any given person an activity is to be meaningful and stimulating, or dull and purposeless. In the case of a skill that takes a considerable period of time to acquire, the desire or will to learn is of immeasurable importance. Without such a desire, learning is ineffective.

The stimulation afforded by a genuine will to learn is an important aspect of motivation in education. An activity is likely to be interesting, in the psychological sense, if it ties in significantly with some meaningful experience or desire on the part of the learner. It is likely to be interesting also to the extent to which progress toward the realization of an aim, goal, or objective, which the learner has accepted as his own, is satisfying, i.e., if the learner feels that he is making progress in the direction in which he wants to go. The unusual, the exotic, the incongruous, or the humorous often make otherwise dull moments more "interesting" by appealing to momentary whimsies or fancies, or to a seemingly natural desire of the human mind to escape from reality at times; but such superficial "interests" cannot be counted upon to serve as more than temporary stimulants to attention, or "springboards" for the development of a more fundamental and enduring will to learn. The necessity for appealing too frequently to interest in the superficial sense of momentary whimsies, moods, or fancies is usually a sign that the learning program itself is lacking in content and objectives of basic significance to the student, or that the learning process is so badly adjusted to the pupil's level of insight as to be more discouraging than encouraging, more discomforting than satisfying. This is often the case in classes in which the content of the program is so sterile that it has to be sugar-coated or enlivened by extrinsic devices, such as parlor games, to prevent the students from becoming listless and bored.

Interest and motivation are especially important factors in any program that normally extends over a period of two or more years, and in which the elementary level is often foundational. There is little need to lay a foundation for anything unless in the process of so doing the pupils also develop a solid and enduring foundation in interest which will make them want to build something of significance upon the foundation that they had laid.   For what is the value of a foundation if in the process of building it the students lose all desire later to erect something of significance upon it?

Motivation through Vital Content.—The fact that the foreign languages have often been rated by a majority of students among the subjects most disliked in high school[1] would seem to indicate that the courses have not always capitalized interest effectively as a factor in motivating learning. The aims of the course of study—such as mental discipline and improvement of English grammar and vocabulary[2]—have often borne little relationship to the immediate objectives of the pupils in learning the language.   Sterile content in the form of insipid reading or composition exercises have dulled the desire to read, write, or speak.   Classics, far beyond the linguistic abilities of the students and remote in time and space from the vital concerns of young people today, have been "read" in advanced classes, and kindergarten stories, far below the maturity level of the pupils, have been read in elementary classes.   Language as communication to an actual speaker, reader, or audience has been lost sight of amid a disproportionate emphasis on form and mechanics to the neglect of meaning.   Inadequate opportunity for practice in applying the rules learned in the grammar book has often served more to encumber than to facilitate the learning process.   The more grammar the student learned, the more mistakes he seemed to make.   A feeling of satisfaction in making progress toward a well-defined goal has been wanting in many cases. In fact, the objectives of the course of study have often been so ultimate and remote that not only the students but also the teachers have at times lost sight of them in their constant preoccupation with laying a foundation which in theory would serve everyone, but in reality served no one in particular.   The result in too many instances has been an omnibus course consisting of a potpourri of grammar, a few dabs of so-called cultural material sandwiched in occasionally

---

[1] Adolph Klein, "Failure and Subjects Liked and Disliked," *High Points*, Vol. XXI, pp. 22–25, January, 1939.   See also the earlier studies by S. S. Colvin and Andrew H. McPhail, "Intelligence of Seniors in the High Schools of Massachusetts," *U. S. Bureau of Education Bulletin* 1924, No. 9, 39 pp.   William F. Book, *The Intelligence of High School Seniors as Revealed by a State-wide Mental Survey of Indiana High Schools*, The Macmillan Company, New York, 1922, 371 pp.; pp. 159–184.

[2] Emma Reinhardt, "A Study of Standards for Immediate or Classroom Objectives, Materials of Instruction, and Pupil Activities for Two Years of French," Unpublished doctor's dissertation, University of Illinois, 1927, 219 pp.

in English, plus a great deal of pin-wheel activity in the foreign language—all motion without direction. Those who survived this type of program were usually pupils with well-established work habits and speech habits before they enrolled in the courses. The 5 to 8 per cent who later continued in college in the language which they began in high school[1] usually did so to round out lower-division requirements, or to prepare to teach foreign languages in keeping with the established tradition.[2]

Some gratifying progress has been made in recent years in the publication of new type combination readers and grammars in which a more unified psychological balance between theory and practice has been attained; but the material in the way of reading lessons and exercises in and through which the pupil is to learn to read, write, or speak the language still frequently lacks content of real meaning for present-day life.   It is still too often material composed primarily to illustrate vocabulary or grammar rather than to convey information or ideas.   There is seldom more than one fact worth knowing on an entire page.   Interest in reading, or in using the language, is hardly motivated by sterile content.   In fact, if a reading lesson does not communicate something of significance or interest it is not likely to lead to increased skill in vocabulary or usage no matter how often the words are repeated in keeping with their merit rating in a scientifically derived frequency list.   Learning does not take place effectively when the mind is dulled by seemingly purposeless verbosity.   The more likely outcome is so thorough a distaste for reading at the elementary level that few young people, indeed, will be thrilled with the prospect of later devoting ten weeks to deciphering or decoding a "classic" which the author originally intended to be read in an armchair, or in bed, in three or four sittings.

The need for motiving and vitalizing the foreign-language program through worth-while content at all levels of instruction is still great. Such content need not, and should not be, material that caters merely to interest in the sense of superficial whims or fancies, but content that has some bearing upon the development of significant insights, atti-

[1] Vera Whittmann, "Are College Preparatory Foreign Languages Justified in Our Curriculum?" *The Modern Language Journal*, Vol. XXV, pp. 470–472, March, 1941.

[2] Coleman D. Frank, "Why Teach French?" *French Review*, Vol. I, pp. 41–52, November, 1927.   G. H. Betts and R. A. Kent, *Foreign Language Equipment of 2,325 Doctors of Philosophy*, Public School Publishing Company, Bloomington Ill., 1929, vi + 151 pp.   M. V. O'Shea, *The Reading of Modern Foreign Languages*, Department of the Interior Bulletin XVI, Washington, D. C., 1927, 78 pp.

tudes, interests, and appreciations in the present-day life of the individual and of the society in which he lives. Since every major foreign culture whose language is studied in school is not without its impress upon our history, population, music, literature, art, science, customs and mores, and commerce, the range of content from which to draw is almost infinite.[1] If this content is chosen in the light of well-defined social or cultural objectives, and organized in some form of unified scope and sequence, it can, over a period of two or three years, make a significant contribution to the basic purposes of American education. Both this opportunity and that of vitalizing the study of foreign languages are often lost at present through the uncritical choice of material primarily for its linguistic rather than for its thought content. The primary purpose of language is to communicate. When it ceases to do so, the study of its structure soon becomes a subject of interest only to a relatively few potential philologists, phoneticians, or grammarians.

Motivation through Audience Situations.—Language as communication, however, requires an exchange of ideas with an audience—a listener, a reader, a correspondent, or a group of listeners. Without an audience, communication is purposeless, and the study of language lacks the motivation characteristic of normal life situations.[2] Most students of foreign languages find themselves in the position of "reciting" for the teacher as critic (usually more concerned with *how* things are said than with *what* is said), or before a group of fellow students who serve as a board of critics, since most of them know the answers as well as the speaker himself. In such circumstances there is little incentive to volunteer information except to make a favorable impression in class. Building audience situations that serve as incentives to learn to read, write, or speak better is essential to effective motivation in any modern-language class. This is not an easy task, but much more can be done than is ordinarily attempted.

An audience situation is usually impossible if everyone in the class knows as much as, or more than, the speaker. Neither is normal communication possible if the subject is devoid of thought content. This means that if the class as a whole is to serve as an audience for a report or talk in a foreign language, the student who is speaking must first of all have something to offer that is not already known to the

[1] Walter V. Kaulfers and Holland D. Roberts, *A Cultural Basis for the Language Arts*, Stanford University Press, Stanford University, Calif., 1937, 115 pp.; pp. 1–16.

[2] Kantor, *op. cit.*, pp. 10–13.

group; secondly, his topic must be presented in language that the class can understand.   If the group, for example, has studied the geography, climate, population, history, or products of Mexico, different students may read and report in Spanish on the same topic as it applies to another Spanish-speaking country—Guatemala, Cuba, Bolivia, Chile, etc.—using as far as possible the same vocabulary as that with which the group became familiar in their study of Mexico.   Words that are likely to be unfamiliar to the class can be defined on the board in the order in which they are to be used during the course of the presentation. A model demonstration by the instructor is usually effective as a guide for students to follow in their own reports.   If each student reporting is responsible for the preparation of 10 completion type exercises in the foreign language, stressing the most important information in his talk, these can be administered to the class as an informal test, or form the basis for an informal review and discussion of the topic later. Reports of this kind have been carried out successfully even in first-semester classes, where the emphasis of the program was primarily on reading for content, and oral and written work centered around the content read.

Corresponding with young people abroad can, in normal times, provide an audience situation to motivate practice in composition, and if guided along profitable channels, can often become an effective means for making a personal acquaintance with the people whose language is being studied.   Wherever foreign correspondence has been made an integral part of the course, and utilized as a means for securing an interchange of ideas and information on topics of common interest, it has proved a highly successful and profitable activity.   Usually it is desirable for students to write to more than one correspondent in order to assure a steady exchange of letters.   If each student takes it upon himself to develop with his correspondent some phase of a topic in which the class as a whole is interested, the translation and discussion of the letters during periods set aside especially for this purpose will serve to extend interest in foreign-language study beyond the four walls of the classroom.   From time to time, some of the letters will be worth translating for use in other classes or for publication in translation in the school paper.   In some schools advanced foreign-language classes have served as translation bureaus in order that any student in the school (regardless of his knowledge of the foreign language) might correspond with young people abroad.   Recent developments in short-wave radio communication give promise of still another means for motivating the study of foreign languages by means of a direct exchange of ideas between classes located in different schools and communities of the United States or in neighboring countries.

Schools located in communities in which there are natives or naturalized Americans who speak the foreign language have an unusual opportunity for motivating the classwork by inviting residents of foreign birth or extraction into the class to answer, in the foreign language, questions previously prepared by the group. If the visitors are young people of approximately the same age as the students in the class, the atmosphere is likely to be more congenial and less formal than if the guests are college professors from some neighboring institution. In the case of first- and second-year classes the teacher or students from advanced classes can serve as interpreters when necessary. This type of class interview has proved more successful than organized talks by outsiders, which even advanced students have difficulty in following. Moreover, it provides for group participation in formulating and asking questions. If the interview is capitalized to throw light on some problem in which the group is interested, it can yield informational as well as linguistic outcomes.

A committee organization of the class, with chairmen to keep the group informed on new books in the library, operas, concerts, art exhibits, lectures, motion pictures, plays, open-forum discussions, important anniversaries, and radio programs relating directly or indirectly to the culture of the foreign country, often provides excellent opportunities for motivating the classwork not only with audience situations but also with content of timely significance. If volunteers can be encouraged to attend concerts, lectures, or plays by distinguished foreigners, the class can ask questions in the foreign language concerning the high lights of the performance. Activities of this kind have been tried out successfully in average public-school classes as early as the second semester and, in rapidly moving classes, as early as the twelfth week of beginning foreign-language work.

Where the school possesses facilities for projecting post cards, mounted pictures, or photographs on a screen, illustrated talks on places of scenic, historical, or cultural interest, prepared and presented by the students themselves, can be effectively capitalized to motivate reading, writing, and oral work in the foreign language. One second-semester class in high-school Spanish voted to divide itself into committees to present illustrated balopticon talks on the different Spanish-speaking countries through which the International Highway of the Pacific passes. The members of the committee on Mexico, for example, divided their report into precolonial Mexico, colonial Mexico,

Mexico in transition, and Mexico today.   Each member collected and mounted pictures obtained by writing to *cámaras de comercio*, automobile associations, consulates, travel bureaus, tourist agencies, and the Pan American Union, and by securing secondhand copies of *Travel*, *The National Geographic*, and other magazines.   Each picture was labeled with a descriptive subtitle in the foreign language.   During the course of the presentation to the class, the members of the committee commented briefly in Spanish on the meaning of each picture, from notes prepared in advance.   The comment on one picture of Chapultepec Castle, for example, ran as follows:

Aquí vemos el famoso Castillo de Chapultepec.   El castillo es la residencia oficial del presidente de México.   Aquí también vivieron el Emperador Maximiliano y la Emperatriz Carlota.

Since the class had already read in common several chapters of a textbook dealing with the geography and history of the Spanish American republics, the background of the group was usually sufficient for a comprehension of the main ideas contained in each report.   Every listener, however, had the privilege of raising his hand at the end of a particular comment if he had difficulty in understanding it, and to ask ¿Qué significa—? ¿Cómo se llama—? ¿Cuándo vivieron—? ¿Dónde está—? etc.

Obviously, activities of this kind require group planning in advance, common background reading by the class as a whole, supplementary differentiated reading by individual students or committees, the division and allocation of special responsibilities, foundation exercises in grammar and syntax, and even occasional workshop or laboratory sessions for the organization of illustrative materials.   The time thus consumed in preliminary work may range from one to ten class hours, but it is time spent with a purpose, and the work done in the way of background reading, grammar, or composition is not just an exercise in vocabulary thumbing, word matching, or pencil pushing.   The opportunities for developing desirable habits of accepting responsibility, cooperation, and ability to organize and present material are probably of greater educational significance than such "disciplines" as might accrue from an equal amount of time spent on memorizing, decoding, or deciphering nonfunctional content in a vacuum.   Among the most important outcomes are a more wholesome *esprit de corps*, a more genuine desire to learn and use the language better, and the acquisition of insights and appreciations of significance in out-of-school life.

Motivation through Vocational Interests.—Although the vocational aims of most junior- and senior-high-school students are not clearly enough defined, and too diverse and too remote in time and space, to form the basis for organizing a complete language program, such immediate opportunities to use the language as may present themselves in connection with out-of-school employment afford excellent opportunities for motivating foreign-language work with usable content.   If a student is assured of employment as a clerk in a store or post office, or as a steward or cabin boy aboard a ship, for example, a careful job analysis of his basic foreign-language needs will reveal that beyond the conventional expressions of courtesy, a specialized vocabulary of 100 to 150 words will usually suffice to cover 90 per cent of the cases in which he will have legitimate occupational use for the language; for it is hardly essential that a clerk, cabin boy, or waiter engage in eloquent conversational repartee with patrons.   The opportunity to make such job analyses and of acquiring a working knowledge of the basic vocabulary, idioms, and expressions needed in performing essential services is already provided in many evening-school classes for employed adults, and in some terminal junior-college classes.

Although the students should be made aware of the potential value of knowing a foreign language in almost any walk of life,[1] emphasis upon its vocational utility in securing or holding positions should be carefully tempered with the advice that the character, personality, professional training, and experience of the individual, apart from language, are of primary importance, for as the French put it: *On peut être fou en plusieurs langues* (One can be a fool in several languages). Full-time positions as interpreters or translators are, in normal times, relatively few in number, often require a ready command of several languages beyond the reach of most high-school and junior-college students, and are therefore usually filled by naturalized Americans who speak English and one or more foreign languages by virtue of extensive residence abroad.   Worst of all, such positions as a rule are badly underpaid.   The best that can be said of the vocational utility of foreign languages is that, *other things being equal*, a working knowledge of one or more foreign languages is a distinct asset in securing and filling such positions in library work, acting, singing, radio announcing, research, foreign commerce, international communica-

[1] William L. Schwartz, Lawrence A. Wilkins, and Arthur G. Bovée, "Vocational Opportunities for Students for Foreign Languages," *Modern Language Journal*, Vol. XVI, pp. 545–582, April, 1932.   Reprinted for general distribution in 1934.   Revised edition, 1941.

tion (train, steamship, airlines, telephonic and telegraph services), foreign news correspondence, diplomatic and consular services, and the like, as require ability to pronounce, read, write, speak, or translate a foreign tongue. Although some vocations in the foreign service require an expert command of a foreign language in reading, writing, and speaking, many occupations, such as radio announcing, require little more than a fair degree of ability in some limited phase of the language, *e.g.*, pronunciation or the ability to translate into English with the aid of a dictionary. It is, perhaps, the failure of the foreign-language program to meet the specific language interests of different students, and to differentiate the activities and content of the courses in terms of a job analysis of language needs in certain professional and semiprofessional types of work, which has led many foreign-language courses to lose the vitality that comes from capitalizing life-career motives.

The principles of reference to experience, insight, learning to do by doing, the transfer of training, and of motivation, which have just been discussed with occasional examples illustrative of their application to the educative process in foreign languages, constitute the psychological foundations upon which any successful learning program must be built.

Psychological Fallacies Inherent in Conventionalized Language Methodologies. The "Natural Method."[1]—In the past, the foreign-language curriculum has often been stampeded in the direction of a specific "method," often highly formalized and seldom based upon anything but psychological speculation. The notion that a foreign language should be learned the way children learn it—the "natural way"—is sound insofar as children learn to do by doing, in motivated life situations, but unsound in its neglect of the principles of reference to experience and transfer of training. The boy, girl, or adult who begins foreign-language study in school is hardly to be compared with a child learning to talk in the nursery, for habit patterns already established in the vernacular either handicap or facilitate the learning of a second language. If a foreign word looks like an English word whose meaning is already known, it is likely to be understood correctly, provided the two words happen to be exact cognates, and incorrectly

---

[1] For a historical survey of methodological systems see Charles H. Handschin, *Modern-language Teaching*, World Book Company, Yonkers-on-Hudson, New York, 1940, vi + 458 pp.; pp. 61–70. Peter Hagboldt, *The Teaching of German*, D. C. Heath and Company, Boston, 1940, ix + 306 pp.; pp. 3–27. Robert D. Cole and James B. Tharp, *Modern Foreign Languages and Their Teaching*, D. Appleton-Century Company, Inc., New York, 1937, xii + 640 pp.; pp. 1–19, 49–70.

if one of the two happens to be a deceptive cognate, *e.g.*, *dormitorio* (bedroom in Spanish, dormitory in English).   Similarly in pronunciation, speech patterns that have become automatic and more or less fixed in the vernacular tend to carry over unconsciously into the foreign language.   Since most foreign languages have an entirely different basis of articulation, this unconscious and inevitable transfer of training is usually more a hindrance than an aid, for exact equivalents in the vernacular and foreign language are difficult to find, and such important factors as liaison, synaloepha, inflection, and intonation are usually sufficiently different to require an almost complete reconditioning of the aural-oral mechanism.

The fact that the speech patterns of younger children are not so fixed as those of older children or adults probably accounts for the still popular illusion that early childhood is the best time to learn a foreign language.   The advantage is probably only on the aural-oral side. The ears of children are probably more sensitive to the sounds of a foreign language only because they do not so readily mistake closely related but different sounds as identical with sounds to which their minds have been tuned in the vernacular.   The aural-oral mechanism has not "set"; consequently, they are less burdened with the handicaps of an involuntary transfer of training.   Nevertheless, a wider background of experience in the vernacular serves the adult to greater advantage in discerning the meanings of many words that are cognates or near cognates in the foreign language.   Moreover, the level of insight of young children, owing to their relatively more limited background of experience, is ordinarily not so highly developed as that of adolescent boys and girls, or adults.   Maturity usually favors older children and grown people with greater ability to generalize.   This is a distinct advantage in the study of a foreign language in school where generalization is often necessary to short-cut the learning process as far as possible to compensate for the handicaps imposed by limitations of time and class size.   The "mother-tongue" fallacy inherent in the natural method makes it fall short as an approach to language at the adolescent or adult levels of schooling.   There is no reason why adults, given equal opportunities for instruction and practice, cannot learn a foreign language as easily and effectively as young children provided sound psychological principles are applied in terms adapted to their levels of insight.   A program of instruction suited to kindergarteners is no more appropriate for adults than a pair of diapers.[1]

[1] For experimental data on adult learning, see footnote references to problem 3 in Appendix A.

Limitations and Virtues of the Direct Method.—A similar miscarriage of methodology in foreign-language teaching can be found in the more absolute forms of the direct method in which direct reference to the vernacular is fanatically ruled out. Although this method provides for more adequate opportunities to hear the language, and thus contributes to the development of a certain measure of *Sprachgefühl*, this advantage is often offset by the circuitous route that teachers and students have to follow to gain an understanding of noncognate expressions (especially where these do not refer to objects or easily demonstrated movements) or of the basic principles governing such matters as tense, moods, agreement, and word order. Moreover, the devotees of the absolute direct method are doing hardly more than making subjective use of the student's background in the vernacular, without recognizing it objectively. Such a sentence as *Ein Fisch kann schwimmen*, for example, can be understood by most beginners on the very first day of German because of its cognate resemblances to English words. Elimination of direct reference to the vernacular is advisable and easy where the meaning is obvious anyway; but it tends to short-circuit the learning process in the case of noncognate situations in vocabulary and usage. Reference to the vernacular in cases of emergency is permitted by advocates of the "modified" direct method, but teachers who try to follow this middle-of-the-road course usually find the number of emergencies so great that they unconsciously become practitioners of the *eclectic* method—of selecting whatever teaching procedure or device seems best adapted to the achievement of a specific purpose.

The chief strength of the direct method is also its chief weakness. The paradox lies in its failure effectively to capitalize the principle of reference to experience, for previous conditioning in the vernacular can often serve to provide a valuable background in terms of which the unknown can be explained by way of comparison or contrast with the known. Moreover, any method, whether it be direct, natural, phonetic, oral, or eclectic can fall short of its goals and even defeat its own ends, if it fails to capitalize the basic principles that underlie the concepts of learning to do by doing, the transfer of training, and motivation.

Logical Organization on the Basis of How Young People Learn vs. Logical Organization within the Subject Itself.—Unfortunately for subject-minded specialists, learning is more psychological than logical. A functional command of language is not gained from practice in memorizing classified categories and fitting them together according to rule, irrespective of the learner's level of insight. A logical organiza-

tion of material within a unit is possible only to the extent to which
the part can be seen in relation to the whole. Since beginners are
hardly in a position to see part-whole relationships, any method that
depends primarily upon a logical organization and sequence of content
from the standpoint of the language itself, rather than from the standpoint of the learner's ability to perceive and understand functional
relationships, is likely to lead either to mental congestion or to a
parrot type of language learning that is as ephemeral as it is superficial.
Logical organization in a new field is meaningful to an individual only
to the extent to which he himself has participated in formulating it.
These principles of modern psychology suggest the advisability of
providing in order (1) abundant opportunity from the beginning to
hear the language in meaningful connected context, (2) adequate
opportunities to read, write, and pronounce the language in connection
with the development of an informational topic or subject, and (3)
occasional linguistic exercises as needed to clarify points of usage, or
to develop automatic control over such mechanical skills as pronunciation, tense formation, and agreement of adjectives.

The primary emphasis throughout is on hearing and using the language in actual communication, *i.e.*, in the sequential development of
some topic, subject or theme, such as *Les Contributions de la France à la
culture des États-Unis*. Objective exercises of the multiple-choice,
completion, or true-false correction type, and completion questions,
carefully constructed to reduce the possibility of making linguistic
errors, are used to provide opportunities for reading, writing, and
speaking the language from the very start. After a few weeks, semioriginal résumés and the like, written by the students from memory
in the foreign language as a summary of the cultural information contained in the unit, provide for the learning and fixation of vocabulary,
idioms, and examples of syntactical construction in connection with
content worth discussing. Note that language and culture are not
separated and that, although specialized practice in usage and mechanics is provided, the emphasis on this phase of language work is distinctly collateral, and exclusively in terms of demonstrated class
needs throughout the elementary and intermediate levels. In
advanced classes, the essentials of form and mechanics which have
been learned on the basis of need in the first two years may be logically
organized by the students themselves, under guidance, as a means for
reviewing and fixing these language concepts; or they may be grouped
according to categories on separate pages of a loose-leaf notebook as
they are developed through the course.

Although learning is psychological and thus requires sequential organization and presentation of content in conformity with the learners' levels of insight, rather than in terms of logical classifications within the subject itself, the learning process does not for this reason have to be disorganized, opportunistic, or illogical. Organization and presentation based on the psychology of learning can be just as logical and unified as organization based on the logic of formal grammar. The reason for the seeming impracticability of organizing elementary foreign-language programs on the basis of the psychology of learning is probably to be found in the fact that most elementary textbooks follow the logic of the subject almost exclusively. Vocabulary, idioms, and syntactical constructions, for example, are presented and emphasized in terms of their frequency of occurrence in frequency counts, and not primarily in terms of the most effective way in which to learn them, or their relative difficulty for students. It is not impossible to find many textbooks in which no more practice material is afforded on relatively difficult items of high frequency of occurrence in current usage than on relatively simple items of low frequency. Effective outcomes cannot be achieved efficiently in such circumstances without an undue amount of mental gymnastics on the part of both student and teacher. Since illustrations of recent attempts to develop more psychologically sound and functional language programs in American education are cited in Chapters VIII and XV, it will suffice here to review briefly the sociological and psychological conceptions underlying recent trends in foreign-language teaching,[1] before turning to a consideration of principles and procedures relating to the development of ability in pronunciation, grammar, reading, vocabulary, and conversation.

Summary.—1. Language, as a vehicle for the communication of feelings, wants, and ideas, is always a *means* and never the end, and should be taught from the point of view of facilitating the expression and comprehension of thought content in audience situations.

2. Primary emphasis on form and mechanics to the neglect of meaning leads to *self-consciousness* in language rather than to language

[1] Walter V. Kaulfers, "Foreign-language Outcomes of the Stanford Language Arts Investigation," *School and Society*, Vol. LII, pp. 235–237, Sept. 21, 1940. Examples of new type foreign-language programs are contained in *A Foreign Language Program for Progressive Schools*, Progressive Education Association, 221 West 57th St., New York, 1938, 86 pp. (mimeographed). See also *Proceedings of the Ohio Workshop on Modern Language Teaching*, Ohio Council on Modern Language Teaching, Ohio State University, Sept. 25, 1940, vi + 60 pp. (mimeographed).

consciousness, or *Sprachgefühl*. Grammar and special practice materials should thus be introduced only when they are absolutely needed to facilitate expression or comprehension in the light of some objective outside and beyond the practice materials themselves. This need can be determined in two ways: first, by the questions that the pupils themselves raise from their own attempts to read, write, or use the language; secondly, by their difficulties or by the mistakes that they themselves make. The latter provide the clues to types of special work needed to help the pupils use the language with confidence and accuracy.

3. To reduce the possible number of errors, the content and exercises should be carefully graded and as "error proof" as possible. Little reliance should be placed on ability to apply explanations involving grammatical terminology.

4. The content and activities in and through which the language abilities are to be developed should be chosen from the start with an eye to their effectiveness in creating worthy attitudes, interests, and appreciations. In other words, the ultimate cultural objectives of the course of study should serve as criteria for the choice of foreign-language content for reading, writing, or speaking from the first week to the last.

5. The best way in which to learn a language is to learn something of significance in and through the language—something beyond vocabulary or grammatical terminology. Knowledge of the grammatical terminology of a language probably has no more relationship to ability to use and understand it with ease or accuracy than ability to name all the intricate parts of an automobile, and to fit them together correctly, has to ability to drive a car efficiently and safely. We learn to do by doing under proper motivation and guidance.[1]

[1] For an overview of recent (1940–1941) research see James B. Tharp *et al.*, "Research and Methodology," *The Modern Language Journal*, Vol. XXV, pp. 717–727, October, 1941. Also "Annotated Bibliography of Modern Language Methodology," pp. 683–702. Walter V. Kaulfers *et al.*, "Along the Foreign-language Frontier," *Hispania*, Vol. XXIV, pp. 353–358, October, 1941.

CHAPTER II

PERSPECTIVE ON THE TEACHING OF PRONUNCIATION

The primary concern is not pronunciation, but something worth pronouncing.

Ability in Pronunciation as a Basic Skill.—A certain measure of facility and accuracy in the fundamentals of pronunciation is generally taken for granted as basically essential to the attainment of the linguistic or cultural objectives of foreign-language teaching. Even institutions that avowedly concentrate on the reading objective at the elementary and intermediate levels provide for a period of intensive preliminary training in pronunciation to facilitate subsequent work in intensive and extensive silent reading.[1] Although ability to pronounce the foreign language is ultimately essential to a satisfactory realization of the ability to read, write, or speak it, this fact does not necessarily mean that practice in pronunciation should be the exclusive concern of the teacher and student during the first few days of the beginning course. Indeed, until the beginner has had sufficient opportunity to *hear* the language correctly in meaningful context, it is doubtful if his ears will be a reliable guide in helping him to imitate or reproduce its sounds. Mental sound patterns already established in the vernacular tend unconsciously to color what one hears in a foreign language. Sounds that are superficially similar in the native and foreign languages are likely to be mistaken for identical sounds, and physical articulation patterns tend to carry over involuntarily in the pronunciation of such sounds as the *u* in French, or the *ü* and *ö* in German, unless proper guidance is given in listening as well as in producing the sounds correctly. The development of a "perfect" pronunciation—one indistinguishable from that of well-educated natives—involves in effect an almost complete reconditioning of the auditory and speech apparatus, for it requires the development to the point of automatization of new neurophysiological associations with respect to differences in bases of articulation, synaloepha, synaeresis, liaison, and intonation.

[1] Otto F. Bond *et. al.*, *French Syllabus*, 7th ed., University of Chicago Bookstore, 5802 Ellis Ave., Chicago, September, 1939, 67 pp.; pp. 8, 15–16.

Handicaps Imposed by the Involuntary Transfer of Training.—The tendency of speech patterns already well fixed in the vernacular to carry over involuntarily into the foreign language is easily observed in the case of identical cognates involving differences in accentuation. Even after having heard the correct Spanish pronunciation of such a cognate word as *doctor,* the beginning student will often persist in accenting the first syllable rather than the last, and pronounce the first *o* as in *hot.* The same unconscious transfer of training is observed in the almost universal tendency of English-speaking students to diphthongize the vowels in the Romance and Germanic languages, or to link intervocalic consonants with the wrong vowels. The most important initial task in the teaching of pronunciation is helping the student to hear correctly what is actually pronounced, and not to confuse what he *thinks* he hears with the actual sounds themselves.[1] This process of reconditioning the aural mechanism can be accomplished in a variety of ways. Comparing and contrasting the pronunciation of letters in certain identical cognates in English and the foreign language serve to emphasize differences that would be obscured if the foreign words chosen to illustrate the sounds were noncognate. The use of cognates makes possible a desirable capitalization of the principle of reference to experience, at the same time "nipping in the bud" the deterrent effects of an involuntary transfer of speech patterns from the native to the foreign language.

Reconditioning the Aural-oral Mechanism.—Suppose, for example, that the teacher wishes to forestall the tendency to diphthongize the closed vowels in French. She might say to the class, "Some words in French and English are very much alike in spelling, sound, and meaning, for both languages have borrowed words from Latin or other sources. I am going to dictate to you a few words which are spelled exactly alike in English and French. Number a separate sheet of paper, and opposite the proper numbers write the words as I pronounce

[1] This illusion has been repeatedly demonstrated by experimentation in psychological phonetics. In his monograph, *Englische Lautdauer: eine experimental-phonetische Untersuchung,* E. A. Meyer reports having recorded repetitions of the nonsensical combination *sórragis,* which he recorded phonographically, pronouncing the combination each time with the accent on the first syllable. On reversing the disk, he heard, not an accented *ó,* but an accented *a, i.e., sigarros,* instead of the *actual* inverted sound *sigarrós.* For this illusion, two factors—one physical, the other psychological—were responsible: the greater sonority of the *a* as compared with that of the *o,* and the fact that the sound combination, as played in reverse, suggested the familiar word *cigar.* See *Englische Lautdauer,* Upsala, Leipzig, 1903, pp. 51, 181, 228.

them in French.   You will usually be able to tell whether or not you understood the French word correctly, if what you write on your paper looks exactly like some English word.   For example, suppose I dictate the French word *rose;* what English word does it sound like?   Yes, *rose* and *rose* mean the same thing in French and English, and the two words are spelled in exactly the same way.   Do the words sound exactly alike too?   No, they do not.   In just what way does the French word *rose* sound different?   What do you suppose causes the differences in the sound of the *r* and of the *o* which you have just mentioned?"

By such inductive leading questions, capitalizing specific, concrete examples, the teacher can sensitize the minds and ears of the students to important differences in bases of articulation, tongue positions, and the like.   The inability of the class to explain exactly what causes specific differences in sound will provide opportunities for the teacher to explain the exact ways in which the sounds are produced.   For example:

"The difference between the French *o* in *rose* and the *o* in our English word is caused by making the sound without moving the tongue, lips, or jaw while pronouncing the letter.   Say *o* now, keeping the tongue, lips, and jaw absolutely still until you have cut off the breath . . . like this . . . (demonstrates).   Now pronounce the *o* in *rose* in exactly the same way, and for the time being pause briefly before adding the *z* (-se) . . . like this: *ro:'z* (writes the phonetic transcription of the word on the board).   The : means prolong the *o*-sound slightly; and the ' means pause for a split second.   Now let us all repeat the word three times in succession . . . very good.   Now perhaps you can see that the French *o* does not fade into an o͞o sound as in English.   All the vowels in French, as in most foreign languages, are pure vowels, without vanishing sounds.   Let us now pronounce the French vowels *a, é, i,* and *o,* without moving the tongue, lips, or jaw while sounding them."

With this preliminary explanation the teacher may proceed to the oral dictation exercises.   Sample units of these are reproduced below in French, German, Spanish, and Italian for use during the first two or three days of beginning work.   Each sample unit consists of aural true-false or completion exercises to be read to the class orally by the instructor.[1]   To these the pupils may respond with the foreign words

[1] Walter V. Kaulfers and Dorothy Sonzogno, "Aural Comprehension-exercises for Beginners in Italian," *Italica*, Vol. XVI, pp. 23–29, March, 1939.   Walter V. Kaulfers and Arabella J. Moore, "Aural Orientation Exercises for the First Week

for *yes* and *no* to indicate whether the statements are true or false, or with such answer-words as are needed to make the statements complete and true.   Since the primary purpose of the exercises is ear training, information that is not a part of the common knowledge of a large majority of the class is ruled out.   The procedure stresses the principle of "impression before expression" with a view to orienting the beginning students in the aural background of the language prior to oral recitation.   After such orientation, work in pronunciation can usually be undertaken with considerable economy in time and effort and with generally superior responses from the pupils because of the training in aural discrimination which they have received during the orientation period.   Unless the procedure is too highly formalized or too prolonged, it can serve as an interesting and painless initiation to foreign-language study, and secure the voluntary participation of almost every member in the group, even of those who otherwise would be lacking in self-confidence.   If it is desirable to organize the work in such a way that a written response may be obtained from each pupil as a matter of class record, the students can readily be directed to number a sheet of paper in columns, and to write their reactions (*yes* or *no* in the foreign tongue) opposite the numbers of the respective statements as they are read by the instructor.   The work of correction can then easily be done by the students themselves through the simple exchange and correction of papers.

It will be noted that if pronounced distinctly, every sentence, except possibly a few in the later sections, can be understood by a majority of beginning students after two or three repetitions.   Instead of reading the sentences slowly, the instructor should repeat them two or three times in succession, in the normal tempo of conversational speech, stressing the cognates.   This suggestion is important for two reasons: first, because it focuses the attention of the students on the meaning of the sentence as a whole, thus preventing the class from getting lost among the words; and secondly, because it avoids the danger of so habituating the ears of the students to a slow classroom style of articulation that they are bewildered when confronted by the normal tempo of speech in daily life with its many liaisons, vowel groupings, and varieties of intonation.   In general, no more than

---

of German," *The German Quarterly*, Vol. XIII, pp. 1–6, January, 1940.   Walter V. Kaulfers and Isabel M. Arata, "Aural Comprehension Exercises for Beginners in French," *The French Review*, Vol. XI, pp. 378–384, March, 1938.   Walter V. Kaulfers, "Launching the Beginning Foreign Language Class," *Modern Language Forum*, Vol. XV, pp. 128–132, October, 1930.

twenty minutes should be devoted to this type of activity at any one sitting—not just to avoid boredom and fatigue, but to allow time for the formation of new neurophysiological association patterns. The principle of spaced learning is important here.

AURAL COMPREHENSION EXERCISES FOR BEGINNERS IN ITALIAN

FORM I. TRUE-FALSE

NOTE: Statements to be made orally. Comprehension can often be facilitated by means of gesticular suggestions.

Directions: Reply to the following statements with *Sì* if they are *true*, and with *No* if they are *false*.*

A

1. La tigre è un animale.
2. Roosevelt è il presidente degli Stati Uniti d'America.
3. Il football è uno sport.
4. Lincoln fu assassinato.
5. Joe Louis è un artista italiano.
6. Chicago è in Italia.
7. La rosa è un errore.
8. L'oceano Pacifico è in Francia.
9. Greta Garbo è un'attrice famosa.
10. Longfellow è un gran poeta italiano.

B

1. La banana è una frutta.
2. Hitler è il duce d'Italia.
3. La Francia è in Europa.
4. Il violino è un metallo.
5. Il Generale Pershing è un esploratore.
6. La Statua della Libertà è a New York.
7. Madrid è in California.
8. Roma è la capitale d'Italia.
9. Shakespeare è l'autore di "Gone with the Wind."
10. "Rigoletto" è un'opera.

C

1. Eddie Cantor è un professore.
2. Sacramento è il centro d'America.
3. Marconi inventò il telegrafo.
4. Jeannette MacDonald è un'attrice.

---

* To rule out the factor of chance guesses, the papers may be scored by subtracting the number wrong from the number right. See C. M. Ruch, *The Objective or New Type Examination*, Scott, Foresman and Company, Chicago, 1929, 478 pp.; p. 185.

5. Il fonografo è una medicina.
6. Grace Moore è una soprano.
7. L'Italia è un continente.
8. Hollywood produce cinematografi.
9. L'Austria è una parte della Germania.
10. Mussolini è un patriota italiano.

D

1. Cristoforo Colombo è francese.
2. Leonardo da Vinci è un medico.
3. Marco Polo inventò gli spaghetti.
4. Il dentista è un medico.
5. Genova è un porto.
6. Il Canadà è una parte dell' America.
7. Il telegrafo è un modo di communicazione.
8. L'America del Nord è immensa.
9. Shakespeare è un autore inglese
10. L'Africa è un continente.

Form II. Dictation

A

Directions: The following words are spelled exactly alike in Italian and English. Number a separate sheet of paper, and opposite the proper numbers write the word dictated.   *Il, la, lo,* and *l'* (the article) mean "the."   If what you write does not look like some English word, you will know that you have made a mistake.

1. l'arena
2. l'aroma
3. la soprano
4. il piano
5. l'idea
6. la banana
7. il casino
8. la villa
9. la radio
10. il diploma
11. lo zero
12. il gas
13. la zebra
14. il boa
15. lo sport
16. l'opera
17. la gardenia
18. la mamma
19. la saliva
20. America

B

The following words are spelled exactly the same in Italian as in English, except that in Italian an *a, e,* or *o* is added at the end.

Examples:		
music	>	musica
animal	>	animale
monument	>	monumento

(a)

1. il presidente
2. l'arte

(b)

1. l'angelo
2. il despotismo

3. l'errore
4. il canale
5. il cannibale
6. l'oratore
7. l'alligatore
8. il continente
9. la confusione
10. l'altare
11. la questione
12. lo splendore
13. il professore
14. lo studente
15. la regione

3. il fragmento
4. l'armamento
5. il monumento
6. il verbo
7. l'alieno
8. il realismo
9. il documento
10. l'organismo
11. il dollaro
12. il resto
13. il socialismo
14. il porto
15. il violino

(c)

1. la persona
2. il dentista
3. l'artista
4. la logica
5. il poema
6. la forma
7. la tomba
8. il poeta
9. il pessimista
10. la visita
11. la tonica
12. il patriota
13. il socialista
14. la massa
15. la palma

(d)

1. silente
2. stupido
3. fertile
4. federale
5. locale
6. animale
7. inferiore
8. intelligente
9. superiore
10. interiore
11. manuale
12. differente
13. centrale
14. musicale
15. elegante

C

Directions: Number a separate sheet of paper, and opposite the proper numbers answer the questions which I shall dictate in Italian. Choose your answers from the list at the right. *Chi* means *who, Che* means *what, Dov'è* means *where is,* and *Qual'è* means *which is.*

1. Chi è Mussolini?
2. Dov'è San Francisco?
3. Dov'è Hitler?
4. Che è la tigre?
5. Che è la Francia?
6. Chi è un esploratore famoso?
7. Chi inventò il telegrafo?
8. Chi è Roosevelt?
9. Chi è il duce d'Italia?
10. Dov'è Stanford?
11. Dov'è la Statua della Libertà?
12. Chi è un autore famoso?
13. Chi è un autore inglese?

a. a New York
b. il presidente
c. Eddie Cantor
d. il duce
e. Marconi
f. nella Germania
g. Giorgio Washington
h. a Palo Alto
i. in California
j. un animale
k. Mussolini
l. Byrd
m. una nazione

14. Qual'è la capitale degli Stati Uniti?
15. Chi è il patriota Americano?

n. Shakespeare
o. Washington
p. Jeannette MacDonald

D. *Comprehension—Oral or Written**

Directions: Number a separate sheet of paper, and opposite the proper number answer the questions which I shall dictate in Italian, selecting only answers from the column to the right. There are more answers than you can use.

1. Chi è il duce d'Italia?
2. Chi participa negli sports?
3. Chi comincia il concerto?
4. Chi parla italiano?
5. Qual' è un'automobile?
6. Che nazione è nell'Oriente?
7. Chi è l'autore di "Giulio Cesare"?
8. Che animale è feroce?
9. Che inventò Marconi?
10. Chi è un generale?
11. Quale nazione è fascista?
12. Qual'è un monumento?
13. Qual'è una scienza?
14. Qual'è una repubblica?
15. Qual'è una danza?

a. il minuetto
b. l'Italiano
c. Pershing
d. la radio
e. a Palo Alto
f. il musicista
g. l'atleta
h. Roosevelt
i. Mussolini
j. il Ford
k. Michelangelo
l. la Cina
m. Shakespeare
n. il leone
o. il Messico
p. la zoologia
q. nella California
r. l'Italia
s. la Statua della Libertà

OBSERVATION QUESTIONS: SUMMARY OF UNIT

1. Which of the words in the foregoing exercises have we borrowed from the Italian?
2. Which words are spelled *exactly alike* in English and Italian?
3. Mention any other words that have come to us from or by way of the Italian.
4. Why do so many words resemble each other in English and Italian? Is it because the Italians have borrowed many English words from us? Because we have borrowed many words from the Italians? Because both the English-speaking people and the Italians have borrowed words from some third language?
5. Are there any people with Italian names in your class, school, or community? Can you guess what some of the names mean?
6. Mention any words for Italian foods, such as pastes and vegetables, that we have adopted in the United States.

* If the exercises are conducted orally, the columns of answers may be written on the board in advance.

A LINGUISTIC ORIENTATION EXERCISE FOR BEGINNERS IN GERMAN

FORM I.   TRUE-FALSE*

NOTE: Statements to be made orally.   Comprehension can often be facilitated by means of gesticular suggestions.

Directions: Reply to the following statements with *Ja* if they are *true*, and with *Nein* if they are *false*.

A

1. Der Präsident von Mexiko ist Roosevelt.
2. Chicago ist in Florida.
3. Gold ist ein Metall.
4. Der Prinz ist ein Schuh.
5. Kalifornien ist ein Staat in Nordamerika.
6. Ein Nest ist ein Boot.
7. Afrika ist ein Kontinent.
8. Der Eisberg ist ein Busch.
9. Ein Bär kann schwimmen.
10. Die Rose ist eine Blume.

B

1. Ein Fisch kann singen.
2. Eis ist warm.
3. Der Professor ist ein Krokodil.
4. Das Gras ist grün.
5. Der Vater ist ein Mann.
6. Das Haus ist ein Park.
7. Kristopher Kolumbus war ein Mann.
8. Greta Garbo ist eine Maus.
9. Eiswasser ist kalt.
10. Kolumbus war in Genua geboren.

C

1. Der Nordwind ist kalt.
2. Das Saxophon ist ein Sofa.
3. Die Henne gibt Butter.
4. Ein Ring ist rund.
5. Der Mississippi ist ein Mann.
6. Das Horn ist eine Maschine.
7. Ein Ball ist rund.
8. Die Sonne ist warm.
9. Edison ist (war) Präsident.
10. Der Eisbär ist grün.

* To rule out the factor of chance guesses, the papers may be scored by subtracting the number wrong from the number right.   See Ruch, *op. cit.*, p. 185.

D

1. Bittere Medizin ist gut zu trinken.
2. Mexiko ist in Europa.
3. Das Papier ist grün.   (Hold up a piece of paper.)
4. Der Mississippi ist in England.
5. Der Ochs gibt Butter und Milch.
6. Das Konzert macht Musik.
7. Braunes Haar ist grün.
8. Kaffee ist gut zu trinken.
9. Der Wolf ist ein Instrument.
10. Im Sommer ist es kalt in Florida.

E

1. Eine rote Blume ist grün.
2. Ein Boot kann auf Land sinken.
3. Der Hammer ist ein Land.
4. Die Hand hat sechs Finger.
5. Tee ist gut zu trinken.
6. Der Elefant hat eine lange Nase.
7. Winter bringt Eis und Schnee in Alaska.
8. Die Deutschen trinken Bier und Wein.
9. Das Herz und die Nase sind im Arm.
10. Der Student studiert in der Schule.

Form II.   Completion

Directions: Number a separate sheet of paper, and opposite the proper numbers answer the questions which I shall dictate in German.   Choose your answers from the list of words at the right (on the board).*

1. Was ist gut zu trinken?	*a.* das Gras
2. Was ist grün?	*b.* ein Mann
3. Was schwimmt im Wasser?	*c.* braun
4. Was ist der Vater?	*d.* der Tee
5. Was ist ein Automobil?	*e.* eine Maschine
6. Was ist das Saxophon?	*f.* der Fisch
7. Was macht das Konzert?	*g.* ein Instrument
8. Was ist eine Rose?	*h.* Musik
9. Was hat der Elefant?	*i.* eine Blume
10. Was ist Afrika?	*j.* Bier
11. Was trinken die Deutschen?	*k.* eine lange Nase
12. Was ist kalt?	*l.* Schnee
13. Was bringt der Winter?	*m.* Eiswasser
14. Wie ist oft das Haar?	*n.* in der Schule
15. Wo studiert der Student?	*o.* ein Kontinent

Form III.   Dictation

Directions: The following list of words are spelled *exactly* like the English.   *Der,* *die,* and *das* (the article) mean *the.*   All names of things (nouns) will be written

* A review of the pronunciation of the list should precede the exercise.

with a capital letter. Number a separate sheet of paper, and opposite the proper numbers write the words dictated, spelling them with capitals except after number 32.

1. die Rose	15. der Hunger	27. der Wolf
2. der Hammer	16. die Minute	28. das Instrument
3. das Horn	17. der Name	29. der Frost
4. der Arm	18. das Nest	30. die Dame
5. der Ball	19. der Park	31. das Museum
6. die Butter	20. der Plan	32. das Echo
7. die Hand	21. der Ring	33. oft
8. das Land	22. der Sack	34. mild
9. der Student	23. der Sand	35. wild
10. der Humor	24. der Strand	36. warm
11. das Deck	25. der Wind	37. blond
12. der Fall	26. der Winter	38. still
13. der Finger		39. so
14. das Gold		40. blind

OBSERVATION QUESTIONS: SUMMARY OF UNIT

1. Why is it that so many words are spelled so nearly alike in English and German? Did we borrow these words from the Germans? Did the Germans borrow them from us? Did both the Germans and the English (or Americans) borrow them from some third language?

2. From your knowledge of history, can you tell *when* or *why* this borrowing took place?

3. Mention any other words that have come to us from, or by way of, the German.

4. Do you know any local family names that look or sound as if they might be German? How many can you find right in your own class or school? In your own community? Can you guess what some of the names mean?

A LINGUISTIC ORIENTATION EXERCISE FOR BEGINNERS IN FRENCH

Form I. True-False

Note: Statements to be made orally. Comprehension can often be facilitated by means of gesticular suggestions.

Directions: Reply to the following statements with *Oui* if they are *true*, and with *Non* if they are *false*.

A

1. Le tigre est un animal.
2. Le football est un sport.
3. Roosevelt est président.
4. Lincoln fut assassiné.
5. Joe Louis est un artiste français.
6. Chicago est en Italie.
7. Le zinc est un métal.

8. Le Ford est un automobile.
9. L'Océan Pacifique est en Californie.
10. Greta Garbo est une actrice célèbre.

B

1. L'orange est un fruit.
2. Hitler est le dictateur en Italie.
3. La France est en Europe.
4. La rose est une fleur.
5. L'Amiral Byrd est un fameux explorateur.
6. La statue de la Liberté est à New-York.
7. Madrid est en France.
8. Mme. Osa Johnson va dans la jungle pour ses bêtes.
9. Victor Hugo est l'auteur de "Roméo et Juliette."
10. Le train est une cage.

C

1. Groucho Marx est professeur.
2. Sacramento est la capitale de l'Amérique.
3. Les Français adorent Jeanne d'Arc.
4. La machine est utile.
5. L'Afrique est un continent.
6. Le lion est cruel.
7. Le Mexique est un fruit.
8. Le musicien commence le concert.
9. Les Français admirent les films américains.
10. Stanford est une université en France.

D

1. Les enfants Dionne—Marie, Annette, Émilie, Cécile, Yvonne—habitent le Canada.
2. Einstein est une grammaire.
3. Le vase est fragile.
4. Le Général Pershing est mexicain.
5. Lindbergh est allé par aéroplane de New-York à Paris.
6. Mussolini est une cigarette.
7. Le violon est un instrument.
8. Le vice est un crime.
9. En route un accident est arrivé à Mme. Earhart.
10. New-York est un grand port.

Form II. Dictation

Directions: The following words are spelled *exactly like* the English. *Le, la* and *l'* (the article) mean *the*. Number a separate sheet of paper, and opposite the proper numbers write the words dictated.

(a)

1. la rose
2. la page
3. la cigarette
4. la date
5. la cage
6. la minute
7. la dame
8. la fortune
9. la machine
10. la solitude
11. la route
12. la statue
13. la nation
14. la cause
15. la table

(c)

1. le courage
2. le prison
3. le camp
4. le compliment
5. le boulevard
6. le vase
7. le continent
8. le sport
9. le monument
10. le port
11. le champion
12. le crime
13. le fruit
14. le train
15. le concert

(b)

1. l'avenue
2. l'importance
3. l'accident
4. l'ambition
5. l'automobile
6. l'accent
7. l'air
8. l'altitude
9. l'encouragement
10. l'importation
11. l'action
12. l'orange
13. l'animal
14. l'impatience
15. l'engagement

(d)

1. horrible
2. long
3. fragile
4. intelligent
5. rare
6. terrible
7. excellent
8. certain
9. absent
10. central
11. adorable
12. brave
13. impossible
14. cruel
15. distinct

FORM III. WRITTEN*

Directions: Number a separate sheet of paper, and opposite the proper numbers answer the questions which I shall dictate in French.   Choose your answers from the list of words at the right.   "Qui" means *who*, "Qu'est-ce qui" and "Quel" mean *what*, and "Où" means *where*.

1. Qui regarde la grammaire?
2. Qu'est-ce qui est utile?
3. Qui commence le concert?
4. Où est la France?

a. à New-York
b. président
c. Shakespeare
d. dictateur

* The pupils should be directed to choose the answers from the column to the right, which may be written on the board.   In this case, the answers will consist only of the responses given in the list.   The subsequent repetition of the exercise in written form may serve as a reading preparatory exercise to weld the aural images to their graphic symbols.

5. Qui parle français?	e. le musicien
6. Qui participe aux sports?	f. le professeur
7. Quel animal est cruel?	g. en Californie
8. Qui est Roosevelt?	h. le lion
9. Qui est dans la jungle?	i. la machine
10. Qui est Mussolini?	j. Tilden
11. Où est le statue de la Liberté?	k. l'explorateur
12. Où est Sacramento?	l. le soldat
13. Qui est dans le camp?	m. en Europe
14. Qui est champion de tennis?	n. le Français
15. Qui est l'auteur de "Roméo et Juliette"?	o. les athlètes

FORM IV. MATCHING—ORAL AND WRITTEN

Directions: Number a separate sheet of paper and opposite the proper numbers, write the following sentences in full in French, from dictation substituting for the X whatever information, as found in the column to the right, is needed to make the sentences complete and true.

1. La machine est X.	1. utile
2. La statue de la Liberté à New-York est X.	2. crime
3. Admiral Byrd est un fameux X.	3. courage
4. Sacramento est la X de la Californie.	4. université
5. L'animal est dans la X.	5. adorable
6. Mme. Johnson va dans la X pour ses bêtes.	6. métal
7. Les X adorent Jeanne d'Arc.	7. animal
8. Les athlètes participent aux X.	8. longue
9. L'avenue est X.	9. explorateur
10. Les Américains admirent le X de MacArthur.	10. fameuse
11. L'éléphant est un X.	11. capitale
12. Le zinc est un X.	12. cage
13. Le vice est un X.	13. sports
14. Shirley Temple est X.	14. Français
15. Stanford est une X en Californie.	15. jungle

The list of answer-words may be written on the board. In any case, a review of the pronunciation of the words should precede the exercise.

FORM V. COMPREHENSION—ORAL OR WRITTEN

Directions: Number a separate sheet of paper, and opposite the proper number answer the questions below in complete sentences in French. For example: *Qui est président? Roosevelt est président.* Use only words that are spelled exactly alike in French and English. (To the right is a column of suggested words that may be written on the board.)

	Suggested List
1. Qui est président?	1. le tennis
2. Quel animal est cruel?	2. l'orange
3. Qui est le dictateur en Italie?	3. Mussolini
4. Qui est l'auteur de "Roméo et Juliette"?	4. le concert
5. Qui est intelligent?	5. Roosevelt

6. Quel fruit est sur la table?
7. Qu'est-ce qui est long?
8. Quelle fleur est dans le vase?
9. Quel automobile est populaire?
10. Quel est le sport du champion Tilden?
11. Qui est adorable?
12. Qu'est-ce qui commence?
13. Quelle nation participe aux sports?
14. Qu'est-ce qui est horrible?
15. Qu'est-ce qui est dans une cage?

6. Einstein
7. le lion
8. Shakespeare
9. l'animal
10. Shirley Temple
11. le train
12. le Ford
13. la prison
14. la France
15. la rose

OBSERVATION QUESTIONS: SUMMARY OF UNIT

1. Why is it that so many words are spelled so nearly alike in English and French? Did we borrow these words from the French? Did the French borrow them from us? Did both the French and the English (or Americans) borrow them from some third language?

2. From your knowledge of history, can you tell *when* or *why* this borrowing took place?

3. Mention any other words that have come to us from, or by way of, the French.

4. Do you know any local family names that look or sound as if they might be French? How many can you find right in your own class or school? In your own community? Can you guess what some of the names mean?

AURAL COMPREHENSION EXERCISES FOR BEGINNERS IN SPANISH

PART I. TRUE-FALSE

Directions: Reply to the statements (which I shall read in Spanish) with *Sí, señorita*, if they are *true* and with *No, señorita*, if they are *false*.

A

1. Clark Gable inventó el automóvil.
2. México es una monarquía.
3. Octubre es un animal.
4. La perla es una fruta.
5. El mosquito es una rosa.
6. El tigre es un insecto.
7. Lindbergh es presidente.
8. La gasolina es sólida.
9. Bob Jones es un piano.
10. Roosevelt es gobernador de Colorado.

B

1. El presidente del Canadá es Roosevelt.
2. La capital de Colorado es Denver.
3. Ford inventó el radio.
4. El teléfono es de adobe.

5. El cigarro es de gasolina.
6. La violeta y la rosa son flores.
7. Asia es un animal.
8. Lincoln fué un héroe.
9. El té es una fruta.
10. El elefante es un animal.

C

1. El tomate es un drama.
2. China es parte de América.
3. El coyote es un animal doméstico
4. El tabaco es una planta.
5. Asia es parte de África.
6. Henry Ford es un indio.
7. El chocolate es un líquido.
8. Lindbergh es un aviador.
9. Europa es un continente.
10. El duque de Windsor es un burro.

D

1. El metal es líquido.
2. Se cultiva el té en China.
3. El coyote es un animal feroz.
4. Rómeo y Julieta son montañas.
5. Hay plantas en el parque.
6. El profesor de la clase es John Brown.
7. Hollywood está en California.
8. "Gone with the Wind" es una novela popular.
9. Chicago es una planta.
10. Jeannette MacDonald inventó el piano.

E

1. El Japón es parte de América.
2. Un famoso actor es Robert Taylor.
3. La capital de los Estados Unidos es San Francisco.
4. El automóvil más popular es el Ford.
5. El teléfono y el telegrama se usan para la comunicación.
6. El cigarro es producto del tabaco.
7. Asia es un animal.
8. El río Misisipí pasa por la parte central de Norte América.
9. Lincoln fué asesinado.
10. El campeón de golf es William Powell.

PART II. DICTATION

A

Directions: The following words are spelled exactly alike in English and Spanish. *El* and *la* (the articles) mean *the*. Number a separate sheet of paper in a column to the left, and opposite the proper numbers write the following words from dictation.

1. el actor
2. el adobe
3. el alcohol
4. el favor
5. el animal
6. la capital
7. el gas
8. el color
9. el manual
10. el motor
11. el plan
12. el radio
13. el rival
14. el social
15. el conductor
16. el diploma
17. el drama
18. el final
19. el coyote
20. el humor
21. el horror
22. el interior
23. el material
24. el negro
25. el rodeo
26. el chocolate
27. el doctor
28. el portal
29. el altar
30. la fiesta
31. la idea
32. el ideal
33. el hotel
34. el aroma
35. el metal
36. la labor
37. el cable
38. el terror
39. el cristal
40. el tutor

B

The following words all end in -ión (with an accent over the ó): ·

1. la religión
2. la opinión
3. la decisión
4. la invasión
5. la diversión
6. la unión
7. la división
8. la extensión

C

The following words are spelled with a single s instead of with a double s (ss):

1. el profesor
2. posible
3. imposible
4. el confesor
5. colosal
6. el posesor

D

Directions: The following words have accent marks, otherwise they are spelled exactly as in English. Write the accent mark (') over the letter (a, e, i, o, u) which you hear emphasized or stressed most strongly when the words are pronounced.

1. el cónsul
2. amén
3. el mormón
4. el salmón
5. el sermón
6. el sofá
7. la península
8. el cráter
9. la ópera
10. el menú
11. el álamo
12. México

Uses and Abuses of Phonetics.—After the ears of the students have become sensitized to the general sound patterns of the language, and a certain amount of *esprit de corps*, devoid of tension or self-consciousness, has been developed in the class, the students are ready to begin the development of independent ability in pronunciation—to the extent, at least, of being able to pronounce all but exceptional words at sight without the constant prompting of the teacher or of the phonetic symbol. Those who have worked with the phonetic method are aware that this ability is not necessarily developed through work with phonetic symbols or transcription exercises per se; for in itself no phonetic symbol is, for a beginner, anything more than a peculiar form of letter—sometimes more misleading than helpful. The phonetic symbol x, for example, tells the beginning high-school or college student nothing about the sound for which it stands, nor how to produce it. He is, indeed, likely to confuse the symbol with the alphabetical x: Whatever sound he associates with a symbol such as ϕ, œ, $\int$, θ, etc., will have to be learned either from a descriptive explanation of it in a textbook, or from the teacher. No matter how detailed and scientifically accurate the explanation in physiological and acoustic terms, the way the student *thinks* it sounds when he hears it pronounced by the teacher is destined ultimately to determine the way he will pronounce it himself. That is why even graduate students in French (after having completed specialized courses in French pronunciation and phonetics) will in their practice teaching at times pronounce the word *plume* in such a way as to astonish both their class and supervising teacher: *i.e.*, *plum* instead of *plym*—even though they have no difficulty in writing the word in phonetic script!

Again, it is quite possible for a student to learn to pronounce acceptably any phonetically transcribed word without gaining much in the way of independent ability to pronounce a new term, however, true to phonetic law, when presented in ordinary script. Although phonetic symbols often facilitate the learning of pronunciation for *those who already know them*, they do not necessarily simplify pronunciation in the case of pupils who do not. Even after the beginner has learned to pronounce the *o* and *ɔ* correctly, he is still dependent upon some kind of rule or explanation if he is to know whether the *o* in *rose*, etc., should be pronounced *o* or *ɔ*. These limitations of phonetic script account for the extensive rules given in many texts for the occurrence of these sounds in ordinary print.

The chief difficulty inherent in the use of phonetic symbols with beginners who do not already know them lies in their tendency more often to encumber the learning process with an extraneous script than to simplify pronunciation. To teach a foreign language in terms of symbols that to the student are as foreign as the language itself, and later to describe the language in terms of a grammatical nomenclature equally foreign to most adolescents, is to frustrate the beginner with extraneous mechanics to such an extent that he may not only lose sight of the language itself, but give up hope of ever learning to use it. So much time can be consumed in explaining the meaning of symbols or explanations, that abundant practice, under guidance, in emulation of correct models, without any explanations at all, would probably yield more functional results with less mental fatigue. The validity of any method or device is its effectiveness in achieving results with a minimum expenditure of time and energy, and its psychological effect upon the student: Does it actually facilitate or complicate matters in *his mind?* It is possible so to overburden work in pronunciation at the start with rules, extraneous symbolism, and overcorrection that the psychological effect becomes one of apathetic resignation, self-consciousness, or complete frustration, rather than a constructive sense of progress toward a satisfying goal. The apathy often manifested by unselected classes toward detailed treatments of technical aspects of language (an apathy frequently encountered in large groups interested primarily in language as a means of communication rather than as an entity in itself) suggests the advisability of attacking the problem of pronunciation at the elementary and intermediate levels more concretely and directly, with a minimum of abstract verbal detail, except for such observations as the students themselves, under guidance, may be able to formulate in their own words from direct experience in using the language.

With the aid of a few simple devices, comprehensible at a glance even to junior-high-school pupils, it is possible to classify the principal phonemes in almost any language according to their phonetic categories, and give at the same time a simple and concrete indication of the normal circumstances in which the sounds can be expected to occur.[1] The charts on pages 60–65 present a résumé of the basic phonemes in Italian, French, Spanish, and German in their normal orthographic settings. The purpose of the charts is to help beginners learn to pronounce the foreign language directly in terms of its normal orthography rather than indirectly in terms of an artificial script. Although the phonetic symbol can be given a place, as in the French charts, the chief emphasis is immediately upon the sound groups as they occur in ordinary context—to the extent, in fact, that all reference to the phonetic characters can be postponed indefinitely or omitted entirely without destroying the utility of the materials. Those who

[1] Walter V. Kaulfers and Dante P. Lembi, "An Inductive Approach to Italian Pronunciation," *Italica*, Vol. XVII, pp. 150–157, December, 1940. Walter V. Kaulfers, "Précis of French Pronunciation for Beginners," *The French Review*, Vol. XI, pp. 235–242, January, 1938.

disagree with the nomenclature or the groupings of the phonemes can readily rearrange the charts to suit their preferences. The aim here is to illustrate an alternate avenue of approach, not to advertise any particular norm of pronunciation.

For purposes of classwork it is convenient to copy parts of the chart on the board, or to have the entire chart reproduced on a roller curtain, which can be pulled down at any time in exactly the same way as a roller type wall map. The procedure may then follow somewhat the following order:

1. Preliminary recitation in emulation of the instruction by the class as a whole and by individual students, of examples illustrative of the sound under discussion. (Examples to be selected by the teacher.)

2. Recitation of the orthographic groups illustrating the most common spelling of the sound group in question.

3. Deduction by the class, under the teacher's guidance (usually by means of suggestive leading questions), of the principles governing the occurrence of the sound.

4. Organization of these principles into generalizations by the students in their own words, and notation of these observations for subsequent reference and review.

5. Learning of the orthographic groups that illustrate the spelling and normal occurrences of the sound in question, and memorization of one or more typical examples suggested by the instructor.

Précis of Italian Pronunciation for Beginners
TAVOLA FONETICA

Pronounce as in the English word:	i machine	e they	a father	o potato	u lunatic
1. h (silent)	hi	he	ha	ho	hu
2. chest	(c)ci	(c)ce	(c)cia	(c)cio	(c)ciu
3. card	chi	che	ca	co	cu
4. gentle	(g)gi	(g)ge	(g)gia	(g)gio	(g)giu
5. go	ghi	ghe	ga	go	gu
6. million	gli	glie	glia	glio	gliu
7. onion	gni	gne	gna	gno	gnu
8. nose	∧si*	∧se	∧sa	∧so	∧su
9. see	si†	se	sa	so	su
10. conscious	sci	sce	scia	scio	sciu
11. lets	(z)zi	(z)ze	(z)za	(z)zo	(z)zu

* ∧ stands for any vowel (a, e, i, o, u).
† Usual sound of s when not between vowels.

ILLUSTRATIVE WORDS

1. H (silent)
1. ho
2. hanno
3. hai
4. ha
5. ahi

2. Chest
1. cibo
2. cima
3. cena
4. dolce
5. acacia
6. ciarla
7. gancio
8. bacio
9. ciuco
10. ciuffo

3. Card
1. buchi
2. chimico
3. anche
4. poche
5. casa
6. carta
7. come
8. parco
9. Cuba
10. cura

4. Gentle
1. gita
2. pagina
3. gente
4. genero
5. giardino
6. grigia
7. gioco
8. giorno
9. giusto
10. giurare

5. Go
1. aghi
2. lunghi
3. righe
4. seghe
5. riga
6. gamba
7. gola
8. regola
9. gusto
10. laguna

6. Million
1. egli
2. agli
3. foglie
4. moglie
5. paglia
6. pigliare
7. figlio
8. meglio
9. gigli
10. voglie

7. Onion
1. ogni
2. pugni
3. lavagne
4. montagne
5. vigna
6. cagna
7. legno
8. segno
9. ognuno
10. regnare

9. See
1. signora
2. Sicilia
3. seta
4. sera
5. santo
6. salame
7. so
8. sole
9. sugo
10. subito

8. Nose
1. uso
2. vaso
3. rosa
4. frase
5. viso
6. esame
7. prosa
8. tesoro
9. caso
10. causa

10. Conscious
1. fasci
2. usci
3. scena
4. scelto
5. lasciare
6. sciarpa
7. liscio
8. sciolto
9. asciugare
10. sciupare

11. Lets
1. zio
2. azione
3. stanze
4. ragazze
5. decenza
6. fidanza
7. terzo
8. marzo
9. zuppa
10. zucca

It is perhaps superfluous to mention that the foregoing procedures are not all employed during a single lesson. They represent several types of approach applicable in the teaching of a given unit. As in other fields involving the development of psychophysical skills, brief practice periods daily (averaging about ten minutes in the case of young students) are preferable to longer periods at intermittent intervals.

For variety in classwork, it may be desirable at times—especially in review lessons—to convert the procedure into a form of game. To this end, one student may be designated as "pitcher" and another as "batter." The former pronounces any orthographic combination, and the latter repeats it and identifies it on the board or wall chart.

Précis of French Pronunciation for Beginners
CHART I. PRÉCIS DE PRONONCIATION: LES VOYELLES

Key:
- . stands for a vowel (a, e, i, o, u)
- ^ stands for any consonant
- -ai stands for a consonant *different* from any coming directly in front of it, or for a consonant that is pronounced.
- -ai means when *at the end of a word*
- ai- means when *at the beginning of a word*
- -ai- means when *within a word*

Normal	Open	Nasal	Mixed
1. . i ꞎ I y -ie -ille -itie *imagination**			13. y u û -ue (eu: avoir)
2. é ée -ai: verbs -ed -er -ez dess- eff- oe- *café**	6. ai- -ai- -â- -aî -aie ê ei -ect -et -el -er^ -eo -ef e égg -e-^ è es^	9. ɛ̃ -aim -ain -ein -im -in -ym -yn aim^ ain^ ein^ im^ in^ yn^ yn^ ien^ yen^ -oin(s) oin^	14. ə The places where this sound occurs can be learned best through elimination. Review *the* *cat* sections 2 and 6 (e, ɛ); the ə is the common sound of e in most other cases, and in the exceptions: dessous, dessus, etc.
3. â oie -aille -oid(s) -ar(t)e croi -ase -asion -assion -ation a *father**	7. a emm à oi oy *fast* -age -atie -athie	10. ã -am -an -en -en am^ an^ en^ em^ emm- -aen -aon	
4. o au eau ô os -o-^ -ome -one *potato**	8. o oo o^ os^ oç oee oci *cord* aur -mum	11. õ -om -on om om on	
5. u ou oû oû -oue *prune**		12. œ̃ -um -un -eun um^ un^ eun^	15. œ (o)euf (o)eup (o)eur(e) -eur(s) oeil (o)euv -euille œ *herd* -ueil
			16. φ -eu(x) -eut -oeu(d) -oeufs *hurt* -euse -ieu(x)

* Since English has practically no absolute equivalents for French phonetic values, the English words should be pronounced as a recent French immigrant tends to pronounce them using his native basis of articulation. This practice will enable the learner more readily to distinguish differences which are ordinarily obscured by descriptive analyses avoiding all reference to contrasts with the vernacular.

CHART II. PRÉCIS DE PRONONCIATION FRANÇAISE: LES CONSONNES

Note: *h* is silent in French. Consonants (d, s, t, x, z, etc.) are usually silent when they stand at the *very end* of a word, except the consonants in *careful* (c, r, f, l), which are ordinarily pronounced.

Les consonnes	Les voyelles															
Les symboles	α	a	e	ɛ	i	y	u	o	ɔ	ə	œ	ø	ã	ɛ̃	ɔ̃	œ̃
1. Silent h	ha	habile	hé	hai	hiver	humide	houe	hôte	holà		heure	heu	hampe	hein	honte	humble
2. S: s-, ss, ç	sabre	ça	ces	cette	ici	sur	sou	seau	sol	ce	soeur	ceux	sans	saint	son	
3. ʃ: ch	châle	chat	chez	chère	chiche	chu	chou	chose	choc	chemise	pêcheur		chant	chinche	marchons	
4. K: ca, co, cu, que, qui	cas	carte	quérir	quel	qui	cure	cours	côte	corps	que	coeur	queue	camp	quint	conte	
5. ʒ: j, ge, gi	Jeanne	jade	j'ai	gel	gipsy	jus	jour	jaune	joli	je	jeune	jeu	Jean	gindre	jonque	jeun
6. G: ga, go, gu, gue, gui	gare	garde	gué	guère	guide	gutte	goût	gogo	golf	guenon	gueule	gueux	gant	gain	gond	
7. ɲ: gn		gagne		peigne	vigne				Bou-logne							
8. j: ie, -ille -il	taille	ail	lier	hier	fille	livre	piou-piou	idiot	idiote		deuil	lieu	diantre	bien	lion	
9. ɥi: ui					lui huile huis hui		Exception: oui									

Précis of Spanish Pronunciation for Beginners
TABLA DE PRONUNCIACIÓN*

	i machine	e they	a father	o go	u food
1. Key					
2. h: silent	hi himno	he heno	ha halo	ho ahora	hu humo
3. c, z > th(in) (s in Latin America)	ci cima	ce cera	za zarza	zo zona	zu zumo
4. c, qu > k	**qui** quinto	**que** queso	ca cama	co coma	cu curso
5. g, j > h (panted)	**gi** giro	**ge** gente	ja paja	jo ojo	hu justo
6. g > g(o)	**gui** guiso	**gue** pague	ga gas	go goma	gu seguro
7. ll > y	lli alli	lle lleno	lla llama	llo lloro	llu lluvia
8. b > v(w)	ib libro	eb sebo	ab cable	ob lobo	ub nube
9. d > th(e)	id nido	ed seda	ad lado	od moda	ud nudo
10. ñ > (ca)ny(on)	ñi añil	ñe muñeca	ña soñar	ño señor	ñu (rare)

*Roller type pronunciation charts in French, German, Italian, and Spanish (see illustration) can be obtained from the author. See Appendix, reference 152.

If time permits, sides or teams may be chosen and innings played after the manner of baseball. The necessity of artificially stimulating attention by such devices, however, will be slight if the application of the chart work to actual growth in ability to pronounce words, to visualize their spelling on hearing them, or to read orally, is self-evident from a close integration of work on the chart with dictation exercises, oral reading, and the analytical resolution of difficulties in spelling and pronunciation in terms of the orthographic groupings in the table.

Obviously, only the normal pronunciation of the sound groups of most frequent occurrence is indicated in the charts. It is quite

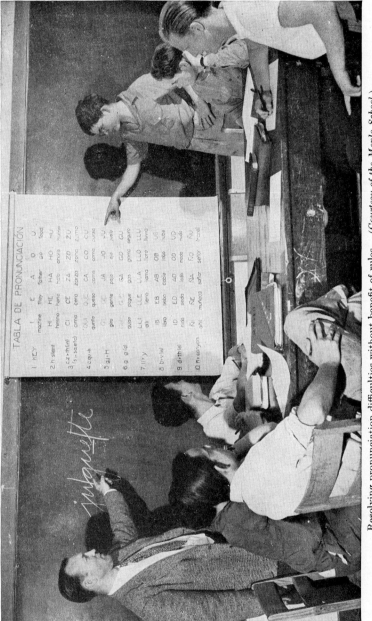

Resolving pronunciation difficulties without benefit of rules. (*Courtesy of the Menlo School.*)

Précis of German Pronunciation for Beginners

A. Die Endkonsonanten*

-i(e)b	-i(e)d	-i(e)g	-ich	-i(e)v	-i(e)tz
-üb	-üd	-üg	-üch	-üv	-ütz
-eb	-ed	-eg	-ech	-ev	-etz
-öb	-öd	-ög	-öch	-öv	-ötz
-ab	-ad	-ag	-ach	-av	-atz
-äb	-äd	-äg	-äch	-äv	-ätz
-ob	-od	-og	-och	-ov	-otz
-ub	-ud	-ug	-uch	-uv	-utz
-eub	-eud	-eug	-euch	-euv	-eutz
-äub	-äud	-äug	-äuch	-äuv	-äutz
-eib	-eid	-eig	-eich	-eiv	-eitz
-aib	-aid	-aig	-aich	-aiv	-aitz
-aub	-aud	-aug	-auch	-auv	-autz

B. Die Anfangskonsonanten*

ji(e)-	pfi(e)-	qui(e)-	si(e)-	schi(e)-	spi(e)-	sti(e)-	wi(e)-	vi(e)-
jü-	pfü-	quü-	sü-	schü-	spü-	stü-	wü-	vü-
je-	pfe-	que-	se-	sche-	spe-	ste-	we-	ve-
jö-	pfö-	quö-	sö-	schö-	spö-	stö-	wö-	vö-
jä-	pfä-	quä-	sä-	schä-	spä-	stä-	wä-	vä-
ja-	pfa-	qua-	sa-	scha-	spa-	sta-	wa-	va-
jo-	pfo-	quo-	so-	scho-	spo-	sto-	wo-	vo-
ju-	pfu-	quu-	su-	schu-	spu-	stu-	wu-	vu-
jeu-	pfeu-	queu-	seu-	scheu-	speu-	steu-	weu-	veu-
jäu-	pfäu-	quäu-	säu-	schäu-	späu-	stäu-	wäu-	väu-
jei-	pfei-	quei-	sei-	schei-	spei-	stei-	wei-	vei-
jai-	pfai-	quai-	sai-	schai-	spai-	stai-	wai-	vai-
jau-	pfau-	quau-	sau-	schau-	spau-	stau-	wau-	vau-

* Practice reading the columns vertically, later horizontally, and finally the individual combinations at random.

possible, for example, that after the fricative form of the letter *b* has been studied in Spanish, some observant pupil may remark, "You have just taught us to pronounce the Spanish *b* something like a *v*, but when you said *buenas tardes* this afternoon you pronounced it more like the *b* in English.   How do you explain that?"

Such questions provide an opportunity for the teacher to impart incidentally insights into some of the finer points of pronunciation. After duly complimenting the student on the merits of his question, the instructor may say to the class:

"You will remember that we did not say that the *b* has only one sound in Spanish.   We merely indicated that it is almost always pronounced in the same way when it occurs in the combinations *-ib*, *-eb*, *-ab*, *-ob*, *-ub*.   In most other cases it has a sound very much like that of our English *b*. To keep ourselves from becoming confused, let us concentrate for the time being on the exceptionally peculiar pronunciations of each letter; the others we can easily learn as we go along, since they are not very different from our English letters.

"Always try to see a word as a combination of the phonetic groups in the table, never as a collection of individual letters each to be pronounced separately. Then sound each combination in the same way that we have been pronouncing it in practicing with the chart."

Although the charts do not cover the entire field of pronunciation, they contain as much material as most beginners can learn to apply correctly at the elementary level in high school or college where time must be reserved for other activities besides pronunciation. A more detailed treatment of exceptions and special points should probably be reserved for more advanced stages, lest the novice, confused with too many details at the start, become discouraged with the overwhelming difficulty of the subject. Ability in pronunciation is, in a sense, a function of general growth in the language, and not without a physiological period of adjustment and adaptation as regards the aural-oral mechanism. Unduly to force this process is to invite discouragement. A more thorough understanding of the importance of this principle in foreign-language teaching would result in a more psychologically spaced distribution of emphasis on pronunciation over the student's entire career in the language, rather than over-emphasis to the point of frustration during the first few weeks of elementary instruction.

Attainable Norms of Pronunciation.—So far, nothing has been said concerning the standards of performance in pronunciations which teachers may keep in mind as criteria for judging the quality of the pupil's achievement. The tendency is to expect too much at the beginning and too little in the later stages of the course. The notion that a skill involving a reconditioning of the aurisensory and speech apparatus can be developed through intensive study and concentrated drill for two or three weeks at the beginning of the course runs counter to reality. Once the tongue, lips, jaw, and soft palate have been habituated to certain relative positions in one language, new coordinations of these organs are not developed to the point of automatization except over a considerable period of time, varying in the length with the learner's auditory acuity, muscular control, and previously established speech patterns. The use of adult standards of perfection as criteria for accepting or rejecting pupil responses at the start leads to overcorrection, which in turn may beget a sense of futility on the part of the learner.   What incentive is there for any boy or girl to so much as open his mouth if he is certain in advance that almost every word will be overruled with corrections—to such an extent that he cannot remember the words, much less the thought of what he intended to say?

It should be taken for granted that no matter **how** perfect the model, or how clear the explanation, errors will occur either through lack of ability properly to control the muscles of the lips, jaw, tongue, and soft palate in their new coordinations, or through inability to perceive the new sounds accurately.   Every skill, whether it be tennis, golf, dancing, shorthand, or typewriting is susceptible to the same involuntary errors.   At the start, therefore, the teacher will do well to let the students express themselves as best they can in reading or answering short true-false or completion questions in which the mind-set of the pupil is primarily on the thought rather than on the mechanics of speech.   During the course of this oral work, she will note, without comment whatsoever, those sounds which seem to cause the students to hesitate or to feel uncomfortable, and those sounds which are most "out of tune" with the norm of pronunciation absolutely essential to intelligibility.   At the end of the recitation she may remark to the class,

"If I am not mistaken, some of you seem a little uncomfortable and uncertain with respect to the pronunciation of certain letters and combinations.   Which sounds bother you most?"

The response of the class will usually bring forth requests for help on the very sounds that are the most troublesome or the most "out of tune."   On the basis of the difficulties that the members of the class themselves feel are troublesome, the teacher will provide special examples, explanations, and practice in keeping with the procedures suggested in the foregoing paragraphs, dealing first with those difficulties which are the most offensive and most widely experienced by the class as a whole, and later in the course with those difficulties which are less common and less jarring to the trained ear.   A sensible criterion for satisfactory performance in the very early stages of the course is that of intelligibility—*would a native listening to the students be able to understand what they are trying to say?*

Obviously, the beginning student is not always aware of his mistakes or appreciative of the difficulties that handicap him.   In such cases, the teacher may well take the initiative and say,

"I note that some of us are having difficulty with the pronunciation of the *ch* in German.   I think that I can help you.   Smile and relax your jaw, and try panting like a dog.   Note how freely the air passes through the open throat.   Now say *i* as in *it,* and end the sound by exhaling as in a short pant.   Be sure to keep the back of the throat relaxed and open . . . Now let's try it again with a smile!"

If a student persists in mispronouncing the combination *ik,* the two sounds *i* and *ch* (pant) may temporarily be sounded separately: *i-ch.* Some students may have to follow the latter method for several weeks before control of the process becomes automatic.   The same procedure, of course, can be followed with the remaining vowel combinations: *ich, ech, ach, och, uch,* etc.

Note that all specialized practice begins with the felt needs of students, proceeds to the gradual elimination of off-key sounds in order of the degree of their offensiveness to the trained ear, and reserves special details of pronunciation for the more advanced levels, except in the case of students whose ability is such that they can progress more rapidly.   These students, like the "problem cases" with which every class is destined to be endowed, can be given special help occasionally in small groups, meeting around the teacher's desk or in a corner of the room during the supervised study period while the remainder of the class are engaged on the assignment for the following day, or in silent reading.

Note also that the standard of performance during the early stages is that of physical intelligibility.   From here the standard can be raised gradually in keeping with the abilities of the class toward the ideal of inability to distinguish their pronunciation from that of a native.   Since few American-born teachers can boast of this level of perfection unless they have been favored by unusual opportunities, such as residence abroad, a practical criterion for the acceptability of pronunciation at the advanced levels might be *inability to identify the pronunciation of the student in French, German, Spanish, or Italian with that of a particular nationality group; i.e.,* would a native Frenchman, be unable to identify the pronunciation of the student of French as that of an American, in the same way that many foreigners in the United States can be identified by certain characteristic speech patterns as being of Swedish, German, or Italian origin, even though they have learned to speak English fluently and intelligibly?   This standard is a relatively reasonable one to keep in mind as a practical goal.   That it is not a low standard is evident from the fact that it is not too frequently attained even by graduate students who have majored in a foreign language.   A higher standard might be desirable, but probably attainable only at a sacrifice of other outcomes of equal or greater importance.   For what is the functional value of a perfect pronunciation if a student is so deficient in vocabulary or usage that he is unable to say or understand anything?

Use of Mechanical Aids for Developing Aural Discrimination.— Since it is not impossible for one to develop a very acceptable pronunciation without being able to understand people whose intonation patterns and tempo in speech are different from those to which one's ears are accustomed, it is desirable to hear the speech of native men, women, and children of different ages as often as possible.   Conversational records now on the market help to solve this problem, provided the school is equipped with a modern phonograph with volume and tone controls.   Natives who speak the language well can often be invited to the class to answer, in the foreign language, questions prepared in advance by the students.   Interviews of this kind provide valuable opportunities for the students to try out their own pronunciation, and to accustom their ears to different voices and normal variations in oral speech.

Since it is very difficult for an individual to hear himself as others hear him, recordings of the pupils' voices from time to time provide a valuable teaching aid by "holding the mirror up to nature."   Recording attachments are now so readily obtainable at relatively little cost that the item of expense can no longer serve as an excuse for failure to capitalize the resources of modern science and invention.   An increasing number of schools are establishing speech laboratories for use by teachers of English, public speaking, dramatics, music, speech correction, and foreign languages, with facilities not only for diagnosing and recording voices, but also for enabling pupils to make test records from time to time to evaluate their progress in speech.   Such instruments as the Magnetic-Tape Recorder are a valuable aid in practicing pronunciation, since they record and reproduce sound almost instantaneously with high fidelity, and do not require the use of recording disks.   The same recording can be repeated indefinitely until the tape is demagnatized.   Occasionally, practice with a Dictaphone or Ediphone is practical since the records can be shaved and used for several recordings.   All the instruments mentioned above are portable, but a suitable environment is essential if students are to make effective use of them in individual practice.   Such space facilities as are necessary can usually be obtained if teachers of English, public speaking, music, dramatics, speech correction, and foreign languages cooperate in pressing the need.

Although the foregoing discussion of pronunciation has not made specific mention of such important associated topics as syllabification,

accentuation, synaloepha, synaeresis, and intonation, it is taken
for granted that these aspects of oral speech are important, and will
be given increasing attention after the students have developed a
certain measure of confidence and facility in forming the basic sounds
of the language intelligibly.   Everything cannot be accomplished at
once.   The important thing is that the teacher facilitate the learning
process for students, rather than complicate it with mental hazards
or activities which might be mistaken by the pupil for meaningless
busywork without purpose or direction beyond the activity itself.
Too intensive an emphasis upon pronunciation, apart from other
abilities equally important in learning a language, is as likely to bore
or befuddle the learner as to encourage him.

Motivation through Integrative Activities.—Psychologically spaced
practice, with meaningful context chosen on the basis of need and the
pupil's level of insight, can, if properly varied through the use of
appropriate devices and techniques for applying the functional principles of learning, convert an essential activity into an intrinsically
interesting and profitable experience.   Foundational work in pronunciation can often be motivated through the judicious choice of
content material for practice in the early stages.   Place names and
foreign terms and expressions used in English are examples of functional content materials for practice in pronunciation, and for the
development of vocabulary in meaningful context during the first
few days of beginning instruction.   Short, tuneful songs provide
similar opportunities for developing ability in pronunciation and
vocabulary in informal context.   Songs are especially useful in developing notions of liaison, synaloepha, and word grouping, since the
rhythm and melody often make the observance of these linguistic
changes necessary.   No matter what specific device, procedure, or
content is used in developing ability to pronounce, however, the
sequence of the learning process should be organized to capitalize
effectively the psychological principles which, on the basis of the
empirical experience of many able teachers and considerable experimentation, have proved efficacious in achieving the best results.
These principles, in the normal sequence of their application to the
development of the aural-oral abilities in language, are

1. Orientation before specialization—the whole before the part.
2. Hearing before speaking.
3. Speaking before seeing.
4. Seeing before writing.[1]

[1] For aural aids in the teaching of pronunciation see Appendix, references 61,
112, 152, 188, 196.

CHAPTER III

PERSPECTIVE ON THE TEACHING OF GRAMMAR

Grammatical robots and slave-scribes—moving hands that write for a master.
—HOLLAND DeWITTE ROBERTS, President, National Council of Teachers of English, 1937

Language is made by the needs of men and grammar is made by professors.
—HAROLD BENJAMIN

The Function of Grammar in Language Learning.—The role of grammar in any functional program in foreign languages is primarily to facilitate readily intelligible communication in reading, writing, or speaking. Correctness is of importance only to the extent to which it makes comprehension easier on the part of a listener or reader by enabling him to concentrate upon the idea or information expressed without being disturbed, inconvenienced, confused, or distracted by deviations from the conventions of language to which he is accustomed; for a slip in grammar is often as distracting in speech as a "sour note" in music. Grammatical correctness, by which is meant conformity to conventionally accepted patterns of speech, can be developed in two mutually complementary ways:

1. Through guided practice with informative content in emulation of correct models of good usage, and

2. Through insights into the *raisons d'être* of language patterns that are different in the vernacular and foreign language.

The importance of worth-while thought content in the way of information or ideas cannot be overemphasized in language teaching. If the content is sterile or immaterial, or not intended to communicate anything worth mentioning, the need for correctness to facilitate effective communication is relatively unimportant. Practice then becomes, in reality, not practice in effective communication, but a kind of linguistic drill for its own sake, or for some extrinsic purpose, such as knowledge of English grammar, improvement of work habits, or mental discipline, quite remote from the original purposes for which modern-language instruction was introduced into the schools, and even more remote from the primary objectives of the students in taking the courses. Correctness is important only to the extent to which one bears in mind the question: Correctness for what? For if the *matter* does not count most, it is doubtful if the *manner* need count at all.[1]

Much foreign-language teaching has been inoperative because it has emphasized correctness for its own sake as a kind of discipline or eternal verity, and has thus lost sight of the primary purpose of language in life: the communication of feelings, wants, or ideas. The result has often been formalized drill with deadening content, over-correction of students to the point of frustration, a grossly disproportionate emphasis on the theory of form and mechanics at levels of maturity where linguistic abstractions cannot be readily understood, much less applied by young people, and a futile expectation that the mastery of the parts of a language will *de facto* guarantee ability to use the language as a whole in normal communication where the mind-set should primarily be, not on form and mechanics, but on the thought expressed. Unless the part is learned in the light of its relationship to the whole, neither its meaning nor use can be fully appreciated. The piecemeal learning of language according to classified parts has caused many a student to become entangled in a mass of grammatical details, to forget one part the moment the emphasis in learning shifted to another, and eventually to become discouraged with the difficulty of synthesizing a seemingly infinite number of parts into an instrumental unit.

Worse than this, preoccupation with correctness in form and mechanics to the neglect of meaning has led to the use of a very scientific, but very difficult, terminology as the medium for describing the structure of language. Granting that grammatical terms are convenient, concise, and accurate labels for those who know how to make use of them, the fact remains that grammatical terminology is for most students a highly abstract and abstruse medium, as foreign at times as the foreign language itself. Although any normal boy or girl can *memorize* the verbal definitions of such terms as "dependent clause" or "predicate adjective," to teach them to identify "dependent clauses" or "predicates" in actual speech requires much figurative pulling of teeth. Most young people seem to find it next to impossible to think about language in such terms. The difficulty lies in the fact that the nomenclature is too abstract and too generalized to fall within the adolescent's ability to make effective use of it in his *own* writing or speech. All the investigations into the practical value of formal grammar and its associated activities (diagraming, parsing,

---

[1] S. A. Leonard, *Current English Usage*, National Council of Teachers of English, Chicago, Ill., 1932, 232 pp.; p. xx.

sentence analysis, etc.) in English have proved the inefficiency of this method as a means for improving the pupil's *own* personal use of language.[1] It is doubtful if a foreign language can be taught successfully by methods which in the case of the vernacular have more often proved to be a disciplinary instrument for the frustration of children than a means of facilitating effective communication in everyday life.

Standards of Correctness.—The standard of correctness that can reasonably be applied in any learning situation is not that of perfection. In the case of language, a degree of accuracy sufficient to ensure intelligible communication of the thought or idea expressed is a reasonable standard to keep in mind at the elementary level, provided the content is compatible with the learner's level of insight. In advanced courses, a degree of accuracy sufficient to avoid distractions to the ears or eyes is probably as much as can be expected, and far more than is ordinarily attained. Naturally, the practical application of any relative criterion in evaluating the work of students depends upon the specific nature of the circumstances. If the activity involves merely copying material correctly, perfection to the last detail of spelling, punctuation, and the like is not too much to expect even at the beginning of the course. In such cases, the correct indication of accent marks, regardless of their importance in determining the pronunciation or meaning of a word, may be insisted upon, whereas in activities involving more than a coordination of the eyes and hand, only those mechanics which would lead to miscomprehension or noncomprehension need be made the object of special attention. Errors in mechanics might at the start be indicated incidentally for subsequent correction by the student, but the time and energy of pupil and teacher alike might profitably be saved at the beginning for the development of insights into those essentials of language which are most important from the standpoint of intelligible communication. The diffusion of attention over a wide range of details without regard for their relative importance leads to mental indigestion.

The importance of using reasonable standards of correctness in guiding the growth of young people in a foreign language can be appreciated when one realizes that beginners often have difficulty just in copying material correctly. Their powers of discriminating

[1] T. H. Briggs, "Formal English Grammar as a Discipline," *Teachers College Record*, Vol. XIV, pp. 251–343, September, 1913. Ellen Frogner, "Clarifying Some Facts," *The English Journal*, Vol. XXIX, No. 8, pp. 653–655, October, 1940. L. J. O'Rourke, *Rebuilding the English-usage Curriculum to Insure Greater Mastery of Essentials, A Report of a Nation-wide Survey*, The Psychological Institute, Washington, D. C., 1934, x + 98 pp.

observation in language are either not adequately developed, or language patterns already impressed upon the visual memories of the learners cause them to mistake what they actually see for what they are accustomed to seeing. It is futile to begin work in syntax and grammar when the learner has not had the opportunity to acclimate himself to the language sufficiently to be able to hear and see it correctly. Abundant opportunities to hear the language in meaningful context, reinforced by practice in copying it correctly to the point where the mechanics no longer cause serious difficulty, should precede specialized work in language usage.

Reducing the Possibilities for Error. Third-person Context.— Obviously, opportunities for error can be reduced materially through a careful selection and organization of learning materials and activities. The development of an informational topic in the third person in terms of reading content composed of cognate and near-cognate words, simple questions, and exercises of the completion, multiple-choice, matching, or true-false correction type, usually involve no excessive strain upon the student's level of insight or attention span.[1] An informational theme, such as *Les Contributions de la France aux sciences et aux inventions*, first presented orally by the teacher with the aid of a vocabulary of cognate words and definitions on the board, then in writing or print, and later in the form of a review enlisting the aural, oral, visual, and kinesthetic participation of the student in answering simple questions, and writing out in full exercises of the type indicated above, usually provides an effective medium for developing the various language abilities collaterally in a unified context.

The use of third-person material is desirable at the start since it makes possible the treatment of grammatical factors and elements, such as adjectives, verbs, and tenses, almost exclusively as vocabulary. Such third-person questions as: *¿Cuál (what) es la capital de la Argentina?* can usually be answered correctly (if one knows the name of the capital) simply by changing the order of the words in the question (*e.g.*, "*La capital de la Argentina es Buenos Aires*), whereas such questions as *¿No es usted peruano?* require not only changes in word order, but also a command of such grammatical elements as the personal pronouns and verb forms. It is unwise in the early elementary stages, while the student is still insecure in pronunciation and still likely to be handicapped by the involuntary intrusion of aural and visual language

[1] For the technique of constructing such exercises and for illustrative examples, see C. M. Ruch, *The Objective or New Type Examination*, Scott, Foresman and Company, Chicago, 1929, 478 pp.

habits from the vernacular, to tax his mind with grammatical variables. The emphasis might more profitably be on such correlated aural, oral, visual, and kinesthetic activities in the third person as will help to develop, simultaneously, ability to hear the language correctly, to pronounce it intelligibly, to increase the vocabulary, and to give insight into the mechanics of spelling, punctuation, and word order. If the content medium is informative and in the third person, these abilities can be developed side by side in context which has some semblance to language as a means of communication in real life, and something to offer in the way of information that can serve as a springboard for the development of cultural interests in the foreign country and its people.   There is no reason whatsoever why content of this kind cannot be used from the start, especially if comprehension is facilitated by the use of cognate words, or occasional definitions in parenthesis.   The use of worth-while content in simple language on the third-person level makes possible the orientation of the student in the language as a whole as a means of communication.   In the light of this orientation the part can then be studied with greater assurance of an understanding and appreciation of its relationship to the whole. In the early stages, first- and second-person material may well be confined to short conversational dialogues in a dramatic setting where almost everything can be learned as vocabulary in connected context.

Importance of Meaningful Content as a Linguistic Medium.—In addition to reducing opportunities for error to a minimum and providing for an orientation in the language as a whole prior to specialization, the use of meaningful content furnishes the teacher with a criterion for judging the immediate language needs of the students. The questions that the pupils themselves ask regarding the reason or nature of certain constructions and usages afford opportunities to give such theoretical attention to problems of form and mechanics as the pupils themselves sense the need for, a more patent *raison d'etre*, and thus circumvent the danger of losing the class by theorizing in grammatical terms about phenomena whose importance has to be accepted on faith if first encountered in isolation or in fragmentary sentences devoid of meaning.   For example,

1. Is the pencil red?
2. The house is white, but the roof is green.
3. Who is the oldest girl?
4. Is the teacher under the table?

If sterile content of this kind is used as the medium for developing ability in language, the work can scarcely become more than a disciplinary exercise in form and mechanics—word matching, parrotlike recitation, and pencil pushing—and the chief outcome, except for a relatively few students, is likely to be an attitude of apathetic resignation. Linguistic material, examined in isolation without specific regard for what it communicates, or to whom, and practiced in ways in which it is seldom used in real life, is hardly language at all.

Palacio Valdés, in his novel *La Hermana San Sulpicio*, gives a classic illustration of emphasis on form and mechanics gone to seed in modern-language teaching. On his honeymoon in Paris the hero leaves the speaking of French to his sprightly wife, saying that his language work had been limited to such questions and answers as

> "Have you seen my sister's cheese?"
> "No, I have seen the cook's carving knife."
> "Have you the maiden's book?"
> "No, I have the lawyer's underwear."

Limitations of Grammatical Terminology as an Aid in Language Learning.—Although correctness can at times be achieved through abundant guided practice in emulation of models of good usage, security and confidence in a foreign language are often greatly strengthened by insights into the way the language works and into the reasons why it works as it does. Facilitation of accurate communication in a language, and the reinforcement of self-confidence in its use with an understanding of the principles underlying form and function, are the chief justifications for the study of what is generally known as grammar. Naturally, neither purpose is likely to be served effectively if the language of the explanations is one in which young people are not secure. A serious objection to the conventional grammar approach is its unwieldy terminology. Instead of facilitating communication and reinforcing self-confidence, it often frustrates the learner with the frequently impossible task of trying to understand the unknown in terms of the unknown. For example,

"In general, conjunctive personal pronoun objects immediately precede the verb as separate words. Such pronouns must follow the infinitive, present participle, and affirmative verb of command, and be attached as additional syllables; and in literary style they may so follow even the finite verb, especially at or near the beginning of a sentence or clause: there is an apparent feeling that the unstressed word should be avoided early in the clause or sentence."[1] To translate

[1] Ronald B. Williams, "Elementary Spanish Grammars and Their Rules," *The Modern Language Journal*, Vol. XX, pp. 85–90, November, 1935.

abstractions of this kind into operational terms is no mean task for anyone not versed in grammatical analysis. Such grammatical magniloquence usually requires that an undue amount of time be devoted to deciphering the "meaning of the explanation" at the expense of opportunity to master the principle through actual guided practice in communication. Indeed, in many cases the pupil has to rely entirely on trial-and-error methods, or upon intuitive deductions based directly on the examples given, in order to gain insight into the mechanics of usage. Complete omission of the explanation would at least avoid making the process seem more complicated than it is in fact.

An analysis of the rules and explanations in eight widely used Spanish textbooks shows that 200 grammatical terms[1] are likely to be encountered by the beginning student of junior or senior high-school Spanish. Such terms as *accusative, elliptical, intransitive, pluperfect,* and *substantive,* constitute 14.5 per cent of the word content of the explanations. That is, to the beginner, approximately one out of every seven words is likely to be one that has little or no meaning in operational terms. In one elementary Spanish grammar, 42.1 per cent of the explanatory word content consisted of grammatical terms or expressions used in a specialized grammatical sense: *future of probability, indefinite future,* etc.—expressions whose meaning is intelligible to young people only in the light of the illustrative examples. Imagine a ninth grader trying to learn Spanish by decoding explanations in which almost every other word is an unfamiliar, abstruse term. Grammar in such cases certainly does not facilitate accuracy or intelligibility in communication. Instead, it erects a word barrage around the language in such a way as to make it less accessible, and unconsciously converts the classwork into a course in which *grammar* is taught as a discipline with the aid of examples from a foreign language. This is quite the opposite of what a foreign-language class should be—a class in which pupils learn to read, write, or speak the foreign language through abundant practice, guided by models of correct usage and by such explanations as are occasionally needed to gain insight into the operational principles governing the relationship between from and function in communicating something to somebody for a purpose.

The foregoing carry no insinuation that grammar or grammatical terminology should be ruled out altogether. The point is merely

[1] Walter V. Kaulfers, "The Grammatical Difficulty of Beginning Spanish Grammars," *The Modern Language Forum,* Vol. XVI, pp. 43–45, April, 1931.

that grammatical nomenclature cannot be relied upon as a medium for explaining anything to people who are not already skilled in grammatical analysis. What, then, are the alternatives? The easiest of all plausible remedies is contained in the suggestion that teachers of English ground their pupils more thoroughly in grammar, so that upon embarking upon the study of German, for example, they will understand at once what is meant by "When coordinating conjunctions connect two independent clauses, the second clause has subject-verb word order." Unfortunately for the advocates of this solution, teachers of English have discovered that such training contributes almost nothing toward the improvement of the pupil's *own* writing or speech, and are therefore devoting the time formerly consumed in this type of formal linguistic busywork to the development of worthwhile reading interests, original writing, and applied semantics—the critical interpretation of language from the standpoint of referents, polar words, ghost words, emotional words, and the like, as they govern thought and action in daily life. Although grammar has not been ruled out of the English curriculum, it is no longer taught as a separate discipline involving diagraming, parsing, or sentence analysis. Grammatical terminology is used only where it facilitates the correction of difficulties encountered by the pupils in their *own* writing or speech. The modern viewpoint of teachers of English is well expressed by Hatfield, editor of *The English Journal*:[1]

All scientific attempts to prove the value of grammar have failed. Yet in grades seven, eight, and nine, grammar is given more time than speech, or written communication, or creative expression—too frequently as much as all three combined. Are curriculum makers and teachers of English perverse, or stupid?

As one of them, who knows a great many of his colleagues, I consider them up to or above the average of the teaching profession in both intelligence and open-mindedness. (And teachers as a whole are in these respects not inferior to the American middle class, from which they are chiefly recruited.) Curriculum makers and teachers of English are neither stupid nor perverse.

The contradiction between theory and practice has a different explanation. The teachers know that they sometimes themselves make use of grammar to test doubtful constructions, and they feel rather sure that they subconsciously use grammatical concepts in building good sentences as well as in maintaining syntactical correctness. Hence they infer that pupils too would profit by a study of grammar.

[1] W. Wilbur Hatfield, "What Grammar? And How?" Public Relations Committee, National Council of Teachers of English, 211 West 68th St., Chicago, Ill., 1937, 4 pp. (mimeographed).

It is in this inference that the mistake must lie. And believing that the specific locus of the mistake is in the kind of grammar study offered, I propose a more natural, instrumental, limited sort of grammar study.

The probable causes of the ineffectiveness of the present type of work suggest the new approach.

First, pupils who learn to define grammatical terms and to analyze sentences do not—frequently cannot—apply this knowledge in speaking, or even in writing. In educational jargon, we say that their knowledge transfers or carries over imperfectly to error-detection tests and still less to actual use of language. Why? Because the definitions were not learned and the analysis was not practiced in connection with their *own* use of language.

Second, the definitions frequently lack real meaning, and the analysis contains a large element of guesswork. . . . The child who learns by way of a logician's definition what a chair or truth is will never thereby know how to use a chair or speak the truth.

Can we, then, teach grammar in such a way as (1) to build real concepts of grammatical relationships, and (2) to connect those concepts dynamically with the pupils' own language? *An Experience Curriculum in English*[1] points the way. It proposes, in brief, (1) that the pupils shall be given exercises in imitating certain constructions which they need to use, and (2) that when through this imitation (perhaps accompanied under some circumstances by the teacher's interpretative comment) the grammatical concept emerges, it shall be given its proper name . . .

Suppose that the difficulty is the use of the adjective for the adverb, as in *John played very good last night.* The teacher may present the incorrect sentence and in contrast the correct form. With these upon the board, other incorrect sentences are offered for correction, or sentences with appropriate blanks are presented. Pupils complete or correct these sentences until attention is thoroughly centered upon these adverbs. The teacher *may* during this process point out that those words show *how* John played, etc. Perhaps he points out, or develops by questioning, that they describe the action rather than the actor. Before the exercise is ended he calls these *how*-words "adverbs," and when the mistake crops up again and further drills are undertaken, he naturally continues to call them adverbs. (This single attack does not, of course, constitute a complete teaching of the concept of adverb; but the other cases are treated similarly.)

Quarrel as much as you like with these particular illustrations; they are, no doubt, open to attack. Find fault with the *arrangement* of the items in the Instrumental Grammar work of the *Experience Curriculum;* it has no claim to scientific accuracy. But focus your attention on the vital idea which these imperfectly illustrate: grammar can be taught inductively *in* and *through* use.

[1] *An Experience Curriculum in English*, a report of a Commission of the National Council of Teachers of English, W. Wilbur Hatfield, Chairman. D. Appleton-Century Company, Inc., New York, 1935, xvi + 323 pp.; pp. 228–238.

When grammar is so taught, four advantages accrue: (1) Useless items, such as transitive and intransitive verbs, the cases of nouns (except the possessive), and the classes of adverbs, are automatically omitted. (2) Most of the time usually devoted to formal grammar is saved for more practice in communication and more motivated exercises in construction and usage. (3) Grammatical terms acquire real meaning, so that they are not forgotten every summer. (4) The transfer problem disappears, since the principles are learned in the actual situations in which they will be needed later. The general adoption of such a procedure, now used at times in some places, would constitute a major improvement in the teaching of English.

Instrumental Grammar.—The foregoing quotation is indicative not only of the fact that the trend in the teaching of English is away from the conventional grammatical method to what might be called the "meaning approach," but also of a technique for overcoming difficulties in usage which can be applied equally effectively at times in teaching a foreign language. This technique, briefly summarized, consists in associating the grammatical label with the language elements for which it stands, not through formal definition and illustration, but through collateral use. The term *noun*, for example, is learned in much the same way as that in which a child learns to associate the word *ball* with the class of objects for which it stands, not by memorizing a verbal definition, but by actually tossing a *ball*, batting a *ball*, rolling a *ball*, etc. The function of grammatical terminology in this approach is not primarily to facilitate learning, but to provide a convenient label for subsequently identifying a generic group of language elements which have already become a part of the pupil's linguistic background. In other words, the label is for convenience of reference and subsequent identification, and not to conceal the contents.

The same principle can be applied to the teaching of the foreign languages. Foreign-language teachers would, perhaps, be less disappointed in the work of their classes if they assumed no foreknowledge of grammatical terminology whatsoever on the part of their students, and taught through incidental association such nomenclature as might be convenient for subsequent reference. To be specific, suppose that a beginning class in Spanish is uncertain regarding the contraction of *de* and *el* into *del*, or of *a* and *el* into *al*. Is there any need for complicating this simple phenomenon with such excess wordage as is to be found in "The masculine singular definite article contracts with the prepositions *de* and *a* to form *del* and *al* respectively." Would it not be simpler and more to the point to say, "*de* and *el* contract to form *del*, and *a* and *el* contract into *al*"? Just wherein is the grammatical description simpler, briefer, more accurate, more intelligible? Just how does it facilitate accurate communication?

In cases such as the foregoing, where the phenomenon is not generic but specialized, the use of grammatical terminology is superfluous. Only in generalized cases, where the principle governs a variety of situations, is its use likely to be convenient for purposes of short-cutting the process of reference and identification. For example, "The definite article is used in Spanish before titles except in direct address." Even here, however, the use of grammatical terms is hardly necessary, *e.g.*, "Before titles such as *señor*, *doctor*, and *profesor*, the words (definite article) *el*, *la*, *los*, or *las* are always used except in speaking directly to the people named." There are relatively few situations, indeed, in which any really necessary grammatical terminology cannot be learned incidentally in one or more of the following ways:

1. *Through illustrative definition*, *e.g.*, the possessive adjectives (*my, his, her, its, your, their*, etc.) must . . .

2. *Through parenthetical identification with the referents*, *e.g.*, the German words (possessive adjectives) for *my, his, her, your, their, our*, must . . .

Explanations of this kind are somewhat longer, but the sacrifice in brevity of wording is small compared with the saving of time in teaching and learning, and the elimination of unnecessary mental hazards. The explanations in many textbooks are useless to students because the language of the explanations is difficult to translate into operational terms.

The Psychosemantic Approach.—A more serious objection to grammatical explanations, however, is their tendency to conceal rather than to reveal the thought processes that underlie linguistic phenomena.[1] Most grammar is merely descriptive of form and mechanics. It rarely affords insights into causal factors underlying semantic relationships in speech. The teacher who is asked such a question as "Why are the endings for the future added to the end of the *infinitive* instead of to the stem of the verb in Spanish (French and Italian)?" is likely to find a satisfactory answer only in a historical reference grammar. For an explanation of the probable reason she will find it necessary to turn to the field of semantics, general linguistics, or the psychology of language. This is unfortunate, for explanations

[1] J. R. Kantor, *An Objective Psychology of Grammar*, Indiana University, Bloomington, Ind., 1936, xvi + 344 pp.; pp. 10–13.

affording insights into the ideological processes underlying language are generally more fascinating, more fundamental, and more likely to be remembered by students than descriptive statements in abstruse terms. Moreover, causal relationships can usually be explained in nontechnical language. For example, instead of "I shall speak tomorrow," people at one time literally said "I to speak *have* tomorrow." In other words, they thought of the "future" in terms of things which they had in mind to do at some later time. Hence the use of the present-tense forms of the verb *have* (*avoir* in French, *haber* in Spanish, and *avere* in Italian):

> je parler ai   > je parlerai
> yo hablar (h)e > yo hablaré
> io parlar(e h)o > io parlerò

In Spanish the *h*, being silent, was easily lost, and an accent mark over the *e* today serves as a reminder of a word (*he*) which was at one time accented separately in its own right.

The psychosemantic approach to language first illustrated is in the long run more effective in developing functional insights into language usage than descriptive rules, and the insights thus gained are more likely to be remembered by students than generalized grammatical formulas. Differences in language, as indicated in an earlier connection, are reflections of originally different ways of reacting to the outer word—of differences in ways of thinking. To obscure this fact behind a barrage of grammatical nomenclature, derived largely on the basis of classifications of form rather than on the basis of function, is to lose some of the most meaningful insights into the nature of language.

Obviously the psychosemantic basis of all language phenomena cannot be easily determined. Its existence, however, is usually sufficiently apparent in generic cases, such as the use of the subjunctive, the idiomatic present, the modal auxiliaries, differences between the imperfect and preterite tenses, and the differentiated uses of *ser* and *estar* in Spanish, to be practical in the very situations where an understanding of the underlying original ideology is most useful. The resources of general linguistics and the psychology of language have not been adequately capitalized to date. Many idiomatic constructions that are likely to cause students difficulty can be grasped easily if the learner is afforded some insight into the semantic etymology of the construction. For example, a semantic translation of the etymology of the French idiom *to marry: se marier avec* (to link oneself with), will clear the seeming superfluousness of the reflexive pronoun and preposition.   Compare the Spanish equivalent *casarse con* (to *house* oneself with—to marry).   Informal experimentation has shown that (given an equal amount of time for practice) students who are afforded insights of this kind gain a firmer grasp of a construction in terms of facility, confidence, and accuracy in its use than those who learn it merely as mechanical vocabulary.

Certainly there is no need for explaining the *raisons d'etre* for every construction or idiom in language.   The irregularities of orthographic or radical-changing verbs, where these follow a specific pattern, can often be learned more effectively if insight is given into underlying causes; but such specific irregularities as are due to analogic radiation, metathesis, and other forms of linguistic change are too numerous, and their case histories too long, to allow time for analysis in terms of historical evolution.   The same limitation holds for grammatical equivalents in the vernacular and foreign language, where the differences are restricted to changes in inflection.   Possessive adjectives, demonstrative adjectives, and the like are often best learned in context as vocabulary with variable endings.

The Principle of Contextual Learning.—The use of the question-and-answer type of conjugation described in a preceding connection provides one of several practical means for introducing and learning grammatical elements in context, and for rehearsing them in a manner more nearly identical with normal communication in daily life than is permitted by the vertical format of the conventional verb paradigm. For example, after the pupils have learned the foreign verb for *to have*, this verb can be reviewed or rehearsed in different tenses with the addition of possessives, later of disjunctive pronouns, etc., in cumulative terms.

Tener: to have

¿No tiene Ud. *su*(s) libro(s)?*	Haven't you your book(s)?
—(yo) no tengo *mi*(s) libro(s).	I haven't my book(s).
¿No tienen Uds. *su*(s) libro(s)?†	Haven't you your book(s)?
—(Nosotros) no tenemos *nuestro*(s) libro(s).	We haven't our book(s).

* tú > tu(s) libros.

† vosotros > vuestro(s) libros.

The principle of agreement in gender and number which is illustrated in the foregoing exercises can be further reinforced through oral and written practice in substituting feminine words for *libro*(s), *e.g.*, *llaves*, and making the necessary changes in the possessives: *nuestra*(s) instead of *nuestro*(s).   Note that the principle of agreement is derived from practice in using it.   No mention whatsoever is made of grammatical nomenclature until *after* the pupils have learned to use the possessive adjectives as inflected vocabulary in imitation of the model. After the exercise has been read by the pupils, the teacher may facilitate comprehension by asking a few leading questions, such as,

1. Can you find the Spanish in the exercise for *your books? your book?*

2. How, then, would you say *your pencil (lápiz)? your pencils (lápices)?*

3. Can you find the Spanish for *our books? our book?*

4. What would be the Spanish for *our car (automóvil)?*

5. When we use a feminine word such as *llaves* (keys), *nuestro(s)* must change to *nuestra(s)*. How, then, would one say *our aunts (tías)? our aunt?*

6. How can you tell when we add *-s* to the Spanish words for *your, my, our*, etc.? When we use *nuestra(s)* instead of *nuestro(s)*?

7. The words *my, your, our*, etc., are called *possessive adjectives*. Pick out the possessive adjectives in the exercise.

Obviously, every student in the class may not be able to answer all these questions correctly, but there will be few students, indeed, who cannot answer a majority of them, and the less alert pupils can always learn from the brighter ones as easily as from the teacher. Where the operational principles governing agreement are difficult to grasp, additional question-and-answer practice, using different nouns and verbs, may be necessary. For example, the class may be asked to transmute the exercise using *aprender* (to learn) and *lecciones* (lessons):

¿No *aprende* Ud. su(s) *leccion(es)* (lessons)?
—(Yo) no *aprendo* mi(s). . . .

Through such practice with different verbs and nouns, the meanings and functions of the possessive adjectives can be generalized gradually until the operational principles of agreement are learned through use in variable context. The amount of practice necessary will depend upon whether the degree of learning desired is to be *active*, for use in conversation or original composition, or *recognitive*, for use on the recognition level in reading or translation into English.

Attention is called to the fact that grammatical nomenclature is not allowed to stand in the way of *learning*. The term *possessive adjective* is introduced only as a summary label for purposes of subsequent reference or identification. Insights into the operational principles of agreement are gained through guided practice, rather than through grammatical formulas, and in question-and-answer context

which bears some relationship to the nature of conversation in daily
life. Moreover, the introduction and learning of the grammatical
material as variable vocabulary in context emphasize both its meaning
and functional relationship to the language as a whole. Naturally,
such correlated learning would be impossible if the pupils did not
already know the verb *tener*, or the present-tense forms of at least a
few regular verbs. Later in the course, the disjunctive pronouns may
be introduced in a similar fashion, by adding them to the exercise:

¿No tiene Ud. su(s) libro(s) *consigo?**   Haven't you your book(s) *with you?*
—(Yo) no tengo mi(s) libro(s) *conmigo.**
No tienen Uds. su(s) libro(s) *consigo?*†
—(Nosotros) no tenemos nuestro(s) libro(s) *con nosotros.*

         * tú > contigo.
         † vosotros > con vosotros.

Inductive Teaching of Instrumental Grammar.—The procedure is
similar to that outlined for the possessive adjectives. Note that
learning is cumulative in terms of an increasingly enlarged functional
whole, and thus serves to link the unknown to the known. Previous
learning is thus reviewed automatically without seeming to be mere
repetition without purpose or direction. In the intermediate stages,
students who have been orientated in this procedure from the start
should have no difficulty in manipulating such question-and-answer
exercises as

     ¿No le dijo que trajera su(s) cuaderno(s) consigo?
     Didn't he tell you to bring your notebook(s) with you?

Although the inductive principle of teaching instrumental grammar
in cumulative context is illustrated above with examples from Spanish,
it is applicable to any foreign language regardless of the fact that the
specific format of the exercises will naturally have to be changed from
language to language. In French, for example, the format may have
to be somewhat more inclusive at the start. Later, however, the conversational (question-and-answer) paradigm may be reduced to basic
essentials. The answers in parentheses may be omitted after the general principle of analogic radiation has been grasped. The *tu* form
of the verb is not essential since it can usually be found simply by
adding -*s* to the *il* form after dropping the last consonant, if any.
Similarly, the last two answers can eventually be omitted since they
involve for the most part, a mere change in word order:

     N'avez-vous pas votre (vos) libre(s)?
       N'a-tu pas ton (tes) libre(s)?
     —Nous n'avons pas notre (nos) livre(s).

N'a-t-il (-elle) pas son (ses) livre(s)?
—Il (elle) n'a pas son (ses) livre(s).
N'ont-ils (-elles) pas leur(s) livre(s)?
—Ils (elles) n'ont pas leur(s) livre(s).

Similar adaptations can be made without difficulty for German, Italian, and other languages.

Rhythm and Rhyme as Contextual Mnemonic Aids.—Although mechanical elements, such as irregular verbs, are often included under the heading of grammar, they are, in reality, little more than inflected vocabulary. Rhymed résumés frequently help students remember verbs that are irregular in a given tense. Where the irregularity is confined, for the most part, to one person, or the irregularity in one form is suggestive of a like irregularity in all the rest, review and recall can be facilitated through versification. In Spanish, for example, the verbs that are commonly irregular in the present tense can be arranged in a rhyme scheme such as the following. Inasmuch as only the first person singular is strictly irregular in the present tense of most Spanish verbs (orthographic and radical changing verbs, being governed by rules, are not strictly irregular), the entire irregular present tense may be summarized as follows:

EL PRESENTE IRREGULAR

NOTE: The jingle is to be read aloud as if it were a verse of poetry (accenting the last words in each line, and omitting the infinitives in parentheses since they are included merely to identify the verb forms):

Ahora yo: *sé* (saber) *pongo* (poner) *quepo* (caber)
                        salgo (salir) *traigo* (traer)
             doy (dar) *hago* (hacer) *veo* (ver)
                        valgo (valer) *caigo* (caer)

                        oigo (oír)   *tengo* (tener)
                        huelo (oler)   *voy* (ir)
                        digo (decir) y *vengo* (venir)
                        soy (ser)   *estoy* (estar)

Similarly, the irregular present-subjunctive forms in French may be rhymed.

LE PRÉSENT DU SUBJONCTIF IRRÉGULIER

If faut que je

sache (savoir)   *fasse* (faire)   *aie* (avoir)   *boive* (boire)
aille (aller)   *vaille* (valoir)*   *doive* (devoir)
meure (mourir)   *puisse* (pouvoir)   *sois* (être)   *prenne* (prendre)
meuve (mouvoir) *veuille* (vouloir)   *tienne* (tenir)
                   * aussi *faille* (falloir).

That the use of rhythm and rhyme to facilitate review and recall is not limited to verb forms is indicated in the following example. Here the *der Wörter* in German are arranged in a rhythmic rhyme scheme.

Die **Der Wörter** *sind*

> dieser mancher jeder
> solcher welcher jener

In the following "poem" the Spanish idioms dealing with the weather are associated with the names of the months. Note that the stanzas can be recited in any tense without distorting the meaning.

¿Qué tiempo hace?

> En *enero* hace frío
> En *febrero* también.
> En *marzo* hace fresco
> En *abril* está bien.

> En *mayo* hay las flores
> En *junio* ¿qué hay señor?
> En *julio* hace viento
> Y en *agosto* el calor.

> En *septiembre* hay neblina
> En *octubre* el tronar
> *Noviembre* trae lluvia
> Y *diciembre* el nevar.

It is, perhaps, superfluous to indicate that versifications of this kind are generally useful *only as aids in fixing for delayed recall that which has already been learned.* Although such a jingle as *¿Qué tiempo hace?* might be useful in teaching or learning the months of the year in association with idiomatic expressions concerning the weather, any attempt to learn the irregular present tense through versified context would be futile from the functional standpoint. Unless the verb forms have been encountered previously in reading, composition work, or practice exercises of some kind, the jingle would be as meaningless as a series of nonsense syllables.

The value of versification as an aid to recall in certain situations is not to be belittled. Thousands of people in many countries (including many teachers of foreign languages) are probably indebted to the little jingle beginning "Thirty days hath September" for their knowledge of the length of the months. Inasmuch as jingles of this kind can usually be learned within ten to twenty minutes, their value in foreign-language classes as a convenient memory aid is usually worth the effort to the pupil, provided he sees the application of the material in terms of his present and future work. Moreover, since versified material lends itself readily to recitation in concert by relatively large groups, it facilitates class reviews of mechanical items that are likely to be easily forgotten.[1] Reviews in the form of oral recitations, first by individual students and later by the class as a whole, can usually be staged at the beginning of the period while such routine details as taking the roll and passing or collecting papers are being handled. If the teacher does not have a flare for composing jingles, one or more pupils can usually be found with talents along this line.

The Principle of Unitary Emphasis.—A general principle worthy of observance in the teaching of any subject, such as grammar, is that of unitary emphasis. A language contains so many details to remember that unless essential items are correlated around a focal point of emphasis, the mind is destined to become gutted, distracted, or befuddled. This is exactly what happens when language is taught in isolated, classified parcels, all seemingly of equal importance. Since the students' background in language is usually inadequate as a criterion for arranging details into a unified whole, synthesis is difficult. Instead, one item is likely to be forgotten before another has been learned, especially if attention is diffused over a wide area of details—articles, possessive adjectives, object pronouns, indirect object pronouns, disjunctive pronouns, relative pronouns, etc.

To prevent students from learning a little about everything; and nothing to the point of mastery, a magnetic core around which details may be correlated is desirable. A unifying focal point of emphasis helps to prevent the dissipation of attention over too diffuse an area of "minimum essentials." In grammar, such a magnetic core may be developed using the verb in the cumulative question-and-answer type of paradigm described above. For this purpose the verb may, figuratively speaking, be likened to the sun as the magnetic center of the solar system. Around the verb move all nouns and pronouns used as subjects or verbal objects, their specific positions depending upon the interrogative, declarative, or exclamatory nature of the sentence. Around the verb, too, move adverbs and certain prepositions; around the nouns move various adjectival satellites. A con-

---

[1] Walter V. Kaulfers, "Facilitating Recall in Language Work," *Hispania*, Vol. X, pp. 257–264, October, 1927. "Method for the Large Foreign Language Class," *Hispania*, Vol. XII, pp. 189–194, March, 1929. Both articles contain additional examples in Spanish.

ception of the verb as the hub of the language system often helps to clarify word order and to establish a magnetic center for other language elements. The ordinary textbook does not provide the learner with a fixed point of reference, nor any unifying core for the synthesis of diverse grammatical details. If new grammatical elements are introduced in meaningful context, where its form and function can be grasped in terms of the previously known, synthesis is almost automatic, for the part is then learned in terms of an expanding whole. If, further, learning is in terms of exercises such as the conversational sentence paradigm, the transfer of training from practice to normal communication is easier owing to the greater degree of similarity in situations.

Material learned in parts is likely to function only in parts, or not at all. The faltering reading and speech habits of foreign-language students who have survived two or three years of language training on the part-by-part basis prove the point. They have seldom been in contact with language as communication. Like the cardplayer who decided, after memorizing a treatise on bridge, that he would not try to play the game because it was impossible to remember all the rules, so language students have often given up the attempt to use a language which any normal six-year-old in France, Germany, Spain, or Italy has learned to speak quite adequately for ordinary purposes of communication, directly through use without benefit of formal grammar.

The principle of unitary emphasis is especially important when the differences between two grammatical factors are to be compared or contrasted as, for example, in distinguishing between the uses of *ser* and *estar* or *por* and *para* in Spanish; the auxiliary verbs *sein* and *haben* in German, *avoir* and *être* in French, *essere* and *avere* in Italian, the *masculine* and *feminine* genders of nouns and pronouns in French, Spanish, and Italian, *direct* and *indirect* objects, etc. The conventional procedure in most textbooks and courses of study involves learning a double series of rules—one set of rules for one factor, and a second parallel set of rules for the other factor. The result is usually a psychological muddle. If the two sets of rules are presented simultaneously, the learning problem is tripled or quadrupled in difficulty, for the complexity of a task, as measured by learning time required for mastery, tends to increase in geometric ratio with the number of variables confronted simultaneously. The set of rules pertaining to one factor is likely to become confused with the set pertaining to the second factor, especially after periods of disuse when the material is no longer fresh in the learner's memory. Similarly, if the two factors are presented in sequence with a view to ensuring a grasp of one factor before the second is introduced, the danger is imminent that the learner, being unaware of the second factor will generalize the first, and tend unconsciously to use it in place of the second factor even after the latter has been studied.

For example, if the beginning student learns *estar* as the verb for *to be* in Spanish, without being aware that *ser* also means *to be*, he is likely to generalize the function of *estar* to cover all cases in which *to be* is used in English. The involuntary transfer of training is here comparable to that noted for the unconscious intrusion into the foreign language of oral speech habits from the vernacular, except that the transfer is here usually attributed more to false generalization than to automatic psychophysical reactions. The introduction of *ser* as *to be* after the pupil has unconsciously generalized the uses of *estar* to cover all the functions of the verb *to be* means, in effect, unlearning a generalization—a process that is likely to be more discomforting and disillusioning than satisfying. Whenever two factors are to be learned separately in sequence, it is important that the learner be aware of the existence of both factors before a specialized study of one of them is undertaken. Otherwise, the part is likely to be mistaken for the whole, *i.e.*, generalization from the vernacular is likely to cause the beginner to use *ser* to cover all the functions of *to be* in English. Preliminary orientation in the case of the foreign languages can easily be provided through reading or questions and answers involving meaningful content on the third-person level where the forms of *ser* and *estar* can be treated as vocabulary in context, *e.g.*,

La capital de México *es* una ciudad (city) de 1,500,000 (un millón quinientos mil) habitantes. La capital *está* situada en el Valle de México. . . .

Questions raised by the pupils themselves regarding such points of usage as "Why do you say '*La capital es*' in one place and '*La capital está*' in another?" will provide the opportunity for introducing a specialized treatment of the verbs. When such a degree of learning readiness has been reached, however, it is just as easy to learn the functions of both *ser* and *estar*, as to learn them separately, provided the subject is presented in keeping with the principle of unitary emphasis.

This principle involves focusing attention on *all* the normal uses of the least difficult factor, in such a way as to leave the mind temporarily free to use the more difficult variable *in all other cases*. To illustrate: since *estar* has relatively fewer functions than *ser* as *to be*, the learner will be confronted only with the uses of *estar* and encouraged temporarily, at least, to use *ser* in all other cases:

Ser and *estar* both mean *to be* (am, is, are, was, were, being, been).   Forms of *estar* are used in speaking or asking about (1) daily health, (2) the location of any person, place, or thing, or (3) any condition which as a general rule can change both *back and forth within twenty-four hours*.   In nearly all other cases, forms of *ser* are used for *to be*.

Compare the foregoing explanation with the formal, grammatical, double sets of rules usually given in beginning textbooks.   Note the avoidance of abstruse technical terminology, or of such ambiguous statements as "*estar* is used to express changeable or transitory conditions."   Following the prescription of such eloquent nonsense, many conscientious students have been taught to make mistakes in sentences like *El muchacho es joven* (The boy is young) and *Es la una* (It is one o'clock); for are not these conditions in a sense changeable or transitory?   By what test is a beginner to know *how* changeable or transitory a condition must be before *estar* can be used to express it?[1]

Naturally, any explanation to be clear requires illustrative examples.   Consequently, it is not assumed that the statement phrased above in nongrammatical terms can be understood without similar models.   The statement (3), "any condition which as a rule can change *both* back and forth within twenty-four hours," requires careful reading and interpretation.   The meaning can usually be made clear through inductive questioning:

Q: Why do you think that *es* is used instead of *está* in *El muchacho es joven* (The boy is young)?
A: Because, although the boy can get older within twenty-four hours, his age is not changeable *backward; i.e.*, he cannot grow *younger*.
Q: Why is *son* used instead of *están* in the statement *Son las dos* (It is two o'clock)?
A: As in the preceding example, time moves only in one direction.   If it is two o'clock at a given moment, time can only become later, not earlier.   In other words, the condition is not changeable *both backward and forward* daily.
Q: Should we use *es* or *está* for *is* in the sentence, "The window is open: *La ventana _____ abierta*"?
A: Use *está*, because as a general rule a window can be opened and closed several times within a day, or from day to day.   It is true that a particular window in an uninhabited house might be locked for months, but in judging whether to use *ser* or *estar* we do not judge from exceptions, but from what is true of windows or doors, etc., *in general*.

[1] Walter V. Kaulfers, "*Ser* and *Estar* in Beginning Classes," *The Modern Language Forum*, Vol. XXI, pp. 87–91, May, 1936.

Note that idiomatic translations of *to be* in statements concerning the weather or personal physical conditions (*e.g.*, in French, Spanish, and Italian) or the use of *ser* to distinguish passive actions from conditions, are not introduced in this connection.   To do so would be to befuddle the pupil through a flagrant violation of the principle of unitary emphasis.   Idiomatic translations of *to be* (as in *faire beau temps, hacer mucho frío, fa freddo, io non ho fame*, etc.) can be presented as separate units, perhaps as vocabulary in dialogue context, or through some device such as the versification of *¿Qué tiempo hace?* cited in an earlier connection.   Similarly, the distinction between *ser* used to express passive action and *estar* used to describe conditions can be reserved until the students are ready to study the passive voice. After the pupils have learned the various ways in which to translate the concept of *to be*, an inclusive simultaneous treatment of the problem, by way of logical organization and review, is desirable.   The learner is then in a position to see the problem sufficiently clearly to be able to identify the relationship between the whole and its component parts, or of the latter to each other.

Enlisting Pupil Participation in Organizing Reviews.—The chief objection to the use of review grammars in this connection is the fact that the student is deprived of one of the most profitable of learning experiences, that of exercising his own intelligence and insight in organizing material in his own mind.   Content that is already logically organized affords the student no more motivating experience than that of rememorizing material in a different classification.   Content so learned is not likely to become so much a part of the learner's personal experience as an organization which the active use of his own intelligence and background in the language has achieved under guidance. In the initial stages, the whole can obviously not be larger at any time than the attention span of the learner, nor beyond the grasp of his level of insight.   Just as a snowball is a whole, whatever its size, which can be expanded with increasing increments, so the unit in learning is, from the organismic standpoint, a cumulative magnetic core.   By the "whole" in language is obviously meant *the language in action as a medium for the communication, as in daily life, of meaningful content in a listening, speaking, or reading situation.*   By the "part" is meant the semantic function of word forms and conventionalized expressions in conveying the current of thought to a reader or listener.   Whereas a strictly logical conception of language teaching from the standpoint of grammatical classifications within the language itself would involve, if carried to extremes, teaching everything pertaining to verbs (forms, tenses, moods, passive voice, idiomatic usages, etc.) in one exclusive unit, the psychological conception involves introducing the part only in the light of a cumulative semantic whole.

The problem of *ser* and *estar* has been analyzed in considerable detail to show the specific application of the principle of unitary emphasis in an organismic conception of learning, because the problem is illustrative of procedures that are applicable to other situations in which a single concept in English is expressed through a duality of form in the foreign language, *e.g.*, *por* and *para* in Spanish, *sein* and *haben* as auxiliaries in German, *essere* and *avere* in Italian, the auxiliary verbs *avoir* and *être* in French, the masculine and feminine genders in French and Spanish, etc. Even where the concept is dual in English, as in the case of direct and indirect objects, the principle is equally applicable. The important thing in such cases is to center attention on the least complicated of the two factors (or sets of factors), and to leave the student temporarily free to use the other in all cases not covered by the first. This procedure reduces the complexity of the learning process, avoids taxing the memory with double series of rules, and helps to prevent confusion or mental congestion. The repeated violation of this principle in so-called basic textbooks has done more to complicate the learning process than to facilitate it.

Frustration of Learning through Unnecessary Shifts in Linguistic Viewpoint.—A second violation of the principle of unitary emphasis of which many textbooks, courses of study, and teachers are guilty, can be observed in the frequent shifts in linguistic point of view from which grammatical explanations are given. Some of the rules are presented from the viewpoint of the vernacular, *i.e.*, of translating English into the foreign language; others are written from the standpoint of translating the foreign language into English. Frequent shifts in linguistic viewpoint unnecessarily complicate and confuse the learning process by demanding a continuous readjustment of the apperceptive mind-set. Unless the learner approaches a problem from the same point of view as that in which its solution is written, neither the nature of the problem nor the solution itself is likely to be clear. The transfer of training from rule to application is destined to be hampered, *e.g.*, if the rule is intended to facilitate translation from the foreign language into English, and the exercises immediately following require translation from the vernacular into the foreign language. Relatively few young people (and none too many adults) find it possible to restate the explanation in operational terms, or to retranslate it in their minds, especially if it is phrased in formal grammatical language. If the work of the class stresses translation from English into the foreign language, original composition, or extemporaneous conversation, the linguistic viewpoint throughout the course may well be "How to say it in the foreign language"; whereas, if the primary emphasis is on reading for comprehension, the grammatical viewpoint may appropriately be "What it means in English." In any case, the viewpoint should be consistent throughout for, although the outcomes might conceivably be equally effective no matter from which angle the foreign language is approached, the learning process is rendered more complicated if the pupil's mind is repeatedly disoriented by unconscious changes in the expository viewpoint of the teacher or textbook.

Except for the occasionally appropriate exercises or incidental reading selections which they contain, many introductory textbooks are ineffective aids to the teacher, and seldom a real help to the student in clarifying problems of usage; for the language of the explanations is either incomprehensible to the learner, or the viewpoint of the explanations shifts from the vernacular to the foreign language and back without regard for the type of work that the pupil is to do, or attention is diffused over such a cumulative mass of classified details that mental indigestion results. Nearly as effective outcomes as are usually achieved in such circumstances could quite conceivably be obtained by trial-and-error activity without benefit of grammar, provided the same criteria of evaluation are used as have often prevailed in measuring the value of conventional foreign-language courses, *viz.*, counting only the successes and disregarding the rest. Any man could easily give the impression of being an expert marksman if he enthusiastically exclaimed, "I made three bull's-eyes today!" and neglected to add that it took 100 shots to do it!

Preventing the Formation of Word-matching Complexes.—If the unifying viewpoint of the grammatical exposition involves the explanation of linguistic phenomena by way of comparison and contrast with equivalents in the vernacular, *i.e.*, "How they say it in the foreign language," caution is necessary to prevent the work of the course from degenerating into a series of mere mechanical exercises in matching words according to rule. The student's resources in his native tongue, developed from childhood in the motivated conditions of actual life, are destined far to exceed such classroom acquirements as he may attain in the foreign language. Yet if conventional textbooks and learning exercises are at all a valid index to present practice in foreign-language teaching, it would seem that the learner is repeatedly forced

into the mental habit of attempting to find in the foreign language
the equivalent of every word and construction in the vernacular.   The
instructional devices in most common use are not, properly speaking,
exercises in the communication or interpretation of thought, but
"matching exercises" in which verbalism is emphasized to the neglect
of meaning.   A sentence is too often marked wrong not primarily
because of its failure to carry the current of thought effectively to a
reader or listener, but for its failure to comply with grammatical
formulas governing form and mechanics.   As a result the student
rarely becomes, even in advanced classes, more than an awkward
"word matcher" as regards ability to restate in his own words the
thought or information of what he has read in the foreign language,
or to communicate an idea of his own in the foreign idiom.   The
exceptions to this rule, if they have not enjoyed practice in the foreign
language outside of class, are usually students who by virtue of mental
alertness and insight have learned consciously or unconsciously to
make the most of the language at their command.

The inability of many students to summarize in English the
information or thought content of a paragraph, page, or chapter without mentally translating every word, and the faltering, labored speech
(punctuated by embarrassing lapses of memory) that is so often
traceable to futile attempts on the part of the students to find just the
right word (even when they have at their disposal other terms adequate
for the communication of the *idea* in point) can be attributed in large
measure to the overuse of disconnected exercises devoid of real meaning, in which form and mechanics are not the servants of effective
communication, but ends in themselves.   The mechanics of structure
and form can be only ends in themselves if the medium of instruction
is an abstruse grammatical language whose rules are to be applied in
finding the exact equivalent in the foreign tongue of such statements as

1. This is not John's book (the book of John), but Mary's.
2. The teacher is not under the table, but in front of it.
3. In winter it is cold, but in summer it is warm.

Neither can form and mechanics become anything but ends in themselves if the reading matter is not written to communicate something
that someone would really care to read, but concocted to illustrate
words, idioms, tenses, and other grammatical phenomena.   Just
what can one do with reading material, such as the following, besides
decode it, or repeat it in translation, oral "reading," or parrot exercises
of the question-and-answer type?   The passage below is an example

of what some foreign-language texts communicate in good English translation:

John and Jane have a dog. The dog does not speak French; he speaks animal language. John and Jane do not speak animal language; they speak French. "Good morning," says the dog in animal language. The dog's name is Beppo. He is two years old. He is not very old. He has two ears, a nose, and two eyes. John and Jane also have two eyes, two ears, and a nose, but they do not have a tail. Only animals have tails. . . .

Are the authors of such reading matter for junior and senior high schools imbeciles, or do they assume that all adolescent boys and girls are? A more plausible explanation is probably to be found in the common habit of mistaking a string of words for language, and in the equally common but erroneous notion that only asinine content can be stated in simple, intelligible words. Whatever the explanation, the effect of such practice exercises and reading materials is distressing, not only because of the dampening influence that they have upon the morale of the class, but also because of the unsound language habits that they beget in students.

To prevent the formation of such inhibitions as often arise from mental habits of word matching, content rich in worth-while information and ideas is essential. Otherwise, accuracy of form for its own sake, rather than for the sake of effective communication, is likely to dominate the learning process to such an extent that the pupil will become more and more bewildered and befuddled instead of more confident and at ease in his own use of the language. When the content medium in and through which the language abilities are exercised is expressive from the start of something worth reading, writing, or talking about, form and mechanics can be appreciated in their proper perspective as aids in effective communication, and attention can then be devoted to principles of usage as the need arises. To start with form and mechanics is to put the cart before the horse—to convert rules and explanations into instruments of frustration and self-conscious inhibition, rather than into means for facilitating and building confidence in the effective use of language.

Instrumental Grammar through Communication Exercises.— Moreover, when the thought content is significant and interesting to the learner, stereotyped word-matching exercises can be replaced with less formalized language activities. Instead of "Translate the first two paragraphs into English," the teacher can say, "Tell me in English, without looking at the book, what the first two paragraphs tell us." She will then listen to see how accurately and completely the pupil understands the thought or information of the paragraphs, and judge his comprehension in these terms rather than in terms of exactness of word matching. Translation will be resorted to, if at all, only to facilitate the comprehension of some essential thought that has been misunderstood or concealed by language beyond the pupil's level of insight. In other words, *interpretation* rather than translation or transliteration is facilitated. Whereas translation and transliteration both stress exactness of equivalent wording, often to such a degree that the pupil's mind is distracted from the thought content to the mechanics of language, *interpretation* focalizes attention on the idea. To avoid the early formation of an inhibitive word-matching complex, recourse to English as a means for measuring comprehension in the elementary and intermediate states should, as far as possible, be in terms of a restatement of the content of the material in the learner's own words.

For the same reason, written work in the foreign language might well be in terms of résumés, précis, abstracts, original questions, or paraphrastic restatements of the content of a series of paragraphs on some unified topic or theme, instead of in terms of isolated sentences disassociated in meaning. The following sample directions to students are suggestive of several possibilities:

1. *Résumés:* Write a summary in French (German, etc.) of the most interesting and important information in each paragraph of the lesson. For the present avoid saying anything for which you cannot find a model in the lesson itself.

In the second semester, the pupils can be expected to write their summaries from memory during the first ten minutes of the following class period. The length of the summaries is defined only in such relative terms as "Write from memory as much as you can remember in ten minutes. In general, it is desirable to include at least one fact from each paragraph." Note that the preparation and learning of a précis involve a critical review of the lesson, comprehension and selection of key statements, organization of key statements into a unified sequence, and the simultaneous learning of vocabulary, idioms, and grammatical constructions in connected informational context. Language and "culture" are not separated. In second-semester classes the length of the précis written from memory by pupils of widely differing abilities and language interests will normally range from 40 to 175 words.

2. *Transpository writing:* Rewrite the chapter on geography, substituting information about our own state (or country) for the facts mentioned about France. For example:

Given: Les montagnes les plus hautes de la France sont les Alpes et les Pyrénées. Les principaux fleuves de la France sont la Seine, la Loire, la Garonne, le Rhône, et le Rhin. . . .

Write (if your home is in California): Les montagnes les plus hautes de la *Californie* sont la *Coast Range* et *la Sierra Nevada.* Les principaux fleuves de la *Californie* sont *le San Joaquin* et *le Sacramento.* . . .

Note that this exercise requires critical reaction, not only to the language, but also to the information of the chapter. Facts that have no parallel in the case of the student's native community, state, or nation are omitted. Since changes in grammatical agreement—especially articles, adjectives, and verbs—are frequently involved in this type of transpository writing, the activity can often serve as an introduction or review of gender, number, negative constructions, and the like. If the content involved is informational and the students are corresponding with one or more young people abroad, the transposed material (*e.g.,* on the geography of their own state or country) may be worthy of inclusion in letters. Material written with a view to communicating something to a definite reader usually elicits better responses than material written for its own sake or to satisfy the teacher. Similar possibilities for recourse to transpository composition often occur in connection with biographical accounts, historical summaries, or reading content in which the information has a close parallel in some aspect of the pupils' own lives or in the environment in which they live.

3. *Semioriginal questions:* Write five good questions in German concerning the information in the chapter, beginning them as follows:

a. Wer war (Who was......................................)?
b. Wann sind sie (When did they.........................)?
c. Warum gingen (Why did they.......................go)?
d. Wo ist (Where is......................................)?
e. Was sagte (What did...............................say)?

The composition of semioriginal questions, based on informational content, is practical as early as the first week of beginning foreign-language study, provided the interrogatives and verbs are given as indicated above. This type of composition requires not only comprehension of the content read, but also some degree of discrimination in selecting the elements of vocabulary needed to complete the questions. The semioriginal question can serve as an introduction to interrogative word order and to the agreement of subject and predicate, in addition to providing material for elementary question-and-answer conversation among pupils from the very beginning of the course. For example, one pupil may ask his questions of another pupil in rotation. Since all the questions will not be identical in wording or information, a more spontaneous language situation is possible than can be expected when a series of identical questions (to which all the pupils can formulate answers in advance) is used as the basis for conversational work. The pupil who answers a semioriginal question written by another pupil has to "think on his feet." Most question-and-answer activity based on completely phrased series of questions usually amounts, in effect, to little more than an oral reading exercise. If conversation is to receive attention in the classroom, students should be cautioned from the start *not to read* their questions or answers, but to use what written material is available merely as a means for refreshing their memories—much as an extemporaneous speaker uses suggestive notes. Otherwise the student may easily become so habituated to the printed word that he cannot understand or say anything unless he sees it in writing. Note also that the *pupil*—not the teacher—asks his own questions. This is the opposite of the usual classroom procedure in which the teacher asks all the questions—and gets almost all the practice! After the pupils have gained insight into such matters as interrogative word order and the agreement of subject and predicate, the instructor may omit the verb from the completion questions and supply only the initial interrogative guide words. Eventually the pupils can write entirely original questions of their own, provided they use as far as possible only the vocabulary and information contained in the lesson upon which the questions are based.

4. *Imitative translations:* Give the Spanish for the following English summary of the chapter. As far as possible, quote directly from the text.

The function of this type of work is chiefly to encourage rapid rereading, and to provide for a review of the content and vocabulary of reading lessons. In beginning courses it involves little more than matching English sentences in the exercise with sentences in the text. As the pupil's grasp of the mechanics and principles of usage increases, greater freedom may be encouraged. In general, however, close imitation of the original text is desirable to prevent too many mistakes from occurring in elementary courses.

Attention is called to the fact that all the writing activities just described are based upon informative content in connected context in the foreign language, and increase in flexibility as the pupil gains insight into the working principles of the language. Form and function are not separated; neither is language decomposed into such isolated particles as vocabulary and tenses, except as the need for special explanations and practice arises. In other words, the pupil uses what language is at his disposal as a unit, and the part is isolated from context subsequently only as it requires special attention. Wherever possible, an audience in the form of a reader or listener is provided to motivate the work. Occasionally the material can be included in letters to foreign correspondents; sometimes it is suitable for publication in translation in the school paper or in a mimeographed foreign-language bulletin. The class as a whole is generally an effective audience only for material concerning which it is interested and seeking additional information. Otherwise the speaker is likely to find himself in the unenviable position of talking to himself before a board of petty language critics.

Although mistakes will always occur, the activities mentioned can be arranged to reduce the possibility for error to a minimum. Mistakes will usually increase with the degree of carelessness with which the original material has been read, and the degree of haste with which assignments are made. When proper precautions in the way of effective guidance are taken, however, the activities can be employed successfully as early as the first week of beginning foreign language in junior-high-school, senior-high-school, and college classes.

Translation as a Language-learning Activity.—The fact that translation has not been included among the types of written work discussed above does not mean that incidental composition involving this skill cannot be introduced occasionally even during the first semester of the beginning course. The interpretative translation into English of famous epigrams or quotations from distinguished foreign writers, or of the words of a foreign song which the pupils are learning, provides motivated opportunities for the exercise of creative expression in language. By interpretative translation is meant a restatement which is designed primarily to preserve the spirit, feeling, and musical qualities of the quotation or poem, in language that is as close as possible, but not necessarily identical with the wording of the original. Many examples of interpretative translation can be found in translations of foreign songs in which some changes in wording had to be made in order to suit the English verses to the music, to retain the original rhythm, or to preserve the rhyme scheme.

Below are two examples of quotations from well-known French writers which have been used incidentally to afford occasional practice in creative translation.   Note that the English meanings for the less familiar words are given after each quotation.

Si nous n'avions point de *défauts*,* nous ne prendrions pas tant de plaisir *à en remarquer*† dans les autres.

FRANÇOIS DE LA ROCHEFOUCAULD (1613–1680)
* faults.   † in noticing them.

S'amuser à *rechercher** les défauts *d'autrui*,† c'est signe que l'on ne s'occupe guère *des siens*.‡
* finding.   † of another.   ‡ with one's own.

Quotations such as the foregoing can be used effectively once or twice a week as a short class exercise in interpretative translation even in beginning courses.   Informal questioning in the foreign language concerning the author can make this activity serve as an introduction in miniature to world literature.   In this respect, the use of quotations is preferable to the use of proverbs, most of which are universal and cannot easily be identified with great names.[1]

The interpretative translation of poems or songs is best encouraged on the volunteer basis in lieu of other assignments.   Formal translation from English into the foreign language, except in close imitation of models in connected context [see activity (4) above], is generally undesirable until after a certain measure of confidence and facility in the new language has been achieved.   Even in upper division high-school classes, translation can hardly be justified except incidentally, in connection with occasional work in commercial letter writing.   The time usually consumed in developing this most difficult of all skills does not represent a profitable investment in terms of the postschool uses to which it is ordinarily put.[2]   Translation from English into a foreign language, except in the case of type-form commercial letters, is a highly technical exercise in two languages, requiring specialized training at the upper division college and graduate-school levels.   The time ordinarily consumed in this type of work in high-school and junior-college classes could more profitably be devoted to the development of facility in reading, and of ability to converse sufficiently intelligibly

[1] Walter V. Kaulfers and Dante P. Lembi, "Instead of Proverbs," *The Modern Language Forum*, Vol. XXV, pp. 138–144, September, 1940.

[2] Clara Altman, "Foreign Language Curricula," *School and Society*, Vol. L, pp. 542–43, Oct. 21, 1939.   Russell J. Fornwalt and Herbert W. Rogers, "An Investigation of the Values of Modern Foreign Language Study in College," *The Modern Language Journal*, Vol. XIX, pp. 161–164, December, 1934.

to be able to fill the limited language needs associated with a specific occupational task or tourist travel abroad.

Foundation Exercises in Instrumental Grammar.—Even practice exercises in which attention is focused on the part can be constructed in such a way as to avoid treating the part in isolation. Note that, whereas the sentences are disconnected in the following sample unit, they deal with a unified topic: words and expressions associated with ordering a meal. Observe also that attention is concentrated, for the time being, on a single center of emphasis—the difference between the future and conditional in Spanish. Word matching, vocabulary thumbing, and the like are reduced by giving the meaning of each exercise in full in English, thus enabling the learner to concentrate on developing control of a single grammatical variable. Practice exercises such as the following can be easily corrected from a key by any pupil, and are adaptable for use at any time as the need for them arises. Since almost all grammatical variables, except the one that is the focal center of emphasis, are kept constant, the course can be organized on the laboratory-workshop plan to enable pupils to progress at their own speed, depending only on the occasional guidance of the teacher, or of able pupils in the class who have already satisfactorily completed the unit.

Sección X: Reconstrucción

Number a separate sheet of paper and, opposite the proper numbers, rearrange the Spanish words in the following exercises, changing the verbs in parentheses to the proper form so as to make complete sentences.

1. ¿Ud. filete el (probar)?
   Will you try the tenderloin steak?
2. ¿leche, té, café ó (desear) Uds.?
   Would you like coffee, tea, or milk?
3. ¿cuál (preferir) el él <u>asado de carnero</u> ó chuletas las?
   Which would he rather have, the roast mutton or the cutlets (chops)?
   The underlined words go together.
4. pan mantequilla (pedir) y.
   I shall order (some) bread and butter. (bread = pan)
5. las mozo bebidas el (servir).
   The boy (waiter) will serve the drinks.
6. nada (comer) no ni (beber).
   I'll not eat or drink anything. (*Ni = nor* in this sentence.)
7. ¿cuchara una (desear) Ud. o servilleta una?
   Would you like a spoon or a napkin? (*napkin = servilleta*)
8. El señor Martínez (preferir) de vaso un leche.
   Mr. Martinex would rather have (prefer) a glass of milk.

   9. ¿no Uds. azúcar crema o (tomar) su café en?
      Won't you take cream or sugar in your coffee?
  10. ¿(pedir) quién cuenta la (pagar) y?
      Who will ask and pay for the bill?   (Use ending for *él* or *ella* in *both* verbs.)

In view of what has been said in this and preceding chapters, it is probably unnecessary to indicate that the value of units dealing with specific linguistic aspects of form and usage depends upon how appropriately the exercises are employed. An elementary course, defined and organized primarily in terms of such units and supplemented only occasionally by illustrative reading lessons, would be just as unmotivated, atomistic, mechanical, and inoperative in outcomes as a course in which grammatical phenomena are illustrated by disconnected examples, matching exercises, and reading lessons devoid of significant thought content. The function of such units is to facilitate individual progress, to make possible recourse to specialized practice as the need arises, and to permit of a more flexible choice of reading materials and learning activities. The conventional basic grammar is not suitable for use in a flexible program in which attention to form and mechanics is determined by the difficulties that the pupil himself encounters in actually using the language in his *own* writing, reading, or speech. The conventional textbook is usually so cumulative that unless the pupil starts at the beginning of the grammar and follows the lessons in careful sequence, he is usually unprepared to do the exercises in any one subsequent section. Moreover, few basic textbooks provide a sufficiently large number of exercises on any one point of usage to develop more than a bowing acquaintance with it.[1]

The use of facilitation exercises of the kind exemplified in the foregoing sample group depends upon whether the immediate language need is a recognition knowledge of variable grammatical forms as vocabulary in reading, an operational knowledge of grammatical variables in making translations or in doing original writing with the aid of a dictionary, or an active command of the variables in extemporaneous or impromptu conversation. The exercises included must vary in type according to the different uses to which the grammatical material is to be put. For a recognition knowledge, only those exercises need be done which are recognitive in nature, *e.g.*, multiple-choice and matching exercises. For an active command of the

---

[1] Walter V. Kaulfers, "The Mastery-unit Plan in Foreign Language Teaching," *Hispania*, Vol. XII, pp. 417–430, November, 1930. For a sample foundation exercise see Appendix C.

material, as many as 50 to 100 exercises may have to be completed, if not as a unit, at least at spaced intervals during the course. Since all students do not need an equal amount of practice to achieve equally effective results, differentiation of practice according to need may be guided by an experimental tryout of the unit. The teacher, for example, may say to the class,

"Some of us have been a little worried by the difference between the uses of *avoir* and *être*, and have asked for help. The unit which I am passing out will clear up some of the points concerning which you are uncertain. It also contains many practical words and expressions which you may wish to add to your knowledge of the language. I suggest that for next time everyone in the class do all the even-numbered exercises (2,4,6,8, etc.) in every section, according to the directions. We shall take ten minutes in class tomorrow to see if we can do a similar group of exercises correctly. Those who pass this tryout test will then continue reading in the various books that they have selected, while those who are still having trouble can work with me on the odd-numbered exercises in each section. Let us see how many exercises we can do correctly before the bell rings."

On the basis of the reactions of the class on the assigned exercises of the unit, or on the diagnostic test (which may be a section not previously assigned to the group), the teacher can judge the need for additional work on different types of exercises in terms of the difficulties of the individual students. Additional practice material is not assigned as a punishment to those who fail the diagnostic test, for no grades or marks need be given. Additional work is assigned merely because certain students need it. Nor is this supplementary work piled on top of any reading which the slower pupils might otherwise be doing. It merely takes the place of it. The only requirement in any class conducted on the differentiated workshop plan is that everyone be purposefully occupied with some profitable activity appropriate to the course. In general, only one-fifth to one-fourth of the total course time, including recitation periods and work outside the class, need be occupied by foundation exercises of the mastery-unit type. The units are nonconsumable in that the work can be done on a separate sheet of paper.[1] Time and energy in scoring the exercises

---

[1] Inexpensive duplicators such as the Gel-Sten Jr., Hectograph, or Ditto, produce 50 legible copies which can be used several times if students are requested to do their work on a separate sheet of paper. The machines reproduce handwriting as easily as typewritten work and can be operated by any child of junior-high-school age. See also Appendix, reference 130.

can usually be reduced through the exchange and correction of papers in class, or by enlisting the help of volunteer students to score the exercises from a key.   A volunteer proofreading committee, whose members are occasionally exempted from other class activities in which they are proficient, can often, with profit to themselves, relieve the teacher of a considerable amount of routine work in checking papers.   Naturally, the actual assignment of grades must in most cases be left to the teacher.

Since everyone can learn from his own mistakes, errors that have been checked on basic units of work should be corrected by the pupil himself, and the papers filed, when completed, in his folder in order of date.   A complete folder of the work of each student is a valuable aid in evaluating his progress and in making reports to parents.   It is also an aid to the pupil himself in gauging his own progress, especially if the responsibility for keeping his folder up to date is gradually transferred to him.   The practical mechanics of conducting a course in which pupil participation in evaluation is enlisted, are discussed in detail in Chapter XIII.

One of the serious obstacles still besetting the effective teaching of instrumental grammar on the basis of need is obviously the absence of basic texts that allow of flexible use with a variety of reading materials.   A different book is generally used from year to year with the result that few students ever become sufficiently well acquainted with any basic textbook to be able to use it in the second or third years as a means for refreshing their memories on topics that they have forgotten.   Indeed, the basic text is often taken out of the pupils' hands at the end of the term.   In such circumstances it is difficult to develop in pupils the habit of referring to previous units of work. This difficulty suggests the need for a vade mecum in the form of a basic, self-instructional grammar, with abundant exercises on specific language problems, which the pupil can use *throughout* four or more years of work in the language—long enough to become sufficiently familiar with its terminology, organization, and contents to be able to use it expeditiously as a helpful companion and guide.   An adequate index of cross references should make such a vade mecum flexible enough for use with an infinite variety of readers, provided the mastery units are organized on the principle of unitary emphasis, *i.e.*, that they treat only one specific topic in any given group of exercises.

Summary.—Although the practical applications of the principles of organismic learning can be understood only in terms of such specific examples as have been elaborated in considerable detail in the present chapter on the teaching of instrumental grammar, the principles themselves can be summarized briefly as follows:

1. Special emphasis on form and mechanics should be on the basis of need as revealed by the pupils' own difficulties or questions concerning usage.

2. Explanations should be in semantic rather than formal grammatical terms. The burden of extraneous grammatical nomenclature should be reduced through recourse to inductive learning procedures, psychosemantic explanations, and parenthetical definitions.

3. Specialized practice should be organized on the basis of unitary emphasis in the light of an expanding whole in which the unknown is linked to the known.

4. Oral and written work should be motivated through the use of informative content in audience situations.

5. Effective communication of meaning, rather than verbal equivalence, should be the primary concern of both pupil and teacher in foreign-language work. The creative interpretation of meaning, rather than mechanical word matching, should be stressed at all levels.

6. Pupil participation in evaluation should be capitalized to motivate progress in the language.

7. Content and learning activities should be organized in terms of levels of insight—on the basis of *how young people learn*, rather than on the basis exclusively of logical classifications within the subject itself.

How would a unit of work embodying these principles be organized? The accompanying outline is suggestive of one of many possibilities. Note that the primary emphasis is on content chosen with specific regard for a definite objective—in this case, an appreciation of the French people and of our own daily life and culture, in terms of the contributions to science and invention that we owe to France. This and similar units have been used successfully in first-semester junior and senior high-school classes in French, German, Spanish, and Italian where an organismic approach to language has been followed. The mechanics of conducting a class on this basis are illustrated in Chapter VII by means of a stenographic report of work with a content unit on the *first day* of beginning foreign language, with junior high-school pupils who had never studied a foreign language in school.[1]

[1] For sample transposition exercises in the teaching of verbs and tenses see Appendix B. For aids in the teaching of instrumental grammar see Appendix, references 8, 13, 14, 19, 20, 24, 25, 60, 71, 72, 73, 112, 152.

Objective: To develop favorable habits of thought and behavior toward fellow citizens of French descent, and toward the French people in general, in terms of the things that France has contributed to the enrichment of present-day life in our homes and communities.

Aspect I	Learning activities	Collateral integrative activities	Materials
French contributions to science and invention which are to be found in our own homes or community A. Inventions: the sewing machine, the cinema, the camera, the gasoline type automobile, etc. B. Scientific discoveries; vaccines, radium, "pasteurization" of milk, etc.	1. Talk in *French* by the teacher, using cognates, pictures, and other comprehension aids 2. Common background reading in French, *e.g.*, in basic text or in mimeographed unit 3. Differentiated reading in French according to varying reading abilities of individual pupils, *e.g.*, Louis Pasteur, Madame Curie, etc. 4. Reports and discussion in class on information gathered through differentiated reading in French 5. Objective comprehension exercises—correction and discussion in class 6. Foundation exercises in instrumental grammar only as needed, *e.g.*, multiple-choice or matching exercises to develop comprehension of *passé indéfini*. 7. Writing, from memory in French, of résumés dealing with French contributions to science and invention	1. Optional reading in English of interesting scientific biographies—perhaps in correlation with work in English, social studies, or science classes 2. Talks in French by competent outsiders, with aid of interpreters, if necessary 3. Interviews with local residents of French extraction, *i.e.*, in class, or by committees during out-of-school hours 4. Reviewing movies having a bearing upon the topic, *e.g.*, *The Life of Louis Pasteur*, or dramatizing excerpts from the moving-picture script in class	1. Basic readers 2. Classroom library of simple texts in French containing information on the unit 3. Mimeographed readings 4. Foundation exercises. 5. Pictures, *e.g.*, of French scientists and inventors, of early French inventions, etc. 6. Bibliographies of interesting books for collateral reading in English or French 7. Moving-picture scripts.

CHAPTER IV

PERSPECTIVE ON THE TEACHING OF READING

If, indeed, "reading maketh a full man," is it not important for the school to ask "full of what?"

Reading as a Linguistic Objective. The "Coleman Controversy." The fact that two years of high-school foreign language were for many decades required for admission to all reputable colleges and universities has had the effect of gradually making the two-year college entrance requirement the standard length of the foreign-language course for 83 per cent of the students enrolled in junior and senior high schools. Faced with the problem of providing offerings of more educative value to young people than two-year preparatory courses in grammar, leaders in the field of foreign language teaching in 1923 inaugurated the *Modern Foreign Language Study*. Of the 18 volumes[1] issued under the auspices of this group, Volume XII, *The Teaching of Modern Foreign Languages in the United States*,[2] sometimes known as the "Coleman Report" gave special attention to the consideration of aims and objectives. Among the most important recommendations was the adoption of "reading" as the central, but not necessarily exclusive, linguistic objective of foreign-language teaching in American education. Although the report summarized the opinions of a majority of teachers as expressed in questionnaires and found favor in many quarters, it was at once berated by a vociferous minority.[3] The discussion of the pros and cons of the reading objective consumed the major attention of specialists in foreign-language teaching for nearly ten years, and was at one time the chief preoccupation of local and regional conventions of foreign-language teachers.

[1] For a summary of the reports see Robert Herndon Fife, *A Summary of Reports on the Modern Foreign Languages with an Index to the Reports*, The Macmillan Company, New York, 1931, 261 pp.

[2] Algernon Coleman, *The Teaching of Modern Foreign Languages in the United States*, The Macmillan Company, New York, 1929, 299 pp.

[3] The controversy over the Coleman Report is well-summarized by Algernon Coleman and Agnes Jacques in *An Analytical Bibliography of Modern Language Teaching*, Vol. I, University of Chicago Press, Chicago, 1933, 296 pp.; pp. 12–16.

Although the report led to the publication of large numbers of new type readers and basic textbooks and thus indirectly influenced foreign-language teaching in the classroom, its direct effect has been more to stimulate discussion than to unify professional thinking toward a constructive solution of problems relating to the place and function of the foreign languages in American education. Although the 18 volumes of the *Modern Foreign Language Study* threw light on such questions as pupil achievement in foreign languages in relation to mental ability, the psychology of reading, prognostic testing, and teacher training, they also served to generate an exceptional amount of heat.

Light generated by heat usually vanishes when the temperature cools. This fact has been admirably demonstrated in the discussion of the "reading objective." Among the many reasons why this subject has proved unusually controversial is the absence of a common referent for the term "reading" itself. The word seems to mean so many things to different people that misunderstanding is inevitable if the speaker or writer does not make abundantly clear the specific sense in which he is using the term at a given time. Certainly the writer who reports that his second-year pupils read "100 words a minute"[1] comprehendingly is not using the term in quite the same sense as the writer who states that his third- and fourth-year pupils "read six to ten lines in an hour!"[2] The many controversies that have been waged over the reading objective and other problems relating to curriculum and instruction in foreign languages are fascinating examples of how linguistically disciplined, logical, and cultured minds can unconsciously become the unfortunate victims of their own specialty, language.

The Reading Process from the Psychophysical Viewpoint.—The term "reading" can easily be mistaken to include all the uses to which written or printed matter can be put in the classroom—vocabulary building, translation, literary appreciation, information getting, etc. Such a variety of referents can easily lead to confusion. Although some progress has been made in distinguishing between "oral" and "silent" reading, and between "extensive" and "intensive" reading, the terms merely describe different types of activity without defining the essential nature of the process itself. For all

[1] Arthur G. Bovée, "An Experiment in Reading," *Modern Language Journal*, Vol. XV, pp. 607–608, May, 1931.

[2] Friedrich Augener, "Wenn die Lektüre beginnt," *Die neueren Sprachen*, Vol. XXXVI, pp. 521–525, November, 1928.

except the blind, reading is basically the process by which meaning (in the nature of feelings, wants, or ideas) is communicated to the mind from the printed page, through the unconscious automatic fixation of the eyes. A person is "reading" only when his attention is tuned to the emotional or thought content of the written language. When the focal center of attention shifts to such extrinsic matters as the mechanics of language, the reading process momentarily ceases, and the activity becomes for the time being something else—translation, reflective thinking, interpretation, "literary" appreciation, or plain mental confusion.[1] Granting that the translation, interpretation, evaluation, or appreciation of the printed page presupposes "reading" it, each of these activities obviously involves additional mental processes. Translation, for example, is an exercise in *two* languages, and hence is something quite different from "reading," which normally involves one language and then only as the unobtrusive conductor of the current of thought which it conveys. Reading in the psychological sense is hardly possible if the mind is distracted too frequently from the thought to the mechanics of the language itself. Material that cannot be understood except by looking up the meanings of one or more words in every line is more an exercise in decoding than an exercise in reading. Although material of this type can be used appropriately at times as a reading-preparatory exercise, a two- or three-year program based on such "reading" matter is not likely to be successful in developing an abiding avocational interest in the reading of worth-while books, magazines, or newspapers in the foreign language. It may increase the vocabulary and it may increase ability to read, but two or three years of vocabulary thumbing may also beget a suppressed desire, as soon as basic requirements have been completed, to thumb the nose at the vocabulary, the textbook, and the teacher.

Reading-preparatory Activities at the Elementary Level.—From the foregoing discussion the conclusion might easily be drawn that "reading," in the sense in which it has been defined, is impossible in the elementary or intermediate stages. This conclusion holds only for certain types of materials. A first-semester student would hardly be able to "read" *Faust, El Quijote, La divina commedia,* or *La Chanson de Roland* in the original. Indeed, he would rarely be able to read connected context in idiomatic language, no matter how simple the thought content. It is quite possible, however, to devise

[1] G. T. Buswell, *A Laboratory Study of the Reading of Modern Foreign Languages,* The Macmillan Company, New York, 1927, xx + 100 pp.

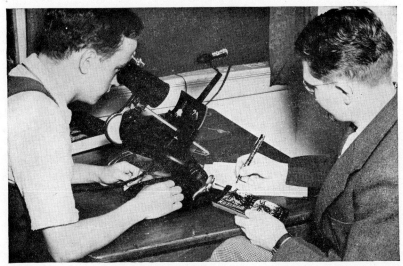

Does this boy need to consult an oculist?

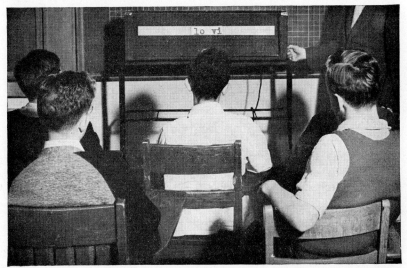

Eye-movement pacing—speeding up comprehension in reading. (*Courtesy of the Menlo School.*)

reading matter for use at the elementary level, which, without violating correct usage, permits of reading, in the psychological sense, without too many distractions from the current of thought. Such "made material" is just as appropriate in the elementary stages of learning a language skill as simple "made" melodies are appropriate for beginning students of piano, violin, or voice. Moreover, this made material need not be infantile in content. It can just as easily be reading matter that is informative but simple in vocabulary and structure.

Obviously, since the meanings of foreign words can be understood by beginners only in terms of their cognate resemblances to words already known in the vernacular, it is natural that the reading matter must at the beginning capitalize effectively the cognate resources of the foreign language. These resources are usually greater in such subject-matter fields as the sciences in which the basic vocabulary is almost universal. The word *automobile* for example, is recognizable in most foreign languages taught in school: *automobile* (French), *automóvil* (Spanish), *automobile* (Italian), *Kraftwagen* (*Automobil*) in German, etc. This fact makes it possible to treat informative topics in language that is fairly comprehensive to the beginner. In general, content written in short third-person sentences lends itself readily to reading at the start. From content utilizing cognate vocabulary, the reading matter can provide for the gradual introduction of non-cognate words. To avoid too great distraction in reading from the thought to the mechanics of the language, parenthetical definition of unfamiliar words in the text proper is to be preferred to vocabulary thumbing. Sometimes new terms can be defined separately at the beginning of each reading lesson. Michael West and others doubt if anything worthy of the name of "reading" is possible if the ratio of unknown words to known words is over 1 in 60.[1]

Comprehension of new words and constructions is obviously facilitated whenever meanings can be inferred from the nature of the passage. Such inference is possible, however, only if the context itself is meaningful and unified. The tense meaning of the verb *declaró*, if isolated, might not be grasped by beginners, but it could hardly be mistaken in such a sentence as:

México declaró su independencia en 1811.

Inference is usually possible if the nature of the whole suggests the

[1] Michael West, "The Reading Approach and the New Method System," *The Modern Language Journal*, Vol. XXII, pp. 220–222, December, 1937.

nature of an essential part. For this reason, an informative subject or topic, developed in sentences that constitute a unified scope and sequence, is preferable to noninformative content composed largely of sentences disassociated in meaning. Within the framework of such material, meanings that cannot easily be inferred can be suggested in one or more of the following ways:

1. Through parenthetical cognate definition in the foreign language.
2. Through parenthetical definition in English.
3. Through parenthetical "hints" in the way of near synonyms, paraphrastic restatements, etc., in the foreign language.

The following passage will serve to illustrate the mechanics of this technique.[1]

LE CONTRIBUZIONI D'ITALIA ALLA MUSICA UNIVERSALE

L'Italia è (is) famosa per le sue (for her) importantissime contribuzioni alla musica classica e (and) moderna. Il violino, il pianoforte, il piccolo, la viola, ed il mandolino sono invenzioni italiane. La città di Cremona è celebre (famosa) per i violini splendidi di Stradivario e di Guarneri. I violini di Stradivario hanno (have) un tono ammirabile e sono considerati un tesoro prezioso fra (among) i violinisti moderni.

Molte (diverse) forme musicali sono (are) d'origine italiana e rappresentano una contribuzione importante alla musica universale. Fra (among) le forme più importanti alla musica universale sono l'opera seria, l'opera buffa, l'operetta, l'oratorio, la cantata, ed il concerto. L'opera seria è una forma musicale interamente (completamente) italiana. Jacopo Peri, "il padre dell'opera," scrisse (wrote) la prima opera, *Euridice*, nell'anno 1600 (mille seicento). *Euridice* fu rappresentata (presentata) in Nuova York nell'anno 1894 (mille ottocento novantaquatro). Nicolo Logroscino sviluppò (originò) l'opera buffa. L'opera buffa è un'opera comica. La commedia musicale americana, la quale (which) è simile all'opera buffa, è una corruzione (degenerazione) dell'opera buffa italiana. Filippo Neri sviluppò (originò) l'oratorio, una forma di musica religiosa dalla quale (from which) si sviluppò l'opera seria. Vincenzo Galilei originò la cantata, una forma di musica vocale. Arcangelo Corelli, famoso violinista, originò la forma musicale del concerto nella quale (in which) il violino è accompagnato dall' orchestra.

La storia (history) musicale ricorda i nomi (names) di famosi compositori ed artisti musicali come Paganini, Corelli, Tartini, e Vivaldi, celebri violinisti; Enrico Caruso, il migliore (best) tenore del mondo; Giacomo Puccini, compositore delle opere *Tosca* e *Madama Butterfly;* Giuseppe Verdi, compositore dell'opera Rigoletto; Gioacchino Rossini, compositore dell'opera *Il Barbiere di Siviglia*, e Vincenzo Bellini, compositore dell'opera *Norma*. Fra i cantanti (singers) moderni più famosi della Metropolitan di New York sono Ezio Pinza, basso; Beniamino Gigli, tenore; Giovanni Martinelli, tenore; e Tito Schipa, tenore. Arturo Toscanini, il celebre maestro (direttore) dell'orchestra NBC, e Bernardino Molinari sono famosi maestri italiani.

[1] Experimental unit developed in collaboration with the author by Dante P. Lembi for use in the Jefferson High School, Daly City, Calif.

I termini (espressioni) musicali italiani sono impiegati (usati) in tutto il mondo e sono un testimonio al genio (genius) musicale italiano. Alcuni di questi (some of these) termini sono falsetto, staccato, trio, solo, prima donna, finale, alto, aria, fortissimo, pianissimo, coda, sotto voce, fine, libretto, virtuoso, andante, allegro, cadenza, arpeggio, intermezzo.

The vocabulary density is obviously greater here than that suggested by Michael West, since the distraction of the eyes and attention in reading is not so great as that which would occur if the pupil were obliged to thumb a vocabulary at the end of the book, or to search for a definition at the side or bottom of the page. Interruptions of this kind are not only annoying and time consuming, but lead to faulty eye movements in reading.

The attempt to justify vocabulary thumbing as a linguistic discipline has many plausible arguments in its favor, some of which are valid if the number of words that the pupil is obliged to look up does not exceed the number that a good reader finds it necessary to consult in a dictionary to satisfy his conscience in reading a non-fiction best seller. In most other respects, the presumed advantages are so heavily outweighed by disadvantages (such as the frustration of interest in reading), that vocabulary thumbing can hardly be justified oftener than once or twice per page.

To date, no reliable investigation has been reported concerning the presumed value of dictionary thumbing as an aid in helping students to remember the meanings of new words, idioms, and constructions. Even if such evidence existed, it is certain that other means, less injurious to the development of effective reading habits and enduring reading interests, exist. Semioriginal types of oral and written composition in the foreign language, based on the content read, have already been described in detail in Chapter III: semioriginal questions, précis, abstracts, summaries, résumés, transpository composition, etc. Appropriately used, these devices can serve not only to fix vocabulary for delayed recall but also to help students remember the information contained in the unit. The rereading and the mental reaction to language and context which these activities require yield far more profitable primary, associate, and concomitant outcomes than can be expected from repeatedly fumbling through the end leaves of a textbook. Indirectly, they also serve as an informal measure of comprehension in reading.

Naturally, oral and written activities based on reading matter are not to be confused with reading. They are associated activities which make possible a close correlation of cultural information with the collateral development of ability in vocabulary, usage, and oral and written work. If the reading matter is itself interesting and purposefully directed toward some specific cultural objective, these activities are less likely to seem dull busywork to the pupils than if the material is lacking in real thought content. Moreover, if collateral activities of this kind are provided in the book, there is little need for the textbook writer to subordinate the thought content to the language, or to dilute meager information with excess wordage, as is so often the case in reading lessons designed primarily to repeat words in keeping with their frequency ratio in standard word counts, rather than to convey information, thoughts, or ideas worth mentioning.

When visual repetition of words in context is relied upon as a means for impressing vocabulary in the minds of the pupils, content must of necessity be diluted with wordage to such an extent that interest is dulled. When meaning is subordinated to form and mechanics, "reading" matter becomes little more than a linguistic exercise. De Sauzé has estimated that some 100 "seeings" of a word are necessary to fix it in the mind with the same degree of retention as would be obtained from 20 "hearings" of it, or from writing the word attentively 5 times![1]   In other words, the textbook writer has to strain himself repeating a key word 100 times to secure a vocabulary outcome that would normally be secured just as effectively through the provision of varied types of supplementary oral and written activities in which key words need be repeated only five times. Vocabulary associated with ideas or information that is significantly interesting to the learner is retained longer than vocabulary learned in sterile context, for vital content often serves as a mental anchor for the vocabulary as long as the information itself is retained in mind. Many teachers have capitalized this principle for decades in requiring students to learn a clever proverb each week as an exercise in vocabulary building.

Uses and Abuses of Scientifically Derived Frequency Lists.— The extension of this principle to the construction of basic readers for the elementary and intermediate levels, however, has been handicapped at times by well-meant efforts to make reading "scientific" through statistical methods. The values of frequency lists (word counts, idiom counts, and syntax studies) have often been lost through an uncritical and unpsychological application of statistics in the

[1] E. B. de Sauzé, *The Cleveland Plan for the Teaching of Modern Languages,* John C. Winston Company, Philadelphia, 1924, vi + 128 pp.; p. 10.

construction of reading matter. Material has been written to illustrate words, idioms, and syntactical constructions in the ratio of their mathematical frequency of occurrence, rather than to provide a content medium through which reading may become a profitable, pleasurable, and informative type of mental growth in language. It is a patent reflection of the constant preoccupation of language specialists with form and mechanics per se and with subject matter for its own sake, regardless of how children learn or of what they can understand and appreciate in terms of their maturity and levels of insight, and without regard for the purposes for which society supports the study of foreign languages in public secondary education.

A salutary trend is to be observed in a few recent textbooks in which the traditional process of writing to illustrate frequency lists has been partly reversed. A unifying theme and frame of reference such as " How Spanish America affects our daily life " has been selected with a view to providing content that has some bearing upon the development of a creative and enlightened Pan-Americanism among the younger generation of Americans, and a more appreciative understanding of our own citizens of Latin-American origin or descent. Aspects of the central theme have been treated as topics for chapters on such subjects as "How Spanish America enriches our daily life through the songs that we sing, through the music to which we listen and dance, through the books which we read or see dramatized upon the stage or screen, through the products which we consume." Each subtopic has then been written from the standpoint of saying something worth knowing, remembering, or discussing. Many of the devices already described for facilitating ready comprehension in reading have been applied where unfamiliar words or constructions might cause difficulty. Wherever possible, vocabulary and constructions of high frequency in standard word counts have been used to communicate the content, but no effort has been made to repeat the words for their own sake. Such repetition has been provided for in supplementary exercises involving a rereading and reconstruction of the material. Starting with content written in short sentences in the third person, the language gradually expands to include the first and second person through the occasional use of such fictions as personal interviews and informative dialogues suitable for dramatic reading in class, or for ready imitation by the pupils in preparing semioriginal dialogues in which the same vocabulary is capitalized to present comparable information about specific Latin-American countries covered in the chapter. Informative reading matter of this kind makes possible a unified language program in which reading, writing, and speaking can be correlated in the service of some social or cultural objective beyond ability in language itself. If this objective is one toward which the efforts of teachers in other areas of the curriculum are also directed, integration of the foreign-language program with work in other fields, and with life, is often possible.

Reading as an Integrative Activity.—Reading matter which, through the nature of the information that it communicates, permits of a close correlation of foreign-language study with other branches of the curriculum is especially desirable at the junior-high-school, senior-high-school, and junior-college levels, where pupil interest in language work can be enhanced through capitalization of interests in other fields.[1] It is also desirable because of the vitality which it gives to such associated activities as oral and written composition in the foreign language. A continuous program of oral and silent reading would, save for a few exceptional pupils, be a monotonous diet at the secondary-school level, where large numbers of children have never acquired a taste for reading as a profitable leisure-time activity.

It is because the percentage of nonreaders and of pupils who are not in the habit of reading for pleasure, is relatively large in the average secondary school[2] that the "reading" objective, narrowly defined to exclude all other phases of language work, is impractical in unselected classes at the elementary and intermediate levels. It is for this reason also that fictional types of reading—short stories, poetry, and the like—cannot be counted upon to maintain the interest of pupils in the first two years, especially if the material contains words and constructions that require frequent recourse to the vocabu-

[1] Belle E. Bickford, "The Practice of Correlation between French and Other Subjects," *The Modern Language Journal*, Vol. XXV, pp. 580–584, May, 1940. Laura B. Johnson, "Correlation through Cooperation," *The Modern Language Journal*, Vol. XXIV, pp. 106–115, November, 1939.

[2] The number of nonreaders varies from 10 to 20 per cent in typical schools. Studies show that reading is seldom mentioned among the favored activities of secondary-school pupils. Of significance for high-school teachers is the fact that twelfth-grade children report reading as a favorite activity much less frequently than ninth-grade children. Even in college, hardly 50 per cent of the students read any material that is not assigned in their courses. Perhaps this condition is more an indictment of the high school and college than of the students. See Paul Witty and David Kopel, *Reading and the Educative Process*, Ginn and Company, Boston, 1939, x + 374 pp.; pp. 12, 83. Ruth Strang, *Problems in the Improvement of Reading in High School and College*, The Science Press Printing Company, Lancaster, Pa. 1940, 423 pp.; pp. 308–309.

lary or footnotes. Most psychologists are agreed that the use of library material as a linguistic exercise is little short of pedagogical crime[1] because of the distaste for reading which it is likely to beget in young people. Although an effectively told short story or biographical anecdote, devoid of too much explanatory or descriptive detail, can be used to advantage at times for plateau reading which introduces relatively few words or constructions not already familiar to the pupils, such material is generally unsuited as a medium for growth in reading ability itself except in the case of gifted pupils who already possess an unusual interest in reading.

Owing to the diversity of pupil interests, abilities, and objectives in elementary and intermediate foreign-language classes, relatively short informational reading units dealing with different aspects of a central unifying theme are preferable to a continuous diet of imaginative fiction[2] which merely entertains or moralizes the obvious. Humorous didactic fables originally intended to be read by parents to children of tender years are not suited for adolescent boys and girls until they have reached a stage of growth in language when this type of didactic fiction can be read rapidly for content, appreciated in terms of its literary merits, and interpreted in terms of the validity of its moral implications for human life. For all but a relatively few students, the elementary and intermediate stages of foreign-language study are not the most appropriate levels for this type of content. For many students the thought itself is likely to be so deeply buried beneath the language that "reading" becomes "decoding," and time is apt to be too limited to permit of an adequate discussion of those literary qualities and human insights which make the material significant. A foretaste of this type of literature, however, can occasionally be provided by the teacher, by gifted readers in the class, or by occasional excerpts adapted for general consumption, with a view to stimulating voluntary collateral reading in the foreign language during the free-reading periods in class or outside of school.

Conducting Differentiated Reading Programs.—Early differentiation of reading along the lines of the students' personal avocational or life-career interests is desirable if a taste for reading is to be developed among as heterogeneous group of young people as are generally

---

[1] V. A. C. Henmon, "Recent Developments in the Study of Foreign Language Problems," *The Modern Language Journal*, Vol. XIX, pp. 187–201, December, 1934. See especially pp. 195–196.

[2] Marion Emory, "Modern Youth and the Classics," *Progressive Education*, Vol. XII, pp. 384–387, October, 1935.

enrolled in elementary and intermediate classes. After a certain measure of facility in language has been developed through work with a common background reader, an hour of class time may be set aside weekly or biweekly for guided free reading under the teacher's supervision in any books or magazines that contain selections within the range of the pupil's interests and background in language. A classroom library of informational readers with vocabularies, simplified student editions of short stories, illustrated magazines in the foreign language on varied current topics, etc., is obviously desirable. While the pupils are reading, the teacher may circulate about the room, pausing occasionally to answer questions or to ask a student such informal questions as may throw light on his comprehension of the material.   For example:

TEACHER: I see that you are reading about the Pyramid of the Sun in Mexico. Does the selection say anything which you think might interest the class?

PUPIL: It says that the pyramid is larger at the base than any in Egypt, but not as high.   The Aztecs used it as. . . .

TEACHER: Does it mention anything about the location of the pyramid, how it was built, or the sacrifices?

PUPIL: I haven't read that far yet, but from glancing over the selection first, I think that it does.

TEACHER: Tomorrow we shall have time to share with each other anything of interest that we have read.   I think that most people in the class would be interested in the pyramids of Mexico.   I wonder if you would volunteer to tell us the most interesting facts which you may come across in your reading today.   If you want to take the book home, check it out with the class librarian before you leave.   If you think that other people would like to read the book, too, try to sell the idea to them.

If the selection that the student is reading is unfamiliar to the teacher, she may ask him to recount briefly the content of what he has read, and occasionally request him to point to the passage that contains the information.[1]   For example:

TEACHER: You say that the pyramid is larger at the base than any in Egypt? Where does it say that?

PUPIL: It says so right here.   (Pointing.)

TEACHER: Yes, which words mean *larger*?

PUPIL: Here; *más ancha*.

TEACHER: Yes, in a sense you are right, but *más ancha* really means *wider*.   In this case, the difference in meaning is probably unimportant.   I'm glad that you are getting along so well.

[1] Walter V. Kaulfers, "Practical Techniques for Testing Comprehension in Extensive Reading," *The Modern Language Journal*, XVII, pp. 321–327, February, 1933.

If a pupil should have difficulty locating a passage, the teacher may interview another student and return as soon as the passage is found. Ordinarily such informal examination is necessary only when the material is unfamiliar to the teacher, or when there is danger that reading, presumably done in the foreign language outside of class, has in reality been reading done in English translation, the movie version of a novel or play that the pupil has seen on the screen, or a book report by another student. Although a classroom with movable tables and chairs is more suitable for guided free-reading periods than one with fixed seats and desks, the procedure described above can be carried out unobtrusively in relatively large classes with no greater confusion or distraction than that which ordinarily prevails in a public library, study hall, or average home where teachers expect their charges to "study the next lesson thoroughly for tomorrow."

The informal discussion in class of interesting material gathered from different magazines or books provides an opportunity for a free exchange of ideas, and serves to motivate the free-reading period not only by providing an audience situation in which reading interests can be pooled and shared, but also by arousing latent interests in nonreaders. A 3 by 5-inch filing card, giving the name of the author and book, the number of pages, and a brief comment (50 to 100 words) concerning the merits of the book usually suffices for purposes of class record. The critical comments are likely to be more intelligent if guided by two or three leading questions on the card itself. For example:

1. Why was the book written? To entertain? To inform? To change people's ideas or opinions? To arouse people to action?

2. For whom would the book be interesting or valuable reading?

The same congenial informality can be maintained in the group discussion of individual reading during the book-chat period. "What did you read, Bob, in which you think some of the other boys in the class would be interested?" is probably a better way of stimulating genuine reading interests than "Robert and Paul were to have book-reports ready today. We shall hear Robert's first. Are you ready?" Formal book reports, oral and written, have done more to surround reading with distasteful associations than to whet the appetite for good books. Moreover, more time and energy have frequently been spent by foreign-language teachers in making sure that the pupil has read every word, than in arousing reading interests or helping students find material suitable to their social maturity and ability in language.

The provision of ample opportunities at the elementary and intermediate stages for purposeful reading for information or pleasure is as important as the development of skill in reading itself. For unless in the process of learning a skill the student experiences in miniature some of the satisfactions that can be his when the skill has been mastered, he is not likely to use it effectively. Experience has shown time and again that skills that are developed apart from insights into their most satisfying and important applications are destined either to function without purpose in later life, or not at all. The development of a taste for worth-while reading is just as important, and often as difficult, as the development of skill in reading itself. The provision of occasional free-reading periods on class time, with opportunities for informal book discussions by the students, is one approach to the solution of the reading problem that has yielded gratifying results wherever the classroom, departmental, or school libraries have been planned with a functional reading program in mind.

Although relatively few materials outside newspapers published for beginning students, and occasional selections in elementary readers, are suitable for individual free reading by the average first-year student in high school, excellent bibliographies of books for first-year college classes are available in such syllabuses as those developed for the extensive reading program in French and Spanish at the University of Chicago.[1] The Chicago syllabuses contain selected lists of books classified according to areas of interest: belles-lettres, music, art, astronomy, history, philosophy, etc. Some of these can be read by able students in second- and third-year high-school classes in which reading has been emphasized from the start as a central objective. The same informal techniques of measuring comprehension that have already been described can be applied to the individualized reading of books, novels, or plays. Informal book-discussion hours are as appropriate and essential to a functional reading program in college as in high school. The need for guided free-reading periods in class, however, would hardly seem great enough at the college level to justify the time.

Reading at the Intermediate and Advanced Levels.—Although the intensive reading of a uniform text is almost unavoidable at the elementary and intermediate levels if a common background in vocabulary and information for collateral oral and written work is to

[1] Otto F. Bond *et al.*, *French Syllabus* and *Spanish Syllabus*, University of Chicago Book Store, Chicago, 1941.

be provided, a certain amount of differentiated reading is possible and desirable at all levels and becomes increasingly important in advanced classes. Nothing is more distressing than to find able students in third- and fourth-year classes reading in lock-step fashion a junior "classic" on the "read-aloud-and-translate" plan. Indeed, it is doubtful if a "classic" read in this way can ever be appreciated as a whole, unless it is reread rapidly in a few sittings. Until facility in reading has developed to the point where abridged novels and plays can be read within a reasonably short period of time, informative selections dealing with the life and culture of the country whose language is being studied is probably the most appropriate material for basic readers in elementary and intermediate classes, when supplemented from time to time by rapidly moving biographical sketches or short stories which give insight into the character and philosophy of the people.

At the advanced levels, literary fiction, supplemented with abundant opportunities for individualized reading along the lines of the student's avocational and vocational interests, may constitute the core of the reading program. At this level, however, it is doubtful if any attempt should be made, as at the elementary level, to correlate vocabulary building, composition work, or the like, with work in reading. To do so tends not only to distract attention from the essential purpose of good literature, but also to frustrate the development of interest in the material through repeated interruptions and delays. A literary masterpiece, originally intended for enactment upon the stage in two or three hours, or to be read by the fireside or in bed in four or five sittings, is not likely to be read with enjoyment or profit when converted into a linguistic exercise for practice in pronunciation, oral reading, translation, vocabulary building, or composition work. If specialized practice along these lines is still necessary, it may well be provided in some connection where it is less likely to eclipse the essential literary and content values of good literature, or to frustrate the development of a strong appetite for good books by surrounding reading experiences with distasteful associations, annoying interruptions, and excessive testing of linguistic minutiae. Language, style, and literary qualities are important only to the extent that they help to communicate the author's purpose more effectively to his audience, for "if the matter does not count most, the manner need not count at all." Unless form is seen in relation to function, it is doubtful if anything worth dignifying with the term literary appreciation can exist. The time usually devoted to reading and translating classics

aloud in lock-step fashion might more profitably be devoted to discussing the significance of the book for human life:

1. Why was the story (play, etc.,) written?

2. What does the author try to make his readers see, feel, understand, or do?

3. How successful is the author in getting his point across?

4. What means does he employ to achieve his purpose effectively—
humor? suspense? effective language (*e.g.*, picturesque speech)? emotional situations?

5. Is the problem or situation with which the author deals of
importance in human life?   Is it a problem that everyone is likely to
face at some time?

6. Have you read any other books, plays, poems, or stories that
deal with the same problem?

7. Could the book be converted into a moving picture?   Would
the picture be popular?   What screen stars would you choose to play
the parts of the various characters?

The correlation of work in grammar, pronunciation, vocabulary,
translation, and composition with the reading of novels, short stories, or
plays is justifiable only in connection with a project of some kind,
such as dramatizations before an audience of parents or students, *after*
the material has been read and discussed from the viewpoint
of its historical, social, or cultural backgrounds, and literary purpose.
Dramatizations presented as puppet shows, pageants, or plays[1] have
been particularly effective with junior-high-school and lower-division
senior-high-school students.

The important concerns of the teacher in any reading program
are the development of ready comprehension of the written language,
of ability to interpret the social or cultural significance of the material
read, and of the habit of enjoying the reading of worth-while books.
For the development of ready comprehension, such contextual devices
and correlated activities as have been described in Chapter III to
fix vocabulary, idioms, and syntactical constructions for delayed
recall, generally suffice at the elementary and intermediate levels.
The discussion of the implications of proverbs, epigrams, poems,
humorous anecdotes, or short stories usually provides many opportunities for guiding growth in interpretation from the beginning of

---

[1] Helen Muller Bailey, "International Understanding Begins at Home";
Dorothy Mae Johns, "Let's Do a French Puppet Show," *Foreign Languages and
Cultures in American Education*, Walter V. Kaulfers, ed., McGraw-Hill Book
Company, Inc., New York. In press.

the course. For the cultivation of an appetite for worth-while reading, however, abundant opportunities to read and discuss a variety of reading materials and a favorable environment are essential. Time is also an important factor, for reading that is perfunctory and discussions that are scaled by the clock always lose in significance.

Oral Reading and Translation.—The problem of finding time to do all the desirable things that should be done is so universal a problem that the same criteria that apply to choices in life apply with equal validity to the classroom. Since there is seldom time for everything, the criterion of selection is obviously one of relative values. Except to set the stage or to orient the class, the oral reading or translation of more than a few opening paragraphs or pages of an unfamiliar selection is of dubious value. Facility in pronunciation and oral reading can be developed in other ways equally effective and less damaging to the development of sound reading habits and interests. Indeed, the time ordinarily consumed in oral reading, even in relatively advanced classes, is quite out of proportion to the need for this skill in daily life, for outside the classroom few people either at home or abroad, find much occasion to read aloud anything beyond short phrases on menus, street signs, or theater programs. Even in business, this skill is usually confined to the rereading of materials that have been dictated. A well-planned foreign-language program can provide adequate practice in oral reading, commensurate with its importance in life, in connection with materials that the pupils themselves have written or that they have occasion to read to the class as audience, *i.e.*, interesting letters received from abroad, dramatized dialogues, short quotations used in connection with reports, etc.

The same observations apply with equal validity to the translation of materials read. As a skill per se, translation involves technical ability in two languages beyond the grasp of the vast majority of students in high school and college who are not preparing for professions in which this skill is absolutely essential. Granting the appropriateness of translating occasional passages that block comprehension, as a linguistic exercise associated with reading, translation probably does more to encourage mental habits of "word matching," and to retard development of speed of comprehension in reading, than to facilitate the development of effective reading skills. At times the "read-aloud-and-translate" procedure even causes the pupils to lose sight of the idea among the words. Although everyone who has understood a passage should be able to state the contents of it in his native tongue, this does not mean that he has to do so in the translated words of the writer. Comprehension can be measured just as effectively through a restatement of the content and often even more effectively through a paraphrastic interpretation of the passage in the reader's own words. After the class has been helped to find its way into the story or spirit of a selection or book, through such preliminary oral reading and translation as may be necessary for this purpose, the teacher may encourage silent reading in class at the learner's own pace, and provide such individual assistance as may be needed by individual pupils. From time to time, part of the class hour may be set aside for group discussion and interpretation of the content read.

Testing Comprehension.—Such actual testing as may be needed to provide a measure of comprehension, beyond that which can be obtained through the less formal means already indicated, can usually be provided through varied types of citation exercises.[1] In its simplest form, the citation exercise involves little more than the citation by the students of the exact place in the text (*e.g.*, by number of the line or lines as counted from the beginning of a paragraph) where certain important items or facts are to be found. The number of items required for validity obviously depends upon the length of the assignment, the degree of comprehension anticipated, and even more upon the nature of the individual exercises. If a very thorough understanding of content is anticipated, the citation may involve specific details, or be stated in such a way as merely to suggest the fact or incident, thus requiring the student to supply from his background in comprehension the associations necessary to locate the passage in the text. In general, eight to ten exercises suffice even for relatively long assignments and, after one or two tryouts, can be administered within as many minutes.

For the administration of the test, the students may be asked to *letter* a sheet of paper in a column to the left (in *a, b, c*, etc., fashion). Then the teacher may say:

"This is an open-book test to see if you can locate certain important incidents, words, or facts in the chapter. I am going to dictate to you a list of ten items to look up. Write these down in order as briefly and quickly as possible opposite the proper letter (*a, b, c*, etc.) on your paper. As soon as we have written down all the items which we are to look up, we shall take ten minutes to find the exact place in the chapter where the information is to be found, and write the *number* of the line or lines containing the information *before* the letter of the corresponding item on our papers. Count the lines from the beginning

[1] Kaulfers, *op. cit.*

of the paragraph where the passage containing the answer is to be found.   Do all the easiest exercises first; then go back to the harder ones.   Here are the items which we are to locate:

    a. The exact line which states that the treasure is found.
    b. The exact lines in which the author shows his contempt for drunkards.
    c. A line that mentions the death of one of the characters.
    d. Three lines that contain an example of humor.
    e. The exact line which contains the word for "cactus-hedge."

That the principle of the citation exercise need by no means be limited to the quotation of line references is easily demonstrated by a few adaptations and extensions, among which may be mentioned the following:

1. *Identification of key words or phrases: e.g.,* "Copy the exact word(s) for *first aid* as they occur in the chapter." In this variation the students write, instead of the line references, the exact forms employed in the text for certain significant words or expressions. These may be new terms that figure prominently in the plot, or that recur sufficiently often in the assignment to be familiar from one attentive reading. Cognates, are, for obvious reasons, usually to be avoided.

2. *Identification of characters:*
    a. From description: e.g., "Write the name of the person, place, or thing described in the following passage." The instructor reads a passage of three to five lines which describes some character, place, or object, and the students write the name of the person (place or thing) concerned.
    b. From actions: e.g., "Write the name of the person who performed the following action." The instructor may quote significant bits of business performed by a character, and leave the students to discover his identity from their knowledge of the plot.
    c. From conversations: e.g., "Write the names of the people who are speaking in the following passage." The examiner may read a conversational passage, leaving out as far as possible, all telltale words or expressions such as "He said."

The foregoing variants of the citation exercise should be conducted with books *closed,* and the descriptions read by the instructor in English translation. In the case of line citations with books open, the examination should also be administered in English lest it become as much a test of aural comprehension of the teacher as of the material read. The administration of citation tests entirely in the foregoing language is appropriate only for relatively small advanced groups.

3. *Identification of literary qualities:* This variation is possible only when the reading matter is characterized by unusually fine picturesque language, effective epigrammatical passages, or striking qualities of style. It consists in locating the exact line references to passages or paragraphs containing choice figures of speech, or unusual climactic, descriptive, or humorous elements.

The facility with which the test can be scored and graded is evident
in the readiness with which all responses can be checked from a uniform key—by the classes themselves through an exchange and correction of papers or by competent students exempted from a part of an
assignment to perform this task.   For practical purposes it will suffice
to count as right all citations that include (or are included in) the
line references in the key, provided, of course that the limits set by
the pupil are not too broad, nor the fact in point expressed entirely
in one line.   When danger of dishonesty intrudes, the students can
be numbered and alternate exercises administered to the odd- and
even-numbered groups.

A scored and graded paper will usually appear somewhat as
follows:

Name
Date
Class and Period

11	a.
1–4	b.
3, 8, 12	c. *
14, 17	d.
21–25	e.
x	f.
5–15	g.
Marie and Jean	h.
x 16	i.
Paul	j.

Number right, 8
Rank in class, +1†

* Occasionally an item of information will be found in more than one place.   The scoring key
must obviously include these possibilities.

† +1 means one point above middle (median) score or norm for the test.

For the measurement of comprehension in independent reading
(when each student reports on a different book) the citation technique
is equally practical.   It is often useful as a check on actual reading,
for when translations, previous book reports, abundant critical comment, or moving-picture versions exist, few other techniques afford
so simple a check on firsthand acquaintance with the foreign text.
As many as six students can be examined simultaneously within twenty
to thirty minutes during a free-reading period in class.   Thus while
pupil A, who has read Tamango, locates the exact passage in which
the hero dies, pupil B locates the exact passage in La Parure that
states that the necklace was made of paste.   Such a generalized

application naturally presupposes some degree of acquaintance with the material on the part of the instructor. When the content of a story, play, or book is vague in the instructor's mind, or unfamiliar to him, a brief individual report substantiated from time to time by direct reference to the text is the only alternative. For example, the teacher may say:

TEACHER: I see that you have read the *Life of Sir Basil Zaharoff* in Spanish. Who was he?

PUPIL: He was a famous munitions king, who became one of the world's most influential and richest men.

TEACHER: What does the author of the book think of Sir Basil? Does he make him out to be a hero, a villain, a victim of circumstances, or a benefactor to humanity?

PUPIL: I think that he describes him as a clever and not-too-honest politician.

TEACHER: Can you find a passage in the book that reflects this attitude on the part of the author?

Independent Reading Programs on the Contract Plan.—In connection with independent reading programs conducted on the contract plan in the Menlo School and Junior College, Menlo Park, Calif., the citation technique has proved exceedingly helpful. Qualified advanced students have carried out successful individualized reading programs formulated in consultation with the reading counselor. A balanced, personalized bibliography of books to be read (usually totaling from 1,500 to 2,000 pages per semester) is developed in writing with the aid of the teacher. This bibliography becomes a contract when signed by the student, and credit is granted whenever the pupil is ready to offer proof of having read the books. The actual completion of the contract is left entirely to the student. Beyond providing help in formulating an independent reading program, and approving desirable substitutions or readjustments during the semester, the counselor's responsibility is limited to announcing occasional consultation hours during his free period (before school or at noon), when the students can report for an informal discussion of their reading, and for such occasional citation testing as may seem necessary. Ordinarily, four to six students can be accommodated at one time. The contract-reading plan is a practical means for providing opportunities to continue work in a foreign language beyond the point for which separate classes can be organized. Students representing various semester levels of previous preparation in different languages, however, can often be accommodated in one class conducted by a teacher with a reading knowledge of the languages taught in school. In states where the law does not define education in terms of number of hours of bench warming, the students can even be accommodated in small groups, or individually, on a modified independent-study and consultation plan. If it is clearly understood that the plan provides an opportunity open to any responsible and well-qualified student, its administration is often as easy as it is delightful.

Although guidance of students in formulating a suitable reading program is desirable and often necessary, experimentation with unrestricted free selection of books has shown that, although some reading matter of questionable worth is occasionally selected, it is usually offset by books of unusual merit. The chief hazard besetting any reading program is the temptation of the teacher to limit the selection of materials to books which she herself has read. This results, at times, in imposing personal patterns of ignorance, or blind spots in reading, upon the student. There is no reason why a teacher should not encourage a reliable student to read a book that looks promising, and to ask for his frank opinion of it as a possible addition to the recommended list. A brief comment on a 3- by 5-inch filing card is the only written record which need be kept by either pupil or teacher as evidence of reading done, provided opportunities for occasional discussion and citation testing are available.

The School's Responsibility for the Development of Reading Interests.—Informal discussions of good books, supplemented by indirect methods of checking comprehension that do not surround reading with distasteful associations, are basic to the success of any reading program. It is because written book reports and formal tests and questionnaires tend to frustrate the development of long-range reading interests with apathetic experiences, to overburden the teacher with papers to be corrected, and to make dishonesty on the part of disinterested students easy, that their value is questionable. Although there is room for the occasional use of such excellent questionnaires as those prepared by Geiger, Hocking, and Soldner,[1] the time required for the administration and correction of these examining devices can be applied more appropriately to activities that make reading for a purpose a profitable and satisfying activity.

Booksellers, publishers, and librarians who have investigated the means by which books become "best sellers" agree that enthusiastic

[1] Elton Hocking, "Outside Reading and a New Way of Testing It," *The Modern Language Journal*, Vol. XXV, pp. 211–214, December, 1940. Karola Geiger, "A New Approach to Checking Outside Reading," *The Modern Language Journal*, Vol. XXIV, pp. 28–30, October, 1939. Dora Soldner, "A Test in Need," *The Modern Language Journal*, Vol. XXIII, pp. 379–384, February, 1939.

personal recommendations given to books during informal conversations at dinner, over the phone, or on social visits, are the most effective of all forms of advertising.   It is doubtful if a program designed to cultivate a lifelong taste for worth-while reading can be effective if it employs methods that are nonfunctional in daily life among the parents of the children who are in school.   After all, *tel père, tel fils.*

In classes in which the pupils represent a cross section of nearly all the social and economic strata of the community, the development of an enduring interest in good books, and of the habit of reading for a purpose, is a challenge to every teacher of the language arts.   In such classes, the number of children who are inactive readers (*i.e.,* children who hardly ever read a book except in fulfillment of a requirement) is unusually large.   To adopt as a central objective a skill that a large number of pupils have no genuine interest in using is futile. The frequent failure of courses of study to provide materials and methods that promote rather than frustrate reading interests and appreciations has often put the reading objective, and the success of reading programs, in jeopardy at the secondary and lower-division college levels.   Among the conditions that tend to thwart interest in reading, and therefore, indirectly to lead to ineffective outcomes in the way of speed of comprehension in reading, are the following:

1. Use of materials that are unrelated to any real concern, desire, or life interest of the pupils.

2. Use of reading materials as linguistic exercises for pronunciation, translation, vocabulary building, and compositions per se, in such a way as to eclipse the content value of the story, play, or book.

3. Methods of testing or checking comprehension that surround the activity with distasteful associations.

4. Frustration of interest through dilatory procedures that delay the completion of a book within a reasonable period of time.   Any program that devotes ten or more weeks to the "reading" of a novel or play (originally intended to be enacted upon the stage or to be read with pleasure or profit in a few hours) is destined to defeat its own ends as often as it achieves them unless reading forms the basis for some creatively motivated group project.

Devices for Facilitating Growth in Reading Interests.—Inasmuch as specific ways and means for circumventing these hazards have been discussed in considerable detail in earlier parts of this chapter, it will suffice to indicate a few suggestions for enlisting the interest of inactive readers. Beyond the choice of appropriate content, the length of the reading unit, and the vocabulary load, are the chief factors requiring attention. When the vocabulary load is difficult, individual silent reading can often be facilitated by writing on the board the definitions of unfamiliar words *in the order* in which they occur in the text. This suggestion obviously applies only to supervised silent reading in class of a common assignment. It is a helpful device, however, in facilitating comprehension of material written in tenses unfamiliar to beginning pupils. For example, irregular-verb forms that are difficult to identify in a dictionary can be treated on the board as vocabulary until the class is ready for specialized work on these elements. In the case of a chapter of considerable scope, the length of the reading unit per sitting can be increased through the use of this device. It is obviously important in dealing with a story, novel, or play to read it in sufficiently large units to be able to feel the spirit of the action. For this reason, short rapidly moving stories are the best introduction to fictional types of literature at the intermediate level, and short readings containing interesting information about the foreign country and its people, at the elementary level. An overview of the life and culture of the country through the medium of the foreign language is not only educationally worth while in itself, but also desirable as a background for the study of literature.

Although long descriptive or philosophical passages are usually omitted from student editions of foreign classics, nonreaders often find it difficult to develop an interest in a book because of the slow way in which the action starts. Rather than risk frustration through boredom at the beginning, it would seem justifiable in such cases for the teacher to tell the students enough about the author, characters, setting, and plot to incite a desire on the part of the students to read the book. Actual reading may start at the point in the story to which the teacher has carried the group. Similar teacher participation would also seem justifiable in the case of relatively dull chapters. Effective but linguistically difficult philosophical or descriptive passages may well be read to the class in translation. If these aids to the development of reading interests and of motivated reading for comprehension are used with discretion, the time and energy which would otherwise be consumed in muddling through language barriers can be devoted more profitably to the vitalized reading of a wider variety of books. To anticipate that the reading of two or three classics during the course of a year will develop a taste for literature, or the habit of reading good books, is naïvely to cherish the impossible.

Interest in independent collateral reading can often be stimulated and guided by the teacher through the medium of book chats in the foreign language. In its simplest form, the book chat is a vivid summary in the foreign language of the plot of a play or book to the point where suspense is aroused. Many teachers have found the device an effective aid in acquainting pupils with the resources of the library and for stimulating pupils to read. As a sales talk, the book chat is most effective if the teacher actually has in hand the book under discussion. As an informal exercise in aural comprehension, it is obviously effective only if carried on in the foreign language.

The Function of Collateral Reading in English.—So far nothing has been said concerning the reading of books in English. The encouragement of voluntary outside reading along lines that will stimulate or reinforce interest in the foreign people whose language is being studied is without question a worth-while concern of every teacher. Such reading can be utilized effectively to motivate class work by placing the study of language in its proper perspective as an aspect of the culture that it represents. Since outside reading is usually an integral part of the work in core courses in English, the opportunity to develop worth-while reading interests can be capitalized to advantage through joint cooperation among teachers of the language arts.[1] In many schools the joint development of reading lists containing a select annotated bibliography of travel books and novels and plays in translation has yielded gratifying results. Reports are prepared by the pupils in the English course, and presented before the members of either class as an audience. Although it is unwise to usurp the outside reading program in English to such an extent that the pupil is confined to travel books or foreign literature in translation, the proportion of time that can legitimately be set aside for reading in these areas usually suffices for all practical purposes. The chief responsibility of the foreign-language teacher is to help

[1] Eleanor M. Hoyle, "The Trend toward Dictatorship: A Third-year Latin Unit for Division L-1940 at George School," *A Foreign Language Program for Progressive Secondary Schools*, Progressive Education Association, 221 West 57th St., New York, 1938, 86 pp.; pp. 51–54. See also the following in *Foreign Languages and Cultures in American Education*, Reports of the Stanford Language Arts Investigation, Vol. II, McGraw-Hill Book Company, Inc., New York. In press: Virginia B. Lowers, "Latin and English Pull Together"; Frances C. Tubbs, "Making Latin Serve Modern Minds"; Helen M. Bailey, "International Understanding Begins at Home"; Florence Sprenger and Erva Taylor, "Streamlined Topsies—Guiding the Growth of Young People through a Unified Program in Social Studies, Spanish, Art, Music, and English."

in the selection of worthwhile books, to encourage reading for a purpose, and to provide an occasional timely audience in class for pupil discussions of books read.

When the content of the reading program in the foreign language itself is suggestive of interesting and informative subjects concerning which the pupils can read books in English as a part of their free-reading activities in core courses, there is little danger that the foreign-language course will become a mere ride on a "cultural merry-go-round." Nothing is more pathetic than stereotyped reports on books or current events motivated only by grade-point requirements, and sandwiched in irrelevantly between dabs of grammar or sterile reading lessons.

The Value of a Unifying Theme.—Without a unifying theme to integrate the work of each semester or year, any program of education is in danger of degenerating into a cultural potpourri with no more unity, and often less utility, than a crazy quilt. The choice of reading content and associated activities in terms of some central objective helps to prevent foreign-language programs from becoming over-burdened with competing interests. One third-year class in high-school French chose as its frame of reference "Seeing Ourselves as the French See Us."[1] The primary aim here was to understand America better by looking at America from abroad. A secondary objective was to gain insight into the psychology of the French mind. It is obvious that the Frenchman, by virtue of his different background in customs, mores, and traditions, has a somewhat different set of values in appraising what he considers important or unimportant in life. This set of values he naturally applies as a criterion in evaluating a foreign culture, just as most Americans tend to set up their own country as the measuring stick for the good, the true, and the beautiful in foreign lands. These differences in criteria of evaluation are often thrown into bold relief when a foreigner writes about our native land—to such an extent, in fact, that they occasionally jar our eyes and ears. To any student who is guided to look for underlying reasons, such reading matter provides not only an illuminating experience, but also excellent training in unprejudiced objective thinking about our institutions and way of life. Conversely, it can also

---

[1] For similar programs see Barbara Clough, "America as Seen by the French," in *op. cit.*, *A Foreign Language Program for Progressive Secondary Schools.* Also the following in *op. cit.*, *Foreign Languages and Cultures in American Education:* Jewell Torrieri, "France Enrolls in the French Class"; Rose Aviña, "Cultural Enrichment of the Spanish Course."

temper with discretion the consumption of reading matter about foreign countries that rolls off our daily press.

The class discussions in this connection centered around such questions as the following:

1. Would a Frenchman reading this book obtain an accurate picture of life in the United States?

2. Is the author fair or prejudiced in his view of our country? Why does he like certain things and dislike others? Is it because he knows only a small part of our country? Because he feels uncomfortable in a different environment? Because he has a different view of what is important or unimportant in life?

3. Are books written by Americans about foreign countries equally sympathetic, accurate, or prejudiced? Can you bring to class any striking examples?

For common background reading and discussion the class chose André Maurois' delightful book *En Amérique*, excerpts of which appeared in *The Reader's Digest* under the title "Advice to a Frenchman Going to America."[1] The reading and group discussion of this book occupied roughly one-third of the pupils' time in class and in preparation at home. Another third of the course time was devoted to supplementary independent reading in correlation with the central objective. The material here varied in degree of difficulty with the students' abilities in language and levels of insight. The supplementary reading program included selections from Paul Morand's *Champions du monde, Magic noire, New York, Air Indien,* and *Bouddha vivant;* from Georges Duhamel's *Scènes de la vie future;* from Paul Bourget's *Outre-Mer;* from Jean Caneau's *Villes et paysages d'Amérique;* and from Chateaubriand's *Voyage en Amérique.* The remaining third of the course time was allocated to free reading along the lines of the pupils' personal vocational or avocational interests (outside the frame of reference for the semester) and to occasional work with language difficulties that handicapped the students. The only exceptions to the program as outlined above were five seniors who were preparing to take College Entrance Board Examinations upon completing third-year French. They worked together as a committee on the contract plan within the regular class, and were exempted from half the reading in order to devote themselves to work with a review grammar. This committee of seniors often met with the teacher during laboratory workshop periods in class, or during class sessions set aside for independent silent reading. Although the class enrolled

[1] *The Reader's Digest*, Vol. XX, pp. 1–3, November, 1931.

more students than are commonly registered in third-year courses, the work of the group was favored by a small but well-selected classroom library, and by an environment conducive to the reading and discussion of books.

Reading programs guided by a unifying central objective to give scope and sequence to the work are naturally easier to organize and conduct in advanced classes than at the elementary or intermediate levels, since the range of suitable materials is usually greater. Nevertheless, the constant increase in the number of books designed for content reading in elementary classes makes possible a more purposeful organization of the reading program than was possible ten years ago. Below is an outline of suggestive topics,[1] organized in terms of a social frame of reference, concerning which elementary reading material is available in French, and to an increasing extent in Spanish,[2] German, and Italian:

FIRST SEMESTER
I. Exploratory preview.
   A. *The spirit of France in America* (*i.e.*, a survey of French influence in American life and culture*); *e.g.*,
      1. In art and music: operas, concert programs, etc.
      2. In language: as observed in words, names, and expressions in current English.
      3. In history: explorers, colonizers, etc.
      4. In commerce: exports and imports to and from France.
      5. In the moving picture and drama.
      6. In population: French-speaking colonies in the New World.
      7. In the daily press: current events, etc.
      8. In fashions and social usages.
      9. In literature: French authors widely read in English translation in the United States.
      10. In government: influence of French political philosophy on Jefferson, etc.
      11. In American foreign diplomacy: our foreign relations with France, Franco-American treaties, etc.

SECOND SEMESTER
II. Orientational survey.
   A. *The French people in world culture*, etc.*
      1. In art: painting, sculpture, architecture, etc.
      2. In music.

[1] Walter V. Kaulfers, "A Program for the Realization of the Cultural Objectives in the Teaching of French," *The French Review*, Vol. XI, pp. 463–470, May, 1938.

[2] Doris K. Arjona and Jaime Homero Arjona, *A Bibliography of Textbooks in Spanish Published in the United States*, Edwards Brothers, Inc., Ann Arbor, Mich., 1939. A useful compilation of texts arranged in 20 classifications according to content.

3. In literature.
4. In science and invention.
5. In world commerce.
6. In philosophy (including political theory).
7. In education.
8. In exploration.
9. In public health and sanitation.
10. In social life: customs and mores.
11. In world diplomacy.
B. *France as a field of foreign travel; i.e.*, places of cultural interest:*
1. Famous cathedral towns.
2. Places of historical interest: Versailles, Fontainebleau, Carcassonne, etc.
3. Famous resorts and watering places.
4. Famous museums, libraries, and art galleries.
5. University centers.
6. Homes of famous Frenchmen.
7. Scenic regions of France.

THIRD SEMESTER, AND BEYOND

III. *Literature in French:** Literature to be defined broadly to include any really worth-while books which have vital significance for life today—not exclusively belles-lettres. Increased opportunity for differentiated reading along lines of individual interest—cultural or professional.

When the reading program in foreign languages is formulated in the light of a significant life objective to give meaning and direction to the work, it can often make an important contribution to the building of American life and culture, and thus help to root the study of foreign languages more securely in American education. The following are examples of unifying objectives around which socially significant reading programs in foreign languages can be built:

1. How does the study of the Spanish and Latin-American peoples (or the people of France, Germany, Italy, etc.) help us understand the meaning of America?

2. How have foreign writers, past and present, thrown light on such problems as democracy and ethics in human relations: Peace and war? Religious or race prejudice? The conflict between scientific progress and reactionary forces in society? Democracy and dictatorship? The meaning for human life of poverty, injustice, and inequality of opportunity?

3. How do foreign writers help us to understand the common ideals, hopes, emotions, and problems of a larger number of people than we

* Foundation exercises as needed to facilitate the acquisition and assimilation of cultural values through the medium of the French language.

can expect to find time to know personally? What can we learn from these writers that will help us solve similar problems in our *own* daily lives?

Topics such as 1 and 2 obviously permit of a ready integration of the reading program in foreign languages with other branches of the curriculum—particularly English and the social studies—in which similar topics are a major concern of both students and teachers. The value of foreign-language work in such cases is directly proportional to the extent to which it supplements or reinforces a study of these problems as reflected in literature—short stories, novels, poems, or plays—by approaching them from a different point of view, or in a broader frame of reference. Topics such as number 3 lend themselves to individualized programs in guided independent reading.

Reading as a Key to Life. Developing Literary Appreciation.— It must already be evident that no reading program can be regarded as functional if it conceives of reading merely as a skill, a form of literacy, or a linguistic exercise. To be worth teaching at all, reading must be regarded not only as a key to life, but also as an essential life activity in itself. For literature, worthy of the name, is the mirror of life and the treasury of human hopes, thoughts, experiences, and ambitions. No really worth-while story, play, or book was ever written just as an exercise in language, nor as an illustration of form, but for a creative purpose. In his famous novel and play, *El Abuelo*, Benito Pérez Galdós protested against the aristocratic Spanish notion that "blood will tell." In *Doña Perfecta* he shows, among other things, the tragic consequences for human happiness when applied science comes into conflict with reactionary stupidity. In *El Gran Galeoto* (*The World and His Wife*) Echegaray dramatizes the way in which the untempered and unreasoning gossip of an unkind society forces a young woman to do the very thing that she was unjustly accused of doing anyway. Similarly, Victor Hugo in *Les Misérables* deals a powerful blow against a bureaucratic administration of justice untempered by mercy. To read a short story such as *Tamango, La Ficelle, La Mort du Dauphin*, or a fairy tale such as *The Emperor's New Clothes*, without being cognizant of the fundamental concern with human life that inspired it, is to miss the real significance of good literature. Literary appreciation that is not primarily concerned with gaining life insight into the meaning behind the word or plot, is little more than busywork in linguistics or the aesthetics of form. For this reason it is important at all times to provide adequate opportunities for reading that will not serve as a mere escape from reality, nor as a mere illustration of rules of grammar, but as a means for intellectual participation in the solution of human problems and in the realization of life's fullest potentialities.

This criterion for the choice of reading content need be tempered only by three considerations: If the social meaning of the material is too remote from the lives of boys or girls or too profound to be understood by young people, it is doubtful if forced attention to the aesthetics of form alone, or to the translation of words as a mental discipline, can make it of value or significance to them.   Secondly, the reading program need not be confined either to contemporary authors or to writers of time-tested classics. The vital problems of human life have been the preoccupation of great thinkers in all times and places, and no generation of minds has ever had a monopoly on the truth by virtue of time or place alone. The organization of reading units in terms of a central unifying objective often permits of the treatment of a problem in terms of contributions from contemporary and past literatures. If time permits, the different literary forms—poems, short stories, novels, plays—through which different writers have expressed themselves on the same issues can provide an educative experience, though circumstances surrounding the teaching of the foreign languages seldom permit of this type of approach below the graduate level of the university. Finally, although reading for enjoyment or pure pleasure, without regard for the significance of the material, should have a place in life, the time which such reading should occupy in a crowded class program, is not so great as that which is ordinarily assigned to reading of this type. In a course that recognizes reading as a central objective and core activity, approximately one-third of the time ordinarily set aside for independent free reading during library periods in class or at home usually suffices to satisfy this occasional need of the human mind to escape entirely from the preoccupations of daily life.

In any creative approach to literature the timely significance of the message for human life which it contains, and the effectiveness with which this message is communicated, are the paramount considerations in the choice of reading materials. The age of a book per se has little to do with its importance. Nor does age-long embalmment in courses of study necessarily make it a classic. After all, the chief difference between a dime novel of the past and a "classic" of today is often just $1.90.

Developing an Appreciative Interest in Poetry.—Owing to the language difficulties that beset the comprehension of versified materials, poetry has rarely occupied a prominent place in junior- and senior-high-school courses in foreign languages. Unfortunately, the number of pupils who have a genuine interest in poetry is relatively small. Indeed, many boys of adolescent age consider poems appropriate only for girls. Building an interest in poetry, therefore, is one of the chief prerequisites to the development of an appreciation of it. This means starting with materials within the range of the adolescent's level of comprehension. It also means affording the learner some insight into the significance of poetry as the most universal and most popular of all forms of vocal expression, some understanding of its early relationship to music, and some knowledge of the important role which it at one time played in the lives of people before history was recorded in books. The following quotation from *Bulletin* 58 of the Stanford Language Arts Investigation develops this subject in terms which most junior- and senior-high-school pupils can readily understand:[1]

Music and literature at one time were Siamese twins. For centuries literature consisted mainly of religious chants, songs about famous heroes, beautiful ladies, etc. You may already have heard of "The Odyssey," one of the finest examples of early Greek literature. It consists of twenty-four cantos (the word "cantos" originally meant "songs") dealing with the adventures of Ulysses. These adventures were recited or sung by a wandering minstrel (supposedly Homer) who usually accompanied himself on a lyre, a stringed instrument of the harp class.

"The Odyssey" of the Greeks corresponds to the famous "Song of Roland" (*La Chanson de Roland*), one of the earliest pieces of French literature. It, too, was originally recited or sung by minstrels known in France as the troubadours. Similarly, the earliest piece of Spanish literature of which we have any record today is the song or poem of the Cid (*El Poema del Cid*), composed by one of the minstrels whom the Spaniards called *joglares*.

Today, the original connection which existed between literature and music has been lost to the extent that few people think of poetry as music. In a few cases, however, the original relationship still exists. Cowboy literature, for example, still consists very largely of songs, or of poems which originally were recited or sung to the accompaniment of a stringed instrument such as the guitar. Perhaps you have already read about poetry contests among the *gauchos* of the Argentine.

To appreciate poetry, therefore, one should think of it as music; for the two most common characteristics of poetry—rhythm and rhyme—had their origin in music, usually in singing accompanied by a stringed instrument.

[1] Walter V. Kaulfers, "Music as Language," *Bull.* 58, Stanford Language Arts Investigation, Stanford University, June, 1938, 13 pp. By permission.

The fact that poetry is suggestive of music has been demonstrated by many able composers who have been inspired to write musical settings for poems. A few examples of poems which have been set to music as songs are given in section II below.

The foregoing excerpt is suggestive of ways and means for developing interest in poetry which teachers have found effective in working with adolescent boys and girls. Musical settings of famous poems such as Victor Hugo's *Si mes vers avaient des ailes*, or Goethe's *Der Erlkönig*, read both in the original and in translation, and then heard as recorded by competent singers, furnish an excellent starting point, especially when two different musical interpretations of a poem exist. The value of music in developing an appreciation of poetry in school is as great as its value in popularizing and preserving poetry in life. How many people, for example, except a few students of Goethe's works, would today be acquainted with his poem *The Erlking* were it not for the musical settings by Schubert and Loewe, which are heard on records and on the concert stage by thousands of people throughout the world? The accompanying exercise from *Bulletin* 58 of the Stanford Language Arts Investigation illustrates how the study of German poetry and music may be integrated. The exercise can be used as soon as the pupils have learned to pronounce the language sufficiently well to be able to read it aloud without undue hesitation. A short humorous poem, such as *The Song of the Flea* from Goethe's *Faust* would, however, be a more appropriate introduction for beginning students in junior- and senior-high-school German.

Der Erlkönig

(The Erlking)

"The Erlking" is one of the most widely known of the poems by the great German writer and philosopher Johann Wolfgang von Goethe (1749–1832). Two English versions by E. A. Bowring and Bayard Quincy Morgan[1] are given below, together with the original German words. Note that four characters speak in the poem: the narrator, the dying child, his father, and the Erlking—the "elf-king" who harms children, often causing them to die. Volunteer to read the part of one of the characters, first in English, then in German, during a dramatic reading of the poem in class. Which of the two translations do you like better? Why? Can you tell which translation follows the original German more closely? Is this an advantage or a disadvantage?

[1] By permission of the translator.

I

Original Version

NARRATOR: Wer reitet so spät durch Nacht und Wind?
Es ist der Vater mit seinem Kind;
Er hat den Knaben wohl in dem Arm,
Er fasst ihn sicher, er hält ihn warm.

FATHER: Mein Sohn, was birgst du so bang dein Gesicht?
CHILD: Siehst, Vater, du den Erlkönig nicht?
Den Erlenkönig mit Kron' und Schweif?
FATHER: Mein Sohn, es ist ein Nebelstreif.

ERLKING: Du liebes Kind, komm, geh mit mir!
Gar schöne Spiele spiel' ich mit dir;
Manch bunte Blumen sind an dem Strand;
Meine Mutter hat manch gülden Gewand.

CHILD: Mein Vater, mein Vater, und hörest du nicht,
Was Erlenkönig mir leise verspricht?
FATHER: Sei ruhig, bleibe ruhig, mein Kind;
In dürren Blättern säuselt der Wind.

ERLKING: Willst, feiner Knabe, du mit mir gehn?
Meine Töchter sollen dich warten schön;
Meine Töchter führen den nächtlichen Reihn
Und wiegen und tanzen und singen dich ein.

CHILD: Mein Vater, mein Vater, und siehst du nicht dort
Erlkönigs Töchter am düstern Ort?
FATHER: Mein Sohn, mein Sohn, ich seh' es genau;
Es scheinen die alten Weiden so grau.

ERLKING: Ich liebe dich, mich reizt deine schöne Gestalt;
Und bist du nicht willig, so brauch' ich Gewalt.
CHILD: Mein Vater, mein Vater, jetz fasst er mich an!
Erlkönig hat mir ein Leids getan!

NARRATOR: Dem Vater grauset's, er reitet geschwind,
Er hält in Armen das ächzende Kind,
Erreicht den Hof mit Mühe und Not;
In seinen Armen das Kind war tot.

II

*The Erlking**

NARRATOR: Who rides there so late through the night dark and drear?
The father it is, with his infant so dear;
He holdeth the boy tightly clasp'd in his arm,
He holdeth him safely, he keepeth him warm.

FATHER: My son, wherefore seek'st thou thy face thus to hide?
CHILD: Look, father, the Erlking is close by our side!
Dost see not the Erlking, with crown and with train?
FATHER: My son, 'tis the mist rising over the plain.

ERLKING: Oh come, thou dear infant! Oh come thou with me!
Full many a game I will play there with thee;
On my strand, lovely flowers their blossoms unfold,
My mother shall grace thee with garments of gold.

CHILD: My father, my father, and dost thou not hear
The words that the Erlking now breathes in mine ear?
FATHER: Be calm, dearest child, 'tis thy fancy deceives;
'Tis the sad wind that sighs through the withering leaves.

ERLKING: Wilt go, then, dear infant, wilt go with me there?
My daughters shall tend thee with sisterly care;
My daughters by night their glad festival keep,
They'll dance thee, and rock thee, and sing thee to sleep.

CHILD: My father, my father, and dost thou not see,
How the Erlking his daughters has brought here for me?
FATHER: My darling, my darling, I see it aright,
'Tis the aged gray willows deceiving thy sight.

ERLKING: I love thee, I'm charm'd by thy beauty, dear boy!
And if thou'rt unwilling, then force I'll employ.
CHILD: My father, my father, he seizes me fast,
Full sorely the Erlking has hurt me at last.

NARRATOR: The father now gallops, with terror half wild,
He grasps in his arms the poor shuddering child;
He reaches his courtyard with toil and with dread,
The child in his arms finds he motionless, dead.

* Translation by E. A. Bowring.

III

*The Erlking**

NARRATOR: Who rideth so late through the night-wind wild?
It is the father, and with his child.
He holds his darling close in his arm
He clasps him tightly, he keeps him warm.

FATHER: My son, why hidest thy face in such fear?
CHILD: Seest, father, not the Elf-king draw near?
The Elfin-king with crown and train?
FATHER: My son, the mist floats o'er the plain.

ERLKING: Thou dearest child, come, go with me
Full lovely games will I play with thee;
Gay-colored flowers adorn the shore,
My mother has golden robes in store.

CHILD: My father, my father, and dost thou not hear
What soft the Elf-king breathes in my ear?
FATHER: Be quiet, be not frightened, my own:
In withered leaves doth the night-wind moan.

ERLKING: Wilt, lovely boy, thou with me abide?
My daughters never shall stray from thy side.
My daughters their nightly revels keep;
They'll rock thee and dance thee and sing thee to sleep.

CHILD: My father, my father, and seest thou not
The Elf-king's daughters in yon gloomy spot?
FATHER: My son, my son, 'tis plain as the day,
'Tis but the old willows that shimmer so grey.

ERLKING: I love thee, thy beauty enraptures me so,
And art thou not willing, I'll force thee to go.
CHILD: My father, my father, he seizes my arm,
Elk-king has done me a cruel harm!

NARRATOR: The father shudders, he rides fast and wild,
He tightly embraces his whimpering child,
Arrives at home in fear and dread.
Upon his bosom the child was dead.

* Translation by Bayard Quincy Morgan.

Now play in succession the two musical settings of the poem by Schubert and Loewe.[1] While listening to the recordings, decide on your answers to the following questions:

1. To what extent is the music appropriate or suitable considering the *subject* and the *spirit* of the poem?
    ____*a*. not at all appropriate
    ____*b*. fairly appropriate
    ____*c*. very appropriate

2. To what extent does the music bring out the "feeling" or dramatic qualities of the poem?
    ____*a*. The poem is just as good without the music.
    ____*b*. The music adds a little to the poem.
    ____*c*. The music makes the poem much more dramatic or more enjoyable.
    ____*d*. The poem is better without the music.

3. Would the *music by itself* be just as enjoyable if it were played as an instrumental number without the singing?
    ____*a*. yes
    ____*b*. no
    ____*c*. doubtful

4. Would the poem be just as effective (entertaining or pleasing) if it were recited or read aloud by an expert without musical accompaniment of any kind?
    ____*a*. yes
    ____*b*. no
    ____*c*. doubtful

5. Would you personally rather read the poem silently than hear it read, recited, or sung, even by a great artist?
    ____*a*. yes
    ____*b*. no
    ____*c*. undecided

6. Could the music of the song be made into a good dance piece for one of our jazz or "swing" orchestras?
    ____*a*. yes
    ____*b*. no
    ____*c*. doubtful

7. Which of the two musical settings of *The Erlking* do you like better?
    ____*a*. Schubert setting
    ____*b*. Loewe setting

NOTE: Ask the teacher to tabulate the reactions of the class on the board.   How do your reactions agree with those of your classmates?   Can you give better reasons for your answers than they can for theirs?

If no musical setting is available, or if the music is too difficult to permit of group singing in class, a dramatic reading of the poem by groups of pupils, chosen according to the quality of their speaking

[1] *Der Erlkoenig*, Goethe-Loewe, sung by Sir George Henschel, Columbia Record 9110-M, in German.   *Der Erlkönig*, Goethe-Schubert, sung by Sophie Braslau, Columbia Record 67431-D, in German.

voices, often provides an effective alternative. The verse-speaking choir technique is readily adaptable to use with poetry that possesses dramatic qualities or unusual opportunities for vocal and rhythmic inflection.[1] In the beginning, poetry containing conversational passages and a strong rhythmic pattern is more suitable for choral speaking than purely lyrical material.

Occasionally, a gifted student of music who is studying foreign languages can be encouraged to try his hand at composing a musical setting for a poem. Unusually fine results have been obtained in schools where teachers of music and the language arts have worked in close cooperation. The encouragement of creative activities is an important responsibility of every teacher of foreign languages, even though not more than one student in two or three hundred may at times respond. Talents appear lacking in many school children simply because they are accorded little opportunity to reveal or express themselves. As a matter of fact, the social and economic background of the average boy and girl is probably at least as high as that of Schubert, Shakespeare, Faraday, or Lincoln.

Teachers of English and the foreign languages can perform no greater service than to enable young people to find inspiration and encouragement in good literature for the continuous re-creation of their lives in keeping with human ideals.[2]

[1] Nina Lee Weisinger, "Choric Treatment of Spanish-American Poetry," *Hispania,* Vol. XXII, pp. 251–253, October, 1939. Anna Balakian, "Choral Reading and the Foreign Languages," *High Points*, Vol. XXI, pp. 63–67, December, 1939. Richard B. Lewis and Holland D. Roberts, "The Director's Part in the Verse Speaking Choir," *Quarterly Journal of Speech*, Vol. XXIII, pp. 63–66, February, 1937; "Foundations of the School Verse Speaking Choir," *California Journal of Secondary Education*, Vol. XI, pp. 98–100, February, 1936.

[2] Holland D. Roberts, "English Teachers Face the Future," *The English Journal* (College Edition), Vol. XXVII, pp. 101–113, February, 1938. For student bibliographies and aids in the teaching of reading for a life purpose, see Appendix D and Appendix references 4, 5, 7, 15, 16, 29, 30, 32, 34, 37, 57, 58, 71, 87, 89–98, 113–116, 151, 153, 155, 159, 166, 191, 193, 197.

CHAPTER V

THE ORGANIC CONCEPTION OF LANGUAGE AND ITS IMPLICATIONS FOR VOCABULARY BUILDING

Good teaching of vocabulary means helping young people to develop a varied and serviceable wardrobe in language, and discretion in wearing it appropriately.

Vocabulary Building in an Atomistic Conception of Language.— Almost since the beginning of foreign-language instruction in schools, words have been considered the foundation stones of language which could be cemented together with grammar into a kind of a semantic conductor of thought. Upon this conception of the nature of language (reinforced by much philosophical speculation concerning the "laws of learning") entire systems of language teaching were built. In terms of this atomistic view the most effective methods of "vocabulary building" were made the subject of detailed research.[1] Was vocabulary learned best when taught directly, *i.e.*, in lists to be memorized, ten words or more at a time? Was the vocabulary recalled better if the meanings of the words were explained in English? In the foreign language? By means of *realia* (pictures, objects, etc.) without verbal definitions? Did flash cards aid vocabulary learning? All these aspects of the problem, and many more of a similar nature, were the subject of minute experimentation dignified by impressively elusive statistical activity.

The net result served to prove that the pupils learned vocabulary *as such* by any method that concentrated attention specifically on the learning of words. With respect to the ultimate superiority of one method over another, however, all this research proved little. The degree of superiority was so slight as to be hardly worth mentioning. Whereas one method seemed to be more efficient than any other in teaching vocabulary in a hurry, it seemed that the pupils also forgot the words in a hurry. Even when the reverse of this situation pre-

---

[1] Recent research has been critically analyzed in the April issue, 1940, of the *Review of Educational Research*, "The Language Arts," Vol. X, No. 2, pp. 73–175. See also Walter S. Monroe, ed., *Encyclopedia of Educational Research*, The Macmillan Company, New York, 1941, 1344 pp.; pp. 446–457, 520–539.

vailed, the pupils did not seem to be able to make effective use of the vocabulary in reading, writing, or speaking. The words that they had learned in isolation tended to function only in isolation. Oral speech as a result was faltering, jerky, and punctuated by embarrassing lapses of memory. Composition work was grotesquely unidiomatic and characterized by patent evidences of mental habits of "word matching"—of trying to find in the foreign language an exact equivalent for every word that occurred to the pupil in the vernacular. Silent-reading habits also showed the retarding effect of this atomistic approach to language in the annoying regressions and unnecessarily long and frequent fixations per line which blocked speed of comprehension. Moving-picture records of the pupil's eyes[1] in silent reading showed that even when the content was phrased in words with which the students were familiar, the process was distinctly one of deciphering, decoding, and transverbalizing, rather than of absorbing the current of meaning conveyed by the printed page.

Language composed of words learned in isolation, and later cemented together with a kind of grammatical mortar, apparently made an extremely poor conductor of thought. The current was interrupted or dissipated by all kinds of short circuits, and any excessive load either caused a fuse to blow out or shocked the pupils into a kind of linguistic paralysis. These dangers were avoided as far as possible simply by reducing the thought current to as low a voltage as possible, so that the pupils could spend their time repairing the circuit, mixing more cement, and replacing the fuses without danger of being annoyed by any current of thought. In this process many of the pupils (and sometimes the teacher) forgot what the circuits which they were constructing were for; but it was taken for granted that if the craftsmanship during the first two years was good, the voltage could be stepped up in advanced classes to any desired degree, short of fire or electrocution, depending upon the use which the pupil cared to make of his perfected power system.

In practice, things did not always work out in quite this way. Although a few students became fairly expert mechanics and repairmen, the material itself disintegrated so rapidly that by the time the pupils started work on the second unit, operations frequently had to cease for repairs on the first. Usually the difficulty was to be found in the lack of cohesive properties in the grammatical cement. Thicker and thicker layers were considered desirable; for no one

---

[1] G. T. Buswell, *A Laboratory Study of the Reading of Modern Foreign Languages*, The Macmillan Company, New York, 1927, xx + 100 pp.

questioned the efficiency of the mortar as a durable and efficient conductor of thought. Even when the power system remained intact long enough to be put to use at the college level, it rarely functioned satisfactorily for all the varied purposes that the language engineers in the university expected it to serve. Indeed, most of the pupils had been so busy in construction and repair jobs in high school that they had almost forgotten why they started to work on the circuit in the first place, or what they would do with it when they finally had everything in working order. But two years of such training in language mechanics was rewarded with a ticket of admission to the university, dignified with the assurance that it improved the memory, disciplined[1] the mind, developed the capacity for hard work, enabled one to become a more effective, logical, and penetrating speaker in English,[2] and helped one to become tolerant and open-minded[3]—all of which, of course, no equal amount of time devoted to work in English, science, art, music, or social studies classes could presumably do. Since the pupils who survived this two-year period of preparatory apprenticeship in language were usually students who already possessed a capacity for hard work, a satisfactory command of English, and a home background favorable to the development of broad social interests, this "cultural" value of foreign-language study was easily proved—provided that one did not take into account the number of pupils who fell by the wayside or were politely ousted by the teachers because they did not already possess most of these essential virtues at the outset.[4] Hence it did not matter much if the pupils actually

[1] Ralph W. Haller, "Developing the Power and Habit of Thinking in the Teaching of Modern Languages," *Clearing House*, Vol. VI, pp. 291–294, January, 1932.

[2] T. H. Briggs, "Formal English Grammar as a Discipline," *Teachers College Record*, Vol. XIV, pp. 251–343, September, 1913. Algernon Coleman, *The Teaching of Modern Foreign Languages in the United States*, The Macmillan Company, New York, 1929, 299 pp.; pp. 107–108.

[3] Report of the Research Council, Modern Language Association of Southern California, "Language Objectives," *Hispania*, Vol. XVII, pp. 290–294, October, 1934.

[4] Every study of foreign-language enrollments has shown that in traditional courses only the fittest survived and that even among a fairly select group of students, failures were high. See Ruth Oxley, "Comparative Study of the Intelligence of Beginners in Senior High School Foreign Language," *School and Society*, Vol. XXXIII, pp. 695–696, May, 1931. Walter V. Kaulfers, "Mental Selection in the Foreign Languages," *Hispania*, Vol. XI, pp. 505–510, December, 1928; "Intelligence and Spanish Failures," *Modern Language Journal*, Vol. XIII, pp. 550–553, April, 1929. Adolph Klein, "Failure and Subjects Liked and Disliked," *High Points*, Vol. XXI, pp. 22–25, January, 1939.

failed to achieve any of the original purposes for which most people study a foreign language, or any of the basic objectives for which society supports the study of languages in its public schools.

Through such rationalizing, a vicious circle was established which was finally broken only by the increasing public demand for efficiency in education after the First World War and during the depression. During the era of efficiency in education, which reached its climax in the late twenties, the job-analysis technique of curriculum building was applied to the scientific derivation of basic vocabularies, idiom counts, and syntax lists.[1] Statistical procedures were applied to the construction of numerous objective tests of reading, vocabulary, grammar, and composition with impressive coefficients of reliability and validity to measure the efficiency of learning in terms of these outcomes.[2] Complicated prognosis tests for eliminating at the start all pupils who lacked "language talent" or "linguistic aptitude" were devised and administered,[3] although no one seemed to know exactly what "language talent" was, or even if it actually existed as an independent ability outside the imagination of language teachers.[4] All this activity led only to two results. The vast amount of testing revealed the poverty of outcomes without connecting them, and the emphasis on the extensive use of tests, usually with norms or group

[1] Among the most valuable of these are the following: Helen S. Eaton, *Semantic Frequency List for English, French, German,* and *Spanish,* University of Chicago Press, Chicago, 1940, xxi + 441 pp. Hayward Keniston, *Spanish Syntax List,* Henry Holt and Company, Inc., New York, 1937, xi + 278 pp. Edward H. Hauch, *German Idiom List,* The Macmillan Company, New York. Hayward Keniston, *Spanish Idiom List,* The Macmillan Company, New York, 1929, xiii + 108 pp. F. D. Cheydleur, *French Idiom List,* The Macmillan Company, New York. See also references 13 and 19 in the Appendix.

[2] V. A. C. Henmon, *Achievement Tests in the Modern Foreign Languages,* The Macmillan Company, New York, 1929, xxvi + 363 pp. Ben D. Wood, *New York Experiments with Modern Language Tests,* The Macmillan Company, New York, 1927, xxii + 339 pp.

[3] V. A. C. Henmon et al., *Prognosis Tests in the Modern Languages,* Vol. XIV, Publication of the American and Canadian Committees on Modern Languages, The Macmillan Company, New York, 1929, xviii + 182 pp. Robert Herndon Fife et al., *A Summary of Reports on the Modern Foreign Languages with an Index to the Reports,* The Macmillan Company, New York, 1931, vii + 261 pp.; pp. 123–124. Walter V. Kaulfers, *Forecasting Efficiency of Current Bases for Prognosis,* Unpublished Ph.D. dissertation, Stanford University, 1933, xxiii + 381 pp.

[4] J. W. Todd, "Is There a Language Talent?" *Modern Language Forum,* Vol. XIII, pp. 7–10, April, 1928.

averages derived from the actual scores of thousands of pupils throughout the country, tended to standardize the *status in quo*.[1]

Rise of the Organic Conception of Language.—Among the practical suggestions promulgated by such educational efficiency commissions as the Modern Foreign Language Study was the recommendation
that foreign-language teachers concentrate their attention primarily
on the reading objective instead of dissipating their energies over
too wide an area in the first two years of foreign-language work.[2]
This alternative, coupled with the hope that pupils lacking in language
aptitude could somehow be weeded out in advance by means of prognosis tests, formed the basis of most curriculum-revision programs
until 1935. By that time it became evident that a modern foreign-
language course stressing reading primarily would have to cater only
to the needs and interests of a relatively small and select group of
students in high school, since a large number of adolescent boys and
girls are inactive readers in the sense that they have never acquired a
taste for good books, or the habit of reading voluntarily for pleasure
or profit even in English. At the same time it became evident that
prognosis tests as a means for selecting or eliminating students were
of little practical value, and dangerous instruments to place into the
hands of anyone but an educational psychologist.[3]

Since efforts to increase the efficiency of foreign-language instruction by fitting students to the courses met with little success, and
often resulted in embarrassing decreases in enrollments, other solutions were suggested. Among these was the introduction of orientation courses in foreign cultures, foreign literature in translation, and
survey courses in language arts, all to be conducted in English by
teachers of foreign languages as a means for meeting the needs and
arousing the interests of young people who could not profit from the
conventional foreign-language program.[4] The decade 1930–1940

[1] Mary K. MacPherson, "Conflicting Aims in the Teaching of Modern Lan-
guages," *The School*, Vol. XXV, pp. 304–307, December, 1936. James B. Tharp,
"The College Entrance Examination Board Looks at Its French Examination,"
The French Review, Vol. XIII, pp. 380–384, March, 1940.

[2] Coleman, *op. cit.*, pp. 109–110.

[3] Walter V. Kaulfers, "Prognosis and Its Alternatives in Relation to the
Guidance of Students," *German Quarterly*, Vol. XII, pp. 81–84, March, 1939. A
critical review and interpretation of experimental research and its practical
implications.

[4] C. O. Arndt and Robert Kirkpatrick, "Exploring Foreign Languages and
Cultures," *The Modern Language Journal*, Vol. XXV, pp. 435–442, March, 1941.
Lilly Lindquist, "General Language," *The Modern Language Journal*, Vol. XXIV,

witnessed a marked expansion of the language-arts curriculum to embrace not only courses in German, French, Spanish, or Latin as such, but also new type semester or year terminal offerings under such headings as *Spain and the Americas Today, French Culture, Introduction to France, German Civilization, World Literature, Social Language,* and *Language Arts Survey.* Although these offerings met with greater success than might be expected from their lowly origin as "dumping grounds" for young people whom foreign-language teachers themselves often politely branded as "language misfits" or "nonacademically minded," they did not contribute, except indirectly, to the correction of weaknesses inherent in the traditional foreign-language courses.[1]   The latter, except for mechanical improvements in the way of visual vocabularies, new types of objective exercises, graded vocabularies, and the correlation of reading with grammar, remained almost unchanged; for the rank and file of foreign-language teachers continued to teach very much as they had always taught and often regarded even minor departures from the traditional with strong suspicion.[2]

The success of the new type orientation courses, however, afforded many clues for vitalizing and enriching the traditional program in foreign languages.   Since the emphasis in the survey courses was primarily on content dealing with the life and culture of the foreign country in relation to our own national and community life, the importance of vital and informative materials and activities as means for motivating the study of the foreign language itself began to be realized.   Inasmuch as no skill is developed except through practice, it seemed that interesting informative material, chosen with due regard for its contributions to the development of desirable insights and appreciations in daily life, might serve as a desirable medium for practice in reading, writing, and speaking.   After all, one cannot learn a language without having something to read, write, or talk about.   Why could not this "something" be material which, among

---

563–567, May, 1940. Walter V. Kaulfers, "Orientation Courses in National Cultures," *Progressive Education,* Vol. XIV, pp. 195–198, March, 1937; "Prognosis and Its Alternatives in Relation to the Guidance of Students," *loc. cit.*; *A Cultural Basis for the Language Arts,* Stanford University Press, 1937, 115 pp.; pp. 56–75.

[1] See Introduction; also Walter V. Kaulfers, "Ten Problems in the Reorientation of Foreign Language Instruction," *The Modern Language Forum,* Vol. XX, pp. 23–31, February–May, 1935; "Magic-wand Solutions to Foreign Language Problems," *The School Review,* Vol. XLIV, pp. 744–752, December, 1936.

[2] Walter T. Phillips, "A Profession of Faith," *The Modern Language Journal,* Vol. XXV, pp. 467–469, March, 1941.

other things, would yield cultural outcomes similar to those which might be expected from a well-planned and competently guided period of residence or travel abroad? Why could it not be material in simple graded language that would help students understand their own country better by becoming more intimately acquainted with the backgrounds of the many people of foreign birth or descent who constitute one-third of its citizenry?[1] Why could it not be interesting and significant material which would help break down prejudices inspired by ignorance, suspicion, or misunderstanding of fellow pupils from non-English-speaking homes? This kind of reasoning gradually led to what has often been labeled the "cultural approach" or "content theory" of foreign-language teaching—of developing the language abilities from the start in and through content of significance for the social and cultural life of the individual as a student in school and as a potential homemaker, voter, wage earner, and creative participant in the social and cultural life of the community.

Moreover, experience with terminal courses in foreign cultures served to convince many teachers that the same methods used in conducting occasional sample lessons in the foreign language could be employed to advantage in regular foreign-language classes. Since the emphasis in the survey courses was primarily on content read and discussed in English, the foreign language was introduced only occasionally in connection with simple but interesting reading lessons, short dialogues rich in practical phrases and vocabulary, songs, and short illustrated talks in the foreign language (making abundant use of cognates written in the order of their use on the blackboard). All formal work in the way of drill or rules was limited to satisfying the pupils' own curiosity concerning the language, or to answering their own questions and requests for help.[2]

Despite the limited exposure to the foreign language which these incidental activities afforded, the pupils seemed to learn more vocabulary, to use what limited resources in language they had at their command more enthusiastically and confidently, and to remember

[1] Walter V. Kaulfers and Holland D. Roberts, *A Cultural Basis for the Language Arts*, Stanford University Press, 1937, 115 pp.; pp. 1–23. Leonard Covello, "Language as a Factor in Integration and Assimilation," *The Modern Language Journal*, Vol. XXIII, pp. 323–333, February, 1939. Walter V. Kaulfers, "Our Creative Role as Teachers of the Language Arts," *The Modern Language Journal*, Vol. XXV, pp. 368–374, February, 1941.

[2] F. J. McConville, "Increasing the Social Values of Foreign Language Instruction," *California Journal of Secondary Education*, Vol. X, pp. 573–574, December, 1935.

such facts about pronunciation or the structure of language as they themselves had requested, better than pupils who were taught to mix their mortar first according to the grammatical recipes in a basic textbook, and then to apply it in cementing words together in jigsaw-puzzle fashion without much regard for the sense. (The exercises rarely contained anything worth mentioning anyway!) Whereas the latter procedure tended to discourage pupils, the former seemed to encourage them. The desire to learn more language better was not satiated, stifled, or frustrated, but stimulated by a sense of power, self-confidence, and satisfaction. This empirical experience, based upon the unconscious application of the principles of modern psychology in language learning, paved the way for a gradual reorientation of the teaching and learning process in foreign-language courses proper. In this reorientation professionally minded teachers in many schools were aided by the consulting services and workshops provided by such curriculum-revision projects as those sponsored by the Eight-year Study of the National Commission on the Relation of Schools and Colleges, and the Stanford Language Arts Investigation.[1] The experimental programs inaugurated under the auspices of these organizations represented a trend away from the atomistic, mechanical view toward a functional approach.

Since the implications of the organismic conception of language for the development of abilities in oral and written communication have already been illustrated in considerable detail in the preceding chapters, it remains only to indicate briefly their application to the problem of vocabulary building.

In terms of the traditional atomistic view of language this problem naturally was a major preoccupation of teachers. Language was conceived as being composed of words. These were the molecules, so to speak, of which language was compounded. Words in turn were composed of syllables, and the latter of such language atoms as vowels and consonants. The cohesive element that bound all these atoms and molecules together was, figuratively speaking, grammar. In keeping with this mechanical conception, language was classified

---

[1] Examples of new type foreign-language programs are described in *A Foreign Language Program for Progressive Schools*, Progressive Education Association, 221 West 57th St., New York, 1938, 86 pp. (mimeographed). See also *Proceedings of the Ohio Workshop on Modern Language Teaching*. Walter V. Kaulfers, "The Foreign Languages in the Stanford Language Arts Investigation," *Hispania*, Vol. XXI, pp. 13–18, February, 1938. Walter V. Kaulfers, ed., *Foreign Languages and Cultures in American Education*, Reports of the Stanford Language Arts Investigation, Vol. II, McGraw-Hill Book Company, Inc., New York. In press.

into neatly labeled divisions and subdivisions. Thus it was not impossible to find elementary textbooks in which the "conjunctive personal pronouns" were boxed off with a heavy black border to insulate them as thoroughly as possible from the rest of the language, and the pupils were expected to "master" them first by memorizing the list as vocabulary, then by studying the rules on agreement and position, and finally by translating exercises containing these elements—all without being able in advance to identify a conjunctive personal pronoun in any language or without ever having come in contact with one, directly or indirectly, in their previous work in the textbook or course.

Vocabulary Building in an Organic Conception of Language.—In contrast with this mechanical view, the organic conception stresses the communication of thought—feelings, wants, information, or ideas—in connected context. The first exposure is aural-oral, then oral-visual, and finally kinesthetic. Language is not regarded as the sum total of all its parts (since it is quite possible to string words together correctly according to grammatical rule and yet fail to make sense), but as a semantic unity. Consequently, such parts of language as words are not considered to be foundation stones, but aspects of the whole which derive their particular form and meaning from the semantic functions which they serve in a specific communication situation. Growth in vocabulary, therefore, is a *derived by-product* of all communication activities involving the use of the language and never an end itself. Although words that cause difficulty in pronunciation, or whose meanings are obscure when encountered in context, are considered in isolation, there is no preoccupation with vocabulary building as a separate teaching or learning activity. Except where foreign words and expressions serve a semantic function when used in isolation in daily life[1] (*e.g.*, French words and expressions used on American menus; Italian terms used in music, etc.), words or idioms are not taught in classified lists or isolated exercises. The nature of the life situation in which the words or expressions are likely to be encountered in isolation is the guiding criterion in such cases.

Contextual Vocabulary Building.—The accompaning unit on French expressions found in American restaurant menus[2] illustrates the application of this principle to a lesson designed for use during

---

[1] Ruth A. Gardhill, "Collector's Item: French Signs," *The Modern Language Journal*, Vol. XXIV, pp. 375–377, February, 1940.

[2] Walter V. Kaulfers and Dante P. Lembi, "French Expressions Used in English," *The Modern Language Journal*, Vol. XXV, pp. 174–180, December, 1940.

the *first week* of beginning French.   It is intended to serve as an orientation exercise to help young people become aware of the influence of France upon even the most commonplace aspects of our daily life and culture, to afford practice in pronunciation with materials that have some concrete application in daily life, and to pave the way for the development of insights into the many interrelationships between French culture and our own.   Note that even in this mechanical unit, the vocabulary serves as the medium for the development of attitudes, interests, and appreciations in a life setting.   Unless a similar frame of reference can be found for classified items of vocabulary that function in isolation in actual life, it is doubtful if specialized vocabulary exercises are justifiable except in the form of occasional review games or diagnostic tests.

LA CUISINE À LA FRANÇAISE

Part I. Vocabulaire

Familiarize yourself with the following groups of French expressions* found on American restaurant menus.   Then, using Part I below as a dictionary, do the exercises in Parts II, III, and IV according to the directions.

A

1. *à la carte:* "from the card" or bill of fare; therefore, the orders on a menu for which one ordinarily pays separately.   The opposite of *table d'hôte* in the United States.

2. *à la française:* "in French style," elliptical for *à la mode française.*

3. *à la julienne:* a clear soup, containing thin strips of carrots and onions.

4. *à la mode:* literally, "in the style."   Pie *à la mode* really means "stylish pie"; usually pie served with ice cream in the United States.

5. *au beurre:* "with butter."

6. *au beurre noir:* "with browned (melted) butter."

7. *au gratin:* with bread crumbs or with grated cheese.   French onion soup *au gratin.*

8. *au jus:* "with juice or gravy."   Roast prime ribs of beef *au jus.*

9. *bisque:* "soup," usually a thick rich soup, such as clam and tomato *bisque.*

10. *bonbons:* corresponds to "goodies" in English.

B

1. *café:* "coffeehouse."   It has come to mean a restaurant in the United States.

2. *café au lait; café noir:* "coffee with milk" (cream, in the United States), "black coffee."

* A few of the expressions are Americanisms coined from French words, and now recognized as being in accepted usage in the United States, although in some cases they are not used in France.

3. *canapés:* toasted bread with anchovies, caviar, mushrooms, etc.   It has come to mean any open-faced sandwiches.

4. *casserole:* "baking dish."   Baked crab *au gratin en casserole.*

5. *champagne:* a white sparkling wine made in the old province of Champagne, France.

6. *chiffon:* literally, "rag" or "scrap."   Anything made from a small piece which becomes larger through cooking.   Orange *chiffon* cake, lemon *chiffon* pie.

7. *claret:* "claret," a red wine.

8. *cognac:* French brandy made from wine produced in the district of Cognac.

9. *consommé; bouillon:* "broth" or clear soup that can be served in a cup.

10. *couverts:* "cover" charge(s).

C

1. *croquettes:* from *croquer,* "to crunch," really means a fried ball of minced meat.   Chicken *croquettes, sauce suprême.   Suprême* is "the best."

2. *croûtons:* literally, "crusts of bread," but really means small toasted cubes of bread.   Cream of tomato soup *aux croûtons* (with crusts of bread).

3. *de luxe:* "of the best."   Chicken salad *de luxe.*

4. *demi-tasse:* literally, "half cup," is a "small black."

5. *en brochette:* on skewers or wooden pins.

6. *entremets:* literally, "between dishes."   Really a side dish or a fancy dish served between the main course and the dessert.

7. *entrée:* in France, a dish served preceding the main course.   In the United States, the term is often used to mean the main course.

8. *à la vinaigrette:* "with vinegar sauce" or with oil and vinegar.   Asparagus *à la vinaigrette.*

9. *filet de sole:* "filet" is a piece of steak or meat without bone.   "Sole" is thin, flat fish.

10. *filet mignon: mignon* is a small tender piece; therefore, in the United States, *filet mignon* usually means a small tender steak.

D

1. *frappé:* something "whipped," especially with ice, as *champagne frappé.*

2. *fricassée:* minced and served with a sauce or cream gravy as *fricassée* of chicken.

3. *glacé:* "iced" or frozen or having a surface resembling ice, as fruit *glacé.*

4. *glace:* "ice" or "ice cream," as *glace aux fraises* (strawberry ice or ice cream).

5. *hors-d'oeuvre:* literally, "outside the work" or extra.   Little appetizers served before a meal.

6. *jardinière:* "pertaining to the garden," means "with a variety of spring vegetables."   Potted Swiss steak *jardinière.*

7. *julienne:* with narrow strips of carrots and vegetables; a soup with vegetables in it.

8. *liqueurs:* beverages (usually sweet) having alcoholic content, served in small glasses.

9. *à la lyonnaise:* "in the style of Lyon."   In France different towns are known in French cookery for special dishes.   Potatoes *à la lyonnaise* are potatoes prepared with sliced fried onion.

10. *maître d'hôtel:* literally "master of the hotel"; chef's special. Grilled steak, *maître d'hôtel.*

E

1. *marron glacé:* "candied chestnut."
2. *mayonnaise:* mayonnaise, a salad dressing made of oil, vinegar, eggs, and various spices.
3. *menu:* menu or bill of fare.
4. *mousse:* a frozen dessert made of whipped cream and fruits; has something of the idea of froth or lather in its original meaning.
5. *nougat:* candy or nuts stirred into a paste made of caramel, honey, or sugar. French *nougat.*
6. *omelette:* omelet.   Creamed chicken *omelette.*
7. *paté de foie gras:* goose-liver paste used as a spread for *canapés,* etc.
8. *paté,* a little pie, often used to mean *croquette* in the United States. Creamed chicken and mushrooms in paté (patty) shells.
9. *petits fours:* literally, "little ovens"; means small cakes, cookies, or pastry.
10. *petits pois:* "little peas," green peas.

F

1. *purée:* soup of mashed or strained vegetables.   Vegetable *purée.*
2. *ragoût:* from *ragoûter,* "to restore one's appetite."   Really a *ragoût* is a highly seasoned stew with vegetables.
3. *petit noir:* "small black," referring to a small cup of black coffee served at the end of a meal.   (See also *demi-tasse.*)
4. *restaurant:* restaurant.
5. *sauted:* Americanized form of *sauté,* "stewed (usually in fat or butter)." Sauted chicken giblets.
6. *sauterne:* a white wine.
7. *sirloin:* from *sur longe,* "on the loin."   Roast *sirloin* of beef.
8. *soufflée:* "inflated" through whipping.   Cheese *soufflée.*
9. *table d'hôte:* "the host's table," means that the meal is served at a given hour and at a fixed price, rather than *à la carte.*   In the United States, *table d'hôte* often means "the complete meal at a fixed price."
10. *pêche melba:* often half a peach served on sponge cake, with ice cream and fruit sirup or fruit sauce.

G

1. *pièce de résistance:* a main dish, or special course, representing the best part or "climax" of the meal.
2. *carottes:* carrots.
3. *pommes de terre:* potatoes.
4. *repas:* meal.
5. *à l'anglaise:* "in the English style."

Part II

Rewrite the following sentences, substituting French words or expressions from Part I for the words that are underlined.   For example:

Given: I'll have some roast beef with juice.
Write: I'll have some roast beef *au jus.*

A

In the following sentences choose words and expressions from group A of Part I.
1. I think I'll order a few things from the bill of fare.
2. I'm getting a little tired of pie with ice cream.
3. Baked potato with butter, please.
4. Did you order this macaroni with bread crumbs?
5. I'm sorry I didn't order the *consommé* instead of this thick rich soup.

B

In the following sentences choose words and expressions from group B of Part I.
1. Would you like the cup of clear soup?
2. How much are the cover charges?
3. Coffee with cream, please.
4. These little open-faced sandwiches are certainly delicious!
5. Just the black coffee, thank you.

C

In the following sentences choose words and expressions from group C of Part I·
1. I prefer the cream of tomato soup with toasted cubes of bread.
2. Bring me just a half-cup, if you please.
3. Their side dishes are better than their entrees.
4. I've decided on a small tender steak.
5. "Chicken livers on sticks" sounds good to me.
6. We'll take the salad with vinegar sauce.
7. Do you prefer the fish steak or the small tender (meat) steak?
8. Their dinner of the best is two dollars.
9. What are they serving as the main dish?
10. You can mince the chicken and serve chicken dumplings (balls) tonight.

D

In the following sentences choose words and expressions from group D of Part I.
1. They serve a large variety of appetizers.
2. Who ordered the potted Swiss steak with vegetables?
3. I think this consommé with strips of carrots and other vegetables is absolutely tasteless.
4. Will you have the baked potatoes or the potatoes in the style of Lyon?
5. For dessert, I'd like the strawberry ice cream.

E–F

In the following sentences choose words and expressions from groups E and F of Part I.

1. You'll like the goose-liver paste.
2. We need some little cakes to go with the ice cream.
3. I recommend the green peas and the soup of mashed vegetables.
4. Shall we order the complete meal?
5. Just a small black, please.
6. Why not take the seasoned stew of meat and vegetables?
7. Perhaps you would prefer the half peach on sponge cake with ice cream.
8. This French nut-caramel candy is the best you can buy.
9. I'm going to have the raspberry dessert made with whipped cream.
10. It will be cheaper to eat at the host's table.

G

In the following sentences choose words and expressions from group G of Part I.

1. Now for the best part of the meal!
2. After their noonday meal, they usually rest for an hour.
3. Potatoes in the English style form a part of almost every meal.
4. He mistook the potatoes for the *entrée*.
5. What do they mean by carrots in the English style?

PART III

Rewrite the menus below using as many of the French words and expressions from Part I as possible.

A

BILL OF FARE

(Cover charge, 3 francs)

| Appetizers | or | Broth with crusts of bread |
| Goose-liver paste | | Vegetable-broth with toasted bread-cubes |

| Omelet | or | Small fish (sole) steak |

Small tender steak, French style
Potatoes in the Lyon style
Green peas

Peach with ice cream and fruit sirup
or
Strawberry ice-cream
Little cakes

Half-cup of black coffee

B

BILL OF FARE
(Cover charge, $2.00)

Appetizers	Clear soup
Open-faced sandwiches	Thick tomato soup

Tomato salad with oil and vinegar

Small tender steak	Roast beef with juice,
	with spring vegetables

Chicken stewed in a cream gravy

Green peas with browned butter
Carrots, English style
Potatoes with butter

Apple pie with ice cream
Whipped cream and fruits
Half peach on sponge cake
Goodies, candied chestnuts
Strawberry ice cream with little cakes

Small black

Make up a good menu for your own using as many of the French words and expressions from Part I as possible.

Make a list, with definitions, of any other French words or expressions that you have seen on menus.

Are there any restaurants, cafés, or hotels in your neighborhood that use French terms on their menus? Persuade the manager to let you bring a copy of the menu to class. What French terms seem to be used most frequently?

PART IV. OBSERVATION QUESTIONS: SUMMARY OF UNIT

1. Why do you think French words and expressions are often used on the menus of our better restaurants and hotels in the United States? Is it because the French words are shorter or more convenient? Is it because we do not have words of our own that are just as good? Is it because they look or sound more "cultured" or "refined"? Is it because they are easier to understand, spell, or pronounce?

2. Which of the French words and expressions that we use on menus in the United States are actually names for foods, recipes, or customs that came to us from France? From your work with this unit, would you say that France has had a direct influence upon our daily life—language, cooking, etc.?

3. Are there any French restaurants in your community, or cafés that specialize in French cooking? Are they popular or not? Why?

4. From your knowledge of European or American history can you tell how, when, or why French cooking became world famous? Tell how or why it has become popular in the United States?

5. From what other foreign countries have we borrowed words for foods, recipes, etc.? From what countries did we borrow the words "tamales," sauerkraut," "macaroni," "potato"?

6. To what extent is it true that the influence of a foreign country on us is reflected in the words that we have adopted into English from abroad?

Sociosemantic Aspects of Vocabulary Building.—Word borrowing as an index of the degree to which a foreign culture has been assimilated into our own, and of the nature of the influence that it has exercised, directly or indirectly, upon our own national and community life, is illustrated in the following unit for the first week of beginning Spanish or general language.[1] The frame of reference is "What we owe to the Spanish-speaking peoples as revealed in the words which we have borrowed from them." Although the exercise serves a linguistic function, the vocabulary is not an end in itself. The unit is designed to help students gain insight into the *life meaning behind the word*. As such, it is an elementary exercise in interpretation. The noun *patio*, for example, does not represent just a word borrowed from the Spanish, but a significant contribution to our Spanish-colonial architecture which came to us from Rome by way of Spain and her colonies. The concrete ways in which Spanish colonial culture has influenced the architecture of many of our homes in the Southwest is revealed in such specific terms as *azotea*, *patio*, *adobe*, and *Monterrey*, which are commonly used in English. Other insights of a similar nature are developed inductively in the several parts of the unit.

FOOTPRINTS OF SPAIN AND SPANISH AMERICA IN THE UNITED STATES—LANGUAGE

Foreword

In this unit are grouped words that have come into our language from the Spanish, either directly from Spain, or by way of her former colonies in the New World. Many of the words are, of course, used only in those parts of the United States which were colonized by the Spaniards—chiefly, California, Texas, Colorado, New Mexico, and Arizona. In these words is revealed the nature of the influence that Spain and Spanish America have had upon life in our Southwest. While examining the nine groups of words, try to decide what contributions they reveal in the way of customs, institutions, or traditions. Then turn to the exercises in Parts II and III.*

[1] Walter V. Kaulfers, A. Marion Ferns, and Dante P. Lembi, "Spanish Expressions Found in English," *Hispania*, Vol. XXIII, pp. 175–184, May, 1940.

* The terms in groups A to I are defined primarily as they have come to be used in English. Comments on etymological origins are based on *Webster's New International Dictionary of the English Language*, *Heath's Pequeño Larousse Ilustrado*, and Harold W. Bentley's *A Dictionary of Spanish Terms in English*.

Part I

A

1. *adobe:* an oblong brick usually about 18 by 6 by 10 inches, made from clay that adheres compactly when mixed with water.

2. *azotea:* the flat platformlike roof of a house built in the Spanish style.   The *azotea* is used as an open-air retreat at various times, particularly for coolness in the evenings.

3. *casa grande:* literally, a "large house," but often means the house of the owner of an *hacienda* or ranch.

4. *hacienda:* a large ranch or landed estate.

5. *patio:* a courtyard, usually an open garden surrounded by walls.

6. *rancho:* a stock-raising establishment for cattle, sheep, or horses; also a farm or an orchard.

7. *corral:* an enclosure, pen, or yard for the larger domestic animals.

8. *hammock:* from the Spanish word *hamaca,* borrowed from the Indian.   It means a swinging couch or bed.

9. *missions:* in the sense of mission churches (California and Texas), this word comes from the Spanish word *misiones.*

B

1. *avocado:* alligator pear; of Mexican-Indian origin.   The Mexican word is *aguacate.*

2. *banana:* a tropical fruit.

3. *barbecue:* from the Spanish word *barbacoa,* borrowed from the Indians of Mexico and Central America.   Barbecued meat is usually cooked over an outdoor gridiron.

4. *cafeteria:* a self-service eating establishment in the United States; a retail coffeehouse in Cuba.

5. *chile* or *chili:* Mexican peppers.

6. *chile con carne:* chile with meat.

7. *chocolate:* a preparation made with cacao, cocoa, and other ingredients; a beverage made by cooking this preparation with water or milk.   This word was borrowed from the Nahuatl (Indian language of Mexico).

8. *frijoles:* beans, usually referring to the Mexican pink beans.

9. *garbanzos:* chick-peas; beans.

10. *potato:* from the Spanish word *patata* taken from the South American Indians.

11. *tapioca:* a word borrowed from the Indians of South America; a kind of starch used in puddings and in thickening soups.

12. *tortilla:* a flat, round, very thin, unleavened griddlecake.

13. *alfalfa:* a species of forage plant.

14. *tamales:* a dish made of cornmeal and meat, probably of Indian origin.

15. *enchilladas:* a Mexican dish made by wrapping meat or other fillings in a tortilla; probably of Indian origin.

C

1. *alligator:* an American crocodile.

2. *armadillo:* from the Spanish word *armado* (armed); a small mammal with a bony shell, found in South America.

3. *barracuda:* a large fish found in the vicinity of Florida and along the Pacific coast of the United States.

4. *bronco:* an unbroken or untamed horse.

5. *burro:* a donkey.

6. *chinchilla:* a small rodent, the size of a large squirrel, with very soft fur of pearly-gray color.   It is a native of the mountains of Peru and Chile.

7. *cockroach:* from the Spanish word *cucaracha;* a species of black beetle.

8. *dogie:* a "scrubby" or anemic calf or other animal.   The cowboys' "dogies" is probably an adaptation of "dobies," being a nickname for a thing of inferior quality.

9. *mosquito:* from the Spanish word *mosca,* meaning a little fly.

10. *mustang:* a horse, bronco, or steed; often refers to the native wild **pony of** the West; from the Spanish word *mesteño.*

D

1. *charro:* a horseman, or one skilled in horsemanship.   The term *charro* is also applied to the national male costume of Mexico.

2. *creole:* a person of European descent but born and bred in the colony; used in Spanish America and the Southern French colonies.

3. *gringo:* an American; a "yankee."

4. *padre:* a priest.

5. *peón:* a servant; a peasant; a day laborer.

6. *pickaninny:* from the Spanish words *pequeño niño;* generally applied to a negro or mulatto infant in the Southern states.

7. *vaquero:* a cowboy; from the Spanish word *vaca* meaning cow.

8. *vigilante:* a member of a volunteer committee of citizens for the oversight and protection of the community.

9. *conquistador:* a leader in the Spanish conquest of the New World.

E

1. *arroyo:* a gorge or ravine cut by water running in the lower parts of a particular region; a canyon.   In Spanish the word *arroyo* is usually applied to a stream.

2. *bajada:* from the Spanish word *bajar* meaning "to do down"; a downgrade in the hill or trail; a sharp descent.

3. *barranca:* a rugged fissure cut in a landscape by the action of running water; a steep and irregular incline or side of a mountain.

4. *cordillera:* a range or chain of mountains.

5. *laguna:* the English modification of this word is "lagoon," a lake or pond; an area of brackish water, especially one near the sea.

6. *mesa:* tableland.

7. *tulares:* a region covered with *tules* (bulrushes).   This word is probably of Mexican origin.

F

1. *alameda:* a street, walk, or drive lined by *álamos* or poplar trees.

2. *EL CAMINO REAL:* the main highway, built by the state or the king. Literally, "the royal road."

3. *plaza:* a public square or park.

G

1. *alpaca:* a thin kind of cloth made from the woolly hair of the *alpaca*, a kind of llama found in Peru.

2. *sombrero:* a large hat with broad brim and high, peaked crown.

3. *sarape:* a blanketlike wrap used by men to throw about the shoulders and body; commonly worn in Mexico by the *charros* and Indians; also spelled *serape* and *zarápe*.

4. *mantilla:* a lace shawl worn by the Spanish ladies for festive occasions. It is worn over a high comb or sometimes just over the head. Originally the *mantilla* was an importation from the Orient.

5. *poncho:* a *sarape* worn by the *peons* of Mexico to protect them from the cold and rain.

6. *huarache:* a Mexican sandal.

7. *bolero:* a short jacket. This type is found in the Spanish bull fighter's costume.

H

1. *adiós:* "good-by," "so long," "I'll see you later," or simply "hello" in passing people.

2. *bonanza:* in Spanish this word originally meant good weather on the ocean. It is now used in connection with a vein or rich ore in a mine. By extension, *bonanza* is applied to an unusually promising enterprise of any kind.

3. *bravado:* boastful behavior; affectation of courage.

4. *bravo:* an exclamation of approval or encouragement.

5. *canoe:* a light boat used by primitive people; from the word *canoa* which the Spaniards borrowed from the South American Indians.

6. *chico:* small or small one; frequently used as a nickname or pet name.

7. *concha:* Spanish for "shell"; used by the *vaqueros* to mean small flat metal plates, shaped in the form of a shell, made of silver or brass and worn on the chaps or belt of the *vaquero*.

8. *filibuster:* from the name of certain pirates who infested the seas of the Antilles during the seventeenth century. The word later became closely associated with the Congress of the United States, and is most commonly used at present to mean an attempt to obstruct or delay legislative action by means of extended talking about some phase of the subject at hand.

9. *hoosegow:* from *juzgado* (judged or sentenced); a court of justice; a jail.

10. *lasso:* a rope used for noosing purposes; from the Spanish word *lazo*.

11. *loco:* crazy; stupid. It was originally applied to cattle.

12. *mañana:* tomorrow, or morning.

13. *presidio:* a military stronghold; a fort; a prison.

14. *pronto:* quickly; suddenly; hurry!

15. *siesta:* rest or nap during the hottest hours of the day, usually after lunch.

I

1. *fandango:* a name brought, together with the dance, from the West Indies to Spain. A lively dance in three-eight or six-eight time, much practiced in Spain and Spanish America.

2. *fiesta:* a holiday or festivity.

3. *rodeo:* a roundup; a show of cowboy stunts involving bronco riding, steer riding, calf roping, etc.

4. *tango:* a Spanish American dance, common especially in Mexico and the Argentine.

PART II.   OBSERVATION QUESTIONS

1. From what foreign language have we borrowed the words given in Part I? Write a short simple heading for each group of words—a sort of title to show what kinds of words they are according to their meaning.   Unless you can think of better headings of your own, choose from the following and tell which group of words they fit best.

    a. Names of types of people.
    b. Words for articles of clothing or wearing apparel.
    c. Topographical (or geographical) terms.
    d. Words for fish, rodents, or other animals.
    e. Words for foods and drinks.
    f. Words for buildings, building materials, etc.
    g. Words for sports, recreations, or amusements.
    h. Words for public squares or public thoroughfares.
    i. Miscellaneous terms.

2. Why do you think we borrowed these expressions and words?   Why did we choose them from Spanish and not from some other foreign language?

3. Judging from these groups of words, what would you say about the kinds of influence Spain and Spanish America have had upon life in America?   Do you think we will continue to adopt words from the Spanish language?   Why?

4. Can you think of any other Spanish or Spanish American words not found in the groups in Part I?

5. Which of the words in the foregoing groups were originally of Indian origin? Judging from these words, what contributions would you say that the Indians of Mexico and of Central and South America made to life in the United States?

6. Which of the words in the foregoing groups have you actually heard used in your community or vicinity?   From your knowledge of history can you tell whether or not these words were ever in common use in your state?   Is the Spanish-colonial tradition dying out in our Southwest?   How could one find out?

7. Mention any communities that have tried to keep the Spanish-colonial tradition alive.   How well have they succeeded?   What effect have their efforts had upon community life?

PART III

Number a separate sheet of paper, and opposite the proper numbers rewrite the sentences below substituting Spanish terms from the groups in Part I for the underlined words.   For example,

    Given: I went to the roundup at Salinas.
    Write: I went to the *rodeo* at Salinas.

A

In the following sentences use terms from group A of Part I.

1. Many of the houses in Monterey are made of mud bricks.

2. We found the family enjoying the evening on the flat part of the roof of their house.

3. After arriving at the hacienda, we went to the owner's home.

4. Tea is being served in the small garden surrounded by walls.

5. The yard for the animals was a long distance from the house.

6. She was reclining in a swinging bed under the tree.

B

In the following sentences use terms from group B of Part I.

1. The salad contained alligator pear and grapefruit.

2. Would you like some chile with meat?

3. Let's buy our dinner in the self-service restaurant.

4. I think I'll order tortillas and Mexican pink beans.

5. At the senior picnic the meat was cooked over an outdoor gridiron.

C

In the following sentences use terms from group C of Part I.

1. I should like to see the American crocodiles in the zoo.

2. At the rodeo the cowboy rode many untamed horses.

3. In Mexico the donkey is the chief beast of burden.

4. The cowboys put the scrubby calves in the corral.

5. She was wearing a coat made from the fur of the small pearly-gray rodent of the mountains of Peru.

6. The mammal armed with a bony shell is found chiefly in South and tropical America, except for one species which is found as far north as Texas.

D

In the following sentences use terms from group D of Part I.

1. In Mexico many men wearing the national costume may be seen at the bull fight.

2. The laborers on the ranchos earn very little money.

3. In New Orleans we saw a small Negro child sitting on the curb and eating watermelon.

4. She waved to the cowboy as we left the rancho.

5. In early days of California history most communities had committees of citizens who volunteered to protect their interests.

6. The Spanish priests established the missions in California.

7. Cortez was a famous leader in the Spanish conquest of the New World.

E

In the following sentences use terms from group E of Part I.

1. Early explorers encountered great difficulty in crossing the deep ravines found along their way.

2. The railroad down the west coast of Mexico crosses some steep and irregular inclines and sides of high mountains.

3. The chain of mountains in the western part of the Americas has some wonderful scenery.

4. Mexico City is located on a tableland over 7,000 feet above sea level.

5. Around the curve there is a downgrade in the road.

F

In the following sentences use terms from group F of Part I.

1. The main highway, No. 101, passes through Palo Alto.

2. Along the drive lined by poplar trees are many beautiful homes.

3. The Zócalo is the principal public square in Mexico City.

G

In the following sentences use terms from group G of Part I.

1. Her dress was of a woolen cloth made from a kind of llama found in Peru.

2. The charro was wearing a broad-brimmed hat.

3. Mexican sandals are being worn for sport this year.

4. Short jackets of contrasting colors are worn for both sport and evening.

5. The peons wear a blanket with a hole cut in the center.

H

In the following sentences use terms from groups H and I of Part I.

1. During the rest hour all the stores close and shopkeepers go home.

2. He visited the military barracks in San Francisco.

3. Come quickly!

4. We said "Good-by."

5. Many pioneers came to California during the days of the gold rush in 1849.

6. Mexico is sometimes called the land of "tomorrow" because no one is in a hurry to do anything.

7. The villain showed a great deal of affected courage.

8. Let's go to the Santa Barbara festival next summer.

PART IV. OPTIONAL ACTIVITIES

1. Write a paragraph in English describing a city, town, fiesta, rodeo, or historical event, using as many words from the groups in Part I as possible. Underline the Spanish words.

Example: In California there are many traces of Spanish influence. Along El Camino Real, Highway No. 101, are located the missions founded by the Spanish

padres.   Many of these missions and other buildings are made of adobe.   Almost
every town name is prefixed by San or Santa meaning "saint," and many are given
other Spanish names such as Sacramento (the sacrament), Fresno (the ash tree),
and Los Angeles (the angels).   Our farms and estates are sometimes called hacien-
das or ranchos.   The Spanish type houses have patios and azoteas.   One of the
most interesting of our fiestas is the rodeo where one can see the vaqueros ride the
broncos with great bravado.   Most of these Spanish influences are contributions
from the Spanish conquistadores or the padres who brought their civilization and
religion to this country.

2. Make a list of Spanish words found in newspapers, books, or magazines,
and give the sentence or article in which each expression occurs.

3. Are there any Spanish names of streets, stores, organizations, or places in
your community or vicinity?   If so, why do you suppose they were given Spanish
names?

4. What evidences can you find in your vicinity of efforts to keep the Spanish-
colonial tradition alive?

Practical Vocabulary in Cultural Context.—If vocabulary is only a
derivative of active experience in using the language for a life purpose
in reading, writing, or speaking, how can one make certain that the
pupils will learn enough "practical" vocabulary to be able to order a
meal, rent a room, or ask their way to the post office?   The fear is
not uncommon that when language is used as a medium for expanding
the mental horizon or for enriching the learner's capacity for appreciation and worthwhile experience in daily life, the study can no longer
be considered "practical."   This fear is probably more imaginary than
real, for it seems to be induced largely by the hypnotic effect of the
words "practical" and "cultural."   In reality, nothing is practical
unless it is put to some life use.   Thus the foreign word for frying pan
(*sartén* in Spanish, *Bratpfanne* in German, etc.) might be learned by
pupils and, because it stands for a commonly used kitchen utensil,
might well be considered a practical word.   But the probability is
exceedingly great that by the time the student found occasion to use
this word in some "practical" life situation he would have forgotten
it entirely.   In what sense then, would the noun *frying pan* be a
"practical" item of vocabulary per se, and to what extent would the
time and effort consumed in learning this noun as a word be a "practical" investment?

A word is seldom practical solely by virtue of the fact that the
object for which it stands is a usable thing.   It is practical chiefly
to the extent to which the word itself is likely to be used with sufficient
frequency, after it has once been learned, to prevent it from being
forgotten beyond possibility of immediate recall a few months after

the pupil has discontinued his foreign-language work in school. Much vocabulary work, which in the past has emphasized the learning of lists of words for furniture, household equipment, and the like, or the clipping of pictures from magazine advertisements to illustrate vocabulary notebooks, has not been, from the practical standpoint, more than an interesting form of nonfunctional busywork—a time-consuming atomistic approach to language illustrated with pictures, leaving little of importance in the way of a linguistic residue, and nothing whatsoever in the way of insights, attitudes, or appreciations that influence habits of thought, speech, and action in human life. In reality, courses emphasizing such activities, and others of a similar nature, were neither practical nor cultural. Like boys and girls enjoying a ride on the merry-go-round, the pupils usually got off only a few feet from where they started—perhaps a little dizzier, but it was fun.

The notion that nothing cultural can be practical, or that nothing practical can be cultural, seems to be attributable to artificial distinctions of purely a verbal nature.   When these mental hallucinations are dispelled, the possibility of developing a functional conception of reality, in terms of which culture is practical in so far as it is translated into the individual's modes of thought, speech, and action as a member of society, becomes less remote.   In terms of such a conception, the criterion for what is worthwhile in language is not the word itself, but the life needs in terms of which it is learned and used.   To be specific, it should make little difference from the language standpoint whether a pupil learns such "practical" French words as *beurre* (butter), *petits pois* (green peas), or *pommes de terre* (potatoes), from a list in a textbook, from a mechanical translation exercise devoid of real meaning, or from an orientation exercise, such as the one already cited, in which these words are put into a social and cultural frame of reference (*e.g.*, menu: *pommes de terre au beurre*) to illustrate our heritage from France as revealed in the terms that we use for those contributions to science and invention, literature, diplomacy, fashions, cuisine, etc., in which France has been a world leader.   The words *beurre, petits pois, pommes de terre*, are just as "practical" per se in any case, but the milieu or frame of reference in terms of which they are learned and used determines their real life significance to the pupils. A life frame of reference is indispensable as a criterion for judging what is worth-while teaching in terms of relative values.   It is also one of the most effective means for motivating the study of language with something more significant in long-range terms than such artificial devices as games, pasting pictures in notebooks, or threatening pupils with grades and tests as a discipline.   (Discipline for *what?*)

The Value of a Frame of Reference and Unifying Theme.—Practical words can be learned with gains rather than losses if acquired in and through activities that have a social or cultural setting and context.   During the first few weeks of beginning work, before ability in pronunciation has been developed to the point where reading and discussion in the foreign language can be used as a basis for vocabulary building, content activities capitalizing the linguistic resources of the social environment as revealed in place names,[1] foreign terms used in English, and the like, can serve a linguistic function for developing ability in pronunciation and vocabulary in a socially and culturally significant frame of reference.

The following unit on Spanish place names in California[2] illustrates ways and means for capitalizing opportunities for developing ability in pronunciation and vocabulary in terms of insights into those aspects of Spanish life and culture which are symbolized in the socio-semantic thought patterns underlying the choice of the names.   The culture that named its communities after saints, flowers, or trees was certainly quite different from the one that called its settlements Gold Gulch, Hangtown, Horse-thief Canyon, Red Dog, or Poker-flat. The study of place names in the introductory stages of junior and senior high-school foreign-language work has often lost in real significance because of its failure *to get at the life meaning behind the word.* Language learned apart from such insights is no more a key to the soul of a people than a list of words learned from a dictionary.

FOOTPRINTS OF SPAIN IN THE UNITED STATES—PLACE-NAMES

On the following pages is a classified list of names given to different places in California by a certain group of settlers who came to this region before 1849.   The names are taken from one of the earliest maps of California.*   Read the names and their meanings carefully, and then answer the observation questions in Part II.

[1] Oswald R. Kuehne, "Place Names in the United States as an Incentive to Foreign Language Study," *The Modern Language Journal*, Vol. XXV, pp. 91–107, November, 1940.   Contains extensive lists, with definitions, of place names in the United States, classified according to language of origin—Spanish, French, Latin, Greek, German, and Italian.

[2] Walter V. Kaulfers in collaboration with Edward J. Trombetta, Bulletin I: "Language as a Socio-cultural Index," Stanford Language Arts Investigation, 1937, 5 pp. (mimeographed).

* H. Kieport, *Mexiko, Texas, und Kalifornien*, 1847.

PART I

Names	Meanings
Agua Sola	Lonely water
Amador	Last name of a family
Antonio de Palo	Anthony of (the) spade
Asunción	Ascension
Bahía de los Esteros	Bay of Estuarios
Buena Vista	Good view
Cabo Concepción	Cape Conception
Cabo de (los) Reyes	(The) Cape of the kings
Calaveras	Skulls
Canal (de) Santa Bárbara	Channel of St. Barbara
Cojo	Lame
Flores	Flowers
González	Last name of a family
Gómez	Last name of a family
Isla (de) San Bernardo	Island (of) St. Bernard
Isla (de) San Clemente	Island (of) St. Clement
Isla (de) San Miguel	Island (of) St. Michael
Isla (de) San Nicolás	Island (of) St. Nicholas
Isla (de) Santa Bárbara	Island (of) St. Barbara
Isla (de) Santa Catalina	Island (of) St. Catherine
Isla (de) Santa Cruz	Island (of the) Holy Cross
Isla (de) Santa Rosa	Island (of) St. Rose
Los Farallones	The small pointed islands
Nieto	Grandchild (also last name of a family)
Ortega	Hazel grouse
Osuna	Bearlike
Pueblo de los Ángeles	Town of the angels
Pulgas	Fleas
Punta (de) Barra de Arena	Point sandy bar
Punta Delgada	Thin point
Punta de Loma	Hill point
Punta de Pinos	Point of pines
Punta de San Diego	Point of St. James
Río de la Merced	River of mercy
Río de las Ánimas	River of souls
Río de los Americanos	River of the Americans
Río del Sacramento	River of sacrament
Río de San Gabriel	River of St. Gabriel
Río (de) San Joaquín	River of St. Joachim
Río (de) San Pablo	River of St. Paul
San Antonio	St. Anthony
San Bartolomeo	St. Bartholomew
San Benito	St. Benedict
San Bernardino	St. Bernard(inus)
Sánchez	Last name of a family
San Felipe	St. Philip
San Francisco	St. Francis

San Francisquito	Little St. Francis
San Juan Bautista	St. John the Baptist
San Juan Capistrano	St. John Capistrano
San José	St. Joseph
San José Monasterio	Monastery of St. Joseph
San Leandro	St. Leander
San Luis Obispo	St. Louis (the) Bishop
San Luis Rey	St. Louis (the) King
San Pablo	St. Paul
San Rafael	St. Raphael
San Simeón	St. Simeon
Santo Tomás	St. Thomas
Santa Bárbara	St. Barbara
Santa Clara	St. Clara
Santa Cruz	Holy Cross
Santa Inés	St. Agnes
Santa Margarita	St. Margaret
Santa Rosa	St. Rose
Sierra Nevada	Snow range
Yerba Buena	Good herb (grass)

PART II. OBSERVATION QUESTIONS

1. What language do you think these settlers spoke?   From where did they come?   When?   Why?

2. Are any considerable number of the place names all of a certain kind? *Suggestion:* Try to arrange the names in groups under a short heading or title to show what kind of names they are according to their meanings.

3. What do you think made these settlers choose those names instead of others?   What must they have had in mind, or been thinking about, at the time?

4. What conclusion can you draw from your answers to these questions as to the character of these settlers as a group?

5. Did these people leave anything in the way of buildings which are still standing today?   If so, is the same influence reflected in the buildings as is reflected in the place names?

6. To what extent is the same influence still important in the lives of people today in the countries from which these settlers came?

7. Are any of the descendants (for example, great grandchildren) of these early settlers still living today?   If so, in what parts of California would you be most likely to find them?

8. Are people still coming to live in California from the same countries from which these early settlers came?   If so, where do most of them make their homes?

9. Do people in California still choose Spanish names nowadays for streets, apartment houses, cottages, real estate subdivisions, etc.?   If so, do they still choose the same kinds of names as the early settlers chose?   Can you explain the reason for any differences that you may find?

10. What are some of the commonest first names of Spanish and Mexican boys and girls?   After whom are Spanish-speaking children often named?   What day do they often celebrate instead of, or in addition to, their birthdays?   Do you see any relationship between the place names in the list and the first names of

Spanish-speaking children?   Can you find your own first name in Spanish among those given in the list?

11. Find a picture showing the skyline (or bird's-eye view) of a typical Spanish or Mexican town or city: for example, Guadalajara or Puebla in Mexico, Burgos or Seville in Spain.   What is it that stands out against the sky?   Is it a factory, hotel, or office building?   Is the same influence that appears in the place names and first names reflected in any way in the picture?

12. To what extent, or in what way, would you say that the following statements are true?

> a. "The kind of place names which the early settlers chose gives us some idea of the kind of people they were."
> b. "Language sometimes reflects the character of a people."

PART III. SUGGESTED ACTIVITIES

1. In one community of California (Palo Alto), many of the streets are named after famous writers (poets, novelists, etc.).   In what would you say the people who chose these names were interested?   What kind of community would you expect it to be: fairly well educated or ignorant?   A community full of saloons, shooting galleries, and public dance halls, or a community with good schools, good libraries, and good playgrounds?

2. What names would you choose if you were to name (a) an apartment house or hotel?   (b) A mountain cabin?   (c) A bungalow on the beach?   (d) A new real-estate tract or residential subdivision?   (e) A street?   (f) A new town? (g) A new school?   Have you any particular reason for your choices?

3. Look over the names of the 48 states.   Can you tell from the names, what people must at some time have lived or settled in them?   As far as possible, prove your points by mentioning such facts as you can remember or find out from American history.

Use of Songs in Vocabulary Building.—Almost all the activities that have been found interesting and worth while in conventional courses can be made to enrich the active or passive vocabulary as a derived by-product of the language experiences that they afford. The problem is one of finding a suitable frame of reference to give meaning and direction to the work.   Songs, for example, are less likely to make a significant contribution to the pupils' total education through language if learned and sung in isolation for pure enjoyment, or as a relief from boredom, than if they illustrate an aspect of some integrating theme such as "How France (Spain, Italy, etc.) has enriched our world of music."

The following unit in Spanish is designed for use in elementary classes[1] in connection with some unifying theme such as the foregoing.   It will be noted that the unit provides for semiconversational

[1] Originally designed for use in first-semester Spanish, Menlo School and Junior College, 1936, by Walter V. Kaulfers.

types of activity involving the vocabulary of the song, and a few other terms relating to music, in such a way as to provide for vocabulary learning through use in an audience situation *after* the song itself has been learned and enjoyed for its own sake.   The words of any song can become an integral part of every pupil's active or passive vocabulary[1] if the singing is not allowed to become a mere vocalization of nonsense syllables in a musical setting.

TE QUIERO, DIJISTE

Canción Popular Mexicana
Letra y Música de María Grever

Read the following verses from the chorus of the song *Te Quiero, Dijiste* with a view to matching the numbered Spanish lines with the lettered English translations of them in group B.

I

A. *Los últimos versos (coro)*

1. Muñequita linda, de cabellos de oro
2.   De dientes de perlas, labios de rubí,
3. Dime si me quieres como yo te adoro
4.   Si de mí te acuerdas como yo de ti.

5. Y a veces escucho un eco divino
6.   Que envuelto en la brisa parece decir:
7. Sí, te quiero mucho, mucho, mucho, mucho,
8.   Tanto como entonces, siempre hasta morir.

B

Number a separate sheet of paper from 1 to 8, and opposite the proper numbers write the letters (*a, b, c,* etc.) to show which of the lettered meanings listed below go with the numbered Spanish verses of the song above.   For example:

d. Which wrapped in the breeze seems to say

This sentence goes with verse number 6 above, so on your own paper write 6-*d*.

a. And sometimes I listen to a divine echo
b. Yes, I love you dearly, dearly, dearly, dearly
c. Teeth of pearl(s), and ruby lips
d. Which wrapped in the breeze seems to say
e. As much as then, forever until death
f. If you remember me as I do you
g. Pretty little doll, with golden hair
h. Tell me if you love me as I adore you

[1] Ethel P. Dickey, "French Songs in the Classroom," *The School* (Secondary edit., Ontario, Canada), Vol. XXVIII, pp. 221–223. November, 1939.

II

A. *Apuntes sobre la canción*

Te quiero dijiste es una canción (song) popular mexicana publicada en 1931 (mil novecientos treinta y uno) por la casa editorial Southern Music Publishing Company, S.A. (Inc.), de Nueva York.   El disco de fonógrafo es número 30078-B (treinta mil setenta y ocho -be) de la compañía Victor, cantada (sung) por Alfonso Órtiz Tirado con acompañamiento de orquestra.   Alfonso Órtiz Tirado es uno de los tenores líricos más renombrados (famosos) de México.   Se le conoce (he is known) como el "Tito Schipa" de México.   La letra y la música de la canción son de la bien conocida (well-known) compositora María Grever.

B. *Acabamiento*

Number a separate sheet of paper, and opposite the proper numbers rewrite the following sentences in full in Spanish, substituting for the X whatever information is needed to make the sentences complete and true.

1. La canción se llama X.   (*Se llama* = is named.)
2. La compositora de la canción es X.
3. La canción fué publicada en el año de X.
4. La casa editorial se llama X.
5. 30078-B es el número del X.
6. La canción es cantada por X.
7. "El Tito Schipa" de México es X.
8. Los discos son fabricados (manufactured) por la compañía X.
9. *Inc.*, en español es X: (Sociedad Anónima).
10. En el disco una X acompaña al cantor (singer).

III. Composición interrogativa

Using only the vocabulary and information of sections I and II, write five good questions in Spanish beginning them as follows:

1. ¿Cómo se llama (what is the name of)...........?
2. ¿Por quién (by whom)........................?
3. ¿Quién (who)................................?
4. ¿Cuál es (what is)..........................?
5. ¿Cuándo (when)..............................?

IV. Sinopsis

Write from memory in Spanish, without notes, a paragraph giving in complete *sentences* the name of the composer and publisher of the song, the date when it was first published, the number of the phonograph record, and the name of the person who sings it.   For the present avoid trying to say anything for which you cannot find a model in section II: A-B above.

V. Dictado

Play the record of the song, and try to write down the words of the remaining verses from hearing them sung.   If necessary, play over again the more difficult parts, setting the machine at a somewhat slower tempo and using a louder needle or volume.

VI. Trabajos opcionales e independientes

1. *Traducción*

Write in English a translation of part of the song, making the words rhyme without seriously changing the meaning or spirit of the poem. If possible, write an English version that will fit the music.

2. *Identificación*

Play the record, and follow the singer by writing on the blackboard the number of each line (verse) as the singer reaches it. If the song is written on the blackboard, point to each line as it is sung.

3. *Presentación original*

Bring to school a record of Spanish or Spanish American music, and before playing it for the class, give in Spanish the same kind of information that is given about the record mentioned in section II. You might begin somewhat as follows:

Tengo aquí un disco Columbia (de mi propia colección). Se llama. . . .
I have here a Columbia record (from my own collection). It is called. . . .

If your record is not a song, you may find it convenient to use the following expressions:

un tango tocado por: a tango played by
una sinfonía tocada por: a symphony played by

una aria de la ópera *Carmen* de Bizet:
an aria from Bizet's opera *Carmen*

un solo de violín (piano, guitarra, órgano) por:
a violin (piano, guitar, organ) solo by

la obertura de la ópera *Goyescas* de Granados:
the overture of the opera *Goyescas* by Granados

VII. Lección o examen de vocabulario

Number a separate sheet of paper, and opposite the proper numbers write the Spanish (as given in the sections indicated) for the words and expressions below:

A. *Sección* I

1. hair
2. gold
3. lips
4. pearls
5. ruby
6. the breeze
7. seems to say (two words)
8. until death
9. as much as (two words)
10. sometimes (at times)
11. tell me (one word)
12. dolly
13. pretty
14. as
15. if
16. yes
17. an echo
18. then
19. the last verses
20. (I) listen (one word)

B. *Sección* II

1. the song
2. was published
3. the publishing house
4. is sung
5. is named
6. the words
7. the music
8. the record
9. sung by
10. phonograph
11. are manufactured
12. Inc.
13. the singer
14. accompanies
15. the company

C. *Sección* III

1. By whom? 2. When? 3. Who? 4. What is?

D. *Sección* VI-3

1. played by
2. the opera
3. a guitar solo (four words)
4. a piano solo (four words)
5. an organ solo (four words)
6. a tango
7. a symphony
8. my own collection
9. here I have (two words)
10. an aria

VIII. Cuestionario personal

1. ¿Es Ud. una muñequita linda?
2. ¿Tiene Ud. labios de rubí?
3. ¿Tiene Ud. cabellos de oro?
4. ¿Tiene Ud. dientes de perlas?
5. ¿Tiene Ud. los cabellos negros, blancos, rubios, ó cafés?

Uses and Abuses of Gouin Series.—Since the days of Comenius, the tendency to classify "practical" vocabulary into groups of words relating to the classroom, the weather, or foods and drinks, etc., has led to much nonfunctional busywork with sterile content whose only unity and frame of reference lay within the artificial limits of the classification itself.[1]   Vestiges of this categorical approach to language are still to be found in certain traveler's manuals, and in textbooks published before 1920.   The possibility of contrasting in simple language a typical high-school classroom with a classroom in a French *lycée* a German *Gymnasium*, a Spanish *instituto*, or an Italian *liceo*, in such a way as to show similarities and differences between the in-school life of an American student and of a foreign student of like age abroad, is not generally appreciated.   Such a description can incorporate

---

[1] Johann Amos Comenius, *Orbis Sensualium Pictus*, Nuremberg, 1658.   Comenius' system for teaching Latin was extended with modifications to the modern foreign languages by Gouin and Bétis.   A series of lessons based on an illustrated classified vocabulary is known as a *Gouin Series*.   See Robert D. Cole and James B. Tharp, *Modern Foreign Languages and Their Teaching*, D. Appleton-Century Company, Inc., New York, 1937, xxi + 640 pp.; pp. 58–59.

nearly all the names of classroom objects which pupils may wish to know, and the vocabulary need not be learned merely as an end in itself but in terms of a cultural objective.   Where a more functional frame of reference is lacking, the comparison and contrast of any aspect of our home, community, or national life with its corresponding aspect abroad can furnish a unifying theme in terms of which any group of words can be learned as a by-product of work with language which has purpose and direction beyond the vocabulary itself.   Content that develops insights beyond the mechanics of language is essential if practice in communication in reading, writing, or speaking is to be effectively motivated and purposeful.

Integrative Vocabulary-building Activities.—Among the many devices for facilitating growth in vocabulary as an aspect of growth in ability to use the language as a whole are the following:

Identification of famous musical compositions, portraits, paintings, or pictures from descriptions read in the foreign language.[1]

For example, while reading an elementary textbook devoted to the cultural development of France, one first-year class made the acquaintance of outstanding leaders in French science, literature, music, art, and politics, for whom colored photographs of famous portraits could be obtained.   These were mounted on cardboard, labeled with the names and life dates of the personnages concerned— François I (1515–1547), Louis XI (1461–1483), Louis XIV (1643–1715), Catherine de Medici Richelieu, Louis Pasteur, Ampère, etc.—and exhibited to the class, using the chalk trays below the blackboards as easels.   A silent-reading unit in French, composed of one hundred 50- to 75-word paragraphs describing the characters, was then distributed among the students with the request that in the blank space, opposite each paragraph, they write the name of the personage described.

JEU DES PORTRAITS

I

Directions: Each one of the sentences below refers to a picture (portrait) on display in the room.   Read the sentence to identify the portrait to which it refers. When you are sure that you have located the right picture, write the *name* of the person whom it represents on the blank line to the left.   If you do not know the meanings of some of the words, look in the vocabulary of your textbook, or in

[1] Device designed by Walter V. Kaulfers for group use in the Palo Alto High School and Menlo School, Calif., 1934–1942, from suggestions received from *Jeu des portraits*, Albums du Père Castor, Ernest Flammarion, Éditeur, Paris, 1934.   For sample music-identification exercises see Appendix D.

the dictionary on the table in front of the class.   A few of the less common words are given in the vocabulary on the front board.

____1. Un grand ruban passe de chaque côté de son cou.
____2. Une couronne dont les bijoux forment une croix repose sur sa tête.
____3. Son chapeau est orné d'une cocarde tricolore, c'est à dire, un noeud ou insigne de rubans à la coiffure qui montre les trois couleurs du drapeau français.
____4. On l'appelle "l'empereur à la barbe fleurie."
____5. Vous pourrez le reconnaître à son visage creusé de rides profondes.
____6. Son visage s'encadre de cheveux bien frisés dont les boucles tombent jusqu'à son col, mais sans toucher son habit ni ses épaules non plus.

II

Write a description in French of some well-known person, using the vocabulary and expressions of part I above.   Can your classmates guess who the person is?

After reading the directions, the students were free to move about the room to locate the portraits corresponding to the descriptions in the paragraphs.   To avoid crowding, the pictures were distributed at convenient intervals along the chalk trays.   Comprehension of unfamiliar words was facilitated by means of a vocabulary of unfamiliar words written on the board.   In case of difficulty, pupils were also allowed to consult the teacher or a committee of three students who had previewed the unit.   Beyond this, no conversation or comparison of notes was permitted until after time had been called.   A subsequent diagnostic test revealed that in addition to affording practice in silent reading for a purpose, experience with the unit had yielded the following outcomes in gratifying degree:

1. A recognition knowledge of vocabulary dealing with facial features, e.g., ears, eyes, mouth, teeth, chin, jaw, eyebrows, eyelids, forehead, cheeks, and associated descriptive adjectives (thick, thin, oval, square, dark, fair, etc.).

2. A recall knowledge of the nouns and adjectives that had been used most frequently in the unit.

3. Ability (a month later) to identify by name the most important characters in French cultural history whose portraits had been described in the picture-identification exercises.

4. A desire for more units of this type.

It is probably unnecessary to indicate that the major linguistic outcome of the unit was a recognition knowledge (aural and visual) of a fairly specialized vocabulary dealing with facial characteristics— words not likely to be encountered sufficiently often in ordinary reading or discussion to be learned incidentally.   The device has been described in considerable detail not only because of its effectiveness in achieving this purpose, but also because of the concrete illustration which it affords of the use of a frame of reference—in this case, the cultural history of France, which had been the focal center of emphasis during the second semester of beginning high-school French. The material provided for silent reading during the process of identifying the portraits, and for oral reading and discussion in French during the subsequent exchange and correction of papers. It also served to refresh the students' recollection of information acquired from their previous reading. Whether ability to identify a portrait of Richelieu in later life is any less "cultural" than ability to identify the aria of an opera, a painting by Raphael, or a quotation from Shakespeare, is obviously a matter of personal opinion.

The principle of the picture-identification exercise can be applied to almost any situation for which a suitable frame of reference and pictorial illustrations can be found to prevent either the device or the language from becoming an end in itself. For example, as an alternative for the stereotyped pictorial wall charts often used to illustrate vocabulary dealing with the rooms and furnishings of a house, one teacher gave in simple French an illustrated talk on the Palace of Versailles, e.g.,

Voici *la chambre à coucher* et *le lit* où le Roi Soleil, Louis Quatorze, est mort. Here is *the bedroom* and *the bed* where the Sun-King, Louis Fourteenth, died. . etc.

Ici j'ai une photographie de *la salle à manger* dans le Palais de Versailles . . . très célèbre pour les . . . (Here I have a photograph of *the dining room* in the Palace of Versailles, very famous for the . . .) etc.

During the talk the various rooms and furnishings of the palace were linked to important incidents in the history of France, e.g.,

Dans ce *salon* fut courronné le premier empereur d'Allemagne . . . (In this *hall*, the first emperor of Germany was crowned . . .) etc.

Sur cette *table* fut signé le fameux Traité de Versailles qui . . . (On this *table* was signed the famous Treaty of Versailles which . . .) etc.

At the end of the talk the instructor reviewed the pictures briefly with the request that the students state, in French if possible, some fact of importance which each picture brought back to mind. The group then repeated orally the subtitle which had been written in French and English at the bottom of each picture. These subtitles were short simple sentences in which "practical" vocabulary was used in "cultural" content, e.g.,

La chambre à coucher et *le lit* où Louis Quatorze est mort.
The bedroom and *bed* where Louis the Fourteenth died.

Ten minutes before the close of the period, the pictures were arranged at spaced intervals along the chalk tray, and the pupils given the following assignment:

During the next ten minutes before the bell rings, will you step to the board and copy in your notebooks the subtitles in French of as many of the 20 pictures as you think you can remember when you come to class tomorrow. We shall take the first ten minutes tomorrow to write from memory in French as many of the subtitles as we can remember. The pictures will be on display again where you will be able to recognize them from your seats; but naturally the typewritten subtitles will not be legible at that distance. Copy first the subtitles of the pictures which interest you most, then as many more as you think you can remember. Watch spelling and accent marks. Step to the board now.

The outcomes of this variation of the picture-identification exercise are essentially the same as those noted for the unit on portraits already described. Students find this type of work interesting and profitable if it is not assigned oftener than once every two weeks.

The writer's experience over a period of eighteen years lends strength to the conviction that the indeterminate assignment (*e.g.*, "as many as you can remember") is better than a definite assignment (*e.g.*, "Come to class prepared to write from memory in French at least *ten* of the subtitles"). A careful check on the outcomes obtained by both methods has shown that the indeterminate assignment seems to provide a greater stimulus to individual initiative, especially on the part of the abler students. A definite assignment is unconsciously interpreted by most students to mean the *maximum* necessary to achieve a grade of 100, *A*, or excellent. Hence it has a limiting effect upon the initiative of able students who at times can easily do twice the amount of work. Similarly, the less interested or less capable student (who has already become habituated to average or passing standards of achievement) uses the determinate assignment as a basis for mentally calculating how far below this "maximum for an *A*" he can go and still get by. Although a few students will not do better under this type of assignment, the composite output of the class, as measured by the total number of words written correctly by the group as a whole, is usually greater if the assignment is flexible rather than fixed.

Twenty pictures can usually be covered in a 30-minute illustrated talk in the foreign language. Ten minutes can then be allowed for an oral review of the pictures and descriptive subtitles, and ten minutes for copying the sentences.   Until the students become accustomed to this type of assignment, however, discouragement can be prevented by reducing the number of pictures to ten or twelve.   Since all work of this type can usually be checked for mistakes from a uniform key, the scoring of papers can often be delegated to able volunteers from the class, and the better papers posted on the bulletin board as a guide to desirable standards of achievement.   Work with this variation of the picture-identification exercises provides a valuable foundation for short illustrated talks in the foreign language by the students on topics of their own choosing.   Where the pictures are small, the use of a balopticon for projecting them upon a screen is desirable.

Among other topics that have lent themselves effectively to vocabulary building in connected cultural context are the following:

1. *Third-semester Spanish.*—A comparison of the paintings of Murillo and Velásquez.   Capitalizing art-appreciation vocabulary of high frequency—*colors, perspective, light* and *shadow,* etc.

2. *First-semester Spanish.   El Palacio de Bellas Artes en México.*—Stressing theater vocabulary.   See sample unit that follows.

3. *First-semester French.*—Principal buildings and monuments of Paris.   Capitalizing an urban vocabulary, especially nouns relating to public buildings—post office, hotel, depot, hospital, city hall, opera house, church, cathedral, bank, street, avenue, park, etc.

4. *First-semester German.   Das Hotel Bristol in Berlin.*—Capitalizing vocabulary associated with the rooms and furnishings of a hotel. Illustrations clipped from advertising circulars showing dining room, reception halls, bathrooms, suites, etc.

5. *Second-semester German.   Das französische Gymnasium in Berlin.*—Capitalizing vocabulary associated with the school and classroom in an illustrated talk stressing similarities and differences between American and German secondary-school life.

6. *Second-semester Italian.   The Opera Balilla.*—Capitalizing vocabulary associated with sports, recreations, and premilitary form of activity to illustrate an important phase in the life of a modern Italian boy.

Although no mimeographed materials or blackboards are essential to the success of the picture-identification technique, these facilities are a distinct convenience in guiding correlated oral and written work. The following unit on *El Palacio de Bellas Artes en México* is suggestive of many types of activities[1] by which vocabulary and elementary

---

[1] Device designed for group use in first-year Spanish in the Menlo School and Junior College by Walter V. Kaulfers, 1940.

principles of usage can be learned in a unified frame of reference. The material is intended for use during the latter part of the first semester of beginning high-school Spanish as an aspect of a larger unit dealing with *La vida social y recreativa de México*. Similar illustrated units on such topics as *L'opéra de Paris, Das Berliner Opernhaus,* or the *Teatro della Scala* are equally practical in French, German, or Italian, respectively.

EL PALACIO DE BELLAS ARTES EN MÉXICO

The Spanish sentences below are the subtitles to the pictures of the Palace of Fine Arts in Mexico which are on display along the chalk trays in the classroom. The Spanish subtitle, with its meaning in English, is given below each picture. After you have looked at the pictures and read the subtitles below them, take a separate sheet of paper, and do the exercises in Part II according to the directions. The *Palacio de Bellas Artes* is the national theater of Mexico and is reserved for operas, symphony concerts, recitals, plays, etc.

PART I. SUBTÍTULOS

1. El Palacio de Bellas Artes da a la Avenida Juárez.
2. Una cúpola de cobre corona el Palacio.
3. En la cima está el águila, emblema nacional de México.
4. La vidriera debajo de la cúpula es una obra maestra.
5. La gran escalera conduce de un piso al otro.
6. Se compran los boletos en las taquillas.
7. Por todas partes se encuentran columnas de mármol y grandes ventanas.
8. Entre actos se puede charlar y fumar en las butacas del vestíbulo.
9. El estilo arquitectural es clásico-moderno.
10. Muchos van a la cantina para tomar refrescos entre actos.
11. Todo refleja limpieza y sanidad.
12. Inmensos candelabros de cristal alumbran las salas.
13. El famoso telón de vidrio oculta el escenario.
14. Un palco particular está reservado para el presidente de la república.
15. Los asientos de luneta son muy cómodos.
16. Hay gabinetes con espejos, lavabos, y mesas de tocador.

PART II

A. *Composición limitada*

Give the Spanish for the following sentences by recombining the words and expressions found in the Spanish subtitles above, or in parenthesis below:

The Palace of Fine arts is the national theater (*el teatro nacional*) of Mexico. (It) faces Juarez Avenue. The Palace is famous for its (*por su*) modern-classical style, and for its copper dome, glass curtain, marble columns, and high stage. Crystal chandeliers and large windows light its (*sus*) halls. From the foyer, where (*en donde*) one finds the ticket windows, a grand staircase leads to the upper floors (*los pisos superiores*). The building (*el edificio*) contains (*contiene*) dressing rooms with mirrors, washstands, and dressing tables, a private box for the president of the Republic, and a bar where (*en donde*) one can smoke, chat, and take refreshments in very comfortable seats or (*o*) armchairs between acts.   The structure is a masterpiece in modern classical style in which (*en que*) everything reflects cleanliness from (the) top to bottom (*al fondo*).   Exceedingly (*sumamente*) beautiful (*hermoso*) is the colored-glass window underneath the cupola.

B. *Composición Interrogativa*

Compose ten sensible questions in Spanish, starting them as follows, and using *only* words and expressions found in the Spanish subtitles of Part I.   Avoid questions that cannot be answered directly from information given in the subtitles.

1. ¿Dónde está (where is)..............................?
2. ¿Dónde se compran (where does one buy).............?
3. ¿Qué conduce (what leads)..........................?
4. ¿De qué *son* (what are the . . . made of).............?
5. ¿De qué *es* (what is the . . . made of)...............?
6. ¿Qué se puede hacer en (what can one do in).........?

C. *Resumen de Vocabulario*

Give the Spanish for the following words and expressions.   In what respects does the Spanish way of saying these things differ in *word order and meaning* from the English?

1. glass curtain (curtain of glass)
2. marble columns
3. crystal chandeliers
4. the main-floor seats
5. a private box

6. dressing tables
7. a copper dome
8. tickets are bought
9. faces (two words)
10. everywhere (three words)

D. *Observation Questions*

1. Instead of *glass curtain* the Spaniard really (literally) says *curtain of glass: telón de vidrio*.   What does he really say (in literal English) instead of crystal chandeliers? copper dome? main-floor seats? dressing tables? gold watch? vegetable soup?

2. What have you learned from working with this unit regarding the position of certain words that tell what a thing is made of?

3. What is the position in Spanish of such descriptive words (adjectives), as *nacional, moderno, clásico, particular, arquitectural*, etc?

4. Give the correct Spanish for the expressions: national theater, modern style, classical style, architectural style, national palace, modern palace, private theater, modern stage, modern dressing rooms, private dressing rooms, modern mirrors, modern washstands.   NOTE: The plural of *moderno* is *modernos*, and the plural of *particular* is *particulares*.

E. *Expresiones sinónimas*

Find Spanish words in the subtitles of Part I that are closely related to the following expressions in meaning.

For example:
Given: la parte superior (the upper part)
Write: la cima (see subtitle 3 in Part I)

1. comfortables
2. iluminan
3. símbolo
4. hablar
5. el bar
6. muy grandes

7. célebre
8. privado
9. lámparas grandes
10. en la parte inferior
11. piso principal de un teatro
12. la forma de arquitectura
13. gran cortina de teatro.

PART III. EXAMEN DE REPASO

Along the chalk trays are distributed the pictures of the *Palacio de Bellas Artes* in Mexico City. Number a separate sheet of paper, and opposite the proper numbers, write from memory, *in Spanish,* the subtitles of as many pictures as you can recognize in ten minutes. Each subtitle should be a complete sentence in Spanish.

Pictures can usually be obtained at little cost from standard agencies, or clipped from illustrated magazines and advertising circulars. A class in Spanish in which the students devoted three weeks to preparing, organizing, and presenting short illustrated talks on South America contributed 483 mounted pictures (with subtitles in English and Spanish) to the class filing case. The pictures had been obtained by the students themsleves from automobile associations, foreign consulates, travel bureaus, the Pan American Union, steamship and railroad agencies, dealers in secondhand magazines, friends, and relatives, etc.

Dramatization of Short Dialogues in a Daily-life Setting.—The memorization of short conversational dialogues for dramatization in class has long been recognized as a practical means for vocabulary building in connected context. The value of this activity can usually be increased, however, if the motivation for learning is reinforced by something more fundamental than the novelty of the experience itself. The following quotation based on notes taken during a visit to a first-semester high-school class in Spanish (which had just completed a content unit on the International Highway of the Pacific) shows the attempt of one teacher to motivate work with dialogues by placing this activity in a suitable frame of reference, and by providing opportunities for using the language skills thus acquired in a life situation:

How many of you are actually planning to go to Mexico via the Pan-American Highway next summer, or to visit some other Spanish-speaking country in the near future? Three? That's splendid! Perhaps others in the class will want to drive to Mexico or Central America soon, now that the International Highway is so near completion. Three boys drove together from San Francisco to Mexico City and back last summer, for less than $50 apiece for gas, oil, and minor repairs en route—and they came back filled with enthusiasm and plans for another trip soon. The class program committee may wish to invite them to speak to us if you care to hear about their trip. . . .

For those who are definitely planning a trip, or seriously considering the possibility, I have had a few short dialogues mimeographed which contain words and expressions which a traveler in a Spanish-speaking country will find convenient to know. The dialogues are entitled "In a hotel," "In a restaurant," "In a service station," etc. I am going to excuse from other work this week those who are planning to go to Mexico in order that they may learn the dialogues. Perhaps our three prospective travelers can form a committee, and practice the dialogues together until they know them well enough to act them out from memory before the class. If any others would like to learn the dialogues, whether they are actually planning a trip or not, they may be excused from other assignments this week also. Please let me know during the supervised study period.

In this connection, some of you may be interested in joining a group of third-year students who have arranged with the office to meet together once or twice a week for lunch at a *mesa española* at which only Spanish will be spoken. Although ten weeks of Spanish is hardly enough to carry on a conversation, many of you may wish to tune your ears to the language by hearing others speak it. Several of the dialogues which I have had mimeographed contain words and expressions which will be useful at the Spanish table. From time to time the members of the *mesa española* will invite guests for lunch to answer questions in Spanish about the countries which they have visited. This week our guest will be one of the boys who drove to Mexico via the Pan-American Highway last summer. . . . For the benefit of those who may not be able to understand everything that the visitors say, their answers to questions will be translated by members of the advanced Spanish class. . . .

Vocabulary Games.—Language games as a means for learning vocabulary are a part of almost every teachers "bag of tricks," for their utility as an entertaining form[1] of practice has long been recognized. The element of suspense, humor, competition, or novelty which they capitalize usually serves to stimulate interest and attention. For this reason, language games are not to be disparaged. Unfortunately, however, their interest value is often attributable not to the thought content of the language, but to the nature of the activity itself. Moreover, their pedagogical function in foreign-language

[1] Joseph A. Corso, "Bingo, a Device in Foreign Language Study," *High Points*, Vol. XXI, pp. 67–68, March, 1939. Amelia H. Anthony, "The Use of Games in the Modern Language Class and Club," *The French Review*, Vol. XIII, pp. 14–25, October, 1939. See also Appendix, references 16, 27, 28.

teaching is limited for the most part to review practice with elements of language that have already been learned. These two limitations usually restrict their use (1) to breaking the monotony of classroom routine and (2) to providing entertaining ways of reviewing and fixing specialized vocabulary.

Where learning cannot be motivated through the interest value of the content itself or through stimulating audience situations in a life setting, games provide a convenient way of deformalizing practice on language mechanics. The need for too frequent recourse to artificial stimulants to attention, however, is usually a symptom either of the mental sterility of the basic core content and activities of the course, or of a poor organization of the learning program. When a foreign-language class provides for growth in language thought content of interest and significance to young people, and capitalizes all the opportunities of the in-school and out-of-school environment for motivating the learning program with varied and stimulating audience situations, there is usually little need for pedagogical hypodermics in the form of games whose interest value lies almost exclusively in the nature of the device itself. Even as artificial stimulants, however, games are a valuable remedy to keep on the pedagogical shelf in cases of emergency—to prevent sleeping on exceptionally hot days, to keep young people out of mischief when half their classmates have been called away to some meeting and nothing new can be attempted, or to provide profitable entertainment at club social meetings and the foreign-language table. From the language standpoint, games are valuable to the extent to which they are re-creative in addition to being recreative.

Summary.—The three approaches that have just been described in detail represent various types of auxiliary devices for facilitating growth in vocabulary in special areas as an aspect of general growth in ability to use the language for a purpose: for acquiring and imparting information, for enriching personal experience, or for broadening the learner's social efficiency as a creative influence in the affairs of the community, nation, or world. When the content and activities of the learning program are organized in terms of a functional conception of language, a more specialized emphasis on vocabulary building than that illustrated by these devices should not be necessary; for all that is done in the foreign language then contributes to growth in vocabulary as a derived by-product. The way in which words so learned will function (whether as aural-comprehension vocabulary, as visual-recognition vocabulary, or as active speaking vocabulary) will obviously depend upon the way in which they are acquired and fixed for delayed recall.

Since numerous integrative activities for developing ability in vocabulary as an aspect of general growth in language have already been described in specific detail in previous chapters, it will suffice to conclude with a brief reenumeration of the basic conceptions underlying the foregoing discussion of vocabulary building:

1. Although words can be learned in isolation as vocabulary by almost any method that focuses attention in this direction, ability to use words effectively in actual oral or written speech is facilitated if vocabulary is acquired as a derived by-product of abundant practice in using the language as a whole in motivated audience situations.

2. Words are not the foundation stones of language, but aspects of language in action. As parts they derive their specific form and meaning from the semantic function that they serve in context.

3. Activities that involve specialized practice with words or expressions in isolation are best limited to words whose pronunciation or variable inflections cause difficulty in communication, and to conventionalized expressions that function in isolation in life outside the classroom.

4. The test for what constitutes a "practical" vocabulary is not primarily the utility of the objects that the words symbolize. It is the extent to which the words are likely to be used sufficiently often in postgraduate life not to be forgotten through disuse a few months after the pupil has discontinued his formal study of the language in school.

5. The organization of the learning program in the light of a unified frame of reference facilitates the acquisition of a practical vocabulary in cultural context.

6. Although basic vocabularies derived from scientific word counts are a valuable guide to teachers and textbook writers in providing for a proper distribution of emphasis on words of high frequency of occurrence, such lists do not, except incidentally, afford an indication of semantic range. At the elementary and intermediate levels the *range* of concepts which a word can express is as important as its frequency of occurrence in oral and written speech.

7. Since the objective function of language in life is the communication of feelings, wants, information, and ideas, the content through which growth in language is to be facilitated should not be designed to illustrate vocabulary or constructions of high frequency, but rather to communicate in words of high frequency something

worth reading, writing, or discussing in terms of a social or cultural objective that lies beyond the mechanics of language itself.

8. In general, 100 exposures to a word in silent reading are no more effective for delayed recall than 20 oral repetitions, or writing the word attentively 5 times.

9. The level of cognition on which a specific vocabulary is to be used should determine the nature and extent of the learning activities through which growth in language is to be facilitated.

10. Rhythm and rhyme facilitate learning for delayed recall, but poems and songs in a foreign language are effective as vocabulary-building materials only to the extent to which the individual words have meaning for the student. Words associated with some incident, fact, or idea of unusual interest or significance are generally remembered better than words that are learned in sterile context. All words tend to be forgotten through disuse, however, unless they have been securely welded to the learner's cognitive experience by some strong emotional or semantic association.[1]

[1] For standard frequency word lists, vocabulary-building aids, and tests, see Appendix, references 8, 13, 14, 16, 19, 20, 24, 25, 59, 60, 71, 72, 79, 112, 148.

CHAPTER VI

PERSPECTIVE ON THE DEVELOPMENT OF ABILITY IN CONVERSATION

Ventriloquist's dummies that cannot originate or express a single idea of their own.

Validity of the Conversational Objective.—The ability to converse in a language is the primary objective of a large plurality of students who enroll in modern-language classes in junior and senior high schools and adult-education centers.[1] Unfortunately this ability is the most difficult of all objectives to attain within the four walls of a crowded classroom, for it presupposes an almost automatic command of pronunciation, vocabulary, and correct usage, as well as facility in aural comprehension. Nevertheless, wherever secondary-school teachers have neglected to capitalize this universal interest or have subordinated it to formal work in reading or grammar, the result has usually been a high rate of discontinuance of foreign-language study, especially after the usual two-year requirement for admission to college has been fulfilled. Evening-school classes in modern languages, in which attendance is voluntary and grades or credits are seldom of interest to the adults enrolled,[2] often close for want of students after 10 to 15 weeks if the teacher uses the same approach as in day-school

[1] Walter Meiden, "People Want to Speak Foreign Languages," *The Modern Language Journal*, Vol. XXV, pp. 864–868, December, 1941. Anon., "Why Pupils Choose the Different Foreign Languages," *High Points*, Vol. X, pp. 41–42, March, 1928. Willis K. Jones, "What Spanish Students Want," *Hispania*, Vol. XIII, pp. 431–434, November, 1930. Emma Reinhardt, *A Study of Standards for Immediate or Class-room Objectives, Materials of Instruction and Pupil Activities for Two Years of French*, Unpublished doctor's dissertation, University of Illinois, 1927, 219 pp. Germaine B. Bouvard, *Does French, Because of Its Practical and Cultural Value, Belong in a Progressive Curriculum for Normal High School Students?* Unpublished master's thesis, New York University, 1928, 69 pp. Anne Z. Moore, "Why I Chose to Study a Foreign Language," *The Modern Language Journal*, Vol. XXV, pp. 181–185, December, 1940. Eleanor H. Carlen, "The Use of French by Graduates of Barringer High School, Newark, New Jersey," *The Modern Language Journal*, Vol. XXV, pp. 199–210, December, 1940.

[2] Bruno Schoemann, "Teaching Foreign Languages in Adult Education," *Modern Language Journal*, Vol. XXIV, pp. 44–52, October, 1939.

courses. The same situation would obtain in many high-school classes were all artificial forms of motivation removed, for adolescent boys and girls are not very different from their parents who attend high school: *Der Apfel fällt nicht weit vom Baume.*

Granting that ability to read and appreciate scientific or literary works written in a foreign language is a valuable asset, this objective is too remote from the lives and primary concerns of adolescent boys and girls to serve as a vitalizing stimulus. The language as heard over the radio, on the screen, or among foreign-born members of the community is likely to be the prime instigator of interest in modern-language work, especially when reinforced by a suppressed desire to travel abroad. The ability to read stories, novels, or plays in a foreign language is not likely to make a strong appeal to the considerable number of pupils who are not in the habit of doing voluntary reading even in English.[1] As indicated in Chapter IV, the development of an abiding interest in worth-while books is as important and difficult a task as the development of reading ability itself. Obviously, if the foreign-language program is to be limited only to those pupils who already possess a voracious appetite for reading, the enrollment is destined to be small indeed. Since no program of study is likely to take root in the minds of young people unless it builds upon interests which they consider important, it is obvious that the conversational objective cannot be entirely neglected. Even if the ultimate linguistic aim is reading, the interests of beginning students in oral communication can serve as a valuable springboard for the development of other abilities.[2]

Dramatization of Dialogues.—In the initial stages of foreign-language study, the need for a working knowledge of the rudiments of pronunciation makes it possible to capitalize pupil interest in oral work by means of short dialogues, rich in useful vocabulary and suitable for dramatization in class. The following sample unit in Spanish is suggestive of types of dialogues that can be learned from memory very early in the first semester. Teachers of high-school and evening-school classes have found very short dramatizations of common life situations useful for developing ability in pronunciation,

---

[1] Paul Witty and David Kopel, *Reading and the Educative Process*, Ginn and Company, Boston, 1939, x + 374 pp.; pp. 12, 83. Ruth Strang, *Problems in the Improvement of Reading in High School and College*, The Science Press Printing Company, Lancaster, Pa., 1940, 423 pp.; pp. 308–309.

[2] M. Margaret Smith," Oral Work as a Means to an End," *The Modern Language Journal*, Vol. XXIV, pp. 585–587, May, 1940.

for vocabulary building, and for capitalizing student interest in conversation. At the start it is important that the dialogues be *short*—rarely over 25 to 50 words—and that not more than one dialogue be assigned at a time. Spacing emphasis by interspersing other activities prevents boredom and prevents frustration by overtaxing the memory. Work with conversational materials has at times defeated its own ends simply because the dialogues were too comprehensive, or the emphasis on this type of activity too concentrated. Capitalizing an interest is not synonymous with satiating it.

Fifteen to twenty dialogues of the type illustrated below can, if learned at appropriately spaced intervals throughout the first year, satisfy pupil interest in practical conversation and, if carefully constructed to include conventionalized expressions of wide application to different life situations, provide a flexible core for meeting such basic language needs as pupils are likely to encounter in travel or the common occupations of clerking in stores or hotels.[1]

CONVERSACIONES INFORMALES*

Choose a partner in the class and rehearse the following dialogues with him until you are able to carry on the conversation aloud from memory.

PART I

1. *De compras*

DEPENDIENTE: ¿En qué puedo servirle? (servirla)?

CLIENTE: ¿Cuánto valen las chaquetas?

DEPENDIENTE: Se venden a quince dólares.

1. *Shopping*

CLERK: May I help you?

PATRON: How much are the (coats) jackets?

CLERK: They sell for fifteen dollars.

2. *En el hotel*

CLIENTE: Quisiera una habitación con baño.

DEPENDIENTE: Las tenemos de dos dólares, tres dólares, y cinco dólares.

CLIENTE: Bien; enséñeme una de tres dólares.

DEPENDIENTE: Con todo gusto. ¡Mozo!

2. *At the hotel*

PATRON: I'd like a room with bath.

CLERK: We have them for two dollars, three dollars, and five dollars.

PATRON: Well, show me one for three dollars.

CLERK: Gladly. Boy!

[1] Ruth Ewald, "Spanish for the Butcher and the Baker," *California Journal of Secondary Education*, Vol. XIV, pp. 108–111, February, 1939.

* Designed for use in the Woodrow Wilson Junior High School (seventh grade), 1925, by Walter V. Kaulfers. For conversational aids see Appendix B; also Appendix, references 71, 72, 112, 151, 153.

3. *En la estación de gasolina*

Mozo: ¿Lo lleno?

Cliente: Veinte litros de gasolina, uno de aceite, y las llantas—treinta libras, por favor.

Mozo: Bien, a sus órdenes.

3. *At the gasoline station*

Attendant: Shall I fill it up?

Patron: Twenty liters (five gallons) of gas, one quart of oil, and the tires—thirty pounds please.

Attendant: Very well, at your service.

4. *En el treatro*

Cliente: Dos boletos para esta noche.

Cajero: ¿Entrada general, o de luneta?

Cliente: Dos butacas.

Cajero: Aquí hay dos de la quinta fila, a setenta y cinco centavos.

Cliente: Muy bien, me quedo con ellos.

4. *At the theater*

Patron: Two tickets for tonight (this evening.)

Cashier: General admission or orchestra?

Patron: Two orchestra chairs.

Cashier: Here are two in the fifth row, at seventy-five cents.

Patron: Very well, I'll take them.

5. *En el restaurant*

Mozo: Aquí tiene Ud. la lista de platos.

Cliente: A ver, tomaré lo siguiente: (Lee la lista.)

Mozo: ¿Hay algo más? Bien; aquí tiene Ud. la cuenta.

5. *In the restaurant*

Waiter: Here is the menu.

Patron: Lets see; I'll take the following: (He reads the menu.)

Waiter: Is there anything else? Very well, here is the check (bill).

6. *Presentaciones*

Tengo mucho gusto en presentarle *al* señor Valdés y a *la* señorita (señora) Romero.

—Mucho gusto en conocerle(s).*

—El gusto es mío.

6. *Introductions*

I am happy to present Mr. Valdés and Miss (Mrs.) Romero.

How do you do? (It's a pleasure to know you.)

It's a pleasure.

* *Conocerla(s):* form for *you, her,* or *them* when the person or people are girls or women.

PART II.   EJERCICIOS

Write an informal conversation of your own in Spanish combining as many different expressions as possible from the six *conversaciones informales* in Part I. Do not try to say anything whatsoever for which you cannot find a correct model or vocabulary either in this lesson or in previous classwork.   You might start your conversation somewhat as follows:

1. *En la estación de ferrocarril*

Cliente: ¿Cuándo parte el tren para . . ?

2. *En la estación de camiones*
3. *En una librería*
4. *En una biblioteca*

1. *At the railway station*

When does the train leave for . . . ?

2. *At the bus station*
3. *In a bookstore*
4. *In a library*

Guidance in Paraphrastic Speech.—Since it is almost impossible for any modern-language student to acquire in school an active vocabulary as large as that which he possesses in his own language, guidance from the start in capitalizing to the widest possible advantage a limited but well-chosen stock of words and expressions is desirable. For this purpose, a vocabulary selected not only on the basis of the frequency of its occurrence in daily life, but also on the basis of its *semantic range*, is important.[1] By semantic range is meant the scope of language concepts which a given word can express in quasi-synonymous terms.   To illustrate, if a pupil has learned the word *commencer* in French (*comenzar* in Spanish, *cominciare* in Italian, *beginnen* in German), he should be encouraged to make this term do the work of a wide range of synonyms or near synonyms: *begin, commence, start* (and by extension) *originate, arise, initiate, inaugurate, introduce,* etc.   A pupil who succeeds in developing even a fair degree of facility in oral speech without opportunity for extensive practice outside the classroom usually does so because he is clever enough to make a few thoroughly familiar terms serve him to the widest possible advantage— in other words, because he consciously or unconsciously capitalizes all the semantic possibilities of the words at his command.   Not being able on the spur of the moment to say "We *started* to run," he says "We *began* to run"; not knowing how to say "It *commenced* to rain," he says "It *began* to rain"; instead of "It *originated* in Italy," he says "It *began* in Italy"; and in place of "He *initiated* the process," he says "He *began* the process."   At times he even makes the same verb serve for *inaugurate, introduce,* or *arise* as in "A new era was *inaugurated*" (= introduced > arose > began).   His diction is not elegant to be sure, but it suffices to communicate the *idea* in terms intelligible and generally acceptable to the auditor, which is probably the basic and most essential desideratum of elementary communication in any language.   At least it is preferable to the faltering, labored speech, punctuated by embarrassing lapses of memory which so frequently characterizes the oral work of pupils who have been wrongly conditioned to rack their brains for just the exact equivalent of some term that occurs to them in the vernacular, rather than to use any available resources in vocabulary that would serve to communicate the *idea* in point.   By the time these awkward word matchers succeed in formulating a question or answer, the occasion for saying anything is likely to be lost.

[1] Walter V. Kaulfers, "Interpretative Vocabulary Exercises for Beginners in French," *The Modern Language Journal*, Vol. XX, pp. 396–402, April, 1936.   See also Appendix, reference 132.

Ineffective communication in such circumstances is often traceable to faulty language habits developed through faulty teaching procedures and materials.   The instructional devices in most common use are not, properly speaking, exercises in the communication or interpretation of thought, but "matching exercises" in which verbalism is emphasized at the expense of meaning.   Sterile exercises in verbalism or word matching are not conducive to effectiveness in the spontaneous oral communication of feelings, wants, or information.   They are more likely to develop eyebound individuals who cannot understand or say anything unless they see it in print—and then only to the extent to which they can match every word with an exact equivalent in the vernacular.

This frequently observed dilemma suggests the advisability of replacing, as far as possible, all types of activities involving mental transliteration, with materials and procedures that encourage the paraphrastic or interpretative communication of *meaning* in terms of a unified subject or topic.   It also suggests emphasizing at the start a limited, active vocabulary flexible enough for use in a variety of situations.   Generic nouns that stand for an entire class of objects, adjectives that have a generic application, and adverbs that can be formed from the latter, usually provide a core vocabulary of wide semantic range.   It is in the nature of things that the generic noun *fruit* is a broader and, therefore, more semantically useful term for most people, than the particular noun *pomegranate*.   Similarly, such an adjective as *nice* is a more generically useful, if less precise term, than the adjective *modest*.   Since the statistical frequency of a word in a standard word count shows a high degree of correlation with its semantic range, words chosen from such a list can appropriately form the core vocabulary of reading, writing, and conversational activities in elementary and intermediate classes, provided the fatal mistake is not made of writing material to illustrate words of high frequency and wide semantic range, instead of capitalizing such words in communicating information or ideas worth reading, writing, or talking about.

Semantic range can usually be inferred from such comparative vocabularies as those presented by Helen S. Eaton in her *Semantic Frequency List for English, French, German, and Spanish*,[1] which lists in parallel columns the words of widest semantic range in English and their nearest corresponding equivalents in a foreign language. Naturally, such terms as *bank* must be ruled out of such a core list, since they are not generic words but multiple words from the semantic

[1] University of Chicago Press, Chicago, 1940, xxi + 441 pp.

viewpoint, *e.g.*, (savings) bank, (river) bank, to bank (a road), to bank (money), etc. Nongeneric terms of high frequency cannot be neglected, but the chief emphasis in developing an active core vocabulary at the start may well be on words of broad generic utility. Other terms may be left for the time being for concomitant learning on the recognitive levels: *aural* (comprehension of the spoken language) and *visual* (comprehension of the written language).

Foundation Exercises in Paraphrase for Beginners.—The unit in Italian below[1] illustrates one way of orienting the student in the concept of paraphrastic or interpretative speech during the *first week* of beginning foreign-language work, before the class is ready to read or answer questions on informational topics that permit of discussion in paraphrastic terms. The practical utility of the vocabulary (common language needs in travel) and the novelty of the language itself, usually compensate for the lack of content interest at this stage.

IN VIAGGIO

In doing the following unit, imagine yourself a traveler abroad who knows only the words in the vocabulary below. The point of the lesson is to get the *thought* across, not to translate mere words. By learning well a few carefully selected words, frequently used in daily life, it is possible to express a considerable variety of feelings, wants, or ideas. This fact is illustrated in the following exercises. The sentences are requests for services often needed in traveling abroad. In order to do the exercises correctly, study carefully the following examples and explanations:

$$\overset{1}{} \quad \overset{2}{}$$

Will you please ⌐*call (get)*⌐ ⌐*a taxi?*⌐

$$\overset{1}{} \quad \overset{2}{}$$

Mi faccia il piacere di ⌐*prendere*⌐ ⌐*un taxi?*⌐

Note that the words grouped under 1 in the example are to be found in the column headed *Gl'infinitivi* of the vocabulary below, and that the words grouped under 2 are to be found in the column headed *Gli oggetti.*

PART I

Using *Mi faccia il piacere di* + *infinitivi* + *oggetti?* as a model, how would you ask or tell some one in Italian to please:

1. Tidy the room?
2. Prepare a meal?
3. Call a porter!
4. Point out the way?

[1] Adapted from Walter V. Kaulfers and Dante P. Lembi, "Escercizi interpretativi per la prima settimana d'italiano," *Italia*, Vol. XVI, pp. 132–138, December, 1939.

5. Fix a watch?
6. Hold the tickets?
7. Go faster?
8. Launder the clothes?
9. Stay where he is?

A. *Gl' Infinitivi*

1.	to close	chiudere	12.	to iron	stirare
2.	to open	aprire	13.	to give me	darmi
3.	to make	fare	14.	to show me	mostrarmi
4.	to carry	portare	15.	to wash	lavare
5.	to check	depositare	16.	to pack	impaccare
6.	to write	scrivere	17.	to hurry	affrettarsi
7.	to wait	aspettare	18.	to change	cambiare
8.	to repair	riparare	19.	to reserve	riservare
9.	to drive	guidare	20.	to come back	ritornare
10.	to send	mandare	21.	to go get	prendere
11.	to clean	pulire			

B. *Gli oggetti*

1.	window	la finestra	21.	bill (account)	il conto
2.	door	la porta	22.	porter	il facchino
3.	bath	il bagno	23.	towel	un asciugamano
4.	trunk	il baule	24.	taxi	un taxi
5.	suitcases	le valigie	25.	physician	un medico
6.	address	l'indirizzo	26.	bank	la banca
7.	watch	l'orologio	27.	guide	una guida
8.	depot	la stazione	28.	clothes	i panni
9.	tickets	i biglietti	29.	transfer	una bolletta
10.	room	la stanza	30.	newspaper	un giornale
11.	suit	il vestito	31.	telephone	il telefono
12.	name	il nome	32.	breakfast	la colazione
13.	key	la chiave	33.	stamps	i francobolli
14.	dishes	i piatti	34.	package	il pacco
15.	bed	il letto	35.	hotel	l'albergo
16.	meal	il pasto	36.	bill (bank)	il biglietto
17.	mail	la pesta	37.	timetable	un orario
18.	shoes	le scarpe	38.	number	il numero
19.	road (way)	la via	39.	check (coupon)	lo scontrino
20.	copy	una copia	40.	supper	la cena

PART II

Give the Italian for the sentences below, starting each one with *Mi faccia il piacere di* . . . and completing it with a suitable word (infinitive) from group A plus another word (noun object) from group B above. Some of the exercises can be stated in more than one way. In such cases ask yourself the question, "Will I get the service or information I want if I ask for it in these words?" Then choose the statement that is most likely *to get results!* This is the test that will be used in sizing up your work. Language that does not say what you mean, or that does not help you get what you want, is of little value no matter how perfect your grammar.   Exercise 50, for example, can be stated correctly in two ways, but both would not get the same results.   Why?

1. May I trouble you to close the window?
2. Will you please open the door?
3. Kindly draw the bath.
4. Take the trunk for me, please.
5. Please check the suitcases.
6. Write down the address for me, if you will.
7. Stay here (qui), if you please.
8. I should like to have you fix the watch.
9. Take me to the station (alla stazione).
10. I wonder if you will please bring the tickets to the hotel (all'albergo).
11. Kindly tidy up the room a little (un poco).
12. Will you press the suit, please?
13. May I trouble you to give me the name?
14. Give me the key, please.
15. Will you kindly show me the room?
16. Please wash the dishes.
17. Will you make the bed, please?
18. Kindly pack the trunk.
19. Bring up the dinner, please.
20. Will you please hurry a little (un poco)?
21. Please let me have the mail.
22. Will you shine the shoes, please?
23. Be kind enough to indicate the road.
24. Show me a copy, if you will be so kind.
25. Please change the bill (money).
26. Will you kindly call a porter?
27. Please fetch me a towel.
28. Order the tickets, please
29. Please call a cab.
30. Get a doctor, please.
31. Kindly wrap them up.
32. Please drive to the bank (alla banca).
33. Show me the trunk, please.
34. Be kind enough to change the seats.
35. Get me a guide, please.
36. May I trouble you to give me the check?
37. May I trouble you to write the name?
38. Will you please hold two tickets (due biglietti)?
39. I should like to have you wash the clothes.
40. Give me a transfer, please.
41. Take me to the Verdi Theater (al Teatro Verdi).
42. Give me a newspaper, will you?
43. Please let me see a timetable.
44. Will you please wait here (qui)?
45. Kindly show me the phone.
46. Please send up the breakfast.

47. Let me have a couple of stamps (due francobolli).
48. I beg you to return this afternoon (questo pomeriggio).
49. May I have the suit cleaned right away (subito), if you will?
50. *I'd like to have the package at once (see sentence 49).

* All the sentences will be *questions* in Italian. Why? Have you forgotten any question marks?

In classes in which these and similar materials in French, German, and Spanish[1] have been used, the units have been substituted for the conventional textbook exercises on the *imperative*, on the assumption that the softened form of expression is generally adequate for all requirements of daily life, in better taste than the imperative (considering the circumstances in which the student is likely to have occasion to speak the language), and easier to master on the active level. Such uses of the imperative as occur in literature are usually recognizable from the context, and require little more than incidental attention in passing. Indeed, many of the better students learn to use the imperative through reading, quite without the necessity of special drill.

To those who would question the advisability of permitting such a free rendition of the exercises as this procedure assumes, the answer is (1) that the materials are intended for use only in the elementary stages of foreign-language work, (2) that meaning is more important than verbalism, and (3) that even in the later stages the teaching of 10 to 15 different types of expressions for the veiled imperative would probably be more boring and confusing than educative. The time thus consumed could be applied to greater advantage in promoting reading ability and interests, or in attaining some of the other objectives of foreign-language study. Since there is never time for everything, the question is always one of relative values as measured by the objectives of the program.

Guided practice in the effective paraphrastic use of a core vocabulary of high frequency and wide semantic range obviously need not be confined to orientation exercises of the type described above. Such practice can be made an integral part of the pupil's experience in reading, writing, and speaking, provided the learning materials and activities are organized with this aim in mind. For example, imitative translation (where the content summarizes the essential thought

[1] Walter V. Kaulfers, *A Cultural Basis for the Language Arts*, Stanford University Press, Stanford University, Calif., 1937, 115 pp.; pp. 88–94. Unit in French. Walter V. Kaulfers, "Exercises in Periphrase for Beginners in German," *German Quarterly*, Vol. X., pp. 161–168, November, 1937.

content of a passage) readily lends itself to guided practice in paraphrase, as illustrated by the italicized words in the following excerpts from a content unit in Spanish on Mexico:

PART I

Sinopsis de la historia mexicana

Read the following account carefully with a view to getting a bird's-eye view of Mexican history. Then do the exercises in Part II below.

. . . y al fin los mexicanos *trataron de ganar* (tried to win) su independencia . . . *Trataron de establecer* una república democrática. . . . La revolución *comenzó* en 1811 (mil ochocientos once) en el pueblo de Dolores. En 1917 (mil novecientos diecisiete) *comenzó* una nueva (new) *época* en al historia política mexicana. . . .

PART II

c. Composición limitada*

Give the Spanish for the following paragraph, using only words and expressions found in the synopsis in Part I.

The Mexicans *endeavored to gain* their independence in 1811. They *attempted to found* a democratic republic. . . . The revolution *started* in Dolores. . . . Finally, in 1917 a new period in Mexican political history *began*. . . .

Developing Ability to Ask, Understand, and Answer Questions.— To the foregoing suggestions for facilitating oral communication in conversational speech may be added a few devices that have already been described in considerable detail in preceding chapters. If a certain measure of ability in conversation is desired as an outcome of the work in foreign languages, even specialized practice on such mechanics as verb forms can be made to contribute effectively toward this end. The question-and-answer paradigm in cumulative thought context can, if used as described in Chapters I and III, serve as an oral-facilitation exercise in addition to providing opportunities for guided growth in grammar, vocabulary, and pronunciation. Semioriginal questions, composed by the students themselves on a topic of common interest to the group, can also provide a medium for guided practice in oral communication in a semiconversational setting. Since the construction and use of semioriginal questions are described in detail in Chapters III and V, the following directions and examples may suffice to recall the discussion:

* The italics are here used merely to indicate paraphrastic constructions. They are not used in classroom copies of the material.

Compose ten sensible questions, starting them as indicated below, and using *only* information, words, and expressions that can be found in the lesson above. Avoid questions that cannot be answered in terms of the information in the lesson.

1. Wo ist (where is...)?
2. Wann war (when was.....................................)?
3. Warum begann (why did...........................begin)?
4. Wer kam (who came.....................................)?
5. Wie hiess (what was the name of.........................)?

The semioriginal question technique obviously can be used as early as the first week of beginning instruction. At the start, the verb and other mechanical elements affecting word order should be included to prevent unconscious errors. After the questions have been prepared, the students may ask them of each other. Since the questions composed by one student will not necessarily be identical either in language or content with the questions composed by another student, the class recitation will more nearly approximate the impromptu circumstances of conversation in daily life than a recitation based on a formal series of ready-made identical questions whose exact answers can be phrased before the questions are even asked. Students who have participated in constructing questions should be able to ask them extemporaneously without using their papers, except to refresh their memories *before* asking a question. In other words, questions should *not* be read orally. The oral reading of questions has little carry-over value for conversational purposes. It is likely to lead to eye-bound language habits which later make it difficult, if not impossible, for a student to say or understand anything unless it is presented in writing.

Although prepared lists of questions in textbooks are useful for purposes of testing comprehension, their value in facilitating spontaneous oral communication is destined to be slight if their use is limited to the question-and-answer cross-examination of pupils by the teacher. In such cases, it is obviously the teacher rather than the pupils who enjoys most of the practice. For every question that a pupil answers in a class of 30 students, the teacher, during the course of half an hour, will ask from 25 to 30 questions, which means that she enjoys from 25 to 30 times the amount of oral practice that any one pupil is likely to receive during the same period of time. The problem is obviously to find practical ways and means for ridding the foreign-language classroom of this grossly disproportionate prima-donna domination of oral work by the instructor. The devices already described suggest one way of providing for a more equitable distribution of oral practice among the pupils. Indeed, the ability to originate questions is one of the skills most essential to effective oral communication, and the one most frequently monopolized by teachers.

If prepared lists of questions in textbooks are to contribute anything at all to facility in conversation, it is important that they at least be asked and answered by the pupils—and *asked* extemporaneously (using the textbook only to refresh the memory, much as a public speaker uses notes) rather than read orally. If the printed questions are too long or involved to be asked *verbatim in toto* (*ad punctuatum!*), the pupils may be encouraged to rephrase the question more briefly before asking it, or to break it into two separate questions. Such mental reactions to language and content often help to prevent question-and-answer recitations from degenerating into a mechanical process by which print is converted into sound without passing through the higher motor centers of the brain. Pupils who ask or answer questions in class as if they were talking in their sleep, or receiving spiritual messages in a trance, are rarely sure of what they are saying, even when their language is correct. Although enabling pupils to ask questions extemporaneously is more difficult and time consuming than permitting them to read the questions, or merely to answer them when asked by the teacher, the additional time and effort are well invested. Pupils who are conditioned from the start to "think on their feet" eventually can restate almost any question at a glance or two as quickly and as accurately as pupils not so trained can read the question orally. The gain is cumulatively in the direction of an increased eye span in silent reading, and of a greater aural-oral retention span in speaking.

It need hardly be indicated that both these abilities are basic to effective communication in actual conversation. Moreover, whereas oral reading tends to retard speed of comprehension in silent reading by reducing the unit of comprehension to the subvocally spoken word, the procedures suggested above tend instead to increase both the visual and aural comprehension spans in silent reading and oral speech. Thus whatever strain on the patience of the teacher the devices described above may impose at the start, the ultimate outcomes are worth the investment of time and effort, and the toleration of such temporary awkwardness in oral recitation with which these procedures may at times be accompanied. There is no virtue per se in mechanically perfect and speedy recitation if the residual values are non-functional or at the expense of efficiency in other respects.

Conversational Ability in an Organic Conception of Language. Levels of Cognition.—It will be noted that the discussion of ways and means for facilitating the development of ability in conversation has so far been in terms of basic activities contributive also to the realization of other linguistic outcomes—pronunciation, vocabulary, grammar, and reading. Such an organic conception of foreign-language instruction is desirable from the viewpoint not only of the psychology of learning but also of economy of time and effort in the learning process itself. The classification of language into compartmentalized elements to be learned in isolation has at times led to a certain measure of efficiency in part learning, but seldom to facility in using the language in synthesis. The memorization of isolated lists of idioms and words has often proved effective in increasing the vocabulary (conceived as a reserve stock of words) but seldom has this increase been accompanied by gains in ability to use the words orally in connected thought context. More often the gains have been achieved at the cost of faulty mental habits of "word matching" in oral and written speech, or of excessive verbalization in silent reading. Facility in oral communication is developed only as language is acquired from the start as an organic unity. In place of the compartmentalized view of language reflected in traditional textbooks and teaching procedures, the organic conception substitutes levels of function.[1] Constant reference to this conception has been made in dealing with different aspects of the teaching and learning process in modern foreign languages, because it is especially helpful in developing ability in conversation, and in preventing a component part of language from being mistaken for the whole. The primary levels of function from the viewpoint of aural-oral communication are the following:

The Recognitive Level.—Informative content, written in connected context in short third-person sentences, furnishes a desirable medium for practice in oral communication in the earliest stages of foreign-language study. Informative topics are desirable to prevent the work from degenerating into a mere vocal exercise, and to avoid the formation at the start of such self-conscious inhibitions in speech as are more likely to undermine self-confidence in the oral use of language than to develop *Sprachgefühl.* Facility and self-confidence in oral expression are possible only to the extent to which the conscious focal center of attention in speech is the *idea* in point, rather than the mechanics of language. If the learner is to be enabled to concentrate as far as

[1] Walter V. Kaulfers, "A Graduated Approach to the Oral Objective," *The Modern Language Forum* (Yearbook), Vol. XVIII, pp. 13–20, April, 1933.

possible on the current of thought which he is trying to convey, linguistic difficulties must obviously be reduced to a minimum at the start. Material written in short third-person sentences, rich in intelligible cognate words, usually provides a suitable linguistic medium for the oral discussion of sequentially developed topics through such devices as the semioriginal question. Grammatical variables (*e.g.*, changes in person affecting gender and verb forms) can usually be kept constant as vocabulary on this level. Moreover, since third-person questions can usually be answered merely by rearranging the words in the question itself (with the addition of whatever information is required), the only variable factors that are likely to cause difficulty are pronunciation and word order.

Abundant practice on the recognitive level is desirable until some measure of confidence and facility in the manipulation of thought units (simple, compound, and complex sentences, both in the interrogative and declarative form) has been achieved. During this stage the occasional introduction of short dialogues stressing useful words and phrases in a first- and second-person setting, where everything can be learned as vocabulary through dramatization, usually suffices to meet "practical" language needs and to facilitate a gradual transition from the recognitive to the cognitive level.

The Cognitive Level.—The cognitive level presupposes ability to originate questions and to answer them in context requiring changes in person. Practice on this level can be begun with short questions-and-answer activity involving at first only changes in the subject (noun or pronoun) and predicate (verb); later, changes in possessive adjectives and, still later, changes in disjunctive pronouns, etc., in cumulative fashion. The conversational question-and-answer type of practice discussed at length in Chapter III can serve as a facilitation exercise in this connection. (See also Appendixes B and C.) Such specialized practice, however, is destined to lose in value unless it is associated with abundant opportunities for guided participation in vitalized conversational activities. By conversational activities are meant extemporaneous oral discussions in audience situations that capitalize the linguistic experience of the learners in a new context, rather than memorized dialogues, reports, speeches, and the like. For example, if the pupils in an elementary or intermediate German class have read and discussed the places of scenic, historical, or cultural interest in Saxony, the same vocabulary and parallel questions may be asked of a committee of four or five pupils who have volunteered to acquaint themselves with the same type of information in German concerning Bavaria, Austria, or other regions of the Reich. Occasionally, pupils of foreign birth or descent in the school, or citizens who speak the language, can be invited to the class to be interviewed on questions submitted to the visitors in advance. In such cases, advanced pupils or the teacher may appropriately serve as interpreters when needed. Activities of this kind are usually more effective in providing lifelike communication situations than activities that involve the dramatization of memorized material or conversational games. The latter, although "interesting" because of the amusement, competition, or suspense that they arouse, are often formalized by rules or lacking in content worth discussing. In an overcrowded program limited by time, it is doubtful if content that does not have some bearing on the development of insights, attitudes, and appreciations compatible with the social and cultural objectives of foreign-language teaching should be accorded more than incidental attention. There is ample opportunity for the use of conversational games during meetings of the foreign-language club, or during class hours when a state of emergency exists—as it often does during the course of a normal school year—on excessively hot days, during exceptionally inclement weather, or on occasions when two-thirds of the pupils are suddenly called to a special assembly.

Use of Audio-visual Aids in Developing Aural Apperception.— Since conversation implies ability in aural comprehension, conversational records are a valuable means for tuning the ears to different voices, tempos of speech, intonations, and dialectal variations, as well as for supplying the learner with models of speech worthy of emulation. Although completely recorded conversational courses are as yet too lacking in flexibility of content and method to be adaptable to varying classroom situations and individual pupil needs, many of the individual recordings are useful. Some schools are supplementing their supply of foreign-language records by means of electrical transcriptions of important broadcasts.[1] Recording machines that transcribe programs directly as received via the radio are now within the price range of the average school. Although the cost of portable talking-picture equipment is still too high for purchase by individual foreign-language

[1] The Menlo School and Junior College, Menlo Park, Calif., has done outstanding work in making school transcriptions of radio broadcasts, as well as local recordings, since 1937 under the direction of Roy Pryor, Douglas M. Whittemore, Holbrook Bonney, and Philip Schultz. See also Willis Knapp Jones, "Riding the Ether Waves," *Nation's Schools*, Vol. XXIII, pp. 31–32, February, 1939; and Appendix, references 35, 89, 123–128, 188, 196.

departments, most visual-education centers are ready to furnish such equipment on call.   Many teachers are finding sound films,[1] accompanied by running subtitles in the foreign language, an exceedingly effective means for speeding up both aural and visual comprehension, especially if the film can be seen and heard several times in succession. Except for advanced students, one showing is often a complete loss from the linguistic standpoint, unless the script has been made the subject of special study.

In 1935, Edward B. Ginsburg reported[2] the increasing extent to which the talking picture is being used by foreign-language departments as an aural-visual aid in the study of the languages, literatures, and cultures of foreign countries.   According to the writer, more than 20,000 high-school students in New York alone attended French, German, and Spanish films during the biennium 1933–1935.   During the period of four years

. . . some two hundred German, seventy-five French, and a dozen Spanish talking films . . . wound their course among the approximately three hundred institutions which exhibited foreign films. . . . Although they have played only a subordinate role thus far, it is the writer's belief that the next stage in the use of sound films in language courses will place the greater emphasis neither upon the dramatic film nor upon the phonetics film, but rather upon a kind of travel film yet to be developed. . . . The film of the near future will be so constructed as to combine with utmost efficiency the various methods of language instruction.   The visual background, which will convey a vivid actual picture of the country studied, will be accompanied by a spoken description which will make the former serve as a visual illustration of the language and grammar.   For example . . . there will appear superimposed on the bottom of the film, at the same time, the printed words which are being spoken.   Thus for example, the student will simultaneously hear the word

[1] W. S. Hendrix, "Films in the Learning of Foreign Languages," *Journal of Higher Education*, Vol. X, pp. 308, 311, June, 1939.   Edward G. Bernard, "Using Films and Slides Effectively," *The Modern Language Journal*, Vol. XXIII, pp. 357–361, February, 1939.   Clifford Parker, "French by Sound Pictures," *The Modern Language Journal*, Vol. XXIII, pp. 367–370, February, 1939.   J. R. Palomo, "A Desired Technique for the Use of Sound Films in the Teaching of Foreign Languages," *The Modern Language Journal*, Vol. XXIV, pp. 282–283, December, 1939.   William W. Brickman, "The Talking Film as a Medium of Instruction in Modern Foreign Languages," *The Modern Language Journal*, Vol. XXIV, pp. 498–506, April, 1940.   Franziska Jauer-Marbach, "Sprachunterricht und Sprechfilm," *International Review of Educational Cinematography*, Vol. III, pp. 432–439, May, 1931.   See also Appendix, references 107–109, 188, 190.

[2] Edward B. Ginsburg, "Foreign Talking Pictures in Modern Language Instruction," *The Modern Language Journal*, Vol. XIX, pp. 433–438, March, 1935.

église spoken in excellent French, see the picture of a church on the screen, and see the word in print. . . . Three years ago scarcely a score of American schools and colleges exhibited foreign films. Today the number must be reckoned in hundreds. That the development will continue seems unquestionable in view of such vitality.

Conversation as an Integrative Activity. Capitalizing Audience Situations.—Inasmuch as a foreign-language course could easily become a mélange of essentially worth-while but heterogeneous activities if all the ways and means for facilitating growth in reading, writing, and speaking were to be utilized in any one class, it is important to establish a frame of reference for every course within which different approaches to a common goal can be unified on the basis of their contribution to a central objective. Integrative activities that afford practice in all phases of language work (reading, writing, or speaking) in terms of subject matter contributive to a common social or cultural aim, are usually well suited to this purpose. For example, the central unifying objective for one first-year high-school class in French was the development of a creative and enlightened American citizenry[1]—a citizenry appreciative of its heritage from abroad (in peoples, customs, literature, language, science, invention, etc.) and one disposed to take an intelligent and active interest in international affairs, open-forum discussions, concerts, worth-while radio broadcasts, travel clubs, literary societies, lectures, civic organizations, or community-theater projects. How was this first-year class in French organized and conducted to make possible some degree of progress toward the realization of this objective through the medium of the French language?

Obviously, any objective such as the foregoing can be realized only through the subject matter or thought content in terms of which the language is practiced and learned, and through participation in worth-while activities to which such subject matter leads by way of suggestion or the stimulation of extracurricular interests. Language materials devoid of essential meaning, except as they illustrate the mechanics of language conceived as a code, are obviously no more contributive to the realization of a social or cultural life objective than reading, writing, or reciting the alphabet. For this reason, the unifying theme "How France enters our daily life" was chosen as one of the criteria for the choice of subject matter and activities for approximately one-fourth of the class time during the first year. To provide for ample opportunities for semiconversational types of oral

[1] French I, ninth grade, Palo Alto High School, Calif., 1935–1936, conducted under supervision of the author.

work in an increasingly extemporaneous setting, the class was organized into committees with rotating chairmen for the purpose of reporting to the class in French on topics falling within the range of their spheres of responsibility.   Among the committees elected by the class every ten weeks were the following:

The Social Committee.—The function of the chairman of this committee was to serve as the class host (or hostess), to introduce and seat visitors, to inform the class of special circumstances calling for messages of condolence, appreciation, or congratulation from the group to absent members, to other teachers, or to visitors to whom the class were indebted.   One member of this committee served as class secretary to keep a record of the minutes of special program meetings. Another member kept a daily record of tardinesses and absences for the teacher.

The Committee on Public Exercises.—The various members of this committee were responsible for reporting to the class in French anything of timely interest in the way of public exhibits, lectures, recitals, concerts, plays, movies, operas, or open-forum discussions having some bearing upon French life or culture (*e.g.*, moving-picture versions of stories, novels, or plays by well-known French writers).   The function of the chairman in this case was to coordinate the work of the committee and to introduce to the class those members of his group who had announcements of public events to make.   A prominent section of the class bulletin board was reserved for the display of printed announcements, news items, critical comments, or programs obtained by the committee.   Usually a member of the committee, or an alternate chosen from the class, attended the public functions as an informal representative of the group with a view to reporting to them his evaluation of the lecture, exhibit, or performance.

The Library Committee.—Interesting magazine articles and new books pertaining to French life or culture, as well as literature in recent translation, fell within the sphere of responsibility of the library committee.   The duties of this body were to interest the class in reading for information and pleasure.   The members consulted city and school librarians, posted colorful book covers, book announcements, and reviews on the bulletin board, read short excerpts (in English) from articles or books of unusual interest, and from time to time invited the school librarian to the class to give informal book chats on the topic "France in Our World of Books."   One of the members of the committee served as class librarian to check the withdrawal and return of books from the classroom library.

The Exhibit Committee.—The members of this body enlisted the cooperation of other members of the class in combing the community for *realia* in the way of pictures, costumes, *objets d'art,* etc., to place on exhibit in the classroom. This committee had complete charge of a glass exhibit case, as well as of floral decorations for the room. The significance of any articles placed on exhibit was explained to the class in French by a member of the committee, who also acknowledged his appreciation of the person from whom the articles were obtained.

The Editorial Committee.—All written reports on topics of interest to the class were reviewed by this committee prior to exhibit on the bulletin board or library table, or to oral presentation in class by the writer. From time to time the members of this committee were exempted from certain assignments to check and score written exercises or tests that could easily be corrected from a uniform key supplied by the teacher.

The Steering Committee.—This body consisted of the class president, vice-president, secretary-treasurer, and the chairmen of the several committees. Its function was to coordinate the work of the various groups, to plan class programs, and occasionally to meet with the teacher in outlining units of work, class standards, and the like. This opportunity for guided pupil participation in course planning and evaluation served to develop a certain measure of *esprit de corps* within the class, and to foster a sense of group responsibility.

The Current Events Committee.—The chairman of this body was responsible for organizing and summarizing, with the help of his committee, the news clippings brought to class by individual students, for helping in the formulation of criteria for the choice of worth-while news items, and for presenting an occasional "news broadcast" to the class. Except in the case of events of unusual importance, news casts were reserved for special days in order that the reports might be indicative of trends in international relations, progress toward the solution of a dispute or problem, etc. One member of the committee was responsible for posting the news items, according to the city or locale to which they referred, on a large map of France which served as a kind of geographical bulletin board. Another member mounted the clippings, classified according to topical headings, in a loose-leaf current-events binder. This student was also responsible for posting, from time to time, a list of the names of students, together with the number of clippings submitted, and the number of items actually found worthy of incorporation into the news cast by the Current

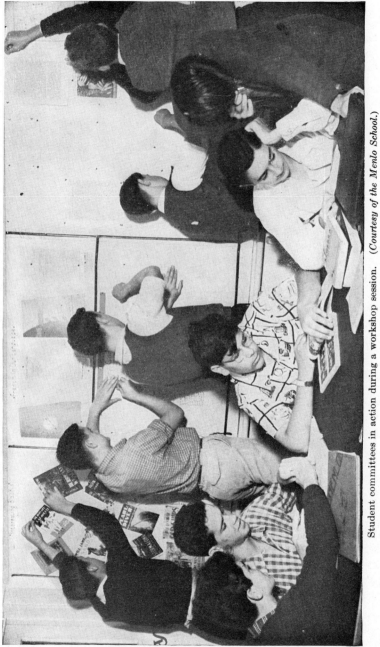

Student committees in action during a workshop session. (*Courtesy of the Menlo School.*)

Events Committee. Since keeping the committee supplied with interesting and informative material was a common responsibility of all members of the class, the posted list served as an index, both to the students and to the teacher, of individual cooperation. For obvious reasons, this committee was permitted to present the major part of its report in English.

The elections of officers and committee-chairman were conducted in French every ten weeks in the manner illustrated by the following "stenographic" report of a model election. Copies of this report were originally used in mimeographed form as an oral reading lesson prior to the close of the tenth week of the first semester of beginning French. Then a mock election was dramatized, using the script only for reference where necessary. The official election was finally held several days later without benefit of notes of any kind. Attention is here called to the integration of oral and silent reading and of vocabulary building in a purposeful setting. Note also that the ultimate criterion of mastery was not mere ability to verbalize (translate, read aloud, etc.) but *to conduct an actual election*. The reelection of officers every ten weeks served as a disguised form of review in a motivated audience situation. A copy of the script follows:[1]

LE BUREAU DU CERCLE

Le président (la présidente).

Le vice-président (la vice-présidente).

Le secrétaire-trésorier (la secrétaire-trésorière)

Le représentant au Club Français.

L'hôtesse du cercle (et de la classe).

L'historien du cercle (chargé des fêtes, des événements, et des anniversaires d'importance historique).

Les porteurs de chaise de

La commission de radiodiffusion (chargée des programmes de la T.S.F.).

La commission des relations publiques (chargée des événements, des fêtes, des conférences, des nouvelles, etc.).

La commission de la bibliothèque.

La commission des beaux-arts (chargée des concerts, des opéras, des exhibitions publiques, etc.).

La commission des arts dramatiques (chargée du théâtre, du cinéma, etc.).

La commission des décorations (chargée des fleurs, des tableaux, etc.).

La commission des exhibitions écolières.

La commission des programmes (chargée des conférences spéciales, des discours, des assemblées, des excursions, etc.).

La commission sociale (chargée des questions de courtoisie).

[1] Designed for use in the Palo Alto High School, Calif., 1935, by Walter V. Kaulfers.

ELECTION DU BUREAU

Dir.: Ce matin (cet après-midi, aujourd'hui, ce soir) il faut que nous élisions les membres de bureau pour le prochain terme. Mais d'abord il faut proposer des candidats. Mlle (M.) Herriot, voulez-vous bien nous servir de secrétaire *pro tempore*, et écrire les noms des candidats sur le tableau noir?

Sec.: Volontiers. N'y a-t-il pas de craie?

Dir.: Si, la voilà; et voici le torchon.

Sec.: Merci!

Dir.: De rien. Eh bien, procédons à la nomination des candidats. Qui désirez-vous proposer comme président(e)?

1ᵉʳ Mem.: Monsieur le Président (Madame la Présidente), je voudrais proposer M. (Mlle) Lebrun comme président(e).

Dir.: On a nommé M. (Mlle) Lebrun. Y a-t-il d'autres nominations?

2ᵉ Mem.: Je propose M. (Mlle) Briand comme président(e).

3ᵉ Mem.: Je propose de clore les nominations.

4ᵉ Mem.: J'appuie la proposition.

Dir.: On a proposé et appuyé de clore les nominations. Que tous ceux qui sont en faveur de la proposition lèvent la main droite (se lèvent, disent *oui*).

Dir.: Monsieur le Secrétaire (Madame la Secrétaire) avez-vous compté les votes?

Sec.: Un moment, s'il vous plaît. Oui, il y en a quinze en faveur de la motion.

Dir.: Maintenant, que ceux qui sont de l'avis contraire lèvent la main (se lèvent, disent *non*).

(Des membres votent.)

Dir.: Voyons! Encore une fois. Bien; il y en a cinq. Adoptée. Les candidats veulent-ils se retirer dans le couloir pendant l'élection?

(Les candidats sortent.)

Dir.: Merci. Que tous ceux qui sont en faveur de M. (Mlle) Lebrun comme président(e) se lèvent.

(Des membres se lèvent.)

Dir.: Combien y en a-t-il?

Sec.: J'en ai compté treize.

Dir.: C'est juste. Maintenant, que tous ceux qui favorisent M. (Mlle) Briand se lèvent.

(Des membres se lèvent.)

Dir.: Comptons les votes.

Sec.: Il y en a seize en faveur de M. (Mlle) Briand.

Dir.: Très bien. Monsieur le Secrétaire (Madame la Secrétaire), voulez-vous bien aller chercher les candidats?

Sec.: Avec plaisir.

(Les candidats rentrent dans la salle.)

Dir.: M. (Mlle) Briand, je suis très content d'annoncer votre élection comme président(e) de notre cercle pour le prochain terme. Je vous cède la présidence à fin que vous puissiez continuer l'élection des autres fonctionnaires.

Prés.: Je vous remercie beaucoup.   Je suis extrêmement touché(e) de l'honneur que le cercle me fait.   Maintenant, procédons à la nominations des candidats à la vice-présidence.   Y a-t-il des nominations?

5ᵉ Mem.: Monsieur le Président (Madame la Présidente), je désire proposer M. (Mlle) Laval comme vice-président(e).

Laval: Monsieur le Président, j'apprécie sincèrement l'honneur que me fait notre collègue, mais malheureusement il faut que je retire mon nom.

Prés.: Nous regrettons extrêmement que M. (Mlle) Laval ne puisse accepter la candidature.   Y a-t-il d'autres nominations?

6ᵉ Mem.: Monsieur le Président, je crois que M. (Mlle) Doumergue serait un(e) bon(ne) vice-président(e).   Je propose son nom.

Prés.: Monsieur le Secrétaire (Madame la Secrétaire) voulez-vous bien noter le nom de M. (Mlle) Doumergue comme candidat à la vice-présidence?

Sec.: Volontiers.

7ᵉ Mem.: Monsieur le Président, je propose que la nomination à la vice-présidence soit close d'office.

8ᵉ Mem.: Je l'appuie.

Prés.: Vous avez entendu la proposition.   Elle est livrée à la discussion. Veut-on la discuter?   (Pause.)   Si personne n'a rien à dire, je vais mettre la motion aux voix.

9ᵉ Mem.: À la question!

Prés.: Eh bien, que tous ceux qui sont en faveur de la proposition disent *oui*.

10ᵉ M.: Pardon, Monsieur le Président, puis-je vous prier de répéter la motion?

Prés.: Certainement.   On a proposé que la nomination à la vice-présidence soit close d'office.

10ᵉ M.: Merci.   Je ne vous avais pas compris.

Prés.: Que tous ceux qui sont en faveur disent *oui*.

(Des membres disent *oui*.)

Prés.: Il y a une grande majorité.   La motion est adoptée.   Au nom du cercle je déclare donc que M. (Mlle) Doumergue est élu(e) vice-président(e).   Que le (la) secrétaire prenne note de l'action dans le procès-verbal.   Y a-t-il d'autres affaires?

11ᵉ M.: Monsieur le Président, ne faut-il pas toujours élire le secrétaire-trésorier (la secrétaire-trésorière), et les porteurs de chaise des commissions?

Prés.: Ah oui.   Je l'avais tout à fait oublié.   Merci de m'avoir fait souvenir de cela.

12ᵉ M.: Monsieur le Président, pour arranger les affaires du cercle dans le temps qui nous reste, je propose que le président choisisse les porteurs de chaise, et que ceux-ci designent eux-mêmes les membres de leurs commissions.

Prés.: Veut-on appuyer cette motion?

13ᵉ M.: À la question!

Prés.: Que ceux qui veulent adopter la proposition disent *oui*.

(Des membres disent *oui*.)

Prés.: Ceux de l'avis contraire, le même signe.

(Des membres disent *non*.)

Prés.: Adoptée.   Comme le temps est court, permettez-moi d'ajourner les nominations jusqu'à la prochaine réunion du cercle.   Y a-t-il d'autres affaires?

14ᵉ M.: Je propose de lever la séance.
15ᵉ M.: Je l'appuie.
Prés.: La séance est levée.

Speaking to an Audience with a Purpose.—How did the group learn the words and expressions needed for conducting the class programs in French? The following "scenario script"[1] dramatizes a class program in action. This script was used in much the same manner as the copy of the foregoing model election. Here again, practice in oral reading and vocabulary building were integrated in functional context. At first, the committee reports were identical in phraseology with those quoted in the script, except for such necessary changes in the italicized information as were required to make the report apply to a real situation. Usually an entire class hour was set aside every two weeks during the first semester as a kind of laboratory period for the preparation of reports in French under the teacher's guidance. In the second year, greater flexibility in the wording and presentation of the reports was possible owing to the background which the pupils had gradually acquired in vocabulary and usage. Pupil needs and difficulties encountered in the preparation of reports were often capitalized as the basis for preparatory, diagnostic, or remedial work in the mechanics of pronunciation, spelling, and syntax. Since class programs were usually presented only once every two weeks, the time devoted to this type of activity, including preparatory workshop sessions, did not exceed 25 per cent of the total time allotment for the course. If collateral reading and foundation exercises in language usage, based upon pupil needs in carrying on this activity, are included, the time allotment probably averaged 50 per cent. The remainder of the class time was devoted to reading, foreign correspondence, short discussions in the foreign language on special aspects of French life and culture in relation to our own national and community life, etc. The only exceptions to this program of work were five senior students who were preparing either to take college entrance examinations or to continue French in college at the end of the year. This group met as a seminar during laboratory workshop or supervised study periods under the leadership of one of its ablest members, and was occasionally exempted from certain activities to devote itself to a more specialized type of college-preparatory work. Their activities were guided by the teacher and organized on the contract plan.

[1] Designed for use in the Palo Alto (Calif.) High School, 1935, by Walter V. Kaulfers.

A typical class program included not only reports from committees,
but also, from time to time, the reading of interesting letters received
from abroad, short reports by students on topics of interest to the class,
outside speakers, illustrated talks in the foreign language on French
art and music, illustrated travelogues, organization of excursions, etc.
During the first year the class was guided by the following script which
may, therefore, be considered as representing a more or less conventionalized stenographic report in French of the proceedings at the
elementary level:

UNE SÉANCE DU CERCLE FRANÇAIS

PRÉS.: Mademoiselle Flandin, comme hôtesse de notre cercle, voulez-vous bien
présenter nos convives (notre convive)?

HÔTESSE: Monsieur le Président (Madame la Présidente), j'ai l'honneur de vous
présenter Mademoiselle (Monsieur, Madame) Bertrand de Stanford.

PRÉS.: Au nom de la classe (du cercle) je voux souhaîte la bienvenue (le bien-
venu). Nous espérons que vous nous visiterez bien souvent. Maintenant,
passons à l'ordre du jour. D'abord nous recevrons les rapports des commissions.
La commission des décorations:

DÉC.: Monsieur le Président, nous sommes très obligés envers Mlle. Doumer des
fleurs (ornéments, décorations, images) qu'elle a apportées. Si vous avez quelque
chose qui puisse servir à orner notre salle, voulez-vous bien le prêter à la commission
aussitôt que possible. Nous vous en serons très obligés.

PRÉS.: Je suis sûr(e) que le cercle apprécie la faveur que vous nous faîtes,
mademoiselle. Maintenant, le comité des exhibitions écolières: Y a-t-il des nou-
veautés ou des curiosités?

EX.: Monsieur le Président, permettez-moi de vous faire remarquer les nouveaux
objets que nous venons de mettre dans la vitrine. La commission en sait gré à
monsieur Barthou et à mademoiselle Pétain. La vitrine contient à présent les
articles suivants: Une poupée normande (parisienne, française) prêtée par Mlle.
L'Enfant; des cartes postales (des photographies, des gravures) prêtées par M.
Bartholdi; des pièces de monnaie française prêtées par M. Rodin; et des timbres-
poste prêtés par M. Millet. Si vous avez quelque chose qui puisse intéresser le
cercle, les membres de la commission seront très contents de le recevoir pour notre
exhibition.

PRÉS.: Nous apprécions vos efforts, mademoiselle (monsieur), et je vous offre
nos remercîments les plus sincères. Y a-t-il un rapport de la commission de
bibliothèque?

BIB.: Monsieur le Président, je voudrais vous faire remarquer ce(s) livre(s)
que j'ai apporté(s) ce matin [que monsieur Poincairé nous a apporté(s)]. Celui-ci
est un livre par Dumas. Le titre est *La Tulipe noire*. Je suis sûr(e) que vous le
trouverez très intéressant. C'est un roman [livre de contes, de poèmes, de voyages,
d'essais, de fables, une pièce] illustré(e) de belles gravures.

PRÉS.: Je vous remercie au nom du cercle. Maintenant nous voulons entendre
le rapport de la commission des relations publiques. M. Proust a la parole.

REL.: Monsieur le Président, les membres du cercle seront intéressés d'appren-
dre que le docteur Main fera une conférence sur la France, jeudi soir, quinze

octobre, à sept heures et demie précises, dans la salle de spectacle de l'Université de Stanford. Le titre de la conférence est La France d'hier et d'aujourd'hui. Je propose que le président désigne des membres comme représentants du cercle, afin qu'ils assistent à la séance pour pouvoir nous faire un rapport du discours à notre réunion prochaine.

Prés.: C'est une bonne idée. Veut-on l'appuyer?

1ᵉʳ Mem.: Je l'appuie.

2ᵉ Mem.: À la question!

Prés.: Que ceux qui sont en faveur disent *oui*.

(Une pause; des membres disent *oui*.)

Prés.: Que ceux de l'avis contraire, disent *non*.

(Une pause; pas de réponses.)

Prés.: La proposition est adoptée. Voyons; combien de membres présents voudraient assister à la conférence comme représentants du cercle? Levez la main, je vous en prie.

(Des membres lèvent la main.)

Prés.: Bien, je nomme M. Ampère, Mlle. Blériot, et Mlle. Pasteur membres de la commission.

Rel.: En même temps, je voudrais annoncer que la fête de Saint-Charlemagne sera célébrée aujourd'hui, vingt-huit janvier, par la colonie française de San Francisco. D'après les journaux il y aura un programme commémoratif spécial.

Quant aux nouvelles, la commission en a trouvé très peu depuis notre dernier rapport. Cependant, je voudrais faire un petit résumé en anglais des nouvelles choisies dans les journaux (les revues) d'hier et de ce matin.

(Le porteur de chaise fait son rapport.)

Prés.: Merci, mademoiselle, c'est très intéressant. Nous n'avons pas encore entendu le rapport de la commission des beaux-arts.

Beaux.: Monsieur le Président, dimanche prochain nous aurons l'occasion d'entendre un concert symphonique par l'orchestre municipal de San Francisco. Ce sera un programme de musique française (espagnole, allemande, russe, italienne, anglaise, américaine, mexicaine, sud-américaine). Le célèbre pianiste (violoniste, chanteur, cantatrice) Iturbi sera le soliste du programme. Le concert aura lieu à l'opéra de San Francisco à trois heures de l'après-midi (à huit heures et quart du soir). Le programme sera diffusé par la station KPO.

Si nous avons le temps, je voudrais annoncer en passant l'opéra *Carmen*, du compositeur français Bizet. Cet opéra sera chanté à San Francisco, mercredi prochain, deux mai, à huit heures et demie. Le principal rôle (les principaux rôles) sera (seront) joué(s) par Ninon Vallin (et Jean Dubois). Sans doute il y aura des membres présents qui voudraient assister à l'opéra. Les billets se vendent à raison d'un dollar jusqu'à trois dollars et demi.

Les autres membres de la commission ont-ils quelque chose à annoncer aujourd'-hui?

3ᵉ Mem.: Monsieur, il est possible que vous ayez déjà entendu parler d'l'exhibition de tableaux (de sculpture, de tapisseries, de documents et de manuscrits historiques, de livres) du célèbre peintre (sculpteur, écrivain) Millet. L'exhibition aura lieu au Musée Municipal (dans la Bibliothèque Municipale) de San Francisco.

D'après les journaux, elle sera ouverte gratuitement au public jusqu'au premier juin, à partir du onze février.

BEAUX.: Merci, mademoiselle.   Monsieur le Président, je pense que c'est tout pour le présent.

PRÉS.: Merci beaucoup.   Nous apprécions votre rapport, et celui de votre commission.   Ils viennent très à propos.   Maintenant nous cédons la parole à la commission de radiodiffusion.

RAD.: Monsieur le Président, je suis content d'annoncer qu'il y aura un discours sur la littérature française contemporaine (une conférence, une comédie, un drame, un programme de musique, de nouvelles, de vaudeville) ce soir (demain l'après-midi, ce matin, après-demain soir, etc.) à sept heures moins le quart, diffusé par le Station KPO de San Francisco.   Le discours sera prononcé en anglais (en français) par le docteur Carré de l'Académie française.

PRÉS.: Je vous remercie.   Nous écouterons le programme.   La commission des arts dramatiques voudrait-elle faire une annonce?

DRAM.: Monsieur le Président, mercredi et jeudi de cette semaine (de la semaine prochaine) nous aurons l'occasion de voir une pellicule (un drame, une comédie) intitulé(e) *Les Misérables*.   La pièce (la pellicule) sera representéé au théâtre Varsity à huit heures et quart.   C'est une pellicule (une comedie, un drame, une pièce) basé(e) sur le livre (le roman, le drame, le poème épique, l'histoire) de Victor Hugo.   Je vous assure qu'il (qu'elle) vaudra la peine d'être vu(e).   Le principal rôle est joué par Frédéric March (Charles Laughton).

PRÉS.: J'espère que quelques membres de notre cercle organiseront une partie de théatre pour l'occasion.   À ce point, s'l n'y a pas d'objections, je transférerai la conduite des affaires à notre vice-président(e).

V.P.: Je pense qu'il nous manque encore le rapport de notre représentant au Club français.   Y a-t-il quelque chose à annoncer?

REP.: Monsieur le Président, comme représentant du Club français je désire vous faire remarquer l'annonce de la prochaine réunion du club, jeudi à midi et quart, dans la salle cinq cent cinquante-cinq.   Il y aura des jeux de salon (des pièces dramatiques, des chansons en choeur, une séance d'affaires, un discours sur la Normandie par M. Carnet de Chicago).   J'espère que vous pourrez assister à la séance.

PRÉS.: N'oubliez pas la date, jeudi à midi et quart, dans la salle cinq cent cinquante-cinq.   Il faut que notre cercle soit bien représenté.   Maintenant, s'il y a une annonce touchant le Club international nous céderons la parole au représentant.

INT.: Monsieur le Président, la prochaine séance du Club international aura lieu vendredi à midi et quart dans la salle cinq cent quinze.   Veuillez noter la date: vendredi à midi et quart, le dix mai, dans la salle cinq cent quinze.   J'espère que ce cercle sera bien représenté.

PRÉS.: Merci beaucoup, mademoiselle; vous êtes bien aimable.   Il ne faut pas oublier le rapport de notre commission sociale.   Y a-t-il un membre de la commission présent?

SOC.: Monsieur le Président, je regrette de vous informer que notre collègue (ami, amie, professeur, directeur, membre) Mlle Dupont est malade depuis samedi. La commission lui a envoyé une lettre de condoléance au nom du cercle.

J'ai une autre nouvelle assez triste.   On m'a dit que nous perdrons bientôt un de nos collègues, M. Chevalier, qui partira pour New York à la fin de cette semaine (de ce mois, de ce semestre, de ce trimestre).

Prés.: Nous sommes extrêmement touchés par ces tristes nouvelles, mais au nom du cercle je désire souhaîter à M. Chevalier le plus grand succès dans ses efforts.   Nous souhaîtons aussi à Mlle Dupont un prompt rétablissement.

Prés.: On m'a dit qu'il y a des membres du cercle qui ont reçu des lettres de leurs correspondents en France.   Le secrétaire (la secrétaire) de correspondence international a-t-il (-elle) un rapport à faire?

Corr.: Monsieur le Président, dernièrement monsieur de Musset a reçu une lettre.   Monsieur, ne voudriez-vous pas nous lire votre lettre?

4e Mem.: Monsieur le Président, la lettre dont vous parlez est arrivée de Tours (Dijon, Nice) la semaine dernière (il y a trois jours, lundi dernier).   C'est une lettre d'un jeune homme (d'une jeune fille) agé(e) de quinze ans qui suit les cours dans le Lycée Descartes.   Je crois que les extraits suivants vous intéresseront.

(Il lit des extraits de la lettre.)

Prés.: Il n'y a rien de si intéressant qu'une lettre de l'étranger.   J'espère qu'à l'avenir d'autres membres auront la bonté de partager leurs lettres avec nous.

Si je ne me trompe pas, il y a un programme spécial ce matin (cet après-midi, ce soir).   Pour cela je voudrais céder la parole au chef de notre commission de programmes.

Prog.: Avant de présenter les conférenciers (les numéros de notre programme) je voudrais annoncer encore une fois l'excursion à la campagne du Club français (la partie de théâtre du cercle) mercredi l'après-midi, le trente janvier.   Nous nous réunirons devant l'école à quatre heures précises.   Il faut que tous ceux qui désirent nous accompagner achètent tout de suite leurs billets des members de la commission de programme ou de notre secrétaire.   Les billets coûtent trente-cinq sous.   Les amis des membres du cercle sont cordialement invités.

Maintenant j'ai l'honneur de vous présenter l'historien du cercle, M. Voltaire.

Hist.: Monsieur le Président, aujourd'hui lundi, vingt-huit janvier est la fête de Saint-Charlemagne, grande fête dans les écoles en France.   C'est aussi l'anniversaire de la signature de l'armistice qui mit fin au siège de Paris par les Prussiens en 1871 (dix-huit cent soixante et onze).

Prog.: Nous vous sommes très obligés de votre rapport.

Notre rapport spécial aujourd'hui sera un discours en français (en anglais) par notre ami(e) monsieur Maurois, de notre cercle (de notre école, de Palo Alto, etc.). J'ai l'honneur de vous présenter M. Maurois.

(Discours par M. Maurois.)

Prog.: Bien de remercîments, monsieur.   Maintenant je suis heureux (heureuse) de vous présenter un (deux, trois) membre(s) de notre cercle (école, de la classe de Mlle Rousseau).   Il(s) nous chantera (chanteront) quelques chansons (il nous jouera quelques solos, il fera une récitation dramatique, il donnera une petite pièce).

5e Mem.: Mesdames, mesdemoiselles, et messieurs.   La chanson que je vais vous chanter (nous allons chanter; la récitation, le poème, que je vais réciter; le morceau que je vais jouer; la pièce que nous allons représenter) s'appelle *Bonjour Suzon*, par le compositeur Délibes.   Les paroles sont d'Alfred de Musset (du célèbre poète, conteur, essayiste, écrivain, dramaturge, romancier; de la célèbre conteuse, compositrice).

(Le cercle écoute le programme.)

PROG.: Au nom du cercle, monsieur (messieurs, mesdemoiselles), je vous assure de notre reconnaissance et de notre gratitude.

Monsieur le Président, ceci termine notre programme. Je désire remercier encore une fois tous les membres qui nous ont aidé au succès de la séance, et surtout notre distingué(e) convive (nos distingués convives).

PRÉS.: Monsieur, nous vous sommes reconnaissants pour un programme de plus intéressant et de plus avantageux, et nous ajoutons un sincère remercîment à nos applaudissements.

Et maintenant, puisque l'heure du départ approche, je déclarerai levée la séance.

The minutes kept in French by the secretary of the class formed a part of this officer's work in composition. In summarizing class programs, the secretary was guided at the start by records kept by advanced students of meetings in previous second- or third-year classes. During the latter half of the second year the minutes represented the more or less free original composition of the student, just as committee reports and discussions centering around them began at this level to approach informal conversation to the extent to which the limitations imposed by the classroom environment permitted of such activity.

To lend spontaneity to the class discussions, special opportunities for guided practice in composing questions were afforded as a regular part of the classwork in connection with reading and writing activities, using the devices previously discussed in this chapter. To originate a question is, from the linguistic standpoint, often more difficult than to answer it. Originating a question always involves an active command of vocabulary and principles of syntax, whereas answering a question (if one knows the answer) often requires little more than ability to rearrange the vocabulary of the question as it is presented to the ear. In many classes almost all the opportunities for developing facility in this important conversational skill are either monopolized by the teacher or converted into a kind of oral reading exercise.

Ability in Conversation in Relation to Other Objectives.—In this as in preceding chapters, the aim has been to suggest concrete ways and means for developing ability in language as an organic whole on the basis of levels of function. In terms of this conception, all the devices discussed in the chapter on conversation may at some time have an appropriate place in any secondary-school class in modern languages, no matter whether the central linguistic objective be ability to read, write, translate, or converse; for the varying language needs and interests of an unselected group of adolescent boys and girls can rarely be met by emphasizing only one phase of language to the neglect of all others.   If the central objective of the course at any particular time is ability in conversation, procedures and activities of the type described in the preceding pages will naturally receive the major share of time and attention, whereas if reading is the primary objective, conversational activities will be used merely to capitalize aural-oral practice as a means for facilitating the fixation of vocabulary, idioms, or content for delayed recall, or to lend variety to the class routine. The concept of levels of function is helpful in approaching the study of language, since it enables one to deal with language from the start as a vehicle for the communication of thought, and to keep language intact while gradually increasing ability to use it as an expanding whole on increasingly higher levels of cognition.

Facilitation vs. Frustration of Self-expression through Language. Finally it is important to bear in mind that the teacher's role is to *facilitate and guide language growth*, not frustrate it.   This implies, first of all, stimulating the desire to communicate by helping young people find something interesting and worth while to say; secondly, creating communication situations that will give them reasons for saying it; and thirdly, providing special opportunities on the basis of actual need for overcoming obstacles that handicap effective communication.   By actual needs are meant the language problems of individual pupils in a particular class as determined by the mistakes that they make, the language difficulties that they encounter, or the questions that they ask on the basis of their *own personal experience* in attempting to use the language as a vehicle for the communication of their own thoughts.   Such needs grow out of the language experiences of the learners rather than out of a rigid predetermined outline of "grammar to be covered."   They are derived by the teacher from the daily work of the boys and girls in her own classroom, not from a list of minimum essentials in a uniform course of study.

The chief function of curriculum committees is to make available to fellow teachers the tried and tested ways and means which in the personal experience of its members have proved most effective in attaining certain objectives with certain groups of students.   A curriculum committee is valuable if it helps to coordinate the work of teachers by developing through discussion and recommendation a community of thought and action in terms of a dynamic unifying philosophy of language and its creative role in the education of young people.   It is a dangerous organization if it indulges merely in retrospective crystal gazing, and on the basis of its visions of tenses, moods, and irregular verbs, formulates *in vacuo*, apart from human life as it is today or as it might desirably be tomorrow, a classified list of minimum essentials of grammar to be covered by children whom the teachers have never seen, by generations yet unborn.

Nowhere has a creative view of language teaching been more effectively expressed than in the presidential address of Holland D. Roberts to the National Council of Teachers of English in Buffalo in 1937:[1]

We are accumulating evidence today that each one of us, if it had not been for certain destructive forces in the environment, would have been a free, ever-growing creative personality. Yet the man on the street and most teachers tell me, "I cannot write." From half a lifetime of teaching writing to people of all ages from kindergarten through the sixties, I know that every person has the potential power to write. There may be those who will disagree, but I will answer: anyone who says a true word of his own has created. He has proved that he has the power to create in words—to say from thought and deep feeling what he knows within himself to be true. Mere repetition of what others have said before does not give our words the breath of truth. We must reaffirm life within ourselves. Every time we speak we have the opportunity to create in words. We may create badly. The important thing is that we create. To originate in writing can be as simple and spontaneous a thing as to speak. Why, then, is the writing of books, songs, plays, and poems so unusual a thing?

We have only to study the natural child at play to find speech growing like mountain flowers and to observe how fortunate it has been that children have learned to speak before they came to school. Otherwise in speech as in writing, humanity would have been schooled to be dumb. Today in scores of schools creative teachers are demonstrating that it is not necessary to infect our children with schoolroom blight in teaching them to write. We have only to prove our interest in the child and what he has to say when he writes, and lose our preoccupation with the form of the writing. Then there is a sea-change that transforms and strengthens everything he does, from original thoughts down to periods and semicolons. . . .

The first fundamental principle is to stress the content of experience—to place emphasis on the act and the idea. We must spend our time trying to help children find something interesting and worth-while to say and building an audience situation which will give them reasons for saying it. The form of their production is to be thought of only in judging the effectiveness of *what* is said and to *whom*.

[1] Holland D. Roberts, "English Teachers Face the Future," *The English Journal* (College Edition), Vol. XXVII, pp. 101–113, February, 1938.

CHAPTER VII

TRANSLATING AN ORGANIC CONCEPTION OF LANGUAGE INTO ACTION

To infinite patience add a little wisdom, carefully strained through profitable experience. Pour in a brimming measure of the milk of human kindness, and season well with the salt of common sense. Boil gently over a friendly fire made of enthusiasms, stirring constantly with just discipline. When it has boiled long enough to be thoroughly blended, transfuse it by wise teaching to the eager mind of a restless boy, and set away to cool. Tomorrow he will greet you an educated man.

—EDWIN OSGOOD GROVER.

An Average Beginning High-school Class.—Although the basic principles of language teaching have already been translated into operational terms by means of concrete examples in the chapters on pronunciation, grammar, reading, conversation, and vocabulary building, it may be helpful to see them at work in a typical classroom situation. The following dramatized report is based upon actual notes taken in a beginning foreign-language class. Although the language is Spanish, exactly the same procedures have been used successfully in French, German, and Italian. The setting is the ordinary public school with standard equipment in the way of blackboards, desks, and wall maps. The characters are 36 unselected beginning students of Spanish (20 girls and 16 boys), an American-born teacher who has learned her Spanish in American schools, and three visitors. It is the first day of beginning (first-semester) Spanish following registration. Thirty-three students have never studied a foreign language before; two have "taken" Latin and one is still taking French; none of them have ever learned any Spanish beyond a few popular loan words, such as *Adiós, vamoose(!), tamales,* and *chile con carne.* Twenty of the pupils are ninth graders (freshmen), ten are tenth graders (sophomores), three are eleventh graders (juniors), and three are twelfth graders (seniors). Nearly all are enrolled in college-preparatory courses because of the prestige value with which the courses have been dignified by academic tradition in the community and school, despite the fact that not over 8 per cent of the pupils enrolled in language classes have ever continued in college in the foreign language which they began in high school—if, indeed, they entered college at all![1]

Fastened above the front blackboard is a roller map of North and South America which has been exposed to view. To the right of the map, the teacher has written some Spanish words and expressions in two parallel columns, headed *A* and *B*. Column *A* contains information which she will attempt to convey to the class *in Spanish* about the Pan-American Highway of the Pacific. Column *B* contains Spanish cognates and semantically related words which will be used to facilitate comprehension, since the pupils have no foreknowledge of the language beyond a few misconceptions based on hearsay.

A		*B*
ciento uno	= 101	comienza (el origen)
catorce	= 14	termina (el fin)
diez mil	= 10.000	ruta
diecisiete mil	= 17.000	forma parte
once mil	= 11.000	capital
Fairbanks		países (repúblicas)
Laredo		millas
Santiago		terminada (completa)
Los Ángeles		partes
Las Pampas		dólares
Chile		costo
la Argentina		por ciento (%)
mundo (globo)		extiende
Buenos Aires		continúa

INTRODUCING THE UNIT

When the class has assembled, the teacher steps to the front center of the room and prefaces the first lesson in beginning Spanish with the following remarks in English to the group as a whole.

NOTE: The comments in the left-hand margin are observations on content, objectives, teaching procedures, and pupil reactions.

The teacher establishes a frame of reference for the unit.

TEACHER: Have any of you ever heard of the Pan-American Highway of the Pacific or traveled over it?

[1] This situation is typical of the country at large. See E. F. Engel, "Why Do Not College Students Continue the Foreign Language Begun in High School?" *The Modern Language Journal*, Vol. XVI, pp. 500–503, March, 1932. Vera Whittmann and Walter V. Kaulfers, "Continuance in College of High-school Foreign Language," *The School Review*, Vol. XLVIII, pp. 606–611, October, 1940.

Two pupils raise their hands. The teacher calls on pupil *A*.

The teacher calls on pupil *B*.

The teacher pauses for a show of hands. Since there is no response she introduces the unit.

The teacher orients the class with respect to procedure.

PUPIL *A*: I haven't traveled over it, but I know that it goes down to Mexico City.

PUPIL *B*: It goes all the way down to South America, doesn't it?

TEACHER: Yes. Do any of you know exactly where the highway starts and ends, how far it is completed, how much it costs, or through what countries and cities it passes?

TEACHER: Suppose, then, that I tell you something in Spanish about the Pan-American (or International) Highway of the Pacific. Listen to see if you can learn something about the highway in Spanish. Do not be discouraged if you cannot understand every word—just try to get the most important facts. From time to time I shall stop to ask volunteers from the class to tell us in their own words in English just what they think they heard. When I stop, please raise your hands if you think you understood anything at all. I don't expect anyone to understand *everything*, but I know that all of you will understand *something*. By stopping to pool our information at convenient points we can learn from each other, in case some of us get lost temporarily. You can help me a great deal by volunteering, since I do not yet know all your names. This will save time and not make our first lesson look like a test. By raising your hands, you can also help me judge whether I am making the talk too easy or too hard. Are you ready? Very well, just remember that everything I am going to say has something to do with the Pan-American Highway—**La Carretera Panamericana.**

The teacher repeats the title three times

DEVELOPING AURAL ACUITY

The teacher takes a pointer and steps to one side of the map. During the talk she stresses the cognate Spanish words to facilitate aural comprehension. She points on the map to all place names as they are mentioned. She points to the starred (*) words in column *B* on the blackboard to facilitate visual comprehension, and to the double starred (**) words in the informational column headed *A*. While finding places on the map, or words and expressions in the column on the blackboard, she periphrases or repeats her remarks in Spanish. She speaks at a normal rate—repeating, paraphrasing, or accenting her remarks instead of slowing down her rate of speech, thus preventing the formation of mental habits of transliteration and accustoming the students' ears from the start to normal rates of articulation.

Bueno, aquí tengo un mapa. El mapa es de Norte América y de Sud América. Pues, la Carretera Panamericana comienza* en Fairbanks,** Alaska. En Fairbanks** comienza* (o se origina*) la Carretera Panamericana. Aquí está el origen* de la Carretera Panamericana. De Fairbanks,** Alaska, la Carretera se extiende (se continúa)* al Canadá. Sigue por el oeste del Canadá hasta Seattle, Wáshington. En Wáshington, Óregon y California la ruta* número ciento uno** es parte de la Carretera. En California, la Carretera pasa por las cuidades de San Francisco, San José, y Los Ángeles. ...

CHECKING COMPREHENSION

The teacher pauses for a show of hands. Over four-fifths of the class raise their hands. Three pupils seem to be especially anxious to volunteer. The teacher calls on pupil *C*. Note that the teacher does not ask for a *translation*, but for a summary of *content in their own words.*

Now let me see the hands of all who think that they understood at least something of what I said. **Señor,** can you give us the gist of our story so far in English?

The teacher encourages the class with signs of approval and satisfaction. Pupil *D* raises her hand and the teacher recognizes her.

The teacher listens approvingly and repeats in Spanish the information which seemingly did not get across to all pupils during her first presentation.

The teacher continues in Spanish, following the same procedures indicated above. She points to all place names on the map.

The teacher facilitates the comprehension of *sube* y *cruza* by means of gestures.

PUPIL *C*: You said that the International Highway begins at Fairbanks, Alaska, goes through Canada; then through Seattle, Washington, down through Oregon, and into California, by way of San Francisco, San José, and Los Angeles.

TEACHER: **¡Excelente! ¡Qué bueno! ¡Este chico es muy inteligente!** Señorita, did you want to add something?

PUPIL *D*: You said that in Washington, Oregon, and California Route or Highway 101 forms a part of the Pan-American Highway.

TEACHER: **¡Sí, sí, sí! ¡Muy bien! En Wáshington, Óregon, y California, la ruta* (carretera) número ciento uno** forma parte* de la Carretera Panamericana. Gracias, señorita. Eso es correcto.** I am glad to see that so many understood almost everything. Now let us go on.

Bien, de California la carretera va para Laredo,** Tejas. En Laredo** la Carretera cruza la frontera y entra en México. De Laredo, la Carretera pasa por México, Guatemala, Nicaragua, Costa Rica, y Panamá. De Panamá atraviesa (pasa por) Colombia, el Ecuador, el Perú, Bolivia, hasta Santiago,** la capital de Chile. De aquí la carretera sube y cruza los Andes** y las Pampas** de la Argentina hasta Buenos

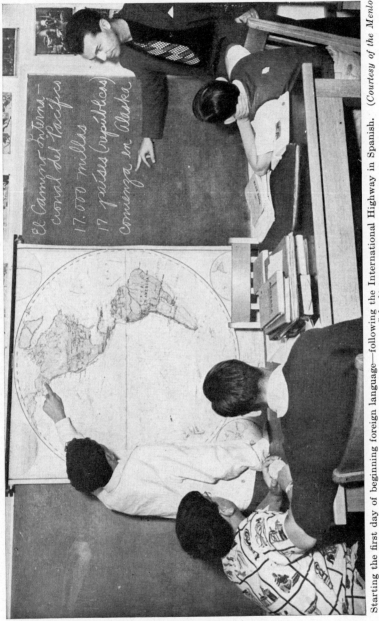

Starting the first day of beginning foreign language—following the International Highway in Spanish. (*Courtesy of the Menlo School.*)

Facing the group, the teacher asks *in Spanish* for volunteers. She facilitates comprehension by raising her own hand as a suggestion, and looks about the class for volunteers. Almost at once hands are raised in every quarter of the room. She looks pleased and calls on pupil *E*.

Aires.** En Buenos Aires** termina* la Carretera Panamericana. Buenos Aires,** la capital de la Argentina, es el fin* de la Carretera.

Bien. ¿Qué he dicho? ¿Quiénes me han entendido? ¡A ver; levanten las manos! ¿Quién lo sabe en inglés? ¡Ud, señor?

PUPIL *E*: I'm not sure that I can remember all the names, but you said that the highway goes from California to some place in Texas, then through Mexico, Guatemala, and other countries between there and Panama; then down along the west coast of South America to Chile, then over to Buenos Aires in Argentina.

The teacher indicates her approval in Spanish with the aid of a visible expression of satisfaction.

TEACHER: ¡Bien, muy bien! Eso es muy bueno. Gracias. Es usted muy inteligente.

I think you understood all the really important points. Does anyone happen to remember the name of the city where the highway crosses into Mexico? Señorita. . . .

The teacher solicits more detailed information and calls on other volunteers.

PUPIL *F*: It's Laredo, Texas.

TEACHER: Sí, precisamente. De Laredo** la Carretera entra en México. Gracias.

PAVING THE WAY FOR CLASS PARTICIPATION IN THE ORAL USE OF SPANISH

The teacher points to the answer-words in column *A* on the front blackboard. Note that the pupils are not encouraged to use Spanish until *after* they have had occasion to hear it. Note also that the

TEACHER: Now let me ask a few easy questions in Spanish, just to see if we can answer them by means of one of these answer-words in column *A* on procedure is from the whole language to the part.

The teacher pronounces the words distinctly (but not slowly) in Spanish, emphasizing the sound of the *d* in *Laredo*, and of the *j* in *Tejas*. She listens to the group response to see to what extent the pronunciation is "off key," but makes no comments or corrections. She proceeds in the same way through all the Spanish answer-words in column *A*.

the board. Volunteer if you have any idea at all what the answer is. There is no harm in trying. After all, this is just the first day of beginning Spanish, and we can't expect too much of ourselves; but we *can* listen carefully, and try to do as well as we can. That's all I expect. But first let us repeat some of the answer-words. I shall pronounce them *three* times in succession in Spanish; then will you all pronounce them *three* times in succession after me.

Bien, Laredo,** Tejas; Laredo, Tejas; Laredo, Tejas. Now three times together:

CLASS: Laredo, Tejas; Laredo, Tejas; Laredo, Tejas.

TEACHER: Bueno; Laredo,** Tejas—donde la Carretera entra en México. Ahora, Santiago de Chile,** Santiago de Chile; Santiago de Chile. Bien, conmigo. . . .

*   *   *   *   *

The teacher calls on pupil *G*, then on successive volunteers for answers to other questions.

Now, let us try to pronounce these words in the same way when we answer the questions. Bien. ¿Dónde (where) comienza** la Carretera? ¡Levanten la mano! Bueno, señorita. . . .

PUPIL *G*.: Fairbanks, Alaska.

TEACHER: Sí, comienza en Fairbanks, Alaska. ¿Y dónde termina la Carretera? ¿Señor?. . . .

Pupil *H*, is a little confused with respect to the answer. His pronunciation of the *a* in Santiago and of the *e* in Chile is decidedly off key, but instead of correcting him, the teacher tactfully repeats the words correctly. Since there are signs of disagreement in the class regarding pupil *H*'s answer, the teacher calls on another pupil. The latter's response shows that he knows the answer, but is a little self-conscious and insecure in his pronunciation. The teacher spares him the embarrassment by simply repeating the answer. She makes a mental note of these and other pronunciation difficulties to guide her in providing practice according to need later on. Instead of "freezing" the students with corrections, she merely repeats the answers correctly after the pupils have finished reciting.

Pupil *H*.: **Santiago de Chile.**

Teacher: **¿En Santiago de Chile? Santiago es la capital de Chile y la Carretera pasa por Santiago; ¿pero es Santiago el fin de la Carretera? ¿Dónde (where) termina* la Carretera?**

Pupil *I*: Boo . . . Boo . . . Booway-nuss. . . .

Teacher: **Sí, Buenos Aires. En Buenos Aires termina la Carretera. Gracias. ¿Y dónde está Buenos Aires—en Chile? en Bolivia? en la Argentina?**

Pupil *J*: Argentina.

Teacher: **Sí, Buenos Aires está en la Argentina. Buenos Aires es la capital de la Argentina.**

This is very encouraging. Let's see how much more we can learn about the Pan-American Highway in Spanish. Raise your hands, as before, as soon as we stop for a summary in English. **Bien: De Fairbanks, Alaska, a Buenos Aires en la Argentina, la Carretera pasa por catorce** países o repúblicas— el Canadá, los Estados Unidos, México, Guatemala, el Salvador, Honduras, Nicaragua, Costa Rica, Panamá, Colombia, el Ecuador, el Perú, Chile, y la Argentina—catorce** países* o repúblicas. . . . Bueno, ¿quiénes saben? ¡Levanten la mano! ¿Señorita?**

Pupil *K*: Fourteen countries.

Teacher: **¡Correcto! Catorce países.** But what about these fourteen countries? What do they have to do with the Pan-American Highway?

PUPIL *K*: The highway passes through them.

TEACHER: ¡**Eso es! La Carretera pasa por catorce** países.*** Let us always link our answers to something about the Pan-American Highway. Can anyone name some of the countries through which it passes— **Alaska, el Canadá, Los Estados Unidos, México—¿qué más?** Can you read the names from the map?

PUPIL *L*: Guatemala, Salvador, Honduras, Nicaragua, Costa Rica, Panama, Columbia, Bolivia, Ecuador, Peru, Chile, Argentina.

TEACHER: **Gracias. Sí, la Carretera pasa por . . . el Ecuador, el Perú, Chile, la Argentina. . . .**

¿Tiene Ud. una pregunta?

PUPIL *M*: How do you pronounce the *g* in Spanish? Is it pronounced like our *h* or how?

TEACHER: That is a very good question; and if you will raise it again a little later when we have finished talking about the **Carretera Panamericana,** I shall be glad to answer it, and any other questions which the class may wish to ask about the Spanish language. We shall try to save the last ten minutes of the period today for this purpose. Will you ask your question again

---

The teacher listens to the pupil's pronunciation and accentuation of the Spanish names. She facilitates pronunciation but does not correct the student directly. After the pupil has finished, she repeats the names correctly, supplying the articles (*el* Perú, etc.) which pupil *L* has omitted.

Pupil *M* has his hand up.

The teacher is pleased with this spontaneous expression of interest in pronunciation—especially with respect to a letter which seemed to be somewhat "off key" in the oral responses of the class. The students are beginning to sense a *need* for help in pronunciation which will gain group acceptance of subsequent oral practice and explanations (provided the latter are in answer to their *own* problems, questions, or difficulties). She tactfully avoids disorganizing digressions by encouraging the raising of questions at a time specifically allocated for this purpose.

then? To stop now would probably cause us to forget all about the **Carretera.** Suppose that you listen carefully between now and then to the way we pronounce some of the Spanish words containing *g*'s, such as **la Argentina,** and perhaps you will be able to answer your own question for us during the question period.

To get back to our story: **Como les he dicho, la Carretera pasa por catorce** ** **países (catorce repúblicas) entre Fairbanks, Alaska, y Buenos Aires, la capital de la Argentina. La Carretera tiene diecisiete mil** ** **millas** * **de largo. Es decir que la longitud de la Carretera es de diecisiete mil** ** **millas.** *

The teacher facilitates the comprehension of largo *by means of gestures and paraphrase.*

En efecto, la Carretera Panamericana es la Carretera más larga del mundo (globo **). ¿Hay manos? ¿Ud., señor?**

PUPIL *N*: The highway is seventeen million miles long.

The teacher calls on pupil N.
There is slight merriment in the class: Pupil N is unaware of his faux pas. *She points to diecisiete mil = 17.000 in column A.*

TEACHER: **Diecisiete millones o diecisiete mil** **

PUPIL *N*: (Smiling sheepishly), seventeen thousand!

TEACHER: **¡Precisamente! Diecisiete mil millas de largo; y es la carretera más larga del mundo (globo).** ** **¿Quién sabe?**

The teacher calls on pupil O. Note that the superlative is perceived correctly on the very first day. Almost all language phenomena, when developed in context suggestive of their semantic *function, can be similarly comprehended*

PUPIL *O*: It's the largest highway in the world.

TEACHER: Yes, it's the largest, but, in what sense—the *widest* or the *longest?*

with the occasional aid of gestures, periphrase, or cognates where necessary. Note that in correcting pupil *O,* the teacher avoids giving him the impression that he ha made a mistake. Her aim is to encourage a feeling of *confidence,* not of frustration. All language teaching should aim directly and indirectly to *facilitate* expression rather than to inhibit it.

PUPIL *O*: The *longest.*

TEACHER: Yes, the *longest.* **Largo** in Spanish can mean largest only in the sense of *longest.* **Muy bien.**

Naturalmente, la Carretera no está terminada (completa)* todavía. La Carretera no está terminada* en Alaska, ni en el Canadá, ni en partes de México o la América Central. En México, la Carretera está terminada* hasta la capital* de México. Hasta ahora, más de once mil** millas* están terminadas, o más de sesenta y cuatro por ciento. La Carretera no está completamenta terminada porque el costo* es grande. El costo* es de diez mil** dólares* la milla. Es decir, una milla* cuesta diez mil dólares. Por eso, la construcción* no está terminada* todavía en partes de Alaska, del Canadá, o de la América Central.

Ahora, a ver. . . . ¿Hay manos?

*   *   *   *   *

The teacher calls on different volunteers for a complete résumé (in English) in the students' own words of the information which she has presented in Spanish. She uses the same techniques (orthographic cognates, gestures, periphrastic restatements, pictorial aids such as the map, etc.) to facilitate comprehension as indicated in the margin above. In the same way she later develops additional information concerning the highway, and eventually expands the topic to include (on successive days) mention of interesting things that can be seen while driving through Latin America via this route: *Los volcanes Popocatéptl e Ixtaccíhuatl, las Pirámides del Sol y de la Luna, la Capital de México, lugares pintorescos o de interés histórico,* etc.

PROVIDING FOR PUPIL PARTICIPATION
IN READING, WRITING, AND PRONOUNCING THE LANGUAGE

The teacher introduces the assignment. In slow-moving classes this work may have to be deferred to the second day. The time limits for units of this type are relative. Much depends upon the length of the class period, the maturity level and backgrounds of the students, and the managerial efficiency of the teacher. Language is a matter of growth which cannot be blocked off into fixed time limits. *A unit may be as long as it can profitably arouse and capitalize the interested attention of students in the service of an objective.*

TEACHER: On the side board I have written a few sentences in Spanish in each of which *one* word is needed to make the sentence complete and true. The X in each sentence stands for the missing word. Look at the first sentence:

La Carretera Panamericana comienza en X. Can you find in column A the word, name, or number that should be substituted for the X in order to make the sentence complete and true?

A ver; ¿manos? ¿Ud., señorita?

PUPIL *P*: **¿Alaska?**

The teacher calls on pupil *P* who has volunteered.

TEACHER: **Sí, muy bien, gracias; pero ¿en qué parte de Alaska? ¿En Nome? ¿Juneau?—¿En qué parte*?**

The teacher points to various places in Alaska on the map.

PUPIL *P*: Oh, Fairbanks!

TEACHER: **Eso es, Fairbanks: La Carretera Panamericana comienza en Fairbanks.**** Now before we do the remainder of the completion exercises, let us review the answer-words in column A. I shall pronounce them in Spanish three times in succession. Then will you pronounce them three times in succession with me? **Bien: ciento uno, ciento uno, ciento uno. Ahora, conmigo.**

The class repeats the answer-word in concert. The teacher listens for pro-

CLASS: **Ciento uno, ciento uno, ciento uno.**

nunciation difficulties and surveys the class, watching closely the lip movements of the students. She repeats all incorrectly pronounced words but makes no comments or corrections. Choral work is used to allow for unembarrassed participation on the part of pupils who are too shy to volunteer in a foreign language at first.

TEACHER: **Muy bien, ciento uno.** And what about **ciento uno?** What does this number have to do with our story? I hope that everyone will try to take part in some way in our first lesson. May I hear from someone who has not had a chance to take part so far? **Gracias; ¿Ud., señorita?**

PUPIL Q: In the United States, Route 101 forms a part of the Pan-American Highway.

TEACHER: ¡**Exactamente! Ud. tiene razón. En Los Estados Unidos la ruta número ciento uno forma parte de la Carretera Panamericana. Bueno;** now let us pronounce some of the other answer-words in column A in the same way—three times —and while pronouncing the items, let us try to recall what each one has to do with the Pan-American Highway. **A ver: diez mil, diez mil, diez mil. Ahora conmigo. . . .**

The teacher develops with the class the pronunciation of the following answer-words from column A in the manner indicated above. After each item has been pronounced she calls on some volunteer to relate the information to the Pan-American Highway:

ciento uno	= 101
catorce	= 14
diez mil	= 10.000
diecisiete mil	= 17.000
once mil	= 11.000
sesenta y cuatro	= 64
Laredo	
los Andes	
las Pampas	
Chile	
la Argentina	

Santiago
Buenos Aires
mundo (globo)

The teacher assigns the completion exercises for individual written work in class.

TEACHER: Now let's number a sheet of paper from one to ten in a column to the left, and opposite each number, write *in full in Spanish* the ten completion exercises that are written on the side board. Remember to substitute for the X whatever answer-words in column *A* are needed to make each sentence complete and true. Let's see how many sentences we can do correctly in fifteen minutes. Head your papers in the upper right-hand corner giving your name, subject, and date as follows:

Me llamo señor *Brown.*
Español I.
Estamos a martes, el dieciséis de septiembre de 19__.

DIAGNOSING PUPIL NEEDS AND DIFFICULTIES

While the class are working on the completion exercises, the teacher moves about the room to see how the pupils are progressing. She calls the attention of individual students to difficulties in spelling and the like with such remarks as "Will you look at sentence 5 again to see if you have left out any word (or how the word *diez* is spelled, etc.)? Occasionally a pupil will ask a question as, "What is that mark over the *a* in *e-s-t-á*?" In such cases, the teacher replies, "That is an accent mark. I think that there are several other students in the class who are wondering what accent marks are. Would you mind asking your question again when we hold our question-box discussion during the last part of the period? That will save me the trouble of having to say the same thing over too often." If her observations suggest the need for a little group guidance, the teacher may caution the class occasionally with such reminders as, "Will everyone make sure to copy all the words correctly? Will you be sure to watch spelling?"

The completion exercises on which the class are working are as follows:

1. La Carretera Panamericana comienza en X.
2. La carretera termina en X.
3. La carretera tiene X millas de largo.
4. La carretera pasa por X países (repúblicas).
5. El costo de la carretera es de X dólares la milla.
6. En California, la ruta número X forma parte de la Carretera Panamericana.
7. Apróximadamente X millas están terminadas (completas).
8. Aproximadamente X por ciento está terminada.
9. Entre Santiago de Chile y Buenos Aires la carretera cruza (pasa por) los Andes y las X de la Argentina.
10. La capital de la Argentina es X.*

HELPING STUDENTS TO GAIN INSIGHT
INTO THE OPERATIONAL PRINCIPLES OF PRONUNCIATION

At the end of fifteen minutes the teacher collects the papers. While collecting them, she solicits questions from the class. The fact that some activity of interest is actually taking place during the collection of papers reduces the danger that this aspect of the mechanics of class management will lead to confusion, unnecessary conversation, or a dissipation of attention. Any superfluous distractions then become a form of discourtesy to fellow pupils—not just an offense against the teacher's personal notions of discipline for the sake of discipline.

TEACHER: From what I have seen, the papers are very good. Even though some of us may not be through, will every one stop now, and relay his paper to the person in front (to the right or left). While the papers are being collected, will you raise your hands if you have any question about the Spanish language which came to mind during our discussion of the highway, or while you were writing the exercises? If I remember correctly, someone

---

* The accuracy of pupil work with exercises of this kind is usually greater if the material is available in mimeographed form. Work written on the blackboard is often difficult to see, and hard for the pupils to copy accurately. Very inexpensive duplicating machines such as the Print-o-matic, Ditto, Gel-sten, or Hectograph, reproduce handwriting as well as typewritten work, and can be operated by any child of junior-high-school age. Fifty copies will usually serve 15 to 20 classes, if the pupils are directed to do their work on a separate sheet of paper, and to return the copies upon completion of the unit. In any case, it is important that the pupils copy each exercise *in full*, not just the answer-words. Otherwise, the potential values of the unit for developing vocabulary, ability in spelling, or notions of word order are likely to be lost.

The teacher surveys the class for questions before answering any one query. By so doing, she can select from among the questions asked those which are most appropriate at this stage in terms of the immediate language needs of the pupils, their levels of insight (*i.e.*, ability to comprehend the *application* of any explanation), and the time available for doing justice to the questions. In this way, too, she can often save time by generalizing an explanation in such a way as to answer two or more questions at once. A piecemeal answering of questions easily leads to mind wandering, irrelevant philosophizing, or a disorganized hodgepodge. Skill in selecting, organizing, and relating questions is essential if the teacher is to lead the class, rather than be disoriented by it.

The teacher writes *la Argentina* on the board, and pronounces the word three times. Then she asks the pupils to repeat the name in concert three times as best they can in Spanish. Note that the examples are chosen from context dealing with the Pan-American Highway. Note also that the part is derived from the whole—not the whole from the summation of parts.

raised a question a few minutes ago on pronunciation. What was that question?

PUPIL *M*: I asked about the sound of the Spanish *g*.

TEACHER: **Ah, sí.** We shall discuss the pronunciation of the Spanish *g* in just a moment. First let me see if there are any other questions. Then, perhaps, we can kill several birds with one stone. **¿Quiénes tienen preguntas? ¿Manos?**

PUPIL *R*: What is that mark over some of the letters, such as the *o* in dollars in Spanish?

TEACHER: Now we have two good questions. Are there any others?

PUPIL *S*: Sometimes you pronounce the *c* like a *k* and sometimes like a *th*. How can you tell which is which?

TEACHER: That makes *three* good questions. I see that there are a great many more that you would like to raise. Perhaps three are all that we shall have time to discuss before the bell rings. Will you save all questions that are not answered today for our question-box discussion tomorrow?

Now with respect to the pronunciation of the Spanish *g*. Listen to the pronunciation of the *g* in **la Argentina: la Argentina, la Argentina.** Now three times with me. Pronounce the word the way you think it sounds. **Bien.**

CLASS: La Argentina, la Argentina, la Argentina.

TEACHER: Múy bien. Pues, señor M, repítalo Ud., si me hace el favor: Pronounce la Argentina, please.

PUPIL M: La Argentina?

TEACHER: Bueno: la Argentina. What does the *g* sound like to you?

PUPIL M: It sounds something like a strong *h*.

The teacher explains and demonstrates the sound in terms of an easily recognized physiological parallel. The pupils feel a little foolish at first, but they join in goodnaturedly.

TEACHER: Correcto. I think you answered your own question. In Spanish the *g* sounds like *h* before *i* or *e*. This sound is produced by relaxing the jaw, tongue, and throat as if we were going to yawn, and then exhaling in a kind of pant. Let's try panting like a dog. Smile, relax your jaw, tongue, and throat as if you were going to yawn. Now pant. Do it with a smile! Come on! It's foolish, but it's fun—and it's the easiest way to learn how!

* * * * *

Sí, sí, sí. Now let's pronounce la Argentina, using the same pant for the *g*. Do it with a smile—and relax the jaw and throat, otherwise people might think you were trying to clear your throat. ¡Bueno! Tres veces: la Argentina, la Argentina, la Argentina,—combine the two *a*'s into one long *ah*: la :rgentina.

The teacher calls on a volunteer from the class.

Pupil *U* has her hand raised. The teacher recognizes her.

The teacher writes the sequences *gui, gue, ga, go, gu* on the board, pronouncing each phoneme distinctly.

The teacher points to different combinations in the sequence in random order, emphasizing the *gui* and *gue*.

The teacher writes the sequence *gi, ge, ja, jo, ju* on the board, pronouncing each phoneme distinctly. She then points to different combinations in random order, emphasizing the *gi, ge,* and *ja,* which are most likely to be confused by English-speaking students. The sequences are arranged on the board as follows:

gui gue ga go gu
gi   ge   ja jo ju

CLASS: **LaArgentina, laArgentina, laArgentina.**

TEACHER: **¡Excelente! ¡Muy español! ¡Casi perfecto! La Argentina. Ahora, pronuncien Uds. Nicaragua.** Listen for the sound of the *g*: **Nicaragua, Nicaragua, Nicaragua.** What does it sound like to you?

PUPIL *I*: Like our *g* in go.

TEACHER: **Sí, como la g en** go. **Correcto. ¿Hay preguntas?**

PUPIL *U*: How can you tell when to pronounce it one way and when another?

TEACHER: **Eso es fácil. Presten Uds. atención al pizarrón un momento. Miren Uds., clase: gui gue ga go gu.** Repeat the combinations after me, paying attention to the sound of the *g* and to the spelling.

CLASS: **gui, gue, ga, go, gu.**

TEACHER: **Bien, otra vez.** Now pay close attention because I shall skip around: **¡Bueno, conmigo!**

CLASS: **go, gui, gue, gu, ga, gui, ga, gue, gui, gue, ga, gu, gue, gui, ga, gu, gue.**

TEACHER: **Gracias.** Note that here we pronounce the *g* very much as in our English word *go.* Now compare the following: **gi, ge, ja, jo, ju.** Pronounce the *g* as in **la Argentina. Bien, conmigo.**

CLASS: **gi, ge, ja, jo, ju, ge, gi, ja, ge, gi, ju, gi, ja, ge, ge, ge, ja, jo.**

TEACHER: **¡Bueno!** Now let us see if we can keep ourselves from becoming confused when we skip from one line to another. Remember that in the top line the *g* has the sound of *g* as in *go*, and that in the second line it has the sound of the *g* in la **Argentina.**

CLASS: **gui, gi; gue, ge; ga, ja; go, jo; gu, ju; ju, gu; jo, go; ja, ga; ge, gue; gi, gui; gue, ge; gui, ga.**

The teacher writes the word *gente* on the board without pronouncing it. She calls on pupil *V.*

TEACHER: How, then, would you pronounce the word **gente** (people) in Spanish? **¿Señorita?**

PUPIL *V:* **¿Gente?**

TEACHER: **Bueno, eso es: gente. Clase, gente, gente, gente.**

CLASS: **Gente, gente, gente.**

The teacher pronounces the word *juguete* without writing it and calls on a volunteer to write it on the blackboard.

TEACHER: Now how would you *spell* the word **juguete,** meaning *toy,* in Spanish? **Ju-gue-te.** Who thinks he can write it for us on the board? Just do the best you can. Don't be afraid of making a mistake. **¿Ud., señor? Bien: ju-gue-te.**

PUPIL *W:* (Writes) **jugete.**

Pupil *W* confuses the sound of the *ge* and *gue.*

TEACHER: That is very close. Listen again: **juGUEte.** Now pronounce after me the following combinations in our table of sounds.

TEACHER and PUPIL *W:* **gi, gui; ge, gue; jo, go; ge, gue; gui, gi; ge, gue.**

TEACHER: Now pronounce the word **ju-gue-te.**

PUPIL *W:* **Juguete.**

TEACHER: Now pronounce these combinations: *ge, gue.*

Pupil *W* sees the point and corrects the spelling of the word on the board. Note

PUPIL *W:* Oh yes, I see; it should be *g-u-e.*

that the teacher has helped the pupil to gain *insight, i.e.,* to see the principle for himself.

The teacher calls on a volunteer from the class to phrase the principle in his own words. The procedure is inductive—from the specific to the generic—and capitalizes the principles of learning to do by doing and of practice in terms of need and level of insight.

TEACHER: **Precisamente. Gracias.** Now suppose someone were to ask you how to pronounce the *g* in Spanish. What would you say? Look at the table of sounds which we practiced pronouncing just a moment ago. **¿Quién sabe?**

PUPIL X: The *g* has the sound of a panted *h* before *i* and *e* and of our English *g* in *go* before *a, o,* and *u.*

TEACHER: **Correcto.** Perhaps it would be a little simpler to say that the *g* has a sound like that of a panted *h* before *i* and *e* and of the *g* in *go in other cases.* That covers all but a few exceptions. **Muy bien.**

The warning bell rings two minutes before the end of the period, and the teacher makes the following suggestions to the class:

TEACHER: During the period tomorrow I shall try to answer some of the questions that we did not have time to discuss today. I notice that almost everyone already has a standard-size loose-leaf notebook which he is using in some of his other courses. Will you reserve a special section of your loose-leaf notebook for this class? Some of the answers to questions which we shall develop together will be worth writing down for future reference. If you already have a notebook, you might head the first page *Pronunciación,* and under this heading write, in your own words, a reminder of the way the *g* is pronounced in Spanish. Will you also bring to class any Spanish expressions, words, or names of places whose meaning and pronunciation you would like to know? We shall reserve a part of our question-box period tomorrow for this purpose.

THE PROSPECTUS OF THE PROGRAM—
METHOD, STANDARDS, CONTENT, AND ACTIVITIES

At the end of the hour, the three visitors accompany the teacher to the faculty room to talk over the program with her. Here the following conversation ensues:

VISITOR *A*: I see that you believe in the natural method and the oral approach.

TEACHER: I am not aware of being a devotee of any special system or method of teaching. It seems to me natural that if a large number of students enroll in foreign languages with the desire to learn to speak them at least a little, we should certainly capitalize this interest in the service of language study, whether we make it our central objective or not. My aim today was to develop an apperceptive basis for learning to pronounce the language, and to do this in terms of content that would provide opportunities for learning to do by doing in a communication situation. Naturally, on the very first day of a beginning language course one has to choose a simple subject that can be developed in concrete terms.

VISITOR *B*: What will you do with the class tomorrow?

TEACHER: During the first part of the period we shall probably review the papers that we wrote in class today. Each pupil will be asked to correct any mistakes that have been checked on his paper. Volunteer students will read the sentences after the teacher in Spanish, pronouncing the words as best they can, and supplying the correct answer-words. Then the class as a whole will repeat the sentence in Spanish. At this early stage, we urge the students to volunteer. We expect only that they do the best they can, and do not interrupt to correct students. If mistakes occur, we merely repeat the entire sentence correctly as a matter of routine before asking the class as a whole to repeat it. Naturally, if a student hesitates unduly for lack of self-confidence or because of uncertainty, we do not allow him to sizzle in his blushes. We unobtrusively supply the correct pronunciation. It has always seemed to me that overcorrection is either a sign that too much is expected at a given level, or that something is lacking in the organization and presentation of the material. Overcorrection is almost synonymous with exposing ignorance before the class. In time, it tends to have a negative effect upon the *esprit de corps* of the group and a dampening influence upon the desire to participate voluntarily.

VISITOR *C*: But don't you think that there is some danger that the students will fix wrong habits of pronunciation if they are left to do just the best they can?

TEACHER: If we depended just on unguided trial-and-error activity, this danger would be a real one. But this is not the case. Pronunciation is a psychophysical skill and, like skill in tennis, golf, or playing the piano, the initial stages will always be characterized by involuntary errors, even when the learner knows exactly what the correct response should be; for it takes practice for mind and muscle to become synchronized. The important thing is to help the students gain insight into what the correct response should be. We start with the language in action—in terms of an informational subject—in order that the student's ears may be tuned to the language as a whole—its intonation patterns, rhythm, inflections, vowel lengths, consonantal modifications, liaisons, and synaloepha—without being conscious of these technicalities as such. Then, when a class atmosphere favorable to voluntary participation, devoid of self-consciousness, has been developed, we introduce activities, such as the completion exercises which you witnessed, to provide for oral participation on the part of volunteer students, supplemented by choral responses from the class as a whole. Although we do not interrupt to correct students, we listen carefully for those sounds which are most off key or for those which seem to cause the students to hesitate or to feel uncomfortable. When given the opportunity to ask questions concerning the language, the students usually raise the very problems which trouble them. We then help them to answer their own questions (in their own words, if possible), and provide specialized practice to strengthen the psychophysical coordinations involved in pronunciation.

You will recall our work with the Spanish *g* as an example. It might seem that much time could be saved by just giving the students the rule, but this is rarely true. In the first place, the wording of a rule is not always comprehended by the students, *i.e.*, they may be able to repeat the wording of the rule but unable to apply it. Secondly, so much time and attention usually have to be given to explaining and illustrating the meaning of the rules that the language is likely to be relegated to the background except for illustrative purposes. It requires very little common sense to realize that ability in language is not developed by theorizing *about* it. Starting with the language in action, developing a favorable attitude toward doing the best that one can, and gradually weeding out in order of degree of offensiveness those deviations from the normal which block intelligible communication or distract from the thought—all help to keep the language intact and to give such theoretical attention or specialized practice as may be necessary, a more patent *raison d'être*. The pupils then see some sense to it. In fact, they may even sense the need sufficiently to ask for it.

VISITOR *B*: How soon do you expect the students to have mastered the rudiments of pronunciation?

TEACHER: The terms "rudiments of pronunciation" and "mastered" are naturally susceptible to many interpretations. I doubt that I can answer your questions directly. Let me add, however, that we conceive of pronunciation as an integral aspect of growth in language over an indefinite period of time; and this rate of growth varies with every individual. To assume anything else, would be as futile as to expect every student at the end of a certain month to jump over a five-foot bar. We do keep in mind certain guiding criteria of growth, however. In the beginning, we aim at least toward *intelligibility:* Would a native listening to a pupil understand what he is *trying* to say? The next level is that of *ready* intelligibility: Would a native *readily* understand what the pupil is saying? When this level is reached, we are ready to work for the elimination of any remaining dissonances that might brand the pupils' speech as being that of a typical *norteamericano* or *yanqui*. A few of our pupils achieve this degree of proficiency by the end of the first semester. Some have difficulty achieving it within three years. We usually give special help in class to problem cases by meeting them as a committee occasionally during the supervised-study period, while the remainder of the group are working independently at their seats. I think you will agree that pronunciation, as an aspect of language, is not something that can be parceled out and "covered" by concentrated drill in a week or two. It is an aspect of growth which should accompany increased ability to read, write, or speak the language. For what would be the value of a perfect pronunciation, for example, if the pupils had no vocabulary with which to say or understand anything? Naturally, if a student of voice is interested merely in being able to sing songs in a foreign language, we afford him the opportunity of securing special assistance as an individual during the supervised-study period, in much the same way that we provide special assistance for problem cases in pronunciation. These pupils are exceptions, however. We do our best to accommodate exceptions, but we do not generalize their needs, or impose them on the class as a whole.

VISITOR *A*: How far do you intend to carry the development of the unit on the Pan-American Highway?

TEACHER: We shall probably continue the unit until the end of the week. We hope that the topic will serve as a convenient "curtain raiser" or "appetizer." Tomorrow we may have time to discuss in Spanish some of the cities and places of scenic, historical, or economic interest which can be seen along the Pan-American Highway. In this way, the pupils will be afforded an overview of Spanish America.

This overview may help them to make intelligent suggestions to a steering committee of their own selection with respect to the content and activities which they would like to choose as a cultural medium for learning to read, write, or speak the language. The remainder of the unit will be presented orally by the teacher in much the same way as today. Pupil participation will be enlisted by means of completion exercises, semioriginal questions, and a concluding résumé in the foreign language. The completion exercises will involve both silent and oral reading (as in the exchange and correction of papers), while the semioriginal questions will provide for informal conversational activity involving practice in pronunciation and vocabulary building with informational content.

Here are a few samples of the semioriginal questions that the pupils are to complete and then ask of each other. The directions to the pupils read as follows:

Compose five good questions in Spanish, starting them as indicated below and using *only* words and information found in the completion exercises of Part I above. Avoid questions that cannot be answered directly from the information given in the completion exercises. Do not separate the Spanish words that start the questions.
1. ¿Dónde está (where is)......................... ?
2. ¿Dónde (where) comienza........................?
3. ¿Qué (which) ruta forma........................?

The composition of semioriginal questions usually gives rise to queries concerning word order, agreement of articles and adjectives, and the like. As in our lesson today, we reserve a special part of the class hour for a discussion of such language problems. Next week, for example, we may have to set aside a day or two exclusively for specialized work on the mechanics of agreement, using a variety of practice exercises involving the concepts of gender and number. During the first two years approximately one-fourth of the pupils' time (including class hours and preparation) is devoted to this type of foundation work *as the need arises from actual experience in using the language.* This is the chief difference between our course as conducted today, and our course of ten years ago. Formerly we used to devote about three-fourths of the class time to formal grammar and grammatical exercises, and about one-fourth to reading or question-and-answer work based upon a short reading selection.

After the class have heard the topic presented in Spanish, and discussed it themselves through the medium of the completion exercises and semioriginal questions they are usually sufficiently familiar with the vocabulary and information contained in the unit to be able to prepare a résumé in Spanish of the most interesting and important points. After review by the class editorial committee, the best of these may be selected for exhibit on the bulletin board, or for publication in the foreign-language section of the school publications. As you may know, our foreign-language classes publish a mimeographed bulletin every semester. After the first few weeks the students are usually able to write their résumés from memory during the first ten minutes of the following class period. In such cases, the résumé serves as a means for fixing vocabulary and information for delayed recall. As in the case of the work with semioriginal questions, the preparation and correction of résumés gives rise to questions of usage, and to correlated practice on such mechanical phases of language as cause difficulty.

VISITOR *A*: If I understand you correctly, no work is done in grammar except as the need for explanations or specialized practice arises. How, then, do the students learn the grammar which they will need to pass college entrance board examinations, or to continue in more or less traditional courses in college?

TEACHER: We are not concerned with college entrance requirements during the first year. Neither are we concerned with entrance examinations in the second year, except in the case of seniors who are preparing to continue their study of foreign languages in some particular college or university the following term. These pupils form a committee under the chairmanship of one of the abler students and operate within the regular class as a kind of college-preparatory seminar. The teacher meets with the group occasionally during the supervised study period to plan differentiated assignments and to answer questions. The work of each student is clearly outlined in advance, and completed on the contract plan. Since senior students are a relatively older and more select group, with at least a year of background work in the language, they are usually able to complete the special assignments without serious difficulty. We find that the measure of responsibility which they are obliged to assume for their progress and achievement under the contract plan is excellent training for work in college—probably better than a grade of excellent achieved by spoon feeding, cajoling, or coddling. By placing seniors on editorial committees and by utilizing them as teaching assistants during the supervised study period to check papers or to assist fellow members of the class who have difficulties in pronunciation, reading, or writing, we are able to capitalize their abilities to the fullest and to make them a responsible, integral part of the class. Naturally, no second-year student is denied the privilege of joining the senior seminar if there happens to be one in his class, but most of the younger pupils prefer the more functional type of foreign-language work.

VISITOR C: You use no grammar text at all, then?

TEACHER: Only with seniors. We make our own grammar as we go along by occasionally copying in our notebooks, under appropriate headings, the explanations (with examples) of any important language problems which are raised in class. Specialized practice on such mechanics as verb forms is provided through mimeographed materials or through exercises written on the board.

VISITOR B: Your only textbook, then, is a reader, I presume. How soon do you begin reading?

TEACHER: As soon as the class have acquired a sufficient background in pronunciation, vocabulary, and notions of word order to be able to read material of an informative nature. Two or three units (such as the present one on the Pan-American Highway) involving practice in hearing, reading, writing, and speaking the language in an integrative setting, usually serve as reading preparatory activities. Each unit may occupy from three to five days, depending upon the reactions of the class. Thus some work in a reader can be begun as early as the third or fourth week. Our chief difficulty is the scarcity of reading materials which contain anything worth knowing or discussing in any language. We find the technique which you saw in operation this afternoon a practical way of compensating for this handicap at the elementary level. Even in intermediate and advanced courses, however, we often skip those chapters or lessons in the basic text which are devoid of real thought content, and devote the time thus saved to integrative units of timely interest or significance to the class. Almost any subject, you know, can be developed in this way by a teacher who is skillful in the use of cognates or paraphrase, provided her professional resources are not limited to a knowledge of the grammar of the language, or to an acquaintance with a few literary classics.

VISITOR A: Don't the preparation and presentation of units of this type require an immense amount of time and effort on the part of the teacher? I should think that she would be a nervous wreck by the end of the first week!

TEACHER: That would undoubtedly be true if the teacher had to conduct every class throughout the day and year on this plan. Obviously, units of this type are employed less frequently at the intermediate and advanced levels, because of the greater amount of printed materials available in the foreign language for reading and discussion in class.   Moreover, after two or three weeks, the presentation of such a unit in class becomes relatively easy, for by that time the students have developed some ability in aural comprehension, vocabulary, and pronunciation.   After the first ten weeks, for example, it is no longer necessary to make preparations on the board.   Such aids to comprehension as may be required can then usually be supplied by the teacher as she discusses the topic.   By the end of twelve or fifteen weeks, the completion exercises and semioriginal questions can often be dictated instead of written on the board; by the end of the first semester the pupils are usually able to compose and answer questions of their own construction.   In fact, by the end of the second year the better students can often take notes directly in the foreign language and write a résumé of the talk without benefit of specialized practice in the way of completion exercises or preliminary question-and-answer activity of any kind.   Thus the teaching load is not so strenuous as it may seem.

VISITOR *B*: But how will a teacher find time to collect the information for the units?

TEACHER: An informative article in a current magazine, or a pertinent chapter in a book, can easily be converted into a unit, once one has mastered the mechanics.   I have even taken notes on radio speeches, or on addresses given by open-forum lecturers, and composed a unit mentally while driving to school.   The presentation next day was probably not so mechanically perfect as if the material and exercises had been phrased in writing beforehand, but it was highly successful, perhaps because of the timely interest of the subject to the group; perhaps also because the unit was developed spontaneously in class.   In this card file are notes taken over a period of years on Spanish painting, music, art, science, invention, customs, historical anecdotes, biography, plots of famous plays, stories, books, etc.   Any of these topics could be converted into a unit on ten to fifteen minutes notice.   Ten to fifteen minutes would allow me to refresh my memory or to collect appropriate illustrative materials in the way of pictures and *realia* from the files.

VISITOR *C*: However, you are a teacher of considerable experience, with a fluent command of the language.   Many teachers, especially beginning teachers, are not so fortunate.   Some find it rather difficult to speak the language.

TEACHER: It is for exactly such teachers that the use of this approach is desirable.   Naturally, the beginning teacher may have to confine herself at the start to very short units—perhaps to material that she can memorize and present with the aid of notes within five to ten minutes. As her ability and confidence increase, the units can be gradually lengthened, until within a year or two she will be able to discuss almost any topic without having to do more than consult the dictionary occasionally for the translations of certain words.

After all, a teacher who conducts four to six classes in a foreign language a day should, if she uses the language to the greatest possible advantage, be able to increase her *own* oral command of the language to any desired degree. It seems to me that if a teacher with a full foreign-language program does not improve her own ability to speak the language in and through experience in teaching it, she is using nonfunctional methods and materials. How can any teacher expect her students to make progress in ability actually to use the language if she uses materials and methods whereby she may even lose whatever original fluency she possesses? If I were to spend five to six hours a day theorizing in English with my students about the form and mechanics of a foreign language, or translating the same books for two to four years at a time, I might eventually find myself tongue-tied outside the verbal confines of the exercises in the basic grammar and readers, or enslaved to a stereotyped class routine as sterile and unmotivated as it would be mechanical.

The unit approach which you saw in operation this afternoon is a convenient and practical means for motivating the study of the language with timely relevant materials, and for adapting the content of the course to the interests of the students when appropriate printed materials are unavailable. Obviously, it is a *device*, not a formalized method of instruction, to be followed religiously in every class every day. It is a helpful means for keeping up one's oral ability in language, and for preventing the courses from going to seed with nonfunctional grammatical busywork or pin-wheel routine. We feel that when our students go on to college they should be able not only to hold their own successfully in advanced composition courses, but also to understand lectures in the foreign language. So far we have not been disappointed. On the contrary, most of our students have been resentful of having to enroll in upper-division college classes in which hardly a word of the foreign language is spoken.

This year we are beginning to enlist the students in our third- and fourth-year courses in the preparation of informational content units for our elementary and intermediate classes. The preparation of such units will be an integral part of the regular classwork. After the juniors and seniors have presented their units in Spanish to their respective classes and revised them according to suggestions from fellow students, they will be invited to present them to our first- and second-year classes. A limited tryout of this plan last semester yielded encouraging results. It served to provide a stimulating audience situation for the work of the advanced students and to motivate the work of the elementary classes with encouraging examples of progress in the language.

VISITOR *B*: What units do you expect to introduce after you have completed the present discussion of the Pan-American Highway?

TEACHER: That will depend upon the specific interests which the unit may arouse among the students. At the conclusion of the unit—probably on Friday—we shall invite the class to select a steering committee to work with the teacher in planning the program for the semester. On Friday we shall take time to discuss in English the significance of the Pan-American Highway for our cultural and economic relations with the Americas, and shall also ask the pupils what they would like to read, write, or talk about in Spanish this semester. If you can visit the class again then, you will see just how our course of study grows out of the needs and interests of the students. As you know, no two classes are ever exactly alike, and with the possible exception of identical twins, one rarely finds two pupils who are exactly alike either.

The Same Class Four Days Later.—The following scene shows the same class in operation four days later. Pupils *B*, *S*, and *Z* have just finished reading the résumé which they have written in Spanish on the Pan-American Highway. The pronunciation of the class is still labored at times. Cognate words that are accented differently in English seem to be the chief nuisance, despite the fact that the matter of accent has already been discussed in class in answer to a question raised by one of the students. A mechanical exercise may be necessary to fix the principle, but the need is not sufficiently great to justify such specialized drill at this time.

The teacher calls on pupil *K*, another volunteer.

Pupil *K* reads in Spanish. The teacher listens for difficulties in pronunciation—especially for deviations that would be unintelligible to a native listening to the pupil read. She makes mental

TEACHER: ¡Excelente, señorita! ¡Y muy bien leído! Gracias. Ahora, ¿quién nos hará el favor de leer su resumen? ¿Señor?

PUPIL *K*: La *Carretera* Pan-americana pasa por catorce

notes of these errors. The words in ( ) show errors in composition. The italicized letters indicate pronunciation difficulties (accent, vowel sounds, etc.).

países entre Fairbanks, Alaska, y Buenos *A*ires en (la) Argentina. (El) es la ca*r*retera más larga del mundo. En California la ruta número 101 forma parte de la ca*r*retera. El costo es (de) di*ez* mil d*ó*lares la mi*ll*a. En (el) C*a*nad*á* y en partes de (la) Am*é*rica Central la ca*r*retera no está *te*rminada. Sesenta y cuatro por ciento de la ca*r*retera está *te*rminada. Entre Santiago de Chile y *Buenos Aires* la ca*r*retera pasa sobre los *A*ndes y las Pampas de (la) Ar*g*entina.

TEACHER: Gracias, señor. ¡Muy bien hecho! I am pleased with the résumés which I have heard, and am surprised that you can pronounce Spanish as well as you do after so very short a time.

Perhaps I can help you with some of the words that seem to cause trouble. They are not so hard to pronounce as you make then out to be. Suppose we pronounce the following words three times together, like this. . . .

The teacher copies on the board the following words from the notes: *la carretera, la Argentina, la milla, terminada, dólares, el Canadá, Buenos Aires.*

The class repeats them each three times in concert. At this time no mention is made of grammatical difficulties. After the résumés have been checked for mechanical errors, the teacher will write on the board those which are common to the group as a whole, and make them the subject of special discussion prior to the correction of papers by the pupils during a workshop session of the class next week. All papers written by the class since the first day will be passed back for correction and discussion at that time. The opening of the workshop session may be preceded by a review of any notes which the pupils have taken during previous question-box discussions on such matters as accent, punctuation, gender, number, or the contractions *del* and *al*.

ENLISTING PUPIL PARTICIPATION IN CURRICULUM BUILDING

TEACHER: From what we have learned about the Pan-American Highway, what effects do you think it will have upon our relations with the other Spanish-speaking countries?

PUPIL *M*: I think it will make it possible for more Americans to visit these countries and for more of the people from there to visit us. That will make them better acquainted and more friendly.

PUPIL *B*: It will probably increase tourist travel and stimulate trade.

PUPIL *S*: More people will probably become interested in Spanish America now that there is some possibility of actually driving down there. I think it will make more people want to learn Spanish and to learn about these countries in school. I think everyone ought to learn more about Mexico and Central and South America in school instead of spending all of their time on Europe.

TEACHER: As you know, the Pan-American Highway has been open for some time as far as Mexico City. How do you suppose we could find out just how the highway is helping to change people's impressions of Mexico?

PUPIL *C*: We might see if we can find someone who has made the trip, and ask him what he thought about Mexico before and after visiting the country.

PUPIL *L*: I know a senior in school here who drove down there last summer with a couple of other fellows and they had a *swell* time. They are trying to get their folks to let them go again this year.

TEACHER: Do you suppose you could persuade them to come to class sometime soon to answer questions about their trip? (To the class) How would you like to have them talk with us?

CLASS: ¡Síiiiiiiii!

TEACHER (To pupil *L*): I wonder, then, if you would care to get in touch with them and let us know as soon as possible, so that the steering committee which we chose yesterday can reserve a date for them. We would like to know sufficiently in advance in order that we may talk over beforehand just what questions we would like to ask our visitors.

PUPIL *L*: I think I can see him tonight or tomorrow.

TEACHER: That would be splendid. Perhaps you can find out just what days he and his friends could most conveniently visit our class.

By the way, if any of you know of other people who have lived or traveled in a Spanish-speaking country, will you please inform me or a member of the steering committee? Later, we might invite some visitors who speak Spanish, and prepare a list of questions to ask them in Spanish about their experiences abroad. Please think about any possibilities between now and Monday.

Yesterday I asked the class to consider what topics of interest and importance we would like to read, write, or talk about in Spanish this semester. Have any of you any suggestions?[1]

GLORIA: I have some Mexican friends here. I'd like to learn something about their country.

WARREN: My aunt and uncle drove to Mexico last summer over the Pan-American Highway. I'd like to know something about that country, too.

JOHN: I used to live in Los Angeles. There are thousands of Mexicans there. I think we should know more about them.

TOM: I worked with some Mexicans last summer. Right here we have Mexican churches, restaurants, newspapers, and movies.

NANCY: After all, Mexico is our closest Spanish-speaking neighbor.

TEACHER: ¡Bueno! You seem to be agreed on Mexico. Mexico it shall be! Now let's see what we already know about our neighbor.

The teacher listens carefully to detect evidences of misinformation, chauvinistic bias, racial prejudices, ignorance, and habits of generalizing from inadequate bases of fact, as well as to gain insight into the cultural backgrounds, personalities, and interests of the pupils. These observations will serve as criteria for the selection of appropriate content and learning activities for the first semester. It is already evident that Pauline, Reginald, Allen, and Henry need to know Mexico and Mexicans better. In all probability, their parents do also.

JIMMY: They have *awfully* pretty music!

DOROTHY: I saw the movie *Juárez*. He was Mexico's greatest president.

PAULINE: They're dirty.

REGINALD: They're lazy. They all take *siestas*.

JOSEPHINE: I think that's a good idea. We Americans rush around too much.

WALTER: I don't think they're lazy. I worked packing fruit with some of them last summer and they work hard. They work on the railroads too.

[1] The following dramatization is adapted from "Cultural Enrichment of the Spanish Course" by permission of Rose Aviña. See Reports of the Stanford Language Arts Investigation, Vol. II, *Foreign Languages and Cultures in American Education*, W. V. Kaulfers, ed., McGraw-Hill Book Company, Inc., New York. In press.

> Besides, it's hot in many parts of Mexico.
>
> JACK: They make a lot of things by hand.
>
> ALLEN: They're always fighting and having revolutions.
>
> TEACHER: Why do you suppose they have revolutions?

ALLEN: I guess they like them.

BILL: In the picture *Juárez* they were fighting for land, and against the French.

TEACHER: Perhaps we should learn something about their past and present problems to find out *why* they have revolutions.

ALLEN: Aw, history is too *dry!*

ROSS: I've read about the early Indians in Mexico. They're sure not dry!

MARILYN: I've read about Cortez too; he was very picturesque.

WARREN: When my aunt and uncle drove down there last summer, there was a lot of poverty, especially in the villages. Lots of people didn't have very nice houses or food.

JOSEPHINE: You don't have to go to Mexico to see poverty do you? It seems to me you can find plenty of people without . . .

MARJORIE: In our social studies class last year we learned that many of Spain's problems were related to her geography. We should study the geography of Mexico.

KEITH: I read that Mexico has a high death rate.

HENRY: Maybe that's because they eat too much chile.

ALLEN: What about the oil they stole from us?

JERRY: American businessmen should stay home in the first place.

ALICE: California used to be a part of Mexico. How did it come to belong to the United States?

TEACHER: Well, now, let's write a list of questions on the board to which we would like to learn the answers. You have already suggested two questions:

The teacher writes the questions on the board in Spanish, giving the translations orally in English while doing so.

1. ¿Por qué hay revoluciones en México?
2. ¿Por qué es diferente la vida en México? What others?

Other questions relating to Mexico are written on the board *in Spanish*, and later reviewed orally in both Spanish and English. The assignment for the following day is to organize the questions into a convenient logical order or outline. Each student is asked to select one question concerning which he would be especially interested in finding information to present to the class during the semester.

TEACHER: I see that we have more questions than we can possibly find time to read, write, or talk about in Spanish this term. Next week I shall bring to class copies of a Spanish book which contains information on some of the questions. Then, too, I have a few units in Spanish on Mexico which will answer some of the questions not covered in the book. Then there are a large number of books, such as this one by Stuart Chase, called *Mexico: A Study of Two Americas*, and this one by Harry A. Frank and Herbert C. Lanks, on the Pan-American Highway.[1] Both contain valuable and interesting information. If you are interested in Mexico, it is possible that your social studies, English, art, and music teachers will be glad to have you read these books in connection with reports or compositions for their classes. Some of you may also like to read a travel book, novel, or play dealing with Mexico for your collateral reading work in English. On the bulletin board is a list of books which other students have found interesting and valuable. All books marked *E* have been approved for outside reading by the teachers of English, and all the books marked *S* have the approval of the social-studies teachers.

The teacher encourages integration and correlation with other areas of the curriculum—English, the social studies, art, and music.

Naturally, if we are to learn to speak, read, or write Spanish, we shall have to save as much of our class time as possible for books written in Spanish, but if in connection with your work in some other class you have occasion to read an interesting book, or to prepare a report dealing with some Spanish-speaking country, I hope that you will let me know. I may be able to help you find material on such topics as art, history, music, science, literature, or living conditions. Moreover, if the book or report contains material of interest to this class, we would appreciate your offering to share it with the group. I remember two very excellent talks which two first-year students of Spanish gave to the beginning Spanish class last year. One talk was a report prepared by a girl as a part of her work in art appreciation. It was an illustrated talk on Aztec, Mayan, and Inca art and architecture. The other talk was developed by a student in connection with

[1] Harry A. Frank and Herbert C. Lanks, *The Pan American Highway*, D. Appleton-Century Company, Inc., New York, 1940. Illustrated.

a course in music.   He illustrated his report with recordings by out-standing Spanish American composers, singers, and pianists.

Similar Possibilities in Other Modern Languages.—At the end of the hour visitor *B*, the only member of the original trio of observers who found it possible to return today, stops to discuss with the teacher the work that she has witnessed.

Visitor *B*: I am beginning to see how you develop your program in terms of the specific needs of a particular group of students, and to tie in their foreign-language work with their activities outside school and in other classes without neglecting the language.   If I understood you correctly, you make the foreign language serve from the start as the medium for realizing the cultural objectives of the course of study.

Teacher: Yes, everything that we do in our foreign-language classes must at least *originate* in the foreign language, except for occasional program periods—perhaps once every two weeks—when we may wish to hear interesting and timely reports developed by students in other classes, to discuss current events, or to listen to appropriate radio broadcasts in English.

Visitor *B*: Do you consider the approach to language which we witnessed last Friday equally practical in other languages?

Teacher: Yes, indeed.   All our classes in French and German, for example, are conducted on the same principles.   Naturally, the content is different.   You can readily see that if the subject of the Pan-American Highway were as appropriate to a French or German class as it is to a class in Spanish, it could be just as easily developed in either language.   For example,

Le Chemin Pan-Américain commence à Fairbanks, Alaska. Il traverse le Canada. . . . À Seattle, Washington, le Chemin Pan-Américain entre dans les États-Unis.   Dans les états de Washington, Oregon, et la Californie la route numéro 101, etc. . . .

or German:

Die Internazionale Autobahn *beginnt* in Fairbanks, Alaska, und *endet* in Buenos Aires.   In Washington, Oregon, und Kalifornien ist die Internazionale Autobahn Nummer 101.   Zwischen Alaska und Buenos Aires ist die Internazionale Auto-bahn siebzehn tausend Meilen lang. . . .

Obviously, this topic is hardly appropriate for a class in French or German.   I am merely trying to show that the *principle* is equally applicable.   Naturally, a topic that can be illustrated is easier to handle at the beginning than one that can only be transverbalized. Cognates help comprehension, of course; but if the possibilities are limited in this respect, gestures and pictorial illustrations will usually suffice. The secret at the beginning lies in choosing appropriate topics—especially topics that deal with concrete things of interest to the pupils. Later, as the pupils' background in language increases, more abstract subjects can be introduced. Some of the topics which we have developed in French and German with beginning students during the first week of instruction are

La France dans les États-Unis
Deutsche Musik: Komponisten, Opernsänger, u.s.w.

Spain and Castilian Pronunciation. VISITOR B: I noted that you used the Castilian pronunciation, even though you are starting with Spanish America rather than Spain.

TEACHER: Yes, until the pupils have acquired a sufficient background in the language to be able to spell unfamiliar words from dictation and to understand simple talks by natives, we use the Castilian pronunciation, since it eliminates most of the orthographic ambiguities raised by the confusion of the c, s, and z in Spanish America. The Castilian Spanish, as you know, is highly phonetic—which means that almost everything is pronounced as it is spelled and spelled as it is pronounced. This fact simplifies the problem of learning to write the language; for there is little or no discrepancy between the sound of a word and its visual form.

However, we feel that no one really knows Spanish until he is able to understand literate Mexicans, Cubans, Spaniards, Chileans, or Columbians as easily as an American of average intelligence can understand a literate Englishman, or a native of Texas, South Carolina, Boston, New York, Idaho, or California. The differences in pronunciation prevailing among the literate inhabitants of the Spanish-speaking people of the world are no greater than the differences prevailing among Americans in different sections of the United States.[1] Consequently, as soon as the students have acquired a background in the language, we invite to class visitors from different Spanish-speaking countries to answer questions in their native tongue; or we listen to radio broadcasts and transcriptions of short-wave radio programs to accustom our ears to variations in pronunciation. Occasionally, we even sing songs or read poems from different countries, imitating, as far as possible, the major differences in pronunciation.

[1] Millard S. L. Rosenberg, "Compatible Diversities of Spanish Pronunciation," *The Modern Language Journal*, Vol. XIX, pp. 15–22, October, 1934. Willis Knapp Jones, "What Spanish Pronunciation Shall We Teach?" *Hispania*, Vol. XXIV, pp. 253–260, October, 1941.

Naturally, we do not attempt to change the pronunciation of any pupil who comes from a Spanish-speaking home, except to improve it in terms of the norms for the country from which his parents come. Neither do we require any pupil to learn more than the Castilian pronunciation in class unless he wishes to do so; for the Castilian is the one norm of pronunciation that is understood universally. A Castilian pronunciation which would not be understood by a literate Mexican, Costa Rican, Cuban, or Bolivian would not be understood by a Spaniard either. Naturally, a Castilian pronunciation is foreign in Mexico, but no more so than the pronunciation of a Mexican from Sonora is foreign to that of a Mexican from Guerrero. Somehow, the pronunciation problem has been unduly magnified in Spanish teaching. It is really no more serious than the pronunciation problem in German, French, Italian, or English, in which equally great, if not greater, regional variations occur. I think we should spend less time worrying about differences in pronunciation and devote more time to helping students learn some Spanish worth pronouncing!

VISITOR *B*: Are you going to make a special study of Spain in the same way that you are taking up Mexico this semester?

TEACHER: Spain will form the background for reference and for comparison and contrast throughout our study of the Americas this year. We shall have occasion to refer to Spain constantly in order to understand the architecture, religion, customs, music, and history of Mexico, as well as the language and cultural antecedents of the people. Last year, for example, the pupils wanted to know about bullfighting in Mexico in connection with a unit on *La vida recreativa en México*. In developing this unit we traced the origin of the bull-fight back to the Roman and Moorish invasions of Spain, and discussed similarities and differences between bullfighting as carried on in Mexico and in the mother country. I think the students who were in the class still remember the *Cid* as being not only the national hero of Spain, but also as probably being the first knight to ride a horse during a *corrida* at a time when the sport was the exclusive prerogative of the Spanish nobility.

Spain, as a historical and geographical unit, is studied in connection with the reading of Spanish novels, short stories, and plays in advanced classes. As a sphere of cultural influence, however, the mother country pervades all our teaching. We find it undesirable to start the study of Spanish with a land remote in time and space from the present-day lives of most Americans, and from the prospective future lives of the pupils in our schools. It seems a little absurd to start with a country which is thousands of miles across the Atlantic when in school the children are often seated next to boys and girls from Mexican homes. Moreover, most of our beginning textbooks about Spain mention little of importance, anyway. So little information of interest or significance is contained in the reading lessons about the people in the places mentioned that, as far as the pupils are concerned, they might as well be people and places in *Moronia Antigua*. To encourage the study of Spanish because of the opportunities open to enterprising young Americans in Central and South America, and then to hide in Old Spain for the duration of the course, is to be guilty of misrepresentation.

We are confident that our approach in Spanish is in keeping with the following resolution unanimously passed by the National Convention of the American Association of Teachers of Spanish in New York City on Dec. 28, 1935:[1]

WHEREAS, Interest in the Spanish-speaking peoples of the Americas is one of the chief reasons for the study of the Spanish language in the United States, and

WHEREAS, The promotion of mutual understanding among the republics of the Western Hemisphere is an important aim of the Spanish curriculum in secondary education,

Therefore Be It Resolved, That the American Association of Teachers of Spanish recommend a greater emphasis upon Spanish American culture, preferably at levels of schooling where it will reach the maximum number of students.

EPILOGUE

It's Work, but It's Fun.—It is the last day of the semester. Eighteen weeks have passed, and some important changes have gradually been taking place in the lives of the boys and girls since they began their study of Spanish with the unit on the Pan-American Highway. Some of the boys' voices have changed. One lad has grown at least an inch, and now carefully grooms the hair which but a few months ago fell unkempt over his forehead. Josephine, who now uses eyebrow pencils and dainty touches of rouge and lipstick, is probably the responsible party. The work on Mexico and Central America has been full of interest to the class. Their progress in Spanish has been gradual but substantial. As a group they passed the *Cooperative Spanish Test*[2] with above-average achievement in reading and

[1] Formulated, and introduced by Walter V. Kaulfers in collaboration with Elsie I. Jamieson. See p. 7 of "The Nineteenth Annual Meeting," *Hispania*, Vol. XIX, pp. 1–8, February, 1936.

[2] The Cooperative Test Service of the American Council on Education, 15 Amsterdam Ave., New York.

vocabulary and without falling below the first-semester norm for grammar. On the cultural information test they did themselves credit. Their teacher was also pleased with their standing on the race-attitudes scales.[1] There were no negative comments during the semester about "those awful irregular verbs" or "What good does all that grammar stuff do you?" A survey made by the school office showed that a large majority of the class ranked the study of Spanish among their favorite subjects.

The teacher is happiest, however, over the responsible role which she has been able to play, along with other teachers, in helping these growing young people to achieve wholesome, integrated personalities— to become human beings capable of thinking with their heads rather than with their prejudices, capable of tolerating and evaluating other points of view, capable of living well-balanced, socially useful lives, capable of living creatively. She is proud of such evidences of growth in this direction as she has witnessed in so short a time, though she is not presumptuous enough to assume that this growth is attributable to her class alone. Occasionally, however, a scene such as the following causes her to feel that she has had at least a small share in the process, especially when she compares the caustic remarks which Pauline, Reginald, Allen, and Henry made about Mexico early in the semester, with their unsolicited comments today.

The group have just returned from an assembly program where they listened to students from an advanced Spanish class discuss the good-neighbor policy in relation to Latin America. Since all books and papers have already been turned in, the teacher decides to let the students discuss the topic for the duration of the short-period class schedule before school is dismissed at noon:[2]

TEACHER: What did you think about the program?

ALLEN: Swell! ¡Excelente! ¡Muy bueno!

WARREN: Sí, muy interesante.

PAULINE: We learned a lot of things.

TEACHER: ¿Qué cosas?

PAULINE: Well, I've heard a lot about Pan-Americanism over the radio lately, but I never realized there were *twenty-one* separate countries in the Union before.

[1] H. H. Remmers and H. H. Grice, *Scale for Measuring Attitude toward Any National or Racial Group*, Division of Educational Research, Purdue University, 1934, Lafayette, Ind.

[2] The following dramatization is adapted from "Cultural Enrichment of the Spanish Course," *op. cit.*, by permission of Rose Aviña, George Washington High School, San Francisco, Calif.

HENRY: Sí, y el Brasil es más grande que los Estados Unidos, y tiene casi tantos habitantes como Francia.

REGINALD: Sí, y el Uruguay (the smallest country in South America) es más grande que Inglaterra.

MARILYN: ¿Cuántos países hablan español?

TEACHER: Pues, vamos a ver. Fíjense Uds. en el mapa: Aquí está *el Brasil*. En el Brasil se habla portugués. Luego hay las tres Guayanas en donde se habla inglés, holandés, y francés. En los demás países se habla español. Cuéntenlos Uds.: El Paraguay, el Uruguay, la Argentina, Chile, el Perú, Bolivia, el Ecuador, Colombia, y Venezuela. ¿Cuántos?

ALICE: Nueve.

TEACHER: Y en el Mar de las Antillas: Cuba y Santo Domingo. En Haití no se habla mucho el español. El idioma principal es el francés. Bueno, ¿cuántos hasta ahora?

PAULINE: Once.

HENRY: ¿Y Puerto Rico?

MARJORIE: Sí, pero Puerto Rico es una parte de los Estados Unidos, ¿no? We learned that in social studies.

TEACHER: Ud. tiene razón. Ahora, echemos una ojeada al mapa de la América Central. Se habla español en todos los países de Centroamerica. ¿Cuáles son?

REGINALD: Hay seis: Panamá, Costa Rica, Nicaragua, Honduras, el Salvador, y Guatemala; y con México, siete.

TEACHER: Muy bien. Entonces, ¿cuántos países?

WARREN: Son *dieciocho*.

TEACHER: Sí, *hay* dieciocho países en que se habla español.

PAULINE: ¿Dieciocho? Eighteen Spanish-speaking countries to the south of us? Gee!

HENRY: Guess that's why the old *español* is kind of important.

NANCY: I wish we knew as much about all these countries as we do about Mexico and Central America now!

TEACHER: How would you like to learn something about these other countries?

CLASS: ¡Me gusta! Swell! Sure! ¡Como no! ¡Buena idea! ¡Magnífico! Can I draw some maps? Can we make reports? I've got some records. Can I bring them to play? What books are we going to read? I can get a movie from the Pan-American Airways! Can we show it at school? ¡Síiiiiii!

TEACHER: And what did you learn about Mexico that makes you want to know about the other Spanish-speaking countries?

PAULINE: We've learned that because of the geography and climate there is little water in the north, and that only a small per cent of the land can be cultivated. So the people often have a very hard time to make a living.

NANCY: The poverty among some of the people leads to a high death rate and to unrest, too.

ALLEN: We've studied the Mexican-American War and know that the Mexicans didn't like us for a long time because we invaded their country and took Texas, Arizona, New Mexico, California, Nevada, and parts of Oklahoma and Colorado from them.

KEITH: Yes, but we also know that this feeling is disappearing, partly owing to Roosevelt's good-neighbor policy.

HENRY: They're still kind of mad about our attitude on the oil question, though.

MARY: Yes, but that expropriation was mostly of British holdings. The Mexican government has already settled with one American company.

ALLEN: There was a lot of justice to their side of the question, too.

WALTER: Now we understand some of the causes of their long revolution, such as the 300-year Spanish domination, the mixture of races, their great poverty and oppression.

JIMMY: Yes, and the large landholdings.

BILL: Cárdenas tried to solve Mexico's problems by his six-year plan. It stresses land distribution, education, and public works such as roads and irrigation.

CAROL: And health and housing, too.

PAULINE: I wonder if Camacho will carry on this plan?

TOM: That is the greatest problem facing Mexico today.

NANCY: I think the most important thing we've learned from Mexico this semester is to be more tolerant, and not judge other people until we know them better.

JOSEPHINE: (Class bell rings.) Is that the bell already? ¡Qué lástima!

"Wish all my courses were like this," remarked Allen as he went out the door. "Yo, también," agreed Henry. "It's work, but it's fun!"

The teacher smiled. She thought so too.[1]

[1] For a specialized bibliography on the teaching of foreign languages to young children (4 to 10 years of age) see Appendix, references 134–140. For a select bibliography on the teaching of non-English-speaking students, see Appendix, references 131–133. For bibliography of teaching aids, see Appendix, references 59–199.

CHAPTER VIII

PERSPECTIVE ON EXTRACURRICULAR ACTIVITIES

If the school cannot give more vital experiences than the child can get anywhere else in the world, it has no valid claim upon his time.

—W. FRANKLIN JONES

What the best and wisest parent wants for his own child, that must be the community want for all its children.

—JOHN DEWEY

Extracurricular Activities as a Bridge between the School and Life.—The effort to bridge the gap between school and life began with the introduction of clubs and other forms of extracurricular activities into the educational program.[1] A reading of Wilds's *Extracurricular Activities* (1926) reveals the optimism with which educators of nearly two decades ago regarded these means for vitalizing the work of the school. Practical difficulties, such as the overloading of teachers and the problem of scheduling suitable activity periods, however, caused enthusiasm to wane in favor of other solutions. Although experimentation with the extracurricular program served to demonstrate the effectiveness of these activities as educative resources, the mechanical difficulties involved were often sufficiently great to nullify their potential values for young people who needed the experiences most—those who could not attend meetings during out-of-school hours or those who had never had the opportunity to develop extracurricular interests, either in school or at home, because the work of the classroom seldom had anything to do with what normal people find pleasurable and profitable avocations in real life. An extracurricular program cannot be effective as a bridge between school and life without a secure foundation on which to anchor the bridge in the classwork of the pupils.

Extracurricular Enrichment of the Foreign-language Course.—The realization of this difficulty in the curriculum of the school led to the gradual incorporation of vitalizing extracurricular activities into the regular classwork. Although the term "extracurricular" is still used

[1] E. H. Wilds, *Extra-curricular Activities*, D. Appleton-Century Company, Inc., New York, 1926, xi + 273 pp. Harry C. McKown, *Extracurricular Activities*, New York, 1927, xxi + 617 pp. Revised ed. 1937, xvi + 734 pp.

to designate certain organized activities that extend beyond the physical and social environment of the classroom or school, they are now almost universally considered integral parts of the curriculum and on a par with book learning in educative value. The ideal toward which frontier workers in education are now working is that of motivating the acquisition of core information and basic skills by organizing the learning program in terms of activities that have their counterpart in the effective social-civic and cultural life of the community, or which the school could help develop as its contribution to community life and culture.[1]

The manner in which this ideal is being realized in the foreign languages today varies with the environmental circumstances that affect the teacher's work. Classes are sometimes organized on the club basis, and biweekly meetings held on class time when programs prepared by committees of students as part of their regular classwork can be presented before the entire group and visitors from other classes. This procedure represents an almost complete integration of the extracurricular with the curricular activities of the foreign-language program, and has proved an effective solution in schools that make no provision for club meetings on school time or in which the enrollment in any one language is limited. The mechanics of conducting such a unified program have already been discussed in considerable detail in Chapter VI.

Since one of the chief functions of extracurricular activities is to bridge the gap between life and the classroom, the complete integration of club work with classwork is destructive of its own ends if the activities do not extend beyond the mental or physical confines of the class or school. The value of a club organization capitalizing the services of responsible student officers is often in making the mechanical arrangements for excursions, for the use of the auditorium and other special facilities, for publicity or advertising, and for the management, under supervision, of finances. Teachers and sponsors of clubs who assume all these responsibilities often deprive young prople of the opportunity to develop a sense of responsibility. Instead, they overburden themselves with tasks which, under guidance, boys and girls can learn to perform with real personal satisfaction when they feel that the club belongs to them rather than to the teacher.

Among the activities that language clubs have sponsored with success in secondary schools are the following:

[1] Paul R. Hanna, *Youth Serves the Community*, D. Appleton-Century Company, Inc., New York, 1936, xiv + 303 pp.; pp. 3–20 and *passim*.

A research committee contributes to plans for a class-written dramatization of the history of Mexico for the school assembly. (*Courtesy of the Manual Arts High School, Los Angeles.*)

Costumes, scenery, stage-settings, Spanish script, and acting are the products of student-initiated reading, writing, and discussion in Spanish and English. (*Courtesy of the Stanford Language Arts Investigation.*)

1. Plays, pageants, amateur moving pictures, and puppet shows written, translated, or adapted by foreign-language classes or club-members for presentation before school and community audiences. (University High School, Westwood, Los Angeles; Allen High School, New Orleans; Wenatchee High School, Washington.)

2. Moving-picture programs presented for school or community audiences. (Pasadena High School and Junior College, Pasadena, Calif., Sullivan High School, Chicago Ill.)

3. Foreign-language community sings open to the public. (Palo Alto High School, Calif.)

4. Lectures and illustrated talks on select aspects of foreign life and culture by observant travelers or foreign-born citizens. (Long Beach Junior College, Long Beach, Calif., Phoenix Union High School, Arizona.)

5. Excursions to places of interest in the vicinity. (Livermore Union High School, Calif., Oakdale Elementary School, La.)

6. Fairs and fiestas to raise money with which to buy special materials and equipment for the foreign-language department outside the budget of the school, or to send delegates to such regional conventions as those of the Pan American Student Forum. (Palo Alto High School, Calif., Roosevelt High School, Des Moines.)

7. Opera and theater parties. (Jefferson Union High School, Daly City, Calif., Westside High School, Newark, N. J.)

8. Publication of student bulletins or newspapers. (Los Angeles High School, Calif., Booneville High School, N. Y.)

9. Publication of translations made by students of interesting literary or historical materials not available in English. (McClatchy High School, Sacramento, Calif.)

10. Translation bureaus to facilitate international correspondence on the part of any individual in the school or community. (Sequoia Union High School, Redwood City, Calif.)

11. Social meetings to develop a friendly *esprit de corps* among students and between students and teachers. (Los Angeles City Junior College, Calif., Pacific University, Oregon.)

12. "Adoption" of underprivileged foreign-born children in the community, or of refugee children abroad. (Manual Arts High School, Los Angeles, Calif.)

13. Assembly programs in commemoration of important anniversaries such as Pan-American Day (April 14) or *El Día de la Raza* (October 12). (New York City Schools, Fargo Senior High School, N. D.)

14. Provision of coaching services for students absent because of illness, etc.

15. Short-wave listening posts for radio communication with amateur radio enthusiasts, and for important foreign broadcasts. (Pupils with recording machines can often make electric transcriptions for club or class use.)

16. Folk dancing and hobby workshops. (Evanston Township High School, Ill.)

17. Competitions and contests. (The University High School, Carbondale, Ill.)

18. International contests, *e.g.*, athletic contests between Mexican and American teams. (Long Beach Junior College, Calif.)

Prerequisites to an Effective Extracurricular Program.—Clubs that are guided in these directions and closely correlated with the activities and needs of the community, school, and classroom, usually develop in time into strong and effective organizations. Granting the need for the provision of opportunities outside of class for hearing and speaking the language, this need can usually be filled by voluntary section meetings for interested members, rather than by subordinating the entire plan and purpose of the extracurricular program to the linguistic objective. Clubs that spend most of their time playing language games usually degenerate into social meetings for teachers' pets—especially if eligibility is limited to pupils with high grades in their foreign-language classes. It is doubtful if specific standards of academic attainment should be made the basis of participation except on the part of candidates for club officers. Even here the ability to sense and fulfill responsibilities is an equally important qualification. Fortunately, the two prerequisites are closely correlated.

The following principles are frequently mentioned by writers on club activities as essential to the building of a strong *esprit de corps* among students:[1]

1. Faculty sponsors capable of guiding young people without dominating or depriving the pupils of a personal sense of responsibility for their own organization.

[1] Ruth Strang, *Group Activities in College and Secondary School*, Harper & Brothers, New York, 1941, xvi + 361 pp. C. K. Fretwell, *Extracurricular Activities in Secondary Schools*, Houghton Mifflin Company, Boston, 1931. E. H. Wilds, *Extra-curricular Activities*, D. Appleton-Century Company, Inc., New York, xvi + 273 pp. C. V. Millar, *The Organization and Administration of Extracurricular Activities*, A. S. Barnes & Co., New York, 1930.

2. A conviction among students that the organization is their own and that it has the interested support of faculty members.

3. A unifying purpose, defined and accepted by the membership, that will give continuous direction to the work of the club over a considerable period of time.   Many of the activities suggested above lend themselves to a constructive long-range activity program.

4. Cooperative participation or affiliation with clubs in other communities.   A feeling of identity with a youth organization which enlists the participation of young people of like age in the service of a constructive objective often helps to build club morale, and to guide the adolescent mind into the social stream of the world.   Organizations such as the International Student Forum, The Pan American Student League, the Pan American Student Forum, and the Pan American League[1] provide opportunities for the development of a feeling of unity among young people of secondary-school age in different parts of the Western Hemisphere.   The notion that young people within four years of voting age can learn to participate effectively in community, state, or national life without opportunity to contact the present-day world outside the classroom, is no longer tenable in an era when the clash and death struggle of armies on different continents, or the pronouncements of dictators, can be heard in almost every home in America.   By keeping alive in the minds and hearts of young people within the Western Hemisphere the spirit of cooperative action for the common good, foreign-language teachers can help prevent the disappearance at home of the democratic way of life which the nation is endeavoring desperately to revive abroad.   The extent to which such a benign effort on the part of teachers may meet with apathetic indifference may well be accepted as a sign that American life has begun to disintegrate far behind its front-line defenses—because the graduates of the schools rarely had the opportunity to discuss or investigate in the classroom any of the vital problems on which as citizens they are expected to express an intelligent opinion either directly in voting on issues, or indirectly in voting for candidates for office whose stand on important issues is known and understood.

Although small schools may find it necessary to provide for club activities within the scope of the regular classwork,[2] schools with large

[1] International Student Forum, 521 Phelan Building, San Francisco, Calif. The Pan American Student League, Board of Education, New York.   The (Junior) Pan American League, Board of Education, Dallas, Tex.   Pan American Student Forum, Yuba City Union High School, Calif.

[2] Elsa M. Tyndall, "Intracurricular Spanish Clubs," *Hispania*, Vol. XXII, pp. 240–242, October, 1939.

foreign-language enrollments cannot afford to forego the opportunity to supplement the intraclass activities with a strong extracurricular organization in which special committees or sections are charged with fulfilling different responsibilities within the framework of the unifying purpose of the club. In such cases, the extracurricular program requires the active attention of all foreign-language teachers at regular departmental meetings if it is to succeed; for the creative efforts of a group of enthusiastic students and their faculty sponsor can easily be sabotaged by the apathetic indifference of teachers lacking insight into the purposes, activities, and values of the organization.

Some Outstanding Extracurricular Programs.—Although effective extracurricular programs are in existence in many schools which have not reported their work in professional journals, the number of articles dealing with successful club projects is sufficiently large to indicate an increasing appreciation among foreign-language teachers of the potential-values of club activities as educative resources for vitalizing and motivating the language-arts curriculum. Among the schools that have reported successful ways and means for capitalizing the extracurricular interests of young people the following deserve special mention:

The Evander Childs High School, New York City.[1]—The first Pan American Club was organized in the James Monroe High School in New York City in September, 1930, and the second in the DeWitt Clinton High School, New York, a year later. By 1932 nineteen schools, including the Evander Childs High School, had joined to form the Pan American Student League which soon evoked appreciative comments in both the United States and Latin America. The superintendent of schools in New York City then requested that all schools implement through education the nation's Pan American good-neighbor policy. In 1939 a Council on Pan American Activities was formed in the Evander Child's High School, which decided to plan activities, not as the effort of the Spanish department alone, but as the joint project of a number of departments. Together all departments observed Pan-American Day, and the week of April 14 was proclaimed Pan-American Week. The Spanish, accounting, art, English, Latin, health-education, mathematics, mechanical arts, music, biology, homemaking, physical science, secretarial training, social science, and speech departments undertook special Pan-American programs. One group of Spanish students contributed a joint letter

[1] Joshua Hochstein, "Inter-American Education at Evander Childs High School," *High Points*, Vol. XXII, pp. 54–65, September, 1940.

of greeting to the students of Hispanic American countries.   The Pan-American program of the Evander Childs High School embodies the philosophy of the Superintendent of Schools of New York City:

The most effective way . . . of making sure that "it can't happen here" is to lead the children of today to know and esteem the other Americans with whose present and future destiny our own is inextricably woven, and with whom our youth of today must collaborate tomorrow in maintaining intercontinental peace, amity, and solidarity.

The Yuba City Union High Schools, Calif.[1]—In January, 1935, the Spanish Club of the Yuba Union High School affiliated itself with the Pan American Student Forum as Chapter 22.   Previous to that time there had been no chapter west of El Paso, Tex.   Through the initiative of this active and enthusiastic group of young people the movement rapidly spread to neighboring high schools.   In March, 1936, the Spanish students of the Yuba City Union High School were the hosts to delegates from nine high schools for the first state convention of the Pan American Student Forum in California.   The following report written for *Hispania* by the state President, Edwin McLaughlin, then a student in the Yuba City High School, gives a brief account of the second two-day state convention held in Yuba City in 1938:

The guest speakers were Dr. Hubert Phillips of Fresno State College and the Honorable Bolívar Aviles Alfaro, Consul General of Ecuador.   The convention opened with the Mexican-made movie, *Allá en el Rancho Grande* on Friday afternoon, and an informal get-together in the evening.   The main session, open to the public, was held the following morning.   Dr. Phillips spoke on "A Changing Monroe Doctrine" and explained President Roosevelt's good-neighbor policy to cover the present attitude of the United States toward the Latin-American nations.   Supplementing Dr. Philips' viewpoint, Señor Aviles Alfaro told the delegates of the feeling towards the Monroe Doctrine in South America.   He also discussed the seizure of oil lands by the Mexican government.   Before concluding his address the speaker told many interesting things about Ecuador, his native land.

The convention was judged a great success by the 150 delegates representing 12 different high schools.   The week following the convention Chico High School was granted its charter as Chapter 51.

The work of the Spanish Club of the Yuba Union High School is an excellent illustration of the constructive leadership which an active foreign-language club, located in an agricultural area, can exercise on a state-wide basis.

[1] Walter V. Kaulfers, "Along the Foreign Language Frontier," *Hispania*, Vol. XXI, pp. 214–215, October, 1938.

The McClatchy Senior High School, Sacramento, Calif.—During the school year, 1940–1941, 16 members of the Spanish club *Los Hispanistas*, in the McClatchy Senior High School, Sacramento, cooperated with students enrolled in art, printing, and book-binding classes to publish a translation (from Spanish) of Ms. E67, No. 3, by Enrique Cerruti, from the Bancroft Library of the University of California. This appeared in a limited edition of 125 copies, under the title *Narrative of Guillermo Fitch and Blas Piña.* The work was done voluntarily outside of class as a club activity without course credits of any kind. The actual division of the work was made at a club meeting conducted by the president, who happened to be one of the 16 members who volunteered to work on the project. The manuscript was divided into eight parts, thus making it possible for two individuals to collaborate on each unit. The participating students, most of whom had completed at least two years of Spanish, borrowed dictionaries from the school to take home. Three members of the club worked over the translations after they had all been turned in and made revisions where necessary. The completed work was checked by the faculty sponsor, Miss Saima Regina Koski, as consulting editor, before being turned over to the print shop for publication. The historical notes that document the translation were written by one of the translators working under the guidance of his social-studies teacher. No grades or credits were awarded for this work since it represented a project which the students themselves considered interesting and worth while, as the following excerpt from the *Foreword*, written by the club president, indicates:

The Narrative of Guillermo Fitch and Blas Piña is a story of California in the days preceding the coming of the Yankees. Fitch and Piña reveal life as seen through the eyes of the *Californianos*. Fitch's father was an American and his mother a member of California's famous Carrillo family. Piña, the uncle of Fitch, throws light upon California's domination by the Americans.

With our translation we have included the Spanish text, following the original as closely as possible, with spelling and grammar just as in the manuscript itself.

The book has been an enjoyable undertaking for those who have participated in its making. We have done our best; and realizing our shortcomings as students, we humbly present this, our contribution to the history of California.[1]

[1] The Nugget Press, C. K. McClatchy High School, Sacramento, Calif., 1941, x + 35 pp.

The Bennett Junior High School, Piqua, Ohio.[1]—Although the Bennett Junior High School does not offer courses in Spanish, it has experimented successfully with a Spanish club for ninth-grade boys and girls who have never studied the language. For this reason the extracurricular program of the school is significantly indicative of possibilities in other communities and in other languages. Experience with this type of club has proved its value in creating interest in foreign languages and cultures. A part of the meeting is usually devoted to the use of practical foreign words and phrases, and the remainder to the reading in translation of short stories and excerpts from famous books, or to singing songs and listening to good music. All the activities involve a discussion of the life and times of the writers or composers.

The Porterville High School and Junior College, California.—The integration of classwork with extracurricular activities has perhaps been achieved more successfully in Porterville than in any other community of like size. Anita Risdon, sponsor of the club in 1939, wrote,

Vitality of the language experience in class prevents linguistic poverty. In Porterville we have Spanish for lunch on Fridays. Coming is voluntary and there is no appeasement diplomacy with grades. Another group publishes a Spanish paper and puts news in Spanish in the school sheet. Thursdays a Spanish motion picture appeals to others. The film is advertised in class the day before and reviewed the day after. Student's questions on why the hero did or didn't, or why the audience laughed, develop into comparisons and criticisms if one is wise enough not to pounce on the offending verb in their questions for being foolishly out of tense. The Spanish club offers parties with games in Spanish, gives a yearly dance, and sponsors programs of songs, plays, and folk dancing for school assemblies, Patron's Days, the P.T.A. carnival and dinner, and for down-town organizations. Exhibits, a reading table of publications in Spanish, and bulletin boards are arranged. Some students correspond with young people of Mexico and South America. A listening schedule of radio programs in Spanish is popular with a few. Certain holidays are observed and on *Los lunes culturales* easy reports relay interesting material picked up in books, magazines, and over the radio.

[At the elementary and intermediate levels] the aim is not grammatical correctness but adequate communication, expression clear enough to be understood. The essential growth in confidence comes only when correction is done in terms of what the traffic will bear, when pleasure in getting the idea across, and not frustration at forgetting some concordance, is the result of those early efforts. . . . There is no evidence here of the pedagogical passion

[1] Nancy J. Simpkinson, "A New Kind of Spanish Club," *The Modern Language Journal*, Vol. XXIII, pp. 168–171, December, 1938.

to compensate for not beginning the teaching of foreign languages early enough, nor continuing them long enough, which usually makes a brutally hard ball of compactly organized analytical detail that is thrown with (drilled) force and precision into the unsuspecting hands of the student, who had just thought it would be fun to talk Spanish. His is really a noble sentiment, and it should be permitted to condition every method—even one based on use![1]

Junior High School, No. 73, Queens, N. Y.[2]—The success of the community sing sponsored by the foreign-language club in Junior High School, No. 73, is suggestive of possibilities in other languages besides German. In 1938, Max Leive wrote,

We attempted a "community sing." The immediate aim was not only to bring well-known songs to the pupils, but also to have them sing with us. . . . Mimeographed sheets were distributed in the assembly, and on these the pupils found the text of *Ach, du lieber Augustin, Wiegenlied* by Brahms, and the popular *Schnitzelbank*. On the stage not only members of the club, but also many pupils of the various German classes, regardless of their academic standing, first set the melody. These pupils knew the text and melodies from their classwork, their club work, and practice with our music teacher. . . . The procedure was as follows: An English summary of the first song was given; the poem was translated, the words were read in German; the pupils on the stage sang the song; and finally it was sung in German by the assembly of pupils. They enjoyed the first song so much it was sung twice. A similar plan was followed for the *Wiegenlied*. For the *Schnitzelbank* the pupils on the stage displayed large drawings on which the German for the pictures appeared: *Schnitzelbank, Kurz und Lang, Geissenbock, Winterrock*, etc. The pupils enjoyed this song very much because of the humorous nature of the drawings.

The foreign-language community sing provides not only an active form of pupil participation, but also a strong incentive to the pupils to know more about foreign languages and cultures. The success of this form of extracurricular motivation is attested also by the experience of other schools. The Palo Alto (Calif.) High School, for example, has from time to time invited townspeople to participate in foreign-language community sings held in the evening. The advantages of developing a favorable rapport between the school and the community hardly require comment. Moreover, the motivation that a community audience provides for the work of the classroom is as

[1] Anita Ridson, "Alternative to Waste in Teaching Spanish," *California Journal of Secondary Education*, Vol. XIV, pp. 230–231, April, 1939.

[2] Max Leive, "The Foreign Language Community Sing," *High Points*, Vol. XX, pp. 61–62, March, 1938.

important a factor in language learning as in other fields of the curriculum. This motivation is often greater if the pupils are given the opportunity to play a leadership role in an informal group activity such as the community sing. Music departments are usually delighted to cooperate.

Integrating Curricular and Extracurricular Interests. The Bronxville Experiment.—The extent to which the integration of extracurricular with curricular activities can motivate and enrich the foreign-language program is demonstrated by the work of the Bronxville schools in French and music:

The study of French is started in the seventh grade by those pupils who by their elementary school record gave evidence of ability to undertake the study of a foreign language. During the first year the pupil sings and becomes familiar with a large number of folksongs, many of which are memorized. These simple folksongs have a double value in the teaching of elementary French. They present a vocabulary of practical, workaday words in vivid combinations and stories that appeal to the imagination of the youngsters. In the first year of French more time is spent in the singing of songs than in listening to music. The children often enjoy dancing and dramatizing these songs. The physical activity involved provides a healthy and profitable outlet for the nervous energy which is so abundant in the adolescent. At the end of the first year the pupils have a definite sense of achievement. Their knowledge of and familiarity with a large repertoire of folksongs serves as a rich background for further study.

In the second year there is an increasing interest in the stories and music of the operas. *Carmen, Faust, Samson et Dalila, Les Contes d'Hoffmann,* and *Mignon* provide an abundance of material of the most consuming interest and value. There are many airs and choruses which can be sung in unison and by rote if necessary without becoming too involved musically. . . . In Bronxville we are able to take groups of pupils to the Metropolitan Opera House in New York where they may see and hear French operas sung by some of the world's finest artists. This experience is a liberal education that gives new meaning and purpose to the necessary routine of classroom work.

In the third year French the student is introduced to some of the simpler art songs of Debussy, Fauré, and Ravel. This is a new adventure and leads to a study of the poetry which has inspired the music. . . . The work that is done during the first two years in French prepares the pupil to listen to and enjoy music in the production of which he is not actively engaged. This enables him to include in his repertoire of art songs many which are too difficult for classroom singing.[1] Much time is given to French instrumental

[1] Many teachers have found the verse-speaking choir technique, with musical accompaniment, admirably adapted to art songs which are difficult for untrained voices. See Nina Lee Weisinger, "Choric Treatment of Spanish-American

music and its development during the past centuries. . . . In our aim to develop cultured American citizens with an appreciation and understanding of the cultures and civilizations of other peoples, we dare not neglect the arts, for it is through these mediums that races and nations express themselves.

The enrichment of the three-year French program in Bronxville has been made possible through the close collaboration of the music and foreign-language departments.[1]

The Student Newspaper.—Many schools have found the student-written newspaper an effective means for capitalizing the extra-curricular interests of students in the service of foreign-language study.[2] Noteworthy examples are the Los Angeles High School and the Jamaica High School, New York. Harry C. Theobald of the Los Angeles High School wrote in 1937:

> For over ten years, our paper has been read by some five hundred students each semester, and has gone out to several other schools. We find ourselves now in the middle, almost, of our eleventh year of continuous publication, a record, we believe, not approached by any high school foreign-language paper west of the Rockies and second only to our Latin paper the *Nuntius*, which preceded *El Romano* by several years. Since our struggles with the first number, we have come out eight or nine times each semester. . . . We feel that our Spanish paper is a real help to the students in several ways. In the first place, it puts the study of the language in a more practical light, giving the student an immediate use for his knowledge of Spanish. . . . The appearance of a new issue of *El Romano* is always an event which brightens the Spanish hour for a considerable body of our students.[3]

The mechanics of publishing a successful student news magazine are discussed by Seymour Janovsky of the Jamaica High School. Because the language students found it insufficient to publish only a once-a-term magazine, they devised a plan to run a series of biweekly language publications:

Poetry," *Hispania*, Vol. XXII, pp. 251–253, October, 1939. Anna Balakian, "Choral Reading and the Foreign Languages," *High Points*, Vol. XXI, pp. 63–67, December, 1939. Richard B. Lewis and Holland D. Roberts, "The Director's Part in the Verse Speaking Choir," *Quarterly Journal of Speech*, Vol. XXIII, pp. 63–66, February, 1937; "Foundations of the School Verse-speaking Choir," *California Journal of Secondary Education*, Vol. XI, pp. 98–100, February, 1936.

[1] Willard Rhodes, "The Use of Music in the Teaching of French," *The French Review*, Vol. XI, pp. 37–43, October, 1937. See also Appendix D.

[2] Anita Risdon, "*Hoy Dia*—Publishing a School Paper in Spanish," *Hispania*, Vol. XIX, pp. 361–367, October, 1936.

[3] Harry C. Theobald, *The Modern Language Forum*, Vol. XXII, pp. 52–55, February, 1937.

A representative was appointed for each class. It became his duty to collect articles on class activities from his fellow students. . . . Cartoonists have been enlisted from the various classes and language students with art experience contribute the headlines. Typing students rotate in cutting the stencils and prepare the paper for mimeographing by Friday morning. Up to this point we have succeeded in activating the entire class; we have helped pupils to branch out from the set forms of grammatical translation to creative work. In addition, we have stimulated them towards using talents developed in other classes, which otherwise might lie fallow.[1]

It will be noted that the most successful club programs are those in which the extracurricular and curricular activities are integrated in terms of a unifying objective that welds the work of the classroom with real life and provides the pupils with someone to write or talk to besides the teacher. The integration of classwork with important club activities usually offers a practical solution to the problem of overloading, from which teachers who attempt to isolate extracurricular activities from curricular activities usually suffer. Complaints of overloading are usually symptomatic of two difficulties: Either the teacher is depriving the students of the opportunity to grow in ability to sense and shoulder responsibilities by dominating rather than guiding the club work, or the work of the club is conducted as something entirely separate from, or additional to, the regular classwork. In either case, the probability is strong that the basic purpose of the extracurricular program—that of bridging the gap between the school and life—is being defeated, and that the school is losing an opportunity to make a contribution to the effective cultural life of the community as it is, or as it might desirably be. If this purpose is kept constantly in mind as an operational principle, the foreign-language program can be motivated and enriched with gains rather than losses in any of the linguistic abilities which are of any consequence to anyone in real life— and without imposing excessive burdens upon the teacher.

The supercilious criticism often directed against extracurricular activities as being artificial "fads and frills" may at times be justified when aimed at clubs which are little more than parlor-game societies for teacher's "pets," but as a generic condemnation of the entire extracurricular program it bespeaks a lamentable ignorance of the philosophy of education and supporting psychology of learning which underlie the movement. In many cases it springs from the negative

[1] Seymour Janovsky, "A New Type of Activity Program for Modern Language Students," *High Points* (Board of Education, New York City), Vol. XX, pp. 51–53, November, 1938.

conception of life and learning inherited from the Middle Ages.   The notion that nothing that is learned with interest or personal satisfaction can possibly be as educative as something dull or distasteful learned with pain is fast being discarded into the dustbin of the past.   The truth of the matter is that nothing learned *without* interest or personal satisfaction is likely to be used after the pupils are released from their last required exercises in pencil pushing and vocabulary thumbing—to enjoy the opportunity of thumbing their noses at the exercises, the textbooks, and the teacher.   The emphasis in education today is on the development of human beings who will *live what they learn*—not just render lip service to their ideals.   This emphasis merely represents a growing realization of the fact that education through intimidation, whether in the form of the rod or in the form of grades, credits, or examinations, is often destructive of its own ends; for "there is nothing like alluring the appetite and the affections; otherwise you make nothing but so many asses laden with books, and by dint of your lash, you give them their pocketful of learning to keep; whereas, to do well, you should not only lodge it with them, but have them espouse it."[1]

[1] Michel de Montaigne, *Essay on the Education of Children*, 1580.   For a select bibliography of teaching aids in carrying on an effective extracurricular program, see Appendix, references 70, 151, 153, 156, 160, 171, 178, 189.

CHAPTER IX

ORIENTATION COURSES IN FOREIGN CULTURES

That person is most cultivated who is able to put himself in the place of the greatest number of persons.

—JANE ADDAMS

The Need for Curriculum Differentiation.—The impossibility of doing justice in the conventional foreign-language course to all the social and cultural values which the study of foreign languages, literatures, and cultures presumably has to offer young people, has emphasized the desirability of providing, wherever possible, differentiated offerings to meet the life needs and interests of boys and girls who lack the time or incentive to profit from courses in which ability to read, write, speak, or translate a foreign language is a major concern.[1] In American communities where almost every doctor, barber, lawyer, grocer, businessman, or bootblack is represented by a son or daughter in high school,[2] every child should at least enjoy the privilege of capitalizing to advantage his interests in foreign languages and cultures in an educational institution which his parents help to support. There is no democracy in education unless such equality of opportunity exists in the public school.

The need for differentiating work within the foreign-language class to accommodate these young people, or for providing entirely separate classes where enrollments justify them, is exceedingly great.

---

[1] Emilio L. Guerra, "What Shall the Foreign Language Teacher Do about the Pupil of Lower Linguistic Ability," *The Modern Language Journal*, Vol. XXV, pp. 521–530, April, 1941. R. Blount Ralls, "Selectivity or Simplification," *The Modern Language Journal*, Vol. XXII, pp. 325–326, February, 1938. Clark Keating, "The Incompetent Student Raises a Problem for the Language Teacher," *The Modern Language Journal*, Vol. XXII, p. 38, October, 1937. Walter V. Kaulfers, "Some Recent Trends in the Reorientation of Foreign Language Instruction," *Hispania*, Vol. XVIII, pp. 87–102, Feburary, 1935; "Magic-wand Solutions to Foreign Language Problems," *The School Review*, Vol. XLIV, pp. 744–752, December, 1936.

[2] Grayson N. Kefauver, Victor H. Noll, and C. Elwood Drake, "The Secondary School Population," National Survey of Secondary Education, *Monograph* No. 4, *U. S. Office of Education Bulletin*, 1932, No. 17, Washington, D. C., 58 pp.; p. 51.

The attempt to fit students of varying backgrounds, needs, interests, and life destinations into a single regimented type of foreign-language course, with uniform assignments, textbooks, and standards for every child, has failed miserably.   In practice, this policy has merely meant maladjustment, high rates of elimination, mediocre achievement, and the continuous necessity of justifying foreign-language teaching. Those who, because of their ignorance of the social composition of the modern secondary school, have urged that every boy and girl should be obliged to take a foreign language for six to nine years as in Europe, have contributed little but confusion to every constructive attempt to make the study of foreign languages, literatures, and cultures a really significant medium of educative experience in the lives of young people.   In actual practice such ex-cathedra pronouncements have done little more than to inspire futile attempts to fit all children with exactly the same style and size of shoe.

In any unselected group of young people some children can always be found whom a particular style and size of shoe will fit to perfection; but this number will be relatively small compared to those whose feet are longer, shorter, wider, or narrower.   To insist that a particular child wear a certain "number" just because it is the "average for his age" can lead to nothing more certain than nervous irritation and foot trouble of such magnitude that he will neither want, nor be able, to make progress toward any objective and probably be glad to take off the shoe at the earliest opportunity.   The attempt to abstract human nature into a mythical "average child," and to organize courses in terms of such verbal abstractions, entirely divorced from reality, has been in large measure responsible for the failure of education in the sense of schooling to "take" with young people, or to carry over into the solution of really crucial problems of individual and group life.

Dr. Helen B. Pryor, Professor of Hygiene in Stanford University, tells the story[1] of a group of scientists who once decided to find the perfect diet for the "average" dog.   In keeping with this objective, they studied the food habits of every kind of dog from the great Dane to the tiny Chihuahua, and computed a scientific calory ratio for each member of the canine family, carefully analyzed in terms of proteins, vitamins, and carbohydrates.   Then they pooled their findings, added all the proteins, vitamins, and carbohydrates together, divided them by the number of dogs examined, and arrived at a theoretically "perfect diet for the average dog."   Being scientifically minded, they decided to validate their findings by administering this diet to an

[1] Paraphrased by permission of the author.

unselected number of canine quadrupeds.   To the amazement of the scientists, the diet yielded unusual results: the great Danes died because there was not enough meat in their food and the little Chihuahuas succumbed because there was too much.   However, among the canine group were some dogs whom the diet suited to per-fection, and the latter succeeded in leading healthy, well-balanced, wholesome, and productive canine lives to the end of a ripe old age. The scientists were satisfied.   They had at last succeeded in finding the perfect diet for the *average dog!*

Foreign-language teaching in the American secondary school owes its limited success to much the same kind of procedure in course of study building, with the exception that the diet is one which has been more or less imposed upon the school by university specialists in the language and literature of the Middle Ages, the Renaissance, or the Romantic period, who on the basis of their amazing scholarship in tracing the origins of the Alphonsine Lapidaries, or the macabre element in Goethe or Dante, are thereby qualified to prescribe from their ivory towers standards of achievement for thousands of school children whom they have never seen—or are ever likely to see—for generations yet unborn.   Even an animal trainer realizes that he can't teach a dog he doesn't know.

Failure of Procrustean Methods.—Realizing from experience that the conventional foreign-language course did not suit more than a relatively small number of the children who enrolled in their classes, foreign-language teachers set about to discover children who would profit from the prescribed diet.   In their search they enlisted the services of psychologists and statisticians.   Prognosis tests were devised to discover in advance which children had the necessary aptitude for the particular kind of foreign-language work which had become crystallized by college entrance board examinations, regents examinations, textbooks, standardized tests, and tradition.   Explora-tory tryout courses in general language were introduced[1] in which the children's aptitudes, interests, and general fitness for language study were estimated from the ability and enthusiasm which they displayed in reading about "John's family" in four or five languages. The result of this attempt to find students who would fit the courses was such a marked decrease in foreign-language enrollments that many teachers were in danger of having to take charge of study halls or other responsibilities in order to have enough to do to retain their status as full-time employees.   Moreover, the forecasting efficiency

[1] See Chap. X.

of the most elaborate and expensive prognosis tests proved to be almost nil for all practical purposes.[1]   The mere possession of ability

[1] In 1938 the author reviewed the literature of aptitude testing since 1900 for the national convention of the American Association of Teachers of German in New York City.   The following conclusions have not been invalidated by any studies available at the present writing:

"A comprehensive survey reported in 1931 revealed that even seven years ago achievement in foreign-language grammar, reading, and vocabulary had already been correlated by 48 investigators with 67 bases, including such factors as ability to think in abstract grammatical terms, memory span for visual and nonvisual material, general intelligence, etc. . . .

"In 1933 a doctor's dissertation completed at Stanford University reported the results of one of the most comprehensive and detailed pieces of research in the field of foreign-language prognosis.   The author selected from the vast number of investigations reported between 1900 and 1933 those bases which seemed to yield the most promising correlations with subsequent success in the several phases of foreign-language work. . . . The results showed that the highest degree of accuracy which could be expected in forecasting foreign-language achievement would be . . . far too unreliable as a basis for denying any child the right to undertake foreign-language work. . . . Moreover, it was found that several of the so-called tests of 'linguistic aptitude' predicted ability in science and mathematics as well as (or better than) work in foreign languages!

"Although the problem of prognosis has been further explored by at least fifteen investigators (Brock, Canty, Finch, Jones, Law, Richardson, Michel, Wadsworth, Wagner, Young, Bement, Gabbert, Maronpot, Seagoe, Tallent) since 1933, none of their results has added materially to the solution of the problem. Indeed, had the authors taken the trouble to consult the previous studies in the field, they would in most cases have saved themselves much busywork.

"It is finally becoming evident that prognosis as a panacean solution to foreign-language problems is destined long to remain in the limbo of wishful thinking.   Even if a perfectly valid test of foreign-language aptitude existed, there would still be no way of knowing how effectively a pupil would use such 'language talent' as it revealed.   It requires only common sense to realize that mere possession of an ability does not give the slightest indication of the efficiency with which it will be capitalized in actual class work.

"Again, it is inconceivable that any one test, however comprehensive, could predict achievement in a field in which such a variety of methods, materials, and objectives abound.   A test designed to predict achievement in a course following a strictly direct method cannot be expected to predict success equally well in a course following a so-called eclectic method.   Neither can a prognosis test designed to forecast success in a beginning course featuring grammar be expected to forecast success in a course which features the 'reading approach' or the 'oral approach' or the 'cultural approach,' or any of the many other 'approaches' to a foreign language.   This is precisely why prognosis tests which originally yielded fairly substantial correlations with achievement in the courses on which they were standardized, have often yielded insignificantly low correlations with achievement in curricula in which different textbooks, methods, and 'approaches' were used.   The results of the actual tryout of such prognosis tests as those developed by Symonds, obviously provided no guarantee whatsoever that the individual would actually use it to advantage.

In these circumstances, school counselors charged with the educational guidance of students began to advise incoming freshmen of the high mortality rate in foreign-language study, and to encourage them to think twice before enrolling in a foreign-language course unless they were definitely planning to go to a college or university requiring foreign-language work for admission. College requirements were the only tangible excuse for justifying the continuance of a formal course which so many pupils dropped at the earliest opportunity.[1] Obviously, this practice served to reduce materially the registrations in beginning classes—the concentration point of foreign-language enrollments, and the only source of recruits for intermediate and advanced courses. Moreover, it served to limit foreign-language work in many schools to two years for all but a few students, many of whom were interested in the courses only as a means for satisfying college entrance requirements.

Todd, Solomon-Orleans, Briggs, Clem, Barry, Wilkins, Handschin, and others abundantly illustrate the point.

"The failure of prognosis tests to provide an adequate basis for educational guidance in the foreign languages has led to a shift of emphasis in the direction of curriculum re-orientation. . . . As an alternative to the elimination of pupils on the basis of prognosis tests or other predictive criteria, the expansion of the foreign-language curriculum in the secondary school to include offerings in the field of language appreciation, world literature, and foreign cultures, comparable to those which have long been a part of the regular offerings of outstanding university foreign-language departments, undoubtedly deserves consideration. Unless some alternative offerings of this kind are provided those pupils whose ability to learn a foreign language in terms of abstract grammatical concepts is limited, prognosis will only mean a serious reduction in enrollments in foreign-language departments, with the result that in the average high school of 250 pupils, few, if any, teachers will eventually have enough pupils to provide a full teaching program in any language. It is important in considering any basis for selecting pupils to realize that the inevitable outcome is always fewer pupils, fewer classes, and fewer teachers, unless some provision is made for those students who are rejected.

"For the sake of American education it is hoped that the policy of foreign-language departments will always be directed toward strengthening rather than weakening the position of foreign languages and cultures in the curriculum. Having tried rather vainly for three decades to fit our students to our courses, we might profitably try for a time to fit our courses to our students."

See Walter V. Kaulfers, "Prognosis and Its Alternatives in Relation to the Guidance of Students," *The German Quarterly*, Vol. XII, pp. 81–84, March, 1939.

[1] Adolph Klein, "Failure and Subjects Liked and Disliked," *High Points*, Vol. XXI, pp. 22–25, January, 1939.

During the last decade this decrease in enrollments became a matter of sufficient concern to national organizations of foreign-language teachers to warrant the inauguration of defense committees, and the publication of circulars propagandizing for the study of foreign languages.[1] The effort to stem the tide consumed so much energy, however, that little was done through concerted effort to solve the very obvious problem of either accepting the fact of limited enrollments for the relatively small number of boys and girls who actually needed foreign language to get into college, or of providing an enriched, differentiated type of foreign-language program which would not be a mere vest-pocket edition of a first-year course in college grammar, diluted with just enough cultural busywork to make it palatable.

The Movement toward Curriculum Revision.—Among the teachers of foreign languages who were not too busy wondering how anyone could achieve the magnificent results which the propagandists for the foreign languages advertised, or too absorbed in listening to the ridicule and contempt heaped upon educational psychologists and "educators" by the apostles of culture and international understand-ing in the universities, a few found time to attend summer workshops[2] sponsored by the Stanford Language Arts Investigation and the Eight-year Study of the National Commission on the Relation of Schools and Colleges, or to enroll for credit in curriculum work with specialists in foreign-language education at a reputable university, where they were able to bring recent research in psychology, curriculum construction, and evaluation to bear upon the development of specific learning programs for the young people in their very own foreign-language classes.   The primary aims in each case were to make foreign-language courses more effective in terms of linguistic and cultural outcomes of value in present-day life, to find practical ways and means

[1] Committee on the Place of Modern Foreign Languages in American Educa-tion, "Suggestions for State and Local Committees," National Federation of Modern Language Teachers, Washington, D. C., 1941, 14 pp.   The Committee on Public Relations, *Why Spanish?* American Association of Teachers of Spanish, 1936, 800 E. Gunhill Road, New York, 39 pp.   Commission on Trends in Educa-tion, *Language Study in American Education*, The Modern Language Associa-tion of America, New York, 1940, 40 pp.

[2] Progressive Education Association, *A Foreign Language Program for Progres-sive Schools*, Rocky Mountain Workshop, 1938, 86 pp.   Reports of the Stanford Language Arts Investigation, Vol. II, *Foreign Languages and Cultures in American Education*, McGraw-Hill Book Company, Inc., New York. In press.   Ohio Council on Modern Language Teaching, *Proceedings of the Ohio Workshop on Modern Language Teaching*, Ohio State University, 1940, 60 pp.

for providing qualified pupils the opportunity to study a foreign language so successfully in the lower years that they will want to continue it at least until graduation.

Realizing the impossibility of reaching through a single type of foreign-language course as large a number of young people as could profit, if not from language study, at least from an acquaintance with the foreign backgrounds of contemporary American life, from literature in translation, or from a study of language as a way of thinking, some teachers followed the precedent set by professors of foreign languages in reputable universities, of introducing courses in applied linguistics, world literature in translation, and foreign cultures, to accommodate those young people who lacked the time or incentive to do effective work in courses in French, German, Spanish, or Latin. As semester or year offerings, these courses would be terminal,[1] *i.e.*, complete and worth-while in themselves in terms of life values—and without foreign-language prerequisites of any kind. It is with the last-named type of program—the civilization-course—that the remainder of the chapter deals.

Language Appreciation in Civilization Courses.—Although the emphasis in the civilization course is upon the development, primarily through reading and discussion in English, of such insights, attitudes, and appreciations as will contribute to balance and perspective in human relations, activities involving the use of the foreign language are capitalized whenever they can be appropriately enlisted in the service of this central objective.   In no case, however, is the language permitted to become a hurdle or an end in itself.   Such activities as the following are usually effective in developing insights of value in daily life, provided they are guided by some purposeful objective to prevent them from becoming a mere ride upon the merry-go-round. None of the activities require more than such a working knowledge of pronunciation as can usually be developed in and through the activities themselves, without special preliminary drill.

1. Making effective use of the contributions of foreign peoples to life in our country as reflected in words and expressions which we have borrowed from abroad, *e.g.*,

[1] Mildred Menhinick, "A Non-college Course in French," *The Modern Language Journal*, Vol. XX, pp. 269–274, February, 1936.   Nellie D. Moehlman, "Non-college Preparatory Courses in French and German," *The Modern Language Journal*, Vol. XIX, pp. 537–545, April, 1935.   Walter V. Kaulfers, "Cultural Orientation in Lower-division Foreign Language," *Hispania*, Vol. XVIII, pp. 365–374, December, 1935.

a. French military terms as a reflection of the importance of France in military science prior to 1940, *e.g.*, lieutenant, etc.
b. French diplomatic terms as a reflection of the importance of France as a world power, *e.g.*, attaché, corps, etc.
c. French place names in the United States as reflections of the contributions of France to the exploration and colonization of the New World.
d. French literary terms as a reflection of French genius in the field of belles-lettres.
e. Similar observations for words and expressions reflecting French contributions to American and to world culture in science and invention, art and music, the theater, cuisine, etiquette, etc.

Pupil participation in the collection, organization, and socio-semantic analysis of foreign words and expressions used in English has proved a valuable means for approaching the study of a foreign people in terms of their contributions to human culture as reflected in the pupil's own language, home, or community. Among the linguistic outcomes which this work has yielded are increased ability to pronounce, spell, understand, and use correctly loan words and expressions that have populated our language but have not as yet become completely naturalized. The sample units on place names and loan words in Chapter V are as appropriate for use here as in connection with vocabulary building and pronunciation work during the first week of a beginning foreign-language course.

2. Learning to understand, appreciate, and enjoy the contributions which foreign people have made to our world of poetry and music, *e.g.*, by

a. Singing songs of foreign origin which are world famous. Where the music is too difficult the words of the songs can often be recited to music in verse-speaking choir fashion. Since the number of songs for which translations exist far exceeds the number which can be used in the classroom, the problem of facilitating comprehension does not present insuperable difficulties.
b. Interpreting poetry. The verse-speaking choir technique can also be used effectively with short dramatic poems for which translations can be found to permit of oral renditions both in English and in the foreign language.

3. Learning to understand, appreciate, and enjoy great thoughts of great men, *e.g.*,

a. Famous quotations from foreign writers, statesmen, or philosophers.
b. Effective epigrams.

A study of short quotations and epigrams that embody effectively expressed truths or ideas can often serve as an introduction in miniature to world literature, to the names of great thinkers and their writings.   For this reason short quotations and epigrams are often of more educational significance than anonymous proverbs.

4. Why foreign people speak, spell, or write as they do, *i.e.*, how differences in ways of saying things reflect originally different ways of interpreting or symbolizing reality:

   a. The psychosemantic basis of word order, *e.g.*, how it accounts for the use of the inverted exclamation and interrogation marks at the beginning of Spanish exclamations and questions; how it explains the position of certain attributive adjectives, etc.
   b. The double negative in Spanish.   In English negatives are *multiplied algebraically* to yield a semantic *positive;* in Spanish, negatives are *added* to give a more emphatic *negative.*
   c. The idiomatic present.
   d. Differences in original ways of thinking as reflected in a comparison of English and foreign idioms.
   e. Historical influences reflected in the evolution of language, *e.g.*, the origin of the block-letter script in German, from the probable custom of scratching symbols on the bark of a beech tree.

Although there is naturally little time in a course in civilization to teach the grammar of a foreign language, interesting and significant insights into the group mind of a foreign people can often be afforded by means of a comparative study of different ways of symbolizing the same concept in different languages, *e.g.*,

English: To put the *cart* before the *horse.*
French: Mettre la charrue devant les boeufs (to put the *plow* before the *oxen*)

It should not require much inductive questioning to enable students to see for themselves the significance of this difference.   The idiom reflects a difference in agricultural economy.   In France, oxen are still in more common use on farms than horses for many reasons, most of which can be discovered through simple deduction.   Obviously, only language phenomena that yield key insights into the thought life or collective ideology of a foreign people are selected for study.   A more detailed treatment of the sociosemantic bases of language than that indicated above would probably be more appropriate for a course in applied semantics.   Except for activities such as the foregoing, the major emphasis in the civilization course is on the *people* and culture of the foreign country in relation to our own daily lives.   Some idea of the possibilities of the field can be obtained from the following accounts of orientation courses that have proved successful in junior high schools, senior high schools, and junior colleges.

Cultural Programs in Action.—In his article "Increasing the Social Values of Foreign Language Instruction," F. J. McConville describes the courses in foreign cultures offered in the ninth and tenth grades of the San Mateo High School, California.[1]

A stock argument of the teachers of foreign languages has been that their pupils acquired a certain amount of cultural background which they could not otherwise have obtained. . . . The belief has been prevalent among parents that the argument of the teachers was valid. . . . In our search for background courses on broad cultural lines suitable to the capabilities of our students there is a wide field in which the well-trained and enthusiastic language teacher can be of immense usefulness. The great stream of our culture flows from European sources, and properly to understand its flow, it is necessary to have some knowledge of the life and customs, the art and history of the peoples from whom we spring. . . . We offer, at the present writing, four courses which for want of better names, we designate as Italy, France, Germany, and Spain. In these courses we endeavor to give the student a conception of the life of the peoples in these countries, and the contribution which each has made to the development of Western civilization. We use no textbook, for none are available. Students . . . make their own notebooks. We have found that much material within the grasp of students is obtainable . . . for the asking. . . . This semester we have assigned a room exclusively for the use of these classes. The room is equipped with tables and chairs. The walls are decorated with pictures and posters. It has its own library and ample closet space for storing teacher's aids. There is a piano and phonograph and equipment for showing films. The popularity of the course is attested by the fact that we cannot accommodate all who would enroll. Those students who have taken one of the courses generally go on.

More recently, the San Mateo High School has attempted to introduce a course in American culture in which will be brought out the contributions of the United States to art, music, and literature.[2]

An interesting example of the increasing emphasis on *Kulturkunde* in the lower division of our colleges and universities is afforded in E. Heyse Dummer's article "The Teaching of German Civilization in First-year and Second-year College classes."[3]   According to the writer,

[1] F. J. McConville, "Increasing the Social Values in Foreign Language Instruction," *California Journal of Secondary Education*, Vol. X, pp. 573–574, December, 1935.

[2] Aubrey A. Douglass, ed., "What's Happening in California Secondary Schools," *California Journal of Secondary Education*, Vol. XXII, p. 501, December, 1937.

[3] E. Heyse Dummer, "The Teaching of German Civilization in First-year and Second-year College Classes," *The Modern Language Journal*, Vol. XXI, pp. 179–185, December, 1936.

. . . The success of the undertaking at Elmhurst was dependent to a large extent on the co-operation accorded by colleagues in the various departments of the college. Members of the social science division and the religion, philosophy, speech, music, and science departments responded to the invitation to lecture on their respective subjects as pertaining to Germany. Thus it was possible to set up the following program of lectures:

First month: (1) Important men and events in German history. (2) Touring Germany (illustrated films employed here and in subsequent lectures were loaned by the German Tourist Information Office).

Second month: (1) German society. (2) The German system of education.

Third month: (1) and (2) Customs and manners (illustrated).

Fourth month: (1) Handwork. (2) Germany, the land of music (a lecture recital).

Fifth month (second semester): (1) German painters of renown (illustrated). (2) Old and new architecture in Germany (illustrated).

Sixth month: (1) From Paganism to Barthianism. (2) Germany's contribution to the theater.

Seventh month: (1) Germany's great thinkers. (2) The German government.

Eighth month: (1) German scientists. (2) Famous German-Americans.

The foregoing offerings are typical of many others in effective operation in many other schools and colleges—principally in the junior and senior high schools of Los Angeles, San Francisco, Detroit, and Sacramento, in the Glendale (Calif.) Junior College, and in the Los Angeles City (Junior) College.[1] In some institutions the introduction of such offerings has been responsible for a significant increase

[1] *Los Angeles*: See Elizabeth N. Reed "Mexicans Became Friends," *Foreign Languages and Cultures in American Education*, McGraw-Hill Book Company, Inc., New York. In press.

San Francisco: "The Culture of the Nations," George Washington High School and Balboa High School.

Detroit: Lilly Lindquist, *New Type Courses in Foreign Language*, Detroit Public Schools, File No. 9831, April, 1939 (mimeographed).

Sacramento: Beth Hughson and Oda Gostick, *In Foreign Lands*, D. C. Heath and Company, Boston, 1934, 362 pp.

Glendale: H. H. Wiebe, "Products of Modern Language Study," *The Modern Language Forum*, Vol. XXII, pp. 237–242, September-December, 1937.

Los Angeles City College: Meyer Krakowski, "The Practice of Correlation between the German Language and Other Subjects," *The Modern Language Journal*, Vol. XXIV, pp. 452–456, March, 1940.

Newark, N. J. (Westside High School): Morris Brenman, "A Modern Modern Language Course," *The Modern Language Journal*, Vol. XXVI, pp. 275–287, April, 1942.

in enrollments in foreign-language departments.   The introduction of courses in German civilization and literature in translation at Stanford University, for example, increased enrollments in the German department to its highest figure in five years.   To quote from the *Annual Bulletin of the German Department* (1938–1939):

The enrollment in spring quarter, 581, our largest figure in five years, shows that there is student interest in German civilization and literature and encourages us to develop further our courses in English.   The present course in contemporary German literature has enrolled 50 students, the course in German civilization, over 100.

Values and Limitations of Current Programs.—Unfortunately, no data are available to indicate the success of the programs in realizing their central objectives.   This, perhaps, is natural in view of the newness of the offerings.   The absence of data on evaluation may also be attributed, however, to the extreme difficulty of measuring cultural outcomes, and to the even more patent fact that very few of the programs give evidence of having any really significant cultural objective beyond the acquisition of cultural information.   The colloquial American question "So what?" would be difficult to answer on the basis of the descriptions of courses found in current articles. A modern program of education should not ask that its right to exist be accepted on faith, but offer verifiable evidence of the growth that young people make in following it.

The following comments from students enrolled in the course in German civilization and culture in the Glendale (Calif.) Junior College, however, may be indicative of the potential value of culture courses to interested young people from their own viewpoint:

A young embryo lawyer wrote: "This course has helped my study of social science courses, and besides has enabled me to take an active part in international discussions outside of school. . . . "
A young Swedish candidate for the ministry had this to say: "This course has afforded me the opportunity of peeping behind the curtains of the German nation and of learning to understand the people themselves.   The course has been an excellent supplement to my history study. . . . "
The following statement by a young Syrian art student is helpful.   He wrote, "I have learned in this course to be more patient, tolerant, and fair-minded. . . . "
The following music major made a real discovery when he reported, "The knowledge of the background of anything or anyone makes one more tolerant. Applying this course in German civilization and culture to my study of music,

I find that knowing the conditions of the times in which these musicians lived makes their work more meaningful. . . . ”

An English major stated, “ . . . the course . . . has whetted my appetite, and I am quite resolved to learn more about it.”

Although offerings of the type just described represent desirable developments in American education, the programs still fall far short of their possibilities.   Most conspicuous of their deficiencies is the lack of a unifying purpose to give meaning and direction to the work beyond the acquisition of factual information.   There is little evidence in most of the programs of a significant criterion for the choice of content.   Geographical boundaries or chronological divisions seem to be the only unifying elements.

Moreover, few of the programs seem to make any but incidental efforts to tie in the work with American life and culture, even where these have been (and often still are) influenced by the foreign country whose civilization is being studied.   It would seem that the influence that the foreign country has exercised on our culture in the arts and sciences, in customs and mores, and on our philosophy of life should furnish an excellent criterion for the selection of significant content for a program in foreign civilizations.   Courses in foreign cultures need a more dynamic unifying basis than that afforded by geographical or chronological limits if they are to yield something more than a syllabus of cultural information or a compendium of miscellaneous facts.

The degree to which a country's contributions to music, for example, is reflected in *our own* radio programs, church music, symphony concerts, recitals, dance music, and operas is a very reliable measure of its importance in the musical world.   Certainly, a contribution to culture that has traveled thousands of miles across the seas, often through decades or even centuries of time, is a more important contribution than one that has had merely local appeal.   Since there is never time for everything, the major emphasis might well be placed on those contributions which have significantly affected the building of America and which continue to do so in the present.   Acceptance of this principle would make mastery of the origin and meaning of the music, dance, architecture, fashions, literature, and history of our daily environment the core of the curriculum and the fundamental concern of our teaching.   We would not continue to rattle the dead bones of our ancient pedagogical stock in trade but turn to life for our guide to what is worth teaching.   The question would be always:

"Of what value is what I learn and teach in the solution of crucial personal and social problems?" If such a criterion were selected, the offerings could make a really significant contribution to one of the basic purposes of education—the building of a creative and enlightened Americanism—one that is aware and appreciative of its heritage from present and past civilizations, and disposed to capitalize its best resources effectively for the enrichment of individual and group life in the present and the future.

Content and activities chosen on such a basis would be more functional and meaningful, for learning rarely possesses value for molding attitudes, interests, appreciations, or modes of behavior, unless it is related directly and immediately to the life experiences of the individual. Lacking such a tie-in with life in the present, "culture" is likely to remain a mere subject for parlor discussions between sips of tea, or something to be looked at, catalogue in one hand, a lorgnette in the other. At the present time there is no real need for enlarging the quota of parlor dilettantes. They have rarely been creative in translating learning into action. The history of dictatorships shows that in the past, as in the present, the culture of our schools has too often been inoperative, and that the solution of the really important problems of the world has of necessity fallen to the culturally illiterate.

A second deficiency of a large majority of the educational offerings is their isolation from life in the community. Too many culture courses are still "taught" in a vacuum. At the end of the program the foreign people who created the civilization are still as remote in time and space as they were at the beginning. Thus it is quite possible for a group of high-school students to spend a semester or a year studying the "culture" of Spain and the Americas, and still feel just as prejudiced or indifferent as before to the descendants of those countries who live in their own communities, or even attend the same classes. Clearly there is little sincerity, and certainly no depth, to the study of "Spanish culture" if it indulges in mere fact collecting or nonfunctional romanticism when in the pupils' own community the immediate descendants of that civilization are barred from public swimming pools except on the day before the water is changed.

Two Outstanding Exceptions.—Among the few programs that have utilized human and community resources in foreign cultures extensively are the sophomore course, "Builders Together," developed in the Santa Barbara Senior High School, and the course in German civilization in the Los Angeles City College, Calif.

In the course in "Builders Together" a student-managed census of the entire high school gave the classes the figures that they needed for knowing the chief heritages of the community. From this census developed the impetus for the study of the backgrounds of our peoples. In this were naturally included the social history, the arts (both fine and practical), the literature, the home life, science and invention, and the manners and customs of the people of the countries. . . . Then back to the local community came the students to learn how individuals and groups from these nations had influenced Santa Barbara and to discover how their racial gifts could be used to build an even better Santa Barbara. . . . Somewhat to their surprise the students found many organized groups of the foreign-born even in the comparatively small city of Santa Barbara. And to their great joy the students found these groups, and many individuals, more than ready to help them understand the countries being studied. So many heirlooms and articles of worth were loaned to the class at various times that six students had to spend an entire afternoon arranging them effectively for a meeting of the P.T.A., at which the 'Builders Together' program was explained and the loaned articles, all carefully labeled by the students, exhibited.[1]

The success of the program in the Santa Barbara Senior High School led to the inauguration in 1938 of a series of community intercultural forms under the auspices of the curriculum department. These are held in the public library under the leadership of Mary O. Kittrell, cultural coordinator for the city schools. Community organizations representing Americans of foreign birth or extraction cooperate in planning and conducting the programs. Naturalized citizens representing these culture groups survey the community for heirlooms and art treasures brought from overseas. These are placed on exhibit in the public library for inspection by excursion groups of school children, teachers, and townspeople, and are explained by representatives of the cultural groups. Programs in costume presenting the folkways, folk songs, and folk dances which Santa Barbara has inherited from foreign cultures in each case accompany the exhibits, in order to make it possible for teachers, pupils, and parents to meet the local descendants of the foreign countries in person.

Those who are acquainted with the outcomes of the programs agree that the result has been the development of a genuine interest in the cultural backgrounds of the community, an increased appreciation of human personalities, and a more wholesome attitude in human relations.   It is remarkable what a little appreciation will do in encour-

[1] Louise Noyes, "Builders Together," *The English Journal*, Vol. XXVIII, pp. 258–260, March, 1938.

aging a local foreign colony to bring together its best singers, speakers, dancers, musicians, storytellers, painters, sculptors, and writers, and to collect its finest heirlooms and art treasures to place on exhibit for the benefit of groups of school children, teachers, or civic clubs. It is eloquent proof that everyone in this world likes to feel that he has something to contribute—something that others appreciate.   Santa Barbara has so far proved that it is much better to approach the building of a 100 per cent American culture constructively by drawing upon the best that is in the human backgrounds of its people, than by driving half its population, through supercilious ridicule or contempt, into introverted alien colonies, none of them filled with any too great a love for a country that belittles or insults the culture of its ancestors.[1]

The effective use of school and community resources in a civilization course has been discussed in concrete and convincing detail by Meyer Krakowski of the Los Angeles City (Junior) College:[2]

For a period of ten years I have been practicing correlation at the Los Angeles City College between the subject of German and the fields of music, drama, art, dance, literature, philosophy, and science.   I found that teachers of these subjects were pleased to be of service to our students, for they knew that they would be received with sincere enthusiasm. . . . When I was preparing my students for the first *Weihnachtsfest* on our campus, I asked the chairman of that department to assist me in training a double quartet.   That was in 1929, the year our institution was founded, and he has since lectured to my classes and our *Deutscher Verein* on various aspects of German music, from Bach to Schoenberg, and played for us both as soloist and with the string ensemble. . . . Last year, the same instructor gave us a program of *Lieder*, with a former pupil of his, a Viennese opera singer, as soloist.   He commented on the songs in German. . . .

Some time later, we also had a lecture on Reinhardt's contribution to the modern theatre by an actress, who had an intimate knowledge of Reinhardt's work and whose father had been a leading actor of the naturalistic school in Germany.   When my class was reading Schiller's drama *Wilhelm Tell*, I invited an Austrian actor, in exile, to read selections from the play.   Several years ago, before a similar class, the Swiss Consul spoke on the government and schools of his country, and a Swiss student, who was enrolled in a neighboring university, spoke on the life and customs of his people.   On occasions of

[1] National Council of Teachers of English, *Educating for Peace*, D. Appleton-Century Company, Inc., New York, 1940, xiii + 275 pp.; pp. 148–161.

[2] Meyer Krakowski, "The Practice of Correlation between the German Language and Other Subjects," *The Modern Language Journal*, Vol. XXIV, pp. 452–456, March, 1940.

this nature one or two other classes are invited to join with mine, and the talks are usually followed by questions from the students. . . .

One project in drama, which was carried out this term, will be of interest here. ' We read in class Mannfred Kyber's little play *Der Tod und das kleine Mädchen*.   When I asked my students how many would be interested in seeing this playlet produced, half out of a class of thirty-eight showed a keen interest. They tried out for the different parts, and the class used good judgment in its choice of the main characters. . . . The students were so enthusiastic over the results of their efforts, that they expressed a desire to do a similar project next fall.   Here is a case of correlation accomplished by the students themselves. . . .

Before leaving the subject of drama, I shall tell about the presentation of a leading German impersonator at a students' assembly, under the sponsorship of the director of our college.   The selections from Lessing and Goethe thrilled the young people as much as the familiar selections from Shakespeare.

The most ambitious literary activity we ever undertook was developed around the one-hundredth anniversary of the death of Goethe.   The different activities included a lecture on Goethe by a professor from the state university, the presentation of a bust of Goethe to the German Club by a local German sculptor and its presentation by the club to the college, and an essay-music-and-art contest on Goethe, sponsored by the club, in which all students of German on the campus were invited to participate.   Among the judges were a music instructor and an English instructor.   The results were most gratifying. Essays, translations of poetry, pen and ink sketches of Goethe, and a musical composition were submitted, and prizes were given away to the winners. Some of the material was printed in the Literary Supplement of our college newspaper. . . .

Art and dance likewise invited our interest.   We heard lectures on modern German art by an art instructor and on architecture by two Austrian-American architects of our city, and the Chairman of the Art Department set aside for us a room when we exhibited the works of two local German artists.   Now and then we visit the Henry E. Huntington Library and Art Gallery.   On one occasion we had as our guest a German artist who interpreted for us some of the English masterpieces on exhibit there.

Our college has its own treasure room, and upon the invitation of its curator we arranged an exhibit, which illustrated the story of the book in Germany through early editions of German authors, original leaves from Chronicles and Bibles of the fifteenth and sixteenth centuries and recent editions of the classics and contemporary writers. . . .

The modern dance has been influenced by the German technique.   Several times I went with some of my students to see demonstrations of the new technique at the studio of a German lady who had taught the dance in Germany.   Both she and her husband, an artist, talked to my students informally about the dance, and later this lady actually conducted a class for us, near the campus. . . .

We know, of course, that many of our students, if not actually a majority, study German because of their interest in the sciences. We, therefore, visited several times the California Institute of Technology and the Seismological Station in Pasadena. At the station, a leading scientist, formerly of Germany, explained to us the significance of the recording instruments found there. On our own campus we had a lecture by a science instructor on the life and work of Robert Koch. . . .

Hiking in the mountains has been among the happiest experiences of our students of German. It was quite natural, therefore, that when the Youth Hostels came to California that they should have found ardent supporters among our students. They know that the movement springs from Germany and that the words "house-mother" and "house father," in use in this country, are of German origin. . . .

Recently the Chairman of the Cultural Arts Department invited us to offer a course in English on Goethe and Faust, which will be given for the first time next fall. It should also be noted here that to some of the literary activities of both club and classes, members of the college administration and faculty are often invited as guests. When we had a lecture on folklore, for instance, we had among our guests members of the English department and colleagues from other departments as well. . . .

The results of correlation are certain to be favorable, if the language teacher emphasizes only the enduring values of the culture represented by the language he is teaching—those values which add to the enrichment of a student's life and of American culture—and if he has full regard for the whole personality of the student and has an abiding faith in American youth and in the American way of life.

A Suggested Criterion for the Choice of Content and Learning Activities.—To be functional, every culture course may well concern itself with the building of desirable attitudes, insights, and appreciations in human relations. Evidences of misconceptions and prejudices that have been acquired from the social environment and reinforced by habits of mistaking the exception for the rule may serve as the focal centers around which content and activities may be organized to give meaning and direction to the work in terms of a significant life objective.[1] There is no need in secondary education at this time for intro-

[1] Rachel Davis-Dubois, *Adventures in Inter-cultural Education*, The Progressive Education Association, 221 West 57th St., New York, 1938, 215 pp. Los Angeles City Schools, *World Cultures: Ninth and Tenth Year Social Studies*, School Publication No. 283, 1936, 158 pp. Council Against Intolerance in America (New York City) *An American Answer to Intolerance*, Teachers Manual No. 1, Junior and Senior High Schools, 1939, 130 pp. Alfred Kirshner, "A Scientific Approach to the Development of Tolerance," *High Points*, Vol. XXIII, pp. 11–22, September, 1941.

ducing vest-pocket editions of university courses in which the humanities are studied without humanity.   Authentic, anecdotal biographies of great artists, musicians, writers, scientists, and inventors often help to humanize the work and to make it contribute to changes in attitudes toward the people whose culture is being studied.

Since a culture course can hardly contribute effectively to the life of the student as a member of the community if the work consists merely of topics to be "covered," or of subjects to be taught in a vacuum by the lecture method or by the read-recite-test routine, activities that capitalize the human as well as cultural resources of the community and its environs are desirable as a means for bridging the gap between life and the school.   Among the tested ways and means for facilitating this integration are the following:

Making a Survey of the Foreign Backgrounds of the Community.—A student who has a hobby in photography, for example, can be encouraged to photograph such concrete evidences of foreign backgrounds as are revealed in the architecture and furnishings of homes and buildings, in city planning, or in parks and gardens.   Another student whose interest is in the field of business and commerce can be encouraged to investigate and report on the extent to which articles imported from the foreign country are sold in the vicinity.   Again, a student with an interest in social-service work or intercultural relations may contact the foreign colony of the community and report upon its contributions and activities.   Such actual contacts with people are primary and, whenever possible, should be stressed as the significant experiences that give meaning to the reading of books, listening to music, looking at art, and the use of products.   It is a people who make a culture.   It is not assumed that any two students need do exactly the same type of work.   Within the unifying framework of the survey, individual interests and abilities can usually be capitalized to advantage.   It is assumed, however, that all findings of the individual students will be reported to the class.   The class discussion of the reports may lead to the selection of an editorial committee to combine the most significant findings from each report into an illustrated booklet under such a title as "What Our Community Owes to Spain," or "How My Daily Living Has Been Influenced by French Civilization."   The work of the survey may well culminate in a group excursion to the places cited in the reports.

Becoming Personally Acquainted with the Foreign People.—A survey such as that described above should yield the names of citizens and fellow students of foreign birth or descent who are competent to share with the class their experiences as children, students, travelers, artisans, farmers, or professional workers abroad. Since all people are not gifted speakers and since young people are not always receptive listeners to ineffective speeches, it is often desirable for the class to prepare for the visitors in advance by formulating questions which they would like to ask their guests. A copy of the questions can be given to the visitors in advance as a guide to the interests of the group. When this is done the rapport between the visitor and his audience is usually more intimate than in the case of a formal talk. If the visitor can be entertained by the class steering committee at luncheon or at a reception in the afternoon, open to all interested students and teachers, the value of the contacts is destined to be even more significant in the promotion of friendly attitudes toward the people whose culture is being studied. In general, young people of the same age as the students in the class are the most desirable visitors from the standpoint of building friendly human relations. In no circumstances should such contacts be limited exclusively to foreign-born professors in some neighboring college or university.

Short-wave radio communication and correspondence with young people abroad are additional ways of becoming personally acquainted with foreign people. It is by no means necessary that letters be written in the foreign language if they are sent to students of English abroad. Often the most effective correspondence[1] (where the promotion of friendly human relations rather than practice in composition is the dominant aim) is that in which each student writes in his own native language. In the case of culture courses conducted exclusively in English, advanced classes in the foreign languages can serve as a clearinghouse or translation bureau for international correspondence with interest and profit to themselves. Since interest in foreign correspondence often lags unless the interchange of letters is fairly regular, it is desirable that students write to more than one correspond-

[1] Addresses of students abroad can be obtained from the agencies listed below. A charge per student is usually made to defray secretarial costs. Applications should be accompanied by a short biographical sketch giving age, sex, race, year in school, and scholastic, vocational, and avocational interests. Letters are translated by the Red Cross into the language of the countries to which the letters are sent.

International Correspondence Club, 132 East 65th St., New York.

International Bureau of Foreign Correspondence, Peabody College for Teachers, Nashville, Tenn.

My Friend Abroad, Dr. S. V. Knudsen, 248 Boylston St., Boston, Mass.

Junior Red Cross, Washington, D. C. Primarily for junior-high-school students.

ent to ensure themselves against the possibility of writing to a "dead" address.   It is also important that the exchange of letters be guided into interesting and profitable channels.   To this end the class should, from time to time, discuss subjects of common interest concerning which they may seek information from their correspondents.   Without a significant purpose, interest in correspondence is destined to wane.

The ways in which European and American history have been interwoven since the colonization of the New World is one example of an approach that has a common basis.   It may lead very naturally to whatever discussion of present conditions abroad and in America would be permitted by the censorships: available food, clothing, shelter, and social services; attitudes toward the peoples of other nations; working plans for promoting the mutual welfare of young people of all countries.[1]   Time for the reading and discussion of letters received from abroad should form an integral part of the class program, otherwise the significant values of the activity are likely to be lost.   Unless correspondence is made an integral part of the class program, it may as well not be started at all.   Conducted as a purely incidental extracurricular activity it usually dies out for want of guidance and motivation.   Where foreign correspondence has been capitalized effectively, it has not only contributed to a more personal acquaintance with foreign people but has also provided a highly successful stimulus for the study of their language.

Participating in the Social and Cultural Life of the Community.— Although it is not always possible for a group to attend a play, movie, lecture, concert, exhibit, or opera en masse, it is usually possible to encourage individual pupils, or small committees of students, to attend these activities as representatives of the class with a view to reporting them the following day.   Certainly every class in foreign cultures should make provision for committees to keep the group informed on impending community events, radio programs, and local, state, or national festivals featuring some aspect of foreign life and culture. Wherever possible, the work of the course should be correlated with these community activities.

The foregoing illustrations are but samples of the ways and means by which a program in foreign civilizations can be made vital in terms of life in the present and future.   To these illustrations might be

[1] War conditions suggest the desirability of encouraging correspondence with the many Free French, Free German, and Free Italian peoples of the Western Hemisphere or with other students of foreign languages in the United States.

added assembly programs presented or sponsored by the class, panel discussions on timely issues, the use of the moving picture and short-wave radio in the classroom, individually illustrated reports on selected aspects of foreign life and culture, community singing of foreign songs, choral speaking based on poems (in the original or in translation), dramatizations, current-events programs, and the like. Many of these activities and countless others are in effective operation in many classes.   It is unfortunate, however, that too often the fundamental significance of these activities is lost because they are not guided by a conscious unifying purpose.   Without purpose beyond the activity itself, outcomes are seldom more than accidental or incidental by-products, and the activities themselves easily degenerate into a pleasurable form of busywork or pinwheel activity—all motion without direction.

Culture as the Cult of Form vs. Culture as a Way of Life.—The need for a new conception of culture as a creative, dynamic, socially centered disposition of mind and behavior has never been greater than it is today.   Who can deny that the people of the world have too often been obliged to face the alternatives of suicidal wars, of enslavement and plunder, or international conferences for the common welfare?   The leaders of the nations—many of them trained in all the potent disciplines of "humanistic" culture—have too often displayed their own bankruptcy by their successive steps in the destruction of peace.   Out of a need for a just and lasting peace without which cultural advance is a mockery, the peoples of the earth must build a new creative leadership pledged not to defend systems or forms of government as ends in themselves, but to guarantee to all human beings the democratic opportunity to live wholesome, socially useful lives regardless of race, color, rank, or station.

The quest of knowledge for knowledge's sake, like the quest of art for art's sake, can doubtless be made an interesting and commercially profitable activity for some people; but in the history of mankind, knowledge pursued for its own sake has seldom led to the development of a generation of citizens competent to translate their learning into constructive action for the solution of the really crucial problems either of their own lives or of the society in which they live. As Maeterlinck has indicated: *Nous ne pouvons nous flatter d'avoir compris une verité que lorsqu'il nous est impossible de n'y pas conformer notre vie.*   A culture course that is not primarily concerned with removing the mental hazards which turn men against their neighbors is not concerned with anything of greater significance for human life than embalming the past upon its throne—and the minds of young people with it.[1]

[1] For a select bibliography of teaching aids in conducting civilization courses, see Appendix, references 30–40. See also Verna A. Carley, "Inter-American Friendship through the Schools," *Federal Security Administration Bulletin* 1941, No. 10, U. S. Office of Education, Washington, D. C., v + 61 pp. Studies in Intercultural Education, *Americans All*, Yearbook of Department of Supervisors and Directors of Instruction, N.E.A., National Council of Teachers of English, and Society for Curriculum Study, 1201 Sixteenth St., N.W., Washington, D. C., 1941.

CHAPTER X

PERSPECTIVE ON GENERAL LANGUAGE AND EXPLORATORY LANGUAGE

No one is exempt from talking nonsense; the misfortune is to do it solemnly.

—MICHEL MONTAIGNE

Ghost words rule the world.

—BERTHA FRANCES KAULFERS

Overemphasis on Prognosis in Early General-language Courses.— During the decade and a half between 1910 and 1925, the rapid rise of the junior high school as a connecting link between elementary and secondary education led to the introduction of "broadening and finding courses" in which young people entering upon the early stages of adolescence could explore their interests and abilities, and secure an overview of the main fields of human knowledge—science, mathematics, social studies, and language—prior to specialization in the senior high school.[1] Offerings entitled general science, general mathematics, social science, and general language appeared in the curriculum of the seventh, eighth, or ninth grades, along with classes in "vocations" to help young people find themselves in terms of an intelligent overview of what the world has to offer, not only as means for earning a living but also for enriching life itself. Although such offerings as general science, general mathematics, social studies, vocations, and homemaking served both an exploratory-guidance function and a terminal function, the general-language course became unduly concerned with the selection of pupils for foreign-language classes.[2] Whereas the general-science course dealt with concrete life situations in which a knowledge of scientific principles in the field of chemistry, physics, or biology is essential to human safety and intelligent living, the general-language course consisted primarily of primer type exercises in a variety of languages, presumably with a view to helping pupils

[1] Calvin Plin Davis, *Junior High School Education*, World Book Company, Yonkers-on-Hudson, New York, 1924, xi + 451 pp. Leonard Vincent Koos, *The Junior High School*, Ginn and Company, Boston, 1927, xiv + 506 pp.

[2] Helen M. Eddy, "Instruction in Foreign Languages," *Bulletin* 1932, No. 17, *Monograph* No. 24, U. S. Office of Education, Washington, D. C., pp. 56–61.

decide for themselves which foreign language, if any, they would like to learn later.

Although some of the earliest textbooks[1] included occasional chapters on the history of language or on the cultural geography of the foreign countries whose languages were sampled in the course, the major emphasis was on the twofold aim of enticing gifted pupils into foreign-language classes and of discouraging the nongifted from taking any foreign language at all. Thus, whereas the courses in general mathematics and general science could be justified on the basis of their consumer-education function as being complete and worth while in themselves, general language usually had few terminal values specifically to its credit. Beyond such work in vocabulary building as was provided by work with Latin and Greek roots, prefixes, and suffixes, there was little that the less gifted pupil could carry away with him except the satisfaction of knowing that he was not good enough to take a foreign language, or that foreign languages were hardly worth his time. As a result of this overemphasis upon the prognostic function, to the neglect of terminal values of life significance in themselves, general-language courses fell into disrepute[2] in many schools, both among teachers of foreign languages and among school leaders. Indeed, had it not been for the vigorous efforts of such frontier workers as Lilly Lindquist, Wilton W. Blancké, and James B. Tharp[3] in reorienting the program in the direction of consumer education in language, it is not unlikely that the offering would have died a lingering death in the public schools.

The Increasing Demand for Consumer Education in Language.— Since 1938 the popularization of the work of I. A. Richards, C. K. Ogden, and Alfred Korzybski, by Stuart Chase, S. I. Hayakawa,[4] and others has aroused widespread interest in the study of language, not

[1] Lucy M. Bugbee *et al., An Exploratory Course in General Language*, Benj. H. Sanborn & Co., Chicago, 1926.

[2] Walter V. Kaulfers, "Observations on the Question of General Language," *The School Review*, Vol. XXXVI, pp. 275–283, April, 1928.

[3] Lilly Lindquist, "General Language," *The Modern Language Journal*, Vol. XXIV, pp. 563–567, May, 1940. Wilton W. Blancké, "General Language as a Prognosis of Success in Foreign Language Study," *The German Quarterly*, Vol. XII, pp. 71–80, March, 1939. James B. Tharp, "The General Language Course and its Administration," Proceedings of the Ohio Workshop on Modern Language Teaching, Ohio Council on Education, 1940, Ohio State University, pp. 24–30.

[4] C. K. Ogden and I. A. Richards, *The Meaning of Meaning*, Harcourt, Brace and Company, New York, 4th ed., 1936, xxii + 363 pp. Alfred Korzybski, *Science and Sanity*, Science Printing Press Company, Lancaster, Pa., 1935, xx + 798 pp. See also revised edition, 1940. Stuart Chase, *The Tyranny of Words*,

solely as a means of communication or code, nor merely as a medium of thought, but also as a hypnotic influence in the thought life of the individual and of society.   The fact that people can be hypnotized by emotionally charged words to die for or against "-isms" which they cannot even define, and often apply interchangeably to the same overt act (depending entirely on who does it), has revealed the need for examining the hypnotic effects of language, and the ways and means for preventing people from confusing the existence of a word with the existence of something in fact.

In his cogent article "Changing Concepts of the Mind," Lawson[1] has called attention to the way in which human progress, even in the sciences, has been handicapped by "bad language"—language that does not at all correspond to what exists in reality.

The supposition seems valid that early thinkers, save for the true philosophers, did not attempt to delve deeply into the subject.   The very lack of definite knowledge admitted of no beginning place.   Yet here a strange paradox appears: Man had little knowledge of the mind but he had a considerable vocabulary built about it; and this very fact of having so extensive a vocabulary probably acted as a deterrent to careful analysis of the problem.

Man, when possessed of an accepted terminology with which to refer to supposed conditions of a phenomenon, may feel little need to question its nature further.   He naturally accepts with more or less confidence those things that appear to bear the approval stamp of long acceptance.

Language as a Behavior Switchboard.   An Introduction to Psychosemantics.—The habit of coining "ghost words" to explain the unknown, and of later mistaking the existence of these words for reality itself, has been responsible for much irrational behavior.[2] Language is basically man's way of symbolizing reality for purposes of communication.   When the language symbols do not evoke identically the same concepts of reality in the listener as in the speaker, or in the writer and his reader, confusion or misunderstanding inevitably results.   To use Korzybski's analogy, language is like a map of reality—it is not reality itself.   The same confusion which is likely to beset a motorist who tries to follow an inaccurate map is likely to beset the

Harcourt, Brace and Company, New York, 1938, xiv + 396 pp.   S. I. Hayakawa, *Language in Action*, College Typing Company, Madison, Wis., 1939, 100 pp.

[1] Douglas E. Lawson, "Changing Concepts of the Mind," *Phi Delta Kappan*, Vol. XX, p. 42, October, 1937.

[2] For a brief overview of irrational behavior associated with language see *Readings in the Foundations of Education*, Vol. II, Bureau of Publications, Teachers College, Columbia University, New York, 1941, "Words and Things," by Max Schiferl, pp. 316–321.

individual who tries to act upon inaccurate language. Anyone who has tried to follow verbal directions and became confused in the process needs no proof of the many annoying inaccuracies to which language is susceptible when used as a guide to action. As a mirror of reality, language often yields very distorted images. It is a dangerous fact that speech functions most fluently and painlessly when it is not used as a guide to action at all, but as an escape into a world of verbal mirages, a world in which ghost words are substituted for real persons, places, or things—a kind of dreamworld which sometimes becomes so much more attractive or satisfying than the reality which it displaces, that the individual is hypnotized into it. Harmless cases exist in great numbers among highly introverted individuals; extreme cases are usually accommodated in psychopathic wards.

Faulty language habits are synonymous with faulty thinking— faulty mental images of reality—which in turn may lead to irrational views and erratic behavior. Certainly, all this does not mean that language cannot be used to project, visualize, or symbolize that which does not actually exist. No invention of note, no important step toward a world without slavery, illiteracy, or disease would have been possible without abstracting reality through symbolization, and then projecting the reconstructed map into the future as a guide to action. As a means of symbolizing, interpreting, and mentally reconstructing what is, language makes possible the projection of the past into the present and of the present into the future. To the extent to which this process of mentally abstracting a real world of real people, places, actions, and things is in keeping with the facts, language is both a faithful mirror and a reliable directional guide. To the extent to which it misrepresents what actually exists, it is a subtly deceptive instrument—a mirage that gradually recedes and finally disappears when actually approached. The mirage effects of language are as dangerously elusive in daily life as the atmospheric mirages of the Sahara.

These effects are the products of a combination of circumstances. A very common pitfall is that of *unconsciously mistaking the existence of a word for the actual existence in fact of whatever the word is supposed to mean.* Such phrases as "100 per cent *Moronian*," for example, are difficult to translate into operational terms unless the "someone" referred to, *i.e.*, the *referent*, is defined so that he or she can be identified from verifiable facts concerning his person or behavior. Without this realistic basis in fact, the term is only a verbal ghost. If, however, what is mean by a "100 per cent *Moronian*" is defined in terms of a specific code of action—what a person who is "100 per cent *Moronian*" actually does in given circumstances, then it can have meaning as a guide to action, provided the code of behavior is understood and accepted as a desirable goal.   Without such a common understanding, the expression is likely to lead, not to concerted action, but to mere vocal confusion and contradictory forms of activity.   Sometimes the effects of verbal slogans are socially and psychologically detrimental, especially when the only identifiable referent is a physical characteristic or fact of birth beyond the control of the individual himself. Nothing more than lines of cleavage or psychological barriers are achieved by such verbalization, for in such circumstances no one can be changed in reality except to be made to feel more important or less important than he really is as a human being per se.   Either one can qualify as being a 100 per cent *Moronian* because one happens to have been born according to specifications, or one cannot.   Education for a 100 per cent *Moronianism* in such cases is obviously mere busy-work.   All slogans that have as their criteria realities that cannot be changed consciously by all individuals through their own efforts, seldom do more than to place halos of prestige around those who qualify anyway through no efforts whatsoever of their own.   As incentives to constructive action, slogans are valueless unless they symbolize specific modes of behavior to which people can learn to conform *in similar circumstances*.   The same observations apply with equal validity to educational aims and objectives.

Examples of other verbal fictions that are too often treated as realities, and thus cause irrational behavior even among "educated people," are such terms as "the average child."   Courses of study that are organized for the benefit of these verbal ghosts rarely fit any real children except those who seem to resemble the verbal ghost in some verifiable respect—perhaps a special characteristic such as chronological age, which may very often misrepresent the child as a whole if taken as the sole basis for estimating his ability to learn, his likes and dislikes, his mental and physical health, or even his height and weight.   The fact is that no two children, with the possible exception of identical twins, are psychologically alike in all particulars. Illusions of similarity are often created by adding up different abilities into a whole.   Such synthetic wholes are usually meaningless as a key to a child's reactions or behavior in specific situations.[1]   The whole is

---

[1] Successful experiments in teaching French to the feeble-minded support this view.   See Paul F. Angiolillo, "French for the Feeble-minded: An Experiment," *The Modern Language Journal*, Vol. XXV, pp. 266–271, April, 1942.

always something more than the sum of all its parts. *This "something" is the element of organic unity, or the characteristic which makes it possible for the whole to do what the parts by themselves cannot perform.* This point is important in attempting to predict pupil achievement in a foreign language from partial samplings which do not characterize the learner's behavior as a "whole person." Every child differs from every other child, if not as the synthetic average of all his parts, at least as an organic unity—*i.e.*, as a human being—and elementary and secondary education is concerned primarily with guiding the growth of young people as individuals in the direction of socially useful lives.

Verbal fictions that remain ghosts or mirages until they are defined in terms of referents identifiable in reality—something, somewhere, at some time—are as useless directional guides in teaching as they are in achieving "social reform," "everlasting peace," or other "verbal topics" that stimulate vocal behavior to the point where it is satisfying in itself, and gradually hypnotizes the individual into accepting the existence of a word for a fact.

Sanity in Language.—Linguistically sane people use their projected dreamworld as a guide to efforts to attain it in reality. Highly introverted people substitute it for reality. Linguistically insane people lose themselves in it and act as if it existed in fact, violently resenting all real things that contradict it, or bringing them into conformity through mental metamorphosis. Sometimes one wonders with Echegaray whether talking and acting as if certain verbal mirages created by writing foreign-language objectives were real outcomes, whether resenting bitterly all presentations of facts to the contrary, and whether merely attempting to bring the contradictory facts into conformity with the dreamworld through a process of verbal rationalization or compensation (instead of by doing something in reality to synchronize and integrate the two worlds) is a case of *locura o sanidad.*

These "touchy" examples, deliberately chosen for their bearing on curriculum and instruction in foreign languages, literatures, and cultures, may suffice to give a superficial insight into the verbal mirages in which even specialists in language at times unconsciously lose themselves for lack of insight into the psychological effects of habitually using empty symbols to the point where they are mistaken for reality. Obviously, there is nothing new in this superficial discussion of a phenomenon of which even the Romans must have been aware when they coined the phrase *facta non verba* (deeds not words). To belittle any attempt to analyze this psychological problem concretely in such a way as to be able to do something about it, however, is to show a lack of appreciation of its subtle but significant effect upon that aspect of the thought life of the individual and groups of individuals which eventually conditions overt behavior. To the educator and psychologist, the problem of doing something about it is of primary concern, for it has an important bearing upon the major task of his profession, that of helping human beings to achieve in reality socially acceptable, verbally conceived projections of individual and group life in its various avocational, vocational, and social aspects.

Since thought life is impossible except through the medium of some form of symbolization (musical, mathematical, spacial, verbal, etc.) the process by which reality is abstracted into symbols and the degree to which these symbols are accurate guides to a real world are of importance to anyone professionally concerned with bringing into being that which does not yet exist. Creating verbal mirages— whether in the form of aims, objectives, or societal Utopias—is a necessary and desirable use of the only significant characteristic that distinguishes a human being from an animal—the ability to abstract reality into symbols, and mentally to rearrange these symbols into a conceptually reconstructed map of the environment which, being more potentially satisfying, serves as an incentive actually to *do* something in order to realize this conception in fact. Indeed, the ability to do conceptual thinking—to create verbally attractive reconstructions of reality is so basically essential to motivated problem solving in individual and group life, that education may well recognize the development of this ability as one of its major objectives, provided it is constantly and keenly aware of the following realistic limitations—limitations that should be common sense but are too seldom acted upon as such.

Word Magic. Conceptual Thinking with Empty Symbols.—Conceptual thinking done through the medium of empty symbols, or ghost words that do not stand for anything that actually exists, cannot of itself change reality. It can at best only distort one's view of the facts or change the nomenclature of reality, a change which may be confusing to those who have not been informed of it. As a pleasurably harmless pastime, playing with ghost words has a place in life; but it never changes reality itself. As more than an occasional game it is undesirable in view of the time consumed in talking about ghosts, and in view of the fact that such prolonged discussion often causes people to act as if ghosts existed—much as children often acquire a fear of the dark from verbally manufactured creatures. The chief difference between the verbal ghosts that haunt the minds of children, and those that occupy the minds of adults, is in the fact that the mental creations of grown people are not content to live modestly in abandoned houses.   They rule the world, often depriving "ideals," "virtues," "self-evident truths," "happiness," "freedom," and "the average child," of their physical means of locomotion and existence in a real world of real people, real places, and real things.

Conceptual thinking to be effective as a basis for action must be done through the medium of symbols with specific physical referents— actions, conditions, people, or places verifiable and identifiable in the environment.   A conceptual reconstruction of the environment in terms of such referents can be made the basis of action necessary to bring what actually exists into conformity with the way it is recon- ceived to be.   Putting real meanings into empty symbols is essential if action is comtemplated.   This process of trying to make ghosts materialize, however, is a difficult task, as anyone who has participated in formulating objectives for an educational program cannot fail to appreciate.

Motivating Action through Language.—Sometimes it is best to start with reality—with what actually exists in contrast with what might desirably be—and let the words grow out of the necessity of describing what verifiable changes are to be expected in fact when reality has been brought into conformity with its conceptual reconstruction.   This is often the wisest procedure if the environment has become charged with electricity in the form of emotional symbols of such high voltage that one must guard himself against electrocution.   Conditions that have become electrically charged with emotional symbols can rarely be seen through language as they really are.   Emotional words always throw the conceptual reconstruction of reality out of focus, either by making it appear better or worse than it actually is, depending upon whether the electrical charge is positive or negative.   Rational behavior is usually impossible in such circumstances, for emotional symbols do not illuminate the way to action; they generate heat rather than light. The function of emotional language is to motivate action *after* the course has been charted in terms of concrete ways and means to a real goal.   Where the process is reversed, "creative thinking" leads to little more than a rearrangement of prejudices accompanied by heat.

People who are interested in seeing that something involving human behavior is actually accomplished without coercion usually secure the best results by using language in conformity with the following prin- ciples of procedure:

1. Contrasting, through language with identifiable referents in time and place, what actually exists with what could actually be brought into existence through a reconstruction of these referents.

2. Making the projected reconstruction of reality seem more desirable by indicating its advantages in terms of what desirable things can then be done or made available that are now difficult or impossible.

3. Stimulating action, where necessary, by charging the reality as it actually exists with the electricity from unfavorable emotional symbols, and the conceptual reconstruction of reality with the electricity from favorable emotional symbols.

The intelligent housewife who wishes to secure her husband's consent and help in rearranging the furnishings in the living room usually applies these principles in the proper order. The social demagogue, on the contrary, usually confines himself to step 3, the use of emotionally charged symbols to secure acceptance of a mirage created through words without a specifically identifiable counterpart in reality. That is because he is either ignorant of ways and means, or not so much concerned with securing a reconstruction of the environment as with reinforcing his privileged position within it. By analyzing the writings and speeches of social-civic leaders in terms of the principles of psychosemantic behavior in language, one can roughly determine whether, in spite of their words, they are actually trying to maintain things as they are or to change the *status in quo*. Obviously, these principles have been too superficially discussed above to be serviceable for this purpose without special training in the recognition and psychosemantic analysis of ghost words, polar words, emotional words, ambiguous words, and such verbal techniques as creating diversions through language.[1]

Mistaking Differences in Words for Differences in Fact.—Because of the emotional charges that certain words carry, it is possible to label the same physical fact with different words in such a way as to hypnotize people into behaving differently with respect to the fact itself. In other words, in the minds of people, reality itself is linguistically camouflaged to the extent that they behave differently toward the

---

[1] Robert H. Thouless, *How to Think Straight*, Simon and Schuster, Inc., New York, 1939, viii + 246 pp. Korzybski, *Science and Sanity, op. cit.* P. W. Bridgman, *The Logic of Modern Physics*, The Macmillan Company, New York, 1932, xiv + 228 pp.; pp. 28–31. H. R. Huse, *The Illiteracy of the Literate*, D. Appleton-Century Company, Inc., New York, 1933, x + 273 pp.; Chaps. IV to VIII. Irving J. Lee, *Language Habits in Human Affairs: An Introduction to General Semantics*, Harper & Brothers, New York, 1941, 278 pp.

act itself and toward the executors of it—which is the important point for the psychologist and educator to keep in mind.   This linguistic hocus-pocus, by which reality is linguistically, but not *really*, transformed in such a way as to change people's behavior, is made possible chiefly by the use of hypnotic symbols charged with favorable or unfavorable emotional associations.   Criminal lawyers are aware of the suceptibility of the human mind to this verbal legerdemain.   Most people recognize it in obvious circumstances; but few are aware of its daily occurrence in ordinary conversation, news reporting, political campaigning, or advertising.   It is for this reason that people who are masters of language in one field are often unconscious victims of it in another.   To this generalization the most highly schooled university graduates are rarely exceptions.[1]

The Importance of Consumer Education in Language.—Because of the rapid increase in improved means of communication by which people's minds can be hypnotized through language to see things that do not actually exist or to view the world through distorted glasses, educators have realized the need for providing training, not only in the correct use of language as a code, but also in the sane use of language as a medium of thought, and as a basis for projecting plans of action that can be realized in fact because the word symbols are accurate descriptions of what actually exists.   Accuracy in expression and comprehension has always been a major preoccupation of language teaching; accuracy in detecting ghosts or distortions in language has not; and only distorted behavior can result from language that throws reality out of focus—especially when people act as if the *symbols* were true rather than the *facts* which they misrepresent.

To assume from this discussion that only prosaic scientific language should be used by human beings is nonsense.   Language that is intended to portray a landscape in such a way as to arouse in a reader as far as possible the same emotion that the writer felt in contemplating it, is obviously effective to the extent to which it uses symbols that accomplish this purpose.   There is certainly no need for purely objective language in such cases.   In news reports, however, it is important to distinguish between what *actually* happened and the writer's *feeling* toward what he thought happened.   Any use of words with definitely favorable or unfavorable feeling tones provides one of several clues to what may be termed a biased distortion of reality.

Consumer Education through General Language.—In the new type general-language course, consumer education along the lines just

[1] Huse, *The Illiteracy of the Literate, op. cit.*

discussed has become an important part of the program[1] and has served to enhance the terminal values of the offering for all students regardless of whether they continue in a regular foreign-language class or not. The place of the foreign languages in this new type of program is readily apparent from the following leading questions around which consumer education in a general language or language-arts survey course may be organized:

1. Why do people (Americans and other nationalities) speak, write, read, and spell as they do?

2. How does language affect people (Americans and other nationalities) in daily life?

3. What can be done to make language a more reliable servant and a less deceptive master of our thoughts, feelings, and actions?

In dealing with these questions, English and the foreign languages are drawn upon for illustrative examples, but no aspect of language is studied as an end in itself.   Although incidental practice may at times be necessary to pronounce intelligibly words and expressions used to illustrate psychosemantic analysis, the amount of such practice is limited by the degree of proficiency required for intelligibility.   The annotated outline[2] below may suffice to suggest content and activities through which the language-arts survey course may be made to yield terminal values of significance in daily life without sacrificing its exploratory-guidance function.   It is just as possible to observe pupil interest and aptitude for foreign-language study while the students are working with materials that afford an insight into speech as a way of symbolizing and interpreting reality, as it is to observe their reactions to content that stifles ability to get at the life meaning behind the language.

Prospectus for a Language-arts Survey Course.—Why do people—Americans and other nationalities—speak, read, write, or spell as they do?

---

[1] Walter V. Kaulfers, "An Integrative Approach to the Social-cultural Aspects of Language," *The School Review*, Vol. XLVI, pp. 737–744, December, 1938. Reports of the Stanford Language Arts Investigation, *Foreign Languages and Cultures in American Education*, Vol. II, "Language Detectives—Two Orientation-courses in the Social-cultural Aspects of Language," McGraw-Hill Book Company, Inc., New York.   In press.   In 1940 the American Youth Commission of the American Council on Education, strongly endorsed general language in its report "What the High Schools Ought to Teach," Washington, D. C.

[2] For a more comprehensive outline, see Walter V. Kaulfers and Holland D. Roberts, *A Cultural Basis for the Language Arts*, Stanford University Press, Stanford University, Calif., 1937, 115 pp.; pp. 60–75.

Since this topic is too broad to be treated in detail, it is important that the work be unified by using a single language as a basis for similarity and contrast in explaining the casual factors underlying various types of linguistic change and semantic shift.   Otherwise, the program is likely to degenerate into a series of purposeless exercises in baby philology.   Because of the many foreign languages that have contributed to English, the pupils' own language obviously provides a more appropriate unifying core for illustrating and contrasting the operation of linguistic factors than does a language that has not been enriched to the same extent by foreign cultures.   Content and activities that enable young people to see how language reveals the way human beings think, and to realize that it is almost as difficult to freeze language as it is to formalize and standardize their thoughts, are especially appropriate in paving the way for an understanding of the subtle role that language plays in conditioning the thought life and behavior of the individual.   Such content and activities are also desirable in developing a creative attitude toward language in which *effectiveness of function* rather than "fascinating" details of form are paramount.   Much language teaching has been so preoccupied with developing an appreciation of language as a code or set of symbols, without reference to any criterion derived from the basic functions of language in human life, that it has actually taught many young people to "appreciate" efficiency and inefficiency in language as objects equally worthy of uncritical adoration and perpetuation.

Among the topics for investigation and discussion by which young people may be afforded vivid insights into the psychological foundations of language without falling into the error of mistaking language to be of divine origin (and therefore fixed for all time), are the following:

A. Why do we write as we do?

1. How did the letters of our alphabet originate?

2. Why are the letters of our alphabet different from those of foreign peoples, *e.g.*, the Germans, the French, the Spanish, or the Chinese?

3. How have the mechanics of handwriting and printing been improved through the centuries to make written communication more efficient, *i.e.*, more rapid and more readily intelligible?

    a. What insights do early ways of graphically symbolizing reality give into the thought life of the people?

    b. Why was the phonetic alphabet invented? What are its advantages and effects?

    c. Modern improvements in systems of penmanship and stenography: Why were they invented? What are their advantages and effects?

4. Why do we punctuate and capitalize differently from the Germans, Spanish, French, or Italians? Of what value are punctuation marks, capitals, accent marks, etc., in language?

B. Why do we spell as we do?

1. Why is the same sound often spelled in different ways in English? Is this fact true to the same extent in Spanish, German, French, Italian, Latin, etc.?

2. What effect does the fact that some languages are highly phonetic, and that others are not, have upon the lives of the people who use different languages?

    a. What effect does it have on the ease with which children can learn to pronounce written words, and to spell spoken words correctly?

    b. What effect does this fact have upon the time which pupils must devote in school, at the expense of other activities, in order to learn to read, write, and pronounce correctly?

    c. What effect does this fact have upon the ease with which foreigners can learn the language?

    d. What effect does this fact have upon the cost of printing?[1]

C. Why do we speak as we do?

1. Why do we speak differently from the Spanish, French, Germans, or Italians, etc.?

    a. Why does the English *i* in *kite*, for example, rarely have this sound in other languages?

    b. Why do we say "I *have been* here (for) ten years" instead of "I *am* here (since) ten years" as in French, German, Spanish, and Italian? Je *suis* ici (depuis) dix ans; Ich *bin* (schon) zehn Jahre hier; *Estoy* aquí desde hace diez años.

    c. Why do we say "I *am hungry* (thirsty, afraid, etc.)" instead of "I *have hunger* (thirst, fear, etc.)" as in French, Spanish,

---

[1] Because of the typographical complexity of the French language, the cost of typesetting, proofreading, and paper has run into hundreds of millions of francs annually above the estimated cost of printing the language phonetically. If a phonetic system were adopted, such a word as *bureaux* could be shortened to **byro,** with a material saving in cost of typesetting, proofreading, and paper consumption. Moreover, hundreds of hours of human time and energy now consumed in embalming the language could be saved by foreigners in learning French, and by French children in learning the language which should be theirs as a natural birthright. The complexities and responsibilities of human life today make too many demands

German, and Italian? *J'ai faim; Tengo hambre; Ich habe Hunger.*

d. Why do we say *"a round table"* instead of *"a table round"* as in French, Spanish, and Italian? *Une table ronde; una mesa redonda; una tavola retonda.*

e. Why do we sometimes say *rub-a-dub-dub* to imitate the sound of a drum instead of *rataplán* as in Spanish?

f. Why do we usually use *it* in speaking of a pencil or pen when in similar circumstances the Germans, Spaniards, French, or Italians would use the same words which they use for persons (she, he, him, her)? Compare:

English: I shall write with *it* (meaning the pencil or pen).
French: J'écrirai avec *lui* (pencil) or *elle* (pen).
Spanish: (Yo) escribiré con *él* (*ella*).
German: Ich werde mit *ihm* (*ihr*) schreiben.
Italian: (Io) scriverò con *esso* (*essa*).

g. Why do we sometimes say "put the cart before the horse" when in similar circumstances the French usually say "put the *plow* before the *oxen*"? Mettre la *charrue* devant les *boeufs.*

h. Why is it incorrect in English, and correct in Spanish, to say "I haven't done *nothing: Yo no he hecho nada*"?

i. Why is it that in English most people say *you* in speaking to a president or a beggar when in French, Spanish, German, and Italian two different words are used in such cases?

j. Why is it that in English we often say "Raise *your right hands,* boys," when in Spanish, French, German, and Italian one usually says "Raise *the right hand,* boys"?

Spanish: Levantad la mano derecha, muchachos.
French: Levez la main droite, garçons.
German: Hebet die rechte Hand, Knaben.
Italian: Alzate la mano destra, ragazzi.

It will be noted from the foregoing outline that the emphasis is on the life meaning behind the word—on the psychosemantic factors that underlie, and to a large extent determine, the external form and syntactical format of language. In dealing with the *whys* of language one must return to the fact that language is basically man's way of

upon the development of insights, attitudes, interests, and appreciations to justify the consumption of so much human time and energy on mastering the tools of civilization.

abstracting and symbolizing reality, and seek the answer by way of such questions as: How did those who originally set the pattern for the language see things, feel about them, react toward them, or use them? A satisfactory answer can never be found in a rule phrased in grammatical terms, for grammatical terminology is not based on causal interrelationships between reality and man's mental or emotional reactions to it, but almost exclusively on the relationship between form and function within the language itself.[1] Grammatical rules are, therefore, descriptive rather than explanatory. More often than not they obscure the real significance of language as a way of thinking behind a word barrage of classificatory labels unintelligible to the novice.

The question "Why do the French and Spanish consider certain things as being masculine and others as being feminine?" certainly cannot be explained satisfactorily merely by stating that words ending in certain ways are almost always feminine and words ending in certain other ways are almost always masculine. Such a "rule" does not answer the question *why* at all. At best, it merely answers the question *when*. The causal reason for the phenomenon of gender in relation to inanimate objects is to be sought in the ideology of primitive cultures. The story is a long one, and a very old one, but not without interest:

Primitive man's inability to explain the behavior of fire, thunder, lightning, cloudbursts, trees, flowers, rain, earthquakes, the sun, moon, stars, etc., probably caused him to invent reasons satisfying to his curiosity. These reasons usually involved personifying the objects—considering them unusual people of the male or female sex, or monsters having the characteristics of both sexes (*i.e.*, neuter). As primitive man became more enlightened he gradually revised his rationalizations of reality, explaining the behavior of the inanimate environment as being controlled by a god (masculine), a goddess (feminine), or a supernatural being without specific sex (neuter). The sex of the controlling deity then became identified with the word label for the water, fire, or thunder, etc., which the deity controlled. This process can be made clearer by comparing it to the primitive Eskimo custom of calling little boys by such names as "Grandmother" or "Mother," in honor of the deceased member of the family whose spirit presumably entered the child's body to guide it to maturity.

By the time animism, deism, and other ways of rationalizing the unknown disappeared with the increase in human knowledge, the sex

[1] J. R. Kantor, *An Objective Psychology of Grammar*, Indiana University, Bloomington, Ind., 1936, xvi + 344 pp.; pp. 10–13.

labels (gender) had already become securely welded to a sufficiently large number of core words to establish a pattern for the future growth of the language. New words that were related to existing words in certain ways (*e.g.*, sounded like them or rhymed with them) were assigned to the same classification, which now became merely one of gender in the linguistic rather than in the biological sense.

The process of analogic radiation, by which the language characteristics of an established stock of words became the criterion for imputing these characteristics to new words having something in common with them in sound or meaning, is important. It is one of the explanations for such a seeming incongruity as the use of a neuter word for *girl* in German. The noun *Mädchen* (girl) is neuter simply because the diminutive ending *-chen* has neuter associations within the language itself. This case in gender is an excellent illustration of the way in which symbols become detached from their physical referents, and begin to behave according to the language-system—a symbolic world independent of reality—rather than according to physical fact. It is amusing to speculate what would happen if the gender of the word became confused with the sex gender of its physical referent, and people actually mistook this characteristic of the symbol to be a characteristic of the individual—as is so often true of peoples' behavior with respect to ghost words where the incongruity between the symbol and that which is symbolized is not so obviously ridiculous.

Although analogic radiation and personification through animism, deism, empathy, etc., probably account for the origin of gender in language, seeming exceptions can usually be explained in terms of the foreign origins of the words in point or on the basis of semantic differentiation or assimilation. For example:

Exceptions Attributable to Foreign Origin.—In Spanish, as in other Romance languages, certain words borrowed from the Greek or Latin retain the gender which they acquired in the parent language: *el programa, el cometa, el planeta, el mapa*, etc., have all kept their original gender since their adoption into Spanish.

Exceptions Attributable to Semantic Assimilation.—Sometimes a word takes on the gender of a word which it has replaced. Originally, *the capital* was *the capital city*, "capital" being an adjective: *la (ciudad) capital, la (citta) capitale*, or *la ville capitale*. Similarly, the terms *vowel* and *consonant* are feminine in Spanish because they replace the noun *letter: la (letra) vowel, la (letra) consonante*.

Exceptions Attributable to Semantic Differentiation.—In Spanish, as in other languages, gender sometimes serves to distinguish two different words which are phonetically and orthographically identical: *la pez* (pitch from a tree) and *el pez* (a fish).

The foregoing explanation of the phenomenon of gender is the kind of explanation that students in general-language courses should develop through reading and discussion guided by leading questions of the type contained in the outline. The aim is always to get at the life meaning behind the word, not just to learn the grammatical names for things. Although the discussion of gender above is phrased in language beyond the reach of many junior-high-school pupils, the psycho-semantic principles are not at all beyond their grasp when illustrated in simple language. The mental reactions of primitive man were seldom too complex for young people to understand.

In dealing with the psychological and sociological foundations of language, no opportunity should be lost to indicate concretely how such phenomena as gender have a bearing upon the translation of thought from one language into another. In his poem *Trees*, for example, Joyce Kilmer personifies a tree as being feminine:

> A tree that looks at God all day
> And lifts *her leafy arms* to pray,
> Upon *whose bosom* snow has lain,
>
> .   .   .   .   .
>
> A tree that may in summer wear
> A nest of robins in *her* hair.

In French, German, Spanish, and Italian, however, the word tree is masculine: *un arbre, ein Baum, un árbol, un albero.* Consequently, in translating this poem into the foreign languages mentioned, a tree would have to be personified as a *male* being. This difference in personification would certainly have a peculiar effect upon the foreign reader. Imagine,

> A tree that looks at God all day
> And lifts *his* leafy arms to pray,
> Upon *whose bosom* snow has lain,
>
> .   .   .   .   .
>
> A tree that may in summer wear
> A nest of robins in *his* hair.

It will be noted that when the study of language is approached from the standpoint of casual psychological factors, it can be made to yield significant insights into language as a key to the thought life of the people who developed it. Insights of this kind are probably of greater significance for an intelligent study of a foreign language later than a preparatory course in grammatical terminology. Although teachers without training in general linguistics and the psychology of language will find themselves handicapped in developing such insights among children, a reading of the books listed in Appendix E–G will to some extent compensate for lack of specialized university preparation in these areas.

Social Perspective in Language versus the Cult of Inefficiency.— The following compositions written at the conclusion of a unit of work[1] dealing with the topics in sections *A* and *B* of the outline will serve to illustrate how the history and psychology of language can be related to problems of significance to young people in such a way as to stimulate creative thinking about language in present-day life instead of a blind worship of inefficiency in the tools of communication.

WHY NOT STREAMLINE ENGLISH?

Have you ever tried to write a composition, and found it hard to put your thoughts down on paper, even when you thought you knew just what you wanted to say?   If you have, perhaps it is because your handwriting cannot keep up with your ideas.   Most of us think in language, and when we get an idea, it enters our mind in the form of a silent stream of words that flows approximately as rapidly as we are in the habit of speaking; but by the time we have written down the first few words we have fallen far behind the stream of our thought.   Then we have to stop to recall what we intended to say, and to connect it up with what went before. The crude system of long-hand which most of us still use is so slow that it often tends to retard or block fluent thinking when we try to write.

How much better it would be if we could be taught from the start to use a kind of shorthand that would make it possible for anyone to write down an idea as fast as we could think it out.   How much easier writing would become then.   There would be less blocking of ideas by an awkward system of writing that drags upon one's ability to think in words.   Why, after all, should the school continue teaching a system of handwriting so inefficient that it has very little place in modern business?   A good shorthand writer can take dictation as fast as the average person speaks.   Why not, then, develop a new kind of shorthand suitable for use in the schools, and teach it to everyone from the start?   That would do away with the many months and even years we spend on spelling, for in shorthand almost everything is written the way it sounds.   How strange it is that we should still be obliged to write a capital Q in very much the same way that the ancients made it 5,000 years ago—and for no better reason than that they somehow took it into their heads to draw a picture of a monkey with his tail hanging down!

Yours for less monkey business and more common sense in language!   *Why not streamline English?*

OUR UNNATURALIZED ALIEN LANGUAGE

When foreigners come to this country we naturalize them before we allow them to become voters, but when foreign words come into our speech we do nothing before allowing them to take root in our language.   To the contrary, we usually

[1] By permission of the Stanford Language Arts Investigation.

insist that these newcomers remain dressed in the very same costumes that they wore in the old country, and we keep patching up all the worn places instead of clothing the words in the latest American fashions.   We have thousands of words in our language that still go around in the same old clothes that they wore when they first came to this country!   Now all this may be very interesting and picturesque to those who like old lavender and lace, but everyone is not interested in being a museum curator of language.

Is it not high time that we naturalize our language by adopting a simple, uniform system of American spelling?   Just think how much time is spent in school learning the ten or more different ways in which the single sound of $\overline{ee}$ is spelled in such words as *me, tree, sea, Caesar, receive, believe, people, Phoenix, biology, machine,* or the *twenty* different ways in which the single sound of *sh* has to be spelled in such words as *sugar, nation, fuchsia, session, fashion, ocean, anxious, nature,* simply because some foreigners started spelling them that way—often centuries ago, and often for no sensible reason at all!   Then consider the time wasted in trying to remember that *procedure* is spelled with *one e,* and that *proceed* (which certainly belongs to the same family) requires *two.*   It is hardly an exaggeration to say that the untaught spelling of a third grader has more sense to it than that.   Of course, you can point out that many of the words are spelled as they are because the Romans wrote them that way two thousand years ago; but why should the English-speaking people of the world be among the few peoples that have to study a foreign language in order to make sense of their own?

Compare our muddled system with the highly phonetic spelling of the Spaniards.   In Spanish, the sound of $\bar{e}$ (as in *me, tree, sea, Caesar, receive, believe, people, Phoenix, biology, machine,* etc.) is always represented by an *i.*   Moreover, when the Spaniards or Spanish Americans borrow foreign words they immediately naturalize them and dress them in the latest Spanish fashions.   Take for example the words *fútbol, béisbol,* and *biftec* which they have borrowed from us.   Observe how much easier the Spanish language is to spell, read, and pronounce than ours.   Think of how much more time the Spanish youth has in school to spend on really worth while and important things instead of on mechanics.   In fact, in those countries in which languages are spelled as they are pronounced, and pronounced as they are spelled, the students are about two years ahead of American boys and girls in school work.

About the only people who are much worse off than we are the Chinese.   It is said that the Chinese student at the age of twenty-five cannot read his own language any better than a bright American boy can read English at the age of ten. That is because he has to learn an "alphabet" of some 4,000 to 5,000 symbols, while we have to learn only 26 letters.   This comparison may be consoling to some, but personally I derive little comfort from comparing our troubles with those of the Chinese.   For my part, I think it only common sense that we stop spending so much time in school on mechanics when a thorough overhauling of our language would make it a more efficient means of communication.   Turkey overhauled her language almost overnight—why can't *we?*

How Does Language Affect People in Daily Life?—Reading and discussion centering around the reasons why people read, write, spell, or speak as they do should pave the way for a clearer understanding of the subtle role that language plays in the mental life of the individual and in the social and economic life of society.   The annotated outline below contains leading questions for making reading, discussion, and correlated activities contribute to the development of social intelligence through language:

1. How is progress in science and invention dependent on language?

2. How does language affect the progress of young people in school?

3. How does lack of ability in language create social problems?

4. How does language affect the religious lives of people?

5. How does language in advertising affect the lives of people?

6. How does the language of news editors, radio reporters, foreign correspondents, and political figures affect the lives of people?

7. How does language in diplomacy affect the lives of people?

8. How effective is spoken or written language in comparison with other means of communication?

9. How does language in law and legal documents affect the lives of people?

10. How does language affect the social or cultural life of the individual?

11. How does language in everyday conversation affect the lives of people?

12. How does thinking done in terms of "bad" language lead to erratic behavior on the part of individuals or groups of individuals?

13. How can people often be hypnotized through language to live or die for reasons that they do not understand and cannot explain?

14. How is language often used to disguise, conceal, dignify, excuse, or justify faulty behavior?

15. How does language provide a key to the social and economic background of the individual?

Since the subtopics above are not altogether self-explanatory, the following annotations may be suggestive of content and activities appropriate for the development of each aspect of the central theme.

Mathematics as the Language of Science.[1]—The fact that the mathematical expression $2 \times 2 = 4$ may be translated into the verbal expression "two times two equals four" is but a proof that all mathematical symbols are but another form of language.   The need for a more accurate and convenient set of symbols than words as a means

---

[1] Tobias Dantzig, *Number—The Language of Science*, The Macmillan Company, New York, 1930, viii + 260 pp.; pp. 38–41.

for thinking in quantitative terms, however, is seldom realized until one faces the limitations that verbal language imposes on one's ability to deal accurately with problems of amount or size.   Try multiplying the following "figures" *without* translating the Roman numerals into the cardinal numbers (1, 2, 3, etc.):

MCMCCCXLVIII by CMMCMLXXIX

Write your answer here in Roman numerals: _____.

Now *divide* the following without translating the problem into cardinal numbers:

MCCLVII by CLXXIV

Write your answer in Roman numerals here: _____.

Can you do it?   If you can, you are better than the Romans were! They usually had sense enough not even to try—for it is impossible to use these symbols for purposes of multiplication or long division. The Romans had to content themselves with laborious adding or subtracting—usually with pebbles!   The term *calculate*[1] you know, comes from the word *calculus*—diminutive of *calx* (limestone).   The reason why the Romans could not do much with their number system was because they used abbreviations for words without a zero point to give them exact meaning in terms of a fixed scale of values or "yardstick."   *M*, for example, was their abbreviation for the word *mille*, meaning *thousand*, and *C*, the first letter of the word *centum* (hundred). But nowhere in this number system did they provide a symbol for *zero*.   Owing to these imperfections in their mathematical language, they lagged far behind the Arabs who, having acquired a reliable language of size, were able to measure a degree on the earth's surface with astonishing accuracy at a time when all Europe insisted that the world was flat!

Because their language of size was more highly developed than that of any other peoples, the Arabs were the leaders in science after the decline of Greece; for mathematics is, after all, the language and cornerstone of science.   Even that phase of the "science of education" which claims to be "scientific" in any objective degree is based entirely on mathematical conceptions, *e.g.*, I.Q.'s, coefficients of reliability, test scores, etc.   Without an accurate and convenient language of size there would be no automobiles, radios, telephones, airplanes, steamships, refrigerators, X rays, weather forecasts, or moving

[1] *Picturesque Word Origins*, G. & C. Merriam Company, Springfield, Mass., 134 pp.; p. 38.

pictures as we know them today, for these inventions require tools of production accurate to the smallest fraction of a millimeter, elaborate mathematical estimates of stress and strain, or detailed measurements in terms of horsepower, volts, amperes, ohms, etc.   Indeed, progress in science and invention has been dependent more than anything else upon improvements and refinements in the language of quantitative thinking.

The correlation between progress in science[1] and progress in the language of mathematics is revealing and significant for human life. At one time the number *three* was the largest quantitative figure in the vocabularies of primitive peoples.[2] If the hunters of the tribe returned from the hunt with more than three deer, they had no way of stating the exact number.   In fact, the question "How *many* deer did you kill today?" would never have been raised.   If anyone was interested in the size of the kill, he would ask instead "How *much* deer did you kill?"   To this the answer would be "We killed enough deer to cover the ground of this enclosure."   The concept of *three* as the largest number probably had its origin in the referent "I + you + the other fellow."   Beyond *three*, quantity or size became relative, *e.g.*, "abundant as the sands of the sea," "abundant as the leaves upon the trees"— language that was poetically beautiful at times and usually adequate to the needs of the day, but useless as a basis for the precision that is required in balancing a budget or running an airplane.   Some authorities have attempted to trace the concept of the Holy Trinity (Father, Son, and Holy Ghost) to the primitive conception of infinity which was attached to anything beyond the number *three*, *i.e.*, to anything beyond the "I + you + the other fellow" relationship.   The equivalent of the modern expression "Three's a crowd" would probably have conveyed more than a polite hint to the minds of primitive peoples.   It would have come very close to being "gospel truth" in their number language.

By the end of the thirteenth century, the language of size in Europe had become sufficiently developed to make the symbol *thousand* the highest number needed for quantitative measurement and thinking. The life needs and aspirations of the day did not require a longer measuring stick.   It was not until the thirteenth century that the process of multiplication was added to the grammar of quantitative

[1] Dantzig, *op. cit.*

[2] Levi Leonard Conant, *The Number Concept*, Macmillan & Company, Ltd., London, 1896, vii + 218 pp.; pp. 1–7.   Florian Cajori, *A History of Mathematics*, Macmillan & Company, Ltd., London, 1919, 2d ed., revised and enlarged, viii + 514 pp.; p. 55.

thinking in mathematics.   Long division, as we know it today, did
not come into common use until about the time Columbus discovered
the New World.   Once these concepts became operative, progress in
higher mathematics became cumulatively rapid, and with this progress
came the increase in scientific knowledge and inventions which have
made it increasingly possible for people to live by controlling or changing the physical environment instead of by living in obedient conformity to it; to control disease rather than to resign oneself to its ravages;
to store and distribute goods for delayed consumption rather than to
move to new pastures; to add to the store of human comforts in life
rather than to accept discomfort uncritically as the price of an admission ticket to a paradise after death.   From the number *three*, which
was the highest number to most primitive peoples, and the number
thousand, which was the *ne plus ultra* to most people in the days of
Alfonso el Sabio, society has come to think in terms of *millions* and
billions.   When an understanding of the real meaning of such a numerical concept as "a thousand trillion light-years away" is involved,
however, the ordinary doctor of philosophy is almost as lost as the
primitive Bororo[1] beyond the number *three*, or the average Castilian of
the thirteenth century beyond the number *thousand*.   "It's just
awfully, awfully far away, if it is still there now" is about all this
astronomical figure can be translated into by you or me.   And perhaps
until we feel that we simply must do something about it, there is no
need for doing much more than expressing a due amount of awe in the
face of its incomprehensibility, like the ancient Egyptians whose only
symbol for *million* was the picture of a man looking astonished.[2]   Even
today, the term *billion* is still so incomprehensible to most Spanish-
speaking people that "a thousand million" is the only idiomatic equivalent that is meaningful to most men on the street.

   The reason for the rapid progress in science and invention is
traceable to three factors: the exactness of the quantitative language
that science employs; the faithfulness with which its verbal abstractions of the physical world identify and describe reality; and the
universality of its terminology.   The fact that the symbolized expression $2 \times 2 = 4$ is comprehensible and productive of exactly the same
answer almost the world over has freed scientific progress from the
barriers to communication which the verbal equivalent "two times
two equals four" might raise in the minds of those accustomed to

[1] Conant, *op. cit.*, p. 23.
[2] Louis Charles Karpinski, *The History of Arithmetic*, Rand McNally & Company, Chicago, 1925, 200 pp.; pp. 1–2.

seeing or hearing: *deux fois deux font quatre, zwei mal zwei sind vier, dos por dos son cuatro*, ad infinitum.   Moreover, the use of a common descriptive terminology (usually based on Greek or Latin roots) has facilitated international cooperation in research, in nearly all the natural sciences.   The word *biology*, for example, is much the same in French, German, Spanish, Italian, and many other languages: *biologie, Biologie, biología, biologia*, etc.   Contrast the tremendous advantage that the natural sciences have had over the social sciences—especially political economy—in being able to operate in and through a language that mirrors reality faithfully, instead of a language that is susceptible to all manner of distortions because it is only partly anchored in fact, and then only in relation to time and place.

The significance of this advantage can be made clearer through a concrete example.   The word *meter* is comprehensible among literate people almost the world over—as *mètre* to the Frenchman, *metro* to the Spaniard, *Meter* to the German, etc.—and to all it means exactly the same thing: one ten-millionth of the distance on a meridian from the equator to the pole, or about 39.37 inches.   To give this term a precise, practical, and nonvariable definition anchored in reality, the countries subscribing to the metric system have in their possession one or more copies of the platinum-iridium bar which is under double lock and key in the temperature-controlled vaults of the International Bureau of Weights and Measures near Paris.   This precious bar, never touched by human hands lest it expand or contract, is the definition of the word *meter*.   The United States has two duplicates of this master bar—Nos. 21 and 27—which are kept in the National Bureau of Standards in Washington.   From time to time these copies are taken abroad for comparison with the original.   No. 21 was sent to Paris for this purpose in 1932.   Thus does science make sure that its words mean something definite and, as far as possible, invariable in fact. Because of this effort on the part of a relatively small group of human beings to think and express themselves in terms of a language that mirrors reality accurately, the world today owes an increase in human comforts—better balanced meals, more appropriate clothing, less pain and disease, and more comfortable homes—which would be even greater were it not for the social approval and prestige attached to the mouthing of empty symbols.   The substitution of the latter process for constructive action has led cumulatively to the perversion of the potential benefits of scientific progress into instruments of frustration and destruction under the cloak of sublime language.   It is a notorious fact of abnormal psychology that the more sordid the defects of reality, the more beautiful the synthetic world of words devised to disguise it or compensate for it. In times of widespread social hysteria, this attempt to transform a sordid reality into a thing of beauty by means of verbal hocus-pocus—*i.e.*, hypnotic sublimation—can be observed on a national or even international scale. The language of the opposing rooting sections at a football game is an illustration in miniature, except that the activities of two teams on an athletic field are relatively harmless and voluntary, and few people feel called upon to dignify them as acts of bravery, self-sacrifice, loyalty, patriotism, or heroism, in defense of the cultural rise of mankind from barbarism. Even in the excitement of a football game, the crowds are sane to that extent.

Insights into the effects of language on human thought life and behavior are significant in terms of social living in the present and future, and give the study of language a concrete frame of reference. The business of the general-language course is to help people put life meanings into their verbally conceived ideals—to use a language which, as Carl Sandburg says, "takes off its coat, spits on its hands, and goes to work!"

Language in Legal Documents and Law.—In 1917 the following lawsuit, typical of many legal cases in which the central problem is the meaning of a single word or phrase, was tried before the Missouri Supreme Court:[1]

A man named Hedrick was arrested for stealing *hogs* in Reynolds County, Missouri. Upon being sentenced in his first trial to three years in the state penitentiary, he appealed to the state supreme court—arguing that he had not stolen *hogs* but only the *carcasses* of hogs, which (he claimed) was an entirely different thing.

The judge in the supreme court agreed with Hedrick, saying: "Defendant was charged with stealing *hogs* in Reynolds County. The proof was that they were dead before they were taken into that county. . . . He cannot be convicted of stealing hogs in Reynolds County, because the hogs, as hogs, were never in that county. He cannot, in this case, be convicted of stealing the carcasses of hogs, because he is not charged with such an offense. The *carcass of a hog, by whatever name called, is not a hog*. The dictionary says that a *hog is an animal*, and that *an animal is a living being*." (p. 193)

The judge then declared Hedrick innocent of the charge of hog stealing.

The foregoing illustration of the role of language in law may suffice to indicate the difficulties that arise in life from the use of words or phrases that fail to identify exactly the same concepts of reality in the minds of two or more people. It is because words have a tendency to add, drop, or change meanings over periods of time

[1] Paraphrased from *State v. Hedrick*, 199 Southwestern 192, Missouri, 1917.

(thus making their exact meanings as guides to action ambiguous in certain instances) that one of the major problems in the writing and interpretation of laws and legal documents is the problem of language. Just exactly what do the words mean when it comes to collecting insurance for *collision* on an automobile insurance policy, to dividing an estate "equally between my son and three daughters," to securing action on a signed contract?   The problem in such cases is that of identifying facts with the labels for facts—a no mean task.   The largest unabridged dictionary is inadequate for many situations. Most law libraries contain specialized dictionaries to help judges and lawyers determine the exact semantic range and limits of such ordinary words as *between, among,* and *across.*   Language becomes exceedingly important when it is intended to function as a conceptual guide to action in a real world, rather than to facilitate escape into a verbal mirage of the past, or into a synthetic dreamworld so divorced from reality that one can do nothing in fact to attain it.

The following example from a consumer-education unit in general language suggests ways and means for vitalizing the study of applied semantics among young people in terms of content chosen from the field of law—a field that affects everyone at some time during his life span, whether it be in the form of contracts, wills, deeds, insurance policies, income taxes, liability for damage, or ordinary traffic ordinances.   The fundamental problem is always, "What do the *words* of the law mean in terms of *action?*" and "Was what actually happened identifiable in time and place with the intended real meaning of the language of the law?"   Attention is called to the way in which etymology, dictionary work, and semantic analysis are integrated in terms of content with a definite meaning for individual and group life:

HOW LANGUAGE AFFECTS US IN DAILY LIFE.   LAW[1]

Below are reports and descriptions of cases which have actually been tried before courts in the United States.   Read each case carefully with a view to answering the questions which follow it.

I

Crowley v. Chicago, St. P., M. & O. Railway Co., 99 Northwestern 1016 (Wisconsin, 1904)

In Chippewa Falls, Wis., a city ordinance made it unlawful for a train or locomotive to remain standing across a street or alley for more than five minutes.

[1] Designed for use in the Stanford Language Arts Investigation, 1937, by Walter V. Kaulfers.

One day a train was standing so that the head of the locomotive reached slightly into the cross street.   Joseph Crowley, in order to get by started to drive his team of horses over the tracks in front of the resting locomotive.   Just as he did so, however, the engineer suddenly let off steam, which frightened the horses so that they tipped over the load, throwing Crowley to the ground and hurting him.   He sued the railway company for damages.

QUESTIONS FOR DISCUSSION

1. Just why was the case brought before the court—in other words, exactly on what did the people involved disagree, or what were they trying to settle?
2. Can you find the exact word or words that caused trouble, or on which the decision of the court was based?
3. To what extent was the case purely a matter of law?   To what extent was it merely a matter of settling or interpreting the meaning of words?
4. How would *you*, as judge, decide the case?   Why?
5. Would you favor changing the wording of the law to make it clearer?   If so, how?

II

People v. Keller

161 New York Supplement 132 (New York, 1916)

Julius Keller ran a restaurant in New York City, and to make his place more popular he put on a floor show every night during the dinner hour.   This show consisted of a small orchestra, with dancing and singing.   No admission was charged for the show.   It was a free entertainment feature coming with the meal.

Now the city of New York had an ordinance which made it unlawful for anyone to run a theater or to hold a circus performance without a license.   Keller was arrested and convicted for violating this ordinance with his show.   He appealed to a higher court.

Keller argued that he was running a restaurant, and neither a theater nor a circus (though some of his entertainment acts were like those to be found in a theater or a circus), and that consequently he was not breaking the law.

QUESTIONS FOR DISCUSSION
Same as for Case I.

III

In re Fisk's Estate, 187 Pacific 958 (California, 1920)

A will provided that some property should "be equally divided between my daughter-in-law Maude Bryant Fisk, and the four children of my late husband's sister. . . . " (p. 958)

The daughter-in-law, Maude Fisk, argued that according to this provision the property should be divided into *two parts*, one of which should go to herself, and the other to the four children in question.   The children said that the division should be in *five equal parts*.   It can be seen that by the first plan Maude Fisk would get *one-half* of the property, but that by the second she would get only *one-fifth*.

QUESTIONS FOR DISCUSSION

Same as for Case I.

IV

Succession of Dupre, 41 Southern 324 (Louisiana, 1906)

A man and his wife, living in Louisiana, wanted to adopt a little girl in order to satisfy the terms of a will. In adopting her, they were careful to follow the provisions of a Louisiana law called Act No. 31, with the title: "An Act providing for the manner of adopting children."

Their opponents in the courtroom claimed that the adoption was without force, because certain provisions of an earlier law had not been followed. By meeting only the requirements set forth in Act No. 31, and failing to comply also with the requirements set forth in the earlier law, the "adoption," according to the opponents, was not sufficiently legal to satisfy the terms of the will.

QUESTIONS FOR DISCUSSION

Same as for Case I.

V

Decisions

Below are the court decisions for the cases. Compare your own decisions with those rendered by the judges, and then answer the questions that follow.

Case I: The Supreme Court of Wisconsin decided the case against Crowley simply by pointing out the meaning of the word *across*, which was a vital part of the law involved: "The train in question was stopped and allowed to stand for a considerable length of time on Canal street in such a way as not to obstruct public travel thereon, yet so that the head and the roof reached slightly into the cross street, called *A* street. It was not across a street in any sense of the term. That being the case, it seems that the charge of violating the ordinance entirely failed." (p. 1017)

QUESTIONS FOR DISCUSSION

1. Did the judge interpret the meanings of the words in question correctly? What authority can you quote to show that he did or did not? What authority did *you* consult as a basis for making your own decision?

2. In making a decision, should a judge confine himself to the strict dictionary definition of a word, or should he take into consideration what the person who wrote the document *intended* the words to mean? Do all dictionaries agree on the meanings of words?

3. Was "justice" really done in this case, or did the court merely juggle words in someone's favor?

Case II: The higher court agreed with Keller. "It is plain," remarked the judge, "that a restaurant and a theater are different things. It is equally plain that appellant's (Keller's) place was not a circus. . . . A *circus* is defined in the Standard Dictionary (Student's Edition) as a large enclosure, with parallel sides, with one end rounded for races; a show in which feats of horsemanship, tumbling, strength, etc. are exhibited. . . . " (p. 138) "The word *theater* is defined in the

Standard Dictionary as a building especially adapted to dramatic, operatic, or spectacular representations, a playhouse, and in the Century Dictionary as a building appropriate to representation of dramatic spectacles, a playhouse, a room, hall, or other place with a platform at one end and ranks of seats rising step-wise as the tiers recede from the center, or otherwise so arranged that a body of spectators can have an unobstructed view of the platform. A theater usually has, among other parts, an auditorium, an orchestra circle, parterre row, dress circle, etc." (p. 137)

The judge also pointed out that the chief purpose of a circus or theater is to earn money directly for the management, but that the only purpose of the entertainment set up by Keller was to increase the popularity of a business already established—his restaurant. Thus, the law in question did not apply to any of his activities. He was thus declared innocent of the charge against him.

QUESTIONS FOR DISCUSSION
Same as for Decision I.

Case III: The judge agreed with the four children, saying that although the word *between* really meant a division into two parts only, all the facts together showed that the writer of the will had meant to say *among* where she had carelessly said *between*. "When the word *between* is used in strict grammatical sense," he observed, "it applies to two things, but . . . it is frequently used in the sense of *among* and has been so interpreted in . . . wills by many courts, including our own."   (p. 959)

QUESTIONS FOR DISCUSSION
Same as for Decision I.

Case IV: The court decided that the adoption held good, saying: "That this Act No. 31 was intended to cover the whole subject matter there can be no room for doubt. It says so expressly in its title: 'An Act providing for *the* manner of adopting children.'   *The* manner; not *a* manner, or one of the manners, or part of the manner; but *the* manner; *i.e.*, the exclusive manner."   (p. 326)

The court decided the point at issue in favor of the man and his wife by giving its careful attention to the small word *the*.

QUESTIONS FOR DISCUSSION
Same as for Decision I.

VI

QUESTIONS FOR SUPPLEMENTARY DISCUSSION

1. Do you know of any cases now before the courts that are based to some extent upon disagreement over the meanings of words?   Is either party trying to take advantage of certain loopholes in the wording or language of the case or law? From the reports of the case in the newspapers would you say that the lawyers are thinking only about "justice," or chiefly about clever ways of getting their clients out of difficulty through loopholes in the language of the case or law?

2. Can you think of any particular situations in which a person might get himself into difficulty in life if he were careless in his own use of language, or in signing his name to something that he had not read carefully?

3. How important is a thorough knowledge of language to a lawyer or judge?

4. The following articles in *The Reader's Digest* show how language often gets people into difficulties.   Select one of the articles and report your findings to the class.

> *a.* Olive H. Rabe, "Read—Before you Crash," Vol. XXX, May, 1937, pp. 43–46.   Condensed from *The American Magazine*, April, 1937.
>
> *b.* E. Jerome Ellison and Frank W. Brock, "The Wage Snatchers," Vol. XXX, March, 1937, pp. 99–100.   Condensed from *Today*, Dec. 26, 1936.   (Read before you sign.)
>
> *c.* "Lotteries and the Law," Vol. XIX, June, 1936, pp. 78–81.   Condensed from *Today*, May 2, 1936.   (Fraud through advertising, etc.)
>
> *d.* "Public Easy Mark No. 1," Vol. XXVII, October, 1935, pp. 69–71. (Read before you sign—and keep a copy.)
>
> *e.* Marc A. Rose, "Law and the Little Man," Vol. XIX, February, 1936, pp. 75–76.   Condensed from *Today*.   (How workers often lose their earnings by failing to read carefully what they sign.)

Making Language a More Reliable Servant.—Although space does not permit of a similar discussion of all the subtopics in the outline, the possibilities indicated in the foregoing comments on the life implications of language in science and law may suffice to indicate a practical line of approach in dealing with the remaining aspects of the topic "How does language affect people (Americans and other nationalities) in daily life?"   A consideration of the various aspects of this question through the medium of reading, discussion, and the collection and analysis of pertinent examples from current magazines, newspapers, and radio broadcasts, should pave the way for an intelligent consideration of the third topic: *How are people (Americans and other nationalities) trying to make language a more reliable servant and less deceptive master?*   Since this question covers a large number of organized activities, those aspects of the topic which help direct the thinking of young people into the current stream of national and international thought obviously deserve greater attention than matters that are only of novel interest like the *Believe It or Not* (so what?) information contained in popular cartoons.   Among the aspects of the topic that have been developed successfully by junior- and senior-high-school pupils are the following:

1. How are people trying to overcome the dangers of misunderstanding that often arise between groups of people who speak different languages?   For example,

> *a.* What attempts are being made to solve this problem through the teaching of such artificial languages as Esperanto?

      b. What attempts are being made to solve this problem through the teaching of basic English?[1]

      c. What obstacles lie in the way of these attempts?

2. How are people of different countries trying to make their own languages more efficient and less costly as means of communication?

      a. How successful has Turkey been in revising the Turkish language?

      b. What attempts have been made to make English spelling more efficient, *i.e.*, easier to learn, easier to pronounce, less costly to print?

3. How are people trying to make language in advertising more truthful?

4. What is being done to help people detect clever hocus-pocus in language, in news reporting? In advertising? In political campaigns? In persuasive writing (magazine articles, editorials, books, etc.)?

5. How are people trying to prevent schools from wasting the time of young people in futile attempts to change speech patterns which the large majority of scholars in English now consider established by usage?[2]

6. Why have previous attempts to solve language problems failed?

      a. Why did Latin decline as an international language?

      b. What circumstances favor or oppose the rise of English as an international language in comparison with other languages?

      c. How does the development of such inventions as the radio, radio television, the airplane, and the talking picture influence the prospects for an international language?

7. How can one avoid appearing snobbish toward fellow classmates and fellow citizens who have not had the opportunity to learn to speak English so correctly as we?

---

[1] C. K. Ogden, *The System of Basic English*, Harcourt, Brace and Company, New York, 1934, ix + 322 pp.

[2] Sterling Andrus Leonard, *Current English Usage*, The Inland Press, 1935, xxx + 232 pp. Albert H. Marckwardt and Fred Walcott, *Facts About Current English Usage*, D. Appleton-Century Company, Inc., New York, 1938, viii + 144 pp. Charles Carpenter Fries, *American English Grammar*, D. Appleton-Century Company, Inc., New York, 1940, viii + 313 pp.

8. How adequately is society providing for the education of speech defectives? The deaf? The blind? The stammerers? How can one earn one's living by specializing in some language or phase of language?

Integrated Activity Programs in General Language.—Since many of the topics contained in the foregoing outline have a direct bearing on problems of interest also to teachers of English and the social studies, it is natural that a language-arts survey course should enlist the close cooperation of teachers in these areas, if not in the actual conduct of the class, at least in the planning of units of work. Since 1938 the Menlo School, Menlo Park, Calif.,[1] has incorporated work along the lines outlined above in a three-hour core course for all ninth graders in which the study of English, general language, and social studies is centered around problems of significance in present-day life. Obviously, a program as comprehensive as that suggested in the outline is difficult to conduct effectively in a one-hour course lasting only a semester or year. Where time limits are confining, many of the topics must be reserved for investigation and report by individual students or small committees. The Balboa High School, San Francisco,[2] has been successful in conducting an elective one-semester social language course for seniors on the workshop plan. Classes conducted on this basis usually devote three days to individual work or committee work, and one day to group planning sessions, or to the presentation and discussion of reports before the class as a whole. This procedure makes possible the individualization of work within the framework of a unifying theme, without denying to any member of the class the benefit of information or discussion on subjects falling outside the range of the topic for which he has made himself personally responsible. A wider range of topics can be covered in this way than is possible on the take-the-next-chapter-for-tomorrow plan. Among the activities that have proved successful in language-arts survey courses conducted on the workshop plan may be mentioned the following:

1. Open-forum and panel discussions on live issues in language, *e.g.*, Should the bill (1940) requiring every junior- or senior-high-school student to take Spanish in New Mexico be passed by the state legislature?

[1] Kaulfers, "An Integrative Approach to the Social-cultural Aspects of Language," *op. cit.*

[2] Edith S. Anderson and Walter V. Kaulfers, "Social Language for High School Seniors," *California Journal of Secondary Education*, Vol. XV, pp. 46–47, January, 1940.

2. Collection and semantic analysis of editorials, news reports, and mazagine articles on live issues or crucial events.

3. Collection and semantic analysis of advertisements.

4. Compilation of dictionaries of foreign words and expressions used in current newspapers, magazines, etc. (Illustrated with clippings.)

5. Collection of concrete examples to illustrate difficulties arising from faulty communication in everyday life, *e.g.*, illustrations from newspaper accounts, personal experience, etc.

6. Discussions of foreign broadcasts translated by an interpreter in the class.

7. Semantic comparison of a local newspaper account of a crucial event with an account of the same event translated from a foreign newspaper.

8. Translation of short news articles into basic English as an exercise in the interpretation of real meaning.

9. Keeping anecdotal diaries to illustrate language growth among infant brothers and sisters.

10. Collecting examples of highly effective figurative language.

11. Analyzing (through the medium of literal translations) the significance of differences in conventional salutations (Christmas, New Year's, or Easter greetings) in different languages.

12. Investigating and dramatizing the history of place names, *e.g.*, why were the names California, Nevada, Colorado, New Mexico, Texas, Montana, Louisiana, Florida, etc., chosen as names for our states?

13. Investigating the history of surnames, and the reasons for differences in customs prevailing in different countries.

14. Collecting and analyzing examples of humor dependent upon ambiguities in language.

15. Investigating the work of language specialists in connection with the production of linguistically authentic moving-picture scripts, the detection of forgery or fraud, the translation of secret code messages, the compilation of dictionaries and grammars, the writing of advertisements, the writing of foreign subtitles to accompany talking pictures, etc.

16. Interviewing people who earn their living wholly, or in part, through specialization in some phase of speech or language.

The Problem Approach vs. the Chronological Approach.—It will be noted that the program is organized around language problems of significance in the present-day life of the individual and of society.

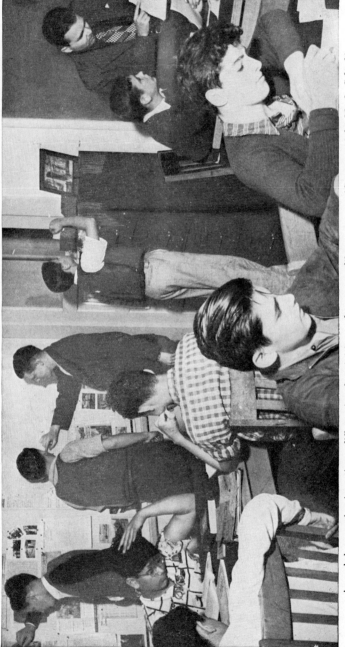

A workshop session in action—differentiated activities replace prayerlike posture. (*Courtesy of the Menlo School.*)

The history of language as such is not treated as a separate unit. Instead, the historical aspects of every language problem are considered insofar as they throw light upon the nature of the problem or the possibilities for solving it.   The organization of items of historical fact into a chronological sequence may be assigned to the students at the *end* of the course as a review exercise, but it does not constitute the unifying framework for the choice of content and activities.   For example, in dealing with the various hypotheses concerning the origins of human speech, onomatopoeic words of common occurrence in English and foreign languages may be utilized as the medium of instruction in context that illustrates the present-day role of such words in vitalizing descriptive language or in heightening the musical effect of poetic verse.

A Sample Unit on the Onomatopoeic Origin of Language and Its Implications for Poetry and Music.[1]—The following unit illustrates one of many ways for making the study of language serve several life purposes simultaneously, *e.g.*, the onomatopoeic origins of language, the appreciation of poetry, and the appreciation of music as a form of intuitive or emotional communication.

I

The following poem tells in verse what the French composer, Saint-Saëns (1835–1921), has told in music in his famous symphonic poem, *Danse Macabre* (The Dance of the Skeletons).   Read the poem aloud, and then answer the observation questions below.   Note that two Latin words are used in the poem. *Duodecim* is the Latin word for *twelve; quattuor* is the Latin for *four*.

DANSE MACABRE

(Récitation onomatopoétique)

How damp, dark, dreary!
Hear the wind's low moan—

The bell in lonely tower,
Tolling woe from hidden bower,
Doling slow the bidden hour,
In rolling tone resounds:

[1] Designed for use in the Stanford Language Arts Investigation, 1938, by Walter V. Kaulfers.   The poem as reproduced here has been used by verse-speaking choirs in the Palo Alto High School.   It will be noted that the macabre element pervading our Halloween traditions gives the poem a timely setting during the last week in October.   Experience with this unit has shown that a competent oral interpretation of the poem (before it is read by the pupils) is almost indispensable.   For recordings see Appendix, reference 201.

Duodecim, duodecim, duodecim . . .

Hark! the sudden mumbling, grumbling,
And the sullen earth's deep rumbling,
'Tis the swollen ground fast crumbling
In the bursting of the mounds;
Mark the opening caskets creaking
'Mid the noise of hinges, squeaking,
And of ghostly voices speaking
As the midnight hour sounds:

Duodecim, duodecim, duodecim . . .

Click, clack, click-click clack
Out they come from crypt and crack
Skipping, prancing, dancing, skipping
Over tombstones lightly tripping.

Click, clack, click-click clack
Oft to side and often back
Spinning first and dipping after
Cackling loud in heinous laughter
(Much like flames on crackling rafter!)
Hither they come by leap and bound,
Thither they run from mound to mound,
Whirling, dipping, skipping, twirling—
Oaths against the living hurling—
So they dance and prance around
Chuckling when their bones resound
Through the vaults half underground . . .
Till with sneaking, slinking pace,
Over far hill's frozen face
Stalks the Dawn's grey wolf to chase
Night's specters to their haunting place.

And now from Death's gloom-shrouded bower,
High in yonder moldy tower,
Slowly rolls the morning hour
In low tolling sound:

Quattuor, quattuor, quattuor . . .

With an ugly guttural mutter
Such as only ghosts can utter
When in ghastly rage they stutter,
With their dangling jawbones chattering
And their feet o'er marble clattering
Back they scurry, scampering, scattering,
Click-click-clack, click-click-clack, click-click-clack!

Hush! the lid's dull thump
And the deads' doleful groan—
How damp, dark, dreary . . .
Hear the wind's low moan.
—WALTER VINCENT KAULFERS,
The La Jolla Journal, 1923

II

OBSERVATION QUESTIONS

1. Is the poem intended for oral reading or for silent reading?   Why?

2. What type of words has the writer chosen to give "atmosphere" to the poem?

3. Words that imitate sounds (for example words like *rumble, gurgle,* or *babble*) are onomatopoeic words.   Pick out all such words in the poem.

4. Has the writer used these words to advantage, or could he have chosen still better ones?

5. Why did the writer use the Latin forms for *twelve* and *four* instead of the ordinary English words?

6. For what time of the year is the poem most appropriate—Christmas? New Year? Easter? the Fourth of July? Halloween?   Why?

7. A large part of the language of primitive man was probably composed of onomatopoeic words.   How many such words can you think of that are commonly used today?   Are they used more frequently by young children or by adults?   Why?

8. Write a sentence or short paragraph describing a sound in such a way that the reader will be made actually to hear it in his imagination.   Put the same idea into verse form.

9. Read to the class any interesting examples from poems or stories to show how the author has made effective use of onomatopoeic words.

10. Play the phonograph record of Saint-Saën's *Danse Macabre* and compare the story as told in music with the story as told in the poem.   In what ways do the two versions of the same story differ?   Which setting of the story—the musical or the poetic setting—do you like better?   Why?   Could one fully understand or appreciate Saint-Saëns' composition without knowing the story which it tries to tell in music?   Suggest any other musical compositions that attempt to tell a story or describe a scene.

Objectives and Outcomes.—What outcomes are to be expected from a course emphasizing consumer education in language?   Over and above the usual "cultural" values in the way of information, appreciation of the mother tongue, insights into the nature of foreign languages, increased vocabulary, and the like, a language-arts survey course, rooted in the language needs of present-day American and world culture, should yield the following outcomes:

1. A mind-set favorable to the effective study of foreign languages as different ways of symbolizing and interpreting reality.

2. Sanity in language as a medium of thought. This implies ability to see life through language without being misled or hypnotized by linguistic distortions of reality.

3. Accuracy in language as a guide to action. This implies ability to use language with specific referents, intelligible in fact to the reader or listener.

4. Ability to discriminate between efficiency and inefficiency in language (*e.g.*, in standard systems of spelling, handwriting, punctuation, etc.) and insight into needed improvements in language as a means of communication and instrument of thought.

5. Discrimination in the consumption of language as used in advertising, news reporting, and editorial comment, or in persuasive articles, books, and speeches.

In a life-centered program in general language, outcomes such as the foregoing are primary, for they have a direct and immediate bearing upon rationality in thought, speech, and action. From the standpoint of the psychology of language, a rational being is one capable of discriminating between language that merely expresses feelings or emotions and language that symbolizes fact. A rational philosophy of language is predicated upon the basic function of speech in human life—the communication of feelings, wants, or ideas. If there is any hierarchy of values by which "good" and "bad" language may be judged in terms of a significant social conception, it is only secondarily one of form. Language is "good" or "bad" merely to the extent to which it helps to unite men in the service of a common purpose, or to drive them apart. Communication is nil when language fails to achieve either purpose. In terms of such a conception, a large vocabulary, for example, is of little value unless it is accompanied by sound judgment regarding the circumstances in which words of rare frequency can be used effectively, and the audience situations in which the use of a rarefied vocabulary merely defeats the purposes of communication. The language with which one clothes one's thoughts in a formal lecture, sermon, or speech at a banquet is no more appropriate on the baseball field than a dress suit.

Developing Social Perspective in Language.—Effective teaching implies helping the individual to acquire and replenish an ample and varied wardrobe in language, and to master the art of wearing it appropriately and unostentatiously at different times and places. The honest soul who through lack of educational opportunity has been unable to acquire greater linguistic resources than those exemplified in such expressions as "That ain't right!" or "Them kids sure done it!" is no more to be disparaged than the God-fearing laborer who can afford no other clothes in which to go to church than a clean shirt and overalls.

From the standpoint of the basic functions of language in life—communication—the difference between "ain't" and "isn't," "those children" and "them kids" is not of sufficient intrinsic importance to be allowed to create a line of demarcation between castes.   Externals of form to the neglect of the honesty, sincerity, and integrity of the content which they adorn are of such momentous importance in life only to those whose culture consists in a kind of grammatical ossification of the higher motor centers of the brain.   If through the medium of the language-arts survey course boys and girls can be led to see that the virtues of one language are often the defects of another and that the important thing in language is after all, *what* is said and to *whom*, the school can rest assured that it has enabled its young people to take an important step in the direction of effective social living through literature and language.[1]

[1] For a select bibliography of references and teaching aids in conducting a general-language course see Appendix, especially references 41–56, 201.

CHAPTER XI

PERSPECTIVE ON THE COLLEGE-PREPARATORY FUNCTION

I have never been more conscious of the need to justify ourselves in a world where the average income of a family of five is less than the expenses of one Wellesley student in a single year.

—MILDRED H. McAFEE,
President of Wellesley College

The Preparatory Function in Historical Perspective.—From the standpoint of public education it is in many respects unfortunate that universities were organized before elementary schools. Instead of growing out of the needs of children from infancy to maturity, the curriculum of the secondary school grew out of the desire of the universities to hand down those mechanical skills and routine learnings which they considered essential but did not care to endure the drudgery of teaching. The first American secondary school—the Boston Latin School—was organized to ground pupils in Latin as a preparation for the study of medicine, law, and religion; and the equivalent of our modern elementary school busied itself chiefly with teaching children enough reading, writing, and grammar to learn their Latin in the Latin School. The fact that many people today still refer to the elementary school as the "grammar school" bears eloquent testimony to this unusual evolution of our educational system.[1]

The effect of this historical development has always caused the lower schools to spend a major portion of their time training children to jump the mental hurdles set up by the institution next above. Owing to the absence of more definite and concrete measures of evaluation, ability to pass entrance examinations, and to get good grades in college, became the criterion by which the work of the lower grades was appraised. Since it is natural for teachers to preoccupy themselves primarily with the development of proficiency in the activities by which their work, and that of their pupils, will be judged,[2] the

[1] For a graphically summarized history of education from 2300 B. C. to A. D. 1900 see Lester B. Sands and John C. Almack, *History of Education Chart*, Stanford University Press, Stanford University, Calif., 1939.

[2] Joseph B. Orleans *et al.*, "Report of the Investigation of Regents Examinations by the First Assistants Committee," *High Points*, Vol. XXI, pp. 14–19, December, 1939.

secondary school became in fact, if not altogether in theory, a coaching school to enable young people to pass college entrance examinations. This university-preparatory function of the early Latin School is preserved in the modern high school in such subjects as foreign languages, science, mathematics, and history.

The public high school, however, is the custodian of another function, that of preparing young people to enter life directly as homemakers, artisans, mechanics, merchants, craftsmen, or semiprofessional workers. This terminal function of the private academy was taken over by the public high school as its major responsibility in 1821. In January of that year, the committee recommending the establishment of the first public high school in America reported as follows:[1]

Though the present system of public education, and the munificence with which it is supported are highly beneficial and honorable to the Town [of Boston]; yet, in the opinion of the Committee, it is susceptible to a greater degree of perfection and usefulness, without materially augmenting the weight of the public burdens. Till recently, our system occupied a middle station: it neither commenced with the rudiments of Education, nor extended to the higher branches of knowledge. This system was supported by the Town at a very great expense, and to be admitted to its advantages, certain preliminary qualifications were required at individual cost, which have the effect of excluding many children of the poor and unfortunate classes of the community from the benefits of a public education. . . . The mode of education now adopted, and the branches of knowledge that are taught at our English grammar schools, are not sufficiently extensive nor otherwise calculated to bring the powers of the mind into operation nor to qualify a youth to fill usefully and respectably many of those stations, both public and private, in which he may be placed. A parent who wishes to give a child an education that shall fit him for active life, and shall serve as a foundation of eminence in his profession, whether Mercantile or Mechanical, is under necessity of giving him a different education from any which our public schools can now furnish. Hence many children are separated from their parents and sent to private academies in this vicinity, to acquire that instruction which cannot be obtained at the public seminaries. Thus many parents, who contribute largely to the support of these institutions, are subjected to heavy expense for the same object, in other towns.

Again, in 1823, the Boston school report emphasized the terminal function of the high school:

Public opinion and the wants of a large class of citizens of this town have been calling for a school in which those, who have either not the desire or the

[1] Elwood P. Cubberly, *Readings in the History of Education*, Houghton Mifflin Company, Boston, 1920, 684 pp.; pp. 580–581, 583.

means of obtaining a classical education, might receive instruction in many branches of great practical importance which have usually been taught only at the colleges. . . . This school was established by a vote of the town in 1820, expressly for the purpose of affording to lads, intending to become merchants or mechanics, better means of instruction than were provided at any of the public schools.

Today, the terminal and college-preparatory functions exist side by side, but with many unfortunate results. Owing to the prestige that has become associated by tradition with college-preparatory curriculums, and by the frequent inability of university-trained teachers to offer anything but vest-pocket editions of offerings which they themselves have taken in college, university-preparatory courses have become crowded with pupils whose personal sense of pride, and that of their parents, would not permit them to enroll in classes in which the teacher's supercilious condescension or poorly veiled contempt for the "dumbbells," "hopeless cases," and "underprivileged" could be felt. Indeed, the large majority of college-trained teachers find it difficult to conceive of any other kind of terminal offering than one in which the pupils are given two to three times as long to digest the sterile content of the preparatory courses. Needless to say, such a diluted diet was too lacking in vitamins to lead to anything but mental scurvy. In these circumstances, "guidance" came into being as a means for distributing and adjusting pupils either to the conventional college-preparatory curriculum, or to terminal courses in which the same content was diluted with time for cultural busywork on the assumption that pupils who often came, through no fault of their own, from homes in which there was inadequate food, inadequate housing, inadequate shelter, and insecurity, had no basis for understanding or appreciating "real values" in education for a decent and human existence on the part of all who desire to realize their fullest capacities in terms of the general welfare.

By 1930 the absurdity of this situation had reached such extremes that something had to be done. The problem, however, was complicated by the following combination of circumstances:

1. The number of pupils who in reality needed a terminal education for effective participation in the economic and social world upon leaving high school far outnumbered those who actually continued in college.[1]

[1] U. S. Office of Education, *Biennial Survey of Education*, 1929–1930, *Bulletin* 1931, No. 20, Vol. II, 833 pp.; pp. 692–693.

2. The only "respectable" courses in high school were college preparatory, and therefore drew many terminal students who did not care to lower their self-respect by enrolling in terminal courses except as electives.

3. With relatively few exceptions, the only teachers available to conduct life-oriented courses in English, social studies, mathematics, or foreign languages were college graduates who had studied the "humanities," but could do little more for humanity than rattle the dead bones of the past as a warning or cultural diversion.

4. Enrollments in the average high school were usually too small to justify the expense of maintaining a separate series of terminal courses for the masses and another set of courses for the "classes."

5. The results of numerous investigations of the records made by high-school graduates in college showed that success in institutions of higher learning is not dependent upon success in any particular subject or combination of subjects in high school, except occasionally in the case of advanced work in the same field. Even in the case of foreign languages, success in an advanced college course can seldom be predicted with any degree of reliability unless the student has previously taken at least three years of work in the same language. In 1935, Byrns and Henmon[1] published the results of an investigation involving 687 seniors in the University of Wisconsin. On the basis of their findings, the authors concluded that

. . . pragmatic sanction may justify the belief that foreign languages and mathematics are valuable instruments of instruction, but the evidence does not indicate that they are sacrosanct. They have probably been valued out of proportion to their significance for success in college. Their prominence both in the high-school curriculum and in college entrance requirements must be justified on some grounds other than mental training, for the facts seem to show that these subjects do not develop a student's capacity for successful college work . . . when mental ability was held constant, the amount of foreign language had no relation to college achievement in science, mathematics, and social science. . . . [Even for students of high ability] there was no relation between the amount of foreign language that had been studied and college achievement in English and foreign language.

In 1941 Bement confirmed the findings of previous investigators that foreign-language achievement in high school has little relationship to success in college language work except in the case of pupils who complete at least three years of work in a language before entering

[1] Ruth Byrns and V. A. C. Henmon, "Entrance Requirements and College Success," *School and Society*, Vol. XLI, pp. 101–104, Jan. 19, 1935.

the university. On the basis of a detailed comparison of the high-school and college achievement of 211 students in French, German, Spanish, Italian, English, and Latin, the writer concluded that "only a preparation pattern containing a three-year sequence, or better, can be very significant as a basis of prognosis, and that prognosis on the basis of the preparation pattern can be very significant only with reference to the elementary course in the new language."[1]

The Trend toward a Unified Curriculum for the Secondary School. A consideration of these circumstances by the Eight-year Study of the National Commission on the Relation of Schools and Colleges, by the Stanford Language Arts Investigation, and by organized groups of teachers and administrators, led to concerted attempts to solve the problem of simultaneous preparation of young people for college and active life through a unified curriculum in the secondary school. The various curriculum-revision programs that resulted from efforts in this direction were guided for the most part by the following considerations:

1. Parallel offerings for noncollege-preparatory and college-preparatory students create artificial distinctions inimical to education for effective living in a democratic society, and destructive of student and teacher interest in worth-while terminal offerings for the majority of adolescent young people. Hence, differentiation of courses on the basis of differences in fundamental interests and life needs, rather than on the basis of preparation or nonpreparation for college, is desirable.[2]

2. Enrollments in the average high school[3] are too limited to make segregation of pupils feasible as a general solution even if valid bases for such segregation existed in intelligence tests or prognosis tests. The safest criterion for segregating pupils on the college-preparatory

---

[1] Newton S. Bement, "Relative Value of Foreign Language Preparation Patterns, as Determined by Achievement in First- and Third-semester College French," *The Modern Language Journal*, Vol. XXV, pp. 394–401, February, 1941. See also C. A. Smith, "High School Training and Freshman Grades," *Journal of Educational Research*, Vol. XXXII, pp. 401–409, February, 1939.

[2] Samuel Everett, Ed., *A Challenge to Secondary Education*, D. Appleton-Century Company, Inc., New York, 1935, pp. 175–176, 193, 237, 324.

[3] Under the caption "What's Happening in California Secondary Schools" (*California Journal of Secondary Education*, Vol. XI, p. 392, October, 1936), Aubrey A. Douglass, State Commission of Secondary Education, quoted the following typical comment of high-school principals: "Our teaching staff is small, and we are limited in the number of classes we can give. Although a very few go on to college, we are forced to keep up a great deal of academic work to stay on the accredited list. These conditions work a tremendous hardship on the small school and make much change practically impossible."

basis is unfortunately the financial and educational background of the home. Since it is neither the business of education to foster social and economic inbreeding nor to prepare pupils for university careers which it may be impossible for them to realize, unified curriculums that meet the life needs of pupils without sacrificing the specialized needs of minority groups are imperative.

3. Preparation for life is as good a preparation as any other for work in college. Such skills in mathematics, science, or foreign languages as have only a deferred value for pupils who continue in these fields in college, can be developed through differentiated assignments or occasional "coaching classes" for seniors who are definitely planning to enter a particular college or university, or to pass an entrance examination at the end of the school year. Such specialized skills do not have to be made the core content or basis for organizing curriculums for all students throughout the secondary school. Basic skills are developed more successfully in and through content illustrative of their importance in meeting crucial personal and social needs than through exercises or problems that afford no insight into their life applications. Skills for which no important application can be found in the life needs of a large majority of our citizens are on a specialized professional level, and as such lie beyond the province of secondary education.[1]

4. Compulsory school attendance on the part of all young people of secondary-school age requires that the needs of those who are obliged to attend be served as effectively as those who could afford to attend private schools if no public high schools existed. It is an educational crime to require school attendance and then sacrifice the educational needs and interests of the large majority of students in order that a small minority may obtain an artificial college-preparatory distinction which does not meet their own fundamental needs, nor the needs of present-day society for the social intelligence that is necessary if democracy is to represent the collective will of the people rather than of small pressure groups.

Identifying the College-preparatory Student.—Many high schools today are effectively using home visitation and conferences with parents in helping teachers to distinguish between those pupils who definitely need specialized training along college-preparatory lines because they will actually continue in certain fields in college, and those pupils who are tempted to enroll in college-preparatory classes

[1] Walter V. Kaulfers, "Magic-wand Solutions to Foreign Language Problems," *The School Review*, Vol. XLIV, pp. 744–752, December, 1936.

merely because they bear the approval stamp of academic tradition. Questionnaires requiring the signatures of parents are distributed to pupils by their home-room teachers and followed by personal visits to the parents in case the response is unsatisfactory. The following questionnaire contains sample questions of value in guiding pupils with respect to college-preparatory work:

The High School is anxious to secure the cooperation of parents in helping their children lay a solid foundation for work after graduation, or for advanced study in a business college, junior college, liberal arts college, or university. Since entrance requirements vary from college to college, and often according to the kind of work for which the student expects to prepare himself, your assistance in approving the answers to the questions below is urgently requested. All information will be kept strictly confidential.

Name of Student_____
Class: Freshman, Sophomore, Junior, Senior_____

1. What school, college, or university do you expect to attend after graduating from high school?
_____

2. For what field of work do you expect to prepare yourself in college?
_____

3. When do you expect to enter college?   Give year._____
4. Do you expect to work before going to college?_____
   How long?_____
5. Do you expect to work for expenses while attending college?
_____

6. If you are not planning to go to college, what occupation do you expect to enter upon graduating from high school?
_____

7. Are you taking a foreign language now?_____If so, do you want to continue the same language in college?_____

The foregoing information is correct to the best of my knowledge. I shall be glad to cooperate with the school by notifying the office of the Vice-principal at once of any necessary changes. Please add any comments on the reverse side of this sheet.

Approved and signed_____
                              Parent or Guardian
Date of signature_____
Comments_____

Planning Individual Programs of Study for College-preparatory Students.—On the basis of the foregoing information, the school counselor and the advisory teachers can help the pupil plan a program of study in terms of the requirements of a particular institution, or of a particular department within an institution. For teachers of foreign languages, adequate guidance of pupils is impossible except as the requirements of a particular college or university are known. Although colleges *recommend* two years of foreign language for admission,[1] many full college standing is often granted without regard for this recommendation provided the student's record is satisfactory in whatever work he has done, and is accompanied by a recommending statement from the principal. Whether or not a student can graduate from college without taking one or more years of foreign-language work in college depends entirely upon the college or, in the case of the university, upon the school in which the student plans to major. Unless the foreign-language teacher has access to the latest catalogues of the institutions to which particular students are planning to go, reliable college-preparatory guidance is impossible. A departmental meeting devoted to the examination and discussion of yearly changes in college-entrance requirements in the institutions to which a majority of the students go is a professional obligation of every language faculty. Usually the school counselor can assist by supplying catalogues or by answering questions. Students who are attending distant colleges can be requested to write for catalogues in case copies are not available in the school.

In guiding students, the information on the questionnaire is valuable, especially as regards the choice of a college or university. In general, the probability that a student will actually attend a distant institution without first completing part of his work in a neighboring college or junior college is slight if the father's occupation identifies him with a relatively low economic level,[2] or if the number of dependents in the home is such as to lower the standard of living for the family unit. Facts of this kind can usually be obtained without embarrassment from the students themselves, or by a trained teacher on her visits to the home. For the foreign-language teacher such information is of value in appraising the true educational needs of young people. It is far more humane to help boys and girls realize in high school ways and means of enriching life, and of finding effective means of self-support before or while attending college—if that is their true ambition —than to set up college preparation as an artificial social distinction, especially if the probabilities are four to one that this goal will not be

[1] In 1937 only half of 146 American colleges required foreign languages for admission: M. E. Gladfelter, "Status and Trends of College Entrance Requirements," *The School Review*, Vol. XLV, pp. 737–749, December, 1937.

[2] "Schools and the 1940 Census," *Research Bulletin*, National Education Association of the United States, 1201 Sixteenth St., N. W., Washington, D. C., Vol. XIX, No. 5, pp. 203–231, November, 1941.

achieved before the "preparatory" work has become too rusty to be useful.

Providing Differentiated Work for College-preparatory Seniors in Advanced Classes.—Where the evidence is strong that the large majority of the students are likely to forget their "grammar" before entering college, the central criterion for the organization of courses and the choice of content and learning activities may well be the life needs of the students, rather than their possible academic needs in a vague and indefinite future.   When courses are not defined in terms of "minimum essentials" in the way of sterile exercises in a conventional grammar (and its anemic "reading" lessons), differentiated types of work, laboratory-workshop organization of classes, and numerous integrative activities of the kind described in preceding chapters, become possible.   On the basis of the information on his questionnaire, a senior who is definitely preparing to enter a particular college or university can then be given differentiated assignments (within whatever class he is enrolled) in terms of the specific requirements of the institution which he plans to attend.   If there are several seniors in a second- or third-year class, they can be organized into a committee or seminar without subjecting all pupils from the start to the specialized type of formal work that may be required by a conservative institution of higher learning.   This plan has proved feasible and effective in operation for the following reasons:

In the first place, college-preparatory seniors are usually a relatively select and mature group capable of developing and accepting responsibility for guided independent work.   Secondly, seniors who are not capable of developing or accepting responsibility in the light of an immediate objective are not likely to do well in college regardless of the high-school grades that they might achieve through prodding or coddling.   Indeed, lack of initiative or interest is usually a sign that the student will either avoid foreign-language work in college, if at all possible, or start over in a different language.   Where rigid requirements allow of no other alternative, the latter procedure may even be recommended in the case of "problem" students in language who otherwise would make good college material.   The teacher's "reputation" is usually safeguarded automatically by the pupil himself in such cases.

Again, the foundation in language which the student has acquired before reaching his senior year—whether it be two, four, or six semesters—is usually an excellent basis for the organized study of such grammar as may be needed to pass formal examinations.   Experience has shown that because of this background in functional-language activities, and the relatively greater maturity of the student, the conventional minimum essentials can be covered in at least one-third, and often in one-fourth, the usual time.[1]

Finally, formal work in grammar remains fresher in the minds of pupils if delayed until their senior year than if presented from the start and allowed to fall into disuse for one or more years before the language is continued in college. If a pupil completes his college-preparatory requirements in his freshman and sophomore years and then discontinues the language in his junior and senior year, the value of his preparatory work for successful language study in college is likely to be as great as the cost of the ink required to record the credits on his transcript of record. The probability is strong that he will prefer to enroll in an entirely different language in college (if such work is required) rather than spend time in a review course without credit or a satisfying sense of progress. No sensible student ever risks debasing his college record with a low grade in a course for which his high-school preparation is no longer secure.

The practice of encouraging any and all students to enroll in foreign-language courses, and to prepare them indiscriminately without regard for any of the fundamental problems analyzed above, has resulted in a waste of human time and effort which all the philosophizing about mental discipline, improvement of English grammar, and the like, is no longer able to rationalize convincingly. There is no reason why, with a modification in the mechanics of class management and a suitable reallocation of content and emphasis, a high school, regardless of size, should not in time be able to provide any and all interested pupils with as many years of work[2] in a foreign language as they can take with interest and profit to themselves—quite without sacrificing the specialized needs for formal work in language which no pupil really needs unless he is a senior definitely planning to continue in the same language in a very conservative college the following year.

[1] Rupert Eichholzer, "Creating Instead of Crushing Interest in German," Reports of the Stanford Language Arts Investigation, Vol. II: *Foreign Languages and Cultures in American Education*, McGraw-Hill Book Company, Inc., New York. In press.

[2] Grace McGuinness and Bessie W. Bankhead, "Three in One—A Mixed Class in Which French is Taught by One Teacher to Students Representing Three Different Levels of Previous Preparation," Reports of the Stanford Language Arts Investigation, Vol. II, *Foreign Languages and Cultures in American Education*, McGraw-Hill Book Company, Inc., New York. In press.

Election vs. Prescription as a Basis of Curriculum Organization.—
The attempt to solve the college-preparatory problem by means of
prescription has not yielded constructive results in practice.   On the
basis of long-range experience with the two-year foreign-language
requirement, it is safe to say that the effects of compelling all pupils
to take three or four years of foreign-language work in high school
before going to college would be educationally disastrous for many
reasons.   In the first place, requirements tend to saddle schools with
a uniformly regimented type of foreign-language course prescribed
from above, rather than organized and conducted in terms of what
adolescent boys and girls can do effectively with interest and profit
to themselves as human beings or as prospective homemakers and
producers or consumers of goods and services.   Secondly, the types
of ability required to pass "entrance examinations" prescribed by an
outside agency become in reality the objectives of the program and the
major concern of instruction in the classroom.[1]   This leads to the
use of sterile content and methods selected primarily for their coaching
or drill value in passing examinations, rather than on the basis of their
effectiveness in helping young people to grow in ability to use a foreign
language for worth-while life purposes.   Thirdly, uniform examinations lead to uniform textbooks, uniform assignments, and uniform
methods.   Since children are not uniform, the result is maladjustment
and futile attempts to fit pupils to courses through various types of
ability or aptitude tests of dubious validity.   Fourthly, since a
mechanical textbook-centered course is easier to teach than a pupil-
centered course, poor teaching (whose failures are excused by "high
standards") are perpetuated at the expense of creative ability in
guiding the educational growth of young people.   Finally, since it is
almost impossible to prepare young people effectively for college
courses in which such a variety of temperamental idiosyncrasies of
method, content, objectives, and standards prevails, the most conscientious high-school teacher is seldom destined to receive encouragement or inspiration for her labors.   Among the hundreds of articles
that have been written since 1900 concerning the shortcomings of
high-school students in college, hardly one can be found that expresses
praise for the task to which both pupils and teachers have for decades
given almost their entire attention.   It has seemingly never occurred
to college departments that the students who continue in college

[1] Orleans *et al.*, *op. cit.*   James B. Tharp, "The College Entrance Examination
Board Looks at Its French Examination," *The French Review*, Vol. XIII, pp.
380–384, March, 1940.

foreign-language work are usually their own educational grandchildren coming home to roost.

The extent to which college entrance requirements dominate the thought and action of high-school teachers of foreign languages is revealed in the mental disturbances which changes, or contemplated changes, in the requirements of a state university produce among secondary-school language staffs.   The underlying fear that the removal of admission requirements will result in a loss in enrollments is a regrettable indication that prevailing courses do not stand on their own merits but depend upon subtle coercion for patronage.   The test of the degree to which a learning program is educationally worth-while to young people is the extent to which it can sell itself through the satisfying results that it yields.   It is unfortunate that a field of human culture, so potentially rich in educative experiences, should have to depend upon subtle compulsion or highly sublimated advertising for patronage.   It is not visionary to conceive of a foreign-language program which can sell itself to young people, and retain their good will, by no other means than the profitable and satisfying outcomes which it enables them to achieve to the extent to which the offering is pursued.

A Lesson in Gains without Losses.—Among the public schools which, as a result of reorienting their curriculums in conformity with this conception, have experienced marked increases in purely voluntary enrollments to the extent of a full four-year foreign-language program is the Jefferson Union High School in Daly City, Calif.:

In the fall of 1938 the enrollment in Spanish in the Jefferson Union High School, Daly City, Calif., was only 59, and in Italian, 31.   The rate of elimination in both languages was so high that third-year classes could not be offered for want of students.   Up to this time the program in Romanic Languages had been conducted along traditional lines emphasizing grammar primarily, with occasional reading lessons in a college-preparatory textbook.

In 1938 the writer undertook a radical reorganization of the course of study in Spanish and Italian in conformity with an organic conception of language suited to the social and cultural needs of young people in Daly City.   Emphasis was placed upon an activity-program capitalizing reading and conversation on such topics as Daly City's heritage from abroad, why the Italians and Spanish-speaking people live, think, and behave as they do, how to get the most out of a visit to Italy or Latin America, etc.

Music was one of many integrated activities which extended beyond the confines of the classroom.   The singing of songs in the foreign language served to develop an interest in composers and their works.   The stories of famous operas were read and discussed in the foreign language, and illustrated with recordings and drawings of stage-sets by members of the classes. Over 175 students attended the opera parties sponsored by the foreign-language students at the time of the opera season in San Francisco. Emphasis in all classes upon creative abilities in musical, artistic, or poetic expression served to vitalize the program. Instead of writing book reports for outside reading, students were given the option of making illustrated cultural maps of the foreign countries, of dramatizing episodes, or of illustrating significant passages.

As a result of reserving the emphasis on college-preparatory grammar exclusively for seniors enrolled in third- or fourth-year classes, the enrollment has increased from 59 in Spanish in 1938 to 171 in 1941, and from 31 to 176 in Italian. More significant is the phenomenal increase in the demand for third- and fourth-year work. In 1941 the advanced class in upper-division Spanish enrolled 22 students a compared with none in 1938! The corresponding enrollments in Italian rose from 0 in 1938 to 30 in 1941!

This increase has been accomplished with significant gains in the morale of foreign-language students and without sacrifice whatsoever of ability in language as measured by departmental tests or grade-point averages of graduates in the State Colleges. No student who has continued in college Spanish or Italian under the new plan has received less than grades of A or B in his college foreign-language work.

The increase in demand for Spanish and Italian in Daly City is revealed by the fact that only 12.8 per cent of the student body were enrolled in Spanish or Italian in 1938 as compared with 50 per cent in 1941. It is doubtful whether any public school in which foreign-language work is purely an elective (as in Daly City) can boast of a similar interest in foreign-language work among young people who in the large majority of cases come from homes in which economic factors do not always permit of advanced study in college.[1]

It will be noted that the success of the Daly City program is attributable in large measure to freeing the courses from the cramping effects of college entrance requirements without sacrificing the needs of senior students for specialized preparatory work within the framework of the regular advanced classes. This reorientation has made it possible to organize courses in terms of the needs, abilities, and life interests of individual groups of students, and to sell the program to them directly through results which they sense and appreciate. Certainly the high-school teachers of foreign languages deserve a more inspiring position in education than that of tagging doggedly at the heels of the university ahead, while being pecked at by the "educators" from behind.

[1] Report of Dante P. Lembi, Chairman of Romanic Language Department, Jefferson Union High School, Daly City, Calif., to the Language-arts Section of the Annual Conference of California Secondary-school Principals, Oakland, Calif., Apr. 8, 1941.

CHAPTER XII

AIMS, OBJECTIVES, AND OUTCOMES IN RELATION TO MODERN NEEDS AND POSSIBILITIES

Ideals are like stars, you will not succeed in touching them with your hands. But like the seafaring man on the desert of water, you choose them as your guides, and following them you will reach your destiny.
—CARL SCHURZ

The world turns aside to let any man pass who knows whither he is going.
—DAVID STARR JORDAN

The outcomes of any learning program involving the development of ability to read, write, speak, or translate a language may be grouped under the three headings:

Concomitant Outcomes.—These embrace all demonstrable values that are realized through experiences afforded by the *process* of acquiring the content or skills emphasized in the learning program, as distinguished from factual knowledge or mastery of the skills themselves. In the case of the foreign languages, mental discipline[1] has often been listed among the values accruing, not from the foreign languages nor from the potential life uses to which they can be put, but from *experiences* afforded by studying them. By mental discipline, language specialists usually have in mind such ability to reason and to think logically, penetratingly, and critically in language as might be expected to accrue from experiences in analyzing, comparing, contrasting, translating, interpreting, or memorizing linguistic materials. Consequently, some writers even emphasize the value of foreign-language *study* in developing the memory; and justify the assignment of vocabulary lists to be memorized, and of paradigms or conjugations to be learned and recited from memory, largely because of their confidence in the "disciplinary" values of work of this type. Other writers associate mental discipline with ability to apply one's self conscientiously to a task until it is completed, to concentrate and work hard even on distasteful problems in which one has no special interest, and to work independently on one's own initiative without constant "spoon feeding," "coddling," or "prodding." Because of the cumu-

[1] John J. Weisert, "Foreign Languages as Mental Discipline, a Survey," *The German Quarterly*, Vol. XII, pp. 61–70, March, 1939.

lative nature and length of the learning program, foreign-language study is considered by many people to be uniquely endowed with these "disciplines"—to such an extent in fact, that it can be justified on this basis alone, regardless of whether the students ever use the language later or even learn enough language to forget.

Among other concomitant outcomes that have often been mentioned as accruing from experiences associated with learning a foreign language in school are the following:

1. Habits of neatness in written work.

2. Habits of attention to such language mechanics as punctuation, spelling, capitalization, and handwriting.

3. A critical attitude toward correct usage in language, both English and foreign.

4. Insights into the mechanical structure of language.

5. Habits of consulting the dictionary.

6. Better speech habits, pronunciation, and diction.

Associate Outcomes.—In the case of the foreign languages, associate outcomes include all demonstrable values that can be attributed primarily to the *content* used as the medium for learning to read, write, speak, or translate a language. Knowledge, attitudes, interests, and appreciations derived from the thought content, or information contained in practice exercises, reading lessons, and the like, fall into this category. So also do interests, appreciations, attitudes, and information acquired through the medium of such cultural activities as excursions, foreign correspondence, dramatics, art, or music, when they involve the use of the foreign language. The list of the associate outcomes that teachers have long associated with foreign-language study is unusually comprehensive, since obviously all kinds of information on an infinite variety of topics can be expressed in language—the only serious practical limitation being the learner's level of insight, and the necessity of using words and constructions that fall within the range of his progress within the language itself. Obviously, content dealing with a foreign country and its people, or with language as a means of communication and medium of thought, has in the very nature of things been considered more appropriate as a basis for oral and written activities in foreign-language work than content that has no apparent connection with the life, literature, or culture of the country whose language is being studied. The same observation naturally applies to the kind of activities that have usually been considered appropriate for pupils enrolled in foreign-language courses.

Among the large number of *associate outcomes* that have been widely publicized by foreign-language committees and individual writers are the following:[1]

A. Associate outcomes contributive to *the worthy use of leisure* through such activity interests as the foreign-language program may develop in

1. Travel, *e.g.*,
   a. Enjoyment of books and magazines on foreign countries.
   b. Enjoyment of lectures on travel.
   c. Enjoyment of travel films.
   d. Actual travel abroad.
2. Foreign literature, whether in the original or in translation; plays by foreign dramatists, etc.
3. Foreign-language study as a hobby or avocational pursuit.
4. Foreign correspondence.
5. Radio programs, songs, and operas broadcast in whole or in part in a foreign language; sound pictures and news reels containing foreign dialogues, etc.
6. Evidences of foreign culture in the immediate environment, *e.g.*,
   a. Enjoyment of concerts, recitals, or exhibits by foreign musicians or artists.
   b. Enjoyment of "fiesta" programs, fetes, and celebrations staged by local foreign colonies.
7. Participation in open forums, literary societies, international good-will organizations, foreign-correspondence clubs, travel clubs, or foreign-language study groups.

[1] For a summary of the literature on objectives in foreign-language methodology to 1936 see Walter V. Kaulfers, "Outcomes as Objectives," *The French Review*, Vol. IX, pp. 224–230, February, 1936.   For more recent statements see Edward O. Sisson, "Foreign Language as an Educational Problem," *School and Society*, Vol. LIV, pp. 369–375, Nov. 1, 1941.   George R. Havens, "The Modern Language Teacher in a Troubled World," *The Modern Language Journal*, Vol. XXV, pp. 306–313, January, 1941.   Olivia Russell, "The Place of Modern Foreign Languages in the Curriculum," *The Modern Language Journal*, Vol. XXV, pp. 385–389, February, 1941.   Henry Grattan Doyle, "A Program for More Effective Teaching of Modern Foreign Languages in the United States," *The Modern Language Journal*, Vol. XXV, pp. 531–534, April, 1941.   Edith E. Pence, "Economic and Social Trends in the Teaching of Modern Languages," *The Modern Language Journal*, Vol. XXIV, pp. 542–543, April, 1940.   Peter Hagboldt, *The Teaching of German*, D. C. Heath and Company, Boston, 1940, ix + 306 pp.; pp. 188–216 and *passim*. Charles H. Handschin, *Modern Language Teaching*, World Book Company, Yonkers-on-Hudson, New York, 1940, vi + 458 pp.; pp. 31–56.

8. Language as an art, *i.e.*,
    a. A greater enjoyment of style and usage in speech and literature.
    b. A greater interest in the psychology, history, or science of language.

B. Associate outcomes contributive to increased *ability to understand, adjust to, and cooperatively improve the social environment.* These embrace such attitudes, appreciations, and insights as the foreign-language curriculum may develop through content and activities stressing:

1. A more sympathetic understanding and fairer treatment of fellow students and fellow citizens of foreign birth or descent.
2. The possibility of building a more creative and enlightened American way of life by integrating our human and cultural heritage from other nations and cultures—our heritage in people, customs, mores, religion, science, invention, art, music, literature, architecture, philosophy, education, language, law, the dance, etc.
3. Worthy ideals for the motivation of ethical conduct as revealed in the literature, philosophy, and customs of foreign peoples.
4. Open-mindedness and tolerance in human relations, personal and international.
5. A realization of the essential oneness of human nature—of the fact that all people, not just ourselves, cherish the right to life, liberty, and the pursuit of happiness as conceived in terms of their philosophy of life.
6. Increased ability to *understand* instead of depreciate, languages, standards of values, and customs that may be different from our own.
7. Increased ability to understand the causal relationships between the social and physical environment as they are revealed in the customs, standards of living, and vital statistics of foreign peoples, *e.g.*, the effects of climate on customs, diet, architecture, recreations, etc.
8. Increased ability to understand the significance of education, literacy, unity in language and cultural traditions, for individual and group welfare insofar as the influence of these factors is revealed in the life of a foreign people.

C. Associate outcomes contributive to increased *ability to understand, appreciate, adjust to, and improve the physical environment.*

These embrace such knowledge, attitudes, and insights as the foreign-language curriculum may develop through content and activities stressing:

1. A greater appreciation of our material environment in terms of the contributions that foreign peoples have made through science and invention to the improvement of living conditions— to personal and public health, to more efficient means of communication and transportation, and to the increase in human comforts throughout the world.
2. A greater insight into the causal relationships between the natural physical environment and the man-made material environment as reflected in the industries, systems of transportation and communication, economic influence, living and working conditions, and technological progress of foreign peoples.
3. A greater insight into the causal interrelationships between the physical, social, and political environments as revealed in the life of a foreign people.
4. Increased ability, through knowledge of the foreign language, to make ready use of foreign contributions in the field of science and invention.

D. Associate outcomes contributive to the building of desirable physical and mental health. These embrace such knowledge, attitudes, interests, and habits as the foreign-language curriculum may develop through content and activities stressing:

1. An appreciation of such wholesome traits of foreign people as have a bearing on emotional and physical health, and as deserve emphasis in our own daily life, *e.g.,*
    a. Temperance and moderation in personal habits.
    b. Enjoyment of simple pleasures.
    c. Community encouragement of music, folk dancing, games, and other arts as popular recreation.
    d. Unhurried attitude toward life.
    e. Appreciation of nonmaterial values.
    f. Wholesome home and family life.
2. An understanding and appreciation of the importance of the problems of sanitation and public health insofar as these manifest themselves in the life of a foreign people. For example, health problems in relation to climatic factors, levels of

literacy, superstitions, organized health services, popular food habits, etc.

3. Worthy attitudes toward the value of a sound mind in a healthy body insofar as they are reflected in the life of a foreign people.
4. Insights into the causal interrelationships between mental health, physical health, and social adjustment as portrayed in literature.

E. Associate outcomes contributive to increased *vocational and prevocational efficiency.*[1] These embrace such knowledge, attitudes, interests, and appreciations as the foreign-language curriculum may develop through content and activities stressing:

1. Linguistic abilities required by vocations in which work with foreign languages is the major responsibility, *e.g.,*
   a. Professional translation and interpretation.
   b. Linguistic research; lexicography, etc.
   c. The teaching of foreign languages and literatures.
2. Linguistic abilities highly desirable in vocations involving frequent contacts with foreign languages, *e.g.,*
   a. Foreign commerce.
   b. Foreign (news) correspondence.
   c. Foreign travel service.
   d. Foreign consular, diplomatic, and secret service.
   e. Acting and directing: as a background for character portrayal.
   f. Singing: concert, opera, radio, etc.
   g. Scenario writing and adaptation of foreign literature.
   h. Scientific research, and foreign expeditions—geographical, archaeological, geological.
   i. Foreign propaganda agencies, etc.
   j. Miscellaneous occupations, *e.g.,* service on board international steamship, railway, or airlines; social-service work in foreign quarters of American communities; clerking in stores located in foreign sections of American communities; customs inspection; service in large metropolitan hotels; occupational placement bureaus in certain localities; teaching Americanization classes, children of the foreign-born, English to foreigners, etc.

[1] William Leonard Schwartz, Lawrence A. Wilkins, and Arthur Gibbon Bovee, *Vocational Opportunities for Foreign Language Students.* *The Modern Language Journal,* Washington, D. C. 1941, rev. ed., 34 pp.

Direct Outcomes.—In the case of the foreign languages, these usually embrace the degrees of ability that are achieved in reading, writing, speaking, or translating them. Direct outcomes are those over which teachers usually have primary control through the choice of method, content, or activities in the classroom. They are the linguistic outcomes for which most people study a foreign language, as distinguished from the *uses* to which they expect to put the language *after* it has been learned. In the conventional elementary and intermediate foreign-language courses of a decade ago, these outcomes were the almost exclusive preoccupation of teachers and students, as revealed by the methods of instruction, the contents of the textbooks, and the tests used as a basis for evaluating achievement. They were in reality the central and dominating objectives of the foreign-language curriculum, regardless of the cultural aims listed in the preambles to the courses of study. In the main, they continue to be the central objectives of foreign-language teaching except that in recent years[1] increasing attention has been given to the enrichment of courses with content and activities contributive to a fuller realization of associate and concomitant outcomes of the kind described in the preceding paragraphs.

This enrichment has been in part a natural development and in part a conscious attempt to justify foreign-language teaching in the face of criticism that the ability to read, write, speak, or translate a foreign language does not represent so urgent a need for some students as an equal amount of time[2] and effort devoted to work in English, art, science, the social studies, or music might conceivably be.

Until recently, this enrichment of the foreign-language curriculum with content and activities designed to increase the realization of concomitant and associate outcomes, has been primarily through the medium of reading materials, project work, reports, and discussions carried on almost exclusively in *English*. To a large extent this situation still holds true today. An examination of the elementary and intermediate basic textbooks most frequently used in classes in which "cultural enrichment" has been attempted, shows that the reading material that contains the chief source from which such enrichment might be expected is in the form of essays written in *English*. If these were excluded, there would be little difference

[1] See references on p. 351.

[2] James B. Tharp, "The Allotment for Foreign Language Study: Internecine Competition or Conciliatory Compromise," *The Modern Language Journal*, Vol. XXV, pp. 598–608, May, 1941.

between many of these modern grammar-readers and those of two decades ago, insofar as the cultural value of the foreign-language content is concerned. In neither case do the reading lessons in the foreign languages reveal much consideration for the development of attitudes, interests, knowledge, or human insights and appreciations of real significance for life outside the classroom or parlor.

Although the interspersion of informational content and activities in English served to familiarize the pupils with many aspects of foreign life and culture that otherwise might have been lost to them, and often helped indirectly to reinforce interest in the study of the language, it contributed relatively little to the enrichment or improvement of work in the foreign language itself. Working under the mental hazards[1] of college entrance board examinations and requirements, teachers found it difficult to spare time for these cultural activities, even though the objectives that they served were often accepted by curriculum specialists, laymen, and teachers of foreign languages themselves as being as important as ability to read, write, speak, or translate the language. This effort to justify the study of foreign languages in terms of culturally significant outcomes which, if they were attained in any really significant degree, were ordinarily not realized through the medium of the foreign language at all, but through reading and discussion in English, naturally gave rise to serious mental confusion. To date, efforts to find a tenable and constructive solution to this dilemma have led to three important developments, all of which have met with varying degrees of success in actual operation: (1) the enrichment, especially of beginning, elementary, and intermediate courses, with reading content *in the foreign language*, and integrative foreign-language activities, to make possible a fuller realization of associate and concomitant outcomes; (2) the introduction of independent orientation or survey courses in which the life, literature, and culture of the foreign country are studied in English in relation to our own daily life; and (3) the reorganization of what are still commonly known as *general-language*[2] courses to include practical work in applied semantics.

[1] Joseph B. Orleans *et al.*, "Report of the Investigation of Regents Examinations by the First Assistants Committee," *High Points*, Vol. XXI, pp. 14–29, December, 1939. James B. Tharp, "The College Entrance Examination Board Looks at Its French Examination," *The French Review*, Vol. XIII, pp. 380–384. See also Chap. XI.

[2] James B. Tharp, "General Language: An Appreciation Course in the Study of Foreign Languages," *Secondary Education*, Vol. VIII, pp. 3–6, January, 1939; "The General Course and Its Administration," *Proceedings of the Ohio Workshop on*

Enriching Concomitant, Associate, and Direct Outcomes in Terms of Life Objectives.—It is with the new type foreign-language course, in which the language abilities are developed from the start in and through content and activities rich in potential associate and concomitant outcomes, that this book is primarily concerned. All the preceding chapters have been written from the viewpoint of helping the foreign-language curriculum to achieve more effective linguistic results in and through content and activities which have some direct bearing upon the development of attitudes, interests, appreciations, and insights conducive to cultivated living. Although the place of orientation courses in foreign cultures, of survey courses in the broad field of language, and of offerings in world literature in translation, is appreciatively recognized in Chapters IX, X, and XV, the primary concern here, as in preceding parts of this book, is with the *life objectives* that can legitimately be proposed as criteria for the choice of content and learning activities in a modern foreign-language course at the secondary-school level.

Attention is called to several important differences between life objectives and such "aims and objectives" as are commonly listed in the preambles to courses of study. The latter are in reality often "classroom objectives," emphasizing information or skills per se without serious concern for the ways in which the knowledge and skills acquired in school will be used in actual life or if, indeed, they are likely to be used at all. An increasing number of able thinkers in all walks of life have come to realize that making knowledge and skill serve constructive, wholesome purposes in the social and cultural life of the individual and of the community in which he lives, is as important for individual and group life as the "diffusion of knowledge" or the development of skills; for one can find approximately as many keen minds with college degrees (and the intelligence needed to earn them) in penitentiaries and insane asylums as in *Who's Who*. Wherein lies the difference between the two groups? The answer is probably to be found in the way in which the knowledge and skills were acquired in school, in the way in which they are put to use, and in the subsequent life purposes which they are made to serve—to enrich life for the individual and group, or to defraud, unbalance, frustrate, or debase it.

Modern Language Teaching, Ohio State University, Columbus, Ohio, 1940, 60 pp.; pp. 24–30. According to the Biennial Survey of Education 1933–1934, courses in general language were in operation in 122 schools in 26 states. See C. A. Jessen and L. B. Herlihy, "Offerings and Registrations in High School Subjects," *U. S. Office of Education, Bulletin* 1938, No. 6, Washington, D. C.

Today the school is concerned as much with the development of constructive life uses for the information, insights, and skills which it helps young people to achieve as with the "diffusion of knowledge" itself; for in reality the diffusion of knowledge has too often proved synonymous with the dissipation of it.   In its effort to make the work of the school and of young people more effective and more operative in life, American education is seeking in the present and future needs of the individual and of American culture the objectives that will serve as criteria for choosing the content, activities, types of curriculum organization, and means of evaluation that will make education more effective in meeting its responsibilities and in justifying the confidence and the faith which the majority of our citizens in all walks of life have in the regenerative power of the school as a dynamic influence for the individual and common good.   The extension of educational facilities in many communities to include parental education, adult education, and preschool guidance indicate the magnitude of this responsibility, and the seriousness with which it is being assumed.   Whether or not the foreign languages have anything to offer to more than a small, relatively select group of students at these levels depends entirely upon the significance of the purposes, beyond the skills themselves, which this branch of the curriculum can be made to serve.

In discussing this vital problem, it is important to keep in mind the distinction between associate, concomitant, and direct outcomes, and the distinction between these and *objectives*.   The latter are *life-derived criteria* for the content, activities, organization, and evaluation of the learning program; the former are the actual results obtained through the medium of an educational program organized and conducted in terms of certain guiding objectives.   Since any aims defined in terms of life needs (in the way of knowledge, attitudes, interests, insights, skills, or human understandings, which give direction to individual and group living) are destined to lie beyond the medium or content of the instruction itself, and to coincide with similarly derived aims of other school subjects, the problem will always arise why certain objectives cannot be achieved just as effectively, if not more so, through the medium of content read and discussed in English than through the medium of a foreign language.   Since this problem strikes at the root of many controversies over the role of the foreign languages in American education, it is important to give attention to the underlying question—why foreign languages?

Why Foreign Languages?—Obviously, the answer is not to be sought in objectives, however desirable, which could be achieved just as effectively through the medium of the vernacular, but in exactly the same sources from which all valid educational objectives in a democratic society are derived in the first place—from the felt needs and interests of the individuals, young and old, who constitute its citizenry. Every superintendent of schools in every community of any size is aware of the popular interest in foreign languages which in normal times expresses itself in the demand for evening-school classes in French, German, Italian, or Spanish. He is aware also of the equally great interest among children and young people expressed in the voluntary enrollments in foreign-language classes where such enrollment is not deliberately discouraged by the counselors, and of the surprising interest at times manifested in them even in transient camps for itinerant boys.[1] The fact that few city superintendents have been able to suppress foreign-language work successfully without suffering serious criticisms and reactions from many quarters of their own communities is but one measure of the strength of this popular interest. To these manifestations of social or cultural need, should be added the even greater demand for foreign-language offerings in private elementary and secondary schools, the considerable number of foreign-language classes in commercial colleges and special foreign-language schools, and the number of teachers of private lessons whose existence is largely supported by popular demand. Even radio stations and newspapers,[2] at times offer foreign-language lessons in response to popular request. It is doubtful if any change in such artificial stimuli as college entrance requirements would seriously affect this source of interest.

The most conspicuous long-range effect of the traditional two-year college entrance requirement in foreign languages has seemingly been to contract the foreign-language program to a very limited, stereotyped two-year course which could not possibly serve the varied life needs and interests of as many young people as commonly profess a genuine desire to learn a foreign language, and which consequently succeeds in defeating its own ends as often as it achieves them. For some strange reason, the two-year requirement for admission to college

---

[1] George E. Outland, "Educational Desires of Transient Boys," *Sierra Educational News*, Vol. XXXI, pp. 31–32, April, 1935.

[2] Among them the San Francisco and Los Angeles *Examiner* (Spanish) 1940, 1941, and affiliated stations.

has been interpreted by many school administrators to mean the maximum amount of time which any student or teacher should require to gain ability to read, write, and speak a foreign language comparable to that achieved in his native tongue by a pupil who lives in and through the English language during all his waking hours in and out of school. In reality, two years of a foreign language usually represents less than 350 hours, and in a class of 35 pupils this means at best only 10 hours of opportunity to speak in class! The cause for wonder is not to be found in how little pupils learn in the limited type of program to which teachers have been confined, but in the fact that presumably intelligent people, capable of crystal-gazing far into the future, should expect miracles. If language ability could be developed by hypnotic suggestion, such expectations would be legitimate, but the fact is that language is a matter of growth, and growth is always a function of time as well as of nature and nurture.

Although the long-range effect of college entrance requirements has been largely in the direction of frustrating popular interest in foreign-language study by confining it in most secondary schools to a very limited type of college-preparatory course, supercharged with formal exercises and rarely related to the language needs and interests of young people, neither the restrictive influence of these barriers nor the apathetic attitude of school administrators has been sufficient to do more than dampen this interest after the students enroll in school. For the true source of popular interest in foreign-language study, as expressed in voluntary enrollments in evening schools, extension classes, commercial colleges, private modern-language classes, radio lessons, and correspondence schools, is not to be found in university bulletins. It is to be found in such subtle environmental influences as the radio, the moving picture, the operatic and concert stage, or relatives who speak the language at home, and the large number of foreign words and expressions occurring in our books, newspapers, place names, and menus. Perhaps it is to be found even in the primitive sense of satisfaction that children often find in inventing codes and sign languages, or talking "pig Latin." Radio advertisers, newspapers, and Boy Scout leaders, if not the school, have recognized and capitalized this language interest to advantage.

Indeed the "average" man is in more frequent contact with foreign languages today than the elite of a few decades ago. As Henry M. Wriston has indicated:

It is a paradox more puzzling than any so far, that as long as the United States was really isolated, with a minimum of international trade, no cables, no telephones, no radios, no steamships, no airplanes, no motion pictures, and relatively few immigrants who did not speak English, every well-educated man was trained in the foreign languages.   Now, with twenty million daily radio listeners, with ten million more in daily contact with foreign languages, with all the modes of present-day contact, many disputants insist that foreign languages are not important.   They are taught grudgingly, therefore poorly, and then it is declared that the results do not justify them.   The cold fact, stripped of all wishful thinking, is that the "common man" has more direct contact with foreign languages today than ever before in history.[1]

Frustration of Personal and Social Needs in the Foreign-language Arts.—Fortunately, the chief criticism of foreign-language teaching in the schools is not directed against the potential value of knowing a foreign language, nor against the increasing need for them in modern life, but against the ability of foreign-language departments to realize all the values claimed for the study.   To this criticism, foreign-language teachers have commonly replied with the explanation that it is impossible to meet the varied needs and interests of young people in a single type of program—usually restricted to two years—and often dominated by college entrance requirements and examinations.

Until 1935 the situation, briefly described, was about as follows:

1. A popular interest in foreign languages, reinforced by educational tradition.

2. An increasing need for knowledge about foreign countries and foreign peoples, owing to the rapid increase in facilities for international communication and transportation, and their effect upon politics and economics.

3. A uniform type of foreign-language course, usually limited by virtue of competing requirements to two years for all but foreign-language "majors," and organized and conducted primarily in favor of students preparing to pass college entrance board examinations, or to continue foreign-language work in the university.

Since 1935, growing international tension and social unrest at home have served to emphasize the need for developing a unified, creative, and enlightened Americanism as a prerequisite to the ultimate success of any program of national defense and regeneration.   The conspicuousness of this need for the cultural unification of our citizenry —one-third of which is of foreign birth or foreign parentage[2]—began

[1] Henry M. Wriston, "Perspective upon Education," *The Educational Record*, Vol. XXI, pp. 90–101, January, 1940.
[2] Leonard Covello, "Language as a Factor in Integration and Assimilation," *The Modern Language Journal*, Vol. XXIII, pp. 323–333, February, 1939.

to shift the emphasis from the disciplinary and college-preparatory values of foreign-language study to its potential values as a medium for the integration of our cultural heritage from the world into a creative, unified, American way of life.

The Foreign Languages in the Stanford Language Arts Investigation.—In 1937 this frame of reference for the role of foreign languages in American education was established for the high schools participating in the Stanford Language Arts Investigation.   The life objectives selected as criteria for the choice of content, learning activities, and means of evaluation were formulated in the following terms:

The conscious purpose is to understand and appreciate American civilization as an integral part of present and past world civilizations, and to develop cultural integration in the present and future by effective communication of socially significant content through the mediums of the foreign languages and English.   The enabling objectives are

1. To evaluate the various contributions of foreign peoples to the building of American life and culture, and to create favorable conditions for such contributions in the future.

2. To understand the part America has played in developing the cultures of other peoples, and of world culture, and to participate actively in the development of more important contributions in the future.

3. To gain insight into the cultural meaning of the major civilizations of the world irrespective of their interrelationships with our own people in the past.[1]

In thus tying the foreign-language curriculum into the long-range core needs of American life, the teachers representing the participating schools subscribed to a specific platform for approaching the solution of the complicated problems of meeting the diverse language needs and interests of young people, of satisfying college entrance requirements, and of making foreign-language instruction more effective in long-range terms.

With respect to the concomitant outcomes frequently proposed as justifications for the study of foreign languages, the teachers participating in the workshops of the Stanford Language Arts Investigation (1937–1940) agreed that their realization depended almost entirely upon the *method* of instruction used in teaching the foreign language, and only incidentally upon the foreign language itself.   Almost any subject from history to automechanics could conceivably be made "disciplinary," if neatness in written work, straight thinking, accurate

[1] Walter V. Kaulfers, "The Foreign Languages in the Stanford Language Arts Investigation," *Hispania*, Vol. XXI, pp. 13–18, February, 1938.

grammatical usage, and habits of consulting the dictionary and sticking to a task until it is finished, were deliberately set up as objectives, and the work of the courses organized with these aims primarily in view. Without disparaging the value of these "disciplines," the participating teachers agreed that the development of desirable work habits and of accuracy in the use of English was a common responsibility of *all* teachers in every school, and not the unique responsibility of teachers of foreign languages. As a common responsibility of all teachers throughout the educational system these outcomes could not be used to justify a special place for the foreign languages in the curriculum in priority over other subjects.

With respect to the purely linguistic disciplines (*e.g.*, accuracy and clarity of expression in English, increased English vocabulary, critical thinking in language, etc.) the participants agreed that these were important outcomes, but that these values could be achieved more effectively if content of real significance for the life needs of the student, rather than formal disconnected exercises devoid of information or ideas worth mentioning, were made the medium for learning to read, write, speak, or translate a foreign language. In recognition of the importance of applied semantics in daily life, the participants favored the organization of special courses in which the phenomenon of language both as a *means* of communication, and as a *medium* of thought, could be investigated from the point of view of the following leading questions:[1]

1. *Why* do people (Americans and other nationalities) speak, read, write, and spell as they do?

2. *How* does language affect people (Americans and other nationalities) in daily life?

3. *What* are people (Americans and other nationalities) doing to make language a more reliable and obedient servant and a less elusive master?

The conviction was strong that the foreign-language course was already too overtaxed with other responsibilities to permit of stressing these values to the extent to which they deserve recognition in their own right as vital educational needs. For this reason, special language-arts survey courses, or revised general-language programs, were recognized as constituting essentially integral parts of the foreign-language curriculum. In offerings of this type the representatives of the participating schools noted numerous possibilities for a joint sharing of responsibilities with teachers in other fields—particularly

[1] See Chap. X.

teachers of English, the social studies, mathematics, art, music, stenography, penmanship, and commercial law.

With respect to the associate outcomes of foreign-language study (attitudes, insights, knowledge, and appreciations apart from language) the participating schools recognized the importance of these values for individual and group life, but realized that they could be achieved in foreign-language courses only through the medium of the thought content of the learning materials, or through such integrative activities as could be carried on primarily in the foreign language. This conviction led to the conclusion that language and content could not be separated at any level if the associate outcomes were to be realized without sacrificing time needed for practice in reading, writing, or speaking the language. However, since reading, writing, or speaking always implies something in the way of feelings, wants, ideas, or information to read, write, or talk about, why could not this "something" be content contributable to the realization of associate outcomes of value for individual and group life, and suggestive of activities for relating foreign-language work to life outside the classroom? A survey of practical ways and means revealed many possibilities for making the foreign-language course contribute simultaneously to the development of ability in language and to the development of insights, attitudes, and appreciations of significance for the individual as a constructive influence in the life of the community. The sample unit dramatized in practical detail in Chapter VII is illustrative of but one of many ways for translating this conception into operational terms during the very first week of beginning classes of varying size or intelligence levels. Numerous other devices and procedures have been described in concrete detail in the chapters on pronunciation, reading, grammar, conversation, and vocabulary building. The nature of the results that have actually been achieved in terms of this conception are reported in the chapter on evaluation.

While recognizing the value of ability in a foreign language as a vocational asset, the teachers of the participating schools realized the impracticability of attempting to use the vocational objective as the primary criterion for organizing foreign-language curriculums in secondary schools. The number of vocations in which knowledge of a foreign language is desirable is too diverse to permit of organizing a learning program for young people whose futures are unpredictable even as regards their probable continuation in school or college. Moreover, every vocation requires a specialized vocabulary peculiarly associated with it. A course of study attempting to provide a vocabu-

lary equally useful to prospective research workers, to foreign news
correspondents, to commercial secretaries, or to stewards on board
steamship or airlines is almost impossible except in specialized courses
which the average secondary school can seldom afford to maintain.
Since all the remunerative professions in which ability in one or more
foreign languages is a distinct, if not indispensable asset, are vocations
requiring an almost perfect command of a foreign language beyond
the reach of most pupils in high school, and the equivalent of at least
four or five years of college training, it seemed desirable to focus attention primarily on social and cultural needs common to all individuals
in a democratic society, regardless of rank or station.   By conducting
classwork as far as possible on the workshop plan, it was felt that such
immediate vocational needs as might be felt by students actively
employed in remunerative work, or definitely assured of employment
in some occupation involving contacts with a foreign language, could
be met individually, or in small groups, within the regular class and
within the framework of the unifying theme for the foreign-language
course.

In practice this involved exempting students with definite vocational responsibilities from certain types of work in order that they
might make a job analysis of the specific language needs associated
with the performance of specific tasks; and (with the occasional aid
of the teacher in locating and organizing materials) to learn the special
vocabulary, idioms, and routine expressions thus derived.   Beyond
a few students employed in stores patronized by Spanish-speaking
people, an occasional student of voice anxious to sing songs in a foreign
language, and a small number of pupils who were definitely planning to
travel abroad during the summer vacation, the actual need for this
type of specialized practical work was slight and easily satisfied without
subordinating the needs and interests of the class as a whole to the
exceptional needs of a few.

With respect to the linguistic outcomes, the participating schools
accepted the thesis that language is always a *means*, and that as means
it is best acquired in terms of the *ends* which it should desirably serve
in postgraduate life.   It was felt that unless in the process of learning
a language, a pupil experiences some of the satisfactions that can be
expected ultimately to accrue from being able to use it, the desire to
capitalize it later may be slight for want of insight into its most
important applications.

While recognizing the linguistic objectives as definite responsibilities of foreign-language teachers, the participating schools realized

that outcomes in the way of ability actually to use a language for some purpose beyond the completion of classroom assignments could not be developed except in terms of specific life objectives.   These became the central guiding criteria for choosing the foreign-language materials and activities in and through which the linguistic abilities were to be developed.   They also served as criteria for evaluating the program in terms of associate outcomes insofar as these could be appraised by means of information tests, by changes in pupil attitudes as registered on batteries of race prejudice scales, by concrete evidences of desirable changes in pupil attitudes and behavior, and by increased voluntary use of the cultural resources of the community—library facilities, open forums, lecture series, concert series, travel clubs, Pan-American societies, etc.[1]

Although the measurement of ability in reading, writing, aural comprehension, and oral expression formed an integral part of the evaluation program, achievement on tests of technical proficiency served primarily a guidance function in providing objective evidence as a basis for counseling senior students with respect to continuance in foreign-language work in college the following term.   In the case of freshmen, sophomores, or juniors, such mechanical tests served only as aids in diagnosing pupil difficulties, and in determining individual and group levels of achievement as bases for choosing foreign-language materials and activities suited to the language abilities of the students.

Like other branches of the curriculum, the foreign languages were regarded as fields of educative experience that owe their places in American education primarily to the interests of young people and their elders.   The educational values of the field were not construed to be exclusively linguistic, nor exclusively in the form of skill outcomes, but also in the nature of insights, attitudes, and appreciations of significance for cultivated living.   For those students who on the basis of their actual progress in a foreign language during a trial period of a semester or year professed a genuine interest in continuing the work, adequate opportunities for further study of the language throughout high school were provided.   In schools too small to support separate advanced classes, these opportunities were provided through individualized reading or study programs conducted on the contract plan or by means of seminar groups within a regular class.

[1] For an excellent survey of community agencies and facilities see Lyle Flanagan, Alice Myers, and Geraldine Rendleman, *Community Resources*, Des Moines Public Schools, 1940, 157 pp.; pp. 59–64.

For students who professed no original interest in a foreign language as such and for students who after a trial period of study in a foreign-language course decided that their primary interest was in becoming acquainted with the foreign country directly through reading and discussion in English, the Investigation recognized the desirability of providing semester or year terminal courses in foreign civilizations, using foreign contributions operative in contemporary American culture as the unifying frame of reference. The place and function of terminal courses of this type have been described in Chapter IX.[1] Where introduced they served to arouse interest in foreign languages and cultures among students who otherwise would have had no occasion to develop an interest in this field, and provided suitable alternative courses[2] for students who after a tryout in a foreign-language class failed to profit from the work. In addition, they afforded students majoring in semiprofessional subjects such as book-keeping, stenography, office management, home economics, or applied arts and crafts, an elective course that would yield approximately the same outcomes as might be expected to accrue from a well-planned, carefully integrated, and competently guided sojourn abroad. Where the introduction of offerings of this kind exercised any appreciable effect upon enrollments in regular foreign-language courses, the result was uniformly in the direction of gains rather than losses.

The conception of the role and function of foreign languages, literatures, and cultures in American education, as translated into operational terms by the school participating in the Stanford Language Arts Investigation, has been described in considerable detail since it affords clues to practical ways and means for approaching the solution of foreign-language problems in institutions of different sizes and types, in communities in which there is a wide variation in the soil and climate of the educational environment. Since this conception has to date[3] yielded the most satisfactory solution that has so far been reported in the literature of long-range curriculum planning in foreign languages, it may be desirable to restate briefly the underlying working hypotheses:

[1] See also C. M. Purin, "A Year's Course in Foreign Civilizations for High School Students," *Monatshefte für deutschen Unterricht*, Vol. XXXI, pp. 96–103, February, 1939.

[2] Elizabeth N. Reed, "Mexicans Become Friends: An Elective Course in Mexican Life and Culture," *Foreign Languages and Cultures in American Education*, McGraw-Hill Book Company, Inc., New York. In press.

[3] Walter V. Kaulfers, "Foreign-language Outcomes of the Stanford Language Arts Investigation," *School and Society*, Vol. LII, pp. 235–237, Sept. 21, 1940.

1. The basic *raison d'être* of foreign-language teaching in American education today is to be found in the widespread interests aroused by such environmental influences as the radio, moving picture, and the foreign backgrounds of contemporary American life and culture as revealed in people, history, customs, architecture, language, place names, music, and the like.

2. These interests are too diverse to be satisfied by a single type of foreign-language course, uniform in objectives, content, methods, or criteria of evaluation for all students.

3. Increasing world interdependence makes it desirable to capitalize these interests in the new program of education for cultural unification and progress by democratic evolutionary means.

4. Since learning to read, write, or speak a language means active practice in reading, writing, or speaking about *something*, the contextual medium for the learning of the language should desirably be content in the way of information or ideas of immediate significance for present-day life outside the schoolroom. The content and activities that give promise of contributing to a better understanding of the meaning of America in terms of its cultural heritage from abroad, and to the development of a creative, enlightened American way of life, might well be chosen as the primary (though by no means exclusive) thought medium in and through which the linguistic abilities are to be developed and exercised from the start. The implications of this conception for methodology have already been discussed in preceding chapters.

5. Inasmuch as the marked increase in facilities of communication—the radio, printed matter, and the sound picture—has intensified the need for consumer education in language, the expansion of courses in general language to include training in the semantic analysis of radio discussions, magazine articles, speeches, books, and news reports is desirable. In such reorganized general-language courses, the study of the growth and development of the English language in relation to other languages, and of the latter as different ways of interpreting and symbolizing reality, can be made to serve a life objective as necessary and as significant as that of consumer education in science or home economics.

6. Since the potential outcomes of foreign-language study in the way of knowledge, attitudes, and human insights and appreciations are considered by many people to be as valuable as ability to read or speak a foreign language, terminal orientation courses in foreign cultures, conducted in English, deserve a place in the curriculum for

students who lack the time or incentive to learn a foreign language. A survey course dealing with Mexico, for example, would obviously be appropriate for sociological reasons in a community which has a large unassimilated Mexican colony.

7. For the same reasons, alternative offerings in world literature, carrying full college-preparatory credit in English, deserve a place in the curriculum of the secondary school. Where these courses are conducted by foreign-language teachers with a reading knowledge of two or more languages, students who are able to read foreign novels, plays, or short stories in the original may be granted foreign-language credit. No foreign-language prerequisites of any kind, however, need be attached to these courses for students who cannot read a foreign language.

8. The function of survey courses in foreign cultures, of orientation courses in language and applied semantics, and of classes in world literature in translation, is not to serve as dumping grounds for students who are sometimes branded as "language misfits," nor to provide substitutes for the regular foreign-language courses, but to make possible a fuller realization of linguistic and cultural values for which there is seldom time in a foreign-language class, and for which adequate provision is seldom made by the secondary school.

9. In all these fields foreign-language teachers, by virtue of their training in language and their background in foreign literatures and cultures, have a unique opportunity to make a significant contribution.

10. Although it is generally admitted that all the desirable outcomes listed at the beginning of this chapter are impossible of attainment[1] in a single uniform type of foreign-language course enrolling young people of widely different interests, backgrounds, maturity levels, and life destinations, the conviction is growing that these outcomes can be realized by larger numbers of students through an appropriate differentiation of offerings. For those pupils who have special interests or purposes in learning a foreign language, or who could be enabled to develop such interests and purposes with ultimate profit and satisfaction to themselves, the foreign-language course is obviously the most appropriate medium for developing simultaneously ability actually to use a foreign language and insights and appreciations desired of socially effective citizens.

An Organic Social Philosophy of Language.—Obviously, ability actually to use a language is not developed merely by picking words

[1] Charles E. Young, "Tumult and Shouting," *The Modern Language Journal,* Vol. XVII, pp. 73–77, November, 1933.

or sentences apart, examining them, and putting them back together
according to rules.   Neither is it developed by discoursing learnedly
in English about grammatical, phonetic, etymological, or philosophical
phenomena *in vacuo*.   Such activity leads to proficiency in picking
words and sentences apart and putting them back together again,
and to proficiency in discoursing learnedly in English about grammatical, phonetic, etymological, or philological phenomena *in vacuo*.

Such work is often interesting to students, just as crossword puzzles
have a certain fascination for some people and are not at times without
some indeterminate linguistic value.   In fact, teachers often justify
teaching more formal grammar to pupils than they ever learn to
apply effectively in their own reading, writing, or speech, on the
grounds that the pupils want it and like it.   Whatever truth lies in
this justification for the continued teaching of formal grammar as a
preliminary foundation is, in reality, a strong condemnation of what
teachers have *taught* pupils to like, or of a subtle policy of ridding
themselves as quickly as possible of young people who did not like it.
For if pupils have been taught to like what has been repeatedly proved
to have little or no carry-over value in their *own* reading, writing, or
speech, except as a means of weeding out those who do not already
possess the mental qualifications[1] which the program sets up as objectives, then it is plain that pupils have been taught to like the nonfunctional or at least have been sidetracked into worshipping the
means without regard for the ends.

[1] Hare R. Douglass and Clifford Kittelson, "The Transfer of Training in High
School Latin to English Grammar, Spelling, and Vocabulary," *Journal of Experi-
mental Education*, Vol. IV, pp. 26–33, September, 1935.   Joseph E. Barber,
"Finds English Grammar of No Benefit to Pupils of Foreign Language," *Nation's
Schools*, Vol. XVII, p. 25, January, 1936.   For a close parallel from experimental
data obtained from Latin classes see Willard W. Beatty, "What is the Future of
Latin in the American Secondary School?" *Progressive Education*, Vol. XII, pp.
329–332, May, 1935.

Owing to the fact that well-disciplined minds are required to master the
foreign languages as traditionally taught, and to the fact that only such minds are
usually acceptable to foreign-language teachers, it is easy to commit the fallacy of
thinking that the study of a foreign language produces well-disciplined minds.
Moreover, since pupils with cultural interests usually come from homes with a
superior social and economic rating, it is easy to take credit for environmental
influences and advantages outside the school.   By using the kind of logic that
is conventionally applied to proving the disciplinary values of foreign-language
study it would easily be possible to prove that the longer a pupil studies a foreign
language the higher will he boost his father's salary, for length of schooling is
positively correlated with family income.

The fact that pupils can be taught to take an active interest in the formal mechanics of language, and to make high scores on formal tests without improving their own personal use of language, has long been noted by creative teachers of English and the foreign languages. The following vignette by Ethel Anne McDonald is an excellent illustration of the failure of formal grammar to accomplish the life objectives which it intends to serve:

A TRUE STORY OF THE GOOD OLD DAYS
WHEN THEY KNEW ALL THE RULES[1]

Jim and I were friends. He used to come in often before school to talk with me. This Monday I was especially glad to see him because I had good news for him. *He had passed the 7A grammar test at the head of his class* and I was proud of him. However, I could tell by his eager face that he had something to tell me, so I let my glad tidings wait.

"Hello there, Jim."

"Hi, Mrs. McDonald! You know what?"

"No, what?"

"Me and my dad, we hiked clean over to Paradise yesterday."

"Oh, Jimmy!"

"Well heck, what was wrong with that?"

"Nothing was wrong with the hike; but, Jimmy, your grammar!"

"Oh yeah, I know, I know! Don't tell me, now—'*My dad and I*'—is that better?"

"Much!" I sighed and relaxed. "Go on, Jimmy."

"Well"—slowly—"my dad and I hiked over to Paradise Camp and when we was about half way back, we seen a snake."

"You what?"

"We seen a snake—a rattlesnake! Gosh, Mrs. McDonald, it sure was a whopper."

"I understood you the first time, Jim, and that must have been a real thrill, but what *verb* have we been working on for the last *month?*"

"I know—*saw*—but, gosh! if you're going to razz me about my grammar all the time, I can't tell you nothin'."

"Of course you can't, Jim. I'm sorry. Go ahead. Let me hear all about it!"

And I listened, smiling a bit ruefully at the thought of my own "glad tidings," as he sailed into his story—his eyes bright and his tongue loosened—on through the "seens" and "dones" and double negatives clear to the triumphant finish:

"And when my dad seen it, he grabbed a rock and landed it right on the bean and I tied a string around its neck, and drug it all the way home!"

[1] Ethel Anne McDonald, by permission of the author and of the Stanford Language Arts Investigation.

Technical training in general linguistics is often of value to teachers in explaining the underlying reasons or causal principles, but it is not synonymous with ability actually to comprehend or convey feelings, wants, ideas, or information in a foreign language. Such ability comes only through abundant guided practice in actually communicating something to somebody, or in learning something from someone, and in appropriately capitalizing the resources of linguistic science when and where they are specifically needed by the pupil to facilitate effective communication in his own personal use of language. Teaching *about* a foreign language and teaching a foreign language to students are two different things. Neither is synonymous with helping young people to grow in ability to use a foreign language for worthy life purposes.

Making Ideals Materialize.—A language may be compared to an electrical circuit in which meaning is the current. It is useless when the flow of meaning is turned off. It is useless also if the current is dissipated. Its life value ultimately depends on the *work* that the current flowing through the circuit accomplishes. The objective may be destructive as in setting off a bomb, or constructive as in lighting a beacon or a traffic signal. It is the business of the school not only to help young people build efficient communication circuits, but also to generate enough thought current to do constructive work in bridging the mental gulfs that separate man from reality and from his neighbor. Over 400 years ago, Johannis Ludovicus Vives, greatest authority on foreign-language teaching produced by the Renaissance, seems to have had in mind this dynamic conception of the value and role of language and literature in life:[1]

But let those who study remember that if nothing is added to their knowledge . . . by the study of the language, they have only arrived at the gates of knowledge or are still hovering in the entrance hall. . . . No language is in itself worth the trouble of learning if nothing is sought beyond the linguistic aspect.[2]

[1] Dorothy M. Kress, "Juan Luis Vives: A Study in Renaissance Theories in Methodology in Foreign Language Instruction," *The Modern Language Journal*, Vol. XXV, pp. 19–25, October, 1940.

[2] For problems and issues for discussion see Appendix A.

CHAPTER XIII

PERSPECTIVE ON EVALUATION AND SUPERVISION

Even if it be true that everything which *does* exist could be measured if we only knew how, that which does *not* exist cannot be measured; and it is no paradox to say that the teacher is deeply concerned with what does not exist. —MERLE CURTI

All criteria of evaluation must be visionary enough to include what is projected as *ideal*, lest that which happens to be become standardized as inevitable.

A Life-centered Philosophy of Evaluation.—Evaluation is that aspect of education which is concerned with the effectiveness with which a pupil or group of pupils is achieving the aims of the learning program, and with the effectiveness of the content, activities, and methodology of the program itself in enabling young people to achieve outcomes of significance in terms of the life objectives for which education in its various phases is provided by society. The fundamental questions are always, "What kind of human being will experience with this method, content, activity, test, or learning incentive condition a growing boy or girl into becoming?" and "How does the learning program help young people to grow in ability and determination to apply what they learn in solving crucial personal and social problems constructively?" In other words, the criteria of evaluation are the *life activities* of individuals, not merely in the classroom or school, but also as members of a family or community unit, and as members of an increasingly interdependent society, in which almost every human act of speech or behavior has either a direct or an indirect effect upon some other person or people. Inasmuch as formal discipline and the transfer of training cannot be counted upon to guarantee the translation of "schooling" into a way of life any more than centuries of formal churchgoing have been able to eliminate wars, the emphasis is upon "living what one learns while learning it." Otherwise, the danger is real that what knowledge one acquires will not change what one really is; for people are far more likely to become what the kind of *means* they employ actually give them practice in becoming, than what their mentally projected objectives are. Consequently,

373

unless the actual practice or experiences afforded by the *means* definitely partake of the nature of the *ends*, it is not at all unlikely that
the "ideals" envisioned by the objectives will ultimately serve merely
as a sublimated disguise for one's real thoughts, motives, or actions.
Means that do not partake of the nature of the ends are not likely to
do more than to develop a certain degree of cleverness in bringing
egocentric behavior into conformity with the ideal through verbal
rationalization.   The frequently observed discrepancy between verbal
culture and actual life behavior, even among educated people, is but
a sign that schooling sometimes succeeds merely in inducing a socially
tolerated form of schizophrenia, popularly known as hypocrisy,
intellectual dishonesty, rationalizing, "whitewashing," etc.

Since the carry-over of in-school learning into out-of-school life
has not always been so great as desired, leaders in foreign-language
teaching and education have shifted the emphasis from measuring
skills exclusively as ends in themselves to appraising the life values
of that which is done or accomplished in the process of learning or
using the skills.   The basic principles that underlie this concept of
evaluation may be summarized briefly as follows:

Three Working Hypotheses.—1. Skills are of life value only insofar
as the purposes for which they are used in out-of-school life are worth
while.   Since the term "worth while" is a polar word, it may be
desirable to indicate the philosophical premises in terms of which the
worth-whileness of the life uses to which such a skill as reading, for
example, may be put.   Here the consensus of expert judgment available at any given time is obviously the final arbiter in cases of doubt.
With respect to reading, the following life purposes are generally
accepted as valid and worthy of encouragement:

Reading that is helpful in enabling young people to find themselves—to formulate personalized conceptions of socially useful, wholesome, productive, and satisfying lives, and of the means for attaining them.

Reading that is helpful in enabling young people to secure guidance and
encouragement for making satisfying progress toward the realization of their
personalized conceptions of a productive and happy cultivated life.

Reading that gives insight into the life problems of other people in such a way
as to make it possible for the individual to gain the human understandings essential
to working or living effectively with others.

Reading that helps to guide nervous tensions resulting from worry, fear, ill
health, frustration, or sorrow, into constructive channels.

In comparison with the foregoing life purposes to which skill in
reading can be applied, the following are either profitless or harmful:

Reading that deals with abnormal, atypical, or psychopathic characters in which the element of distortion is the center of attention rather than cause and effect in relation to possible solutions.

Reading that substitutes wishful thinking and introvertic day dreaming for purposeful action, or leads to the vicarious feeding of neurotic tendencies.

Reading that misleads, deludes, or deceives the individual, or hypnotizes him into behaving hysterically rather than rationally.

2. Skills that are not learned in and through content and activities that give insight and practice into their most important applications in out-of-school life are likely to function either without purpose in life or not at all.   Worse than this, a skill that is not developed in the light of a constructive purpose may easily become the tool of a destructive force, in which case the welfare of the individual and of society alike would be better served if the individual had not acquired the skill at all.   Of what value is mechanical skill in reading, for example, if this ability leads to paying two to fifty times the true worth of an article advertised to accomplish the impossible?   Of what value is skill in reading if this ability is consumed in acquiring misinformation from the irresponsible pages of a "yellow" tabloid?   Of what value is ability to read if it is applied to printed matter that stimulates neurotic tendencies into antisocial or criminal acts of behavior?   The proposition could easily be defended that in such cases the welfare of society and of the individual himself would be better served if he had not learned to read at all.

The fact that reading ability, like any other skill, can be applied to serve either constructive or destructive purposes, and that the opportunities are sometimes equally great in both directions, emphasizes the responsibility of the school for developing skill and satisfaction in reading for a beneficial life purpose.   If, indeed, "Reading maketh a full man," is it not important for the school to ask "Full of what?" The concept of evaluation thus includes the appraisal not only of outcomes in the way of technical proficiency in the use of skills, or amount of information learned, but also of the probable effectiveness of the content and activities (through which the skills or information are acquired) in making these learnings serve wholesome life purposes.

3. Any learning program is destructive of its own ends if in the process of developing a skill it crushes all subsequent desire to use it voluntarily.   There is no need for laying a foundation for anything unless that foundation includes building a deep and abiding interest that will encourage the individual to create something of significance upon the foundation which he has laid.   Unless this self-evident

truth is capitalized as a guiding principle in the organization and conduct of foreign-language study, in the writing of textbooks, and in the choice of learning activities and procedures, the outcomes of instruction in the language arts, from the standpoint both of proficiency in the skills themselves and of their application to worthy life purposes, are destined to be so insignificant that all manner of rationalized justifications (mental discipline, improvement in English grammar, etc.) will have to be devised to support the study in the schools.   Justifications irrelevant to the primary purposes of language in life, irrelevant to the reasons for which most people study languages, and irrelevant to the cultural objectives in the field of human relations which the teachers themselves advertise, are usually verbal mirages designed to conceal the sterility of an impoverished reality, or the incompetence of those who are unwilling to cooperate with others in removing the mechanical obstacles that frustrate progress in the field.

Evaluation as an Integral Phase of All Aspects of the Educative Process.—The foregoing discussion of the operational principles underlying the concept of evaluation as an integral part of the educative process may serve to provide a background for the criteria and ways and means by which the effectiveness of a learning program in foreign languages may be appraised from the standpoint of its objectives, content, activities, methods, and abiding outcomes.   Unless an evaluation program is concerned with every aspect of the educative process in the light of the immediate and long-range needs of the individual in society, it is not likely to amount to much more than an impressive routine exercise in counting and filing—after it is too late to do anything more important about the results than to brand them as failures.   The shelves of libraries are already crowded with books and monographs full of impressive statistical reports concerning which relatively little is done besides quoting them in articles and speeches or making them the basis of minor changes in school routine.   The translation of these data into operational principles of action would doubtless be easier and more effective if a community of understanding prevailed among pupils, parents, teachers, supervisors, administrators, and university professors concerning the place and function of the foreign languages in American education.   The avenues for cooperatively developing such a community of understanding have long been available through the medium of national and regional organizations of foreign-language teachers, national and regional education associations, parent-teacher associations, and the like.

Unfortunately, owing to a blind preoccupation with language and literature as scholastic worlds in and of themselves, apart from the lives of children and from the changing real world in which they live, little use has been made of these agencies in considering what the study of a foreign language does to or for people, as human beings, in helping them to achieve in reality, for themselves and others, the kind of world in which they wish to lead genuine, wholesome, productive, and friendly lives. Instead, the major preoccupation during the past twenty years seems to have been upon finding Procustean ways and means for fitting humanity into a rigidly defined course of study and for casting aside all human material that would not fit the traditional mold. In the light of its humanitarian objectives, there is no other area in the entire field of public education in which human life, as it actually faces the teacher in the classroom, has so often been regarded with such irrelevancy and, at times, supercilious contempt. It is a patent illustration of the fact that it is always easier to know "culture," and to talk "culture"—especially about a culture several thousand miles from home—than it is to translate learning into action in living and working creatively with others. Culture as a way of life, in which human needs and values are paramount, is the only kind worth educating for at public expense in a society willing to risk life and property to guarantee such a way of life to the entire world.

In view of the crises created by long periods of social and economic maladjustment and by the incompatibility of changed realities and ideological patterns inherited from a cultural era without radios, airplanes, automobiles, sound pictures, or machines to replace human hands in large numbers, the problem of evaluation from the point of view of objectives, content, activities, methods, and immediate and long-range effects and results, is the most significant problem facing teachers today. Although acceptable criteria of evaluation can only be cooperatively defined after a realistic examination of fact in relation to societal needs and goals, the following statement of principles may throw light upon the magnitude of the problem and such concrete ways and means as have so far been found effective in solving it.

Criteria for the Evaluation of Objectives.—Are the life objectives of the program in conformity with the basic purposes for which schools are maintained in a democratic society? For example,

1. To enable people to earn a comfortable living through socially useful work? Are the vocational opportunities in the field of language within the reach of the high-school pupil and sufficiently prevalent to

be capitalized as incentives in learning on the part of any considerable number of young people?

2. To help people work and live effectively with others in the home, school, or community?

3. To help people develop and maintain desirable mental and physical health through proper diet and sleep, proper health habits, a wholesome use of leisure time, etc.?

4. To help people become creative participants in one or more aspects of the social and cultural life of the community?

5. To help people become intelligent and responsible participants in solving social problems affecting life needs in health, food, shelter, employment, education, and recreation by rational means before they lead to national or world crises?

Unless the aims of foreign-language teaching give evidence of being enabling objectives contributive to the realization of the basic purposes for which education is provided at public expense, their validity is doubtful unless foreign-language offerings are intended for more than a very small percentage of the public-school population. Such cultural values as knowledge of English grammar, mental discipline, and the like, can be developed just as effectively through subjects contributing to these central purposes. To date, the vocational utility of foreign-language training and its college-preparatory values have been the almost exclusive objectives which in practice have actually determined the choice of content, examinations, and methods for the courses. Granting the validity of these objectives for some students, the wisdom of capitalizing them as the dominant criteria for the organization and conduct of classes is seriously to be questioned as long as only 5 to 10 per cent[1] of the students who begin foreign-language work in high school continue the same language in college. Moreover, since college training in languages is usually required to develop the proficiency needed in remunerative vocations requiring a command of a foreign tongue, and since too few foreign-language teachers possess the degree of proficiency required to earn a comfortable living exclusively through language, outside of teaching, the central problem in foreign-language teaching today is that of organizing and conducting learning programs on the basis of objectives

[1] E. F. Engel, "Why Do Not College Students Continue the Foreign Language Begun in High School?" *The Modern Language Journal*, Vol. XVI, pp. 500–503, March, 1932. Walter V. Kaulfers and Vera E. Whittmann, "Continuance in College of High School Foreign Language," *The School Review*, Vol. XLVIII, pp. 606–611, October, 1940.

that will be valid for as large a population of students as usually profess a genuine interest in foreign-language study, and of relating the core content and activities of the classroom directly to these objectives from the start, without sacrificing the needs of the relatively few students who are likely to be able to prepare for foreign-language vocations or to continue in college in the same language which they began in high school.   In recent years, the conviction has grown that a unifying objective stressing the development of insights, attitudes, and appreciations that govern rational behavior in human relations within the home, school, community, nation, and world, should be the central (though not necessarily exclusive) objective of modern-language teaching.   Since the nature and scope of this objective have already been discussed in another connection,[1] it is unnecessary to carry the analysis further.

Criteria for the Evaluation of Content and Activities.—Objectives have no other purpose than that of serving as criteria for the choice of content and activities in and through which the skills, and the purposes for which they are taught, are to be attained.   Unless what is read, written, or said in the classroom has some direct and immediate bearing upon the objectives, the outcomes are destined to be accidental or incidental by-products, and the objectives themselves are not likely to serve as more than a decorative preamble or window dressing to a sterile outline of "minimum essentials" to be covered. The following leading questions provide a basis for evaluating a learning program in a foreign language:

1. What information or ideas are contained in the material read, written, or discussed in the foreign language which will contribute to the development of insights, attitudes, appreciations, or habits of behavior that are in keeping with the central objective?   Is the major part of the pupils' time and energy consumed in working with appropriate material, or in analyzing, deciphering, decoding, or transverbalizing mechanical exercises with no purpose beyond illustrating certain facts of language itself?   If pupils are temporarily engaged in what seems to be mechanical work, can they state confidently, in their own words, for what specific reason or immediate purpose beyond the assignment itself, they are doing the exercises; or are their answers limited to such statements as "because we didn't do so well on our test on verbs," "because we have to know pronouns in order to speak the language"?   Are seniors in the class given differentiated assignments to prepare them for college entrance board examinations,

[1] See Chaps. XV and XVI.

or are the specialized needs of this relatively small group imposed through uniform assignments and examinations upon all pupils in the course from the start?

2. Is life outside the classroom contacted through the medium of activities involving the use of the foreign language?[1] Are lectures or open-forum discussions relating to the foreign country announced and discussed in the classroom? Are local art exhibits, operas, movies, concerts, recitals, and fiestas featuring some aspect of a foreign culture, announced and discussed in the classroom? Are important international events affecting the foreign country discussed in the classroom from the point of view of their probable bearing upon our *own* national and community life? Are important anniversaries, such as Pan-American Day, celebrated in the classroom or through school programs sponsored by foreign-language classes? Are the experiences and abilities of resident citizens of foreign birth or descent capitalized from time to time? Is there an active foreign-language club affiliated with some constructive youth organization such as the International Student Forum or the Pan American Student League?[2] Is it working in cooperation with other clubs for some constructive purpose besides holding entertaining meetings? Is it functioning for some constructive purpose within the school and community? Is foreign correspondence for an informational purpose an integral part of the regular class work? Are appropriate short-wave radio programs heard and discussed in the classroom? Do the pupils visit and understand the evidences of foreign culture in their own community in architecture? city planning? customs? language? foreign "colonies?" history and traditions? permanent art collections?

3. Are pupils guided in accepting and filling increasingly larger responsibilities for their own work, and for the work of the class, in group activities of the kind described above, or are these activities assigned and executed at the will of the teacher without opportunity for group initiative or participation in the discussion, formulation, and cooperative execution of plans? Does the teacher conduct these activities in such a way as to provide young people with the opportunity to grow in ability to sense needs, to accept responsibilities, and to cooperate with other people in seeing that a common task is effectively done? Is teacher commendation or group approval the criterion of the success or failure of individual efforts in class activities? Is the teacher concerned with guiding the growth of young people in character

[1] For tested ways and means see Chaps. VI, VII, and VIII.
[2] See Chap. VIII, pp. 265–267.

and personality through language experiences, or is she concerned with covering certain minimum essentials with a particular score or grade?

Criteria for Evaluating the Appropriateness of the Learning Program for the Learner.—The effectiveness of any learning program depends upon the degree to which it keeps abreast of the pupil's level of insight as he matures as a human being and as a student in the class itself. The ability to perceive relationships, especially relationships symbolized through words rather than things, depends less on chronological age than upon the richness of the linguistic environment and the social and cultural interests of the home and community. The latter also influence the vocational and avocational interests and ambitions of the children in school. To be specific, a class composed of boys and girls from homes in which the parents have had little opportunity to secure an education, in which there is little time or money for good books and magazines, in which conversation is limited to very personal problems or comments on popular movie or radio programs, or in which the prospects for a job after school or during vacation are more pressing than a career after college, the pupils' levels of insight in situations involving language are destined to be limited or stunted regardless of latent potentialities. Compared with pupils from more favorable home and community environments, this lack of fertility in the soil and climate of the pupils' lives outside the school manifests itself, with few exceptions, in a relatively smaller active and passive vocabulary in the vernacular, in relatively low speed of comprehension in reading, and in a lack of interest or distaste for the reading of books. Cases are not infrequently found in which a pupil has never read a book except under the pressure of a collateral reading assignment.[1] Where reading interests are developed, they often tend in the direction of exciting material which serves as a psychological compensation for the limitations of an impoverished reality. Interest in people outside the pupil's social environment is likely to be limited to such individuals as have been made interesting by the newspapers, the movies, or the radio.

Pupils whose levels of insight are retarded or stunted by limitations of the kind indicated above usually develop signs of maladjustment in a foreign-language course in which the medium of instruction is a highly abstracted verbal symbolism. They are also likely to show

---

[1] Paul Witty and David Kopel, *Reading and the Educative Process*, Ginn and Company, Boston, 1939, x + 374 pp.; pp. 12, 83. Ruth Strang, *Problems in the Improvement of Reading in High School and College*, The Science Press Printing Company, Lancaster, Pa., 1940, 423 pp.; pp. 308–309.

signs of maladjustment if the purpose of the mechanical preparatory
work is to enable them to read books, plays, or poetry in a foreign
language before they have had the opportunity or encouragement to
develop an interest in such reading in English.   Unless the medium of
instruction is changed and an apperceptive basis[1] for the purposeful
reading of good books is built up *while skill in language is being developed,* whatever outcomes are likely to accrue in the way of ability to
use the language for some worth-while and enduring interest are
destined to be relatively insignificant.   Among the symptoms of a
state of incompatibility between the curriculum (content, methods, activities, and examinations) and pupil levels of insight are the
following:

*The Relative Number of Pupils Dropping the Study of a Foreign
Language through Dissatisfaction or Failure.*—Ordinarily, dropouts
due to a mobile school population, changes in classes, illness, or
incapacity for regular school attendance, do not exceed 3 to 5 per cent.
Where the rate of elimination exceeds this number, the percentage
becomes progressively symptomatic of curricular maladjustment
insofar as it can be traced to voluntary discontinuance through dissatisfaction.   The fact that rates of elimination have averaged four
times this number in the first-year high-school courses in foreign
languages[2] during the past two decades is not symptomatic of high
standards nor of lack of ability on the part of the students, but rather
of the inappropriateness of the content and methods for the levels of
insight and fundamental needs and interests possessed by the boys
and girls enrolled in the classes.

*Strong Dislike for Foreign-language Courses by Pupils Who Are
Taking Them, or Have Taken Them.*—One of many simple devices
for securing an estimate of the relative favor or disfavor with which
courses are regarded by students is that of asking pupils to list in
order, from "like most" to dislike most," the courses that they are
taking or have taken.   If unsigned reactions can be secured by a
nonforeign-language teacher outside the foreign-language class, the
collective evidence can be accepted as significant.   The fact that to

---

[1] See Chap. IV, pp. 116–117.

[2] Adolph Klein, "Failure and Subjects Liked and Disliked," *High Points*, Vol.
XXI, pp. 22–25, January, 1939.   See also the earlier studies by S. S. Colvin and
Andrew H. McPhail, "Intelligence of Seniors in the High Schools of Massachu-
setts," *U. S. Bureau of Education Bulletin* 1924, No. 9, 39 pp.   William F. Book,
*The Intelligence of High School Seniors as Revealed by a State-wide Mental Survey of
Indiana High Schools*, The Macmillan Company, New York, 1922, 371 pp.; pp.
159–184.

date every thorough study of pupil likes and dislikes has shown that foreign-language courses are often rated among the subjects *most disliked* in high school, rather than among the subjects liked most, is an unfortunate sign of curricular maladjustment, considering the potentialities and infinite resources of the field.

Dissatisfaction with the Worth-whileness of the Courses.—Unsigned pupil statements indicating in order of merit the courses that they considered most helpful, important, or valuable to themselves, yield significant measures of curricular adjustment provided they are obtained in circumstances similar to those indicated in the preceding paragraph. The presence of any sizable percentage of pupils who see little purpose, point, or value to the course is not necessarily a sign that the offering is without purpose, point, or value, but that the teacher has failed to reveal these values, or to capitalize them as motivating factors. It hardly requires training in psychology, however, to realize that learning is destined to be listless, careless, or ineffective if the pupils see "no sense to it," or fail to experience the satisfaction that usually comes with progress toward objectives that individuals accept as their own.

Criteria for Evaluating the Effectiveness of the Teacher in Conducting the Class.—Although the physical environment in which the classes are conducted and the facilities in time and equipment that are at the disposal of the teacher have a direct bearing upon the efficiency of a learning program, the effectiveness with which whatever available resources are capitalized is within the control of the teacher herself. The following leading questions apply to procedures in teaching regardless of extrinsic factors. Since the supporting ideology behind these criteria has already been developed in considerable detail in Chapters I to VII, they are presented without detailed comment below:

1. Does the teacher ask all the questions or does she guide question-and-answer discussion among the pupils?

2. Does the teacher constantly interrupt students to correct them or does she wait until they have finished reading or speaking?

3. Does the teacher encourage students by expressing appreciation of their good points before indicating ways and means for improving weaknesses?

4. Does the teacher phrase her criticisms in such a way that they are accepted as helpful suggestions of ways and means for overcoming difficulties in pronunciation, grammar, reading, composition, and study habits, or do her criticisms suggest personal annoyance or

public exposure and denunciation of ignorance or laziness before the class?

5. Does the teacher appear to be conducting a class in comparative grammar, in which principles of agreement and mechanics of form are the core of the program, or is she conducting a class in which human insights, attitudes, interests, and appreciations are developed through reading, writing, and discussion in the foreign language, facilitated where necessary by comments or special practice on such mechanics of language as cause difficulty, *i.e.*, that cannot be learned through abundant guided activity in emulation of meaningful connected context in an audience situation?

6. Does the teacher explain problems of form and mechanics by recourse to grammatical rules or does she enable the learners to see the life meaning behind the language, *i.e.*, does she explain differences in language as originally different ways of symbolizing or interpreting reality?[1]

7. Does the teacher rely on the memorization of rules and examples for increasing the pupils' understanding of the working principles governing the language, or does she guide and stimulate growth in ability to perceive and grasp relationships by asking the pupils pointed leading questions?[2]

8. Does the teacher facilitate insight into a problem by relating new elements through comparison or contrast, to what is already known?[3]

9. Does the teacher use the present-day social, cultural, and economic needs of life outside the school as her criterion of what content and activities are worth emphasizing and testing in the classroom, or does she teach language in a vacuum as an end in itself?

10. Does the teacher appear to be concerned with correctness for its own sake, regardless of what is written, read, or said, or with correctness only insofar as it might distract the thought or cause confusion?

11. Are the examples used to illustrate the working principles of language chosen from informative context with which the pupils are familiar, or are they examples unrelated in meaning to any larger unit of work (such as a story, cultural essay, or short talk in the foreign language)?

12. Are facilitation exercises based on the actual verbatim difficulties which the pupils have encountered in their *own* writing, read-

---

[1] See, also pp. 8–11, 81–83, 281–282, 283, 300*ff*.
[2] See pp. 83–84, 90–91.
[3] See pp. 19, 83–86.

ing, or speech, or are they exercises that are not connected in any way with what the pupils themselves have written, read, or said?

13. Does the teacher employ procedures that will help pupils grow in ability to develop personal standards of self-evaluation, a sense of personal responsibility for their own progress, or does she deprive the pupils of this opportunity for growth by playing the role of Jehovah in assigning grades ex cathedra on the basis of standards (scores or percentile averages) decreed in advance?

14. Do the pupils show initiative and contribute voluntarily to the class discussion, or is the procedure exclusively one of question-and-answer cross-examination between teacher and pupil on previously assigned lessons?[1]

15. Is the use of English in the classroom by the teacher confined exclusively to the explanation or discussion of grammatical principles, or to occasional asides in English where the vocabulary is new to the pupils?

16. Is the use of English in the classroom by the pupils confined exclusively to the occasional discussion of topics beyond the language resources of the class, to the occasional translation of difficult passages, or to the informal interpretation of an oral reading or talk (*i.e.*, summarized in the pupils' own words)?

17. Are the pupils encouraged to read good books on travel or literature in translation as part of their collateral reading responsibilities in English classes?

18. Is an occasional audience provided in the class for reports on relevant topics developed by members of the group in other courses?

19. Are opportunities encouraged and capitalized for translating, for use in other classes, foreign editorials, letters received from abroad, or informational materials available only in the foreign language?

20. Is the work of the class facilitated by efficiency in the mechanics of class management?

Criteria for Evaluating Efficiency in Class Management.—Whenever two or more people are working in close proximity on a common task, the problem of finding a *modus operandi* becomes important. That is why an army of 10,000 cannot be moved simultaneously en masse unless the soldiers know how to march, to keep abreast, and to interpret ordinary commands. Marching drills have as their chief purpose the development of efficiency in the collective movement of men. Although marching is rarely an end in itself, it is so important as a means to an end—to getting somewhere—that it is practiced to the point of automatization; for if every man in a group

[1] See Chap. VI.

of 10,000 were to walk at his own speed, pace, or gait, the result would be chaos and an eventual riot.   Just as an army of men has to become automatic in certain mechanics before anything of consequence can be accomplished efficiently by the group as a whole, so a class of pupils has to become habituated to performing automatically certain necessary routine operations—collecting or passing papers, coming to order, sharpening pencils, reporting absences or excuses, and the like.   Although these routine operations are relatively simple and unimportant in themselves, unless they are subordinated to the point where they become unconscious and inconspicuous habits, they lead to the same frustration of efficient group work which a regiment of soldiers would experience if only a few of the men knew how to march or to interpret simple marching commands.

Symptoms of inefficiency in the mechanization of routine are usually to be found in irrelevant noise or conversation, inattentive behavior, random movements, or habitual drowning out of the voices of individual pupils by collective interruptions from the class, *i.e.*, "all talking at once."   Although these evidences of disruptive behavior may be attributable to far more fundamental causes than poor class management, an evaluation of the learning program in terms of the following diagnostic questions will aid in determining whether the source of difficulty is to be found in the way in which the class is conducted, in the environment, or in the fact that the content and objectives of the program itself are unsuited to the abilities and needs of the pupils:

1. Does the teacher capitalize the services of volunteers from the class as efficiency experts to assume responsibility for proper lighting, heating, and ventilation of the room for the semester?   For taking and recording attendance?   For keeping the blackboards in order and supplied with erasers and chalk?   For recording the withdrawal and return of books from the classroom library?   For passing or collecting papers, books, and materials?   For seeing that all members of the class are supplied with sharpened pencils or pen and ink before the class begins?

2. Is the work of the foregoing assistants mechanized in relation to time and place and is it carried out unobstrusively with dispatch?

3. Do the pupils behave as if they knew that there is a time and place for everything—for sharpening pencils, filling pens, etc.?

4. Does the teacher ask one or more pupils to restate any group instructions or assignments to make sure that everyone has been able to hear her voice or to understand the language in which the directions were phrased?

5. Does the teacher work out with the class one or more examples to illustrate the assignment and methods of procedure in carrying it out?

6. Does the teacher allow sufficient time in class for work on the assignment as a means for detecting and correcting in advance inefficient work habits or evidences of misunderstanding?

7. Do the pupils know exactly how their work on a specific unit will be tested, if at all? By what criteria and by whom their work in the course will be judged?

8. Do the pupils secure the recognition of the teacher or chairman, or wait until others have finished speaking, before they talk?

9. In conducting group work, does the teacher stand and speak facing the class as a whole, or does she carry on a private tête-à-tête with one pupil while the rest of the class sit idly by?

10. Are the pupils' reactions boringly slow because the teacher fails to encourage the participation of volunteers? Because the teacher lacks discretion in calling on individual pupils for what they are *not* likely to know rather than for what they may be able to contribute?

11. Are the pupils listless or restless because the temperature and humidity are high (about 70 degrees) or the ventilation poor? Because the teacher is spending too much time on a specific subject without providing for variety in methods of approach?

12. Is the atmosphere of the class tense, funereal, cowed, or congenial because of the voice, mannerisms, dress, or personality of the teacher?

13. Are the pupils inattentive or restless because the teacher does not seem to know what she wants to say or do next?

14. Are the pupils inattentive or restless because the teacher has difficulty in approaching learning problems from the viewpoint of the pupils?

15. Does the teacher redirect the disruptive behavior of problem cases by helping them find something that they can do with interest and profit to themselves? Does the teacher enable problem cases to find something worth while to do that they can share with the class as a means for securing recognition through desirable forms of group approval rather than through bravado, affected difference, or insolence that may be symptomatic of a disguised inferiority complex?[1]

16. Does the teacher conduct the class discussions as if she were cross-examining the pupils or testing them orally? Or does she guide

[1] Winifred V. Richmond, *Personality: Its Development and Hygiene*, Farrar & Rinehart, Inc., New York, 1937, vii + 279 pp.; p. 183 and *passim*.

the class discussions through leading questions and encourage volunteers to participate on the basis of what they know or would like to know?

17. Do the pupils become noisy or unruly because there is nothing to occupy their attention during the performance of such routine operations as the passing of papers?   Or does the teacher make certain, before such mechanical operations are performed, that the pupils are attentively occupied, either in their own work or in listening to a fellow member of the class?   For example, does the teacher ask a member of the class to recite the days of the week, months, numbers, or other mechanical learnings which may need review, and then, after a pupil has begun to recite, quietly ask the class to pass the papers? If this is done, any conversation or unnecessary noise on the part of other members of the class becomes a discourtesy against the person who is speaking, rather than an offense against the teacher's personal notions of strict discipline.   There is no more need for pupils to maintain absolute quiet in a classroom when nothing important is going on, than there is need for the elite at the opera to cease talking or visiting before the orchestra begins to play the overture.   Mechanical elements of language, such as the numbers, days of the week, months, etc., can be reviewed briefly during the process of taking the roll or collecting papers.

18. If the class is conducted on the laboratory or workshop plan, are talking and moving about relevant to the performance of a specific task, or are they random movements symptomatic of poor planning, of lack of organization, or of incompatibility of the unit of work with the pupils' backgrounds in interest and experience?

19. Are the students inattentive, apathetic, or inactive because lock-step procedures occupy too large a portion of the class time? For example, is too large a portion of the class hour devoted to "read-translate" recitations in which one pupil performs while the rest await their turn to be cross-examined?

It is doubtful if asking 25 or more students to listen to the mistakes or difficulties in oral reading of one student represents an efficient use of class time. Supervisory visits to hundreds of classes conducted on the "read-aloud-and-translate" plan have revealed the following conditions to prevail without exception when this procedure was followed over a period of time: Observation of the eye movements of the pupils showed that only those who felt that they would soon be called on actually followed the text. The pupils who had already recited, either lapsed into a coma or began to draw doodles, to whisper to close neighbors, or to gaze out of the window. Some of the best pupils "lost the place," usually because they were reading ahead to escape the boredom of the mediocre mechanical recitations. Although "good discipline," in the sense of quiet, usually prevailed, the efficiency of learning was exceedingly low. It is easy for a teacher to mistake prayerlike attitudes of posture for active learning. It is doubtful if more than ten minutes of group work of this type is justified, and then only as a means for orienting the class as a whole with respect to a common assignment in a new reading unit (chapter, story, or one-act play). If a few students are deficient in their oral reading, it is preferable to call them aside and to work with them as a small committee while the remainder of the students read silently. When this latter procedure is followed, not less than 25 per cent of the time which pupils spend in foreign-language classes is saved for more profitable and functional types of work. Oral reading in foreign-language classes is usually far out of proportion to its social utility in normal life situations. As a means for improving pronunciation or ability to speak, it is relatively inefficient as a class activity compared with other learning procedures. Such values as it may have in these respects can be conserved by means of the devices suggested above.

Criteria for Evaluating Proficiency in the Skills—Comprehension and Expression.—Numerous objective standardized tests have appeared in the last twenty years to measure vocabulary, speed of comprehension in reading, and ability in grammar.[1] Recently, some attempts have been made to measure ability in pronunciation and ability to speak and understand the language.[2] Although uniform standardized tests have real values, less emphasis is being placed upon their use in modern schools today owing to their detrimental effects upon the initiative of teachers in developing learning programs

[1] Critical reviews and descriptions of published foreign-language tests are available in *The Mental Measurements Yearbook*, Oscar Krisen Burns, Ed., Highland Park, N. J., 1941, xxiii + 674 pp.; pp. 157–197. See also the 1938 edition, French, pp. 81–82; German, pp. 85–87; Latin, pp. 114–116; Spanish, pp. 152–154. See Appendix for a select annotated bibliography of tests that have been given superior ratings in the *Yearbooks*.

[2] For sample tests see Ernest J. Hall, "Oral Examinations in Spanish for Undergraduates," *Hispania*, Vol. XIX, pp. 461–466, December, 1936. Agnes L. Rogers and Frances M. Clark, "Report on the Bryn Mawr Test of Ability to Understand Spoken French," *The Modern Language Journal*, Vol. XVII, pp. 241–248, January, 1933. Lawrence W. Ross, "Pronunciation Quiz for French," *High School Journal*, Vol. XX, pp. 96–97, March, 1937. Walter V. Kaulfers, "Objective Tests and Exercises in French Pronunciation, " *The Modern Language Journal*, Vol. XXII, pp. 186–188, December, 1937.

adapted to the soil and climate of the local educational environment.[1]
Among the detrimental effects that are inherent in the use of standardized tests as the exclusive means for evaluating outcomes are the
following:

1. The tests become in reality the objectives of the program for
both teachers and pupils.   When this is the case the skills are learned
and taught as ends themselves, with little or no regard for the simultaneous development of insights into their most important and profitable applications.   Without such a supporting basis in interest and
insight, skills rarely function for any purpose sufficiently significant
to be worthy of the time and effort required to learn them in the first
place.

2. The tests lead to inflexible stereotyped courses, ill-adapted to
the needs and abilities of particular groups of students.[2]   Since most
standardized tests available today are validated on the basis of the
content and methods common to select college-preparatory classes, the
scores have little meaning as an indication of the students' ability
to understand ordinary conversation, to communicate intelligibly
simple ideas of his own in speech or writing, or to summarize in his
own words the salient points of a page or chapter of connected reading
matter.   The scores rarely mean more than that the pupil recognizes
the meanings of a certain percentage of words of high frequency in
college-preparatory courses of study, that he can identify the meanings
of these words in sentences or short paragraph context, and that he
can proofread isolated sentences for mechanical errors of form.   The
correlation between the pupil's ability to score on tests of this type
and his ability to communicate extemporaneously ideas of his *own*
in speech or writing is low unless abundant opportunity for impromptu
conversation and writing has been provided in the classroom.   In such
cases, the correlation may be high, not because of a causal relationship
between the two variables, but because the pupil has applied his
ability to learn with like effectiveness to both types of work.

One of the chief criticisms of all uniform standardized tests available to date is that they do not measure ability to acquire or com-

---

[1] M. Cant and A. Macpherson "The Danger to Modern Studies: A Discussion
at University College," *Modern Languages*, Vol. XX, pp. 112–117, March, 1939.
Arthur Ackerman, "Reading Before Grammar, an Experiment With a Reading
Method in French," *High Points*, Vol. XXI, pp. 31–38, May, 1939.

[2] Geraldine H. Marino, "Projects in the Teaching of Italian in High School,"
Italica, Vol. XVI, pp. 146–147, December, 1939.   L. G. Osborn, "Relative Difficulty of High-school Subjects," *School Review*, Vol. XLVII, pp. 95–100, February,
1939.

municate *ideas* through language, but facility in manipulating the mechanical *parts* of a language (*i.e.*, grammar), or a knowledge of the meanings of words as isolated molecules.   The carry-over of this mechanical part learning into ability to use the language as an organic whole in normal life situations is so slight that its measurement is a waste of time except for diagnostic purposes.   Comprehensive tests of ability to comprehend related information or ideas in connected context of reasonable length are the only tests that provide some indication of ability to use language for purposes of real communication. Inasmuch as ability to translate some other person's language, or to state the meanings of isolated words, does not measure ability to express one's own thoughts or ideas, it is doubtful if grammar-translation tests or vocabulary tests should be used for purposes of evaluating actual ability in *language*.   Their function is primarily diagnostic, *i.e.*, to help the teacher to locate the *causes* for certain deficiencies in ability to use or comprehend the language.   For example, are the pupils' difficulties in reading attributable to lack of vocabulary, to the unintelligibility of certain types of constructions, etc.?

If proficiency in manipulating the parts of a language is taken as the criterion for evaluating ability to use the language itself for purposes of normal communication in connected speech, the danger is real that the sum of all the isolated parts will be mistaken to represent the whole in action or that one part will be mistaken for the universe.   A good test of ability to understand related information or ideas associated with some topic, developed in printed context, is the best measure of ability to read; and a similar test, in which the information or ideas are presented orally instead of in print, is the best measure of ability to understand the spoken language when it actually functions as a means of communication.   Fairly valid and reliable objective tests of these abilities are already available and can be modified to suit local needs.[1]   For the evaluation of ability to converse or write extemporaneously on impromptu topics, only qualitative judgments are possible.   The best that the teacher can do in such cases is to provide a suitable testing environment that will enable the pupil to do justice to himself.   In general, however, the day-by-day observations of the teacher provide a far more reliable basis for valid judgments than are likely to be obtained by means of a single test in an atypical situation.

The foregoing limitations of standardized tests are important to bear in mind in using presumably scientific instruments as a means

[1] For practical illustrations, see Chap. VII and the references in footnotes on p. 389.

of evaluating outcomes. It is easy to mistake a high score on the grammar or vocabulary sections of a test for ability to read, write, or speak the language in normal life situations. The thousands of students who have passed such examinations substantiate the fact that it is quite possible to be an expert proofreader, and to amass a creditable stock of words, without being able to communicate ideas of one's own with any degree of facility in extemporaneous speech or writing.[1] Moreover, the fact that reading ability can readily be developed without recourse to the usually piecemeal methods of language learning[2] lends strength to the conviction that tests of vocabulary, grammar, pronunciation, and the like should be used only for diagnostic purposes—to locate difficulties requiring special attention—and that scores made on such subtests should not be added together into a total score to give a measure of actual ability to use the language for the purposes for which language exists in out-of-school life.

Since most standardized tests available to date are guilty of the error of mistaking the whole to be the sum of its disassociated parts or of overlapping parts, total scores on such tests are meaningless statistical fictions as far as ability actually to use the language for something besides classroom exercises is concerned. Fortunately, this statistical delusion does not invalidate the use of these instruments, provided the results are not misapplied or misinterpreted. If the reading section of a test is valid and reliable, the score may be used with confidence, independently of the remainder of the examination, as a measure of ability in one of the most important life uses of language. In no circumstances, however, should the scores on subtests of grammar, vocabulary, or pronunciation be used for other than diagnostic purposes, nor should they be added together into a "total" score. The intercorrelations between the mechanical subtests and the reading tests show such tremendous overlapping, that total scores obtained by processes of addition are nothing more than statisti-

---

[1] William R. Price, "Shorn Lambs," *The French Review*, Vol. VIII, pp. 5–19, November, 1934. Russell J. Fornwald and Herbert W. Rogers, "An Investigation of the Values of Modern Foreign Language Study in College," *The Modern Language Journal*, Vol. XIX, pp. 161–164, December, 1934.

[2] Arthur Ackerman, "Reading Before Grammar, an Experiment," *High Points*, Vol. XXI, pp. 31–38, May, 1939. J. C. Greenup and David Segel, "An Experimental Study of the Relation Between Method and Outcomes in Spanish Instruction," *The Modern Language Journal*, Vol. XIV, pp. 208–212, December, 1929. Lila Pargment, "A New Approach to the Teaching of the Russian Language," *The Modern Language Journal*, Vol. XXIV, pp. 362–363, February, 1940.

cal fictions whose real meanings defy translation into operational terms.[1]

What, then, may be considered a legitimate testing program for evaluating probable ability to use a foreign language for worthy life purposes in normal life situations?   If a numerical score on a vertical scale is desired for comparative purposes, the possibilities at present are limited to the following types of objective tests:

Comprehensive Tests of Ability to Acquire Ideas and Information from the Printed Page.—Tests that consist of a series of disconnected sentences are usually inadequate for this purpose.   To duplicate life situations in reading, meaningful topics, developed in connected context, are essential.   Five to ten topics, illustrating different types of reading (intensive or extensive), and reading for different life purposes (fact finding, following printed directions, etc.) are usually required if the score is to be of more than academic interest.

Comprehensive Tests of Ability to Comprehend Ideas, Information, or Directions Communicated Orally.—The mechanical arrangement of such a test need not differ significantly from that of the reading test, except that the thought content on which the test items are based will be presented to the students orally rather than in print.   Obviously, if the scores are to be valid for comparative purposes, the examination must be administered by means of easily intelligible electric transcriptions suitable for use in tone-control talking machines. The ready accessibility of such machines in almost all schools today, however, makes this procedure both practical and economical as a means of standardizing testing procedures.

Tests of Ability to Write Connected Paragraphs on Topics for Which the Facts or Information Are Given.—For example,

First-semester Spanish: Write a paragraph in Spanish on the geography of Spain, using the following information together with any additional information of your own, in sentences of your own choosing.   Use only expressions which you feel sure are correct:

límites: Francia, Portugal, la Mancha, el Mar Mediterráneo, el Océano Atlántico
clima: variable como en California
montañas: los Pirineos, la Sierra Nevada, la sierra Guadarrama, etc.
ríos: el Tajo, el Ebro, el Guadalquivir, etc.
habitantes: 26,000,000
capital: Madrid

[1] For tables showing intercorrelations among test parts and total scores, see Walter V. Kaulfers, *Forecasting Efficiency of Current Bases for Prognosis*, Unpublished doctor's dissertation, Stanford University, 1933, 381 pp.; pp. 166–174.

centro industrial: Barcelona
productos: frutas, minerales, granos, etc.

Since only qualitative appraisals on a five-point scale can be obtained with any degree of facility on tests of this kind, their independent use as a basis for evaluating ability to write extemporaneously is unjustified. Six to ten such tests, spaced over a period of a year, however, may in their totality yield a fairly significant estimate of the pupil's ability and progress in this direction, provided the criteria of evaluation are clearly defined and rigorously applied. A homemade test carefully devised to require only the use of vocabulary and constructions falling within the pupil's background in the language, is likely to be more valid than a test devised by an expert unfamiliar with the work of the class.

Rating Scales of Conversational Ability.—Since conversational ability is difficult to evaluate owing to the complexity of this skill, such appraisals as may be desirable or useful are not destined to be more valid or reliable, no matter how formal or complicated the testing machinery, than qualitative observations over a period of time. The number of questions, scaled in difficulty, which a pupil can answer orally within a given time limit, *on topics familiar to him*, however, provides one means for securing a numerical score for a limited aspect of what may be termed ability to converse. The chief limitation besetting the use of such tests is the fact that they require unusual care in preparation and cannot be used to test more than one pupil at a time.

The foregoing devices for evaluating the language skills should suffice to yield an appraisal, adequate for all practical purposes, of ability to use a language for life purposes. Although special tests of ability in pronunciation, functional grammar, and vocabulary have a place in the learning program, their use for other than diagnostic purposes is likely to lead to the delusion that a total score represents ability to use a language. The value of such tests is primarily pedagogical, and their use by any one else than the teacher or supervisor in locating specific sources of pupil difficulties is hardly to be recommended.

Progress in the science of tests and measurements has been almost as rapid as progress in the automobile industry. A test published before 1930 is almost comparable to a 1928-model car. As in the case of the automobile, recent improvements in objective tests have been largely in the direction of maximum power and speed with a maximum of economy in running costs. In comparison with tests developed before 1930, the newer standardized examinations have been stream-lined in such a way as to make them easier to give and score, less costly, and more adequate measures of ability per unit of testing time. An annotated list of recommended tests for use in evaluating the skill outcomes is included in Appendix F.

Criteria for Evaluating Cultural Information Acquired in the Course.—Although numerous objective tests of cultural information have been published in foreign-language journals in recent years,[1] the difficulty of validating such tests has led to few marketed editions. An examination of these pioneer efforts, however, is valuable in pro-viding concrete models for constructing tests of one's own. The chief limitation of such cultural information tests as are available to date is the lack of validity of the items. A miscellany of facts, selected without reference to any criterion beyond their occurrence in readers, is difficult to appraise from the standpoint of its life value to the student. It leads to nothing but academic inbreeding.

It would seem that information that frees the mind from misconceptions, ignorant prejudices, or misinformation, might lay a strong claim to being more functional than information that does not answer the question, "Information for what?" Insofar as the objectives of the foreign-language program stress the development of attitudes, insights, and appreciations of significance for human cooperation and understanding, the criteria for the selection of factual items for a cultural information test might well be the questions:

1. Would knowing this fact give evidence that the pupil knows in what way his own life and that of his community, state, and nation have been enriched by the contributions which the foreign people have made to world progress in science, invention, music, art, archi-tecture, language, literature, education, customs, manufactured products, etc.?

---

[1] For sample tests see Guiseppe Antonio Russo, "A Quiz on Italian Civiliza-tion," *The Modern Language Journal*, Vol. XXIV, pp. 279–281, January, 1940. Hymen Alpern, "A Modern Test in Modern Literature," (Spanish) *The Modern Language Journal*, Vol. XVII, pp. 268–274, January, 1933. Marie K. Neuschatz, *The Comparison of the Amount of French Cultural Information Possessed by French and Non-French Students*, Unpublished master's Thesis, College of the City of New York, 1933, 94 pp. Waldo C. Peebles, "A Test in German Life and Culture," *German Quarterly*, Vol. X, pp. 22–26, January, 1937. James B. Tharp, "A Test on French Civilization," *The French Review*, Vol. VIII, pp. 283–287, March, 1935. Minnie M. Miller, *French Life and Culture* (Test), *Spanish Life and Culture* (Test), Bureau of Educational Measurements, Kansas State Teachers College, Emporia, Kans., 1937.

2. Would knowing this fact give evidence that the pupil is not the victim of a misconception which causes many people to disparage the foreign country or its people?

3. Would knowing this fact give evidence that the pupil understands the *reasons why* the foreign people speak, live, dress, behave, or think differently from others?

Selecting and grouping the items of a culture test according to their merit in contributing to one or more of these three purposes—neutralizing prejudices, building appreciative attitudes, and developing tolerant insights into the *why* of things—would provide a valuable measure of the contribution of the learning program through literature and language to rationality in human relations.   The following are merely examples of items which in sufficient number might yield an indication of the learner's mind-set with respect to insights of significance for life in the present and future.

Directions: Each statement of fact below is explained by five possible reasons. Put an X in the parentheses before the *best* reason.

En muchos países de habla española se echan siestas porque

( ) la gente es perezosa.
( ) no hay mucho trabajo.
( ) hace mucho calor al mediodía.
( ) es obligación religiosa.
( ) es cosa de costumbre.

There have been many revolutions in Spanish-speaking countries because the people

( ) resent government.
( ) are naturally high-strung and emotional.
( ) are too uneducated to live by law and order.
( ) are mostly savage Indians.
( ) have been driven to desperation by extreme poverty and governments which did nothing to help them.

Directions: In the parentheses below put an X before each invention or scientific discovery which we owe to the French more than to any other nation:

( ) photography   ( ) the steamboat
( ) the radio   ( ) the sewing machine
( ) the moving picture   ( ) the steam engine
( ) the telephone   ( ) radium
( ) the automobile   ( ) vaccination

In the parentheses below put an X before each product which we do not produce in sufficient quantity to be able to stop importing from Latin America without inconvenience to ourselves:

( ) iron   ( ) rubber
( ) nitrates   ( ) coal
( ) sugar   ( ) oil
( ) coffee   ( ) cocoa

The tragic effects of racial and religious intolerance are best portrayed by Benito Pérez Galdós in his novel:

( ) El Doctor Centeno   ( ) Electra
( ) El Abuelo   ( ) Gloria
( ) Marianela   ( ) El Amigo Manso

It will be noted that when the questions are phrased in such a way as to emphasize the significance of the information that is being tested, grouping of the items around focal centers of emphasis is possible. Such grouping is desirable if the test is to have diagnostic value as a possible indication of the strength or weakness of the factual background underlying the pupil's appreciation of the foreign people, or of such of their contributions to American and to world culture as are operative in the present. Beyond the first semester, the test items may be phrased in the foreign language, especially if they are based on content read or discussed in the foreign language in class. *In such cases, the culture test and the test of ability to read may be combined into one.* This is the goal toward which teachers may direct their efforts in building a unified program in which language and culture are not separated but reinforce each other in the service of the basic purpose of language in life—bridging the mental gulfs that separate men from their neighbors. Culture tests in which the items are phrased in English are appropriate for courses in foreign civilizations or literature in translation without foreign-language prerequisites; but their use in a foreign-language class is usually a sign that nothing of real significance has been learned through reading, writing, or discussion in the language itself, and that the only cultural information worth testing has been acquired incidentally through collateral reading or discussion in English, unrelated to the major preoccupations of the pupils and teacher in the classroom.

An annotated list of cultural-information tests is included in the Appendix. Although the items are not grouped according to focal centers nor on the basis of any specific criterion of emphasis, teachers of foreign languages will find the tests useful in constructing culture tests of their own.

Criteria for Evaluating Directional Changes in Attitudes, Interests, or Appreciations.—Although pencil-and-paper reactions on attitudes scales are by no means perfect measures of the way in which an individual is likely to behave in real life toward people of certain racial or nationality groups, such recorded reactions are valuable if interpreted as *symptoms* of mind-sets that have been induced by the pupil's social environment. Extreme antipathy toward a nationality group is usually a sign that the pupils have repeatedly heard the group disparaged by their parents, relatives, or friends, or seen them misrepresented in books, plays, movies, or novels. Not infrequently, such antipathy is also attributable to unfortunate experiences with particular individuals whom the pupils have generalized as being typical of the nationality group as a whole. With this background of insight into the mind-set of the class or of particular students, the teacher is better able to bring the content and activities of the course to bear on the problem. Although the chief value of race-attitudes scales is in learning to know the pupils *at the beginning of the course,* their utility in providing an indication of *directional changes in attitude over a period of time* is not to be disparaged. Rough measures of such directional changes can be obtained by repeating the same test at the end of a semester or year, provided neither the scales themselves nor their component items have been specifically discussed in the interim.

Owing to the limited reliability and validity of tests of this kind, differences in group averages cannot be considered significant unless they approximate or exceed at least one-fourth the difference between the highest and lowest ratings possible on the scale. Thus if the maximum possible score is 100, a difference of less than 25 points between the group average on the first test and the group average on the retest should probably not be regarded as highly significant unless other supporting evidence is available. Observations of actual changes in pupil behavior supply one source of such data. The following example from the anecdotal records kept by a participant in the Stanford Language Arts Investigation may serve to illustrate types of supporting evidence for which teachers may look in the actual work and behavior of the students:

M—— asked to have her seat changed so that she would not have to sit beside two Mexican girls. At Christmas time the class decided to "adopt" a group of little Mexican children in the Mexican quarter of the city. M—— took an active part in working with the two Mexican girls on a committee to collect and distribute presents. She now seems to be on friendly terms with the girls near whom she refused to sit at the beginning of the course. She often practices her Spanish with them.

Circumstantial evidence of the kind indicated above is difficult to secure except through observation over a period of time. In its totality, however, it may furnish an excellent basis in fact to validate directional changes revealed by attitudes scales. It is probably unnecessary to indicate that, wherever possible, tests of this kind should be administered in disguised form in a neutral environment (*e.g.*, during the home-room period, by the home-room teacher) rather than in the foreign-language class. Otherwise, the danger that the pupils may react in conformity with the responses which they feel the examiner wants them to give is likely to cast suspicion upon the validity of the findings.

Although other tests of race attitudes suitable for use in foreign-language classes have been constructed since the appearance of the Remmers-Grice *Scale for Measuring Attitude toward Any National or Racial Group*,[1] this scale is probably the most useful and easiest to administer of any available for purposes of group measurement at the present writing. Other scales that can be adapted for use in foreign-language courses, or imitated as a basis for constructing evaluation instruments of one's own, are Thurstone *Social Attitudes Scales*[2] and the Kirshner *Tolerance-Inventory*.[3]

Criteria for Evaluating the Products of Creative Activities Involving the Use of the Foreign Language.—Concrete evidences of achievement, although they cannot always be evaluated in terms of numerical scores, nevertheless often speak for themselves. If a group of students enrolled in a German class, for example, translate and publish an old diary of sufficient historical interest[4] to represent a contribution that is recognized by libraries, historical societies, and citizens in the community, the product of their work and the approval which it is accorded by competent individuals become a proof of creative activity that can stand on its own merits. Score-card evaluation is unnecessary and would probably do nothing more than distract attention from the real significance of the product in terms of the educative experiences afforded in the process of producing it, the worth-whileness of the uses to which it is put, or the degree of technical proficiency in language needed to do the work. Among the questions that a group of foreign-language teachers might keep in mind in formulating an

---

[1] Division of Educational Reference, Purdue University, Lafayette, Ind., 1934.

[2] L. L. Thurstone, Ed., *The Measurement of Social Attitudes: Scale No. 34*, Forms *A* and *B*: Attitude toward War, University of Chicago Press, Chicago, 1931.

[3] Alfred Kirshner, "A Scientific Approach to the Development of Tolerance," *High Points*, Vol. XXIII, pp. 11–22, September, 1941.

[4] *I Knew Sutter*, The Nugget Press, C. K. McClatchy High School, Sacramento, Calif., 1939.

evaluative judgment of the merits of a specific product of the kind indicated above are the following:

1. Was the degree of accuracy and proficiency in the use of basic skills required to carry out the work equal to, or greater than, that needed to do the "exercises" ordinarily undertaken in foreign-language courses?

2. Was the activity initiated by the pupils? By the teacher? By an outside agency?

3. Did the pupils themselves assume the major responsibility for planning, organizing, executing, and evaluating the work, or did the teacher dictate and assign each step of the process?

4. Was the work an integral part of the course work of the pupils, or was it done incidentally on the side?

5. Did the work capitalize the abilities of the pupils in other respects than language?

6. Did the work provide opportunities for learning to work harmoniously and constructively in cooperation with others? To assume and fulfill responsibilities? To develop and exercise initiative? To develop and apply standards of self-evaluation? To secure group recognition and approval in sufficient degree to make such recognition and approval a more effective incentive to whole-hearted achievement than grades, credits, or tests?

7. Was the work reviewed before an audience of readers, listeners, or observers from outside the class, or from within the class itself, or was everything done for the exclusive benefit of the teacher as audience and critic?

8. Did the product represent a unit of work independent and complete in itself, or was it one of a series of units related to a long-range goal?

9. Was the work done by a single student, or was it done cooperatively by a group of students working independently except for the consulting services of the teacher?

10. Was the work done under the exclusive supervision of one teacher, or did it provide for cooperation among several teachers?

11. Did the work provide for educative experiences and contacts outside the classroom or school?

It will be noted that the questions stress the *educative experiences* involved in the process of production, and the *degrees of competence in basic skills* needed to do the work, as much as the product itself. It is hardly necessary to indicate that an object produced by a single student in the course, and involving no significant use of the foreign language, is not to be compared with something whose real values are to be found in the educative experiences, both in and through language, that went into the making. Knowing what criteria of evaluation to use depends upon one's knowledge of young people, of the objectives of education, and of the nature of the learning process. Without such a frame of reference, the evaluator is in danger of making the sad mistake of using a Jersey score card to judge a Holstein cow. Whenever a product of creative individual or group work is accompanied by an authentic account of the educational objective which it served, of the young people who made it, and of the educative experiences that it afforded, a qualitative judgment of its merits is possible. Such an appraisal may not always have the "scientific" appeal of a numerical score, since it is based directly upon the exercise of the same human intelligence that ultimately gives life meaning to a score, mean, median, quartile, or percentile.

Since concrete evidences of creative ability in foreign-language classes are exceedingly numerous, only two examples which rank exceedingly high, in terms of the criteria of evaluation contained in the list of leading questions, can be provided by way of illustration within the limits of the present chapter.

In 1939, in order to commemorate the centennial of Sacramento, a second-year class in German in the C. K. McClatchy High School, Sacramento, Calif., cooperated with students of English, social studies, printing, and bookbinding in translating and publishing an authentic pioneer diary written in German. The greater part of the work was done during the class hour. To facilitate the work of translation, the teacher prepared a vocabulary list for the most difficult paragraphs. Occasionally, the whole class worked on the same paragraph; sometimes a committee assumed the responsibility for a different paragraph. These translations were written on the blackboard, discussed by the group as a whole, and altered where necessary. The final version was copied by a secretary, sent to the cooperating English class for editing, and returned to the German class for a recheck. Since the activity formed an integral part of the course, only the usual credit was allowed for the semester's work. Although the teacher served as a consultant and coordinator, all research on special points was done by volunteers. The edited translation was then turned over to the classes in printing and bookbinding who published a limited edition of 285 copies under the title *I Knew Sutter.*

Encouraged by the favorable recognition given to the work of the German class, sixteen members of the Spanish club, *Los Hispanistas,* volunteered to translate from Spanish an original document (Ms. E67, No. 2) by Enrique Cerruti in the Bancroft Library of the University of California. This work was done entirely outside of class without special grades or credits. The final translation, carefully documented with copious historical footnotes and printed and bound by students in the C. K. McClatchy High School, appeared in 1941 in a limited art-print edition of 125 copies under the title *Narrative of Guillermo Fitch and Blas Piña.*[1]

The following editorial from one of the leading California newspapers, the *Sacramento Bee,*[2] is quoted in full as an illustration of the fact that other means of evaluation than "counting" are often more significant than scores in judging the life values of a learning activity or its products:

Two Latin American nations and many states throughout the United States have given recognition to the C. K. McClatchy High School publication, *The Narrative of Guillermo Fitch and Blas Piña. Romance,* a semimonthly literary newspaper published in Mexico City, gave praise to the members of the school's Spanish club, who, under the direction of Saima Koski, language instructor, translated the book from an old Spanish manuscript of the Bancroft Library at the University of California. Compliments were also given the students who printed the book in the school's print shop under the direction of George Smisor, printing instructor. The review, which will be distributed throughout Latin America, also mentioned two earlier manuscripts of this type which were published by the C. K. McClatchy High School. The first was a German translation about John A. Sutter; the second was an anthology. José F. Arias, general director of industrial education in Uruguay, and G. M. Echániz, known throughout Mexico for his work in ancient books and manuscripts, were both impressed by the school's latest publication which deals with early Spanish California. Señor Echániz especially was lavish in his praise, saying in a letter to Smisor, "This sample of printing will serve to encourage our teachers to follow your example."

Attention has been given to the manuscript by such well-known persons in the United States as Dr. Herbert Priestley, director of the Bancroft Library, Joseph Henry Jackson of the *San Francisco Chronicle,* and Holland Roberts of Stanford University. Dr. Mildred Struble Carpenter of the University of Southern California, head of the department of comparative literature, in a letter to Smisor, said, "You are to be congratulated for this unusual achievement." George A. Hill, Jr., president and trustee of the Museum of Fine Arts in Houston, Texas, and president of the San Jacinto Museum of History, was greatly impressed by the work of the California school and is trying to encour-

---

[1] The Nugget Press, C. K. McClatchy High School, Sacramento, Calif., 1941, x + 34 pp.

[2] *The Sacramento Bee,* Sept. 20, 1941.

age Texas high school students to do something similar. Mention also was given the publication in the *New York Times*.

The book is really a series of interviews with Guillermo Fitch and Blas Piña, who tell about conditions in early California history. The interviews were gathered aboard a boat sailing from San Francisco to Donahue, a little town near Santa Rosa, in April of 1874. The Bear Flag Incident and many stories about Indians and Spaniards in Spanish California are included. Piña was the first Californian whom the Yankees took as a prisoner.

The recognition accorded *I Knew Sutter* and the *Narrative of Guillermo Fitch and Blas Piña* led to the establishment in 1941 of the *Nugget Press* for the yearly publication of simpler products of creative student activity in the McClatchy High School. *I Knew Sutter* and *The Narrative of Guillermo Fitch and Blas Piña* are interesting examples of the use of a foreign language for purposes of sufficient worth to represent a contribution to the annals of community culture. A school could hardly choose a more stimulating or more educationally significant project than an investigation, interpretation, and synthesis of the community's social and cultural heritage as recorded in the original language of the generations that have contributed to the building of America. Many documents, letters, pictures, and newspapers of vital interest and significance for our culture have been discovered by students under guidance. *The past lives when it speaks for itself.*

Among other creative activities whose merit can be judged from the quality of the product itself, and the approval with which it is received by the audience for which it is intended, are the following:[1]

1. Translating short stories, plays, poems, or articles for use in other classes or for publication.

2. Translating letters for pupils in English or social-studies classes who wish to correspond with young people abroad.

3. Adapting short stories or novels for dramatic presentation before the school, the parent-teacher association, or a community audience.

4. Writing dialogues for Pan American Day pageants, radio broadcasts, etc., capitalizing reading done in the foreign language.

[1] Reports of the Stanford Language Arts Investigation, Vol. II, *Foreign Languages and Cultures in American Education:* "International Understanding Begins at Home" by Helen M. Bailey; "Latin and English Pull Together," by Virginia B. Lowers; "Let's do a French Puppet Show," by Dorothy M. Johns; "Mexicans Become Friends," by Elizabeth N. Reed; "France Enrolls in the French Class," by Jewell Torrieri, McGraw-Hill Book Company, Inc., New York. In press. Theodore Huebener, "School Radio Broadcasts," *The Modern Language Journal,* Vol. XXIV, pp. 573–575, May, 1940.

5. Preparing foreign-language materials for use in less advanced classes (*e.g.*, collecting and writing the subtitles for pictures that can be used to illustrate balopticon talks on special topics, etc.).

Criteria for Evaluating the Carry-over of Foreign-language Work in College.—Until recent years the work of students and teachers in foreign-language courses was evaluated almost exclusively in terms of the pupils' scores on objective college-preparatory types of tests, and their subsequent grades in college classes. The fact that not all students who enter high school continue in college, and that only a relatively small percentage of those who enter actually continue in the same language which they began in high school, makes this a very small percentage, indeed, to use as a criterion for judging the success or failure of an entire foreign-language program. The best evidence available today shows that not over 5 to 8 per cent of the pupils who begin a foreign language in high school continue the same language in college—or less than three pupils in an average beginning class of 35![1] Since this low percentage is rarely ascribable to the completion of foreign-language requirements in the secondary school, nor exclusively to the failure of the graduates to continue their education, the reason for this low rate of carry-over is to be found primarily in the common practice of changing to a different language in the university. This tendency is in itself symptomatic of maladjustment in the organization of college-preparatory curriculums in the high school. The grades of the relatively few students who continue in college in the same language which they began in high school are a very inadequate basis for evaluation and likely to distort completely the true condition of things. Such a statement as "All my pupils who took French in college made either *A*'s or strong *B*'s last year" lacks real meaning unless one also has the factual information on the following questions: How does the percentage of high-school graduates continuing foreign-language work in college compare with the total percentage of high-school graduates who continue in college? How many students who entered college changed to another language? How many of the students who changed to another language did so because they were obliged to take their preparatory work during the first two years in high school, and probably hesitated to continue in college in a language which they had had one or more years to forget?

---

[1] Vera Whittmann, "Are College Preparatory Foreign Languages Justified in Our Curriculum?" *The Modern Language Journal*, Vol. XXV, pp. 470–472, March, 1941.

The best evidence available to date indicates that only one out of four high-school graduates who enter college continues the foreign language begun in high school.[1]   The validity of evaluating an entire program on the basis of such a limited sampling is questionable.   The only conclusion possible from such a state of affairs, regardless of grades made in college, would seem to be that the college-preparatory objective serves too limited a group to be justified as an exclusive objective or criterion of evaluation for an entire secondary-school foreign-language program.   Unless the graduate who enters college continues in the same language which he began in high school, his "college-preparatory" work has in reality done little more than paid the price of an admission ticket to the university.   So far the evaluation of the carry-over of high-school foreign language in college has been confined to counting the grade-point averages of a relatively few pupils without reference to the large majority of young people who discontinue the language after fulfilling minimum requirements for admission.

Criteria for Evaluating the Carry-over of Foreign-language Work into Out-of-school Life.—With respect to the evaluation of the carry-over of foreign-language work into out-of-school life, the criteria are difficult to verify statistically.   It would seem obvious, however, that unless the learning program capitalizes the situations in which foreign languages and cultures are operative in the out-of-school environment, the carry-over is likely to be incidental.[2]   The school is certainly derelict in its responsibility for educating young people if it merely places tools and facts into their hands without motivating their most important life uses.   If the course stresses reading or an appreciation of foreign literature and culture as an objective, how many books have been read in their entirety, or in part, by the pupils?   How many books have been read voluntarily?   Are books on foreign countries, or books in translation, withdrawn from the school library or neighborhood library more frequently by students of foreign languages than by pupils who are not taking a foreign language?   How many pupils have made some use of the foreign language outside of school in listening to radio programs?   In talking with natives?   In traveling abroad?   In attending foreign talking pictures, operas, or song-recitals?   In writing to correspondents abroad?   To what extent have these activities

---

[1] This situation is typical of the country at large.   See Engel, *op. cit.*   Whittmann and Kaulfers, *op. cit.*

[2] John J. Weisert, "Foreign Languages as Mental Discipline, a Survey," *The German Quarterly*, Vol. XII, pp. 61–70, March, 1939.

been encouraged by the school through the use of the radio, moving picture, library reading period, foreign correspondence, or phonograph recordings in the classroom?

The answer to the last question is especially important in estimating the extent to which the learning program has been responsible for developing or capitalizing environmental interests beyond the point where the evidence may be attributed to chance or to mere compliance with requirements for a high grade. The accumulated evidence over many years of public-school experience with compulsory requirements and artificial incentives has led educational psychologists and curriculum specialists to question whether work done under compulsion, or for an extrinsic incentive such as a high mark or grade, is likely to be continued voluntarily in post-school life after the compulsory requirements or incentives have ceased to operate. For this reason it is important for the school to enrich the learning program with opportunities for developing an enduring interest in those phases of the social and cultural life of the community which function without compulsion or artificial incentives beyond the personal satisfaction or social recognition afforded by the activity itself.

Any need for making frequent use of tests, requirements, or grades as incentives to do daily work in a course is usually a sign that the content, objectives, or activities of the classroom are not associated with anything vital, necessary, interesting, or useful in the minds of the pupils. When such is the case, the likelihood that the learnings acquired in the course will function significantly in out-of-school life is exceedingly small. Although grades are not harmful when they are used as evaluation symbols whose referents are clearly defined, their use as incentives to achievement is open to serious question if the work of the course is to be evaluated from the standpoint of what it is likely to contribute to the voluntary life interests, activities, and personal code of behavior of the individual as a human being.

Enlisting Pupil Participation in Evaluation.—The ability to evaluate objectively one's own behavior or progress toward a goal is as important a part of the mental equipment of an educated individual as any ability that the school can help young people to develop. It is especially important in a learning program that seeks to develop in boys and girls a sense of responsibility for their own actions and progress. In few classes, however, is the work organized or conducted in such a way as to provide for growth in this direction. The teacher, like Jehovah, passes evaluative judgments on every detail of thought, speech, or behavior, often without indicating to the pupils the bases for her appraisals. In such cases, the opportunity for growth in ability to evaluate one's own work, to formulate personal standards of achievement, or to develop a sense of responsibility for one's progress is limited, since the formulation of evaluative criteria, and the exercise of evaluative judgments, are preempted by the teacher. Symptoms of the failure of the learning program to provide for pupil growth in self-evaluation are to be found in the extreme pleasure or dissatisfaction that pupils sometimes express at the sight of a "grade," in evidences of uncertainty regarding their work, or in such chronic questions as the following:

What do I have to do to get an A?
Why did you give me a C?
What work do I have to make up to bring up my average?

Chronic questions of this kind are usually indicative of the fact that the pupils do not see the relationship between the objectives of the course and the day-by-day assignments, that they have not been helped to develop criteria of evaluation except from trial-and-error experience with the teacher's marking system, or that they hold the teacher more responsible than themselves for their work and grades. In such circumstances it is idle to expect that the pupils will develop ability in self-evaluation or a sense of personal responsibility that stimulates initiative.

In order to facilitate and encourage pupil growth in these directions many devices have been tested experimentally by teachers who have sensed the importance of this responsibility of education, and the value of such growth in a field covering from four to eight semesters of work. The *Guide to Self-evaluation* reproduced here is illustrative of a plan that has proved successful in junior and senior high-school classes of 20 to 40 pupils.[1] Since the *Guide* is self-explanatory, it is presented here without comment beyond the observation that during the first semester it is advisable to set aside frequent workshop periods in class where the work can be done under the supervision of the teacher, with the assistance of an editorial committee composed of three to five able and conscientious pupils selected from the group. The time and patience required to initiate the plan and to gain pupil support in its favor are usually amply rewarded in the later stages. In a course in which learning is cumulative over a period of semesters,

---

[1] Designed for use in the Palo Alto High School and Menlo School and Junior College, Calif., 1935–1941, by Walter V. Kaulfers.

and even years, the time required to initiate the plan is a profitable investment, particularly when viewed from the standpoint of the objectives that it serves. Growth that represents an integral part of the education of an individual is not achieved except over a period of time even in an environment favorable to it. The following *Guide* is placed directly in the hands of the pupils and discussed with the group as soon as enough written work has been done in the course to justify setting aside an hour of class time as a self-evaluation workshop period. During this period the aim is *to help pupils to learn from their mistakes instead of becoming discouraged by them.*

GUIDE TO SELF-EVALUATION

How am I doing? Everyone likes to feel that he is making progress—getting somewhere. This applies to anyone who is sincerely interested in learning something, whether it be to swim, to play tennis, to dance, or to learn a foreign language. Too many slips cause discouragement and leave one wondering "What's the use?" Naturally, no one has ever learned anything of consequence without making some mistakes—many of them, perhaps; for as the Romans used to say, *Errare humanum est*—"To err is human." The difference between a careless beginner and one who is conscientious is simple: The former keeps on making the same mistakes over and over without bothering to find out what the trouble is, or to correct it. The latter profits by his mistakes, and finds out how to avoid them in the future. If he has to make mistakes, he tries at least to be original—that is, to make an entirely *new kind* of mistake each time, unless he is working at something in which he should be expert.

Each mistake in language should be considered a difficulty to be overcome by finding out exactly what causes the handicap, and then doing something to overcome it. Naturally, the instructor will do all that he can to arrange the work in such a way as to reduce the number of possible errors as far as is humanly possible; but since mistakes will occur, and since intelligent people often learn a great deal from their own mistakes, it is often worth while to find out just where the trouble lies.

One way of measuring progress in learning a skill, such as a language, is to see how rapidly one is overcoming handicaps over a period of time. This can be done by graphing or charting the number of difficulties encountered per 100 words written. If this is done by the student himself, it will help him to see how he is progressing, and in what ways he can improve still more. Then there will be little need to depend only upon the teacher's opinion, or to ask, "How am I doing?" The student can become a more independent worker, with enough self-direction to pass judgment upon himself. For the more thoroughly one knows something, the more able one is to see one's own points of strength and weakness without feeling either too cocksure or too uncertain.

The self-evaluation scheme described below requires the conscientious cooperation of every student, or it will be of little value. Words written will have to be counted, and the kinds of difficulties recorded and then changed into per cent. Although the arithmetic is simple, careless arithmetic is hard to avoid. Time will occasionally be taken during the class hour to do the checking and tabulating.

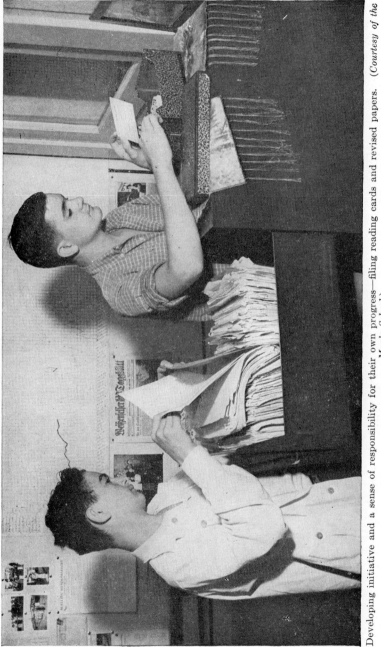

Developing initiative and a sense of responsibility for their own progress—filing reading cards and revised papers. (*Courtesy of the Menlo School.*)

Occasionally the mathematics instructor may allow this work to be done in connection with work in his class.

If the plan is followed carefully, the *per cent* of progress shown by the student's own self-evaluation chart throughout the semester or year will approximately match the progress shown on tests. If the difference is marked, the instructor will recheck the tests carefully, and ask the student to do the same with his progress chart. The plan works somewhat as follows:

Proofreading and revising written work. Papers written in class are checked for difficulties, but the mistakes are to be corrected by the student himself, either outside class or during a workshop period announced in advance. No paper which has been checked for difficulties will be given full recognition until after it has been completed correctly by the owner. In case of uncertainty regarding a difficulty or mistake, ask the instructor for a conference during the independent study period in class, or consult a member of the class editorial committee which will proofread the papers from time to time.

Filing revised papers. All papers which have been checked for difficulties will be filed in a separate folder by each member of the class. Inside the folder, papers should be arranged in the *order of the dates* when they were first written. For this reason, it is not only desirable, but also necessary that the *date* be written on *each* paper. A good way to learn and to remember the days of the week, the months, and the numbers in German is to head each paper in German (in the upper right-hand corner) as follows, spelling out all the numbers except the year (1942, 1943, etc.):

My name is *Charles Brown:*   Ich heisse Karl Braun
Today is *Monday*, the *seventh*   Heute ist Montag, den siebten
  of *October*, 194–.   Oktober, 194–.

The date for each meeting of the class will usually appear on the board.

To avoid congestion or distraction during the class period, members of the class will consult their folders in the filing cabinet only during the independent-study or workshop sessions. Until a paper has been completed correctly, it may be kept by the owner in his personal notebook. The back part of this notebook may well be "sectioned off" as a kind of Appendix for this purpose. This should only be done, however, if there is little danger that the notebook will be lost.

Revising written work. Every difficulty should be corrected on the original sheet. Do not recopy the entire paper unless absolutely necessary and, in any case, always keep the original. Correct omissions and mistakes in punctuation or accent marks in the exact spot where the need for correction is indicated. Rewrite misspelled words, wrong words, and other mistakes directly above the word(s) that cause difficulty. Use 8- by 11-inch paper (typing paper size) wherever possible, and *skip a space* between each line to leave room for corrections. Count the number of words (not including the heading) which you have written, and write the total number of words in the upper left-hand corner, opposite the heading. This total is very important, for it will be used later in finding the *per cent* of difficulties per 100 running words.

Self-evaluation check list. The check list (with spaces for recording various types of difficulties, and proofreading symbols used in checking the papers) follows.

SELF-EVALUATION CHECK LIST

Count the number of difficulties of each kind *separately for each paper* and record the number in the proper box space below:

Key to proofreading	Date 6/9	Date	Date	Date	Date	Date	Total: all papers
Mechanics:							
P Punctuation or capitalization........ 1.	2						
- umlaut missing..................... 2.	2						
S Incorrect spelling................... 3.	3						
? Not clear; handwriting, etc.......... 4.							
Neatness and organization........... 5.							
Number of difficulties in mechanics... 6.	7						
Usage:							
∧ Word missing, or incomplete........ 7.							
↰ Wrong order of words............. 8.	1						
O (circle): wrong word............... 9.	1						
‿ contraction........................10.							
A ending of adjective................11.							
N ending of noun.....................12.	1						
Pr Mistake in pronouns (*sie, uns, mir,* etc.)............................13.	1						
V Verb-ending.......................14.							
Number of difficulties in usage.......15.	4						
Number of German words not including the heading...................16.	210						
% of difficulties: divide total difficulties in rows 6 + 15 above, by number of words in row 16....................17.	5.2						
My greatest difficulty is with (write: *mechanics, verbs,* etc.)...............18.	Mech.						

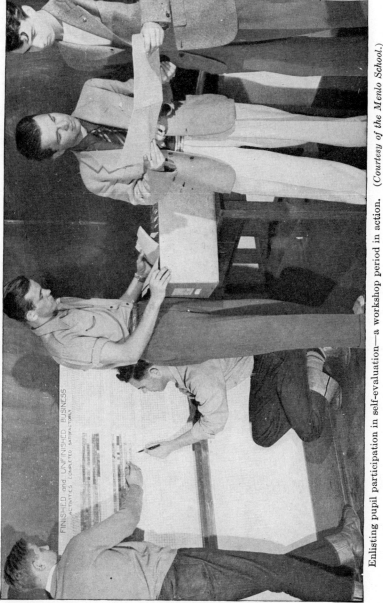

Enlisting pupil participation in self-evaluation—a workshop period in action. (*Courtesy of the Menlo School.*)

If the concept of self-evaluation and of learning from ones' own mistakes is capitalized effectively in the classroom during the initial stages, the time required to do the checking gradually decreases. So also does the proportional number of careless mistakes, especially in mechanics. Although the administration of the plan could easily occupy all the teacher's time in and out of school if she failed to share the responsibilities for its execution with the pupils, it should be self-evident that any such conscientious attempt on the part of the teacher would merely defeat the central purposes of the activity. The following practical suggestions may prevent the teacher from overburdening herself with mechanical proofreading and checking, or from unconsciously frustrating the opportunities for growth that she is attempting to encourage:

1. Enlisting the voluntary cooperation of able pupils in checking or scoring papers for difficulties, accuracy, or completeness of corrections. These pupils may constitute an editorial committee, and with proper guidance from the teacher, may often assist handicapped pupils in correcting their own work, in explaining difficulties, etc. At times, the members of the editorial committee may be exempted from certain units of work to devote themselves to this service.

2. Setting aside occasional class periods for a laboratory workshop in which the pupils can secure the aid of the teacher or members of the editorial committee in correcting and recording their work.

3. Enlisting the occasional cooperation of the mathematics teachers in permitting pupils to perform the tabulations and computations required in the chart.

4. Replacing the teacher's grade book with pupil folders and an achievement chart. The mechanical operation of these devices during a self-evaluation workshop period is illustrated in the picture facing page 412.

All papers that have been checked for difficulties are kept by the pupil in a folder in the order of the date on which they were originally written. These folders are arranged in alphabetical order in a filing case accessible to the pupils. After a pupil has revised a unit of work and tabulated his difficulties on the self-evaluation check list, he is entitled to fill in the corresponding space on the chart entitled *Finished and Unfinished Business* (see photograph). On this chart the names of the units and the dates on which they were initiated are indicated at the top of the horizontal rows. To the left are the names of the pupils, grouped according to teams. The folder containing the tabulation sheet and all the written work that the pupil has done to date (with his original difficulties indicated on the papers, and the corrections that he has made) is a valuable aid in reviewing the pupil's progress at a glance. Such actual evidence is a more valid guide in making reports of progress than a series of grades listed in a roll book. It is also a valuable aid to the pupil and his parents in appraising work done in the course.

The chart entitled *Finished and Unfinished Business* is a visible record of units of work which the pupil has completed satisfactorily and of such units as he has not completed owing to absence or to individualized reading activities. This visible record takes the place of the teacher's grade book, and obviates such pupil questions as "What did I miss?" or "What do I have to make up?" Any extra time required by the self-evaluation plan is thus saved by eliminating other time-consuming responsibilities of the teacher, such as recording grades and personally seeing that work is completed satisfactorily. The danger that this plan will overemphasize written work can be reduced by giving due recognition to other language activities, and by indicating to the pupils that only papers that have been checked for difficulties need be tabulated on the check list. Properly administered, the plan obviates the need for grades, although commendation of good work in the form of a brief word of approval is always in order and encouraging to the pupils. Especially fine papers may occasionally be selected by the editorial committee for posting on the bulletin board. Granting that the effective operation of the plan requires conducting the class as a laboratory workshop on certain days, any overloading of the teacher with mechanical detail is usually a sign that she is defeating her own ends by preempting the very responsibilities that she is trying to help young people to fulfill.

The plan for pupil participation in evaluation described above has been especially helpful in conducting courses designed to enable pupils to work under their own power and under their own speed. Grades of "incomplete," with the opportunity to remove them through additional or equivalent work, have proved an effective substitute for failing marks at the end of a quarter or semester in the case of pupils whose work is seriously deficient for any reason.

Criteria for Appraising the Evaluation Program.—The foregoing discussion of evaluation as an integral part of every aspect of the educative process is predicated on the obvious fact that no matter whether the evidences of achievement be "objective" test scores, samples of pupil work, group activities, subsequent grades in college, or success in actual life, the actual appraisal always depends upon the intelligent exercise of discriminating and *humane* judgment. Such judgment can be refined either by mechanical means, such as statistical norms, or through the development of insight into the significance of an activity or product as an educative experience contributive to effective living in a world in which people are the masters rather than the supine victims of chance and circumstance.

It is doubtful if there is any better way of appraising a school's philosophy, objectives, curriculum, and administrative organization than examining those evidences of pupil growth which the school takes the trouble to evaluate: "Let me see the teacher's testing program, and I shall tell you what her real objectives are, and with what she has been almost exclusively concerned in her teaching." A teacher who justifies the study of foreign languages, literatures, or cultures in terms of their vocational, social, or cultural values, but can provide little evidence beyond test scores of vocabulary or grammar that anything having a significant bearing upon these objectives has ever been done, except incidentally, by the pupils themselves, in the classroom or outside of it, is admitting in fact, if not in words, that she has been operating under a conception of language in education and life that insists on belittling and depreciating the interests of the majority of young people who are not going to college to permit a small minority to obtain an egocentric college-preparatory distinction that does not even meet their own fundamental needs. The extent to which this conception is operative in the course can be gauged by the presence or absence of supporting evidence in answer to the following questions:

1. Does the evaluation program provide for pupil growth in self-evaluation?

2. Does the evaluation program provide for the appraisal of outcomes in the way of cultural insights for some life purpose?

3. Does the evaluation program provide for the appraisal of constructive changes in attitudes toward the people whose language is being studied—especially toward those who are trying to adjust themselves to a creative and enlightened American way of life?

4. Does the evaluation program include the appraisal of successes *in relation to the total number of pupils* who elect (or are required to take) foreign-language work?

5. Does the evaluation program include a critical appraisal of the probable carry-over value into actual life of those interests, abilities, activities, or insights which are developed in school?

6. Does the evaluation program include an appraisal of the extent and effectiveness with which the foreign language has been capitalized as the medium for achieving the outcomes submitted as evidences of success?

7. Does the evaluation program provide for the use of tests that measure the pupils' ability to use a foreign language for other than classroom purposes or "doing" disconnected exercises in a textbook?

8. Are mechanical tests of vocabulary, grammar, phonetics, and the like used primarily for purposes of diagnosing language difficulties, or are these parts compounded into a fictitious total score to represent ability actually to use the language for normal life purposes?

Among the few offerings in foreign languages in which some attempt has been made *to evaluate proficiency in the skills in terms of the ends which they make possible,* are the programs reported by the Stanford Language Arts Investigation.[1] Evaluation programs that are not concerned with the appraisal of knowledge and skills in relation to the degree to which they provide for the realization of the life objectives that they are intended to serve can have no other long-range effect than that of causing means to be mistaken for ends—and eventually to be taught and measured as such in a vacuum insulated against life. The following paragraphs from "Foreign-language Outcomes of the Stanford Language Arts Investigation" are quoted as exemplifying a significant initial step in the direction of a life-centered program of evaluation in the foreign languages:[2]

Although the experimental programs have varied widely in content and activities according to the needs of individual classes, schools, and communities, and according to the degrees of freedom which the teachers experienced in working out their programs in typical school situations, the evidence lends strong support to the following generalizations:

1. In classes in which these principles have been put into operation in the first two years there has been an increase of 100 to 300 per cent in the number of pupils who voluntarily continue into advanced foreign-language classes beyond the two years ordinarily required for admission to college.

2. The number of pupils discontinuing the study of the language by choice or through failure has been materially reduced—in some instances by as much as 95 per cent.

[1] Reports of the Stanford Language Arts Investigation, incorporating statements of practice by teachers in the field, *Foreign Languages and Cultures in American Education,* Vol. II, McGraw-Hill Book Company, Inc., New York. In press.

[2] Walter V. Kaulfers, "Foreign-language Outcomes of the Stanford Language Arts Investigation," *School and Society,* Vol. LII, pp. 235–237, Sept. 21, 1941.

3. Student interest in language study has been maintained at a high level as indicated not only by unsigned student reactions, and comments, but also by such evidences as are reported in the two preceding paragraphs.

4. Ratings made by the experimental classes on batteries of race-prejudice scales indicate without exception a conspicuous gain over the control classes in tolerant and sympathetic attitudes toward the people whose language is being studied. This should be considered significant if the cultural objectives commonly found in courses of study are to serve some more functional purpose than that of providing a decorative preamble to outlines of "grammar to be covered."

5. In the experimental classes in which reading, writing, and speaking centered from the start around cultural reading content, the gain in information about the country and its people (in relation to their contribution to American and to world cultures) was from two to three times as great as the gain revealed by the test scores of pupils who studied foreign languages in the conventional way.

6. The advantages reported in the foregoing paragraphs were achieved without sacrifice whatsoever in ability to use the language correctly in speaking and writing, or to read the language with understanding. The average scores made by the classes on objective measures of ability in reading, grammar, and vocabulary were in every case as high as the averages traditionally made by pupils of like age and ability on departmental examinations, or on such well-known measuring instruments as the *Cooperative* (Spanish, German, French, and Latin) *Tests*.[1]

7. Although valid and reliable tests of fluency in the conversational use of language are not available, the teachers are convinced that the gain has been marked—especially with regard to the development of *Sprachgefühl*, or feeling

---

[1] It is interesting to observe that every scientific study based on actual pupil performance (as measured by test scores rather than mere opinion) has shown that proficiency in the use of language is achieved as well as, or better than before, when learned in terms of *use* in the immediate service of a life objective, rather than through the type of preliminary grammatical work which is presumably justified as a means to the same goals, but has done more than anything else to make the ends inaccessible to large numbers of young people. For abstracts of studies based on objective data see *Review of Educational Research*, Vol. X, "The Language Arts," pp. 126–145, April, 1940. *Encyclopedia of Educational Research*, Walter S. Monroe, Ed., The Macmillan Company, New York, 1941, 1344 pp.; pp. 520–539. Algernon Coleman and Clara Breslove King, *An Analytical Bibliography of Modern Language Teaching*, The University of Chicago Press, Chicago, 1938, xviii + 561 pp.; pp. 397–414. J. Wayne Wrightstone, *Appraisal of Newer Practices in Selected Schools*, Bureau of Publications, Teachers College, Columbia University, New York, 1935, 117 pp. J. Paul Leonard and Alvin C. Eurich (Editors), *An Evaluation of Modern Education*, D. Appleton-Century Company, 1942, 299 pp.; Chaps. V, VIII, IX. *New Methods vs. Old in American Education*, Teachers College, Columbia University, 1941, 64 pp.

for the language, and of security and freedom in oral expression. Outside visitors have repeatedly been impressed with the superiority in oral work—in the desire voluntarily to participate—of pupils enrolled in the experimental classes. The latter seemed to show greater *esprit de corps*.

8. Although the foreign-language teachers felt that their work was severely handicapped by the almost total absence of textbooks and readers containing content worth reading or discussing in terms of the central objectives of the investigation, they nevertheless agreed that they would "never go back to the old plan."

But is it language? If grammar, vocabulary, and reading are conceived of as *means* rather than as ends, then the outcomes reported above in terms of attitudes, interests, abilities, and cultural insights would seem to provide an affirmative answer.

Evaluation as a Creative Process.—In terms of the creative conception of evaluation embodied in the foregoing paragraphs, a specific outcome is viewed not only as an evidence of the pupil's level of achievement, but also as evidence of the effectiveness of the teacher, course, and school in meeting the basic purposes envisioned in the American ideal of universal free education for socially useful, cultivated living as the natural birthright of every human being. Most fatal to any learning program is a concept of evaluation that restricts the exercise of human judgment to a limited type of evidence which can be conveniently counted, but rarely reveals a single significant fact concerning the meaning for human life that lies *behind* the score.

In a world that will continue to change as long as men have the capacity to think, education will have to concern itself not only with what exists, but also with what might desirably exist among people who are not mere victims of change but masters of it. Otherwise the progress of civilization will continue to be a "race between education and catastrophe." Perhaps it is a sad commentary upon the kind of education which the presumably civilized and cultured nations of the world have financed, that their "progress" has seldom been achieved without major catastrophe for millions of people. In helping education to lay the foundations for a just and lasting peace in which the mending of men's minds and hearts will be far more important then the mending of their pocketbooks, teachers of the foreign languages can demonstrate their vision by cooperatively giving attention to the kind of world that might exist, and use this creative foresight as a criterion of evaluation for *all* that they do in working with young people. Those who are the custodians of mankind's ideals must make certain that ideals are acquired in and through use in emulation of encouraging examples, lest they become, not rallying calls for uniting human beings in building a heaven on earth, but mere "sick 'em" words for inciting underprivileged peoples against each other.[1]

[1] Kenneth Gould, *They Got the Blame: The Story of Scapegoats in History*, Service Bureau for Intercultural Education, New York, 1942, 64 pp. Alain Locke and Bernhard J. Stern, *When Peoples Meet: A Study in Race and Culture Contacts*, Progressive Education Association, New York, 1942, 756 pp.

For a bibliography of published test see Appendix, references 59–69.

CHAPTER XIV

PERSPECTIVE ON THE PRE-SERVICE AND IN-SERVICE TRAINING OF TEACHERS

It is hard for an empty bag to stand upright.
—BENJAMIN FRANKLIN
When love and skill work together, expect a masterpiece.
—JOHN RUSKIN
Every teacher is in danger of becoming a czar in his own classroom.
—STUART A. CURTIS

Preparatory Needs in the Field of Professionalized Subject Matter.—The translation of a creative conception of language teaching into action presupposes adequate preparation of teachers[1] for the task of helping young people grow in ability to use a foreign language for worthy life purposes. This preparation must of necessity include more than offerings designed to develop an acceptable degree of proficiency in reading, writing, and speaking; for the mere possession of a skill does not necessarily imply ability to develop such a skill

[1] This vital problem has been the subject of intensive discussion and investigation in recent years. See Henri C. Olinger, "Methodology in Language Teaching," *The French Review*, Vol. XII, pp. 323–348, February, 1939. John L. Tildsley, "Equipment of Foreign Language Teachers in the Senior High Schools," *The French Review*, Vol. XIII, pp. 162–163, December, 1939. Roy E. Mosher, "Merits and Defects in Modern Language Teaching," *Hispania*, Vol. XXII, pp. 19–30, February, 1939. Hugo Giduz, "Good Teaching of French," *The Modern Language Journal*, Vol. XXIII, pp. 508–514, April, 1939. Emilio L. Guerra, "Training the Beginning Teacher of Foreign Languages," *The Modern Language Journal*, Vol. XXIV, pp. 163–168, December, 1939. Mark Waldman, "The Selection of Heads of Modern Language Departments, Appointments of Modern Language Teachers, and Their Supervision," *The Modern Language Journal*, Vol. XXIV, pp. 510–525, April, 1940. A. G. Gutowski, "Survey of Modern Language Teaching in the United States," *The Modern Language Journal*, Vol. XXIV, pp. 431–442, March, 1940. S. A. Freeman, "What Constitutes a Well-trained Modern Language Teacher?" *The Modern Language Journal*, Vol. XXV, pp. 293–305, January, 1941. J. R. Pilley, "National Teacher Examination Service," *The School Review*, Vol. XLIX, pp. 177–186, March, 1941. Geraldine Spaulding, "The Achievement of the Modern Language Candidates in the National Teacher Examinations," *The Modern Language Journal*, Vol. XXV, pp. 361–367, February, 1941. Anna P. McCreary and James B. Tharp, "The 1941 French Teacher Census: Teacher Training," *The French Review*, Vol. XV, pp. 493–500, May, 1942.

effectively in others.   Neither does it give assurance that the means employed in developing the skills will not defeat the ends that they are intended to serve.   It is astonishing at times to find teachers who have taught beginning and advanced classes in a foreign language, four to six hours a day, for ten to fifteen years, yet who cannot themselves boast of any commendable degree of proficiency in actually using the language outside the routine lingo of the classroom.   It would seem idle to expect students to grow significantly in ability under the guidance of a teacher whose methods contribute little or nothing to her own personal proficiency in the language.   In a day and age when radio programs in foreign languages are common, and excellent phonograph recordings available at little cost,[1] it is entirely possible for a beginning teacher with limited proficiency in the active use of a language to adopt procedures whereby she may grow with her own students.   Limited ability to speak, understand, or write a foreign language extemporaneously is not an excuse for evading functional procedures, but the very reason why such procedures should be increasingly used.   It can hardly be expected that students, with only one class in a foreign language available to them each day, will grow significantly in ability to use the language effectively if the teacher with four to five class hours at her professional disposal does not improve in and through her own methods over a reasonable period of time.

Beyond such basic courses as may be needed to develop proficiency in the tool uses of language, every candidate for a teaching position in a secondary school should avail himself of offerings that will develop an intimate acquaintance with the literature and culture of the foreign country whose language he expects to teach.   If this preparation is adequate, it will yield ready answers to such questions as the following:

1. How have great foreign writers influenced world thought through literature?

2. How have great foreign scientists and inventors contributed to the increase in human comforts and to freeing the world from fear, disease, and superstition?

3. How have great foreigners contributed to the source materials for American culture in art, architecture, music, language, science, education, etc?

[1] Anna Balakian, "Radio Broadcasting, and the Teaching of French," *The French Review*, Vol. XIII, pp. 222–224, January, 1940. Stowell C. Goding, "Neglected Treasures?"   *The Modern Language Journal*, Vol. XXIV, pp. 34–42, October, 1939.   See also Appendix, references 112, 196.

4. What novels, plays, short stories, or nonfiction books, edited for student use, are suitable for reading for a life purpose in elementary, intermediate, and advanced classes?

5. In what respects, and *why*, do the foreign people think, live, or behave differently from others?

6. In what respects are the foreign country and the United States interdependent?

7. How can greater cooperation between the United States and the foreign country be enlisted in the interests of the common good? What facilities are now available for this purpose?

If the information and insights required to answer these questions are developed in and through reading and discussion in the foreign language itself, the necessary competence in language and subject matter can be developed simultaneously. The need is not for the introduction of additional offerings, but rather for a radical change in the content and organization of those offerings which have traditionally been required of prospective practitioners in language as distinguished from research specialists in philology, grammar, or belles-lettres.

Since skills and information serve no significant life purpose unless they are put to some constructive use, instruction cannot be effective unless the teacher is competent to guide learning in the direction of socially effective living in a changing world. The development of this competence presupposes insight into the function of the school as an instrument of social control and improvement in contemporary and past civilizations and cultures, and a clear understanding of the role of the foreign languages in American education. For this reason, educational sociology, social psychology, and offerings in the history and philosophy of education as a means of social control are desirable foundation courses for all teachers of any subject. The school cannot be more than a pawn in the hands of a small but powerful pressure group unless the teachers see their vocation in relation to the fundamental needs of *all* the children of *all* the people and of the changing society in which they live.

Since no two children, with the possible exception of identical twins, are exactly alike, offerings that give insight into the psychology of individual differences, into the ways in which children learn most effectively, and into the symptoms and causes of social, physical, or mental maladjustment are a valuable part of the teacher's professional equipment. Such offerings, when accompanied by personal contacts with young people through practice teaching, club work, or community-service organizations will help the prospective teacher develop the personality and social effectiveness which are necessary if his life is to be consecrated to some more creative purpose than drilling young people into becoming subservient grammatical robots: "moving hands who write for a master," or ventriloquists' dummies who cannot originate or express intelligibly a single idea of their own.

To complete this background of professional preparation for teaching, a comprehensive course in curriculum and instruction in foreign languages is desirable as a means for translating the teacher's resources in subject matter and knowledge of young people and education into concrete terms. A study of the materials available for enriching the learning program, of the successful practices of teachers in different school and community environments, and of the ways and means for bringing the learning process into conformity with the pupils' levels of insight, should form an integral part of the professional course.

Developing Social Insight and Perspective through Life Contacts.— If this basic professional preparation can be supplemented by residence or travel abroad, the teacher will be able to vitalize the course through the choice of materials that otherwise she might be tempted to avoid for lack of interest or self-confidence. It is doubtful, however, if mere gymnastics in space abroad contribute significantly to the fundamental enrichment of a teaching program. The tendency on short visits is to take an interest only in things rather than in the lives of people as they are today. If time and money do not permit of effective study, travel, or residence abroad, it is preferable to develop an intimate acquaintance with the evidences of foreign culture in the United States in people, customs, mores, and traditions. Indeed, such a firsthand acquaintance is primary if the learnings of the classroom are to be translated into life interests in people whom the younger generation can contact in person. It may be possible for the student of Spanish, for example, to lend the strength of his voice, pocketbook, vote, and personal example to securing a decent and humane treatment for the American children of Spanish-speaking parents in the United States.[1] It may not be possible for him to do

---

[1] In the Southwest the number of school children from non-English speaking homes, chiefly Mexican, ranges from 20 to 45 per cent. See Algernon Coleman and Clara Breslove King, *English Teaching in the Southwest*, American Council on Education, Washington, D. C., 1940, 307 pp.; p. 4. For the educational needs of these children from underprivileged homes, in communities which discriminate against them socially and economically, see pp. 17–20. Also, E. R. Hutton, "We Mexicans," *Foreign Languages and Cultures in American Education*, Vol. II,

much about the Cathedral of Seville, the Alhambra, or the Cid's coffer, except to read interesting books about them as a pastime.

With this professional equipment the teacher should be able to play a creative role in the lives of young people and in the society in which they live. Voice, appearance, posture, and demeanor—all the external essentials to an effective personality—can be acquired, in some cases almost over night. The philosophy of life that is required to give real meaning and direction to the teacher's own personality and ability, however, is a matter of growth and experience in the social stream of the world.

Facing Changing Realities Constructively.—A teacher fired with a creative conception of her role in education and society will not be dismayed by reactionary conservatism or lack of support even from her own colleagues. She will work quietly without denouncing others or proclaiming a new method from the housetops. She will use whatever materials are available to the extent to which they are useful, replacing them at the earliest opportunity with materials that are better suited to the needs of her own pupils. She will sell her program through the good will of her students and the satisfying progress that they themselves sense and appreciate. She will receive students from other teachers and continue quietly where they left off, justifying any changes in materials or methods on the basis of "the splendid foundation which you have had for the new advanced type of work which we are now ready to do."

From time to time she will invite the principal or parents to witness the class in action on some effective unit of regular classwork, and request the opportunity to discuss the activity with the principal as a means for securing his good will and support of the program in the future. If a unit of work proves particularly successful, a short (1,000 to 1,500 words) article, describing the objectives, content, methods, and results may deserve a place in one of the foreign-language magazines and thus ally the teacher with other pioneers in the field. A few such articles, based on actual classroom experience, will in time either secure a recognition for her work in her own school or open the door to a better position elsewhere. Some of the best experimental programs have been developed without publicizing the fact that what was being done was any different from what any good teacher might do in similar circumstances. Naturally, such extreme caution is

McGraw-Hill Book Company, Inc., New York. In press. Annie Reynolds, "The Education of Spanish-speaking Children," *U. S. Office of Education Bulletin*, 1933, No. 11, Washington, D. C., 64 pp.; pp. 30–33.

imperative only when on the basis of a careful study of the school, the teacher finds that the thinking of her colleagues and principal are still in the dark ages of language teaching. Where opportunities for cooperation in new type programs already exist, the problem of circumventing mental sclerosis is obviously unimportant. Supplying the principal and fellow workers with books and articles which contain constructive solutions to foreign-language problems, and cooperating with fellow workers wherever possible, however, often help pave the way for long-range modifications which require the support of the administration and colleagues.

Choosing between Competing Philosophies of Education.—The novice entering the teaching profession is often faced, like newcomers to the legal, medical, or clerical professions, with the alternative of allying himself with one of two or more groups representing different viewpoints concerning practice in the field. In foreign-language teaching the lines of cleavage are particularly marked. During the last two decades, curriculum revisions necessitated by changes in the nature of the secondary-school population[1] have tended to accentuate the differentiation. At the present writing, foreign-language teachers fall roughly into two schools of thought, the developmental school and the Procrustean school.

The Developmental School.—This group consists primarily of teachers who in addition to the usual preparation in literature and language have studied the history and philosophy of education, educational sociology, educational psychology, and curriculum building. Their own home backgrounds, or their contacts with humanity as it is, have sensitized them to values that are ordinarily eclipsed behind such statistical fictions as the "average child," I.Q.'s, or total scores. Subject matter to them is one of many mediums for helping human beings grow in ability to lead constructive, wholesome, and socially useful lives. The school is conceived as an educative environment[2] which compensates for deficiencies in the child's social, economic, or cultural background—for parents who are a negative or destructive influence, for homes in which there is inadequate food, shelter, and

[1] Grayson N. Kefauver, Victor H. Noll, and C. Elwood Drake, "The Secondary School Population," *U. S. Office of Education Bulletin*, 1932, No. 17, Washington, D. C., 58 pp.; pp. 1–26. Walter V. Kaulfers, "The Challenge of Education to Prospective Teachers of the Foreign Language Arts," in *The Challenge of Education*, McGraw-Hill Book Company, Inc., New York, 1937, xiv + 417 pp.; pp. 259–275.

[2] Franklin Bobbitt, *The Curriculum of Modern Education*, McGraw-Hill Book Company, Inc., New York, 1941, 410 pp.

clothing and little opportunity for recreation or travel, or for the read-ing and discussion of good books, magazines, plays, lectures, or recitals. The developmental group knows not only from books, but also from personal contacts, that a violently expressed contempt for any of the things that "nice people do" is often but the symptom of a defense mechanism against an impoverished reality to which no sane person ever confines himself by choice unless the avenues of escape are unknown or beyond his reach, or so paved with supercilious con-descension that no person with an ounce of individuality in his humble station would care to accept it. Mild symptoms of such disguised defense mechanisms are to be found in almost any class where pupils are intimidated into learning stereotyped lessons in chain-gang fashion from supercilious neuropaths in dull packing-case schoolrooms. Among the antiquated beliefs that the developmental group has successfully challenged, the following have been listed by Roberts:[1]

1. That subject matter is of primary importance and children are secondary.

2. That meeting college entrance requirements is a proper aim for the teacher and the great majority in our schools who are not going to college. That the interests of the majority who are not going to college should be sacrificed to permit the minority to obtain an artificial college-preparatory distinction which does not meet their own fundamental needs.

3. That the curriculums and instruction in colleges and universities are modern. That their courses of study are above criticism and need never change.

4. That teaching by the textbook method can ever educate young people. That teachers who use the ancient Chinese-Prussian method of textbook question-and-answer drill can be considered modern teachers.

5. That children should be taught to work for grades and credits. That teaching children to work for grades and credits is sound psychology and prepares them to meet the demands of life situations.

6. That young people who are in our high schools and colleges know how to read. That it is the business of the elementary school so to teach reading that years later in high school and college they will be able to read adequately problems in advanced algebra, solid geometry, calculus, and physics, and interpret Shakespeare, Chaucer, Milton, Carlyle, Burke, and Gibbon.

7. That in teaching children to read we should make a sharp distinction between work reading and pleasure reading, so that they will understand clearly that they are not supposed to enjoy themselves when their reading has any purpose to them beyond the pleasure of the moment.

[1] Holland D. Roberts, "English Teachers Face the Future," *English Journal* (College Edition), Vol. XXVII, pp. 101–113, February, 1938.

8. That there is any evidence that formal grammar—sentence analysis, parsing, diagraming—is of use in helping anyone speak or write more correctly or effectively.

9. That in teaching people to speak or write, mechanics and style should be emphasized and the ideas, content, and human experiences are of secondary value, or even of no concern, to the teacher. . . .

10. That creative writing is "arty" writing and should deal chiefly with lavender and old lace in a vague and timeless shadowland.

11. That children can learn, and teachers can teach them in poorly lighted packing-case schoolrooms, children crowded together three in a seat, with no bulletin boards and no bookcases except the window sill. That in America, where millions of men are refused the elementary right to earn their bread, we are so poverty-stricken we must continue to use obsolete school buildings. That school buildings need be less modern than factories, theaters, and restaurants.

12. That it is possible to build a secure peace through diplomacy and legislative enactment without building world peace through the curriculums of our schools.

Although recognizing the importance of broad and thorough scholarship as essential to anyone who presumes to use subject matter as a medium for achieving anything of importance in the lives of young people, the developmental group realizes that the means employed are as important as the objectives; for *people become, not what their objectives are, but what the kind of means they employ give them actual practice in becoming.* Thus the individual who tries to become wealthy by illegal means is more likely to end life as a racketeer or a criminal than as a multimillionnaire. And so it is with the means employed for achieving objectives—even in foreign languages. *Young people become, not what the aims of the program are, but what the teachers train them to be by the kind of means—methods, activities, content, or examinations—which they use.* For this reason, ways and means for providing more effective learning environments are of as much concern to the teachers of foreign languages who belong to the developmental school as scholarly papers on "Lope de Vega's Dramatic Use of Women" or "Some Neglected Aspects of the Imperfect Subjunctive in Sixteenth-century French." Although the foreign-language sections of educational associations and summer workshops (such as those occasionally provided by Ohio State University, Stanford University, Mills College, and the University of Colorado) constitute the only avenues of cooperation that have so far been open to the developmental school, the vigor of this relatively small group has been responsible for the few changes in foreign-language teaching which have provided more constructive solutions to foreign-language problems than the Procrustean method of simply chopping off those groups of young people who do not fit the stereotyped mold—and then rationalizing as valid outcomes, the qualities and abilities that the pupils are expected to possess before entering the courses.

For in reality, few teachers of foreign languages develop disciplined minds, effective study habits, or good English in young people; they simply wait for the most convenient opportunity to get rid of pupils who lack these qualifications. Otherwise the reasons most frequently given by teachers for failing pupils would not be so dangerously similar to the presumed values of foreign-language study as a "discipline." The developmental school questions the validity of claiming as evidences of success qualities which are frequently insisted upon as prerequisites. The conviction is growing that the study of foreign languages, literatures, and cultures can serve some more constructive purpose in public education than providing a sieve for weeding out young people who may need education most—not to discipline their minds, but to compensate for the lack of encouragement or opportunity to participate outside of school in all the fine things that "nice people" approve.

At the present time the adherents of this school are a numerically small but highly influential minority. The increasing opportunities offered by forward-looking institutions of higher learning to do graduate work for the M.A., Ph.D., and Ed.D. degrees in curriculum and instruction in foreign languages will in time furnish this group with more effective leadership. The School of Education of Stanford University, for example, provides individualized programs in curriculums and instruction in foreign languages leading to the M.A., M.Ed., Ph.D., and Ed.D. degrees in language-arts education. These programs are open to all graduate students possessing adequate scholarship in the language, literature, and culture of at least one foreign country. In addition, the university offers workshop courses on the seminar or independent-study plan, carrying up to ten units of graduate credit, in which teachers in service can develop materials, methods, or courses of study specifically adapted to their *own* schools. In these projects the teacher has access to the library of the Stanford Language Arts Investigation and to the consulting services of a staff of experts in psychology, evaluation, curriculum building, and foreign languages. With the gradual increase in similar opportunities in other colleges and universities, the trend in foreign-language teaching is swinging definitely in favor of the proponents of the developmental school. Already the impress of their influence is to be felt in the newer textbooks and new type courses[1] which this group have successfully sponsored. As yet, however, the conduct of foreign-language organizations and the official organs that they publish remains very largely in control of the Procrusteans.

The Procrustean School.—The adherents of this school believe in knowledge for knowledge's sake on the theory that facts and skills have intrinsic values for human life independent of the way in which they are used. Such questions as "Information for what?" or "Correctness for what?" are either considered impertinences or evaded altogether. All the instrumentalities of experimental psychology, such as intelligence quotients or prognosis tests are used by this group, not for diagnosing educational needs, but as excuses for inability either to recognize or meet them. The entire hierarchy of cultural values is based upon subject matter and externals of form as ends in themselves rather than upon their effectiveness in solving important personal and social problems on an intelligent and humane basis. Education is narrowly conceived as formal "disciplinary" schooling rather than as embracing all those agencies of mental suggestion, the family, friends, the radio, the press, the church, the sound picture, or the playground, which hypnotize human beings into behaving differently from animals—or like them.

Instead of viewing the work of the school in relation to these educative forces, the Procrusteans insist on teaching content to students in terms of a supporting ideology which developed during an age when the controlling influences governing the life application of classroom acquirements were the church and the home. In general, the adherents of this school are devotees of the eighteenth-century conception of education as the kind of training becoming "the scholarly gentleman"—a person of "quality" (means) competent to take part as graciously in a parlor discussion of Plato or Voltaire as in a fox hunt, and to maintain and defend with exclusive dignity the inherited blue-blood tradition of his family. Foreign languages as means for obtaining a firsthand acquaintance with "the best that has been

---

[1] Ellen Gail Babbitt and James B. Tharp, "The French Grammar Text Grows Socially Minded," *The French Review*, Vol. X, pp. 293–298, February, 1937. Lawrence A. Wilkins *et al.*, *Auxiliary Syllabus in Modern Foreign Languages, Foreign Civilization, and Visual-aural Aids*, Board of Education, New York, 1939. Lilly Lindquist, *New Type Offerings in Foreign Language*, Detroit Public Schools, File No. 9831, 1939.

written or said" were special badges of culture, since the development of ability to do anything about the problems portrayed in the writings of the masters was distinctly taboo. Indeed, young people were permitted to read and discuss "radical" writers only a century or two after they were dead. The same conception of education as a disciplining of the mind in the great literature of the past dominates the thinking of the Procrustean school. The "classics," together with the preparatory work in grammar necessary to read them, become the content of the curriculum, and children either fit the logically organized scope and sequence of the program, or they fail.

A decade ago, the adherents of this school found themselves the victims of their own negative methods of solving educational problems by eliminating relatively large numbers of pupils through exploratory tryout courses, prognosis tests, and standardized examinations with a stereotyped national norm—a kind of five-foot hurdle which every child was expected to clear when the stop watch was set after a uniform period of training in linguistic gymnastics. Although demanding their fair share of the increasing school enrollments[1] brought about through the extension of educational facilities at public expense to all the children of all the people, the Procrustean group refused to recognize the different educational needs of thousands of young people who no longer represented only the professional or semiprofessional levels of American society. *In extremis*, they merely diluted the traditional pabulum with time, often giving young people with entirely different educational needs a twice- or thrice-prolonged exposure to deadening materials for which they could see little reason and which they would not, therefore, be likely to master anyway. The thought that what these young people might need was not more time to digest materials to which they were allergic or apathetic, but an entirely different diet, was foreign if not heretical. The defense of a foreign-language curriculum originally designed for a select group of young people who, in case of necessity, could afford to attend private schools, became the major preoccupation of the vested-interest group. The tragically low level to which this controlling element sank in the estimation of teachers and administrators outside the foreign-language field is revealed in the remarks of Paul B. Diederich to the foreign-language section of the National Education Association in St. Louis in 1936:[2]

[1] James B. Tharp, "The Allotment for Foreign-language Study: Internecine Competition or Conciliatory Compromise," *The Modern Language Journal*, Vol. XXV, pp. 598–608, May, 1941.

[2] Quoted from James B. Tharp, Ed., "Foreign Language Integration: Extended

An audience which is attracted by the prospect of learning how the foreign languages may be adapted to the program of a modern school is likely to be disappointed. Unless something is done about it, the discussion bids fair to degenerate into the customary irritable defense of the vested interests of the foreign-language teachers against every hopeful modern tendency in education.

Out of fairness to the audience this simply must not happen. It springs from the basest of psychological motives: the inflation of the ego which makes one's own interests seem the most compelling and important in the world, while the competing interests of other teachers seem not only lacking in common sense but wilfully malicious; from insecurity in one's position, which makes one exclaim, on the one hand, against any lowering of the requirements in foreign languages, and on the other hand, against the unfitness of one's students for the study of foreign languages; from an inability to see the students' needs and interests except in the light of one's own; from an inability to understand and adjust to the different conception of education exemplified by an integrated curriculum; from the primordial law of life, "increase and multiply," and from the American tradition that one must always "boost" one's own line. Any such tendencies as these cropping up in the discussion should be rigorously gaveled. . . .

"The good old days" in secondary education are still too close at hand in the programs of the majority of secondary schools to take on any romantic glamour. Let us look at them by way of contrast. They consist of a program planned, in every essential respect, by a group of ten college professors and their like in the 1890's, in terms of their own academic interests: their psychological adjustment to the materials of education inherited from the Middle Ages. They consist, more specifically, of 45 minutes of English, 45 minutes of Latin, 45 minutes of either French, German, or Spanish, 45 minutes of mathematics, and 45 minutes of either physics, chemistry, or history. A few students are able to substitute a pitifully meager course in one of the fine or practical arts or music. This work is largely dictated and examined by a little group of college and boarding-school men who have no connection with the public schools.[1]

The sheer horror of the existing program in secondary education should drive every intelligent educator to the support of any promising attempt to improve it. Yet the movement toward integration has encountered the most obdurate and implacable resistance from the teachers of foreign languages and mathematics. In many schools they have blocked every effort to improve

---

Remarks of the St. Louis Panel Members," *The Modern Language Journal*, Vol. XXI, pp. 115–121, November, 1936.

[1] The more modern viewpoint of boarding-school men is reflected in "A Report of the Conference on Modern Foreign Languages," Boston, Dec. 28–30, 1940, Secondary Education Board, Milton, Mass., 1941, 32 pp. See also Nicholas Moseley, "Language Teaching: Practice and Theory," *The French Review*, Vol. XIII, pp. 289–294, February, 1940.

the quality of the educative experience. They have insisted on their ancient prerogative of five mortal periods a week to do what they please without regard to the rest of the curriculum. It has taxed the ingenuity of every progressive administrator to schedule these periods at times which will not conflict with the large blocks of time required for the connected, thoughtful work of an integrated curriculum. In their teaching methods and point of view they have been utterly hostile to the spirit of the newer programs. Thus far they have distinguished themselves as the most formidable obstacle to integration or to any attempt to improve the traditional curriculum. "The Place of Foreign Languages in an Integrated Curriculum" has been that of the dog in the manger.

It will be tragic if the Panel continues this futile and antisocial resistance to the inevitable course of modern education. The educators who attend the conference will be half persuaded already that it is impossible to humanize the foreign languages; that they can only be endured and prevented whenever possible from doing harm until they can safely be omitted from the program of secondary education. If the Panel displays the same chip on the shoulder that is worn by the rank and file of language teachers, or if it dodges the issue of integration altogether, or fails miserably to understand what it is all about, these suspicions will be confirmed. The intelligent way to safeguard the interests of the foreign-language group—to say nothing of the interests of boys and girls—is to make an honest attempt to find out what the study of foreign languages may contribute to educational objectives. . . .

Building Professional Morale.—By 1940, the provision of increasing facilities for the preparation of foreign-language teachers in schools of education, and thorough regional workshops for teachers in service, served to reorient thinking and practice in the foreign-language field. Progress, however, has been slow. As yet, ways and means for bringing curriculum and instruction in foreign languages into conformity with present-day needs receive only passing attention on the programs of foreign-language organizations. Concerted action is still largely in terms of committees for defending the *status in quo* in foreign languages against its "enemies," instead of in terms of cooperative group discussion and evaluation of needs in the field of curriculum revision. The constant preoccupation with defense still leaves little time for participation in educational conferences or curriculum-revision programs. As late as February, 1941, Leo L. Rockwell[1] noted with keen disappointment the habitual absence of foreign-language teachers from educational conventions and discussions:

[1] Leo L. Rockwell, "Dead Teachers of Living Languages?" *The Modern Language Journal*, Vol. XXV, pp. 359–360. February, 1941.

Recently a conference of delegates from a score of colleges and teachers colleges in one of our largest states spent a week together discussing teacher education. Professors of physics, chemistry, mathematics, philosophy, English, education, and other subjects, and lesser fry such as college presidents, deans, and other administrators were appointed by their colleges to participate. But not a single man or woman now teaching a modern foreign language was present. Why?

Last year a regional meeting of a state education association was held in a large eastern city. One morning was devoted to group meetings in the various subject-matter fields. After passing room after room filled with people assembled to discuss the problems in various other fields, one came to the large room set aside for modern language teachers. One didn't need to hunt for a seat. When at the end of the program the question was asked how many of those present were public school teachers of modern languages in the large host city, only eight hands were raised. Why?

Some time ago a certain university established a conference on education. Sections were arranged devoted to problems of the various subjects in the curriculum. After a few years, the section devoted to modern foreign languages was quietly dropped. Why?

In short, why do foreign-language teachers seem to be elsewhere when discussions of education are going on? Do they know all the answers? Have they no problems? Or are they being unjustly discriminated against in never being asked? To one observer who is seriously concerned with the problem as to why languages are losing out in the schools of this country it seems that there is no single answer. But it does seem clear that part of the answer lies in the indifference of great numbers of modern language teachers to the general problem of American education and to some of the urgent particular problems in their own field.

Why should the president of a great university say, as one did at the conference on teacher education mentioned above, that language classes are the most insolvent classes in the curriculum? Is that mere prejudice? Is the frequent attitude of hostility of students to foreign language merely pig-headed ignorance? Every teacher of modern languages knows that a great deal of the opposition does come from ignorance of the values of foreign-language instruction, but can that be the whole story?

Let anyone who thinks it is ask himself a few questions. How much have I thought recently on the problem of education in a democracy? How much have I read on it? Specifically what books and articles? How many conferences have I attended at which I can talk over with men in other fields our common problems? How interested am I really in my responsibilities as a teacher, as distinguished from my devotion to my subject for its own sake? How intelligent am I about my classroom procedure as related to the particular students I have, their needs and abilities? How many students go out from my classes enthusiastic about the thing I teach? How many go out failing to see that it has in any way benefited them?

Was the retreat from the classics due altogether to their inability to compete with "soft education"?   Was the hatred of English grammar the result of the difficulty of that subject or of the stupidity of teachers who slavishly followed a foolish tradition and refused to do their own thinking?   A new emphasis in grammar teaching, which owes more to sociologists and psychologists than to language teachers for its inception, is revivifying that subject. Students of English are learning that their subject can be actually exciting.

Granting all the difficulties which confront modern languages, and granting that there are many alert and stimulating teachers in the field, it is nevertheless probable that there is a great mass unleavened by broad intellectual interests.   The expanding programs of the Modern Language Association of America furnish no argument in rebuttal.   Except insofar as this organization is a pleasant social club ("I really go to see my friends and to avoid hearing papers" is a common remark) it represents narrowly restricted scholarly (some would question even that adjective) interests.   The regional affiliates of the National Federation of Modern Language Teachers are too often paper organizations or sustained only by the vigorous efforts of a small minority of thoroughly interested men and women.   It seems clear that many so-called modern language teachers are dead above the mouth.

Shall these dead awaken?

On entering the profession of foreign-language teaching the novice has the opportunity to join hands with those creative personalities who continue to grow by working creatively with others, or to align himself with those whose inspiration comes not from the needs and opportunities of the present and future but from the halo effects of the past.   Only the aged in mind and spirit, for whom the future has nothing in store, live exclusively in their yesteryears.   The opportunities for creative leadership and for continuous professional growth in foreign-language teaching are numerous.   Most urgent at present are forward-looking teachers who will help transform such organizations as the American Association of Teachers of French, the American Association of Teachers of Spanish, and comparable organizations in German and Italian from university-dominated literary-debating societies into professional organizations for the cooperative investigation, discussion, and support of such research and experimentation as may be required to keep instruction in the foreign languages in tune with the ever-changing needs of a rapidly changing world.

Among the activities that might well be undertaken by organizations of foreign-language teachers as ways and means for meeting the professional needs and interests of teachers in service, are the following:

1. Sponsorship of investigations in current language usage, *e.g.*, pronunciation, vocabulary, grammar, and syntax.

2. Cooperative discussion and development of new type teaching materials, *e.g.*, annotated bibliographies of books actually read with interest and profit for given life purposes by pupils of given levels of insight; units of work centering around key objectives in foreign-language teaching; tests for measuring directional changes in attitudes and gains in cultural insights.

3. Demonstration of ways and means for conducting new type units of work formulated through cooperative discussion and group planning.

4. Panel discussions among teachers actively engaged in experimenting with varied approaches to similar objectives, with pupils of different social or cultural backgrounds and different maturity levels.

5. Reviews of current foreign literature to replace research papers which are of interest only to literary historians.

6. Demonstration of the uses of such facilities as the radio, recording machine, and sound pictures in foreign-language teaching.

7. Maintenance of libraries of *realia*—pictures, models, phonograph records, radio transcriptions, etc. (The visual- and audio-education departments of local school systems are usually willing to cooperate.)

8. Group discussion of recommendations for institute programs, changes in college entrance requirements, etc.

9. Cooperative development of recommendations to publishers setting forth the needs of teachers in service for new type textbooks and teaching materials on basic educational problems.

10. Panel discussions among foreign-language teachers and teachers in other fields of the curriculum.

11. Cooperative formulation and discussion of recommendations to universities and teacher-training institutions for desirable improvements in professional and preprofessional offerings, standards, and requirements.

12. Maintenance of editorial committees of teachers in service for the review and publication of articles, units of work, bibliographies, or tests contributed by fellow members or research workers in curriculum and instruction in foreign languages.

13. Maintenance of service bureaus for language teachers through which the materials, services, and facilities of different social, cultural, and educational agencies may be made available and coordinated.

14. Sponsorship of summer workshops for foreign-language teachers in collaboration with university specialists in language, literature, and curriculum building.

In recent years the work of the Modern Language Association of Southern California has contributed effectively through its Research Council toward the constructive solution of local foreign-language problems. Valuable aid has also been extended to teachers through the agency of the Service Bureau conducted by the Modern Language Association of Northern and Central California. Similar efforts to meet the professional needs of teachers in service have been made by language teachers in various parts of the country. To date, however, the majority of foreign-language associations and their regional chapters have no long-range plans or definite purposes. Meetings are infrequent and consist for the most part of literary papers by university professors, with little opportunity for participation by teachers in the pooling of constructive suggestions for the solution of the problems facing them in the classroom. The isolation of foreign-language teachers into separate associations has deprived the field of the vitality of such organizations as the National Council of Teachers of English which has been responsible in recent years for the most significant contributions to cooperative curriculum building in the history of American education.[1]   While the foreign-language associations are still competing with each other or defending themselves against the administrators and educators (whose language they do not at times understand any better than these "enemies" at times understand foreign languages), teachers in other areas of the curriculum are finding a common meeting ground in the educational needs of young people, and enlisting the aid of all individuals—parents, laymen, subject-matter specialists, administrators, educational psychologists, curriculum specialists and, at times, even young people and alumni— who can contribute to the development of ways and means for making the schools a more effective agency for the continuous re-creation of life in conformity with democratic ideals.

[1] Among the cooperatively written publications of the National Council of Teachers of English, which have enlisted the immediate participation of successful teachers in elementary and secondary schools, are the following: Nellie Appy, *Pupils Are People*, D. Appleton-Century Company, Inc., New York, 1941, iii + 303 pp. Max. J. Herzberg, *Radio and English Teaching*, D. Appleton-Century Company, Inc., New York, 1941, viii + 246 pp. *Conducting Experiences in English*, D. Appleton-Century Company, Inc., New York, 1939, xvi + 394 pp. *An Experience Curriculum in English*, D. Appleton-Century Company, Inc., New York, 1935, xx + 323 pp. *A Correlated Curriculum*, D. Appleton-Century Company, Inc., New York, 1936, xv + 326 pp. *Educating for Peace*, D. Appleton-Century Company, Inc., New York, 1940, xiii + 275 pp.

The Challenge of the Future.—It is because few teachers of foreign languages have more than a bowing acquaintance with the history and philosophy of education, or educational sociology and psychology, that a common meeting ground for cooperative curriculum planning has been difficult to establish.   Indeed, the very nature of the foreign-language teacher's training has often been such as to make him even less familiar with the history, literature, education, and social problems of his own country than with the grammar and literature of the foreign language that he is teaching.   The problem now facing the teacher of foreign languages is that of rooting his specialty in the soil and climate of American democracy in a joint effort to weld our human heritage from abroad in people, customs, language, literature, and the arts and sciences into a creative and enlightened American way of life that will survive the vicissitudes of international chaos and conserve for war-torn peoples a leadership capable of implanting and nourishing in the minds of men the seeds of a just and lasting peace in which a decent and humane existence is the guaranteed birthright of every child.   Such a constructive conception is economically possible and far less costly than conscripting the best resources in people and property, with which men might create a heaven on earth, to create a hell on earth instead.   If nations can conscript and pool their best resources to make death rain from the skies on women and children in homes, schools, hospitals, and churches, why can they not conscript and pool their resources to eliminate the breeding grounds of disease, crime, poverty, and economic insecurity?   The answer lies in the kind of mind-set that the adult generation of tomorrow receives in the world's schools of today.[1]

[1] The question is not, "Can education be effective," but "How soon will teachers with the courage of their convictions join with others in educating and harnessing the forces which frustrate its work under the cloak of highly sublimated language or hysterical name calling?"

Ruth Hirschmann, "*The Effect of School and Other Selected Social Factors upon the Attitude of High-school Students toward War*, Unpublished Ph.D. dissertation, Stanford University, 1937, 172 pp.   For names and addresses of language-study groups, foreign-language hostels, or centers for accredited study abroad (for teachers wishing to improve their active command of a foreign language) see Appendix, references 113–118, 123–128, 156.

CHAPTER XV

A RECONSTRUCTED CURRICULUM FOR THE FOREIGN-LANGUAGE ARTS

There are one-story intellects, two-story intellects, and three-story intellects with skylights. All fact collectors, who have no aim beyond their facts, are one-story men. Two-story men compare, reason, generalize, using the labors of the fact collectors as well as their own. Three-story men idealize, imagine, predict; their best illumination comes from above, through the skylight.

—OLIVER WENDELL HOLMES

Why People Want Languages.[1]—In any discussion of the place of the foreign languages in American education the curriculum maker is usually confronted with two fundamental questions: "Why should foreign languages be taught at all?" and "Why cannot the presumed social and cultural values of foreign-language study be achieved more readily through the medium of English?" The answer to the first question is simply, "Because people want to study them—often with a view to learning to read, write, or speak them." One need only consider the voluntary enrollments in foreign-language classes in evening schools, private study groups, commercial colleges, and even transient camps for itinerant boys to find evidence of a widespread popular interest which even correspondence schools, newspapers, and radio stations have frequently sought to capitalize. Naturally, this interest varies in intensity with the social and cultural needs stimulated by the local environment—a relatively greater interest in Spanish in Texas, New Mexico, Arizona, and California, in French and Spanish in Ohio and Louisiana, in German in Kansas and Wisconsin, etc. During an era in which all the major languages of the world enter the average home via the short-wave radio, however, this interest is no longer confined exclusively to regions in which the language is spoken by foreign settlers, or to people who patronize the opera or concert stage. The average man is in more intimate contact with foreign languages today than were the elite of a century ago.

The answer to the second question is not that social and cultural values can be achieved best through the study of a foreign language,

---

[1] This question is treated at greater length in Chap. XII.

436

but that a foreign language cannot be learned effectively for any worthy life purpose except in terms of content of social or cultural significance. Skill in reading, writing, or speaking is developed through *practice* in reading, writing, or speaking, and it should not impose too severe a strain upon the imagination to realize that none of these activities is possible in any significant degree without content in the way of ideas or information. To separate language from content is to mistake a copper wire for an electric current.[1] In seeking to develop ability in a foreign language from the start in terms of content and activities chosen for their potential bearing upon the development of attitudes, insights, and appreciations of real meaning for human life in the present and future, frontier workers in the language arts merely recognize the desirability of enriching the contribution of foreign-language study to the basic purposes for which schools exist— the building of cultural unity and the development of wholesome, well-balanced, and socially effective personalities.

The answer to the question, "Why cannot the presumed social and cultural values of foreign-language study be achieved more readily through courses taught in the vernacular?" is, therefore, simply, "They can if you do not want to learn the foreign language." For those students who are not interested, or cannot be interested, in learning to read, write, or speak a foreign language, courses might well be offered in which foreign civilizations and cultures are studied through the medium of the vernacular. Chapter IX deals exclusively with offerings of this type.[2]

What Foreign Languages Should Be Taught?—In view of the widespread interest in foreign-language study, however, adequate opportunities to learn foreign languages in school should be provided wherever the felt needs and interests of the population justify the maintenance of classes in terms of adequate voluntary enrollments.

---

[1] Edward O. Sisson, "Foreign Languages as an Educational Problem," *School and Society*, Vol. 54, pp. 369–375, November, 1941. This dichotomy dates from mediaeval feudalism and Renaissance Ciceronianism when the problem in education was to yield to the educational demands of the rising middle class without "spoiling" them. Learning was made as inaccessible and sterile as possible, locked in foreign tongues, as a means of frustrating reforms through vitalized education. By draining content from literature and language and "disciplining the mind" on form in a vacuum insulated against the life of the day, education was rendered impotent as a constructive means for solving human problems, and reserved as a veneer for the leisure class to wear in its desperate attempt to find some external means of impressing "the aristocracy of blood" upon unbelievers.

[2] See pp. 275–297.

The consensus is growing that increasing opportunity should be afforded by the school[1] for instruction in Scandinavian, Oriental, Italian, Portuguese, or Slavic languages and cultures in localities where the social environment is particularly rich in untapped human resources.

The number of languages that any one school can offer will depend upon the size of the community and the degree to which local interest and need create a sufficient demand. Small schools will probably be obliged to concentrate on the languages and cultures that best serve the educational demands of the vicinity. Accommodation of pupils of varying needs and interests in foreign languages and cultures can be facilitated by means of a flexible arrangement of course offerings and through differentiation of work within each class.

Who Should Study Foreign Languages?—In the light of two decades of experience with prognosis tests, exploratory-tryout courses, and homogeneous grouping on the basis of intelligence quotients, it is evident that effective guidance of students in the choice of language offerings is possible only insofar as provision is made within each course for varying degrees of interest, ability, and need. Certainly a school cannot expect to serve any considerable number of young people if it limits itself to a single type of offering with uniform texts, assignments, and standards for all who enroll. The answer to the question "Who should study foreign languages and cultures?" is, therefore, "All young people whom the school can genuinely interest and accommodate through appropriate differentiation of methods, content, standards, and activities." The degree of ability that a pupil is likely to develop in speaking a language is no more appropriate as a criterion for selecting or rejecting students interested in the foreign-language arts than such a criterion would be appropriate in the field of consumer education in art, music, or science. As in all branches of learning, some pupils develop only an avocational appreciation of the field, others become occasional performers on an amateur level, and a few develop skill sufficient to serve professional needs. This holds true for all areas of human experience and for all subjects taught in school. The foreign languages can claim no dispensation from this rule.

The chief concern of the teacher of foreign languages and cultures should be the enrichment of the program at all levels with stimulating content and activities that have a high surrender value in terms of

[1] "A Report of the Conference on Modern Foreign Languages," Boston, Dec. 28–30, 1940, Secondary Education Board, Milton, Mass., 1941, 32 pp.

insights, attitudes, and human understandings of significance for creative, cultivated living in the present and future; and, wherever community interest in learning to communicate through a foreign language is sufficiently strong to justify foreign-language instruction, to make such vital content and activities the medium for developing and exercising the linguistic abilities from the first day to the last. Among the surrender values that an appropriate choice of content methods and activities can yield are a better understanding of the nature of language, increased ability in English vocabulary and usage, and insights into the lives of people of different racial, environmental, or historical backgrounds. Although the opportunities afforded by foreign-language study for comparing and contrasting different modes of thinking and communicating in language are numerous, relatively few students enroll in foreign-language classes for this purpose. Moreover the evidence tends strongly to support the conclusion that improvement in English vocabulary and usage is achieved far more effectively and economically through orientation courses in language arts of the type described in Chapter X. Similar conclusions hold for the study of foreign civilizations and cultures in English by young people who have no real desire to learn a foreign language.

Fiddling and Quibbling While Rome Burns.—In times of national and international crises, the question confronting all teachers of young people is not "How can I make my students master the minimum essentials laid down in the course of study for this semester?" nor "How can I find students who will learn the minimum essentials without driving me to desperation?" but "How can I use most effectively all that I know, from books and from actual life, about young people, the psychology of learning, the history, sociology, and philosophy of American education, and about foreign languages, literatures, and cultures in providing a fertile educative environment, and the kind of guidance needed to aid young people to grow in ability to live creatively in the kind of world that they must help rebuild for themselves and others?"

Following Blind-alley Leadership.—The well-trained foreign-language teacher has always had much more to contribute to the education of boys and girls than disciplinary grammar courses whose only real value is often merely that of an admission ticket to the university.[1] Indeed, many able foreign-language teachers have long

[1] Thornton C. Blayne and Walter V. Kaulfers, "College-entrance Requirements —Hazards to Curriculum Revision," *School and Society*, Vol. 55, pp. 421–422, Apr. 11, 1942.

resented the servile position to which they have often been relegated by the pressure of college entrance examinations or requirements. Although these external pressures have at times been a godsend to the less competent teachers—a kind of refuge for those who would be at a loss to know what else to do if external requirements were removed— the rigidity of entrance examinations and requirements has often forced the ablest and most creative teachers into slavish imitation of instructional procedures—none too appropriate even for university students, much less so for adolescent boys and girls—and into the use of content and materials which in practice as often defeated the objectives of instruction as they contributed to their realization. For the fact of the matter is that elementary classes in foreign languages in the lower divisions of many colleges and universities have too frequently been placed in the hands of part-time teaching assistants[1]— usually without university rank—young and inexperienced graduate students who almost without exception, if they have any professional ambitions at all, are looking forward to more creative work as university professors, or as instructors in high schools or junior colleges. The realization is growing that there is little hope for the foreign-language curriculum in secondary education if teachers continue to devote all their professional energies to slavish imitation of the least experienced, the worst paid, and the most hamstrung of their colleagues.

New Frontiers for Foreign-language Teachers.[2]—The foreign-language teachers who are making the most effective contributions to education today are finding their opportunities for service in the interests and needs of young people and of the society in which they live. If they look to the university at all, they are more inclined to identify themselves with the role of the abler professors of foreign languages, than with that of their part-time assistants in instruction. They know that very little of the professor's time is devoted merely to drill courses in grammar. His teaching responsibilities, outside research, are primarily in the field of foreign literature and culture. Moreover, many of our most distinguished professors of foreign languages do not hesitate to conduct courses in comparative and world

---

[1] Mark Waldman, "The Selection of Heads of Modern Language Departments, Appointments of Modern Language Teachers and Their Supervision," *The Modern Language Journal*, Vol. XXIV, pp. 510–525, April, 1940.

[2] Henry Grattan Doyle, "A Program for More Effective Teaching of Modern Foreign Languages in the United States," *The Modern Language Journal*, Vol. XXV, pp. 531–534, April, 1941.

literature in translation, in foreign civilizations, and in the sociological implications of language, open to any and all students without foreign-language prerequisites of any kind.[1]

The abler foreign-language teachers possess a versatility comparable in scope and degree to that of the abler teachers of art and music.[2] Just as the well-trained music teacher's competence is not limited to rote instruction in the *do re me fa so* of the various major and minor keys, so the competence of the abler foreign-language teacher is not confined to drill on paradigms or to the translation of proofreading exercises. Within his field of interest and competence lie offerings in world literature in translation, survey courses in national cultures, and orientation courses stressing the social and cultural implications of language and communication in individual and group life. These offerings lie within his field of interest, training, and experience to the same extent that courses in music appreciation, music history, or bands, orchestras, and glee clubs fall within the field of professional interest and competence possessed by the better qualified music teacher. Although these offerings cannot be labeled "foreign language" in the strict subject-matter sense, they may form as appropriate a part of the foreign-language *curriculum* as offerings in music appreciation usually form an integral part of the curriculum in music. Indeed, the precedent for such a broad concept of the foreign-language program is thoroughly established in the practice of foreign-language departments in many of our most reputable universities. The question of terminology here is of importance only among those who adhere to a rigid subject-matter conception of curriculum organization.

World Literature in Translation.—In many secondary schools it is already possible to find—in addition to functional courses in the foreign languages themselves—offerings sponsored by teachers of English or foreign languages in the field of world literature in translation.[3] Planned in joint collaboration with teachers of English, social studies, and such other representatives of the arts and sciences as are interested, these offerings make a real contribution to the basic objectives of education, for the fundamental problems of individual and group

[1] For example, see Walter V. Kaulfers, "Expanding Scope of the Foreign Language Curriculum," *Education*, Vol. LVII, pp. 432–441, March, 1937.

[2] For an overview of the duties and responsibilities of teachers in other areas see Stanford Education Faculty, *The Challenge of Education*, McGraw-Hill Book Company, Inc., New York, 1937, xiv + 471 pp.; pp. 79–276.

[3] For concrete examples, with reading lists, see Ruth Mary Weeks, *et al.*, *A Correlated Curriculum*, D. Appleton-Century Company, Inc., New York, 1936, v + 326 pp.; pp. 132–155.

life are almost universal. With respect to these problems, the most fertile minds of the world have expressed their fears, hopes, ideals, and ambitions in literature.

It would be unfortunate if, through a narrowly restricted program in literature, the youth of our land should somehow gain the mistaken impression that the only creative thinking that has been done by human beings with respect to the problems of life has been confined to the geographical limits of the United States or England. Such a notion would be biased in favor of a very limited portion of our heritage, to the blind neglect of many other cultures that have affected and are continuing to affect the building of America and the progress of civilization in the world. It would make our citizenry either naïvely ignorant or indifferent to the cultures of other peoples with whom we shall henceforth have to live in the community of nations perhaps more intimately than the farmer of a century or two ago had to live with "city folks" in any of our states. And it would hardly be complimentary to the new curriculum in secondary education if the only contact with world literature as the treasury of human hopes, thoughts, experiences, and ambitions should continue to be made by our young people almost exclusively through the movies. Whether world literature is conceived as a strand running though the entire core program of the school, or as a special offering, the teacher with a first-hand acquaintance with one or more foreign literatures and cultures is usually qualified to make a potentially significant contribution.[1]

The usual criticisms[2] against the use of translations obviously do not hold for secondary schools. The number of good translations available is greater than any group of high-school students can read in a year course and, whereas an acquaintance with the original is undoubtedly preferable to an acquaintance with its translation, the point should not be stressed to such an extent that foreign-language teachers must blush to admit that their only acquaintance with the most influential book of all times—the Bible—is based on the reading of a *translation!* If any book comparable to the Scriptures in cultural value is read in translation in the classroom, the teacher as the authority on the original should be able, like the scholarly clergyman, to point out weaknesses or misinterpretations. The difficulty of securing translations of recent books suggests the possibility of using the

[1] Walter V. Kaulfers, "The Contribution of the Foreign-language Teacher," *Curriculum Journal*, Vol. X, pp. 168–171, April, 1939.

[2] Edwin H. Zeydel, "Can We Rely on Translations?" *The Modern Language Journal*, Vol. XXV, pp. 402–404, February, 1941.

creative abilities of upper-division college classes in making translations for school use. At the risk of lese majesty it might be added that if high-school students in Sacramento can learn their Spanish and German through the translation and publication of original documents of historical import from the Bancroft Library of the University of California,[1] then there is little reason why the *flor y nata* of our college youth cannot learn their foreign languages in terms of something more valuable than papers that are dumped into the wastebasket after the grades have been recorded in the professor's roll book.

Although courses in world literature in translation are not recommended as substitutes for foreign-language courses for pupils who have the time and ability to learn to read foreign literature in the original more understandingly than literature in translation, it must be remembered that there are many pupils in high school who even in advanced classes seldom attain a level of competence in language sufficient to permit them to read more than abbreviated adaptations of a very small number of classics—so cut and revised according to basic-vocabulary specifications that it is doubtful if the school editions are as good as the translations—at least the kind of translations that young people usually make with the aid of the vocabularies at the end of the texts. The question at the secondary-school level is probably not that of translations or no translations, but the intelligent use of this resource according to the needs of the pupils, *e.g.*, as collateral means (at the elementary and intermediate levels) for whetting the appetite for the reading of literature in the original in advanced classes, and as a means of developing an appreciation of foreign literature on the part of pupils who are not enrolled in foreign-language courses. Certainly there can be no objection to conducting a course in world-literature in which some pupils read books in the original and others in translation, and each receives credit according to the language in which his reading is done.

This middle-of-the-road attitude toward the use of translations has been cogently expressed by L. Denis Peterkin. Although the writer has reference primarily to classical literature in translation, his

---

[1] *I Knew Sutter*, and *The Narrative of Guillermo Fitch and Blas Piña*, The Nugget Press, C. K. McClatchy High School, Sacramento, Calif., published in 1939 and 1941, respectively. Described in Chap. XIII. The most recent contribution (1942) published by the McClatchy High School is a translation by students from the French of *Six French Letters: John Augustus Sutter to Jean Jacques Vioget 1842–1843*.

observations would seem to apply with equal validity to the modern foreign languages:[1]

I wonder if the method we have been pursuing in the teaching of the classics has not been a putting of the cart before the horse. We have insisted on a study of the language first, and have assumed that an understanding of the peoples and an interest in their achievements would naturally follow. In practice it has worked out that little save language study was done in the schools, and anything further was reserved for college. So the majority of students go to college with but the haziest ideas on all that is implied by Greek and Roman civilization, and in many cases pursue the matter no further. . . . I suggest, therefore, that we revise our present process, and begin with a course in Greek and Roman civilization, either preceding or accompanying the beginning course in Latin in schools. . . . Today in the Loeb and other series, so many good translations are available that it is foolish to ignore this avenue of approach. I am afraid that if we continue our shortsighted opposition to the reading of the classics in translation the time will come when they will be read only in translation.

Sherman P. Young of Drew University has long been actively engaged in successful experimentation with courses of this type. In 1937 he announced,

The classics department will continue to offer full concentration in the original tongues but will recognize the validity of modified requirements permitting the option of courses in translation. . . . The specialist in Greek and Latin should be ready to offer courses in English translation as basic work in his own department. . . . The new courses can open wider horizons of ancient culture than two or three years' halting study of the original tongues has provided. This is the usual testimonial of students who have had the chance to make the comparison.[2]

Comparable offerings in the Germanic and Romance languages are now an integral part of many college and university curriculums.[3] The precedent for literature courses conducted in English has thus been set by some of our leading institutions of higher learning. This fact is significant for secondary-school teachers of foreign languages; for the reasons that justify the introduction of such offerings into the

[1] L. Denis Peterkin, "The Classics in School and College," *The Classical Journal*, Vol. XXXI, pp. 89–98, November, 1935.

[2] Sherman P. Young, "The Classics in Translation," *The Journal of Higher Education*, Vol. VIII, pp. 221–244, 228, May, 1937.

[3] For example, see B. Q. Morgan, *Annual Bulletins of the German Department*, Stanford University, 1938–1942.

college curriculum apply with even greater validity to junior high schools, senior high schools, and junior colleges, where the range of pupil needs, interests, and abilities is in the very nature of things much greater than at the university level.

Life-centered Programs in Foreign Civilizations and Cultures.— In an increasing number of schools it is also possible to find able foreign-language teachers sponsoring offerings, similar to those described in Chapter IX, in whatever foreign cultures are prominently represented in the community, state, or nation. The most significant contribution to education in these cases is in the field of human relations—the development of a rapport with those Americans of foreign birth or extraction who need to be understood appreciatively if they are to be integrally woven into the cultural fabric of a creative and enlightened Americanism. In a sense, the contribution is toward a more wholesome Americanism, not exclusively on the part of so-called aliens or foreigners, but more particularly of our own youth who cannot presume to know their own country's human resources and cultural possibilities, or even to understand their own fellow citizens or parents at times, without understanding the world cultures of which America is both the product and the heir.[1] When offerings in the field of foreign civilizations and cultures are planned in close cooperation with representatives of the social studies, English, the arts, and the sciences they can easily make a direct contribution to one of the basic concerns of education in all times and places—the development of that degree of community in ideals, customs, and mores among the people which is indispensable to the orderly progress of society in the interests of the common welfare.

Indeed, there should even be a place in the curriculum for offerings that might afford young people the opportunity to secure an intrinsically worth-while substitute for an ideally planned period of travel or residence abroad. The incidental reading of a few miscellaneous travel books in satisfaction of a collateral reading requirement in English, or the incidental study of some limited phase of a foreign culture in connection with a "problem" in the social studies is hardly a compensation for the lack of opportunity on the part of the large majority of our boys and girls to share in the benefits of actual residence abroad in educationally profitable circumstances. It is hardly more

[1] Edwin H. Zeydel, "America Needs Us," *The Modern Language Journal*, Vol. XXV, p. 83, November, 1940. Walter V. Kaulfers and Holland D. Roberts, *A Cultural Basis for the Language Arts*, Stanford University Press, Stanford University, Calif., 1937, 115 pp.; pp. 1–14.

significant than the impressive gymnastics in space which some tourists perform when they take a trip around the world in sixty days.

There is need for an acquaintance with our neighbors as *people*— as people very much like ourselves—as homemakers, as inventors, and as producers of art and music, rather than exclusively as abstract illustrations of social "problems," historical "movements," or "institutions." It is probably needless to indicate that such an offering can make a rich contribution to the broadening of the individual's social intelligence, cultural interests, and capacity for appreciation in the many phases of daily life—the moving picture, the radio, the drama, the concert stage, the magazine and daily press, the open forum, the opera, and the lecture and concert platform where the culture of the nations is in almost constant parade. Here again the interested foreign-language teacher can make a significant contribution. Many of them are already successfully engaged in this type of service. (See chart on page 447.)

Life-centered Programs in General Language.[1]—Not least among the contributions of foreign-language teachers to the new curriculum are the insights and appreciations that are being developed through orientation programs in the language arts—programs dealing with language and communication as subtle conditioning factors in the everyday lives of individuals, communities, states, and nations. In spite of its unfortunate origin as a course in baby philology, or as a tryout in a variety of foreign languages, general language has finally become in the hands of the abler teachers a program intimately related to the problems of modern life as they are dependent upon, reflected in, or affected by the very fact of language. In the new type general-language program[2] prominent attention is given to the role of language—native and foreign—in the lives of people and nations. Where the offering has been expanded to include the broad field of communication in modern life, worth-while units dealing with music and art as forms of intuitive or emotional communication have been successfully integrated into the program.

Through these various types of offerings—courses in foreign languages, orientation courses in foreign civilizations and cultures, world literature in translation, and general language, frontier workers in the foreign languages are capitalizing their resources in training and

---

[1] For an overview of recent trends in general language see Walter S. Monroe Ed., *Encyclopedia of Educational Research*, The Macmillan Company, New York, 1941, 1344 pp.; pp. 545–546.

[2] See Chap. X.

Grade Levels

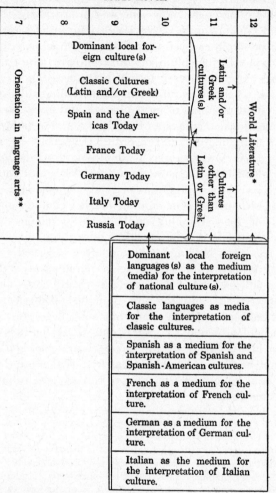

* World Literature: For both juniors and seniors. Offered as a 2-year course when enrollments are adequate. Although the course utilizes primarily literature in translation, students with special competence in reading foreign languages may be encouraged to capitalize their abilities. Courses of this type are offered in the Lincoln School, Teachers College, Columbia University and in the Palo Alto High School, California.

** Orientation in Language Arts: A course stressing appreciations in the growth and development of language, cultural facts of word derivatives, foreign origins of the mother tongue, differences in psychology underlying the foreign languages, etc.

→ indicates the many possibilities of transferring from one type of program to another.

experience in meeting the changing educational needs of young people. The accompanying chart shows one way of organizing these offerings in a six-year (junior-senior high school) program of secondary educa- tion. The possibilities open to particular schools obviously depend upon the type of curriculum organization prevailing in the school system, and upon the degree to which the assistance of teachers in other areas can be enlisted, if not in the actual conduct of courses, at least in the joint planning of units of work and in the cooperative use of such educational facilities as the library, radio, phonograph, slide projector, moving picture, and recording machine.

Despite their lowly origin as dumping grounds for noncollege preparatory "misfits," the new type courses have won for themselves a significant place in the programs of many schools and colleges with gains[1] rather than losses in enrollments in regular foreign-language classes. That more thinking needs to be done on the place and function of these offerings in secondary education, however, is evident from the fact that they are still too often reserved for noncollege preparatory students. It would seem paradoxical, indeed, if such offerings as culture courses and world-literature courses conducted in English (and considered fit for students in our most select universities) should not be considered fit for any but noncollege-preparatory pupils in high school. Is one to understand that "culture" should be reserved in high school only for those who are *not* going to college? Might it not be more reasonable to assume that more than one route to the same ultimate objective may at times be desirable when traffic becomes congested?

= indicates fields utilizing foreign languages as media of instruction. For a description of this type of course, see Chapter VII, pp. 220–260.

— - — indicates fields utilizing English as the primary medium of instruction. It is important to note that such an offering as "France Today" is not a 3-year course. The chart should be interpreted to mean that a student may enroll in the subject for a semester or year at any level from the low eighth through the high tenth grade and follow it with "Spain and the Americas Today," or any other survey course. In large schools in which a wide range of offerings is pos- sible, a student might have the opportunity to enroll for a semester in each of six different fields. For description of courses offered in the San Mateo High School, California, and elsewhere see Chapter IX, pp. 275–297.

[1] F. J. McConville, "Increasing the Social Values of Foreign Language Instruc- tion," *California Journal of Secondary Education*, Vol. X, pp. 573–574, December, 1935. Quoted in Chap. IX. B. Q. Morgan, *Annual Bulletins of the German Department*, 1938–1940, Stanford University, Calif. Meyer Krakowski, "Practice of Correlation between German Language and Other Subjects," *The Modern Language Journal*, Vol. XXIV, pp. 452–456, March, 1940.

New Highways for Increased Traffic.—Less than a generation ago the only road directly connecting the writer's community with San Francisco was a relatively crude and narrow highway known as El Camino Real, or Highway 101. Since then three highways have been constructed to accommodate the rapid increase in traffic. Today, if the motorist wishes to stop at communities along the road, he ordinarily chooses El Camino Real; if he is in a hurry to reach San Francisco, he generally selects the Bayshore Route; if he wishes to entertain guests with a sightseeing trip to the city, he may often prefer the longer but more scenic Skyline Boulevard. Which route he chooses depends entirely upon his needs and purposes at the time. There are no signs saying, "This highway reserved for Cadillacs and Packards, Fords take this detour"—and nothing in the way of social or intellectual prestige is necessarily attached to the choice of one highway in preference to another, yet all roads lead to the same destinations: San Francisco or points north. Indeed, the system is so flexible that it is possible at convenient intervals to cross from one highway to another with little or no sacrifice in time and without serious risk of being stigmatized for making the change.

In pursuance of our American faith in universal education as a means for promoting the continuous recreation of life in conformity with democratic ideals,[1] traffic has increased on the educational highroads even more rapidly than on the highways of life, yet in many communities only one road—the narrow college-preparatory route—to educational goals exists, with the result that a considerable number of learners find the narrow traditional route too circuitous or too encumbered and congested with traffic hazards to make the time and effort of the trip worth while. The effect has been an inevitable waste of educational effort in policing the thoroughfares, in erecting *Stop* and *Go* signals, and in maintaining ambulance patrols—not to mention the social cost in the frustration of human ambitions and hopes.

The Reconstructed Curriculum in Action.—In view of these considerations it is gratifying to note the example that many high schools and colleges are setting in demonstrating the feasibility of providing

[1] Educational Policies Commission of the National Education Association, *Education and Economic Well-being in American Democracy*, 1201 Sixteenth St., N. W., Washington, D. C., 1940, 227 pp. George E. Axtelle and William W. Wattenberg, *Teachers for Democracy*, Fourth Yearbook of the John Dewey Society, D. Appleton-Century Company, Inc., New York, 1940, xii + 412 pp. John Dewey, *Education Today*, G. P. Putnam's Sons, New York, 1940, xiv + 373 pp.

differentiated approaches to educational goals through such new type curriculum offerings as have been discussed in detail in Chapters VII to X of this book.   The leadership of such outstanding universities as Harvard in providing courses in which the linguistic abilities are developed functionally rather than theoretically, and in terms of content that has a wider intellectual appeal than content limited exclusively to belles-lettres, is reflected in the freshman courses entitled "Introduction to France."   The problems around which the courses are organized are as follows:

(A) What is a Frenchman, and who are the French?   (B) French centralization and the role of Paris in national life; (C) looking at a map of France; (D) human life and its different aspects in the territory of France; (E) France as an organized nation—how is the country governed?   (F) national defense and its problems; (G) national education; (H) the French language; (I) landmarks in French culture and civilization.

On the basis of their experience with the course, its sponsors André Morize and Howard C. Rice concluded " . . . we are convinced of one thing: that is, the absolute necessity of an 'Introduction to France.' "[1]

Among other institutions of higher learning that have demonstrated the feasibility and value of providing functional courses in foreign languages are Bennington College, the University of Redlands, Calif., New College, Columbia University, and the University of Chicago.   At Bennington, beginning courses in foreign languages are classified as tool courses:

They are studied not as separate disciplines in themselves, but are undertaken only when there is some specific end to be attained for which they are simply instruments. . . . One of the literature experiments which has worked out best . . . is the study of contemporary literature in the introductory group for freshmen.   Almost all the freshmen are excited about studying Joyce, Mann, Gide, Proust.   These difficult authors rarely fail to prove to the students that they need to study older literature.   It would be a more natural course, according to Bennington, to have Gide, for example, lead a student to Nietzsche, Nietzsche lead to romanticism, and romanticism to classicism, than to begin with the historical survey approach.   In the Senior Division the literature major works out her project under the guidance of her counselor who will see to it that she takes courses which will throw light on her main work, such as courses in foreign literatures, philosophy, and history.   Each student presents a paper before the literature seminar composed of the students and

[1] André Morize and Howard C. Rice, "Introduction to France: an Experiment," *Education*, Vol. LVII, pp. 427–432, March, 1937.

faculty. This paper is based on some phase of her work. After the reading of the paper there is a discussion of content and methods. . . . The groups in French literature are conducted in French, but the emphasis in the teaching is not at all a linguistic emphasis.[1]

At the University of Redlands the integration of French with the study of history and music has met with singular success:

During the last few years we have had real success at the University of Redlands in integrating the work of the second-year French classes with that of some of the other departments. All students in the second-year reading class are requested to do some two hundred pages of collateral reading. Of course the majority of them read the usual novels and plays in French, but anyone with definite interests is encouraged to read along those lines. This idea of cooperation appealed particularly to the professor of European history. We came together, compared our class lists, and made our plans accordingly, selecting periods or topics upon which he wanted reports, suggesting interesting books in French which presented these periods from a new or different angle, details or points of view not readily found in English, and then assigned readings to the different students. The technicality of credit was easily adjusted. . . .

Another field in which cooperation proved well worthwhile was music. Several students have read in Romain Rolland's musical biographies, and others have enjoyed lives of Chopin and Liszt . . . they found in Thierry's *Temps Mérovingiens*, in Michelet's *Jeanne d'Arc*, in an article from a recent magazine, an approach slightly different from that of their textbooks; they found that French was not just a page to study, but a living, breathing language.[2]

Perhaps the most outstanding college program in foreign languages in America was that inaugurated at New College, Columbia University, under the guidance of Peter Sammartino. The following description of the program is quoted not only as a model for high schools and junior colleges, but also as a sensible solution to the transfer problem involved in placing high-school students of different degrees of preparation in appropriate college classes:

To start with, the students are not required to take a language if they don't wish to. . . . So far, all students have taken at least one language. Once having made a choice, there are no requirements as such. If a student has already begun the study of language elsewhere, he is given a comprehensive

[1] Wallace Fowlie, "The Bennington Experiment," *The French Review*, Vol. XI, pp. 93–101, December, 1937.

[2] Dorothy Page, "Experiments in Integration at the University of Redlands," *The Modern Language Journal*, Vol. XXII, pp. 47–48, February, 1937.

examination which includes a conversation test, a dictation test, an aural test, and a standardized test. . . . A pronunciation test is also being tried out. . . . On the basis of these tests . . . the student is placed in that class where he can accomplish most toward the satisfaction of his goal. . . . Once in the course there are no requirements of any sort. No two students do the same work; no two students spend the same amount of time on their work. . . . The idea of failure is non-existent. The student is simply encouraged to accomplish as much as he is able to and to cover that subject matter which he feels is necessary for the attainment of his goal. . . . Periodically, standardized tests are administered so that any readjustment may have at least one objective basis. These results are not used primarily for the score obtained, but for their diagnostic qualities. The independent reading group comes together once a week in order to discuss its readings. . . . Opera projects are very successful. For instance, if *Faust* were the opera, the German instructor would explain the literary sources, the music instructor would talk on the music, the French instructor would go over the libretto, and the students themselves would sing some of the arias.[1]

The significance of the first-year program in French and Spanish at the University of Chicago lies in its successful approach to the reading objective through the use of content from the start which has an intimate bearing upon the student's avocational or vocational interests. Teachers of junior-college or upper-division high-school classes will find the classified reading lists exceedingly helpful in selecting books in other areas besides belles-lettres, *e.g.*, music, history, art, archaeology, etc.

Although the number of colleges and universities that have expanded their reading programs in beginning and elementary classes to include more than the traditional classics is relatively small, the desirability of providing a more varied and better balanced reading diet is now generally recognized by all institutions of higher learning. Professor Edward F. Meylan of the University of California wrote in 1937,

In my estimation neither the non-college-preparatory nor the college-preparatory group should be sacrificed. . . . Specifically, I mean that in the first two years of language the textbooks used, including the basic text, should have a cultural background. . . . New second-year reading courses were established about five years ago. Any student with two years of high school language may take these courses, the aim of which is the proper understanding of a foreign text, and in which grammar is studied only incidentally. Also

<hr>

[1] Peter Sammartino, "Foreign Language Work at New College," *The Modern Language Journal*, Vol. XIX, pp. 271–277, January, 1935.

students with less than two years of a foreign language may repeat part of this work without loss of units toward graduation. This last answer shows that, as far as the transfer of High School students to the University is concerned, practically all difficulties have been eliminated. There remains, however, the problem of what should be done within the High School.[1]

In the field of literature in translation the work of Stanford University has been outstanding,[2] e.g.,

The Romantic Movement.—Lectures in English giving a comparative view of romanticism in European and American literatures; assigned readings in English, French, or Spanish to meet the needs of the student. Open to graduates and undergraduates.

The Contemporary Theater in France, Spain, Italy.—Lectures in English, readings, and reports. . . .

In the field of survey courses in foreign civilizations, open to all students without foreign-language prerequisites of any kind, the work of the foreign-language departments of Stanford University, the Glendale Junior College, and the City College of Los Angeles has been particularly successful. With few exceptions, these elective offerings have often drawn larger enrollments than basic courses without decreasing the usual enrollment in regular language classes. Thus the introduction of survey courses in English boosted the enrollment in the department of Germanic languages at Stanford in 1938 to its highest figure in five years—despite the downward trend in other institutions.[3]

The Movement toward Curriculum Revision and Differentiation.— In keeping with these trends, school systems such as those of Detroit, Los Angeles, New York City, San Mateo, Phoenix, San Francisco, Tulsa, and Seattle have experimented successfully with various kinds of new type offerings in foreign cultures and general language while revising their regular foreign-language courses. Thus in an increasing number of secondary schools today the student interested in foreign literatures and cultures, who does not have the time or ability first to master a foreign tongue, has his choice of a variety of offerings suited to his needs and purposes quite on a par with such of his fellow students as may wish to approach the same objective via the foreign-language

[1] Quoted by permission from a letter to the author. See A Visit with a Teacher of First Year Foreign Language by Walter V. Kaulfers, School Publication, 314, Los Angeles City School District, June, 1938, 23 pp.; pp. 20–21.

[2] See The Challenge of Education, Stanford Education Faculty, McGraw-Hill Book Company, Inc., New York, 1937, 471 pp.; p. 260.

[3] See references in footnote, p. 285.

route.   Indeed, it is not unusual for some students to enroll in both types of courses—especially if their major interest in school is in the foreign languages, or if a latent interest in foreign languages is aroused through the medium of the orientation courses in general language or foreign cultures.

As in every field of human life, any deviation from the traditional is bound to meet with opposition.   That is why new type offerings that withstand the test of criticism in practice often prove so superior to the traditional that they tend ultimately to react favorably upon a reevaluation of the conventional programs.   Sometimes the main highways of the past are even relabeled "alternate" routes.   An increasing number of foreign-language teachers, like the majority of our citizens, realize that whenever traffic increases as much as 600 per cent, one traditional route to any destination will rarely suffice.   The exigencies of modern economic and social life have increased the traffic on the educational highroads as on the thoroughfares of the world outside.   The conclusion is obvious:

Old roads must be paved and broadened, and new highways must be built.

CHAPTER XVI

ROOTING THE FOREIGN-LANGUAGE CURRICULUM IN AMERICAN LIFE AND CULTURE

THE ROLE OF THE FOREIGN-LANGUAGE TEACHER DURING THE NATIONAL EMERGENCY AND AFTER

The genius of a people does not exist exclusively in originality, but in distinguishing the best wherever it is to be found and perfecting its adaptability.

The mere teaching of tolerance is not enough, for who enjoys just being "tolerated"?

At the entrance to New York harbor stands the symbol of American democracy, the Statue of Liberty. On a bronze plaque at its base is the following inscription—a poem by Emma Lazarus.

THE NEW COLOSSUS
Not like the brazen giant of Greek fame,
With conquering limbs astride from land to land,
Here at our sea-washed sunset gates shall stand
A mighty woman with a torch, whose flame
Is the imprisoned lightning, and her name
Mother of Exiles. From her beacon hand
Glows world-wide welcome; her mild eyes command
The air-bridged harbor that twin cities frame.
"Keep, ancient lands, your storied pomp!" cries she
With silent lips. "Give me your tired, your poor,
Your huddled masses yearning to breathe free,
The wretched refuse of your teeming shore.
Send these, the homeless, the tempest-tost to me,
I lift my lamp beside the golden door."

By people such as these has America been created from the first landing of the Pilgrim fathers to the present day. The entire group of the foreign born and their children constitute one-third of the total population of the United States.[1] Out of a total population of about 7,500,000, over 73 per cent of the people of New York City are either of foreign birth or of foreign origin. America is indeed the heir to

---

[1] Leonard Covello, "Language as a Factor in Integration and Assimilation," *The Modern Language Journal*, Vol. XXIII, pp. 323–333, February, 1939.

the cultures of all ages and all peoples. The potential resources lying fallow in the cultural background of the large numbers of our population of foreign birth or descent could, if effectively capitalized rather than neglected or suppressed, be made to yield a New World culture of infinite variety and fertility. This Old World heritage is as rich as any endowment with which nature has favored us in the form of natural resources, and its effective utilization is destined to grow daily in significance.

Unfortunately, in the past our approach toward the building of a dynamic unified Americanism has not always been the most tactful or constructive, either psychologically or socially. Not infrequently it has been negative in effect—at times even chauvinistically suppressive.[1] Rarely has it sought to capitalize the social heritage that we have received from all parts of the world. Instead, we have often cast aspersion upon those who left foreign lands to become Americans. At times we have gone as far as to invent deprecative names for these groups—derogatory epithets that unfortunately have found their way into the vocabularies of our youth. The result of such antisocial name calling has not infrequently been an enforced introversion of our foreign population into isolated colonies,[2] with a consequent increase in the problem of achieving American unity and a destructive loss to the development of a creative Americanism. Yet, by virtue of its diverse social composition, its youth, and its size in area and population, the United States is probably as vitally in need of a unifying cultural objective as any country of the Western Hemisphere. In

[1] Unfortunately, we do not change human behavior merely by appraising or condemning it in terms of our ideals, but by enabling people to experience more satisfying alternatives. Without constructive alternatives, condemnation merely makes what is condemned "unseen," and therefore more difficult to change. To wit: during prohibition, drinking in public places was almost invisible. Today, immorality is practically *unseen*. If this is progress, then it is also progress that leads to clever hypocrisy and to the growth of a social, political, and economic underworld, not to mention "escapist" personalities among the so-called cultured groups.

[2] Sociologists and social-psychologists have called attention to the close correlation existing between degree of race prejudice and the degree to which the nationality group or culture group is strong enough to be a controlling or competitive economic factor in the life of the community, or to inconvenience local arrangements without profit. Where the social group can readily be distinguished by its physical characteristics, speech habits, mannerisms, or dress, the development of prejudice under stress of economic competition is usually rapid and more intense. When such distinguishing features are lacking, and no competition exists in business or the labor market, prejudice is less pronounced or deep-seated.

the days of sparse populations and unlimited opportunities for social and economic expansion, the need for such an integrating factor was not always apparent; but in our era of increasing world interdependence, it grows daily in social significance. Europe and Asia adjoin our doorstep. We are an indissoluble part of the world.

Does not all this have meaning for the teacher of foreign languages, literatures, and cultures, in a period of national and international confusion when the building of a dynamic unified Americanism is so urgent? Those who think it does are seeking to make the building of America the dominant emphasis in their teaching. The contents of books, the topics for discussion, and the activities of the classroom are being selected with this immediate aim in mind as a criterion for building the program of instruction from the very first day to the last.

One public-school class conducted under the auspices of the Stanford Language Arts Investigation started its first day of beginning French with a simple talk by the teacher *in the foreign language* on the contributions of France to science and invention which are found in almost every home and community in America: the automobile, the sewing machine, the camera, the moving picture—to mention but a few of the many.[1] The aim here was the development of an appreciation, through the medium of the foreign language, of our own people of French descent in terms of the things that we and the world owe to their native land. *Language and culture were not separated.*[2] Cultural content of significance in terms of the objective served as the medium in and through which the language abilities—reading, writing, and speaking—were developed from the start. Problems of usage were solved as they were encountered by the pupils, and revealed in their *own* questions or needs when they were preparing to communicate something of interest and significance to an audience. Later this group made a survey of the community and produced in French an illustrated booklet under the title "What Our Community Owes to France." Citizens of French origin or descent were invited to the class, not to give formal talks but to answer questions about life abroad that interested the group, or about the difficulties that they experienced in becoming Americans. These questions were prepared by the students in French and were answered in the language with the aid of advanced students and the teacher as interpreters when needed. Activities, of

[1] See Chap. III, pp. 106–107.
[2] Walter V. Kaulfers and Holland D. Roberts, *A Cultural Basis for the Language Arts*, Stanford University Press, Stanford University, Calif., 1937, 115 pp.; pp. 1–14.

which these are but samples, served more to create a desire to learn French better than any amount of formal drill with lifeless content material could ever achieve. For, what is the use of developing a foundation for anything if in the process we crush all subsequent desire to build anything of significance upon it?

A recent study of the continuance of high-school foreign languages in college shows that out of a class of 35 beginning students not more than three ordinarily continue the same language in college, and not more than *one* majors subsequently in the language which be began before entering the university. To what extent, then, are high-school courses in foreign languages college preparatory in any significant sense?[1] The last stronghold of the conservative forces in foreign-language teaching—preparation for college—is, to say the least, rather shaky. The implications are obvious. Either teachers are not building a foundation in interest sufficient to create a strong desire on the part of students to continue their language study (even on the part of those whom they pretend to serve), or they are not sufficiently concerned with removing the mechanical obstacles[2] that prevent the continuance of the study. Moreover, the successes that they achieve are often attained over the dead bodies of the rather large number of students who fall by the wayside.[3]

The difficulty seems to lie in the absence of a clear conception of the role that foreign languages, literatures, and cultures can play in American education. The assumption that a foreign language is a skill to be developed through drill without regard for the purpose which the skill is to serve is dangerous. Certainly the experience of those European countries in which the foreign languages have been taught the longest and to the most "select" people do not arouse much confidence in the belief that the mastery of any language will in itself contribute much toward understanding and good will. Perhaps the

[1] E. F. Engel, "Why Do Not College Students Continue the Foreign Language Begun in High School?" *The Modern Language Journal*, Vol. XVI, pp. 500–503, March, 1932. Walter V. Kaulfers and Vera E. Whittmann, "Continuance in College of High School Foreign Language," *The School Review*, Vol. XLVIII, pp. 606–611, October, 1940. Vera Whittmann, "Are College Preparatory Foreign Languages Justified in Our Curriculum?" *The Modern Language Journal*, Vol. XXV, pp. 470–472, March, 1941.

[2] "Long interval between high-school language course and college course" was listed by Engel among the chief reasons why 80 per cent of 666 college students failed to continue the language begun in high school. See Engel, *op. cit.*

[3] Adolph Klein, "Failure and Subjects Liked and Disliked," *High Points*, Vol. XXI, pp. 22–25, January, 1939.

contribution of foreign-language study abroad could have been greater had the languages been learned from the start in and through content dealing with the lives and problems of foreign peoples in relation to the pupils' own native land. To learn a language through sterile content, and later to apply it exclusively to the reading of a few classics which afford no insight into the lives of foreign peoples as they are today, or into the ways in which past generations have influenced our *present* modes of thinking and living, is not likely to have more than a parlor-culture significance.

The foreign-language teachers of America have the rare opportunity of tying the study of foreign languages, literatures, and cultures into our own national and community life, and to make the study serve not merely as a parlor-culture veneer, but as a dynamic influence in welding our human resources and our cultural heritage in peoples, customs, mores, and the arts into a creative and enlightened Americanism. International understanding can with profit to ourselves begin right at home. By learning to understand our own people of foreign birth or extraction we can better learn to understand ourselves, and in the process of so doing we can bring foreign languages, literatures, and cultures, both past and present, into closer rapport than if we started thousands of miles away and stayed there. For what nation can presume to be a creative influence for world peace if it cannot even tolerate or understand the foreign-born citizens in its own midst?

No subject is more in need of a secure mooring in American education than the foreign languages. Unless they can find a more secure anchorage, they will remain adrift without any more tenable footing than that which is temporarily afforded by such very debatable justifications as vocational utility, mental discipline, improvement in English vocabulary and usage,[1] or the satisfaction of college entrance

---

[1] Ruth Byrns and V. A. C. Henmon, "Entrance Requirements and College Success," *School and Society*, Vol. XLI, pp. 101–104, Jan. 19, 1935. Arthur F. Engelbert, "A Modern Language Program in the Modern Curriculum," *School and Society*, Vol. XLVII, pp. 83–85, Jan. 15, 1938. John J. Weisert, "Foreign Languages as Mental Discipline, A Survey," *The German Quarterly*, Vol. XII, pp. 61–70, March, 1939. Harl R. Douglass and Clifford Kittelson, "The Transfer of Training in High School Latin to English Grammar, Spelling, and Vocabulary," *Journal of Experimental Education*, Vol. IV, pp. 26–33, September, 1935. Joseph E. Barber, "Finds English Grammar of No Benefit to Pupils of Foreign Language," *Nation's Schools*, Vol. XVII, p. 25, January, 1936. For a close parallel from experimental data obtained from Latin classes see Willard W. Beatty, "What Is the Future of Latin in the American Secondary School?" *Progressive Education*, Vol. XII, pp. 329–332, May, 1935.

requirements which are subject to change.[1]   Unless foreign-language teachers can develop a mere creative conception of their role in society, the foreign-language curriculum is in danger of becoming an omnibus course consisting of a potpourri of grammar, a few dabs of so-called cultural material sandwiched in occasionally in English, plus a great deal of pin-wheel activity in the foreign language—all motion without direction.   To make the study of foreign languages, literatures, and cultures serve as a dynamic unifying influence in the building of a richer American life and culture is not inconsistent with any traditional objectives of education in the foreign languages.   It merely means putting these objectives to *use* as more than decorative preambles or window dressings which bear little or no relationship to the activities of the classroom or the contents of the textbooks.[2]

It means teaching languages for a life purpose, not the mere theory of language.   It means teaching language from the very start

[1] In 1937 only half of the American colleges and Universities required foreign-language work for admission.   See Millard E. Gladfelter, "Status and Trends of College-entrance Requirements," *The School Review*, Vol. XLV, pp. 737–749, December, 1937.

[2] The marked difference between the actual practices of foreign-language teachers and the values claimed in their objectives has led many people to wonder by what metaphysical process of metamorphosis these verbally conceived ghosts could be made to materialize.   See Paul B. Diederich, "Report of the Panel Discussion on the Appraisal of Teaching for Cultural Objectives," *The French Review*, Vol. XI, pp. 471–477, May 1938:

"Here was the audience [annual convention of the American Association of Teachers of French in Chicago] in full flight from one of the most widely advertised objectives of the study of French.   To avert panic, it was explained that members of the panel were only indicating what these 'cultural objectives' meant to them individually and what kind of questions they asked to find out whether they were getting anywhere with their pupils."

See also Charles E. Young and John Guy Fowlkes, "To Teachers of Foreign Languages and Professors of Education," *School and Society*, Vol. XLII, pp. 231–233, Aug. 17, 1935:

"Though many fail to admit it, the problem of the function of foreign language in education is one of the roots, perhaps the taproot, of the dilemmas, dissents, minority reports, round robins, and what not.   That this function can remain the same in times that are fluid as it was in times that were relatively static is out of the question.   Equally absurd are the claims for foreign language advanced by language enthusiasts.   Making claims for any subject that are out of all line with [actualities] merely renders the subject ridiculous.   That has been done for foreign language, and critics have not failed to make the most of it. . . . The teacher shares in making [the curriculum] only when he so conducts his classes that his subject commends itself to the public.   Tradition is a powerful force in education, and thus far foreign language is coasting comfortably along with tradition.   To count too much on tradition is likely to prove a mistake."

not as an end, but as the medium for the attainment through meaningful content of objectives that have some direct bearing upon human behavior in the present and future. When the activities in and through which language is acquired have some discernible relationship to the lives of the pupils or to the environment in which they live, language has meaning and the resulting incentive to learn to read, write, and speak better gives such theoretical attention as is needed for improvement in grammatical usage a more patent *raison d'être*. The pupils then see some sense to it. The questions that they ask concerning the *whys* and *wherefores* of certain constructions and usages will indicate their interest in language and their need for guidance in learning it and communicating through it.[1] The fundamental principle is to help young people "to find something interesting and worthwhile to say and then build an audience situation that will give them reasons for saying it. The form of their productions is to be thought of only in judging the effectiveness of *what* is said and to *whom*."[2]

The reading, writing, or translating of such meaningless material as is still too often found in beginning readers and grammars is for most people an unprofitable use of time. Although made material adapted to the language abilities of the pupils has to be used at the start, it does not have to be material devoid of information or ideas significant in terms of a basic social objective. It can just as easily be made material which, through the ideas and information it develops in simple language, contributes to an appreciation of our foreign-born citizens and neighbors in terms of what makes them what they are and in terms of what they and their native lands have contributed to the building of America and of the world. Unless this is done from the very start, before the large majority of the students have discontinued the study of foreign languages, it will not be impossible, for example, to find students who have studied Spanish two, three, or four years who still harbor the same prejudices and intolerant attitudes toward the citizens of Mexican descent in their own community, and

[1] This viewpoint has been cogently expressed by Harold Benjamin in *Phi Delta Kappan* for November, 1941: "The logical and scientific tradition of foreign language teaching seems to clog the wheels of learning. . . . Yet there are teachers in growing numbers who, while recognizing the value of grammar and using it as an appropriate instrument of learning, know that language is made by the needs of men and grammar is made by professors. . . . They believe in the teaching of grammar *only after* there exists in the learner's experience something upon which grammar can be based."

[2] Holland D. Roberts, presidential address for the National Council of Teachers of English, Buffalo, Nov. 25, 1937.

toward their own Mexican classmates in school, which they had before beginning the study of the language.

Clearly there is no integrity and certainly no depth to the study of a people—their language or their civilization—that operates only in a vacuum by remote control. It is a tinsel culture which, guidebook in hand, reveres the Parthenon and disdains the sons of the men who died at Thermopylae. Whatever is worth giving our lives to in public education must be rooted in a deeper regard and friendliness for the man who is our fellow townsman and our neighbor. Otherwise, we shall merely be augmenting the ranks of those who "time and time again will prate of their country, but have no time to waste on their countrymen."[1]

Culture becomes a mockery when used merely as a decoration to conceal an eyesore, or to counteract the stench of reality with highly perfumed phrases. As specialists in the chief medium of mental suggestion, language, teachers of the arts of communication can well afford to give attention to the uses to which their specialty is put. Human hopes and ambitions can be frustrated by the sword; but this method is hardly less treacherous than smothering them to death with Judas kisses or sanctimonious phrases uttered with the same degree of sincerity that the Devil quotes Scripture.

The functional study of foreign languages, literatures, and cultures can yield outcomes beyond mere skills in language or information. It can lead to the development of a generation of citizens who will be active, creative participants in open forums, library study groups, travel clubs, community-theater projects, civic organizations, art, music, and literary clubs, or national and international societies for the constructive solution of basic human problems. It can lead to a generation of citizens who are not mere curators of culture but producers of it. For the culture of an age is never to be measured exclusively by its heirlooms, but also by its own original contributions to the welfare and progress of mankind. Over a century ago Horace Mann emphasized this dynamic interpretation of education for culture:

We want no men who will change like the vanes of our steeples, with the course of the popular wind; but we want men who, like mountains, will change the course of the wind. We want no more of these patriots who exhaust their patriotism in lauding the past; but we want patriots who will do for the future what the past has done for us.[2]

[1] José Hernández, *El Gaucho Martín Fierro.*
[2] Mary Mann, Ed., *Life and Works of Horace Mann*, Walker, Fuller and Company, Boston, 1867, Vol. II, Lectures on Education.

Obviously, the development of a creative and unified Americanism can be approached via more than one route.   Teachers of English, the social studies, the arts, and the sciences can make as great contributions as teachers of the foreign languages.[1]   Indeed, unless the efforts of *all* teachers in *all* fields are consciously focused in this direction, the contribution of education is likely to be inadequate in terms of the need.   Daily it is becoming more apparent that unity amid diversity can exist only insofar as all groups of citizens feel that they have something to contribute to the common good—something that others appreciate.   Name calling, browbeating, and deprecative epithets can silence people and drive them into isolated, mutual-consolation societies, but beyond securing outward conformity through lip service, these negative devices rarely beget anything but negative results. Psychologists, sociologists, and frontier workers in education are beginning to realize that no aspect of American culture is sufficiently broad to include all the rest.   The ideals that constitute the Plymouth Rock tradition in American education constitute a body of ideals worthy of perpetuation as the unifying factor around which American life and culture can be integrated.   In a figurative sense, they may serve as a magnetic core to draw out the best that lies fallow in the human backgrounds of our citizens who are not of New England descent.

No one who has stood beside Plymouth Rock, however, will be foolish enough to maintain that it is large enough to support all that is now America.   It cannot presume to support the culture that became ours along with the purchase of Florida or Louisiana, or the annexation of those vast territories which (politely speaking) we obtained from Mexico.   In the southwest, the Spanish colonial tradition is far stronger than the New England influence, and in the Middle West, the Germanic, Scandinavian, and French cultures have left an

[1] For examples of the work of teachers in other areas of the curriculum see Council against Intolerance in America, *An American Answer to Intolerance*, Teacher's Manual No. 1, Junior and Senior High Schools, Experimental Form, 1939, Lincoln Building, New York City, 116 pp.; Los Angeles City School District, *World Cultures:* Ninth- and Tenth-year Social Studies, School Publication No. 283, 1936, 158 pp.   Rachel Davis-Dubois, *Adventures in Intercultural Relations*, A Manual for Secondary School Teachers, Progressive Education Association, 221 West 57th St., New York, 1938, 215 pp.   Reports of the Stanford Language Arts Investigation, *Foreign Languages and Cultures in American Education*, Vol. II, McGraw-Hill Book Company, Inc., New York.   In press.   Alfred Kirshner, "A Scientific Approach to the Development of Tolerance," *High Points*, Vol. XXIII, pp. 11–12, September, 1941.   Also see Appendix, references 182, 183, 189, 195, 202, 204.

indelible impress.   Los Angeles has a Mexican population equal to
that of the third largest city in Mexico, and New York City houses
more Italians than Rome, the largest city in Italy.   Facts such as
these underlie American democracy.   That is why it is unsound
psychology so to stress a limited portion of our heritage as to make
large numbers of our people think that it is useless to try to become an
American unless they had the discretion before birth of choosing
English-speaking ancestors.

The teaching of history and of English literature in our schools
has often succeeded less in developing a creative and enlightened
Americanism, in the building of which young people feel qualified to
participate, than in making thousands of young people ashamed of
their parents.   In days of social and economic insecurity, when front-
line defenses are no stronger than the morale that prevails at home,
teachers of foreign languages, literatures, and cultures can play an
important role in helping to build an understanding of the meaning of
America among natives and nonnatives in terms of the human backgrounds of her people.   It is well that everyone love the "rocks and
rills, the woods and templed hills," but it is also important that everyone show a genuine appreciation for those things which did not already
exist in even greater splendor before the first white man set foot on
American soil.   After all, it is a people who make a culture, and the
most significant things about people are often things one cannot touch.

In dealing with young people in a community it is important to
realize that youth draws its inspiration from the possibilities of the
present and the prospects of the future, while age nurses its memories
of the past.   The creative teacher is one who can help young people
to build castles in the air, and then, utilizing the best resources of the
past and present, to *put foundations under them*.   She is one who can
lead her children to realize that there is no final America yet, that our
national life and culture are still in the building, and that in the
development of this culture we can all be builders together.   She will
say to her young people: "Here is the finest that the genius of mankind has so far produced.   It is well that we understand and appreciate
this heritage.   It is still more important that we *use* it in building
our own contribution to the progress of mankind.   For nothing has
been done so perfectly that it cannot be done better.   The finest
music has not been composed even by Wagner or Bach; the greatest
plays have not been written even by Shakespeare; the best pictures
have not been painted even by Raphael—the best we have today,
perhaps; but greater plays can still be written, finer music can still be

composed, and better pictures can still be painted—and, what is more, the world *needs* them, and they *will* be produced, someday by somebody, and why not by some of *you?*

"For Beethoven was the son of a drunken father and of a consumptive mother, herself the daughter of a cook. Schubert was the son of a peasant father and of a mother who had worked as a maid. Faraday, one of the greatest scientists of all time, was born over a stable, his father an invalid blacksmith and his mother a common drudge. Shakespeare was the son of a bankrupt butcher and a woman who could not write her name. That is why we must everlastingly believe in democracy, in ourselves, *and in those who have faith in us.*"

Somehow, when people go to school, they often obtain the foolish notion that the world is all finished, that everything is settled and done, that the finest conceivable art has already been achieved, that the last word on making a living or how to live had already been said, and that there is nothing left for anybody to do but to sit down and memorize it or appreciate it. And of course it is all a lie! Apparently this false notion is by no means rare; for one still finds many citizens who spend all their energies embalming the past and themselves with it, rather than utilizing its contributions for the enrichment of life in the present and future. We are still training too many of our youth to be museum curators and undertakers, knowing full well that culture is a living thing that thrives only through the creative genius of the race. That is bad for any society. What has youth to live for, except for its own selfish ends, if everything in the world is settled and finished? What is to become of democracy if it closes the door of opportunity to do better?

We must enable young people to travel the road of American culture as far as we have built it; but having directed their gaze to the past, we must make sure that they turn their eyes to the future; and we must encourage them to continue the building of the highway as their opportunity to make a contribution of their own to human culture. Given this guidance, they will discover for themselves that this opportunity is not a task, but a creative use of human endeavor whose satisfactions can lie not only in its achievements, but also in the joy of the doing itself. This is our creative role as adults in life and as teachers of the language arts.

For America's road to culture is still the broad road of democracy. The supreme law governing traffic by this route is the old maxim, "The welfare of *all* the people is the highest law." Therefore this road can never be just a military road or a commercial highway. The origin of the road is in the past, but it does not rise from the tomb. It is peopled with the living, not haunted by the dead, and its goal is not the grave.   It is the highway of youth facing the morning star and the sunrise.   It is *America's* road to culture and of all who are ashamed to die until they have won "some victory for humanity."

APPENDIX A

PROBLEMS AND ISSUES FOR DISCUSSION

The aim of discussion is not to win arguments, but to find solutions—to generate *light*, not heat.

Chapters I and II

1. Some courses of study have advocated the use of the direct method throughout the program (in order to eliminate as far as possible the use of English in the classroom) and at the same time have set up increased knowledge of English as an *objective*. Can such a course of study be considered sound in the light of the objective evidence yielded by numerous investigations in the field of the transfer of training?

2. "Disciplinary values—by which most teachers seemingly mean habits of application, persistence, attention to detail, neatness, mental perspicuity, and the like—depend far more upon the *method* of instruction employed than upon the subject itself. Consequently, the claims of any field to a place in the curriculum on the basis of outcomes which represent little more than by-products of a *method* of instruction can hardly take precedence over offerings which yield significant outcomes in their own right."

   a. How valid is this viewpoint?
   b. What implications does it have for the postulation of "disciplinary" or transfer values as *objectives* in foreign-language teaching?
   c. How sound is it to found a curriculum on dubious values?
   d. Is it conceivable that there may be other outcomes of more widely acknowledged significance which deserve stress as aims in preference to such highly debatable issues as disciplinary or transfer values?

3. It is frequently asserted that childhood is the best age level for learning a foreign language.

   a. How do the supporters of this view justify their position when in reality they usually allow junior-high-school pupils at least *four or five semesters* to cover work equivalent to only *one semester* in college?
   b. To what extent is this view substantiated by the findings of Thorndike, Cheydleur *et al.?*[1]

[1] No controlled experimental study has revealed significant differences in achievement of young people (age 10 to 18) and adults (age 20 to 60) in foreign-language work when method and time factors were held constant. See Irving Lorge, "Psychological Bases for Adult Learning," *Teachers College Record*, Vol. XLI, pp. 4–12, October, 1939. Edward L. Thorndike *et al.*, *Adult Learning*, The Macmillan Company, New York, 1928, x + 335 pp.; Chap. IV. F. D. Cheydleur, "An Experiment in Adult Learning in French," *Journal of Educational Research*,

c. What implications does the fact that junior-high-school pupils are given at least *four* times as long as university freshmen to cover the same ground have for the *appropriateness* of the content and methods commonly employed in teaching lower-division high-school classes? Is it possible that there are other phases of language, or other learning procedures, than those prevailing today, which might prove better adapted to the adolescent's level of insight?[1]

4. What implications do recent technological advances in radio communication have for the importance of stressing the oral and aural aspects of language? For popular interest in learning to speak the language or to understand the spoken language?

5. What aural aids in the teaching of pronunciation do teachers now have at their disposal which were either unknown or too costly for school use at the time the "Coleman Report" was compiled (1924–1928)? See Appendix, references 107–110, 112, 123–128, 190, 196, 197.

Chapter III

6. A questionnaire yielding returns from 273 college graduates[2] who had studied foreign languages indicated that only 5 per cent were interested in, or felt

---

Vol. XXVII, pp. 259–279. See also Bruno Shoeman, "Teaching Foreign Languages in Adult Education," *The Modern Language Journal*, Vol. XXIV, pp. 44–52, October, 1939.

[1] Even the feeble-minded often learn to pronounce and converse in foreign language classes taught by nonacademic methods—an ability often considered impossible to achieve in conventional courses. See Paul F. Angiolillo, "French for the Feeble-minded: An Experiment," *The Modern Language Journal*, Vol. XXVI, pp. 266–271, April, 1942. A. F. Tredgold, *Mental Deficiency*, 5th ed., William Wood & Company, New York, 1929, Chap. XV: "Idiots Savants."

For methods of teaching foreign languages to elementary-school and primary-school children see Elia Boudreaux, "Some Aims and Methods in Teaching French in the Elementary Schools in Louisiana," *The Modern Language Journal*, Vol. XXIV, pp. 427–430, March, 1940. Idabelle Yeiser, "The Why and How of French to Little Children," *The Modern Language Journal*, Vol. XXIII, pp. 591–593, May, 1939. Hosea Phillips, "Foreign Languages in the Grades in Louisiana," *The French Review*, Vol. XIII, p. 71, October, 1939. James W. Bishop, "Observations on Teaching Elementary Pupils Spanish," *The Modern Language Journal*, Vol. XXV, pp. 138–139, November, 1940. Hélène F. Farrère, "The Creative Teaching of French," *The French Review*, Vol. VI, pp. 114–122. Reports successful experiments in teaching French to children in such a way as to capitalize creative impulses. Helen B. Rosgate, "French and Young Children," *The French Review*, Vol. II, pp. 173–174, December, 1934. Methods and devices for teaching French to children four to eight years of age. E. M. Stokes, "The Teaching of French," *The Modern Language Journal*, Vol. XVII, pp. 80–82, February, 1936. A French program for children of five or six years of age.

[2] Russell J. Fornwalt and Herbert W. Rogers, "An Investigation of the Values of Modern Foreign Language Study in College," *The Modern Language Journal*, Vol. XIX pp. 161–164, December, 1934. For more recent supporting evidence see Clara Altman, "Foreign Languages in College Curricula," *School and Society*, Vol. L, pp. 542–543, Oct. 21, 1939.

any need for, composition (*i.e.*, translation from English into the foreign language, etc.). What implications do these findings have for foreign-language instruction—content, methods, instructional emphasis, etc.?

7. It is an accepted principle of learning that knowledge which is constantly used, and facts of experience which are frequently relived, are not readily forgotten. In third- and fourth-year high-school classes, when time is devoted for the most part to reading in the foreign language and to the discussion of books read, pupils often become exceedingly "rusty" in their "grammar" (*e.g.*, ability to translate correctly from English into the foreign language, to recite conjugations of irregular verbs, to recall the rules for the use of the subjunctive, etc.). Indeed, teachers often consider it necessary to devote at least one day a week in such courses to grammar review lest the pupils forget the work of the first two years entirely. What implications do these facts have for

    a. The need for a thorough preliminary grounding in theoretical grammar as a basis for learning to read?

    b. The amount and value of the grammar often taught in the first two years?

8. Extensive research in the field of curriculum and instruction in English indicates that drill in diagraming, parsing, recitation of paradigms, identification of grammatical elements, etc., does not improve the adolescent's ability to use English accurately in his own oral or written speech.[1]

    a. What implications do these findings have for content and methodology in foreign languages?

    b. In the light of these findings, to what extent can curriculum specialists be expected to appreciate the claims of foreign-language specialists that the study of foreign languages increases pupil knowledge of English grammar?

    c. How valuable is a knowledge of grammatical nomenclature per se considering the other educational needs of youth, and the proved inability of the large majority of adolescents to apply grammatical abstractions in their own writing and speech?

    d. Who talks about "substantives," "finite verbs," "conjugations," etc., besides schoolteachers?

Chapters IV to VI

9. It is frequently asserted that foreign literature cannot be appreciated in translation. By some this argument is seemingly advanced as the chief reason for studying a foreign language.

    a. If this argument is valid, why is translation so frequently employed when other means, more economical of time and effort, are available for testing comprehension?

    b. If the argument is valid, to what extent is it justifiable to resort to translation as a means for *facilitating* comprehension?

    c. To what extent does the argument hold for adolescents—thirteen to nineteen years of age?

[1] For parallel findings in the foreign language see Frederic D. Cheydleur, "The Relationship between Functional and Theoretical Grammar," *The Modern Language Journal*, pp. 310–334, January, 1932.

10. Even those high-school pupils who are destined to have the opportunity some day to travel in foreign countries are not likely to be able to remain abroad for more than a few weeks or months. Indeed, foreign-language teachers (who seldom have more than eight to ten weeks during the summer in which to travel) often find it convenient to enroll in standard "tours," conducted by English-speaking guides, in order to cover the country with a minimum of expense. In view of these circumstances is a command of the language per se of more importance as a preparation for foreign travel than a foreknowledge of the cultural backgrounds of the people in the countries to be visited?

11. What type of content for reading and discussion can serve appropriately both as a preparation for travel or as a substitute for it, without sacrificing growth in ability to read, write, or speak a foreign language?

12. International understanding is often postulated as an objective of foreign-language teaching. Observe that in Europe this ideal is far from realized despite the fact that in most secondary schools six to nine years of foreign language study has been required for generations.

> *a.* To what extent can this objective be realized through the study of language as a body of organized linguistic material? Through the translation of a few approved classics?
>
> *b.* What changes in content or instructional emphasis are required if this ideal is to be achieved at least partly under the conditions prevailing in the average American high school?

13. The "Coleman Report" recommending *reading* as the central linguistic objective of foreign-language teaching was based on questionnaires sent to teachers between 1924 and 1926 when the radio was in the earphone stage and local programs were accompanied with as much static as short-wave broadcasts from Russia or the South Pole. Is it possible that a new survey of teacher opinion would yield the same results today?

Chapters VII and VIII

14. What philosophy of language underlies the demonstration lesson in Chapter VII? Can you cite specific procedures in the lesson that illustrate the principle of inductive learning? Of learning to do by doing? Of instrumental grammar when the need arises? Of reference to experience? Of the whole before the part? Of motivation through audience situations? Of differentiation? Of integration with life interests and objectives?

15. What is the central guiding objective of the teacher in the demonstration lesson? How are skills in reading, writing, or speaking made to serve as contributory or enabling objectives to this central purpose?

16. What evidences of growth in attitudes or linguistic abilities are revealed in the Epilogue? Compare the remarks of Pauline, Henry, Bill, Allen, and Reginald at the end of the semester with their remarks at the beginning of the course.

17. How can a teacher with limited facility in speaking a modern foreign language develop the skill necessary to conduct occasional lessons of the type illustrated in Chapter VII?

18. To what extent is the teacher in Chapter VII an educational "faddist"? A specialist in "soft pedagogy"? Who shall decide what is a "fad" or a "frill"? By what standards?

19. Can you cite any evidence in the demonstration lesson that the course work will be integrated with out-of-school life through extracurricular activities?

20. How can teachers enrich their courses through integrative extracurricular activities without suffering nervous breakdowns from overwork? How can teachers improve their ability to speak and understand a foreign language while teaching it?

Chapters IX and X

21. Recent announcements of leading universities indicate that survey courses in foreign literatures and cultures, open to all students regardless of previous preparation in foreign languages, are now among the standard offerings of foreign-language departments.

    a. By what right can such offerings be considered as "foreign language"?

    b. On what grounds is their incorporation into the university foreign-language curriculum justified, *i.e.*, how would university professors sponsoring such courses answer objections that these courses belong more properly in the department of English, social studies, or art?

    c. To what extent could the arguments in defense of these offerings be capitalized to justify the introduction of similar courses (adapted to the adolescent's level of insight) in the public secondary school?

    d. Would such offerings fall more nearly within the field of interest, preparation, and experience of foreign-language staffs than courses in ancient history, English, or physical education which foreign-language teachers are often obliged to take over in order to complete a teaching load?

22. Travel abroad is often considered to have significant values; yet the traveler on returning home is not ordinarily expected to be able to speak any foreign language fluently, nor even to know specific facts concerning the population, industries, or history of the places visited.

    a. What values, then, must those who favor travel have in mind when they recommend it as an educationally desirable form of experience?

    b. If foreign travel is truly of as great educational value as popular opinion supposes, why would it not be within the legitimate province of the secondary school to offer a program of educative experiences, simulating those of a *well-planned* trip or period of residence abroad— especially when the large majority of pupils are not likely to have the opportunity to visit foreign lands?

23. In secondary schools where new type survey courses in foreign literatures and cultures, paralleling those of many universities, have been introduced, the classes have often been reserved for pupils of "lesser academic ability." On what logical grounds can offerings considered worth-while for upper-division and graduate students in our leading universities be considered suited only for the less intelligent and near morons in high school? What are the *real* reasons for this practice?

24. Many citizens who confess that they have "forgotten" their foreign languages nevertheless defend the traditional curriculum on the grounds that the courses yielded real cultural benefits in the way of appreciations of foreign peoples

—their customs, contributions to world progress in the arts and sciences, etc. If these appreciations are acknowledged to be of such educational significance in afterlife that even as by-products they seemingly justify two to three years of work devoted primarily to the mastery of grammar, is there room in the curriculum for an additional type of offering in which these appreciations are made paramount? In view of the limited period for which many adolescents are likely to continue in school, would such an offering yield more socially significant outcomes than a preparatory course devoted for the most part to the mastery of language as a tool?

25. "As Latin forms the root of approximately 50 per cent of all English words, it is entirely natural that a mastery of Latin could improve one's understanding and utilization of this fraction of the English language. However the Beaver County Day School at Chestnut Hill, Massachusetts, has shown through several years of teaching that a greater power with the English vocabulary can be obtained in one year through a vitally interesting and intensive study of all English roots."

  a. What bearing do these findings have upon the validity of postulating "increased knowledge of English vocabulary" as an *objective* of modern-language teaching? Are such contributions as foreign-language study makes to ability in English sufficiently great to warrant consideration as being more than *by-products*?
  b. Can instruction in any area be justified solely in terms of by-products that can be achieved as effectively, and perhaps more directly, in other fields or in other ways?
  c. To what extent are foreign-language specialists inclined to attempt such a justification?

Chapter XI

26. Of every 100 pupils who enter the high school, only one in four is likely to enter the university, and only one in twelve to graduate from an institution of higher learning. Of 100 pupils beginning a foreign language in high school, only one in ten continues the same language in college, and only one in a hundred becomes a college major in the language. In view of these facts, on what grounds can exclusively college-preparatory work be justified in the *lower division* of the high school? What is a *practical* solution?

27. It is frequently asserted that university entrance requirements necessarily limit foreign-language offerings in the secondary school to the conventional type of course. What are the objections to reserving the preparatory training for seniors to the end that the freshmen and sophomores may be free to do more functional types of work? What factors basically determine whether a pupil will continue in college or not? Is a boy or girl likely to work enthusiastically in a strictly college preparatory course if the chances for his being able to afford a college education are very remote or uncertain?

28. The results of experiments with new type courses show very clearly that pupils can learn to read a foreign language at least as effectively (and in most cases more effectively) as pupils in conventional courses, without the conventional preparatory emphasis on grammatical principles of usage. In many colleges and universities, upper division and graduate offerings are conducted in English, and both term papers and theses are acceptable if written in the mother tongue—a reading knowledge of the foreign language being the only ability seemingly pre-

requisite for advanced work. In other institutions of higher learning, class lectures are in the foreign language, but students are permitted to conduct their discussions in English, and to submit both theses and term papers in English. On what basis can such institutions justify entrance examinations in grammar and composition?

29. The public secondary school now enrolls from 50 to 90 per cent of all children old enough to attend. Of this number, nearly half are enrolled in foreign-language courses. To what extent can a uniform preparatory course, standardized on the needs and abilities of students of a generation ago (when the public high school enrolled less than 20 per cent of the chronologically eligible population) serve as wide a range of social and intellectual backgrounds and prospective vocational destinations as prevail at the secondary-school level today? What is a *practical* solution?

Chapters XII and XIII

30. Because of the increasing complexity of life in contemporary society and the growing complexity of the curriculum itself, guidance is generally taken for granted as one of the primary responsibilities of education at the adolescent level. If helping students to find themselves with respect to the in-school and out-of-school world in which they live is a fundamental obligation of the secondary school, to what extent is the failing of pupils by teachers justified in the elementary stages of any course for which adequate bases for the prediction of prospective success do not exist? (Note that extensive research shows that an actual tryout of pupils in foreign-language work is the only safe means for the discovery of abilities and latent interests.) What implications do the limitations governing the prediction of pupil achievement in foreign languages have for beginning courses with respect to choice of content, methods, standards, organization of classes, etc?

31. Studies of withdrawals from foreign-language classes (dropouts and failures) show a relatively high rate of elimination among boys as compared with girls. Although a balance of sexes ordinarily prevails in beginning classes, girls as a rule far outnumber the boys in advanced classes.[1] What implications do these facts have for the foreign-language program in locations where such a situation obtains?

 a. Is such a differential elimination inevitable? To what extent?
 b. Would it be to the advantage of the foreign-language curriculum, as a potential field of cultural influence in American education, to consider modifications directed toward a more favorable adjustment of content and learning activities to the needs and interests of boys?
 c. How can such a reorientation of the instructional program be accomplished?

32. Repeated investigations of the effect of foreign-language study upon English usage have shown that the benefits are negligible.

 a. In the light of these findings what justification is there for postulating increased knowledge of English grammar as an *objective* of foreign-language teaching?
 b. What proportion of the students who enroll in foreign-language courses have this purpose in mind?

[1] L. G. Osborn, "Relative Difficulty of High-school Subjects," *School Review*, Vol. XLVII, pp. 95–100, February, 1939.

Chapters XIV to XVI

33. If a policy of limiting foreign-language enrollments specifically to "college material" is favored, then

> a. By what means can the vocational and academic futures of pupils be prophesied?
>
> b. On what basis can aptitude for the study of foreign languages be predicted? (Note that the best prognosis and intelligence tests available to date assure accurate predictions of prospective success for less than 30 per cent of the cases.)
>
> c. How can such a policy be reconciled with the widely accepted concept that orientation and guidance are among the most significant functions of education, especially at the junior-high-school and lower-division high-school levels?
>
> d. How can such a policy be reconciled with the democratic tradition of American secondary education in which the high school is conceived as "the people's college"?
>
> e. How valid is it to refuse pupils admission to "required courses"?

34. During the first year from 20 to 40 per cent of high-school freshmen who enroll in beginning foreign-language courses drop out (or fail) owing to apathy toward the work or to inability to profit therefrom. At the close of the second year only 17 per cent of the pupils who begin a foreign language elect to continue the study. By the beginning of the fourth year, 97 per cent of the pupils have dropped out of foreign-language classes.

> a. What implications do these facts have for the appropriateness of content and methods conventionally employed in high-school foreign-language courses?
>
> b. What grounds do those who oppose the introduction of more liberal differentiated offerings have for insisting upon a rigid maintenance of the *status in quo?*
>
> c. If the traditional foreign-language course were the only type of offering that the secondary school could provide, what per cent of the total high-school enrollment, as now constituted, could be expected to profit from the work, *i.e.*, actually attain outcomes directly associated with the objectives commonly set up for the program?

35. It is frequently asserted that foreign-language courses should be limited to pupils who are definitely "college material."

> a. What ultimate implications would the inauguration of such a policy have for foreign-language enrollments, and for the range and number of course offerings that would be possible in the average high school?
>
> b. How would this policy eventually affect the position of the foreign-language curriculum, broadly conceived, as a field of cultural influence in American education? Why would such a policy eventually lead to social and economic inbreeding?

36. The average high school enrolls less than 500 pupils, of whom nearly half drop out before the beginning of the junior year. What implications does this fact have for

    a. The number of foreign languages that the average high school can offer?

    b. The number of *years* of any one foreign language that can be offered in separate classes?

    c. The number of different teaching preparations that are likely to fall to the high-school instructor?

37. In conformity with our democratic tradition in education, high-school attendance has now been made compulsory in practically every state—in many localities up to eighteen years of age. On what basis, then, is it justifiable to organize and conduct curriculums (especially in fields possessing potential values of acknowledged educational significance for all interested youth) in such a way that only the relatively small fraction of the total secondary-school population which is especially academically minded can profit therefrom? Who need public education most, the pupils who are favored with educated parents and favorable home environments, or the pupils who lack these advantages?

APPENDIX B

SAMPLE TRANSPOSITION EXERCISES

The following exercises illustrate contextual learning of grammatical variables in a conversational setting, and *can be transposed as a whole to any tense or person* without distorting the meaning. *A* and *B* represent two different speakers. The exercise may be used as an auxiliary device in learning irregular verb forms. The exercise should be dramatized as a dialogue between two people—*A* and *B*— in different persons and tenses.

Exercice de prononciation: Des Verbes irréguliers

Read or recite in (1) French and (2) English, as a dialogue between *A* and *B*, in any person, number, or tense suggested by the teacher. Only the underlined words may require changes.*

    A. 1: Quand allez-vous au travail?

    B. 2: Je pars de la maison vers sept heures.

    A. 3: Y allez-vous (marchez-vous) à pied, ou prenez-vous l'autobus?

    B. 4: Je mène ma propre automobile.

    A. 5: À quelle heure en revenez-vous?

    B. 6: J'en reviens (j'en retourne) à quatre heures.

    A. 7: Et puis, qu'est-ce que vous faites?

    B. 8: Après d'être arrivé chez moi je me divertis un peu en jouant au tennis.

    A. 9: N'êtes-vous pas fatigué quand vous rentrez chez vous?

* Future and conditional constructions will often require translation as the future or conditional of probability in English.

B. 10: Naturellement je n'en peux plus (je meurs presque de fatigue) mais c'est la récréation en plein air qui vaut mieux.

A. 11: Vous avez raison. À propos, qu'est-ce que vous savez de la première de "Hernani" de Victor Hugo? Qu'est-ce que les critiques en disent (écrivent)?

B. 12: Ils en disent qu'elle vaut la peine d'être vue. La Compagnie Royale la représente (produit).

A. 13: Elle monte (croît) rapidement en faveur, ne le croyez-vous pas? Combien de représentations y en a-t-il par jour?

B. 14: Il y en a deux, je crois. Ne voulez-vous pas m'accompagner à celle de ce soir? Les portes s'ouvrent à sept heures précises. Nous pouvons aller ensemble.

A. 15: À coup sûr, j'ai envie de la voir.

B. 16: Néanmoins (cependant) comme vous savez (voyez, pouvez-vous imaginer) de ce que les journaux en disent, la compagnie ne couvre pas ses dépenses.

A. 17: Eh bien, à quelle heure venez-vous chez moi? Connaissez-vous mon quartier? Vous rappelez-vous mon adresse?

B. 18: Je me la rappelle parfaitement. J'y vais à sept heures au plus tard: il faut que nous allions de bonne heure.

A. 19: Pour acheter les billets d'avance? Alors, en ce cas-là, je dois écrire un cheque et le faire changer à la banque.

B. 20: Très bien. À bientôt.

A. 21: À ce soir.

Ejercicio de transposición—verbos irregulares

Read or recite in (1) Spanish and (2) English as a dialogue between two people, in any person, number, or tense suggested by the teacher. Only the underlined words may require changes.

A. 1: ¿Cuándo va Ud. a la obra?

B. 2: Pues, salgo (parto) de mi casa a eso de las siete.

A. 3: ¿Anda Ud. o va (sube) Ud. en camión?

B. 4: No; porque llevo (traigo) mi coche conmigo.

A. 5: ¿A qué hora vuelve (regresa) Ud.?

B. 6: Vuelvo (regreso) a las cuatro.

A. 7: Y luego, ¿qué hace Ud.?

B. 8: Juego al tennis por cosa de hora y media.

A. 9: ¿No está Ud. muy cansado al volver a casa?

B. 10: Como no; casi me muero de cansancio; pero más vale el ejercicio al aire libre.

A. 11: Tiene Ud. razón. A propósito, ¿qué sabe Ud. del estreno de "La Malquerida" de Benevente? ¿Qué escriben los críticos de él?

B. 12: Dicen lo usual; que es digno de verse. La Compañía Real lo produce (representa).

A. 13: ¿Cuántas funciones hay por día?

B. 14: Ponen dos. ¿No quiere Ud. acompañarme a la función de noche?
Las puertas se abren a las siete en punto. Podemos ir juntos.

A. 15: Claro. Me da ganas de verla. Oigo hablar tanto de "La Malquerida."

B. 16: Sin embargo, como ve Ud. de lo que dicen los periódicos, no cubren
los gastos.

A. 17: Bueno, ¿a qué hora viene Ud. por mí?

B. 18: A las siete a más tardar.

A. 19: Bien, hasta luego.

B. 20: Hasta luego.

APPENDIX C

SAMPLE FOUNDATION EXERCISE

This illustrates semiinductive self-instructional procedures for the contextual
learning of grammar on the basis of need.

LAVARSE LAS MANOS

[To wash one's (self the) hands]

PART I

Observe carefully the forms, meanings, and position of the underlined Spanish
words in the following model sentences. Then read the notes below, and *on a
separate sheet of paper* do the exercises in Parts II, III, and IV according to the
instructions.

¿No se ha lavado Ud. las manos?	Haven't you washed your hands?
—(Yo) no me he lavado las manos.	I haven't washed my hands.
¿No se han lavado Uds. las manos?	Haven't you washed your hands?
—(Nosotros) no nos hemos lavado las manos.	We haven't washed our hands.

NOTES: The *-se* on the end of *lavarse* (to wash one's self) means that the verb
is *reflexive,* and that the words (reflexive pronouns) *se, me, nos,* etc., should be
used with the verb, as shown in the model above.

2. With "*-se* verbs" (reflexive verbs) the forms (possessive adjectives) *your,
my, our,* etc., are ordinarily not used in speaking of parts of the *body* or articles of
clothing.

3. *Mano* (hand) is feminine in Spanish, because the word *manu(s),* from which
it was borrowed, is feminine in Latin.

PART II. OBSERVATION EXERCISES

Reread carefully the model sentences and the notes; then complete the following exercises, substituting for the ? whatever word or information is needed to
make the sentences true.

1. In the model above, the reflexive pronouns are *me, nos,* and ?.

2. *Lavarse* is a reflexive verb because it ends in ?.

3. In the model, the words (reflexive pronouns) *se, me, nos*, come   ?   the complete verb (where   ?).

4. In the model above, *no* comes directly   ?   the reflexive pronouns (where ?).

5. *Se* may be used with *él, ella*(*s*), *Ud., ellos*, and   ?.

6. *No nos hemos lavado las manos* really (literally) says "We haven't washed ourselves   ?   hands."

7. *¿No se han lavado Uds., las manos?* really (literally) says "Haven't you washed   ?   the hands?"

8. With reflexive verbs, the words (possessive adjectives) *your, my, our*, etc., are ordinarily not used in speaking of parts of the   ?   or articles of clothing.

9. Hasn't John washed his hands?   ¿No   ?   ha lavado Juan las manos?

10. The following words are in the *wrong* order: ¿se no ha Ud. lavado?   The first word in the correct order should be *no*, and the last word should be   ?.

PART III. RECONSTRUCCIÓN

Rearrange the words of the following exercises in the proper order, so that they will form correct sentences in Spanish.   Remember that in questions the words (subjects) *Ud., él, ella, Juan*, etc., go *after* the verb form that ends in *-do*.

> *Given:* ¿se no ha Ud. acostado *todavía?* *
>   Haven't you gone to bed (retired) *yet?*
> *Say:* ¿No se ha acostado Ud. *todavía?*

1. ¿no se ha Ud. levantado *todavía?*
   Haven't you got up *yet?*
2. pero sí me no bañado he *todavía.*
   Yes, but I haven't bathed *yet.*
3. nos no rasurado hemos nosotros *todavía.*
   We haven't shaved *yet.*
4. dientes no los limpiado se Ud. ha.
   You haven't cleaned (brushed) your teeth.
5. cabellos peinado no he me los.
   I haven't combed my hair.
6. ¿se no han quiénes vestido *todavía?*
   Who haven't dressed *yet?*
7. ya no hemos los pulido nos zapatos.
   We haven't shined our shoes yet.   (Begin sentence with *Ya no.*)
8. el Juan José y peinado pelo no se han.
   John and Joe haven't combed their hair.
9. ya no han se desnudado.
   They haven't undressed yet.   (Begin sentence with *Ya no.*)
10. ya no secado me las manos he.
    I haven't dried my hands yet.   (Begin sentence with *Ya no.*)
* Put all *italicized* words at the end of the sentence.

PART IV. RECONSTRUCCIÓN Y ACABAMIENTO

The words of the following exercises are in the wrong order, and the reflexive pronouns *se, me, nos*, are missing.   Rearrange the words to form complete sentences when the forms *se, me, nos* are inserted in their proper places just before the complete verb. Observe that only verbs whose infinitives end in -*se* (as for example *lavarse*) require the reflexive pronouns *se*, *me*, or *nos*.

Examples

desayunarse: a. ¿no han Uds. desayunado todavía?
                 Haven't you had breakfast (breakfasted) yet?
            a. ¿No *se* han desayunado Uds. todavía?
But, *almorzar:*   b. y yo él almorzado no hemos.
                 He and I haven't had lunch (lunched).
            b. *El y yo no hemos almorzado.*
despertarse: 1. los despertado muchachos no han todavía.
                 The boys haven't awaked yet.
dormir: 2. ¿han Uds. bien dormido?
                 Have you slept well?
acostarse: 3. niños han los acostado.
                 The children have gone to bed (retired).
llamar: 4. ¿alguien llamado ha?
                 Has somebody called?
comer: 5. Ud. y él comido han no todavía.
                 You and he haven't eaten yet.
quitarse: 6. la quitado ha americana.
                 He has taken off his coat (jacket).
desayunarse: 7. Rosa yo y hemos no desayunado.
                 Rose and I haven't had breakfast.
lavar: 8. ¿he no lavado vajilla yo la?
                 Haven't I washed the dishes?
desvestirse: 9. ¿han Uds. desvestido ya?
                 Have you already undressed? (Begin sentence with Ya.)
estar: 10. ¿enferma estado su ha madre?
                 Has your mother been sick (ill)?

Recheck your work: There is a mistake somewhere if you have more than *five* sentences with the reflexive pronouns *se*, *me*, or *nos* in Part IV.

APPENDIX D

SAMPLE INTEGRATIVE UNITS ILLUSTRATING LANGUAGE LEARNING IN LIFE CONTEXT

DIE MUSIK ALS SPRACHE[1]

PART I

Für den Komponisten[1] ist die Musik eine Ausdruckweise,[2] genau so wie das pathetische[3] Sprechen für uns ist. Der Dichter zeigt seine tiefsten Gefühle in besonderen Ordnungen von Wörtern, die wir Dichtung nennen. Die Formen, die er braucht, helfen ihm zu sagen, was er meint. Der Maler braucht allerlei Farben,

[1] Designed as an illustrated reading unit for use in first- and second-year German classes, Menlo School, Menlo Park, Calif., by Dorothea Lange and Walter V. Kaulfers, 1939.

einen Baum zu schildern, und der Verfasser[4] braucht beschreibende[5] Wörter, die sorgfältig[6] geordnet sind.   Folglich finden wir, dass der Künstler immer eine besondere[7] Technik braucht, um sein Gemälde zu bilden.   Der Komponist legt seinen Baum mit Tönen aus.   So hören wir das Knarren[8] eines alten Eichenbaumes,[9] der von einem starken Wind gepresst wird.   Oder vielleicht will der Komponist uns eine ruhige Landschaft beschreiben, wo es kein menschliches[10] Leben gibt—nur das Wandern der Schafe.[11]   So haben viele Komponisten versucht, Geschichten zu erzählen oder die Landschaft zu schildern durch die Musik und sie können unsere verborgenen[12] Gefühle mit der wunderbaren Harmonie der Töne zum Ausdruck bringen.

[1] composer	[5] descriptive	[9] oak tree
[2] method of expression	[6] carefully	[10] human
[3] emotional	[7] special	[11] sheep
[4] author	[8] creaking	[12] hidden

PART II

The instructor will play a few compositions for you without telling you their names.   Each of the selections will deal with one of the subjects in the list below. While the first selection is being played, try to decide with which subject it deals. Then write the number 1 in the space before it.   When the second selection is played, write the number 2 opposite the proper subject, etc.

_____*a. Ein behendes* Menuett:* Viele Männer und Damen sind am Hof† versammelt‡ und tanzen vornehm.   Wir sehen das Bild eines Hofs mit seiner Festlichkeit.‖

> * light   ‡ are gathered
> † court   ‖ festivity

_____*b. Ein schlimmes Gewitter** wütet; nachdem es die Schale† seines Zorns‡ über die Welt ausgegossen hat,‖ wird es schwächer und schwächer.   Bald ist eine Stille überall.   Auf Regen folgt Sonnenschein.

> * thunderstorm   ‡ wrath
> † vessel   ‖ has poured out

_____*c. Ein Wiegenlied,** das schläfert das Kind ein.

> * a cradle song

_____*d. Ein Walzer:* Hier ist eine romantische Szene, wo höfliche Männer und Damen in bunten Kleidern zu dem lustigen* Rhythmus des Tanzes sich drehen.†   Es ist in einer alten Stadt, die für ihre Liebeslieder,‡ Serenaden und Walzer berühmt ist.

> * merry   ‡ love songs
> † whirl

_____*e. Ein Trauermarsch;** er ist langsam und ernst.

> * funeral march

_____*f. Das fröhliche Schweizer* Leben* wird geschildert† und wir hören Kuh-glocken,‡ Schweizer Hörner und die lustige Tanzmusik der Bauern.‖

* Swiss	‡ cow bells
† is pictured	‖ of the peasants

_____*g. Ein Schwert* wird gemacht:* Ein eingeschrumpfter† Zwerg‡ arbeitet in einer Höhle und schmiedet‖ das Schwert mit kräftigen Schlägen.¶

* sword	‖ forges
† wizened	¶ blows
‡ dwarf	

_____*h. Ein königlicher,* feierlicher Zug*† führt den König durch das Gedränge‡ zu der Krönung‖ mit Pomp und Glanz. Er wird von Musikkapellen begleitet.¶

* regal	‖ coronation
† procession	¶ is accompanied
‡ crowd	

Part III

Suggested Recordings

Mozart: *Symphony No. 40, in G minor*, third movement, Minuetto, (K550), Victor, Serge Koussevitzky, London Philharmonic Orchestra.

Beethoven: *Symphony No. 6, in F major* ("Pastoral"), Victor, Arturo Toscanini, The British Broadcasting Company Symphony Orchestra.

Brahms: *Wiegenlied*, recorded by Cortot at the piano, Victor 1271.

Strauss: *Wine, Women and Song; Wiener Blut; Artists' Life Waltz*, Decca 1776–77.

Beethoven: *Symphony No. 3, in E flat major* ("Eroica") 5-8, *Marcia funebre;* Victor, Willem Mengelberg, Philharmonic Symphony Orchestra of New York; or Wagner, *Siegfried's Funeral March.*

Happy Swiss Memories, folk song, Victor.

Wagner: Siegfried—Synthesis, *The Forging of the Sword;* Victor, Leopold Stokowski, Philadelphia Orchestra.

Meyerbeer: *Coronation March*, Victor, Philharmonic Symphony Orchestra of New York. See also Appendix, reference 84.

Part IV

Write a few short descriptions in German of compositions by German composers for which recordings are available, and then try out the descriptions on your classmates to see if they can identify the pieces.

AN ILLUSTRATED READING UNIT IN FRENCH, FEATURING MUSIC BY FRENCH COMPOSERS[1]

Part I. Identification

The instructor will play a few compositions for you without telling you their names. Each of the selections will deal with one of the subjects in the list below.

[1] Designed for use in first- and second-year French classes, Menlo School, Menlo Park, Calif., by James S. Neill in collaboration with Walter V. Kaulfers, 1941. For bibliography of recordings, see p. 483.

While the first selection is being played, try to decide with which subject it deals. Then write the number 1 in the space before it. When the second selection is played, write the number 2 opposite the correct subject, etc.

_____a. À minuit La Mort appelle les squelettes* pour une danse. Ils dansent toute la nuit, jusqu'au chant du coq.†

> * skeletons   † crowing of the cock

_____b. L'amant se trouve aux champs. Il entend les bergers qui chantent l'un pour l'autre. Mais la nuit vient et alors un orage éclate.*

> * bursts

_____c. Une imitation du sifflement* d'une toupie† qui tourne.

> * whirring   † top

_____d. Un après-midi de dimanche dans une gaie ville alsacienne.* Deux amants se promènent à la campagne . . . une composition calme et joyeuse.

> * Alsatian

_____e. L'apprenti sorcier* ordonne à son balai† de se tenir debout‡ et d'apporter l'eau pour le bain du sorcier. Mais l'apprenti oublie le mot magique et le balai commence à inonder‖ la maison. Saisissant une hache,¶ l'apprenti fend en deux** le balai, mais maintenant les deux parties s'enfuient†† pour chercher l'eau. Enfin il faut que l'apprenti implore son maître à l'aider.

> * sorcerer's   ¶ axe
> † broom   ** splits
> ‡ to stand on two legs   †† scurry off
> ‖ flood

_____f. À travers des nuages qui pirouettent* nous voyons bien de gens qui dansent. Peu à peu les nuages se dispersent et l'on voit les gens plus clairement. Une scène de la cour impériale environ 1885.

> * whirl

Part II

_____a. C'est un thème de beauté calme et pastorale, qui devient de plus en plus triste et finit sur une note sinistre.

_____b. La mort est un ménétrier qui convoque les squelettes. On entend le tic-tac des squelettes et un autre thème, symbolique* de la nuit et de la solitude du tombeau.†

> * symbolical   † grave

_____c. Les bouffonneries bizarres de l'apprenti sorcier après s'être sauvé* du service de son maître sont dépeints d'une manière pittoresque.

> * after escaping

___*d*. Les violons dépeignent le sifflement d'une toupie, accompagné d'une mélodie de danse, fournie* par les bois† et les pizzicati.‡

> * furnished   ‡ pizzicato violins
> † woodwinds

___*e*. L'auteur rappelle les souvenirs d'Alsace en montrant le calme d'un joyeux après-midi de dimanche.

___*f*. Premièrement exécutée à San Francisco le 28 octobre, 1921, le compositeur a desiré faire "l'apothéose* de la valse." Il a voulu exploiter la danse viennoise de Johann Strauss.

> * apotheosis, deification

Part III. Suggested Recordings

Saint-Saëns: *Danse macabre*, Symphonic Poem (Op. 40), Victor, Record 14162, Stokowski, Philadelphia Orchestra.

Berlioz: *Symphonie fantastique* (Op. 14), Album M-662, Third Movement, Bruno Walter, Paris Conservatory Orchestra.

Bizet: *Jeux d'enfants*, Ballet Suite (Op. 22), Victor, Record 12374, Artal Dorati, London Philharmonic Orchestra.

Massenet: Suite, *Scènes Alsaciennes*—Third Movement, *Sous les tilleuls*, Victor, Record 36026, Victor Concert Orchestra.

Dukas: *L'Apprenti sorcier*, Victor, Record 7021, Toscanini, Symphony Orchestra of New York.

Ravel: *La Valse*, Victor Records 7412–7414, Koussevitsky, Boston Symphony Orchestra. See also Appendix, reference 84.

Part IV

Write a few short descriptions in French of some compositions by French composers for which recordings are available, and then try out the descriptions on your classmates to see if they can identify the pieces.

APPENDIX E

A MINIMUM KEY LIBRARY
FOR MODERN FOREIGN-LANGUAGE TEACHERS

A. A Must List for Teachers

1. *The Modern Language Journal*, The National Federation of Modern Language Teachers, 450 Ahnaip Street, Menasha, Wis.

   Articles on curriculum, instruction, and research in modern foreign-language teaching, book reviews, notes and news, meetings of associations, departments on radio, visual aids, etc.

2. Coleman, Algernon, and Clara Breslove King: *An Analytical Bibliography of Modern Language Teaching*, Vol. I, xiii + 296 pp., 1933; Vol. II, xviii + 561 pp., 1938, University of Chicago Press, Chicago.

   Abstracts, with evaluative comments, of 1,695 articles, tests, books, monographs, pamphlets, and bibliographies published between 1927 and 1937. Classified for ready use. An indispensable reference for all teachers.

3. COLE, ROBERT D., and JAMES B. THARP: *Modern Foreign Languages and Their Teaching,* D. Appleton-Century Company, Inc., New York, 1937, xxi + 640 pp.

    Excellent chapters on *realia,* tests, and measurements, new type courses, and reference materials.

4. HANDSCHIN, CHARLES H.: *Modern-language Teaching,* World Book Company, Yonkers-on-Hudson, New York, 1940, vi + 458 pp.

    Valuable chapters on *realia,* visual aids, student activities, recent trends.

5. KAULFERS, WALTER V., GRAYSON N. KEFAUVER, and HOLLAND D. ROBERTS, EDS.: *Foreign Languages and Cultures in American Education,* Reports of the Stanford Language Arts Investigation, Vol. II, McGraw-Hill Book Company, Inc., New York. In press.

    Incorporating 20 readable and realistic statements of actual practice by teachers in the field. Written by teachers in public high schools of different types. Shows students at work—why, how, and with what results.

6. Progressive Education Association, Rocky Mountain Workshop, *A Foreign Language Program for Progressive Secondary Schools,* 221 West 57th St., New York, 1938, 86 pp. (mimeographed).

    Materials prepared by teachers in service for use in their respective foreign-language classes, *e.g.,* courses stressing student-teacher planning, America as seen by the French, the trend toward dictatorship, a source unit on Mexico, development and evaluation of attitudes, etc.

7. OLIVER, THOMAS EDWARD: *The Modern Language Teacher's Handbook,* D. C. Heath and Company, Boston, 1935, vii + 706 pp.

    A valuable source book for securing the addresses of agencies, importers, publishers, societies, etc., in purchasing books, *realia,* films, pictures, phonograph records, translations, and the like, or in making foreign contacts. Arranged alphabetically by topics with cross references.

8. EATON, HELEN S.: *Semantic Frequency List for English, French, German, and Spanish,* University of Chicago Press, Chicago, 1940, xxi + 441 pp.

    Gives the first 6,000 words in each language, correlated and alphabetically arranged in four parallel columns. Valuable to teachers in constructing tests, exercises, or teaching materials with valid vocabulary content.

9. GULLETTE, C. C. *et al.: Teaching a Modern Language,* New York, 1941, 136 pp.

    A brief manual of conventional methods for French, German, Italian, and Spanish.

10. SCHWARTZ, WILLIAM L., ARTHUR G. BOVÉE, and LAWRENCE A. WILKINS: *Vocational Opportunities for Foreign Language Students,* The Modern Language Journal, Washington, D. C., 1941, 34 pp.

    Opportunities and practical limitations in the field of business, foreign commerce, diplomacy, etc. Essential to teachers in giving reliable advice to students.

B. Additional for Teachers of French

11. *The French Review.* The American Association of Teachers of French, 228 East 45th St., New York.

    Occasional articles on curriculum, instruction, and research in the teaching of French. Regular departments: book reviews, phonetics, film and theater news, meetings of the A.A.T.F., communications, and notes.

12. BAKER, FLORENCE M.: *The Teaching of French*, Houghton Mifflin Company, Boston, 1931, 260 pp.

Practical devices and techniques for classroom use.

13. THARP, JAMES B.: *The Basic French Vocabulary*, Henry Holt and Company, Inc., New York, 1939, 222 pp.

Containing 80 to 90 per cent of the vocabulary of the ordinary French prose reading book. Valuable to French teachers in constructing tests, exercises, or teaching materials with a valid vocabulary. Part III classifies the words into semantic categories, *e.g.*, adjectives of degree, size or quantity, shape, time, etc.

14. CHEYDLEUR, FREDERICK D.: *French Idiom List*, The Macmillan Company, New York, 1929, ix + 154 pp.

Based on a running count of 1,183,000 words. A valuable list of French idioms arranged alphabetically and in order of frequency of occurrence (use). Of value to teachers in selecting or constructing valid tests and teaching materials.

15. BOND, OTTO F. *et al.*: *French Syllabus*, The University of Chicago Bookstore, 5802 Ellis Ave., Chicago, 67 pp.

Valuable bibliography of books *in French* suitable for reading in lower-division classes. Classified according to content—belles-lettres, art, biography, geography, travel, history, music, sciences, etc. Books are arranged in the order of their popularity with students who have actually read them.

16. JAMESON, RUSSEL P.: *Le Cercle français*, D. C. Heath and Company, Boston, 1932, 228 pp.

A valuable aid in conducting profitable extracurricular activities in French. Excellent calendar of dates and anniversaries in French history. Good chapter containing directions in French for playing games, bibliography of books for collateral reading in French and English, proverbs, anecdotes, poems, etc. See also references 32–34, 36, 44, 57, 60–62, 66–69, 71, 73, 79–81, 89, 92, 93, 96, 99, 104, 107, 111, 112, 115, 117, 119, 127, 134, 144, 146, 152, 153, 158, 160, 190, 197, 198.

C. Additional for Teachers of German

17. *The German Quarterly*, American Association of Teachers of German, 450 Ahnaip Street, Menasha, Wis.

Frequent articles on curriculum, instruction, and research in the teaching of German, meetings of the A.A.T.G., book reviews, etc.

18. HAGBOLDT, PETER: *The Teaching of German*, D. C. Heath and Company, Boston, 1940, ix + 306 pp.

Excellent chapters on methodology, use of cultural materials, and testing. The special bibliographies on cultural readers, periodicals, scientific readers, tests, etc., alone are worth the price of the book.

19. MORGAN, B. Q., and WALTER WADEPUHL: *Minimum Standard German Vocabulary*, F. S. Crofts & Co., New York, 1934.

Words of most frequent use in German arranged in dictionary form. Based on scientific studies of range and frequency of occurrence.

20. HAUCH, EDWARD F.: *A German Idiom List, Selected on the Basis of Frequency and Range of Occurrence*, The Macmillan Company, New York, 1929, xi + 98 pp.

Useful to teachers in selecting or constructing tests or teaching materials with valid linguistic content in German. See also references 31, 32, 34, 37, 38, 40, 44, 57, 60, 65, 68, 69, 71, 73, 79, 80, 94, 95, 98, 102, 104, 107, 111, 112, 114, 123, 144, 147, 156, 160, 190.

D. Additional for Teachers of Italian

21. *Italica*, American Association of Teachers of Italian, George Barta Publishing Company, Menasha, Wis.

Occasional articles on curriculum, instruction, and research in the teaching of Italian, book reviews, meetings of the A. A. T. I. See also references 31, 35, 57, 60, 69, 80, 85, 102, 104, 107, 111, 112, 117, 144, 146, 147, 152.

E. Additional for Teachers of Spanish

22. *Hispania*, American Association of Teachers of Spanish. George Washington University, Washington, D. C.

Occasional articles on curriculum, instruction, and research in the teaching of Spanish. Regular departments, book reviews, reviews of professional literature, chapter news, announcements.

23. WILKINS, LAWRENCE A.: *Spanish in the High Schools: A Handbook of Methods*, Benjamin H. Sanborn & Co., Chicago, 1925, 284 pp.

Useful and practical teaching devices without reference to other than linguistic objectives.

24. KENISTON, HAYWARD: *Spanish Idiom List Selected on the Basis of Range and Frequency of Occurrence*, The Macmillan Company, New York, 1929, xiii + 108 pp.

Helpful to teachers in selecting and constructing tests or teaching materials with valid linguistic content.

25. KENISTON, HAYWARD: *Spanish Syntax List: A Statistical Study of Grammatical Usage in Contemporary Spanish Prose on the Basis of Range and Frequency*, Henry Holt and Company, Inc., New York, 1937, xi + 278 pp.

An invaluable aid to teachers in allocating time and emphasis to constructions, tenses, etc., on the basis of frequency of use.

26. JONES, WILLIS KNAPP: *Calendar of Latin American Anniversaries and Calendar of Spanish Anniversaries*, Tardy Publishing Company, Dallas, Tex., 1935.

Two paper-bound pamphlets giving annotated dates of historical events, holidays, etc., for each month in the year.

27. ROACH, ELOISE: *Spanish Club Manual*, Tardy Publishing Company, Dallas, Tex., 1935, 108 pp.

A useful book in conducting extracurricular activities in Spanish. Suggestions for various types of club programs. Models for minutes, lists of proverbs, mottoes, games, poems, anniversaries, source materials for programs.

28. SPARKMAN, COLLEY F.: *Games for Spanish Clubs*, Instituto de las Españas, New York, 1926, 108 pp.

Ice-breakers and mixers, singing games, circle games, counting-out rhymes and forfeits, tricks, pencil-and-paper contests, spelling and other matches, drills. Directions and source materials.

29. Arjona, Doris K., and J. H. Arjona: *A Bibliography of Textbooks of Spanish Published in the United States*, Edwards Bros., Inc., Ann Arbor, Mich., 1939.
    A usable classification of texts according to more than twenty categories. See also references 31, 32, 39, 44, 57, 60, 62, 64, 67–69, 71, 73, 75–77, 79, 80, 82, 86, 87, 89–91, 97, 99, 100, 104, 107, 109, 111, 112, 116, 117, 120–122, 124, 128, 133, 144, 147–152, 155, 159, 160, 189, 192–200, 203–204.

F. Additional for Teachers of Civilization Courses

30. Division of Secondary Education, Los Angeles County Schools, *A Guide to Articles in Reader's Digest*, 1937–1940.
    A valuable index of titles arranged according to such topics as "Foreign Countries," "International Relations," "Literature and Language," etc.
31. Commission on Intercultural Education, Progressive Education Association, 221 West 57th St., New York.
    The Commission on Intercultural Education serves as a clearinghouse for pamphlet material on immigrant groups in America, and prepares and distributes mimeographed lesson sheets, suggestions, and bibliographies in mimeographed form. Materials available on German, Italian, Latin-American, and other culture groups.
32. Wilkins, Lawrence A. *et al.*: *Auxiliary Syllabus in Modern Foreign Languages, Foreign Civilization, and Visual-aural Aids*, Board of Education, New York, 1939.
    Materials for each of four years of French, German, Italian, and Spanish.
33. Lindquist, Lilly: *New-type Offerings in Foreign Language*, Detroit Public Schools, File No. 9331, 1939.
    Includes a detailed outline of a one-year survey course in French culture, and somewhat less specific accounts of similar courses in German and Spanish cultures.
34. Stanford Language Arts Investigation, *Annotated Student-bibliographies on Foreign Peoples and Cultures*, Bulletin 17 (France), Bulletin 50 (Germany), Bulletin 35 (Scandinavian countries), Bulletin 40 (Greece and Rome).
    Books in English about the foreign people, including literature in translation.
35. Office of Education, U. S. Department of the Interior, *Americans All—Immigrants All.*
    Twenty-four radio scripts, adapted for use in the classroom, on the stage, or before the microphone. May be supplemented with 24 recordings on 12-inch or 16-inch disks. The latter contain all the programs.
36. Morize, André, and Howard C. Rice: *An Introduction to France*, The Macmillan Company, New York, 1938.
    A syllabus of readings in French with references for class use.
37. Handschin, Charles H.: *Introduction to German Civilization, An Outline*, Prentice-Hall, Inc., New York, 1937.
    A syllabus for courses stressing German civilization and culture.
38. Krakowski, Meyer: *Syllabus for German Civilization and Culture*, Los Angeles City College, Los Angeles, Calif.
39. Lili Heimers: *Pan-Americana*, Visual Aids Service, New Jersey State Teachers College, Upper Montclair, N. J., 1940, 29 pp.

Visual and teaching aids on Spain, Spain in the United States, and Latin America. Bibliography of charts, exhibits, films, pictures, slides, and publications.

40. *The American-German Review* (Bimonthly), Carl Schurz Memorial Foundation, Inc., 420 Chestnut St., Philadelphia, Pa.

   Although many of the articles are too scholarly for high-school students, the magazine is beautifully illustrated with photographs and photostats of important documents, etc., which are invaluable to teachers of German. See also references 44, 57, 58, 63–67, 69–89, 99–130, 141–145, 147, 152, 155, 159, 160, 190.

G. Additional for Teachers of General Language

41. THARP, JAMES B., WALTER V. KAULFERS *et al.: General Language Abstracts*
   An indispensable item for the teacher of general language, exploratory language, or courses in applied semantics. Contains abstracts of nearly all that has been written on the subject to October, 1941. Background reading for teachers of new type general-language courses.

42. JESPERSEN, OTTO: *Language, Its Nature, Development and Origin*. Henry Holt and Company, Inc., New York, 1922, 448 pp.
   A masterful historical study of language which emphasizes the fact that "language is activity, purposeful activity, and we should never lose sight of the speaking individuals and of their purpose in acting in this particular way."

43. VENDRYES, JOSEPH: *Language: A Linguistic Introduction to History*, Alfred A. Knopf, New York, 1925, xxviii + 378 pp.
   An important study of the development of language with emphasis upon the psychological and sociological aspects.

44. WILSON, P. G.: *The Student's Guide to Modern Languages: A Comparative Study of English, French, German, and Spanish*, Sir Isaac Pitman and Sons, Ltd., London, 1930, vii + 190 pp.
   Shows how the virtues of one language are often the defects of another. Affords many interesting insights into languages as mediums of thought and as different ways of symbolizing or interpreting reality.

45. ARNOLD, THURMAN W.: *The Folklore of Capitalism*, Yale University Press, New Haven, 1937, 400 pp.; Chap. VII.
   The book is helpful in understanding the key concepts of the American ideology and the language habits upon which it is based. Chapter VII deals with "polar words."

46. BRIDGMAN, P. W.: *The Intelligent Individual and Society*, The Macmillan Company, New York, 1938, 305 pp.
   Applies "operational definition" to social problems.

47. CHASE, STUART: *The Tyranny of Words*, Harcourt, Brace and Company, New York, 1938, 396 pp.
   Popularization of the work of Ogden, Richards, Korzybski, and others into a nonfiction best seller. A painless, slightly sensationalized, introduction to psychosemantics. Chapter II summarizes the disastrous effects of using "bad language" in discussions of political and economic problems, and reviews the major verbal spooks in the United States. Chapter III shows how we use language to interpret our environment, and how misinterpretation endangers our survival.

48. HAYAKAWA, S. I.: *Language in Action*, College Typing Company, Madison, WIS., 1939, 100 pp.

A readable introduction to applied psychosemantics with practical illustrations of irrational behavior induced by linguistic pitfalls. Suitable for upper-division high-school and junior-college students. Includes practical exercises.

49. KANTOR, J. R.: *An Objective Psychology of Grammar*, Indiana University, Bloomington, Ind., 1936, xvi + 344 pp.

A criticism of logical systems in which language is treated as if words were things rather than aspects of the communication process.

50. KORZYBSKI, ALFRED: *Science and Sanity: An Introduction to Non-Aristotelian Systems and General Semantics*, Science Press Printing Company, Lancaster, Pa., rev. edit., 1941, xx + 798 pp.

A comprehensive discussion of the language habits that cause people to be maladjusted, and an outline of a system of general semantics that frees language from the sources of maladjustment. Difficult to comprehend without thorough study.

51. LEE, IRVING J.: *Language Habits in Human Affairs: An Introduction to General Semantics*, Harper & Brothers, New York, 1941, 278 pp.

A brief and authoritative book for the layman.

52. OGDEN, C. K.: *Basic English: A General Introduction with Rules and Grammar*. Kegan Paul, Trench, Trubner & Co., London, 1935, 95 pp.

Basic English is important in the study of interpretation not only because its use eliminates the source of much misinterpretation, but also because Ogden and Richards have studied the relation of words to things. Their analyses of the various "parts of speech" show how different kinds of words are related to the sensory world.

53. OGDEN, C. K.: *The System of Basic English*, Harcourt, Brace and Company, New York, 1934, ix + 322 pp.

The most complete general account of basic English. Part II is a "simple step by step account of the 850 words, the rules and grammar, including special uses; all in basic."

54. OGDEN, C. K., and I. A. RICHARDS: *The Meaning of Meaning: A Study of the Influence of Language upon Thought and of the Science of Symbolism*, Harcourt, Brace and Company, New York, 1936, xxii + 363 pp.

A very difficult book to read, but one that represents a highly important contribution to the study of psychosemantic behavior in language.

55. THOULESS, ROBERT H.: *How to Think Straight*, Simon and Schuster, Inc., New York, 1939, viii + 246 pp.

A general discussion of some of the common linguistic barriers to straight thinking. Includes a practical discussion with illustrations, "of emotional meanings," "dishonest tricks in argument," "logical fallacies," "tricks of suggestion," "tabloid thinking," and "a discussion illustrating crooked thinking." In the footnotes to the sample discussion the author explains why statements are misleading, and why the participants in the discussion use them.

56. DANTZIG, TOBIAS: *Number—The Language of Science*, The Macmillan Company, New York, 1930, viii + 260 pp.

The mental processes underlying quantitative concepts of reality are effectively traced. See also references in footnotes to Chap. X, and references 62, 69, 70–89, 99–130, 146, 152.

H. Additional for Teachers of World Literature

57. Stanford Language Arts Investigation, *Foreign Literature in English Translation: An Index to Collections*, Bulletin 63, 1938, 52 pp.; *Spanish and Spanish American Literature in English Translation*, Bulletin 60, 1938, 33 pp.; *Popular Foreign Literature in Translation*, Bulletin 26, 1937. (See also reference 34.)   Usable classified bibliographies.
58. WEEKS, RUTH MARY, Chairman: *A Correlated Curriculum*, D. Appleton-Century Company, Inc., New York, 1936, xv + 326 pp.

    Pages 129–155 contain outlines of successful secondary-school courses in world literature with reading lists.   See also references 64, 68, 69, 102–104, 107–116, 123–128, 160, 192, 193, 199.

APPENDIX F

A SELECTED BIBLIOGRAPHY OF MODERN TESTS AND MEASUREMENTS

59. BUROS, OSCAR KRISEN, Ed.: *Mental Measurements Yearbook:* 1940, Highland Park, N. J., 1941, 674 pp.

    A critically annotated bibliography containing descriptions and evaluations of published tests, scales, and other evaluation instruments.   A book that should be accessible to all teachers in the school's professional library. For reviews of foreign-language tests see pp. 157–197.

A. Tests of Ability in Vocabulary, Silent Reading, Grammar, and Aural Comprehension[1]

60. *Cooperative Foreign-language Tests*.   Cooperative Test Service, 15 Amsterdam Ave., New York.

    Available for French, German, Italian, Spanish, and Latin in several forms for each language.   Measure vocabulary, reading, and grammar objectively.   Advanced forms for use in classes that have had four semesters or more of high-school foreign language or two or more semesters in college.   Elementary forms for use in the first three semesters of high-school foreign language, or first-semester college.   Testing time 40 minutes for short editions, 90 minutes for long editions.   Probably the best tests available to date from the viewpoint of comprehensiveness per unit of testing time, objectivity, reliability, validity, and ease of administration and scoring by machine.
61. LUNDEBERG-THARP: *Audition Test in French*, College of Education, Ohio State University, Columbus, Ohio, 1934.

    Probably the best available test for measuring ability to comprehend oral French.   Two forms: for high school and college.

B. Prognosis Tests

62. SYMONDS, PERCIVAL M.: *Foreign Language Prognosis Test*, Bureau of Publications, Teachers College, Columbia University, New York, 1930.

[1] For uses and abuses of achievement tests see Chap. XIII, pp. 389–399.

Two forms for grades 8 to 9; testing time about one hour. Should be used only as a means for grouping pupils homogeneously in beginning classes taught by formal methods in old-fashioned schools.

C. Cultural Information Tests

Since the question, "What information is of most worth?" can be answered only in relation to time and place, the following titles are suggested merely as samples of ways and means by which teachers can measure cultural information which they expect pupils to acquire. Permission to mimeograph the tests in whole or in part can usually be obtained from the authors or editors of the magazines in which the tests were published. For the theory and practice of cultural information testing, see Chap. XIII, pp. 395–399.

63. Russo, Guiseppe Antonio: "A Quiz on Italian Civilization," *The Modern Language Journal*, Vol. XXIV, pp. 279–281, January, 1940.
64. Alpern, Hymen: "A Modern Test in Modern Literature" (Spanish), *The Modern Language Journal*, Vol. XVII, pp. 268–274, January, 1933.
65. Peebles, Waldo C.: "A Test in German Life and Culture," *German Quarterly*, Vol. X, pp. 22–26, January, 1937.
66. Tharp, James B., "A Test on French Civilization," *The French Review*, Vol. VIII, pp. 283–287, March, 1935.
67. Miller, Minnie M., *French Life and Culture* (Test), *Spanish Life and Culture* (Test), Bureau of Educational Measurements, Kansas State Teachers College, Emporia, Kans., 1937.
   For two years of high-school or first-year college. Reliability .73, validity dubious.
68. National Committee on Teacher Examinations, American Council on Education, Washington, D. C., 1940.
   The foreign-language examinations include tests on literature and civilization (French, German, Spanish, and Latin). Suitable primarily for upper-division college and graduate students. Testing time 90 minutes. Constructed by experts, the tests are objective and reliable, but open to serious questions concerning their validity, *i.e.*, do they measure something worth measuring?

D. Scales for Measuring Directional Changes in Attitudes

Scales of this kind are suitable only for locating differences in attitudes existing within a given group, and for determining directional changes in attitudes within the same group over a period of time. They are too lacking in reliability and validity for comparative purposes unless the differences are marked. For uses and abuses of attitude testing see Chap. XIII, pp. 397–399.

69. Remmers, H. H. *et al.*: *Attitudes Scales*, Division of Educational Reference, Purdue University, Lafayette, Ind., 1934–1936.
   a. *Scale for Measuring Attitude toward Any National or Racial Group.*
   b. *Scale for Measuring Attitude toward Any Practice.*
   c. *Scale for Measuring Attitude toward Any School Subject.*
   d. *Scale for Measuring Attitude toward Any Teacher.*
   e. *Scale for Measuring Individual and Group Morale.*
   Grades 7 to 16; three to five minutes testing time per attitude variable.

APPENDIX G

SOURCES OF LOW-PRICED ENRICHMENT MATERIALS— TEACHING AIDS, SONGS, PICTURES, DESCRIPTIVE BOOKLETS

70. Study-Travel Club, 1000 Union Trust Arcade, Cleveland, Ohio.
    Posters and decorative travel maps of France at cost.
71. The Thrift Press, Ithaca, N. Y.
    Paper-bound pamphlets of songs, bibliographies of foreign literature in translation, classified practical vocabularies, compact vest-pocket size résumés of grammar, etc., for French, Spanish, German, and Latin.
72. Tardy Publishing Company, Dallas, Tex.
    Inexpensive paper-bound pamphlets containing teaching aids (calendars of foreign anniversaries, question books for conversational practice, subjunctive handbooks, etc.) in Spanish.
73. Cuthbertson Verb Wheels, Department of Romanic Languages, University of Colorado.
    Useful and compact résumés of regular and irregular verbs in all moods and tenses. Easy to use, easy to learn. Separate wheels for French, German, Spanish, and Latin.
74. Friendship Press, 150 Fifth Ave., New York.
75. *En Guardia*, Coordinator of Inter-American Affairs, Washington, D. C. A beautifully illustrated monthly in Spanish featuring hemisphere defense.
76. Grace Line, Publicity Department, 50 Rockefeller Center, New York, *Spanish American Daily*.
    Illustrated radio newspaper distributed on Grace Line "Santa" ships.
77. *Turismo en el Uruguay*, Publicación Oficial de la Comisión Nacional del Turismo, Oficinas Sarandi, 659 Montivideo.
    A magazine beautifully illustrated with fine photographs; Spanish text. Available to foreign-language departments.
78. *The World Almanac and Book of Facts*, *New York World-Telegram*, New York City. Yearly editions. Latest facts on foreign countries.
79. Songs: Collections of foreign songs are published by: Ginn and Company, Boston, D. C. Heath and Company, Boston, Henry Holt and Company, Inc., New York, The Thrift Press, New York.
80. The University Prints, Newton, Mass.
    Prints 5½ by 8 inches: Deal primarily with Italian, Spanish, German, French, Roman, and Greek painting and sculpture.
81. Chambre de Commerce Française des États-Unis, Inc., 4 East 52nd St., New York.
    Illustrated pamphlets and folders on France.
82. Departamento Autónomo de Prensa y Publicidad, Bucaroli 12, México, D. F.
    Illustrated booklets on Mexico.
83. French Government Tourist Bureau, 610 Fifth Ave., New York.
    Illustrated booklets.
84. *Ready Reference Classification of Victor Records*, Educational Department, RCA Victor Division, Camden, N. J. Illustrating music appreciation and music history; also a graded list for home, school, and college.

85. *Americans All—Immigrants All*, The Federal Radio Education Committee in Cooperation with the U. S. Office of Education, Washington, D. C., 120 pp. A handbook for listeners containing interesting and significant facts concerning the contribution of German, French, Italian, Spanish, and other immigrants to American life and culture.

86. National Railways of Mexico, San Francisco; Pacific Electric Building, Los Angeles.
    Illustrated booklets on Mexico.

87. Pan American Union, Washington, D. C.
    Illustrated booklets.
    a. *American City Series.*
    b. *American Nation Series.* Illustrated booklets.
    c. *Ports and Harbors of South America.* pp. 200, 110 illustrations.
    d. *Seeing South America.* pp. 224, 70 illustrations.
    e. *Stories of Commodities:* coffee, chicle, asphalt, nitrates, etc.
    f. *Seeing the Latin Republics of North America.* pp. 185, 73 illustrations.

88. National Service Bureau, Federal Theater Project, 1697 Broadway, New York. Catalogue on request.
    Issues mimeographed playscripts and other materials at cost.

89. U. S. Office of Education. Educational Radio Script Exchange, Washington, D. C.
    "The Script Exchange is designed to serve as a bureau of information regarding the sources of educational radio scripts and as a depository and point of distribution for selected script series. At the present time more than 500 scripts have been collected from various institutions throughout the country. . . . Any individual or group, agreeing to use the material for *non-commercial* purposes, may receive for the asking one complete set of each script series and also one copy of each of the supplementary aids to production available directly through the Script Exchange." See also references 91–95, 113–116, 151, 155, 189, 198.

APPENDIX H

FOREIGN-LANGUAGE PERIODICALS PUBLISHED IN THE UNITED STATES

90. *El Eco*, Doubleday, Doran & Company, Inc., New York, twice a month; quantity rates.
    A periodical edited for beginning and advanced students of Spanish. Illustrated with pictures, cartoons, etc. Cultural readings, short essays, jokes, etc., graded according to language difficulty.

91. *Selecciones del Reader's Digest*, Pleasantville, N. Y.
    Select articles from *The Reader's Digest* in Spanish translation. Although many short items are suitable for reading in first- and second-year high-school classes, the magazine as a whole is suitable for use only in classes that have had two years or more of high-school Spanish or its equivalent in college.

92. *Le Petit Journal*, Doubleday, Doran & Company, Inc., New York. Twice a month from October to May; quantity rates.

A periodical edited for beginning and advanced students of French. Illustrated with pictures, cartoons, cultural readings, jokes, etc., graded in language difficulty.

93. *La Vie*, Banks Upshaw Company, Dallas, Tex.

A student periodical in French; quantity rates.

94. *Das deutsche Echo*, F. S. Crofts & Co., New York.

A ten-month periodical edited for high-school and college students of German. Quantity rates.

95. *Jugent Post* (c/o *Abend Post*), Rochester, N. Y.

A periodical edited for high-school and college students of German.

96. *Le Courier des États-Unis*. Western Newspaper Union, 310 East 45th St., New York. Published Saturday.

A weekly newspaper published for French-speaking readers in the United States.

97. *La Prensa*, 245 Canal St., New York. Daily except Sunday.

A newspaper published for Spanish-speaking readers in the United States.

98. *Staats-Zeitung und Herold*, 24 North Williams St., New York.

A newspaper published for German-speaking readers in the United States. See also references 75, 151, 153, 158, 159, 191, 200.

APPENDIX I

IMPORTERS OF BOOKS, PERIODICALS, MAPS, PICTURES, POSTCARDS, STAMPS, COINS, ETC.

99. Rand McNally and Company, 111 Eighth Ave., New York.

Makers of wall maps and importers of foreign maps.

100. La Casa de Realia, 1204 South 16th St., Chickasha, Okla.

Spanish posters and *realia*.

101. The Economist Stamp Co., 87 Nassau St., New York City.

102. Denoyer-Geppert Company, 5235–5257 Ravenswood Ave., Chicago, Ill.

Importers of charts, globes, maps, scientific models, and pictures.

103. Brentano's, 1 West 47th St., New York.

Books, pictures.

104. George E. Stechert and Company, 31–33 E 10th St., New York.

Foreign books and periodicals.

105. Universal Postcard Company, 115 North St., New York.

106. New York Coin and Stamp Company, 912 Sixth Ave., New York.

APPENDIX J

VISUAL AIDS (FILMS AND SLIDES) AND AURAL AIDS

107. *Famous Foreign Features*, Educational Department, Columbia Pictures Corporation, 729 Seventh Ave., New York.

Outstanding foreign features with superimposed English subtitles for school assemblies, etc.

108. U. S. Film Service, Washington D. C. Catalogue available.

109. Garrison Film Distributors, 750 Seventh Ave., New York.

> Rents and sells films; five one-reel Spanish teaching films released in April, 1941.

110. College Film Center, 59 East Van Buren St., Chicago, Ill.

> Rents and sells sound films.

111. Educational Lantern Slide Service, Inc., 736 South Wabash Ave., Chicago, Ill.

> Slides for rent and for sale, colored and uncolored. See also reference 152.

Aural Aids and Equipment

112. Linguaphone Record Language Courses, Linguaphone Institute, 30 Rockefeller Plaza, New York.

> Courses in French, German, Spanish, Italian, and other languages—including pronunciation, grammar, vocabulary building, with student and teacher manuals. Special conversation courses for travel, etc. Recordings of literary selections by eminent linguists; recordings of songs suitable for class use. Also phonographic equipment. See also reference 196.

APPENDIX K

FOREIGN-LANGUAGE SERVICE BUREAUS

For information, contacts, bibliographies, directories, teaching materials, loan collections, etc.

113. State Teachers College, Emporia, Kans.
114. University of Wisconsin, Madison, Wis.
115. French Information Center, 610 Fifth Ave., New York.
116. Spanish Language Center, 292 Madison Ave., New York.

> For making foreign contacts directly, consult the consulate of the foreign country. See classified telephone directory for address or write to consulate in New York. See also reference 155, 189, 194, 195.

APPENDIX L

INFORMATION CENTERS FOR ACCREDITED STUDY ABROAD

117. Delaware Plan for Study Abroad, University of Delaware, Newark, Del.
118. Smith Plan for Study Abroad, Smith College, Northhampton, Mass.

APPENDIX M

DIRECTORY OF NATIONAL
AND INTERNATIONAL STUDENT SOCIETIES

119. Student Forum on International Relations, 521 Phelan Building, San Francisco, Calif.
120. Pan American Student League, care of Board of Education, New York.
121. Pan American Student Forum, care of Ann Hull, Yuba City, Union High School, Calif.

122. Student International Travel Association, 2929 Broadway, New York.
     Arranges low-priced travel for students under nineteen years of age via freighters, etc.

APPENDIX N

RADIO STATIONS FEATURING SERIES
ON FOREIGN LANGUAGES, LITERATURES, AND CULTURES

Write to stations for prospectus.

123. School of the Air, University of Kansas, Stations KFKV, Lawrence, Kans.
     Presents cultural programs in foreign languages.
124. "Spanish Treasures," Wisconsin Radio Service, Madison, Wis., Station WHA.
     Send for program of broadcasts.
125. N.B.C. "Good Neighbor" Broadcasts of the U. S. Office of Education.
     Weekly series featuring Spanish American life and culture.
126. WNYE (affiliated with WNYC) Brooklyn Technical High School, New York.
     Cultural programs in the foreign languages, some of them prepared and enacted by students.
127. Station WTIC, Hartford, Conn.
     Occasional series in French language, literature, and culture.
128. Ohio State University Broadcasts, Columbus, Ohio.
     Occasional foreign-language series. See also references 85, 89.

APPENDIX O

LOW-PRICED FILING AND DUPLICATING EQUIPMENT

129. Hobart Cabinet Company, Troy, Ohio.
     Four-drawer (green) steel filing cabinets, for filing student notebooks, papers, correspondence, printed materials, pictures, etc., with adjustable arrangements for filing post cards, bibliographical cards, etc. Also a 27-drawer green steel filing case; each drawer 3 inches in depth, size 9 by 12 inches. Both cabinets priced with discounts for teachers.
130. Inexpensive duplicators such as the Gel-Sten Jr., Hectograph, or Ditto, produce 50 or more legible copies which can be used several times if students are requested to do their work on a separate sheet of paper. The machines reproduce handwriting, maps, and drawings as easily as typewritten work, and can be operated by any boy or girl of junior high-school age. For post-card size copies see Print-O-Matic Stencil Duplicator, Print-O-Matic Company, 333 W. Lake St., Chicago Ill. This small portable table model is self-feeding and duplicates 3,000 cards per hour.

APPENDIX P

SELECT REFERENCES FOR TEACHERS OF
NON-ENGLISH-SPEAKING STUDENTS

131. COLEMAN, ALGERNON, and CLARA BRESLOVE KING: *English Teaching in the Southwest*, American Council on Education, Washington, D. C., 1940, xvii + 307 pp.

An authoritative review of the problem of bilingualism, with special reference to the teaching of English to Mexican-speaking children in the United States. Pages 281–307 give a comprehensive bibliography for experimental studies, teaching materials, textbooks, courses of study, etc., in the field of bilingualism.

132. OGDEN, C. K.: *The System of Basic English*, Harcourt, Brace and Company, New York, 1934, ix + 322 pp.

A complete general account of basic English, a system of proved value in the teaching of English to foreigners or to bilingual children. Invaluable to teachers of English in Americanization classes, night schools, etc.

133. ESCUDERO, MARY J.: "Language Difficulties of Spanish-speaking pupils," *California Journal of Secondary Education*, Vol. XIV, pp. 501–502, December, 1939. See also references 150, 152, 157.

APPENDIX Q

SELECT BIBLIOGRAPHY FOR TEACHERS OF ELEMENTARY AND PRIMARY-SCHOOL CHILDREN

134. BOUDREAUX, ELIA: "Some Aims and Methods in Teaching French in the Elementary Schools in Louisiana," *The Modern Language Journal*, Vol. XXIV, pp. 427–430, March, 1940.

135. YEISER, IDABELLE: "The Why and How of Teaching French to Little Children," *The Modern Language Journal*, Vol. XXIII, pp. 591–593, May, 1939.

136. PHILLIPS, HOSEA: "Foreign Languages in the Grades in Louisiana," *The French Review*, Vol. XIII, p. 71, October, 1939.

137. BISHOP, JAMES W.: "Observations on Teaching Elementary Pupils Spanish," Vol. XXV, pp. 138–139, November, 1940.

138. FARRÈRE, HÉLÈNE F.: "The Creative Teaching of French," *The French Review*, Vol. VI, pp. 114–122.

Reports successful experiments in teaching French to children in such a way as to capitalize creative impulses.

139. POSGATE, HELEN B.: "French and Young Children," *The French Review*, Vol. II, pp. 173–174, December, 1934.

Methods and devices for teaching French to children four to eight years of age.

140. MAYS, RUTH: "Teaching Spanish in the Lower Grades," *Hispania*, Vol. XXV, pp. 141–143, May, 1942.

Methods and possibilities in the third grade. See also references 152, 154.

APPENDIX R

INTERNATIONAL CORRESPONDENCE BUREAUS

Addresses of students abroad can be obtained from the agencies listed below. A small charge per student is usually made to defray secretarial costs. Applications should be accompanied by a short biographical sketch giving age, sex, race, year in school, and scholastic, vocational and avocational interests.

141. Junior Red Cross, Washington, D. C. Letters are translated by the organization into the language of the countries to which the letters are sent. Primarily for junior high-school students.
142. International Correspondence Club, 132 East 65th St., New York.
143. International Friendship League Inc., 41 Mt. Vernon St., Boston.
144. International Bureau of Foreign Correspondence, Peabody College, for Teachers, Nashville, Tenn.
145. My Friend Abroad, Dr. S. V. Knudsen, 248 Boyleston St., Boston, Mass.

APPENDIX S

ADDENDA

146. *The News Letter*, Bureau of Educational Research, Ohio State University, Columbus, Ohio.
     Brings information to the teacher about the radio, press, and the motion picture. Contains references to technical equipment for school use, bibliography of pamphlets, books, and studies on the classroom use of these facilities. Monthly except June, July, August, and September.
147. Service Bureau for Intercultural Education, 221 West 57th St., New York.
     Stresses "national unity through knowledge of the contributions of the various culture groups to American life and through the merging of many aspirations in a single national purpose." Publishes *Intercultural Education News* (bulletin) reporting activities in the field, suggestions, bibliographies.
148. SIPP, SOLOMON, and HENRY N. BASSO: *Conversational Spanish for Army Air Forces of the United States*, The Air Corps Spanish Project, Works Projects Administration, Hastings House, New York, 1941, xvii + 168 pp.
     An interesting illustration of a functional (use) approach to Spanish for a specialized purpose in a technical field. Has special appeal for boys.
149. SNYDER, ISABEL: "Vitalizing Spanish Through Movie Production," *Hispania*, Vol. XXIV, pp. 267–268, October, 1941.
     Practical details, advice, and suggestions may be obtained from the sponsors of the project. Address Allen High School, New Orleans, La.
150. MURDOCK, MARY W., and LEAVITT O. WRIGHT: "A Fifth-grade Spanish Club in Oregon," *Hispania*, Vol. XXIV, pp. 261–266, October, 1941.
151. *Norte*, 171 Madison Ave., New York.
     A modified Spanish equivalent of the popular illustrated pictoral magazines *Look* and *Life*. Attractive prices for club or class subscriptions.
152. *Kaulfers Pronunciation-charts*, School of Education, Stanford University, Calif.
     For description see pp. 60–65. Available for French, Italian, German, and Spanish on spring rollers. Cost prices vary according to language.
153. *La Voix de France*, 306 West 105th St., New York.
     An 8-page periodical, 20 issues per year, of which four pages are expressly edited for classroom use, and four pages are devoted to general information and articles. Quiz sheet with each copy. Special quarterly subscription rates.

154. Secondary Education Board, *A Survey of Modern Languages in Elementary and Secondary Schools:* 1939–1940, Milton, Mass., 1941, 25 pp.

Reports statistics on foreign-language offerings in 348 schools, the large majority of them *private* schools.

155. Committee on Inter-American Relations, Department of Secondary School Teachers, National Education Association, 1201 Sixteenth St., N. W., Washington, D. C.

Classroom materials in the form of study units, completely outlined by topics, bibliography, suggested questions for individual report.

156. Foreign Language Camps, Address Warren E. Tomlinson, Department of German, University of Washington, Seattle, Wash.

Orcas Island language camps sponsored jointly by University of Washington, College of Puget Sound, and Reed College. Provide for in-residence language learning in a beautiful scenic setting. For in-residence foreign-language houses on college campuses, see Catalogue, Middlebury College, Vt., Stanford University, California, etc.

157. *Review of Educational Research,* "Education of Exceptional Children and Minority Groups," National Education Association, 1201 Sixteenth St., N.W., Washington, D. C., June, 1941.

Pages 340–360 deal with the education of bilingual children and Indians. Extensive bibliographies.

158. *Voici,* Carmel, N. Y., 12 issues per year; special group subscription rates.

An excellent opportunity for relating social studies and the French language. For mature students with a thorough grounding in French.

159. *Las Americas,* Las Americas Publishing Company, 98–99 65th Road, Forest Hills, N. Y.

A promising newcomer (1941) in the field of Spanish-language periodicals for students. Materials vary in degree of linguistic difficulty. Illustrated. Special group subscription rates. Monthly during school year.

160. Division of Museum Extension, Museum of Fine Arts, Boston, Mass.

Illustrated sets, consisting of 40 large plates (12 by 16 inches) designed to correlate art with the study of different cultural periods in the fields of languages, history, literature, and music. Among the sets of interest to language teachers are "Spanish Ideals in the Golden Age," "Medieval France," "French Renaissance," etc. Entire collection designed to include 6,000 reproductions.

161. Touring y Automóvil Club del Perú. Pabellón Morisco, Parque de la Exposición y Avenida Wilson, Lima, Perú.

Illustrated pamphlets available to department heads in Spanish and English.

162. Junta Nacional de Turismo de Costa Rica, San José, Costa Rica.

Illustrated pamphlets on such topics as "Costa Rica, the Heart of the Americas," "Sightseeing in Costa Rica," "Notes on the Archaeology of Costa Rica," "Visite el Ojo de Agua," "Costa Rica, sus bellos Volcanes," "Costa Rica—Ayer y Hoy," "Costa Rica y la Civilización en el Caribe." Also scenic posters.

163. Comité Nacional de Turismo, Secretaría de Relaciones Exteriores, República de Guatemala.

Booklets and folders on travel in Guatemala available to department heads.

164. Department de Turismo, Avenida B. O'Higgins, No. 1442, Correo No. 8, Santiago de Chile.

Maps, posters, and pamphlets available to department heads.

165. Gerencia, Ferrocarril del Sud, C. Correo 109, Buenos Aires, Argentina.

Illustrated folders, railway maps, and travel posters available to department heads.

166. *Turismo*, revista peruana de viajes, artes, letras y actualidad, Lima, Peru.

Beautifully illustrated with photographs. Printed in Spanish by Touring and Automóvil Club del Perú.

167. *Así*, Avenida del Ejido No. 19, México, D. F.

A popular illustrated magazine on a level comparable to that of *Look* and *Pic* in content. Published weekly.

168. *Phi Delta Kappan*, November issue, 1941. Latin-American Relations and the Schools.

169. Educational Policies Commission, *In These Americas*, National Education Association, 1201 W. Sixteenth St., N.W., Washington, D. C., June, 1940, 16 pp.

A pamphlet emphasizing education for Inter-American friendship.

170. Division of Intellectual Cooperation, Pan American Union. *A Selective List of Periodicals of General Interest Published in Latin America and A Partial List of Latin American Educational Journals.*

Valuable directories available from the Pan American Union, Washington, D. C.

171. True-Vue, Incorporated, Rock Island, Ill. Stereoptican colored views, on automatic roller films. Available for Fontainebleau, the steamship Normandie, Paris, Versailles, in 11 rolls. For use by individual students.

172. Progressive Education Association, *A Report of the Workshop on Latin-American Studies*, 221 West 57th St., New York, 1941, 96 pp.

Bibliographies of source materials for use in elementary-school and high-school classes: books, music, literature, etc. Suggested projects and activities for class use.

173. *Automovilismo*, órgano oficial del Automóvil Club Argentino, redacción y administración: Libertad 1235, Buenos Aires, Argentina.

A beautifully illustrated magazine on touring topics and allied subjects. Available to department heads. Full of photographs. Spanish text. Road maps available from the same agency.

174. GUERLAC, OTHON: *Les Citations Françaises*, Recueil de Passages célèbres, Phrases familières, mots historiques avec l'indication exacte de la source suivi d'un index alphabétique par auteurs et par sujets. Librairie Armand Colin, 103 Boulevard Saint-Michel, Paris, 1933, 458 pp.

175. Franz C. Feger, 70 Fifth Ave., New York. Dealers in Latin-American and Spanish fiction. Send for catalogue of books.

176. Nuestro Mundo, Agencia de Publicaciones, 890 Glen Arden Way, N. E., Atlanta, Ga.

Agency for representative Spanish newspapers, magazines, and reviews.

177. Carl Schurz Memorial Foundation, Inc., 420 Chestnut Street, Philadelphia, Pa. A foundation devoted to preserving our "free" German heritage from abroad and to protecting the welfare of "free" Germans in the United States.

178. Banks Upshaw and Company, 707 Browder St., Dallas, Tex. Publishes inexpensive teaching materials in French and Spanish, such as the pupil periodicals *Le Vie* and *La Luz; Canciones de Navidad* by Ina W. Ramboz, merry-go-round of *Games in Spanish* by Grace D. Vogan, etc.

179. Instituto Panamericano de Bibliografía y Documentación, *Boletín Bibliográfico Mexicano*, Librería de Porrua Hermanos y Compañía esquina Argentino y Justo Sierra, Apartado 7990, México, D. F.

 In addition to publishing its classified bibliography of books in Spanish, the company provides bibliographical information of every kind, secures photostatic and photographic reproductions, copyrights, etc.

180. *The Spanish American*, 247 Park Ave., New York.

 Beautifully illustrated magazine dealing with different Spanish-American countries. In English.

181. Audio-Scriptions Ins., 1619 Broadway, New York.

 Sells transcriptions of radio broadcasts suitable for playing on tone-control phonographs. Transcriptions also made on advance request.

182. CARLEY, VERNA A.: "Inter-American Friendship through the Schools," *Federal Security Administration, Bulletin* 1941, no. 10, U. S. Office of Education, Washington, D. C., v + 61 pp.

 A valuable illustrated pamphlet describing ways and means through which Spanish teachers and others are translating the good-neighbor policy and hemisphere defense into constructive action in the elementary and secondary schools.

183. Studies in Intercultural Education, *Americans All*, Yearbook of Department of Supervisors and Directors of Instruction, N. E. A., National Council of Teachers of English and Society for Curriculum Study, 1201 Sixteenth St., N.W., Washington, D. C., 1941.

 Contains 25 statements of theory and practice by frontier workers activity engaged in cultural relations service in the elementary and secondary schools.

184. DEBOER, JOHN J. *et al.: A Report of the National Commission on Cooperative Curriculum Planning*, D. Appleton Century Company, Inc., New York, 1941, ix + 239 pp.

 Chapter V, pp. 94–114, "The Modern Foreign Languages," discusses sketchily the objectives of foreign-language study, the organization of the foreign-language curriculum, general language, and survey courses in foreign cultures.

185. DIEDERICH, PAUL BERNARD: *The Frequency of Latin Words and Their Endings*, The University of Chicago Press, Chicago, 1939, 121 pp. An important study suggestive of techniques desirable in modern foreign languages. Demonstrates that a thorough mastery of only 18 Latin endings is required for an understanding of the grammatical function of 92.5 per cent of all Latin words used in context.

186. "Educational Cooperatives," *The News Letter* of the Commission on Teacher Education of the American Council of Education, 741 Jackson Place, N. W., Washington, D. C., January, 1942, pp. 1–8.

 Describes in practical detail the organization, conduct, and values of classroom service bureaus for teachers supported by membership subscriptions.

187. University Lithoprinters, 54 East Cross St., Ypsilanti, Mich.
    Syllabi, monographs, and teaching materials (including illustrations, and pictures) lithoprinted and bound for class use at low prices.

188. Erpi Classroom Films Inc., 35-11 Thirty-fifth Ave., Long Island City, N. Y.
    Sells sound films produced under the auspices of leading educators. Erpi films may be rented from the University of California Extension Division, Berkeley, Calif.   Send for catalogue.

189. Information Exchange on Education and National Defense, Federal Security Agency, U. S. Office of Education, Washington, D. C.   Loan packets (IX-G-1, IX-H-1, IX-S-1, IX-E-1, IX-A-1, IX-C-1, IX-C-2, IX-C-3, IX-C-4) may be borrowed without cost for two weeks.   Especially timely is the Inter-American Friendship and Understanding series.   Loan packets consist of pamphlets, bulletins, mimeographed lesson-plans, magazines, charts, etc.   Send for catalogue.

190. Excelsior Pictures Corporation, 723 Seventh Avenue, New York.   Foreign sound films for use in theaters or school auditoriums with standard projection facilities.   Catalogues include Schubert's *Serenade* in French with English subtitles, *Charm of La Bohême* in German with English subtitles, *Orphan Boy of Vienna*, etc.

191. *Pour la Victoire*, Journal Français d'Amérique, 535 Fifth Avenue, New York. Published twice a month from September to June.   Vigorously supports the cause of Free France with timely news.   For mature students with a reading knowledge of French.

192. REID, DORCAS W., "Latin American Novels in English Translation," *The Inter-American Quarterly*, pp. 55–71, July, 1941.   A useful bibliography.

193. JAMES, CONCHA ROMERO, and FRANCISCO, AGUILERA: *Latin American Literature*, mimeographed bulletin of the Pan American Union, September, 1941.   Contains titles of Latin American literature in English translation.

194. Coordinator of Inter-American Affairs, Education Section, Department of Commerce, Washington, D. C.   See reference 75.
    Specializes in Inter-American educational relations and intellectual cooperation between the United States and the Americas.

195. American Association of Teachers of Spanish, George Washington University, Washington, D. C.
    A valuable source of guidance and information on Spanish and Latin American topics.   Official organ, *Hispania*.

196. Hispanophone Course, Castellanos-Molina Music Shops, 45 West 116th Street, New York City.
    Set of 15 double-faced 10-inch records with 150-page textbook and record album.   Course divided into 30 practical lessons.

197. TORRE, EMILIO DE, *et al.*: *The Latin American Song Book*, Ginn and Company, Boston, 1942.   Seventy-two songs with music and English translations, published in cooperation with the Music Division of the Pan American Union.

198. HEIMERS, LILI: *Aids for the Spanish Teacher*, G. E. Stechert & Company, New York, 1941.
    Bibliographical aids, addresses of publishers, and agencies for all types of books, information, and realia.   Emphasis on Spanish America.

199. BARRY and GOETZ, *Children of the Americas*, The Pan American Union, Washington, D. C., 1942.

A comprehensive bibliography for American schools.

200. *The Mexico Magazine*, 614 East San Antonio Street, El Paso, Tex. An illustrated monthly in English and Spanish.

201. *Danse Macabre*, recording of the poem by the author for school use. (See page 331.) Address School of Education, Stanford University, Calif.

202. National Information Bureau of the American Association of Teachers of French, Daniel P. Girard, Chairman, Teachers College, Columbia University, New York.

Furnishes bulletins, bibliographies of classroom aids, etc., for teachers of French.

203. *The Inter-American Monthly*. 912–918 Burlington Avenue, Silver Spring, Md.

An illustrated magazine incorporating the *Inter-American Quarterly* and *Pan American News*. Text in English featuring articles on social, political, economic, and cultural topics of current interest. For adults and upper-division high-school students.

204. *Mexican Voice*, An Inspirational Educational Youth Magazine. 864 South Raymond Street, Pasadena, Calif.

A quarterly eight-page magazine reporting the problems and activities of Mexican youth in our Southwest. In English.

APPENDIX T

FOREIGN-LANGUAGE STATISTICS— ENROLLMENTS AND TRENDS: 1890–1942[1]

TABLE 1.—PERCENTAGES OF HIGH-SCHOOL POPULATIONS STUDYING FOREIGN LANGUAGES

Year	1890	1895	1900	1905	1910	1915	1922	1928	1934
Latin	34.7	44.0	50.6	50.2	49.0	37.8	27.5	22.0	16.0
All modern languages	16.4	17.9	22.1	29.4	34.3	35.6	27.4	25.4	19.7

[1] Tables 1, 2, and 3 are adapted from data supplied by James B. Tharp, Time Allotment for Foreign Language Study, *The Modern Language Journal*, Vol. XXV, No. 8, pp. 598–608, May, 1941. Permission of *The Modern Language Journal*.

TABLE 2.—PERCENTAGE OF RURAL HIGH SCHOOLS, BY SIZE GROUPS, OFFERING ONE OR MORE SUBJECTS IN THE VARIOUS SUBJECT-MATTER FIELDS, 1934*

Subject-matter fields	Size of high schools by number of pupils enrolled					
	40 or fewer	41–75	76–150	151–300	Over 300	All rural high schools
Ancient and modern foreign languages..................	58	77	80	92	99	80
English.....................	100	100	100	100	100	100
Mathematics................	99	99	99	100	100	100
Social science..............	100	100	100	100	99	100
Science....................	96	96	100	100	99	98
Physical education...........	39	47	48	43	52	45
Fine arts....................	31	39	45	59	70	47
Industial arts...............	19	23	18	31	60	27
Commercial arts.............	61	60	76	83	89	74
Agriculture.................	19	30	38	47	41	35
Home economics.............	19	35	49	67	74	47

* Data from a survey (1934) of 1,238 representative high schools located in centers of 2,500 or fewer population.

TABLE 3.—SHIFTS IN DISTRIBUTION OF THE FOREIGN-LANGUAGE ENROLLMENT IN NEW YORK CITY SENIOR HIGH SCHOOLS DURING 23 YEARS

Year	French	German	Italian	Spanish	Latin	Ratio to school population
1917	23.2	27.1	0.1	25.3	24.3	103
1920	30.7	0.1	0.2	45.6	23.4	90
1925	35.8	5.9	1.2	29.3	27.8	81
1936	45.5	10.6	5.1	24.3	14.5	61*
1940	43.7	8.0	7.2	25.6	13.8	57*

* In 1936 there were 1,539 students of Hebrew; in 1940 there were 2,714, or 1.7 per cent of the enrollment.

TABLE 4.—ENROLLMENT IN FOREIGN LANGUAGES IN NEW YORK CITY
HIGH SCHOOLS, OCTOBER, 1941
IN JUNIOR HIGH SCHOOLS
(Total junior-high-school population: 128,185)

Languages	7B	8A	8B	9A	9B	7B-R	8B-R	9A-R	9B-R	Total
French.....	46	126	5,418	5,553	4,874	38	2,163	1,288	1,880	21,386
German....	..	...	314	375	286	..	131	65	137	1,308
Hebrew....	..	...	.....	.....	13	..	.....	.....	.....	13
Italian.....	..	...	928	1,003	766	..	150	128	162	3,137
Latin.......	..	69	373	375	298	..	312	181	222	1,830
Spanish..	..	...	2,897	2,369	1,088	..	926	278	120	7,678
	46	195	9,930	9,675	7,325	38	3,682	1,940	2,521	35,352

IN SENIOR HIGH SCHOOLS
(Total high-school population: 242,358)

Languages	I	II	III	IV	V	VI	VII	VIII	Total
French.......	4,284	4,960	12,980	11,830	7,348	6,781	796	354	49,333
German......	1,452	1,268	1,703	1,654	838	737	40	37	7,729
Greek........	31	11	10	10	5	.....	.....	...	67
Hebrew......	475	383	556	476	267	177	25	6	2,365
Italian.......	1,611	1,386	2,012	1,772	935	671	150	48	8,585
Latin........	4,320	3,494	3,830	3,353	1,580	1,223	265	190	18,255
Spanish......	16,209	11,426	9,320	6,688	1,889	1,380	117	18	47,047
	28,382	22,928	30,411	25,783	12,862	10,969	1,393	653	133,381

For German the corresponding figures as of Oct. 15, 1940, were:

Total in junior high schools............................. 1,699
    (Total school population 133,247)
Total in senior high schools............................. 10,241
    (Total school population 253,676)

For grade placement of modern foreign-language study in 348 schools of the United States, see chart and table 5, page 506.

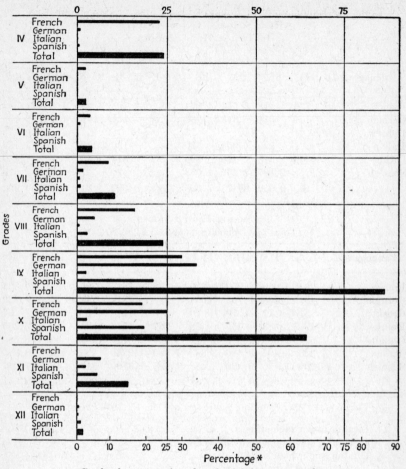

Grade placement of modern foreign-language study.

TABLE 5.—SUPPORTING DATA FOR GRADE PLACEMENT CHART

Type of school	Secondary	Elementary	Totals
Private boys..............................	140	17	157
Private girls..............................	58	0	58
Private coeducational......................	45	15	60
Public schools and public-school systems*.....	71	2	73
Totals.................................	314	34	348

* Includes four boys' high schools, otherwise coeducational. See *A Survey of Modern Languages in Elementary and Secondary Schools: 1939–1940*, Secondary Education Board, Milton, Mass., 1941, 25 pp.; pp. 4–5.

ENROLLMENT TRENDS IN SPANISH IN ELEMENTARY AND SECONDARY SCHOOLS, 1940–1941*

TABLE 6.—DISTRIBUTION BY STATES OF 671 SCHOOL SYSTEMS OFFERING INSTRUCTION IN SPANISH, 1940–1941

Texas	74	Mississippi	7
California	59	Montana	7
Pennsylvania	49	North Carolina	7
New Jersey	47	Wyoming	7
Ohio	38	Arizona	6
Florida	32	Virginia	6
Oklahoma	32	West Virginia	6
Colorado	29	Idaho	5
New York	25	Minnesota	5
Massachusetts	22	Wisconsin	5
Kansas	21	Nebraska	4
Illinois	17	South Dakota	4
Tennessee	14	Utah	4
Missouri	13	Nevada	3
New Mexico	13	Oregon	3
Michigan	11	Rhode Island	3
Washington	10	South Carolina	3
Kentucky	10	Delaware	2
Georgia	10	Maine	2
Louisiana	10	Maryland	2
Arkansas	9	Vermont	1
Alabama	9	New Hampshire	0
Indiana	9	North Dakota	0
Iowa	8	District of Columbia	1
Connecticut	7		

* The data are condensed and rearranged from *Bulletin* 1941, No. 10, of the Federal Security Administration, U. S. Office of Education, Washington, D. C. See Verna A. Carley, *Inter-American Friendship through the Schools*, v + 61 pp.; pp. 7–16.

TABLE 7.—ENROLLMENTS IN SPANISH CLASSES IN GRADES 7 TO 12 FOR THE
FIRST SEMESTER, 1940–1941, REPORTED BY 671 SCHOOL SYSTEMS IN
THE VARIOUS REGIONS OF THE UNITED STATES

Region	Number of school systems reporting	Total enrollment in grades in which Spanish is offered	Number taking Spanish	Per cent taking Spanish
West South Central............	125	146,474	31,722	21.7
Mountain....................	74	66,326	13,065	19.7
Pacific.....................	72	214,899	33,697	15.7
East South Central...........	40	39,866	6,085	15.3
South Atlantic..............	69	85,550	11,042	12.9
Middle Atlantic..............	121	649,839	72,330	11.1
New England................	35	120,700	9,457	7.8
East North Central...........	80	394,810	30,497	7.7
West North Central...........	55	149,346	10,912	7.3
Total....................	671	1,867,810	218,807	11.7

TABLE 8.—ENROLLMENT IN SPANISH COURSES IN GRADES 9 TO 12 IN
671 CITY AND RURAL SCHOOL SYSTEMS, 1940–1941

Grade	Total enrollment in grades in which Spanish is taught	Number taking Spanish	Per cent taking Spanish
9	403,940	74,275	18.4
10	472,312	63,134	13.4
11	406,267	30,470	7.5
12	280,147	10,940	3.9
Total.........	1,562,666	178,819	11.4

TABLE 9.—ENROLLMENT OF JUNIOR-COLLEGE, POSTGRADUATE, AND SPECIAL
STUDENTS IN SPANISH CLASSES OF 671 CITY AND RURAL SCHOOL
SYSTEMS, 1940–1941*

City and rural school systems	Number of "other" students enrolled in the school system	Number taking Spanish	Per cent taking Spanish
Population over 100,000..........	142,508	15,297	10.1
Population 30,000 to 99,999.......	7,942	966	12.8
Population 10,000 to 29,999.......	4,726	429	9.1
Population under 10,000..........	3,685	362	9.7
County and rural school systems...	1,605	146	9.2
Total......................	160,466	17,200	10.7

* Exclusive of adults in evening-school classes.

TABLE 10.—NUMBER OF PUPILS REPORTED TAKING SPANISH FOR THE
FIRST TIME IN 1939–1940 AND IN 1940–1941 IN THE VARIOUS REGIONS
OF THE UNITED STATES*

Region	Number of pupils taking Spanish for first time		Per cent increase
	1939–1940	1940–1941	
West South Central.....................	10,193	15,875	55.7
West North Central.....................	4,286	6,662	55.4
East South Central.....................	2,432	3,117	28.2
New England...........................	1.889	2.354	24.6
Middle Atlantic........................	24,349	29,896	22.8
South Atlantic.........................	3,946	4,842	22.7
Pacific................................	13,741	15,127	10.1
East North Central.....................	13,207	13,695	3.7
Mountain..............................	6,017	6.171	2.6
Total................................	80,060	97,739	22.1

* Recalling the sudden "good neighborliness" of the United States toward Latin America in
1916–1918, and the reaction which followed the stampede toward Spanish, McKendree Petty writes
advisedly concerning the inevitable boomerang effects of overemphasizing the vocational value
of foreign-language study in elementary and secondary schools. See "Reflections on the Prospects
of Another Spanish Boom," *The Modern Language Journal*, Vol. XXVI, pp. 288–291, April, 1942.

TABLE 11.—NUMBER OF YEARS OF SPANISH OFFERED IN 671 SCHOOL SYSTEMS, 1940–1941

Number of Years Offered	Per Cent of 671 School Systems
1	10.0
2	26.2
3	27.7
4	32.1
5	2.8
6	1.2
Total	100.0

TABLE 12.—SPANISH IN THE ELEMENTARY SCHOOLS, GRADES 1 TO 8, 1940–1941

(Based on returns from 671 school systems)

Grades	Number of School Systems
1–6	5*
7	10
8	68

* Victoria, Tex. (grades 1, 2, 3); Corpus Christi Tex. (grades 2–6), a city-wide Spanish program enrolling 6,356 pupils in 1940–1941; Dover, Del. (grade 6); Pearson and Yoakum, Tex. (grade 6 and below).

TABLE 13.—FOREIGN-LANGUAGE TEACHING IN 38 COUNTRIES*

The first modern foreign language taught in 1937 was

French...................................... in 16 countries
English..................................... in 12 countries
German...................................... in 10 countries

The first modern foreign language is begun at the

Age of 9—in 1 country
Age of 10—in 8 countries
Age of 11—in 8 countries
Age of 12—in 17 countries
Age of 13—in 2 countries
Age of 15—in 1 country

Length of required courses:

2 countries have a 2-year course.
1 country has a 3-year course.
5 countries have a 4-year course.
7 countries have a 5-year course.
13 countries have a 6-year course.
4 countries have a 7-year course.
3 countries have an 8-year course.
1 country has a 9-year course.
1 country gave no exact data.

The total of obligatory languages is

0—for 4 countries
1—for 6 countries
2—for 19 countries
3—for 8 countries

* Fritz Thon, "Some Data on the World Situation in Foreign Language Teaching and the Place

The effects of the Second World War on foreign-language enrollments were reported by *Time* (Vol. XXXIV, No. 11, 1942) under the caption "Language Boom." According to *Time*'s data, Texas has issued 75,000 texts for use in the third grade. French has experienced a decrease of 23.5 per cent in college enrollments, and a 90 per cent decline in Berlitz Schools. French seems to have suffered more than German, which dropped only 11 per cent in the colleges. In every case the declining enrollments in German and French have been accompanied by marked gains in Spanish, amounting to 60 per cent in the Berlitz Schools. Portuguese is now taught in at least 48 colleges and universities, but outside Fall River, Mass., high-school classes in Portuguese are hard to find. Realizing the urgent need for adequately prepared teachers, the University of Vermont has inaugurated an intensive teacher-training course in Portuguese.

More alert than the high schools and junior colleges to the demands of the present crisis and to future world needs, Cornell and Harvard are offering Russian, the University of Michigan, Siamese, and seven universities (California, Colorado, Harvard, Michigan, Washington, George Washington, Yale), Japanese. Since December, 1941, enrollments in Japanese have climbed 1,000 per cent. For possible African contacts, courses in Swahili have been introduced by the University of North Carolina.

The conviction seems to be growing that, in the cooperative world order which must inevitably replace the present competitive world economy, that nation will exercise the greatest influence which knows how to appeal to the peoples in other lands in their own languages in terms of problems that are meaningful and significant to them. It is significant to observe that the Axis powers have made the study of foreign languages and cultures an important instrument for propagating their ideologies. Few Americans, on the other hand, have ever had enough proficiency in foreign languages and cultures to convert Italians, Germans, Japanese, or Russians to democracy through an effective appeal to their ideals, hopes, backgrounds, or survival-needs. It seems that the United States has all too often been obliged to rely on stock-market diplomacy or armed marines in Mexico, Nicaragua, Panama, Cuba, China, and elsewhere in order to win the world over to democracy.

---

of the U. S. A. in the World Picture," *The French Review*, Vol. XV, pp. 224–227, January, 1942. Compiled from *Publications du Bureau International d'Éducation* No. 45, L'Enseignement des langues vivantes, Genève, 1937. Fritz Thon's study of 38 countries shows that (1) French is the preferred first language; (2) a majority require the study of a foreign language, starting at age 12 or earlier, for four or more years; (3) the United States stands at the bottom of the list with respect to number of years of foreign-language study encouraged, the number of languages required, and the age at which foreign-language study is introduced. For recent data on foreign-language teaching in Brazil, China, Cuba, and Guatemala see "The Teaching of Modern Languages in Foreign Countries," *Education*, Vol. 62, pp. 330–346, February, 1942.

INDEX

Jauer-Marbach, Franziska, 205n.
Jespersen, Otto, 8n.
Jessen, C. A., 357n.
Johns, Dorothy M., 122n., 403n.
Johnson, Laura B., 116n.
Jones, W. Franklin, 261
Jones, Willis K., 189n., 204n., 255n.
Jordan, David S., 349
Junior Pan American League, 265n.
Junior Red Cross, 294n.

K

Kant, Immanuel, 8
Kantor, J. R., 17n., 30n., 81n., 312n.
Karpinski, Louis C., 320n.
Kaulfers, Bertha F., 298
Keating, Clark, 275n.
Kefauver, Grayson N., 275n., 343n., 423n.
Keniston, Hayward, 148n.
Kent, R. A., 29n.
Kieport, H., 169n.
King, Clara B., 415n., 421n.
Kirkpatrick, Robert, 149n.
Kirshner, Alfred, 292n., 399, 463n.
Kittelson, Clifford, 370n., 459n.
Klein, Adolph, 4n., 5n., 28n., 147n., 279n., 382n., 458n.
Kopel, David, 116n., 190n., 381n.
Koos, Leonard V., 298n.
Korzybski, Alfred, 299, 306n.
Krakowski, Meyer, 285n., 290, 448n.
Kress, Dorothy M., 372n.
Kuehne, Oswald R., 169n.

L

Laboratory workshops (see Supervised study)
Lange, Dorothea, 479n.
Language, and education, 315–316, 317, 426
and law, 323–327
and mathematics, 317–321
nature of, 3, 8–9, 11–12, 30, 311–315, 416
onomatopoeic origins of, 331–333
sanity in, 303

Language, and science, 317–322
social perspective in, 219, 334–335
(See also Foreign languages; Grammar)
Language aptitude, 2, 6, 219, 381–382
among feeble-minded, 302n., 468n.
(See also Prognosis)
Language consciousness, 39–40
(See also Sprachgefühl)
Language talent (see Language aptitude; Prognosis)
Lanks, Herbert C., 253n.
Latin, 443–444, 472, 501
enrollment trends in, 503–505
tests of ability in, 490
Lawson, Douglas E., 300
Lee, Irving, J., 306n.
Leisure, worthy use of, 351–352
Leive, Max, 270
Lembi, Dante P., 20n., 59n., 101n., 112n., 153n., 160n., 195n., 348n.
Leonard, J. Paul, 415n.
Leonard, Sterling A., 72n., 328n.
Lewis, Richard B., 144n., 272n.
Library, use of, 207, 253–254, 405, 506
Lindquist, Lilly, 6n., 149n., 285n., 299, 427n.
Literature, 101, 132–134, 135–144
(See also Poetry; World literature)
Literary appreciation, 136–144
(See also Reading; World literature)
Locke, Alain, 417n.
Lorge, Irving, 467n.
Lowers, Virginia B., 131n., 403n.

M

McAfee, Mildred H., 336
McConville, F. J., 151n., 284, 448n.
McCreary, Anna P., 418n.
McDonald, Ethel Anne, 371
McGuinness, Grace, 345n.
McKown, Harry C., 261n.
McPhail, Andrew H., 4n., 28n., 382n.
Macpherson, A., 390n.
Macpherson, Mary K., 149n.
Magazines, nonprofessional, 493–494
professional, 483, 484, 485, 486
Management of class, 234

Organizations, of students, 265, 495–496

of teachers, 431–434

Orleans, Joseph B., 336*n.*, 346*n.*, 356*n.*

O'Rourke, L. J., 3*n.*, 73*n.*

Osborn, L. G., 390*n.*, 473*n.*

O'Shea, M. V., 29*n.*

Outcomes, 349–358, 462

associate, 350–354

concomitant, 349–350

direct, 355–356

in general language, 333–334

of modern experimental programs, 414–416

(*See also* Objectives)

Outland, George E., 359*n.*

Oxley, Ruth, 147*n.*

P

Page, Dorothy, 451*n.*

Pageants, 263

Palomo, J. R., 205*n.*

Pan American Student Forum, 265*n.*

Pan American Student League, 265

Paradigms, 13–16, 26

question and answer format of, 83–86, 199

Paraphrase, exercises in, 192–199

Pargment, Lila, 392*n.*

Parker, Clifford, 205*n.*

Peebles, Waldo C., 395*n.*

Pence, Edith E., 351*n.*

Performance levels (*see* Cognition)

Peterkin, L. Denis, 443–444

Phillips, Hosea, 468*n.*

Phillips, Walter T., 150*n.*

Phonetics, 8, 57–58

Pictures, sources of, 494, 499

uses of, 177–184

Pilley, J. R., 418*n.*

Poetry, 137–144, 282

and music, 138–139, 282, 331–333

and onomatopoeia, 331–333

Portuguese, teaching of in United States, 511

Posters, sources of, 494

Price, William R., 392*n.*

Prognosis, 339–340, 428, 474

tests of, 6, 278–280, 298–299, 490

Progressive Educational Association, 280*n.*, 463*n.*, 500

Pronouns, teaching of, 85–89, 477–479

Pronunciation, 19, 41–70, 225, 228, 235–239, 240–242, 248–249, 255–256, 498

attainable norms of, 66–69, 242

charts for, 59–66

diphthongization, 42

evaluation of ability in, 69

growth in, 66

transfer of training in, 42

use of mechanical aids in, 69–70

Pryor, Helen B., 276

Pryor, Roy, 204*n.*

Psychology, of foreign language teaching, 1–40

Psychosemantics, 8–9, 10, 11

consumer education in, 300–335

in culture courses, 281–282, 283

in general language courses, 300–335

in law, 322–327

in mathematics, 317–321

in science, 317–321

in teaching of grammar, 81–83

(*See also* General language)

Puppet shows, 263

Purin, C. M., 367*n.*

Q

Questions, in paradigms, 83–86, 199

semioriginal, 199–200

use of, 199–201, 217

R

Race prejudice, 456, 461–462, 463*n.*

tests of, 491

Radio, programs on, 496

uses of, 264, 269, 380, 419

Ralls, R. Blount, 275*n.*

Reading, 20, 33, 108–144, 424

apperception in, 114, 188

collateral in English, 131–132, 253, 445

on contract plan, 127–128

Whittmann, Vera E., 6*n.*, 29*n.*, 221*n.*,
378*n.*, 404*n.*, 405*n.*, 458*n.*
Wiebe, H. H., 285*n.*
Wilds, E. H., 261, 264*n.*
Wilkins, Lawrence A., 34*n.*, 354*n.*, 427*n.*
Williams, Ronald B., 76*n.*
Wilson, P. G., 8*n.*
Witty, Paul, 116*n.*, 190*n.*, 381*n.*
Wood, Ben D., 148*n.*
Word counts, 114
(*See also* Frequency counts)
Workshops, in classroom, 249
for hobbies, 264
for teachers, 426
(*See also* Supervised study;
Teacher training)

World literature, bibliographical aids
for teaching of, 449
courses in, 441–445, 447, 453
in translation, 369, 441–445
Wrightstone, J. Wayne, 415*n.*
Wriston, Henry M., 360–361

Y

Yaller, Ray, 2*n.*
Yeiser, Idabelle, 468*n.*
Young, Charles E., 369*n.*, 460*n.*
Young, Sherman P., 444

Z

Zeydel, Edwin H., 442*n.*, 445*n.*